ASKING QUESTIONS IN BIBLICAL TEXTS

CONTRIBUTIONS TO BIBLICAL EXEGESIS AND THEOLOGY

SERIES EDITORS

K. De Troyer (Salzburg)
G. Van Oyen (Louvain-la-Neuve)

ADVISORY BOARD

Reimund Bieringer (Leuven)
Lutz Doering (Münster)
Mark Goodacre (Duke)
Bas ter Haar Romeny (Amsterdam)
Annette Merz (Groningen)
Madhavi Nevader (St Andrews)
Thomas Römer (Lausanne)
Jack Sasson (Nashville)
Tammi Schneider (Claremont)

Bart J. KOET
Archibald L.H.M. VAN WIERINGEN (eds.)

ASKING QUESTIONS
IN BIBLICAL TEXTS

PEETERS
LEUVEN – PARIS – BRISTOL, CT
2022

A catalogue record for this book is available from the Library of Congress.

© 2022 — Peeters, Bondgenotenlaan 153, B-3000 Leuven

ISBN 978-90-429-4928-7
eISBN 978-90-429-4929-4
D/2022/0602/73

All rights reserved. No part of this publication may be reproduced, stored in a retrieval system, or transmitted, in any form or by any means, electronic, mechanical, photocopying, recording or otherwise, without the prior permission of the publisher.

TABLE OF CONTENTS

ABBREVIATIONS.   IX

Bart J. KOET & Archibald L.H.M. VAN WIERINGEN
Questioning the Phenomenon of Questions: An Introduction to
Asking Questions in Biblical Texts   1

Willem A.M. BEUKEN
Unease as Plaything between Questions and Answers: The Promise
of Progeny for Abraham in Genesis 12–25   7

Penelope BARTER
Questions in Numbers 11   23

Richard J. BAUTCH
Questions Posed in Deuteronomy 6: Learning and Teaching
the Ways of God.   35

Bob BECKING
The Questions in Ezra and Nehemiah.   49

Barbara SCHMITZ
'Who am I to disobey my lord?' (Judith 12:14): Asking Questions
in the Book of Judith   65

Sehoon JANG
Do Contradictory Readings of the Question by Job's Wife Really
Matter?.   81

Harm VAN GROL
In Search of God: Asking Questions in the Psalms   97

Pancratius C. BEENTJES
Asking Questions in the book of Ben Sira: Their Form and Function   111

Joachim ECK
Questions in Isaiah's Woe Oracles against the Rulers of His People
(Isaiah 10:1-4) and Assyrian Power (Isaiah 10:5-15) 125

Archibald L.H.M. VAN WIERINGEN
The Question of the Word of God: The Communicative Function
of the Questions in Amos 3:3-8 149

Ruben ZIMMERMANN
Q Document Means 'Question Document': Form and Function of
Jesus' Questions in the Sayings Source. 163

Geert VAN OYEN
Questions in the Gospel of Mark: Two Examples (1:24; 16:3) . . 183

Bart J. KOET
Counter-questions in the Gospel of Luke: An Assessment. 209

Douglas ESTES
Unasked Questions in the Gospel of John: Narrative, Rhetoric,
and Hypothetical Discourse 229

Arie W. ZWIEP
A Question of Misunderstanding or a Misunderstood Question?:
Exegetical Comments on Acts 1:6 247

Bert Jan LIETAERT PEERBOLTE
An Erōtēsis in Romans 8:31-39: On the Importance of Questions
and Question Marks 263

Ignas W. TILMA
Questions as Rhetorical Tools in 1 Corinthians 11:22 281

Hanna ROOSE
Asking Questions in the Revelation of John 293

Albert L.A. HOGETERP
Asking Questions in Qumran Literature 305

Leon MOCK
Some Observations on the Importance of Questions in Rabbinic
Tradition and Halakhah 321

Eric Ottenheijm
Disturbing Questions: Observations on the Rhetoric of Two
Rabbinic Parables 335

Hanna Roose
Educational Perspectives on Questions in Biblical Texts. 355

Index of References 365

Index of Modern Authors. 389

ABBREVIATIONS

AB	Anchor Bible
ABS	Archaeology and Biblical Studies
AcBib	Academia Biblica
AnBib	Analecta Biblica
ANEM	Ancient Near East Monographs/Monografías sobre el Antiguo Cercano Oriente
AYBRL	Anchor Yale Bible Reference Library
BAFCS	The Book of Acts in Its First Century Setting
BBB	Bonner biblische Beiträge
BECNT	Baker Exegetical Commentary on the New Testament
BETL	Bibliotheca Ephemeridum Theologicarum Lovaniensium
Bib	*Biblica*
BibB	Biblische Beiträge
BibInt	*Biblical Interpretation*
BibInt	Biblical Interpretation Series
Bijdr	*Bijdragen: Tijdschrift voor filosofie en theologie*
BKAT	Biblischer Kommentar, Altes Testament
BN	*Biblische Notizen*
BSac	*Bibliotheca Sacra*
BTS	Biblical Tools and Studies
BWANT	Beiträge zur Wissenschaft vom Alten und Neuen Testament
BZ	*Biblische Zeitschrift*
BZAW	Beihefte zur Zeitschrift für die alttestamentliche Wissenschaft
BZNW	Beihefte zur Zeitschrift für die neutestamentliche Wissenschaft
CBET	Contributions to Biblical Exegesis and Theology
CBQ	*Catholic Biblical Quarterly*
CBQMS	Catholic Biblical Quarterly Monograph Series
ConcC	Concordia Commentary
CRINT	Compendia Rerum Iudaicarum ad Novum Testamentum
DCH	*Dictionary of Classical Hebrew. Edited by David J. A. Clines. 9 vols. Sheffield: Sheffield Phoenix Press, 1993–2014*
DCLS	Deuterocanonical and Cognate Literature Studies
DJD	Discoveries in the Judaean Desert

EANEC	Explorations in Ancient Near Eastern Civilizations
EBib	Etudes bibliques
EHAT	Exegetisches Handbuch zum Alten Testament
EJL	Early Judaism and Its Literature
EKKNT	Evangelisch-katholischer Kommentar zum Neuen Testament
EstBib	*Estudios bíblicos*
FAT	Forschungen zum Alten Testament
FRLANT	Forschungen zur Religion und Literatur des Alten und Neuen Testaments
GKC	*Gesenius' Hebrew Grammar*. Edited by Emil Kautzsch. Translated by Arther E. Cowley. 2nd ed. Oxford: Clarendon, 1910
HBS	History of Biblical Studies
HCOT	Historical Commentary on the Old Testament
HThKAT	Herders Theologischer Kommentar zum Alten Testament
HThKNT	Herders Theologischer Kommentar zum Neuen Testament
HTR	*Harvard Theological Review*
HUCA	*Hebrew Union College Annual*
IBC	Interpretation: A Bible Commentary for Teaching and Preaching
IBHS	*An Introduction to Biblical Hebrew Syntax*. Bruce K. Waltke and Michael O'Connor. Winona Lake, IN: Eisenbrauns, 1990
ICC	International Critical Commentary
Int	*Interpretation*
JANESCU	Journal of the Ancient Near Eastern Society of Columbia University
JBL	*Journal of Biblical Literature*
JBS	Jerusalem Biblical Studies
JHS	*Journal of Hellenic Studies*
JNES	Journal of Near Eastern Studies
Joüon	Joüon, Paul. *A Grammar of Biblical Hebrew*. Translated and revised by T. Muraoka. 2 vols. Rome: Pontifical Biblical Institute, 1991
JQR	*Jewish Quarterly Review*
JSOT	*Journal for the Study of the Old Testament*
JSOTSup	Journal for the Study of the Old Testament Supplement Series
JTS	*Journal of Theological Studies*
KAT	Kommentar zum Alten Testament
KBL	Koehler, Ludwig, and Walter Baumgartner. *Lexicon in Veteris Testamenti libros*. 2nd ed. Leiden, 1958

KEK	Kritisch-exegetischer Kommentar über das Neue Testament (Meyer-Kommentar)
KJV	King James Version
LCL	Loeb Classical Library
LHBOTS	The Library of Hebrew Bible/Old Testament Studies
LLT	Library of Latin Texts
LNTS	The Library of New Testament Studies
LXX	Septuagint
MT	Masoretic Text
NA[28]	*Novum Testamentum Graece*, Nestle-Aland, 28th ed.
NAC	New American Commentary
NAS	New American Standard Bible
NedTT	*Nederlands theologisch tijdschrift*
NETS	*A New English Translation of the Septuagint*. Edited by Albert Pietersma and Benjamin G. Wright. New York: Oxford University Press, 2007
NIBC	New International Biblical Commentary
NICOT	New International Commentary on the Old Testament
NIGTC	New International Greek Testament Commentary
NovT	*Novum Testamentum*
NovTSup	Supplements to Novum Testamentum
NRSV	New Revised Standard Version
NSKAT	Neuer Stuttgarter Kommentar, Altes Testament
NTD	Das Neue Testament Deutsch
NTOA	Novum Testamentum et Orbis Antiquus
NTTS	New Testament Tools and Studies
OBO	Orbis Biblicus et Orientalis
OLAW	Orality and Literacy in the Ancient World
OTP	*Old Testament Pseudepigrapha*. Edited by James H. Charlesworth. 2 vols. New York: Doubleday, 1983, 1985
OTS	Oudtestamentische Studiën
POT	De Prediking van het Oude Testament
PTMS	Pittsburgh Theological Monograph Series
RB	*Revue Biblique*
RBS	Resources for Biblical Study
RNT	Regensburger Neues Testament
RSV	Revised Standard Version
RTL	*Revue théologique de Louvain*
SANT	Studien zum Alten und Neuen Testament
SBB	Stuttgarter biblische Beiträge

SBLDS	Society of Biblical Literature Dissertation Series
SBLGNT	SBL Greek New Testament
SBLMS	Society of Biblical Literature Monograph Series
SBLSBS	Society of Biblical Literature Sources for Biblical Study
SBS	Stuttgarter Bibelstudien
SBT	Studies in Biblical Theology
SCS	Septuagint and Cognate Studies
SHBC	Smyth & Helwys Bible Commentary
SNTA	Studiorum Novi Testamenti Auxilia
SNTSMS	Society for New Testament Studies Monograph Series
SP	Sacra Pagina
SSN	Studia Semitica Neerlandica
StBibLit	Studies in Biblical Literature
STDJ	Studies on the Texts of the Desert of Judah
StPB	Studia Post-biblica
TGl	*Theologie und Glaube*
ThWAT	*Theologisches Wörterbuch zum Alten Testament*. Edited by G. Johannes Botterweck and Helmer Ringgren. Stuttgart: Kohlhammer, 1970–
TKNT	Theologischer Kommentar zum Neuen Testament
TNTC	Tyndale New Testament Commentaries
TOTC	Tyndale Old Testament Commentaries
TSAJ	Texte und Studien zum antiken Judentum
TThZ	*Trierer theologische Zeitschrift*
UBS[5]	*The Greek New Testament*, United Bible Societies, 5th ed.
UF	Ugarit-Forschungen
VT	*Vetus Testamentum*
VTSup	Supplements to Vetus Testamentum
WA	Weimarer Ausgabe
WBC	Word Biblical Commentary
WUNT	Wissenschaftliche Untersuchungen zum Neuen Testament
ZAW	*Zeitschrift für die alttestamentliche Wissenschaft*
ZBK	Zürcher Bibelkommentare
ZNW	*Zeitschrift für die neutestamentliche Wissenschaft und die Kunde der älteren Kirche*

QUESTIONING THE PHENOMENON OF QUESTIONS
An Introduction to Asking Questions in Biblical Texts

Bart J. KOET & Archibald L.H.M. VAN WIERINGEN
Tilburg University

In an earlier joint publication, the subject was Multiple Teachers in Biblical Texts.[1] In that volume, the authors examined the roles of teacher and disciple from a textual perspective. The volume is part of the research programme 'Teaching and Tradition' at the Tilburg University, School of Catholic Theology, which has been focusing on learning processes in biblical traditions. In addition to authors who are affiliated in one way or another with this School, a large number of specialists from other countries participated. Besides contributions on Old Testament and New Testament texts, there were also articles on teacher models in early Rabbinic Judaism.

The focus on the pedagogy of the biblical traditions proved fruitful, and when it became clear that questions as being a part of this biblical pedagogy had so far been under-researched, it was logical to publish a follow-up volume on questions in the biblical tradition. Once again, a core group of authors who are in one way or another connected with the above-mentioned School's research programme 'Teaching and Tradition' have contributed and are supplemented by a selection of specialists from all four corners of the world.

Not only in the biblical tradition, but also in daily life questions and the use of questions surround us everywhere. All day, we all ask questions, and we all are asked questions. A question really is an everyday occurrence. We ask questions to other people ('what is the homework for next week?'), to ourselves ('where am I going on vacation this year?') and

---

[1] See B.J. Koet and A.L.H.M. van Wieringen (Eds.), *Multiple Teachers in Biblical Texts* (CBET 88; Leuven: Peeters, 2017). See also B.J. Koet, G. O'Floinn and A.L.H.M. van Wieringen (Eds.), *Models of Teacherhood* (CBQ Imprints; forthcoming).

even to the objects around us, e.g. the computer ('why are you not doing what I want you to do?').

However, if someone asks what a question actually is, it is not easy to answer that question. It feels rather like what Augustine of Hippo said about 'time:' *What, then, is time? If no one asks me, I know what it is. If I wish to explain it to him who asks me, I do not know* (Confessions XI, 14,17).[2] What is a question? If no one asks us, we know what it is, but if we wish to explain it to someone, we do not know.

In biblical exegesis and cognate studies, remarkably little research has been done into the phenomenon of questions. We do see that already the older grammars of Biblical Hebrew pay attention to more than just the interrogatives. For example, in their English edition of Wilhelm Gesenius' Hebrew Grammar, Emil Kautzsch and Arthur Cowley separately deal with interrogative sentences, i.e. sentences containing a question.[3] The first thing they make clear is that a question can also be asked by intonation without using an interrogative. We see the same approach in the grammar of Paul Joüon and Takamitsu Muraoka, albeit that in the index of their grammar the lemma 'question' refers to the lemma 'clause: interrogative,' due to which 'question' is not present as an independent issue.[4] Modern grammars do not necessarily do better than sound older grammars. Bruce Waltke and Michael O'Connor deal with the phenomenon of questions in the unit about interrogatives; they do not have a separate unit on the syntax of interrogative sentences.[5] Special studies on Biblical Hebrew syntax summarize what is already available in the traditional grammars, without adding really new insights.[6]

The grammars of Biblical Greek actually pay less attention to the phenomenon of questions than the grammars of Biblical Hebrew. The classic grammar by Friedrich Blass, Albert Debrunner and Friedrich Rehkopf has no separate section on the question.[7] However, much information can be found spread over various sections.

In contrast to the grammars of Biblical Greek, modern grammars of classical Greek do deal extensively with the phenomenon of questions,

---

[2] Quid est ergo tempus? Si nemo ex me quaerat, scio; si quaerenti explicare velim, nescio.
[3] GKC, § 150.
[4] Joüon, § 161.
[5] *IBHS*, § 18.
[6] See e.g. B.T. Arnold and J.H. Choi, *A Guide to Biblical Hebrew Syntax* (Cambridge: Cambridge University Press, 2003), 187–188 [§ 5.3.1].
[7] BDF, *passim*.

discussing this issue in a separate section. For example, Evert van Emde Boas, Albert Rijksbaron, Luuk Huitink and Mathieu de Bakker devote a sub-chapter to the phenomenon of questions and related problems, in particular the rhetoric of questions.[8] Steven Runge is especially in line with this development. In his discourse grammar of New Testament Greek, he discusses concrete examples both from the narrative texts of the Gospels and from the discursive texts of the Letters.[9]

Only a small number of monographs has been published on questions. For Old Testament exegesis the most important one is the rhetorical study by Kenneth Craig,[10] for New Testament exegesis the rhetorical study by Douglas Estes.[11] Both studies, especially the one by Estes, have much to offer regarding the understanding of the rhetoric of questions in biblical literature.

However, the grammatical and (limited) exegetical attention given to the phenomenon of questions has not resulted in a generally accepted definition for 'question.' This attention has rather shown that such a definition may not be feasible. Nevertheless, it has become clear that the phenomenon of questions justifiably demands attention. In this volume, we wish to give this attention to the complex phenomenon of questions.

This volume deals with the phenomenon of questions from various perspectives. Since no single definition of question has been imposed on the authors (and as mentioned above, such a definition simply does not exist), a broad spectrum of approaches to research the phenomenon of questions has arisen. We wish to enumerate the most important perspectives here.

A syntactical perspective has old papers, as described above. In contrast to semantics and pragmatics, syntax is the hard material for research. Syntax therefore plays a role in almost all the contributions. However, it is more prominently present in the contributions by Douglas Estes and Archibald van Wieringen.

---

[8] E. van Emde Boas, A. Rijksbaron, L. Huitink and M. de Bakker, *Cambridge Grammar of Classical Greek* (Cambridge: Cambridge University Press, 2017), 474–481.
[9] Steven E. Runge, *Discourse Grammar of the Greek New Testament: A Practical Introduction for Teaching and Exegesis* (Lexham Bible Reference Series; Peabody: Hendrickson Publishers, 2015).
[10] K.M. Craig, *Asking for Rhetoric: The Hebrew Bible's Protean Interrogative* (BibInt 73; Leiden: Brill Academic, 2005).
[11] D. Estes, *Questions and Rhetoric in the Greek New Testament: An Essential Reference Resource for Exegesis* (Grand Rapids: Zondervan, 2017).

From the syntactical perspective, rhetorical questions play a special role. After all, Biblical Hebrew has the special particle הֲלֹא to mark a rhetorical question. However, not every rhetorical question is marked by the particle הֲלֹא, and not every question containing the particle הֲלֹא appears to be a rhetorical question. The particle הֲלֹא rather indicates a preferable answer, but whether that answer is indeed given is an open question. In Greek this is even more complicated, because the Greek language does not have such a particle.[12]

The rhetorical question is dealt with by Joachim Eck for Isaiah 10:5–15, by Panc Beentjes for the book of Ben Sira and by Ignas Tilma, also in dialogue with Estes, as a figure of speech in 1 Corinthians.

Estes' perspective can be called *taxonomical*. He labels the various forms of questions, creating very detailed subdivisions. His labels are based on a combination of observations regarding syntax, semantics and discourse analysis.

In his contribution, Estes elaborates his taxonomy with the category of 'unasked questions,' applied to the Gospel of John. In his analysis of the Gospel of Luke, Bart Koet also develops this taxonomy by focussing on a new kind of question: the counter-question. Albert Hogeterp taxonomically arranges the various kinds of questions in the literature of the Discoveries in the Judean Desert according to the various para-biblical genres.

The presence of questions is not limited to the literature of the Bible and of the Discoveries in the Judean Desert, but questions are also common in Rabbinic literature. Leo Mock makes clear that Rabbinic literature, through all ages, up to the modern responsa-literature, is also characterized by questions.

Erik Ottenheijm's *genre*-perspective demonstrates the importance of questions in some concrete parables in Rabbinic literature. The presence of questions directs the development of the parable and, therefore, the application of the parable as well.

From a *narratological* approach it becomes clear that questions effect the development of the plot. Wim Beuken demonstrates this plot-related function of questions for the Abraham-cycle in the book of Genesis, while Bob Becking does so for the books of Ezra-Nehemiah. Hanna Roose, too, makes a link between the presence of questions in the text and the textual drama that unfolds in Revelation.

---

[12] Van Emde Boas, Rijksbaron, Huitink and De Bakker, *Grammar of Classical Greek*, 480 [§ 38.19] mentions a couple of expressions that could be understood as rhetorical questions.

This narratological approach also applies to the book of Judith, as Barbara Schmitz makes clear. The development of the plot in this biblical book is specifically linked to the question 'who is God, if not Nabouchodonosor?' This question, therefore, not only evokes the narrative plot, but also the theological development. Ruben Zimmerman already sees a combined narratological and theological function of questions present in Q.

Geert Van Oyen specifically demonstrates the narratological function of questions by analysing the opening and closing questions of the Gospel of Mark. These two questions form a kind of inclusion within which the story's plot can take place. The book of Acts also opens with a question that sets the plot in motion. Arie Zwiep goes into this in detail, also against the background of the interpretation history of this opening question 'Lord, is this the time when you will restore the kingdom to Israel?'

A special narratological function of questions becomes visible in the so-called *cameo appearance*. Richard Bautch extensively deals with this for Deuteronomy 6.

In addition to a narratological approach, a *prosodic* approach is suitable for poetic literature. Harm van Grol investigates the phenomenon of questions within the prosody of some concrete Psalms.

Van Wieringen offers a *communication-oriented* perspective, based on the idea that a question presupposes a discrepancy in information between various textual constructs, e.g. the text-immanent reader and the characters. The effect of questions on the reader, although not explicitly formulated in a communication-oriented way, plays an important role in many contributions. The interpretation of a question by the text-immanent reader does not necessarily consist of just one single reading option. Sehoon Jang demonstrates that, in the book of Job, even contradictory reading options are possible.

This communication-orientation functions both synchronically and diachronically. In his analysis of Genesis 18:19b, Beuken uses the communication-oriented perspective in a synchronic way, whereas Penny Barter makes clear in her analysis of Numbers 11 that a difference in reader-oriented functions of questions is a signal to diachronically uncover the textual development.

The last perspective we wish to mention is the *text-critical* perspective. While Biblical Hebrew has no punctuation marks (and therefore no question mark), Greek does. Text tradition with punctuation marks, among which the question mark (the semi-colon in Greek), is complex. The presence or absence of a question mark creates a different interpretation of the text to be handed on. Bert Jan Lietaert Peerbolte unravels this complexity for Romans 8:31–39.

It is important to observe that questions are not restricted to one text type, for example the Old Testament chokmatic literature. Questions arise throughout the Old and New Testaments, as well as in Qumranic and Rabbinic literature. Each time, they play a communicative role that further develops the narrative or discursive text.

Essentially, the phenomenon of questions can be seen as a link between all these religious texts. It is even possible to take a further step: questions are the connecting element in doing theology and in the relationship between theology and other fields of science.[13]

To conclude this volume, Hanna Roose opens a window onto this relationship between theology and another scholarly discipline, namely religious education. The biblical and literary phenomenon of questions provides new insight into the place and function of questions in religious education.

The phenomenon of questions has its own place in the biblical *paideia*: the various biblical texts do not only contain multiple teachers, but they use, at all the different textual levels, the method of asking questions in order to themselves function as teachers. They challenge both the text-immanent reader, e.g. in the development of the chokmatic discourse, and the real reader, e.g. in the text-critical transmission of the biblical text. By asking questions, the biblical tradition of teaching is continued in continually new (textual) contexts.

Many questions. Many kinds of questions. Many definitions of what a question is. If this volume makes anything clear, it is that it is free to ask questions – for everyone, in any form, anytime, anywhere.[14]

---

[13] See for a first example of the connecting function of the phenomenon of questions within theology, A.L.H.M. van Wieringen and B.J. Koet (Eds.), *Vragen staat vrij: Over vragen stellen in oude en nieuwe wijsheidstradities* (Heeswijk: Berne Media, 2020).

[14] We would like to thank Drs. Maurits J. Sinninghe Damsté for correcting the English text of the manuscript and Drs. Leo van den Bogaard for correcting the lay-out of the manuscript.

UNEASE AS PLAYTHING BETWEEN QUESTIONS AND ANSWERS
The Promise of Progeny for Abraham in Genesis 12–25

Willem A.M. Beuken
KU Leuven

1. Introduction

The *toledot* of Terah (Genesis 11:27–25:18) is a composition of its own, even though as a narrative, it is strongly connected to the following *toledot* of Isaac (Genesis 25:19–35:29).[1] Its relative independence, among other aspects, appears if one focuses on the pattern of questions and answers regarding the topic of progeny for Abraham. The textual basis of this item is implicitly contained in God's command to him to depart from Haran: 'I will make of you a great nation, and I will bless you, and make your name great' (12:2). The very concept 'offspring' (זרע), however, occurs, literally and connected to the concept 'land,' no earlier than when Abram has passed through the land of Canaan, namely in Yhwh's promise: 'To your offspring I will give this land' (12:7).

In this contribution, I aim to describe the dramatical context in which questions about that promise arise and answers are given, while taking the sequential connectedness of the eight passages concerned into account. Obviously, it is impossible to digress to matter which lies outside of this focus. The headings of the eight sections follow the pattern of speaker to addressee.

---

[1] J. Taschner, *Verheissung und Erfüllung in der Jakoberzählung (Gen 25,19–33,17): Eine Analyse ihres Spannungsbogens* (Herders biblische Studien 27; Freiburg: Herder, 2000), 11–21.

2. Pharaoh to Abram (Genesis 12:10–19)

The first question in the literary corpus at issue is not raised by Abram, neither after Yhwh's command to depart from Haran (12:1–3), nor after God's promise to give him 'this land' (v. 7), but by Pharaoh when he is punished by Yhwh for having taken Abram's wife into his house: 'What is this you have done to me?' (vv. 18–19). By presenting Sarah in a deceitful way, the patriarch has assured his personal safety and acquired great wealth (vv. 12–16), but he has also risked a specific element of God's promise, namely progeny: 'I will make of you a great nation' (v. 2). In the context, the scene in Egypt serves no other purpose than to describe the gravity of the famine in Canaan, but in connection with the preceding story, it creates a problem. Abram has arrived in the land, where he is in touch with Yhwh who has appeared to him, who has promised him: 'To your offspring I will give this land,' and to whom he has built an altar (vv. 6–8). Why does he not consult his God when there is a famine in the land; why does he travel right away to the granary of Egypt? If he loses his wife Sarai there, his chances of begetting legal offspring run a great risk (vv. 11–20). Only Yhwh guards his chances by afflicting Pharaoh and ordering him that Sarai be delivered to Abram. Surprisingly, Abram does not reply to Pharaoh's threefold question: 'What is this you have done to me? Why did you not tell me that she was your wife? Why did you say: "She is my sister", so that I took her for my wife?' (vv. 18–19). Abram's absolute silence is embarrassing with regard to his personal development in light of God's promise. It twins with the other narrative ellipse regarding how Pharaoh knew about God's punishment.[2] Together they create unease within the story.

3. Abram to Lot (Genesis 13)

The unease is provisionally remedied in the scene of Abram's and Lot's separation (13:1–18), particularly in Abram's question to Lot: 'Is not the whole land before you?' (v. 9). This looks as if it is a rhetorical question, yet in the sequel of the Abraham epos it will become clear that the settlement in the land of Canaan is not trouble-free, neither regarding territory, nor regarding population. Opposed to Abram's lack of concern about offspring in the previous story, his solicitude for a partition of the land

---

[2] From the point of *Wirkungsgeschichte*, the question of how Sarai reacted to the whole procedure arises; for this, cf. A. Wénin, *Abraham ou l'apprentissage du dépouillement: Lecture de Genèse 11,27–25,18* (Lire la Bible 190; Paris: Cerf, 2016), 53–56.

without conflicts is striking here. However, that goal is ill-considered: land and offspring are closely bound to each other. In the problematic context of Egypt, Abram has put aside the issue of offspring, and now he does so again by allowing Lot, the son of his brother and his possible heir, to depart. Therefore, Yhwh takes this up in a new utterance, and does so moreover, by uniting land and offspring, and with more emphasis than he did when he ordered Abram to depart from Haran (12:1–3) and after Abram's entry into the land (12:7). Now he says: 'Raise your eyes now, and look from the place where you are, northward and southward and eastward and westward; for all the land that you see I will give to you and to your offspring forever. I will make your offspring like the dust of the earth...' (13:14–15). God's speaking of 'all the land' is illogical, for in this way, he disaffirms its actual partition between Abram and Lot (vv. 10–12). It is, moreover, exaggerated to speak of innumerable offspring (v. 16: 'like the dust of the earth') while not even the first generation is within sight. Thus, we conclude: Abram's question to Lot seems to be rhetorical, yet it gets an answer at two levels. From the view of pragmatics, it results in the separation of the two immigrants, which will turn very risky for Lot in the next episode. From the narrative point of view, Yhwh awakens an expectation of offspring that remains inconvenient as long as the guarantees for this are totally missing.

4. Abram twice to God (Genesis 15)

Abram's meeting with King Melchizedek and their common confession to 'God Most High, maker of heaven and earth' (14:18–23) ushers in Yhwh's subsequent appearance to Abram (Genesis 15). In this episode, Yhwh raises the matter of the realisation of his initial call to Abram (Genesis 12:1–3) in two movements. Each comprises a self-presentation of Yhwh (v. 1: 'I am your shield...'; v. 7: 'I am Yhwh...'), a question of Abram (vv. 2–3: 'What will you give me?; v. 8: 'How am I to know...?') and Yhwh's reply (vv. 4–5; 9–16). The first panel runs into the second through Abram's act of confidence in Yhwh: 'He believed Yhwh, and he reckoned it to him as righteousness' (v. 6).[3]

In the first movement, Abram raises the question as to who will be his heir by birth, given the fact that he has not got a physical son. Yhwh's

---

[3] See the commentaries and a mass of detailed studies about the syntax of v. 6. The interpretation that Abram reckoned Yhwh's preceding announcement as righteous, i.e. trustworthy, fits the context most and is adopted here; cf. Wénin, *Abraham*, 98.

answer: 'Your very own issue shall be your heir' (v. 4) confirms the earlier promise, but does so in new, yet similar imagery. Compare: 'Look toward heaven and count the stars, if you are able to count them ... So shall your descendants be' (v. 5) with 'I will make your offspring like the dust of the earth; so that if one can count the dust of the earth, your offspring also can be counted' (13:16). The literary form of a progressive comparison, from 'like the dust' to 'like the stars' (*exaggeratio a synonymis*),[4] serves a different constellation in both texts. In 13:17–18, Yhwh commands Abram, after their discussion, to pass through the land, which he does, so as to settle there and to build an altar for Yhwh (v. 18). In 15:5, Yhwh guides Abram, during their discussion, to under the arch of heaven where Abram reacts with an act of confidence: 'He believed Yhwh, and he reckoned it to him as righteousness'. In this way, Abram's initial question is not met in terms of pragmatics, however, from now on, the relationship of Yhwh and Abram forms part of the question of the latter's progeny. The implied reader can hardly go on reading without wondering what the outcome of this conversation will be.

In the second movement, Yhwh broaches the topic 'land': 'I am Yhwh who brought you from Ur of the Chaldeans, to give you this land to possess' (v. 7). The topic was included in Abram's preceding concern about who would inherit his property (vv. 2–3). Now that God himself brings up the topic, Abram raises the question: 'How am I *to know* that I shall possess it (the land)?' (v. 8). In terms of relationship, Yhwh's reply, in first instance, is a command to prepare a sacrifice (vv. 9–11) for the covenant that he will make with Abram (vv. 17–21). In second instance, the reply is a prophecy given during a deep sleep: '*Know this for certain*' (v. 13). In terms of pragmatics, Yhwh describes the particular identity of Abram's progeny: 'Your offspring shall be aliens in a land that is not theirs' (v. 13). Through the *litotes* of the statement, 'not theirs,' God creates a juridical and social problem. He declares Abram to be the testator of a land which his heirs will not inhabit for the time being, and to which they will only return after a long period of estrangement and suppression (vv. 13–16). In this way, the identity of Abram's offspring is determined by a dramatic relationship with the land in which their ancestor himself will conclude his life (v. 15). The revelation of the future is emphasized, first by the mention that Yhwh made a covenant with Abram (vv. 17–18a),

---

[4] W. Bühlmann and K. Scherer, *Stilfiguren der Bibel: Ein kleines Nachschlagewerk* (BibB 10; Fribourg: Schweizerisches Katholisches Bibelwerk, 1973), 30–31; E.W. Bullinger, *Figures of Speech Used in the Bible* (London: Messers, 1898 / Grand Rapids: Baker, [17]1993), 325–338.

next by his description of the scale and population of the land to be inherited (vv. 18b–21).

In sum, the revelatory meeting of Yhwh with Abram remarkably modifies the question-answer structure of the promise of progeny for him. The relationship of the questioner with the person questioned becomes part of the question, while the matter of the question itself becomes questionable.

5. The messenger of Yhwh to Hagar (Genesis 16)

The next question–answer episode in reading sequence is that of Yhwh's messenger to Hagar when she fled from Sarai: 'Hagar, slave-girl of Sarai, where have you come from and where are you going?' (16:8). The questions are rhetorical insofar the messenger seems to know Hagar, for he addresses her by name, perhaps imputatively.[5] His questions 'where from?' (*espace perçu*/'first-space') and 'where?' (*espace conçu*/'second-space') mean, when taken together, that he recognizes her right to a place to stay, yet also that in his view, the desert will not provide her an abode (*espace vécu*/'third-space').[6] The fact that he finds her 'by a spring of water in the wilderness' (v. 7) signifies the utmost frontier of life. Hagar admits this plainly, for she only replies to the question 'where from?': 'I am running away from my mistress Sarai' (v. 8b). This incomplete answer gives the messenger of Yhwh the chance to reconstruct the other question, 'where?,' into advice and a promise. He does not suggest a viable place of refuge but opens a perspective onto another time; he offers a future. The promise consists of three *demarches*, each is announced through a narrative legitimation (vv. 9–12: 'The messenger of Yhwh said to her'). It would be good for Hagar to return to Sarai and 'let herself be afflicted' (v. 9 ענה *hitp*.), for there, in the house of Abram to whom Sarai had consigned her, God will give her many offspring (v. 10). She will bear a son whose name, 'Ishmael' ('God listens'), will testify to the fact that 'Yhwh has given heed to your affliction' (vv. 11–12). So her son will not live in the desert where she, the slave-girl, is now staying but as 'a wild ass of a man ... he shall live over against all his brothers' (v. 13; *espace vécu*/'third-space').

---

[5] B. Jacob, *Das erste Buch der Tora: Genesis* (Berlin: Schocken, 1934 / New York: KTAV, 1974), 412.
[6] For terminology in a theory of space, cf. H. Lefebvre, *La production de l'espace* (Paris: Anthropos, 1974; translated by D. Nicholson-Smith, *The Production of Space*, Oxford: Blackwell, 1991).

With this prophecy, the exchange of questions and answers between Yhwh's messenger and Hagar brings the story to an interim end, however, it flares up when Hagar accepts his command by addressing him under a new name which reflects their encounter: 'You are God of seeing' (v. 13a).[7] The subsequent explanation in the form of a question appeals to an audience, and presents the content as irrefutable: 'Have I really not seen here after he has seen me?' (v. 13b).[8] In this way, she presents the name which she has personally given to Yhwh's messenger, to the larger public, larger even than her own offspring. Thereupon, either the messenger himself or people in general (3rd pers. sing.)[9] elaborate this by integrating Hagar's experience of God in the name of the well: 'Spring of the Living who sees me' (v. 14: 'Beër Lachai Roï'). If it is the messenger, he leaves his footprint 'Living,' besides Hagar's confession, in the name of the well. Thus, this place is more than a geographic indication of Hagar's escape-route. It invites passers-by to reply, in whatever way, to Hagar's self-reflection ('Have I really not seen...?'). With regard to the question of Abram's progeny, the Hagar-scene forms a delay of the denouement. This is embodied in two names: 'Ishmael,' 'God listens,' and 'Hachai Roï,' 'The living who sees me'.

6. Abraham and Sarah to Yhwh (Genesis 17:1–22; 18:1–15)

After Hagar has given birth to Ishmael, Yhwh's intention to grant Abraham a physical son seems to have been achieved (16:15–16), however, the related question, raised by both Abraham and Sarah, revives the topic of progeny. When God promises Abraham in the aftermath of his covenant that he will be given a son from his legal wife Sarah, the patriarch asks himself: 'Can a child be born to a man who is a hundred years old? Can Sarah, who is ninety years old, bear a child?' (17:16–17). Parallel to this, Sarah wonders at the visit of the three men, *alias* Yhwh: 'After

---

[7] I interpret רָאִי in v. 13a as a noun (st. abs.), 'seeing,' and neither as a noun with poss. pron., 'my seeing' (Jacob, *Genesis*, 414), nor as part. with pers. pron., 'seeing me'; cf. Wénin, *Abraham*, 130–131: 'Elle voit celui qui a vu' est le seul personnage biblique qui a l'audace de donner à Dieu un nom inédit'.

[8] An adequate interpretation of the rare expression אַחֲרֵי רֹאִי in v. 13b is complicated (cf. Lev 13:56; 14:36). In my view, רֹאִי is a part. with pers. pron., 'seeing me'. The whole clause is cryptic because two elements are lacking: an object of 'I have seen' and a subject determination of 'seeing me'. Anyhow, the suffix 'me' is the plus of Hagar's explanation (v. 13b) as compared with her naming of God (v. 13a). Wénin, *Abraham*, 395, appropriately refers to Gen 22:14; Exod 3:6–7.

[9] Wénin, *Abraham*, 131.

I have grown old, and my husband is old, shall I have pleasure?' (18:12). Both Abraham and Sarah raise their question while 'laughing' (צחק) and 'saying in his heart/ saying to herself' (אמר בקרב / אמר בלב). 'To laugh' need not stand for rejection or mockery, but rather for the inability to adequately react to something done or claimed by others.[10] The literary form of a question strengthens this embarrassment. What is being announced to Abraham and Sarah, does not square with people's experience of the course of life.

Yhwh's reply to the disbelieving question that Abraham and Sarah share, is reported in two scenes (17:18–22 and 18:12–15).[11] In both, Yhwh refutes the argument of their age by nothing else than his speaking authority. In the first scene, God simply confirms to Abraham that Sarah will bear a son, to be called Isaac, and he adds the promise of an everlasting covenant, even for Isaac's offspring (17:19, cf. 17:16). Abraham reacts to the promise of a physical son in a positive but restricted way by praying for his son Ishmael, borne by Hagar (v. 18), and later on, he does the same by circumcising him and all his house (vv. 23–27). Yet for the moment, he keeps silent concerning a son borne by Sarah. From the rhetorical point of view this means a flight, and from the narrative point of view it creates an 'expectancy'. The narrator has not yet told how it ends; there is still something to tell the reader.

The speech-direction in the second scene (18:1–15) compensates this expectation with a play of 'a question in the question'. To begin with, Yhwh *alias* the visitor asks Abraham to see Sarah, apparently in order to involve her in their conversation (v. 9), and then he delivers his promise: 'I will surely return to you (*sg.*) in due season, and your wife Sarah shall have a son' (v. 10). Thus, the narrator presents Abraham and Sarah together as the addressees of the promise. Next, not Abraham's reaction 'under the tree,' which could be an act of confidence, but that of Sarah 'at the tent entrance' follows: 'Sarah laughed by herself, saying: "After I have grown old, and my husband is old, shall I have pleasure?"' (v. 12). This leads the visitor to ask two new questions: (1) 'Why did Sarah laugh and say: "Shall I indeed bear a child, now that I am old?"' (v. 13);

---

[10] B. Janowski, *Anthropologie des Alten Testaments: Grundfragen – Kontexte – Themenfelder* (Tübingen: Mohr Siebeck, 2019), 164–166; Jacob, *Genesis*, 445.

[11] For an elaborate analysis of the intricate parallelism between the two passages which, at the same time, are connected by narrative progress, cf. Wénin, *Abraham*, 167–172. This thesis relies, moreover, on the research of J.P. Fokkelman, *Narrative Art in Genesis: Specimens of Stylistic and Structural Analysis* (SSN 17; Assen: Van Gorcum, 1975).

(2) 'Is anything too wonderful for Yhwh?' (v. 14a). The two questions cohere; actually, they are statements asking for distancing in such a way that departure from the first opinion relies on departure from the second. Should Sarah, through Abraham, reply to the first question that their age does indeed exclude fertility, Yhwh *alias* the visitor rejects this response in advance by claiming that for Yhwh nothing is impossible. Consequently, the visitor repeats and confirms his preceding promise to Abraham: 'Sarah will have a son' (v. 14b, cf. v. 10).

It is not Abraham who responds to both questions. Sarah, on the contrary, does so, yet not to the second question about Yhwh's omnipotence, only to the cloaked first question: 'Why did Sarah laugh?' (cf. v. 13). She denies the fact itself: 'I did not laugh' (v. 15a); the visitor, however, confirms the fact: 'Oh yes, you did laugh' (v. 15b).[12] The narrator presents the visitor as being right (v. 12), for by way of an excuse, he adds: 'For she was afraid' (v. 15a). In this way, the story gets a remarkably open end, the more so since this is the first and only time that God addresses Sarah. Behind this unsettled question, the main question does not get a response: 'Is anything too wonderful for Yhwh?' (v. 14a). Sarah's denial of having laughed does not mean that she denies God's omnipotence. That question will only be answered 'at the set time ... in due season' (v. 14b anticipates 21:1–7). Therefore, the implied reader can join her in looking forward to that event.[13]

7. Yhwh to himself and to Abraham (Genesis 18:16–33)

There is a fairly broad consensus that the story of Abraham's intercession for Sodom has a literary-historical origin of its own but is redactionally connected to the preceding episode by the opening and the concluding location (cf. v. 16: 'Then the men set out from there, and they looked toward Sodom; and Abraham went with them to set them on their way'; v. 33: 'And Yhwh went his way, when he had finished speaking to Abraham; and Abraham returned to his place'). From the narrative angle, Yhwh's subsequent interior monologue should not be understood as taking place at the outset of the men's journey, but as a looking back on an

---

[12] The text is ambiguous: the subject of v. 15b ('he said') can refer to both the speaker Yhwh and the person addressed in v. 13. According to Ramban, Abraham is speaking here; cf. M. Zlotowitz, *Bereishis: Genesis*, Volume II (ArtScroll Tanach Series; Brooklyn: Mesorah Publications, 1978), 647. However, this hardly fits the refined structure of the speech direction in Gen 17:1–18:33.

[13] Cf. Wénin, *Abraham*, 189–191.

earlier decision of God.[14] It dominates both their preceding visit to Abraham and Sarah, and their actual journey to Sodom in Abraham's company: 'Yhwh *had said* (ויהוה אמר): "Shall I hide[15] from Abraham what I am about to do, seeing that Abraham shall become a great and mighty nation, and all the nations of the earth shall be blessed in him? No, for I have chosen him, that he may charge his children and his household after him to keep the way of Yhwh by doing righteousness and justice" – so that Yhwh may bring about for Abraham what he has promised him' (vv. 17–19). In the last clause of v. 19b, the implied speaker of the story seems to step in, adding what in his view the purpose of God's dealing is: the realisation of his promise to Abraham.[16] In this way, Yhwh's plan to grant Abraham offspring includes serious solicitude about their righteousness. There should be righteous progeny or no progeny at all, and the former purpose would best be served if God took Abraham into confidence.

From the specific angle of this research, however, the question-form requires attention. Why does the narrator mention only now that Yhwh has wondered whether he should inform the patriarch about what he plans to do, namely 'to go down and see whether they have done altogether according to the outcry that has come to me; and if not, I will know' (v. 21)? Is it feasible that Yhwh had an argument not to do so? Abraham cannot be the addressee of this information about God's doubtfulness, for he is the subject matter; only the implied reader can be addressee. He learns that Yhwh might have hidden from Abraham what he intended to do. In that case, the outcome of the story would have gone without saying. Abraham would not have joined Yhwh on his way to the sinful cities and Abraham would not have interceded for them. In other words, by deciding to involve Abraham in his plan to inspect and chastise Sodom and Gomorrah, Yhwh took the risk that Abraham would even meddle in this venture. Thus, seen narratively, the question: 'Shall I hide from Abraham?' is not rhetorical at all. Negatively answered, it might create unease for God himself, because Abraham, as a persistent partner, will

---

[14] Cf. Jacob, *Genesis*, 446–447; M. Buber and F. Rosenzweig, *Die Fünf Bücher der Weisung* (Köln: Hegner, 1968), 48. The speaking direction of vv. 16–23 with the narrative ending in v. 33 argue for this, as well as the word-order in v. 17 (ויהוה אמר; w^e + subject + *qatal*) in contrast with v. 20 (ויאמר יהוה; *wayyiqtol* + subject). For *qatal* as a *past perfect*. cf. *GKC* §106 f, p; 111 g; Joüon §112 c; 118 d.

[15] 'Shall I hide (המכסה)?': the participle stands for the immediately present time.

[16] Assuming a change of speaker is syntactically based on the 3rd pers. for Yhwh from v. 19b on *(courtesy Archibald van Wieringen)*.

come up with the argument: 'Shall not the judge of all the earth do what is just?' (v. 25; cf. v. 28).

8. Sarah and everyone who hears (Genesis 21:1-7)

The topic of Abraham's progeny does not play an explicit role in the story of Sodom's ruin, Lot's rescue and the conflict with Abimelech (Genesis 19–20). It returns in Sarah's question at the birth of Isaac (Genesis 21:1-7). The beginning of this story contrasts with the end of the previous one: 'For Yhwh had closed fast all the wombs of the house of Abimelech because of Sarah, Abraham's wife' (20:18). This story continues the story of Abraham's visitors who promised him a son by Sarah (18:1-15). The narrator resumes its essential elements: 'Yhwh visited Sarah as he had said.... Yhwh did for Sarah as he had promised.... Sarah conceived ... she bore Abraham a son in his old age ... at the time of which God had spoken to him' (21:1-2). New is the mention that Abraham named his son 'Isaac' (v. 3), in connection, of course, with the boy's circumcision according to God's earlier command (v. 4; cf. 17:22). At that occasion, the name Isaac was not explained (17:19), and at the prediction of his birth, it was not mentioned (18:10, 14). Now Abraham, as father, announces the name (v. 3), and Sarah, as mother, explains it (vv. 6–7):

> ⁶ *Sarah said: 'God has brought laughter for me; everyone who hears will laugh with me'.* ⁷ *And she said: 'Who would ever have proclaimed to Abraham: "Sarah nurses sons"'? Yet I have borne him a son in his old age'.*

Sarah's first statement in v. 6 follows the basic pattern of a thanksgiving: 'Yhwh has saved...' and 'Those who hear it will....' So, she announces God's action ('to bring' ['to make'], עשׂה; cf. v. 1: 'to do') 'for her' (*dativus commodi*), and the reaction of the people around: 'Everyone who hears it will laugh (יצחק) with me'. Thereby she refers to her meeting with the visitors *alias* Yhwh and her reply, namely her 'laugh,' to his announcing a son (cf. 18:12-15). The connection between the two events is irrefutable, but the pattern of actors differs. Sarah's laughing now alludes to the name Isaac (v. 3), but also to her discussion then with Yhwh, whether or not she had laughed about what he then said (18:12-15). Sarah does not decide on that moot point, she rather rearranges the dispute: it is anyhow God's work that laughing occurs. What matters is not that she (subject) laughed at that time (*pace* some translations), but rather that people who learn that she has borne a son to Abraham will laugh with her now (indirect object).[17] So this new event of laughing is 'an explanatory expression of praise in derision of her earlier sceptical laughter'.[18]

Sarah's second statement in v. 7 alludes, according to many exegetes, to the ancient custom that the birth of a child is reported to the father so that he may accept it as his progeny.[19] Against this explanation it should, first of all, be argued that the verb מלל, 'to proclaim,' signifies publicly speaking with some authority and certainty (cf. Psalm 106:2; Job 8:2; 33:3; Sirach 35:3).[20] In the case of family-talk about the birth of a single son, one would rather expect the verb נגד *hiph.* with the noun בן in the singular. Secondly, the expression 'to nurse (breastfeed) children' (היניקה בנים) fits more with practical motherhood than with responsible fatherhood. These semantics, together with the literary form of a question, promote the interpretation that the presumed reply to Sarah's question: 'Who would ever have proclaimed to Abraham…?' is not 'no one' but 'God'.[21]

In short, Sarah praises Yhwh in her first statement because he has brought her the recognition ('to laugh with') of all who hear about the birth of her son Isaac, and in her second statement because God has proven what he claimed to Abraham at their meeting: 'Is anything too wonderful for Yhwh?' (18:14). The fact that Sarah, 'old, advanced in age' (18:11–12), can now nurse children, demonstrates that for him indeed, nothing is out of the question. Taken together, Sarah's two statements dispel the unease about her laughing which Yhwh's visitor brought into the open by his twofold question (18:13–14). This unease has accompanied the topic of progeny for Abraham from its very beginning when God ordered Abraham to depart from Haran/Ur (Genesis 12:1). Now that God's promise has been fulfilled, the subject can be concluded, apart from the fact that, nothing being too wonderful for Yhwh, matters may lead to new events. This chance remains open.

---

[17] The syntactical parallelism of צחק עשה לי אלהים with כל־השמע יצחק־לי advises to interpret לי in the second clause as the indirect object of 'to laugh,' i.e. 'to smile at,' i.e. 'congratulate,' not as direct object, i.e. 'to laugh about'.

[18] Jacob, *Genesis*, 749–750.

[19] C. Westermann, *Genesis 12–36* (BKAT 1/2; Neukirchen-Vluyn: Neukirchener Verlag, 1981), 403–410.

[20] Zlotowitz, *Bereishis*, 750.

[21] Concerning מי + verb in *qatal* as a rhetorical question which expects 'God' as the answer, Jacob, *Genesis*, 479, refers to Exod 3:11; 2 Kgs 10:22; Isa 23:8; 40:12, 26; 41:2, 4, 26. This explanation is found with Rashi and Redaq.

9. God's messenger to Hagar (Genesis 21:8–21) and Isaac to Abraham (Genesis 22:1–19)

In the story of God's testing of Abraham, the topic of his offspring turns up. With it, the preceding story, Abraham's dismissal of Hagar and her son, cannot be left out of consideration. In several regards, Abraham's two sons, Ishmael, and Isaac, form a diptych: with them, the survival of Abraham's progeny is at stake. As for Ishmael, Abraham has acknowledged him as his offspring (17:18, 23), and God has explicitly integrated Ishmael into the promise that he will bless Abraham and make his son by Hagar into 'a great nation' (17:20; 21:13). While the respective relations of the two sons with their father differ (16:15; 21:11–13; 25:5–9), each of them plays a role in God's plan with Abraham and is consequently saved (21:15–20; 22:17–18). Since this study concerns questions and answers concerning the topic of Abraham's offspring, we start with the meeting of God's messenger with Hagar in chapter 21, when the slave-mother sat down in the desert with her son:

> [17] *God heard the voice of the boy; and the messenger of God called to Hagar from heaven, and said to her: 'What troubles you, Hagar? Do not be afraid; for God has heard the voice of the boy where he is.* [18] *Come, lift up the boy and hold him fast with your hand, for I will make a great nation of him'.* [19] *Then God opened her eyes and she saw a well of water ... and gave the boy a drink.*

The question of Yhwh's messenger evokes his question at their first meeting: 'Hagar, slave-girl of Sarai, where have you come from and where are you going?' (16:8; cf. *5. The messenger of Yhwh to Hagar (Genesis 16)*). That time, he apparently knew her, but she was surprised by his greeting (16:13). This time, he refers to Ishmael's present situation and name, 'God hears,' which was given then by God himself (16:11) and is now the grounds for his rescue (21:17: 'Do not be afraid. God has heard.'). Hagar, as opposed to Sarah who entered into a dispute with Yhwh *alias* the visitor (18:13–15), simply executes the messenger's command without amazement or any comment: 'God opened her eyes, and she saw a well of water ... and gave the boy a drink' (v. 19). This action fits the purpose of the story: it demonstrates that God effectively puts into practice what he promises, in this case what the boy's name Ishmael signifies: 'God hears' (v. 17; cf. 16:11).[22]

---

[22] J.G. Janzen and J.T. Noble, "Did Hagar Give Ishmael up for Dead? Gen. 21.14–21 Re-visited," *JSOT* 44 (2020): 517–531.

While the event embroiders on the messenger's first intervention (Genesis 16), his question in 21:17 forms a parallel to Isaac's question in the next story, the so-called 'binding of Isaac' (Genesis 22):

> [7] *Isaac said to his father Abraham: 'Father!' And he said: 'Here I am, my son'. He said: 'The fire and the wood are here, but where is the lamb for a burnt offering?'* [8] *Abraham said: 'God will see for himself the lamb for a burnt offering, my son'. So the two of them walked on together...* [14] *So Abraham called that place: 'Yhwh will see'.*

The parallel of Yhwh 'hearing' Ishmael (21:17) with him 'seeing' the lamb (22:8, 14) has an inverse parallel of the 'seeing' and 'hearing' of the beneficiaries of God's acting: 'Hagar saw a well of water' (21:19) and Abraham is praised 'since you have heard to my voice' (22:18 – literal translation). The double semantic parallelism functions in the question that arose with the birth of Isaac: What will be the relationship of Abraham's two sons, Ishmael and Isaac (anticipated in 17:19–21)? Sarah's view regarding that question (21:10: 'The son of this slave-woman shall not inherit along with my son Isaac') is certainly surpassed by the messenger's intervention: 'I will make him a great nation' (21:18). So, God's promise for Ishmael (16:10) is not annulled by the same for Isaac (18:14, 18; 22:17).

Taken by itself, the scene of Abraham and Isaac walking together as father and son, shows that the promise of offspring for Abraham has been accomplished.[23] However, Isaac's question in the intermezzo carries a dramatic load in light of God's command at the beginning of the story: 'Take your son, your only son Isaac, whom you love, and go to the land of Moriah, and have him go up there for a burnt offering on one of the mountains that I shall tell you' (22:2). Many authors have pointed to the plural meaning of 'to have someone go up' (עלה *hiph*.).[24] It comes to the fore in the strange preparation of the journey and the offering itself (vv. 3–9). It arrives at a crucial point in Isaac's unequivocal question regarding the sacrificial animal, and in Abraham's ambiguous reply: 'God himself will provide the lamb for a burnt offering, my son' (v. 8). Suffices for this study: with Isaac's question, the very existence of Abraham's progeny is at stake, however, Abraham entrusts this matter to Yhwh. This comes to light in the conclusion of the story: 'So Abraham

---

[23] The topic of Abraham's progeny returns in 24:7 for a last time in the Abraham composition (not in a question) before passing in 26:3 into the *toledot* of Isaac (from 25:19).

[24] *DCH* 4 (1998): 411–412.

called that place "Yhwh will see"; as it is said to this day: "On the mount of Yhwh it shall be seen"' (v. 14). Consequently, Yhwh gives evidence under oath that he will protect Abraham's offspring (vv. 15–18). He does so in richer phrases than ever before, and with the outspoken argument: 'because you have not withheld your son, your only son ... and have listened to my voice' (vv. 16, 18). The end of the story: 'So Abraham returned to his young men, and they arose and went together to Beer-Sheba' (v. 19) suggests that Isaac remains as an everlasting icon on the mount called by Abraham: 'on the mount of Yhwh it shall be seen' (v. 14).

In reading sequence, the questions of the messenger and Isaac are raised after the promise of a physical offspring for Abraham has come true. As opposed to questions that occur during the implementation of that promise (in Genesis 12:1–22:19), they bear resemblance insofar they initiated events which proved the trustworthiness of what God had achieved in Abraham. Therefore, these questions do not create unease within the story. Hagar went through an ordeal which was appeased by the question of God's messenger, who opened her eyes for the well of water. Abraham went through an ordeal that was initiated by God himself and brought to a climax by his son's question, yet got an answer when he saw the ram on the mountain. The well of 'the God of seeing' (16:13) and the mountain where 'Yhwh will see' (22:14) remain as a guarantee for Abraham's offspring.

10. Conclusion

The composite of Genesis 11:27–25:18 contains some question-and-answer events which link the pledge of Abraham's progeny into a narrative string. Unease surrounds each occurrence, yet it is the spirit leading to the fulfilment of the promise, with the birth of Isaac. From that event on (21:1–7), unease gives way to trust in Yhwh's actual maintenance of the offspring (21:8–21; 22:1–19). This regards, of course, the actants within the story, yet the text-immanent reader is not excluded. This textual construct is, of course, the over-all addressed partner of the narrator, yet at some points, he is, in an aside, aimed at by one of the actors. This does not affect the indispensable structure of the question-and-answer process, yet it is more than an incidental benefit. It bears on the following texts.

First, Hagar's demand for consent, directed to the larger public who may pass by the well she has named: 'Have I really not seen here after he has seen me?' (16:13). The second and third occurrences are intimately connected, for they have to do with Sarah's laughing. The visitor's challenge: 'Is anything too wonderful for Yhwh?' (18:14) together with Sarah's tempting confession: 'Who would ever have proclaimed to Abraham: "Sarah nurses sons"?' (21:7) call for shared amazement about the coming of progeny for Abraham. The fourth occurrence is elicited by Isaac's question: 'Where is the lamb for a burnt offering?' (22:7) and meets the implied reader when Abraham attributes to the place of his offering the name 'Yhwh will provide'. The narrator remarks: 'As it is said to this day: "On the mount of Yhwh it shall be provided" ' (22:14). In short, near Hagar's well, at the entrance of Sarah's tent and on the mountain of Abraham's loyalty, readers are called to share in the unease and give voice to it.

QUESTIONS IN NUMBERS 11

Penelope BARTER
Tilburg University

1. Introduction

Despite the relative obscurity of the book of Numbers, chapter 11 is well known for its engaging story, and the complex interplay of at least two narrative strands. This contribution focuses specifically on the role of questions in Numbers 11, asking how they function within their own narrative strands and in the text as a whole. The received text offers an ambiguous picture, especially of Moses and his role as the leader of Israel, but a focus on the questions posed in the dialogue can offer new perspectives and help to uncover the artistry in the final form.

This study will first briefly discuss the unity and disunity in Numbers 11, before looking more closely at specific questions and responses in the two narrative strands independently. Finally, we will consider the role and function of these questions in the combined text, arguing that a focus on questions can help us to better interpret the enigmatic relationships between Moses and Yhwh on the one hand and Moses and the people on the other. In particular, this analysis of questions in Numbers 11 will demonstrate that the combined narrative paints a more ambiguous picture of Moses.

2. The Problem of Numbers 11

The literary shape of Numbers 11, and the questions it raises, are well-known. The received form of the narrative is a combination of two discrete strands: one concerning the people's desire for meat, and the other reporting the placing of the spirit of Yhwh on the elders, that they might share the burden of leadership with Moses.[1] This unusual text is most

---

[1] A division akin to this has been identified in scholarship since at least 1900, when J. Estlin Carpenter and G. Harford-Battersby, *The Hexateuch according to the Revised Version* (Volume 2, London: Longmans, Green, and Co., 1900), 202 argued that Num 11:4–25 "reveals a dual origin. The communication of the spirit to the seventy elders in 16, 24b–30 is plainly independent of the demand for flesh meat and the plague which punished the voracity of the people."

likely the result of redactional activity, namely the compilation of two independent narratives. Using plot as the primary guideline, the text can be divided into an introduction consisting of the etymology of Taberah (11:1–3), a plague story (11:4–15, 18–24a, 31–35) and an elders story (11:16–17, 24b–30).

Compared to other examples of combined narratives in the Torah (such as Genesis 6–9), the reader is encountered here with an unusual composite, where it appears that two stories with entirely different plotlines have been brought together.[2] One, which I here name the 'plague story' describes the complaint of the people concerning their diet in the wilderness – they wished for meat instead of only manna – and Moses and Yhwh's subsequent anger. As a result, a punishment is brought upon the people: while they are biting into the plentiful meat that they desired, Yhwh strikes them with a plague, and many are killed. The other story, here called the 'elders story,' reports the settling of the spirit on seventy elders, and the unintended consequence that Eldad and Medad begin to prophesy in the camp. The combined text is not completely incoherent, but it seems to be the case that coherency was established on the grounds of the shared theme of leadership, rather than on the basis of plot. Indeed, when these events are referred to in Psalm 78:17–30 and briefly in Psalm 106:14–15, they mention only a plague tradition.[3]

---

[2] This approximate division, as well as the argument that a compositional divide is indicated, is supported by the majority of commentators. See e.g. A. Kuenen, *An Historico-Critical Inquiry into the Origin and Composition of the Hexateuch* (trans. Philip H. Wicksteed; London: Macmillan, 1886), 158; G. Buchanan Gray, *A Critical and Exegetical Commentary on Numbers* (New York: Scribner, 1903), 97–119; H. Holzinger, *Numeri* (Kurzer Hand-Commentar zum alten Testament 4; Tübingen: Mohr, 1903), 41–43; E. Blum, *Studien zur Komposition des Pentateuch* (BZAW 189; Berlin: de Gruyter, 1990), 83; B.D. Sommer, "Reflecting on Moses: The Redaction of Numbers 11," *JBL* 118 (1999): 601–624, here 604; J.S. Baden, *The Composition of the Pentateuch: Renewing the Documentary Hypothesis* (AYBRL; New Haven: Yale University Press, 2012), 82–102. For more detail on this argument, see Sommer, "Reflecting on Moses," 601–602, and Joel Baden's detailed study of the text in *The Composition of the Pentateuch*, 82–102. Although I do not hold to the neo-Documentary Hypothesis, Baden's detailed analysis helps to demonstrate both the coherence of the individual narratives and the elegance in their redaction.

[3] I find Sommer's argument about the importance of the named psalms very reasonable: "It is unlikely that the narrative in Psalm 78 is based on the pentateuchal text. Jacob Milgrom points out that in Ps 78:27, the quail fall within the camp itself, while in Num 11:31, they fall outside the camp. The variation suggests that the Psalm and Numbers depend on an older tradition but not on each other." (Sommer, "Reflecting on Moses," 605). While it is entirely possible to hold to both an originally independent plague tradition and the literary unity of Numbers 11, I consider this supporting evidence for the theory that Numbers 11 is a compositionally complex text.

Of course, this division is not unanimous, and whether this indicates compositional breaks, or simply interwoven elements of a unified story, is still debated. For example, Martin Noth considers this a story from the Jahwist about a complaint and plague, with some additions. He proposes that verses 14–15 belong with verses 16–17, but that all four verses are an addition to the earlier story. In other words, Noth believed that the gathering of elders was a direct response to Moses' complaint about the burden of leading this people, rather than suggesting that the two issues are linked only by the juxtaposition of two different stories.[4] Timothy Ashley also sees multiple verses (namely 14–15, 21–23, and 35) as 'transitions' between the two plotlines, though he goes on to argue that the text must be a compositional unity, on the grounds that what remains of each story is fragmentary.[5] However, since Ashley identifies some key verses as 'transitions' rather than as part of the narrative itself, it is quite natural that the remaining text will appear incomplete.

Since the purpose of this study is not to launch a full defence of redactional activity in Numbers 11, allow me simply to note the starting point: this study assumes a redactional combination of two narratives. However, it is not necessary to hold this view to understand the crucial role of questions in this text. First, even if one assumes the literary unity of Numbers 11, almost all the questions under discussion are clearly tied to, and play an important role in, one of the two subplots. Treating the two subplots independently is thus still valuable. Second, regardless of the composition of the text, a focus on questions can still help to reveal the artistry therein: techniques or motives assigned here to a redactor could be considered the work of the author of the combined text.

3. Questions in the Plague Story (Numbers 11:4–15, 18–24a, 31–35)

Interrogatives play a crucial role in the plague story, with each main character posing one or more questions that reveal interpersonal dynamics and serve to move the story forward. All phrases treated in this study as questions will contain an interrogative pronoun (such as מי or למה/מה) or an interrogative ה. Any ambiguities will be discussed in due course.

---

[4] Similarly, although he sees two distinct themes in the text, B. Levine, *Numbers 1–20* (AB 4A; Garden City: Doubleday, 1993), 327–328 reads Numbers 11 as a single narrative.
[5] T.R. Ashley, *The Book of Numbers* (NICOT; Grand Rapids: Eerdmans, 1993), 207.

3.1. *Numbers 11:4*

After a short narrative about the naming of Taberah in verses 1–3, the plague story begins with the greedy rabble and the sons of Israel asking מי יאכלנו בשר ('Who will feed us meat?').[6] It is possible to translate this interrogative sentence as an exclamation ('Would that we had meat to eat!') but I think there are good reasons to understand this as a genuine question, rather than an exclamatory question.[7] The complaint that follows makes a direct comparison between the apparent plenty of Egypt (fish, cucumbers, melons, leeks, and onions) and the unappetising manna that the people now eat. Yet this complaint – as we will shortly see – prompts an angry outburst from Moses about his leadership, which leads me to favour the more confrontational translation.

However, this question, and the comparison with Egypt that it leads to in verse 5, raise some immediate problems for careful readers, which have been well-documented by other commentators. As Rashi noted, the people's demand for meat makes little sense when the people are often said to be accompanied by a large amount of livestock.[8] Indeed, the phrase used to describe the rabble and introduce the question (התאוו תאוה; 'they craved a craving') already implies that the desire may be excessive: as noted by Baruch Levine, the root אוה in Hithpael 'most often, if not always, connotes an improper or excessive desire.'[9] Further, although the people demand meat or flesh (בשר), they draw comparisons to the fish, fruits, and vegetables they ate in Egypt.[10]

---

[6] All translations from Hebrew are my own.
[7] See also A.B. Davidson, *Introductory Hebrew Grammar: Hebrew Syntax* (2nd ed; Edinburgh: T&T Clark, 1896), 183 [§ 135]; GKC, 476 [§ 151a n3], *IBHS*, 315–316 [§ 18.1a-c]. An exclamatory question is an interrogative with the force of an exclamatory statement (e.g. "Aren't you a big boy!"), and thus one sub-category of rhetorical questions. However, as discussed above, the present study has not rendered it an exclamatory question, which less commonly incite a response.
[8] Exod 12:38; 17:3; 19:3; 34:5; Num 14:33; 32:1. In Exod 17:3, the livestock are at risk of dying from thirst.
[9] Levine, *Numbers 1–20*, 321.
[10] J. Milgrom, *Numbers* (The JPS Torah Commentary; Philadelphia: Jewish Publication Society, 1989), 83 addresses these first two issues neatly, suggesting that verse 4 'seems to stem from a tradition that did not credit the Israelites with possessing livestock' and that the בשר desired by the people 'meant fish ... a plentiful and cheap commodity in Egypt'. The second point is somewhat less compelling than the first: if the author intended בשר to be understood as 'fish,' we need to account for the decision to choose the less specific term (covering meat, sacrificial meat, and both human and non-human flesh) in the people's central statement. Levine, *Numbers 1–20*, 321 discusses the specific foods desired by the people in more detail, calling the list of foods 'entirely appropriate' and 'strikingly realistic.' I interpret his discussion of ancient Egyptian

Despite these issues, or perhaps because of them, this outburst from the people has a crucial function in the story. Without this question, their complaint stands simply as a statement of their perceived hardship, without necessarily inciting a response. Moreover, the question clearly challenges the current leadership, since it is not only a desire for meat, but a query as to *who* will feed it to them, with the implication that Moses either cannot or will not. Whether this question shows a kind of learned helplessness, suggests a food supply issue, or is simply a particular manifestation of a general longing for Egypt, it demonstrates a marked distrust in the current leader: Moses and/or Yhwh cannot be counted on to provide. The issue, to quote Timothy Ashley, is that 'the contrast drawn by the people between the plenty of slavery and the *nothing at all* (except manna) of their freedom ... is seen as rebellion against God the Liberator'.[11]

As we will see, the response to the question confirms this: the narrator's response is to interrupt the story altogether with an aside about the nature of manna, and Moses and Yhwh's responses are to be displeased and angry respectively (though without immediately answering the question).

3.2. *Numbers 11:11–13*

After the complaint of verses 4–6, the story is put briefly on hold to introduce a description of manna's qualities and preparation in verses 7–9. This short pause between question and response is seemingly an opportunity to show the reader that the manna which the people find so unappealing (verse 5) is in fact 'tasty and choice.'[12] That said, there are also clear benefits of this aside for the purpose of storytelling: the question and complaint do not receive an immediate answer, but are left hanging

---

cuisine as supporting his argument that the desire for meat is confusing alongside the people's comparison to non-meat foods. While I agree in part with this overall argument, whether or not the list of foods is realistic seems less relevant unless the text is given a very early date of composition.

[11] Ashley, *Numbers*, 208.

[12] T.E. Fretheim, "7. Numbers," in: John Barton and John Muddiman (Eds.), *The Oxford Bible Commentary* (Oxford: Oxford University Press, 2001), 110–134, here 119. As Gray, *Numbers*, 105 rightly points out, 'Taken by itself the present account does not suggest that the manna was miraculously provided – the prevalent view elsewhere (Ex. 16, Dt. 8^{3,16}, Neh. 9^{15,20}, Ps. 78$^{23-25}$ 105^{40}). The writer speaks of it as a natural product of the desert.' For this reason, I find it difficult to read this aside as a reminder of positive divine intervention on behalf of the complaining Israelites; *contra*, e.g., Dennis T. Olson, *Numbers* (IBC; Louisville: John Knox Press, 1996), 65.

in the air, offering the reader an opportunity to themselves formulate an opinion. When the narrative thread resumes, the response to the people's weeping is anger from Yhwh and disapproval from Moses. What follows is a stream of questions from Moses, directed to Yhwh:

> *Why have you done your servant wrong? And why have I not found favour in your sight, that you place the burden of all this people on me? Was it me who conceived all this people? Was it I who bore them, that you should say to me, 'Carry them in your bosom like the nurse[13] carries the nursing child, to the ground which you swore to their fathers.'*[14] (Numbers 11:11aα₂–12)

and finally, the apparent reason for the conversation:

> *From where am I to get meat to give to all this people? For they weep before me, saying 'Give us meat so we may eat!'* (Numbers 11:13)

The initial two questions are marked as such with למה; the third with an interrogative ה, and the final question begins מאין ('whence?'). The formulation of the outburst, including the questions, is interesting. Moses' self-reference as 'your servant' introduces a deferential tone, as evidenced by similar uses of the expression in both biblical and extrabiblical material.[15] On the other hand, למה often carries an accusatory, defensive, or expostulatory tone, and the content of the questions in these verses supports this interpretation.[16] Instead of a direct response to the people's complaint, or a plea with Yhwh to provide meat for them, Levine notes

---

[13] With an object (as is the case here), the Qal masculine participle of אמן indicates a guardian (2 Kgs 10:1, 5; Isa 49:23; Est 2:7), while the feminine form אמנת is often translated 'nurse' (2 Sam 4:4; Ruth 4:16). Although the masculine form is present here, I see no reason to follow a presumed dichotomy in English, since both 'guardian' and 'nurse' can apply equally to all genders.

[14] Num 11:12aβ-b is often read as a continuation of the question asked in the initial clause (i.e. 'Was it me who conceived all this people, was it I who bore them, that you should say to me…?'). Here I have rendered the two questions separately, partly to highlight the number of questions in the speech, and partly to better display the structure of verse 12 as a whole. The double rhetorical question (that is, where the question appears to be an either/or question, but where both elements are rhetorical) is relatively frequent in Biblical Hebrew prose and poetry – see also M. Held, "Rhetorical Questions in Ugaritic and Biblical Hebrew," *Eretz-Israel* 9 (1969): 71–79, here 72–73.

[15] The expression can be found in Old Babylonian CAD A. 2.25, s.v. *ardu*, e, and letters from Lachish and Arad; see D. Pardee and S. David Sperling (Eds.), *Handbook of Ancient Hebrew Letters: A Study Edition* (SBLSBS 15; Chico: Scholars Press, 1982), 157–159. Useful comparisons from the Torah include Lot addressing the messengers (Gen 19:2, 19), Jacob addressing Esau via a messenger (Gen 32:5), and Moses addressing Yhwh (Exod 4:10) – all three use the phrase to show deference to the addressee.

[16] Other examples of למה introducing this kind of confrontational question in the Torah include Gen 12:18; 27:45; 44:4; Exod 5:15, 22; Num 14:41.

that 'Moses does not castigate the people for their sinfulness, but instead confronts YHWH with the problems caused by his position as leader of the Israelites.'[17]

It seems clear, then, that Moses has interpreted the initial question in v. 4 as one pertaining to his leadership. That said, we need not necessarily distinguish food supply problems from leadership altogether, since one of the roles of a leader is to provide for their people and there are other places in the Torah where the two are combined.[18] More than this, however, Moses cites the initial question not as a query, but as a demand: 'Give us meat so we may eat!' (verse 13).[19] This offers an interesting perspective on Moses as leader. He does not seem to think that his leadership is at risk, since he complains about the people making his role more difficult, rather than expressing concern that they may turn away from him. Yet his reaction is also not to chastise the people for rejecting Yhwh's provision, but to chastise Yhwh for giving him the task of leadership in the first place. The function of these questions, then, seems to be manifold. Within the narrative, they show Moses' perception of both the situation and the pressure he is under. For the reader, they highlight the real issue at hand: a power struggle.

3.3. Numbers 11:22–23

After Moses' outburst, verses 16–17 begin the elders story, and it is only in verse 18 that we return to the matter of feeding the people. In verses 18–20, Yhwh finally addresses the people's initial complaint, including a quotation of their original question (in stark contrast to Moses' misrepresentation!), and explains that the people will eat meat until it comes out of their nostrils and is loathsome to them,

> ... *because you have rejected Yhwh, who was in your midst, and you have wept before him, saying, 'Why on earth did we leave Egypt?'* (Numbers 11:20)

The decision of the author to summarise the people's mention of Egypt as a question here is telling. The למה זה formula is stronger than למה alone, and the use of למה with an imperfect is often deprecating or rhe-

---

[17] Levine, *Numbers*, 322.
[18] See, for example, Exod 15:22–26; 17:1–7.
[19] It was acknowledged in 3.1. above that it is possible to read the question in verse 4 as an exclamatory question. Even if this is the case, Moses still introduces a clear imperative into his report of the people's words: compare מי יאכלנו בשר in verse 4 with תנה־לנו בשר in verse 13.

torically indicating something that should or should not be done.[20] In this way, the author ascribes to Yhwh a more critical interpretation of the people's question than originally expressed in verse 4. While the initial wording (מי יאכלנו בשר) could be interpreted as a genuine question and is at face-value quite limited, this rendering in Yhwh's words shows that their question has been understood as a criticism of the exodus. Further still, as explicitly stated earlier in the verse, it has been interpreted as a rejection of Yhwh himself.

Moses immediately retorts with questions, which Yhwh answers with yet another question: 'The people, among whom I am, are 600,000 on foot; but you said, "I will give meat to them, so that they may eat for a month." Will flocks and cattle be slaughtered for them – would that be enough for them? Or if all the fish of the sea were gathered together for them – would *that* be enough for them?' (Numbers 11:21–22)

> *So Yhwh said to Moses, 'Does the hand of Yhwh fall short? Now you will see whether my word will happen for you or not.'* (Numbers 11:23)

Both Moses' and Yhwh's questions are marked as such with an interrogative ה, with the repeated ומצא להם extending Moses' initial question to ask repeatedly (and idiomatically) whether these things would suffice. These questions could feasibly be interpreted as either sarcastic, asking how the appetites of the people could possibly ever be satiated, or genuine, suggesting that Yhwh does not have the requisite power. However, it seems that Yhwh understands the question to be the latter, namely, a challenge to his power. The opening question of his response ('Does the hand of Yhwh fall short?') expects an answer in the negative. Indeed, Moses' challenge to Yhwh's power will be a crucial turning point in the narrative. Rather than providing for the people – an issue which Moses appears very concerned about, despite having never been directly complained *to* – Moses' questions ultimately invoke punishment and even death (verses 31–34).[21]

---

[20] As with other uses with an interrogative pronoun, זה here strengthens the interrogative by adding a certain force to the question (or, per *IBHS*, 323 [§ 18.3b], 'vividness'). A standard English rendering that suits multiple contexts is extremely difficult to find, but here the addition of 'on earth' indicates some of the forcefulness of the question, highlighting the apparent regret of the people (as opposed to a genuine attempt to gain knowledge).

[21] Sommer, "Reflecting on Moses," 613–614 names this as one of three possible interpretations of this passage, all of which indicate a negative portrayal of Moses. For more on Moses' role in (over)hearing the initial complaint, see G. Coats, *Rebellion in the Wilderness: The Murmuring Motif in the Wilderness Traditions of the Old Testament* (Nashville: Abingdon, 1968), 101.

Although the story is far from over, it seems fitting that this question and challenge from Yhwh are the final piece of dialogue in the plague narrative. The final question is one that summarises the story: the questions as to *whether* the people can or should have meat and *why* Moses' leadership is so exhausting are both answered by asking whether Yhwh's provisions and decisions are adequate and inviting the reader to respond affirmatively, contra Moses.

4. Questions in the Elders Story (Numbers 11:16–17, 24b–30)

The elders story is relatively straightforward: Moses is instructed to gather seventy men from among the elders of Israel, and Yhwh will take the spirit that is upon Moses and share it with the seventy, so that they can help to bear Moses' burden. Note that these elders are already leaders of the people in their own right, but that they are now to receive a temporary ability to prophesy, which they do not do again. Or, at least, sixty-eight of them don't. Two men – Eldad and Medad – have remained in the camp, but the spirit rests upon them nonetheless, and they prophesy in the camp. An eager young man runs to tell Moses, and Joshua asks Moses to stop them. In verse 29, Moses responds with a rhetorical question: 'Are you being jealous for my sake? Would that all Yhwh's people were made prophets, that Yhwh would put his spirit upon them!'

The first question is clear enough: beginning with an interrogative ה, it is used to warn Joshua against over-zealousness for Moses' leadership. However, the second part of Moses' response begins ומי, just like the people's opening question did in the plague story. There, the phrase could be translated as either a question ('Who will feed us meat?') or an exclamatory interrogative ('Would that we had meat to eat!'). This example is much harder to read as a true question: the closest workable option is reading as 'Who will set all the people of Yhwh as prophets…?,' but we would expect a preposition on נביאים and the question would make little sense in context.[22]

Milgrom notes that the choice of נביאים ('prophets') in Moses' wish, instead of מתנביאים ('ecstatics'[23]), is significant, arguing that it suggests

---

[22] GKC, 485 [§ 154b] also reads this as 'a new clause beginning with the formula of wishing' and, indeed, the usual translation of Num 11:29b is as an exclamation rather than a question.

[23] The use of נבא in Hithpael suggests a more ecstatic form of prophecy, as shown by its usage in 1 Kgs 18:29 and 1 Sam 18:10 (where it is often translated as 'raved' rather than 'prophesied'), as well as Jer 29:26, where is it explicitly connected with irrational behaviour.

'a desideratum that all of Israel qualify ... to be prophets like Moses himself.'[24] If so, this further strengthens the power of Moses' opening question in the elders story, making the sentiment strikingly clear: Moses is not threatened by sharing his leadership position or the spirit of Yhwh in the slightest, even if there are now two stray prophets in the camp.[25] Once Joshua is put in his place, the question does not elicit further response – Moses and the elders simply return to the camp. Questions have not played a particularly important role in the story, but simply served to admonish Joshua and pre-emptively put to rest any concerns from the reader that Moses did not want to share his special status.

However, although the role of this short text is straightforward enough in the elders story, this question and wish from Moses raises some issues when read in the context of the combined narrative.

5. Questions in the Combined Narrative

When we consider the role of questions in the received form of Numbers 11, two key issues become apparent. First, let us return to the exchange of questions between Moses and Yhwh in the plague story, which saw Moses have an angry outburst about his burden and Yhwh (mis)quote the people's question as 'Why on earth did we leave Egypt?' (למה זה יצאנו ממצרים). Moses retorted with questions about how much should be slaughtered to feed the people, and Yhwh questioned whether Moses (and thereby the reader) thinks that his power is limited. Described like that, the importance of questions in the heated exchange between Moses and Yhwh is obvious. In the combined text, however, this exchange is interrupted: Moses hurls his questions, but then we pause while Yhwh's speech first introduces the elders plotline (vv. 16–17). This pause in the combined narrative has a significant impact. In the received form, the initial response to Moses' questions about food and leadership is a practical one: Yhwh *first* announces the process for relieving Moses' burden and only *secondly* deals with the issue of food and rebellion. Our redactors, then, have cooled off the exchange somewhat, and placed the promise of help for Moses before the admonition of the people at large. Moreover, the response from Yhwh is now twofold, addressing both issues apparently raised by Moses' speech: the concerns about his leadership

---

[24] Milgrom, *Numbers*, 91.
[25] Gray, *Numbers*, 115 takes this further, stating that 'Moses has more at heart the good of the community as a whole than his own personal honour or continued pre-eminence (…) this fine trait in Moses' character as conceived in early Israel stands out clearly.'

role (verses 16–17, cf. verses 11–12, 14–15) and the people's desire for meat (verses 18–20, cf. verse 13). The drawback is that Moses' response now appears somewhat skewed, since his reaction to Yhwh's speech in verses 21–22 is solely concerned with food and is still questioning Yhwh's power. As discussed in 2.3. above, this powerful repartee has important repercussions within the plague story by itself, which are by no means undermined by this take on Moses' character in the combined narrative.

Second, the final question in the text ('Are you being jealous for my sake? Would that all Yhwh's people were made prophets') seems quite strange when read as part of the combined narrative. Earlier on in the combined story, Moses has either sarcastically asked whether any amount of food could ever satisfy the people, or suggested that Yhwh does not have sufficient power to feed them all. Earlier still, Moses claims he would rather die than continue to carry this burden! In the combined text, then, this question is not a mark of humility – or, at the very least, not *only* a mark of humility. Instead, he is a leader so sick of the people that he wishes they all would suffer like he has. This is, of course, not a unique take on the verse – Benjamin Sommer has already argued this.[26] Yet our specific focus on questions leads to a new perspective. In the combined text, the dialogue opens and closes with a מי question or exclamation: 'Who will give us meat to eat?' (מי יאכלנו בשׂר) and 'Would that all Yhwh's people were made prophets' (ומי יתן כל־עם יהוה נביאים). Although I think that the two are to be understood differently (one as question, one as a wish), the similar formulation draws our attention to the parallel. In the elders' story alone, it could read as a mature response to the shared leadership. In the combined text, the natural comparison of the two מי phrases offers an alternative take. The people want meat, because they are fondly remembering their time in Egypt. But why does Moses want shared leadership? Is he too fondly remembering a time in Egypt when life seemed easier than it is now? The combined text does not give nearly as favourable an impression of Moses as when his statement in the elders' story is treated independently, but instead offers a much more ambiguous portrayal of Moses.

6. Concluding Thoughts

What role(s) do the multiple questions play in Numbers 11? When viewed alongside the issue of the text's compositional development, we

---

[26] Sommer, "Reflecting on Moses," 616.

can see that the two narrative strains use their questions in quite different ways. In the plague story, the questions prompt the reader to respond to Moses' challenges by affirming the adequacy of Yhwh's provision and offer a generally unfavourable picture of Moses. In the elders narrative, the rhetorical question and subsequent wish statement from Moses pre-emptively set aside the suggestion of threat to his leadership, painting Moses in a positive light. In the received form of Numbers 11, the combination of these narratives and important redactional choices in the arrangement of the material serve to portray a version of Moses whose character and motivations are much more ambiguous. Indeed, this study has shown the important role of questions in developing this ambiguity. By interrupting the exchange of questions and answers, and enabling questions to play a role in the structure and wider interpretation of the combined text, the redactor places interrogatives front and centre in the interplay of the two disparate narratives. In sum, both the discrete narrative strains and the combined text play with interrogatives to advance the plot, reveal character, and ultimately leave the reader with even more questions.

# QUESTIONS POSED IN DEUTERONOMY 6
Learning and Teaching the Ways of God

Richard J. Bautch
St. Edward's University

1. Introduction

The sixth chapter of Deuteronomy features two references to children who in their own ways learn what is important about God's ways. In this setting, Israelites are told to inscribe their religious values and beliefs upon their children (6:7). Later, one child in particular enquires into the meaning of the decrees, statutes and ordinances that God has enjoined upon this people (6:20). Because the two references to children are aligned as part of a chiasm (vv. 4–9 = A; vv. 20–25 = A'), they draw the reader's attention to questions of a child's agency, a child's voice and a child's ability to pose questions in the world of Deuteronomy.

The two references to children, however, are challenging inasmuch as the characters are unnamed and minimally developed. There is no backstory to either child, nor is the reader brought to appreciate specific details about the two. Because these children are barely visible, a robust methodology is required for this study. In fact, it is a matter of *methodologies* drawing from three different hermeneutics to shine light on the composite figure of the child in Deuteronomy 6.

- This volume on asking questions in biblical texts provides that methodology which is first among equals. In 6:20–25, the child's question about God's decrees, statutes and ordinances, gives rise to a teaching moment. A close reading of this interrogative will show how the child's question functions to convey a message from one character to another while contributing to the rhetorical tradition of Deuteronomy.
- The children in Deuteronomy 6 are 'cameo appearance members,' a concept that Gina Hens-Piazza applies to biblical characters with shadowy silhouettes.[1] In this approach, Hens-Piazza interrogates the story

---

[1] G. Hens-Piazza, *The Supporting Cast of the Bible: Reading on Behalf of the Multitude* (Lanham: Lexington Books/Fortress Academic, 2020), 65–78.

world and the surrounding narrative of these individuals; she investigates the role such characters play in excess of their limited appearance in the story. This study will gauge the contribution that the children as *dramatis personae* make to the account that is unfolding in Deuteronomy 6.

- Our third methodology is informed by the childist approach of Kristine Garroway, who focuses on young characters in biblical texts and considers the opportunities available to them as well as the ways in which the children may question what they are being taught.[2] In Deuteronomy 6, both the incised child and the questioner represent Israelite society's youngest generation who are learning key elements of their ethnic and cultural heritage. Moreover, they are active learners who apply the lessons of history to their own day and critique contemporary Israel when it is warranted.

2. Questions and Answers

To concentrate on the biblical text of Deuteronomy 6:7, 20–25, we are engaging an emerging methodology based upon the asking of questions. Bart Koet and Archibald van Wieringen have shown that the asking of questions is a major form of teaching and learning both in the relationships between characters in the biblical text and in the relationship between the text-immanent author and text-immanent reader.[3] Questions can be studied in various ways. For example: How do questions function in a certain text? How do questions convey a message from one character to another? In which ways are questions persuasive? How do questions address the text-immanent reader? How are questions part of a biblical text's rhetorical traditions?

In 6:20–25, the child's question (6:20) about 'the decrees and the statutes and the ordinances that the LORD our God has commanded you' occasions an opportunity.[4] A close reading of this text will suggest how the child's question functions to convey a message from one character to another while engaging the rhetorical tradition of Deuteronomy. The engagement is complex as the questioning child ultimately challenges the

---

[2] K. Henriksen Garroway, *Children in the Ancient Near Eastern Household* (EANEC 3; Winona Lake: Eisenbrauns, 2014); K. Henriksen Garroway, *Growing Up in Ancient Israel: Children in Material Culture and Biblical Texts* (ABS; Atlanta: SBL Press, 2018).

[3] For indications of this methodology, see B.J. Koet and A.L.H.M. van Wieringen (Eds.), *Multiple Teachers in Biblical Texts* (CBET 88; Leuven: Peeters, 2017).

[4] Biblical citations follow the NRSV unless otherwise indicated.

grandiloquence of Deuteronomy. First, however, the child's question must be put in context.

Initially (6:1-3), Moses tells the Israelites that he will teach them 'the commandment – the statutes and the ordinances' as God commanded him, so that 'you and your children and your children's children' might keep these dictates and multiply greatly in a land flowing with milk and honey. Moses' teaching is transhistorical in that he indicates a time span of many generations: the Sinai generation, who have largely died out; the subsequent generation(s) gathered at Moab; and the future generations who will occupy the promised land flowing with milk and honey. How, we ask, can this teaching be literally simultaneous across multiple generations? The answer lies in the rhetoric of Deuteronomy itself, which is an uncanny admixture of the time-bound particular (Sinai-Moab-Promised Land) and the universal good, understood in terms of instruction (commandment-statutes-ordinances). Deuteronomy insinuates the particular, here represented by generations of uninitiated persons, into the universal, here expressed through legal norms that the community values and observes. Brent Strawn refers to this dynamic as Deuteronomy's rhetoric of 'inscription:' 'In the transgenerational communication of religious values, ... Deuteronomy commends and commands inscription: narrating the next generation into the story of Israel with its God.'[5] Idealized Israelites are inscribed into the tradition, either the legal tradition or, as Strawn indicates, the narrative tradition of the people's release from Egyptian slavery. The Deuteronomic rhetorical tradition leverages both the book's legal materials and its historiography.

The teaching of the Shema ensues (6:4-5) with emphasis on the unicity of the Lord our God and the need to love the Lord God with all one's heart, soul, and might. Next, Moses states that the people must have this teaching upon their hearts, and they must teach it diligently to their children. The verb pertaining to the children, וְשִׁנַּנְתָּם לְבָנֶיךָ, from the root שׁנן, is relatively rare and has been variously translated.[6] Renderings should approximate the Deuteronomic dynamic of inscription introduced above.

---

[5] B.A. Strawn, "Slaves and Rebels: Inscription, Identity and Time in the Rhetoric of Deuteronomy," in: D.I. Block and R.L. Schultz (Eds.), *Sepher Torath Mosheh: Studies in the Composition and Interpretation of Deuteronomy* (Peabody, MA: Hendrickson, 2017), 161–191, here 170.

[6] While the NRSV reads 'recite [these words] to your children,' Jeffrey Tigay proposes 'impress them upon your children.' J.H. Tigay, *The JPS Torah Commentary on Deuteronomy* (Philadelphia: JPS, 1996), 78. For a discussion of the range of translations as well as the Syrian and Assyrian treaties that require the treaty be taught to children, see J.R. Lundbom, *Deuteronomy: A Commentary* (Grand Rapids: Eerdmans, 2013), 313.

In this vein, Kristine Garroway's 'incise,' based on her reading of the root שנן, is especially apt.[7] In Deuteronomy, the Mosaic teaching must also permeate other spheres of life (6:7b–9): the household as well as its interior thresholds (mezuzot) and similarly one's forearm and forehead (tefillin). The next portion, 6:10–19, anticipates the Israelites' entry into the land, with success contingent upon their following God's commandments, decrees and statutes (6:17).

In this context, 6:20 pronounces:

כִּי־יִשְׁאָלְךָ בִנְךָ מָחָר לֵאמֹר מָה הָעֵדֹת וְהַחֻקִּים וְהַמִּשְׁפָּטִים אֲשֶׁר צִוָּה יְהוָה אֱלֹהֵינוּ אֶתְכֶם

When your children ask you in time to come, 'What is the meaning of the decrees and the statutes and the ordinances that the LORD our God has commanded you?'

Before considering the historical recital (6:21–25) that constitutes the parent's response to the son, let us examine the language that encases the son's question.

It is significant that the son refers to the deity as 'the LORD our God' inasmuch as the expression itself is rare. Moses and other speakers in Deuteronomy typically refer to 'the LORD your God.' One notable exception is the Shema (6:4), the credal statement par excellence that the son here echoes. The child is marked by his belief and his commitment. The child is not outside the community or its faith, but the question remains: is the child to be inscribed with the prior generations, and might the child have something to say about it?

The son's question revolves around Israel's 'decrees, statutes and ordinances.' The reference to the legal tradition is highly Deuteronomic, but it is not identical to those of Moses in 6:1 and 6:17.[8] In each case, the expressions differ from one another by a single word to suggest that the idioms, like the speakers (Moses-the father-the son),[9] are close to one

---

[7] K. Henriksen Garroway, "Enculturating Children in Eighth-Century Judah," in: Z.I. Farber and J.L. Wright (Eds.), *Archaeology and History of Eighth-Century Judah* (ANEM 23; Atlanta: SBL Press, 2018), 415–429, here 418.

[8] In this context, Moses's diction and syntax serve as a model for the older generations and in particular the boy's father.

[9] Rüdiger Lux suggests that the roles of the father and the son also reflect the role of Moses and the people of Israel since Moses as the first teacher of Torah is the "father" of Israel. See R. Lux, "Die Kinder auf der Gasse: Ein Kindheitsmotiv in der prophetischen Gerichts- und Heilsverkündigung," in: A. Kunz-Lübcke and R. Lux (Eds.), »*Schaffe mir Kinder*«: *Beiträge zur Kindheit im alten Israel und in seinen Nachbarkulturen* (Arbeiten zur Bibel und ihrer Geschichte 21; Leipzig: Evangelische Verlagsanstalt, 2006), 197–221, here 198.

another but they are not (yet) perfectly aligned. The child's articulation, 'decrees, statutes and ordinances,' is attested in only one other place, 4:45: 'These are the decrees, statutes and ordinances that Moses spoke to the Israelites when they had come out of Egypt.' That verse, in the judgement of Reinhard Kratz, serves as 'the literary nucleus' of 4:44–49, a pericope added by a postexilic editor of Deuteronomy.[10] Specifically, the term for 'decrees' is typical of late Hebrew (in Psalm 119, verse 2 and 22 additional verses), and the recurrence of Egypt in both verses (Deuteronomy 4:45; 6:20) is noteworthy. The point is that the son's phraseology is neither Deuteronomic boilerplate nor is it highly original and lacking connection to the legal tradition in question. In the wording of his question, the son locates himself liminally somewhere along the edges of the Deuteronomic world.

The child's question is additionally enigmatic in asking 'When, in time to come ... what is the meaning?' The Hebrew reads alliteratively: מָחָר לֵאמֹר מָה. What could be the full import of this expression, especially מָה, 'what is the meaning?' The interrogative מָה fills pages and pages in the lexica of biblical Hebrew, but they do not definitively treat this word as it appears in 6:20. Is it possible that מָה here is equivalent to '<u>what</u> is the meaning of this?' In this scenario, the expression is angrily asking why someone is doing something of which the speaker does not approve. Is the child sharply questioning the Deuteronomists? The possibility must be considered.

Gerhard von Rad was one of the first to point out that the entirety of 6:20–25 is based upon a false analogy: the context of the parent and his child, monarchic Israel, is very different from the legendary realm of Moses. In contradistinction, monarchic Israel involves a king, a stratified civil service, an economy based on currency that is liable to downturns, and vulnerability to empires east and south. Von Rad concluded: 'This Israel has in fact no longer any points of comparison with the Israel that in the past stood at Horeb.'[11] Von Rad may be guilty of hyperbole, but he was right in pointing out a disjuncture between the ideal and real in Deuteronomy. The disjuncture is actually a disturbing reversal that may be summed up thus: 'Yahweh had called Israel 'out of Egypt' because he was the champion of the oppressed peasant class. Yet the scriptures ... [reflect a society of] scribal retainers and an aristocracy that were

---

[10] R.G. Kratz, "The Headings of the Book of Deuteronomy," in: K. Schmid and R.F. Person, Jr. (Eds.), *Deuteronomy in the Pentateuch, Hexateuch and the Deuteronomistic History* (FAT II 56; Tübingen: Mohr Siebeck, 2012), 31–46, here 38.

[11] G. von Rad, *Studies in Deuteronomy*, tr. D. Stalker (SBT; London: SCM, 1953), 70.

wholly subservient to the royal tyranny that Israel had tried to escape.'[12] The result was an acute need to shore up the credibility of the religious system, especially among youth. Strawn writes: 'The child's question [in 6:20] reflects a likely rhetorical situation that calls for (or calls forth) this particular rhetorical move – namely the problem younger generations face when they encounter (often with some measure of dissatisfaction) religious systems for themselves.'[13] If von Rad was guilty of hyperbole, Strawn may be understating the problem, although he names it well. The child clearly had something to question, the legally-normed system of social dictates that was no longer tethered to Israel's halcyon past. Deuteronomy's attempts to reconnect these two by inscribing children into its discourse were grounds for questioning: <u>what</u> is the meaning of this?

Delving into this questioning, one finds a clue in the pronominal distinction that the child makes. In 6:20, the narrator uses the singular to refer to 'your child,' who asks 'you' a question. But the child opts for plural pronouns and pronominal suffixes: 'that the LORD our God has commanded you [plural].' In Strawn's analysis, the shift in pronouns suggests that the legislation and the command to obey it 'applies only to the parents ... the child is asking not simply about the content of the legislation but about its *meaning for* and/or *pertinence to* the child.'[14] The generation gap, here defined as the child's ambivalence over mainline teaching, is typically bridged in Deuteronomy with the topos of Egyptian servitude and the release therefrom (6:21–25). As this well-attested topos (5:6, 15; 6:21; 15:15; 16:12; 24:18) functions to provide motivation and justification for following the decrees, statutes and ordinances, it also creates identity for the people of Israel. The creation of Israelite identity was not a static process and, depending on the historical period in question, it could be more or less subject to scrutiny and even controversy.[15]

---

[12] K. Armstrong, *The Lost Art of Scripture: Rescuing the Sacred Text* (New York: Knopf, 2019), 34–35.
[13] Strawn, *Slaves and Rebels*, 170.
[14] Strawn, *Slaves and Rebels*, 168. Emphasis original.
[15] In his discussion of Israelite identity, Bob Becking notes a major shift between preexilic, or Iron Age III, Judah and postexilic Yehud: 'In the monarchic period Judah was, despite its vassal-relationship with Assyria, an independent and well defined area. On the level of religion, being Judean implied being Yahwistic. All this changed when Yehud became part of a satrapy in the immense Persian empire in which Yahwism was no longer the religion shared by over 90% of its inhabitants. The changed social, political and mental circumstances provoked a religion on the move. To phrase it in an oversimplified way: being Yahwistic was no longer based on tradition but on choice.' B. Becking, *Ezra, Nehemiah and the Construction of Early Jewish Identity* (FAT 80; Tübingen: Mohr Siebeck, 2011), 44.

As ours is not a diachronic study per se, we leave open the question of periodization and simply note the following. If one situates the composition of 6:20 in the monarchic period, the child's question is the exception that proves the rule of Deuteronomic rhetoric; if one situates the verse in the context of Yehud, i.e. the Persian period, the question is more of a challenge and exemplifies the choice increasingly available to individuals in a Yahwistic family.

To sum up these points, a question normally deals with a discrepancy in information. The one who asks the question has a lack of information and by asking the question tries to resolve this discrepancy. But the other way around is possible as well: someone asks a question to make the addressee aware of an information deficit. Such is the case with the famous question in 6:20, posed by the child. At face value, the child asks for information about the Lord in the desert, because he was not present there. But the child already knows many things. His knowledge positions him to ask about the decrees the Lord God has commanded, namely 'to you' (instead of 'to us'). This implies that the question in 6:20 has the function of urging the father to think more critically about the tradition that is imparted from generation to generation. 'What is the meaning of Israel's history with God in the present-day context?' The child is challenging his parent and critiquing Deuteronomy's rhetoric of inscription.

2. The Child Makes a Cameo Appearance

In biblical literature, cameo appearance characters enjoy a single, brief encounter with the reader. After the initial impression, which can be as curt as a single word, the reader receives no more cues or clues about these characters. In the words of Gina Hens-Piazza, 'Mentioned only by the narrator in crafting the conditions or circumstances of the story, these supporting cast characters hardly command our attention. They are 'the crowd,' 'the slaves,' 'the servant girl,' 'the reapers.'"[16] Hens-Piazza adds that such labels may be incorrect and unduly limit the description of these individuals in terms of who they are as well as what they contribute to the story.

Hens-Piazza develops a hermeneutic that takes seriously the cameo appearance characters as persons worthy of notice and not without a certain renown. Although they make only very brief appearances, they should not be passed over but rather recognized. The key to this endeavour

---

[16] Hens-Piazza, *The Supporting Cast*, 66.

is the reader's decision to make the one-time appearance of a character more than a whimsical encounter, *à la* the cinematic cameo. The one-time appearance becomes rather 'a place where readers can choose to dwell' by stopping and asking questions.[17] Hens-Piazza notes, 'We can interrogate the story world and the surrounding narrative about this individual. If we choose, readers can investigate the role such characters play in excess of their limited appearance in the story.'[18] Such characters offer an excess of meaning if they are read astutely.

It is intriguing to think of the questioning child in Deuteronomy 6 as one of Hens-Piazza's cameo appearance characters. He fits the part inasmuch as he appears only once and is given a single line of dialogue. Moreover, he inhabits a complex story world that is built upon traditions of origins, namely Egyptian servitude and Israel's release therefrom. In this story world, the child stands at the juncture of the traditions and present reality, expressed as societal norms and legal practices. The child asks: 'What is the meaning of the [Deuteronomic] decrees, ordinances and statutes?' In few words he speaks volumes, not simply for himself but for his generation.

By coincidence, Hens-Piazza offers a close reading of a biblical story with cameo appearance characters that closely parallel the child in 6:20. In 2 Kings 4:1–7, the prophet Elisha orchestrates a miracle on behalf of a widow and her two children, who are about to be put into debt slavery as the family faces starvation. The story turns on a small portion of oil in the widow's kitchen; Elisha instructs her to gather jars from her neighbours and, with her children, start pouring her oil into all the jars she has collected. The family fills all the jars with oil until the eldest child, a son, announces that there are no more jars (4:6). 'There are no more,' the son says, and then the oil stops flowing.[19] But all that had flowed up to that point was enough for the woman to pay off her debts and feed her family.

---

[17] Hens-Piazza, *The Supporting Cast*, 67. Hens-Piazza's idea of 'cameo appearance members' could be considered as a reader-oriented technique to be added to the five techniques mentioned in A.L.H.M. van Wieringen, "Assur and Babel against Jerusalem: The Reader-Oriented Position of Babel and Assur within the Framework of Isaiah 1–39," in: A. van Wieringen and A. van der Woude (Eds.), *'Enlarge the Site of Your Tent': The City as Unifying Theme in Isaiah: The Isaiah Workshop: De Jesaja Werkplaats* (OTS 58; Leiden: Brill, 2011), 49–62, here 49–50.

[18] Hens-Piazza, *The Supporting Cast*, 67.

[19] It is striking that a negative word (אֵין) is used to express the 'miracle.' In other words, the abundance is expressed by mentioning the limitedness. I am grateful to Archibald van Wieringen for pointing out this paradox in personal communication.

In her analysis, Hens-Piazza emphasizes the children's peril before considering the son's role in the life-giving resolution. Because the children have lost their father, they are 'residents in a society whose <u>laws</u> [emphasis added] do not protect them.'[20] Instead, they become commodities by which debts are settled: 'They are about to be taken from their mother and made slaves.'[21] These prospects are doubly disturbing inasmuch as Israel's lending system was supposed to take into account borrowers such as the widow who need financial assistance: 'Forgoing the profit that came from interest was grounded in the care of the community that God had brought out of Egypt, liberating them from slavery. When one member of the community was in need, a loan without interest was the care to be given in the name of the LORD, who brought you out of the land of Egypt' (Leviticus 25:35–38).[22] It is the bitterest of ironies that emancipation from Egypt here helps form the legal context in which children such as the son and his sibling could be sold into slavery.[23] In the courts, the seminal account of Israelite liberation has become an outdated story, and nothing more. Perhaps a scenario such as this lies behind the question of the child in Deuteronomy 6:20: '<u>What</u> is the meaning of Israel's decrees, statutes and ordinances?' The child might add: 'Why speak of the LORD bringing us out of Egypt with a mighty hand (6:21) if it does not 'keep us alive, as is now the case' (6:24)?'

In her reading of the widow's son in 2 Kings 4:1–7, Hens-Piazza also captures the child's agency as he contributes to the tale's life-giving resolution. First, both children assist their mother as they go to neighbours and collect jars. They then help the mother pour her oil into the jars. The oil multiplies exponentially, and when the process is complete, it is the child who announces this miraculous feat: 'There are no more.' Put differently, 'We have filled every last jar: We are beyond slavery and starvation.' If the drama were staged in a theatre, this cameo appearance character, the son, would stand front and centre for a moment, for the

---

[20] Hens-Piazza, *The Supporting Cast*, 69.
[21] Hens-Piazza, *The Supporting Cast*, 69.
[22] Hens-Piazza, *The Supporting Cast*, 71.
[23] While we have noted that the historical setting of Deut 6:20–25 could be monarchic Israel or the postexilic Persian period, it is the former that serves as the background for 2 Kings 4:1–7. The Elijah and Elisha stories take place in the era of the Omrides, the Northern Kingdom's first real dynasty. The Omride dynasty was expansive in terms of establishing new trade routes and launching building projects that taxed the economy. As Hens-Piazza, *The Supporting Cast*, 71 observes, 'The rise of debt slavery can be attributed to the insolvency among free citizens caused by these shifts in both economic factors and social stratification tied to this monarchy.'

time it takes to announce 'There are no more.' The moment is the turning point, for the child, for the family, and for Israel. In a similar way, the son in Deuteronomy 6:20 acts as a cameo appearance character, marking the moment of his questioning the fathers as a turning point not only for him and the family, but also for Israel.

3. The Child as Child

What difference does it make that *a child* asks the question of 6:20, and not an adult? In this section we consider the different ways of perceiving childhood as distinct from adulthood, all the while respecting the symbiosis between youth and adulthood that inspired Wordsworth to write, 'The child is father to the man.'[24] To support the inquiry, there is a burgeoning literature on children in the ancient world and specifically in the biblical story.[25] We as a research community are well positioned to study the place of children in antiquity and especially their potential to play an outsized role in biblical texts.

In her childist approach, Kristine Garroway identifies young, often silent characters in biblical texts and considers their contributions. Garroway views these children as subjects who are in the process of being encultured and engendered; as such children provide an important window on Israelite society and the values at its foundation: 'This act of passing on information to the next generation is called enculturation, and it is how a society hands down their culture. The process of enculturation is multifaceted, so that there are many ways to help children learn the values, skills, language, and behaviours that their society understands to be normative.'[26] In Deuteronomy, enculturation occurs within a certain context, namely the book's rhetoric of inscription. Appropriately, Garroway translates the verb שנן in 6:7 as 'incised.'[27] As children are incised or inscribed into Deuteronomy, they learn the ways of both God and their community.

---

[24] At the conclusion of his poem *My Heart Leaps Up*, William Wordsworth wrote: 'The child is father to the man.' If this be the case, then women and men gain insight by listening to the child's voice, be it the inner child, as Wordsworth suggested, or the composite who represents the youth of a given society.

[25] See *inter alia* S. Betsworth and J. Faith Parker (Eds.), *Handbook to Children and Childhood in the Biblical World* (London: T&T Clark, 2019); C.B. Horn and J.W. Martens, *"Let the Little Children Come to Me" : Childhood and Children in Early Christianity* (Washington: CUA Press, 2009) and the publications of Kristine Henriksen Garroway listed in it.

[26] Garroway, "Enculturating Children," 419.

[27] See footnote 7.

Our study thus far suggests that the child, at least the questioning child in 6:20, is no blank slate. Because he already knows many things, he is not a passive receptacle of tradition but indeed a subject in the process of enculturation. While the child does not control this process, he is finding that he has a voice in it and can ask questions of it. In Deuteronomy 6, both the incised child and the questioner (6:20) represent Israelite society's youngest generation who are actively learning key elements of their ethnic and cultural heritage. They are taking stock of Israel's origins with respect to Egypt, and they are adopting Deuteronomy's transhistorical perspective to assess the past as well as their own present-day reality.[28] The pedagogical tone that emerges is not adversarial *per se*, but one observes the healthy tension that is engendered by the process. To be clear, the child is challenging and critiquing the Deuteronomic rhetoric of his forebears: 'What is the meaning of Israel's decrees, statutes and ordinances?' But the child is doing so from within, while in relationship to the world of Deuteronomy. The exchange augers growth for all the parties involved, the children as well as the adults.

4. Summary in Five Points and a Catechetical Comparison

In this study, there are five key points about asking questions in the world of Deuteronomy that have emerged.[29]

- In Deuteronomy 6, the youths reflect the Deuteronomic rhetorical tradition, into which Israelites inscribed each subsequent generation of children.

---

[28] In this vein, we consider the work of Melody Briggs on how children read biblical narrative. She reports that child readers have a narrative orientation, and that they focus on the viability of the text's narrative world. They are decidedly less interested in questions about the biblical narrative's factuality. Thus, with regard to Deuteronomy 6, the child's question is not, 'Did this really happen?' but rather, 'Is this happening today such that the story of Egypt remains viable and meaningful?' Briggs further reports that the reading strategies she discerns among children serve young readers and the text itself better than the imposition of a moral framework. That is, Deuteronomy's 'decrees, statutes and ordinances' do not hold great promise for the inculturation of children if they preclude the possibility of youth asking questions about their relevance. M.R. Briggs, *How Children Read Biblical Narrative: An Investigation of Children's Readings of the Gospel of Luke* (Eugene: Pickwick, 2017).

[29] These points are exegetical rather than historical. The basis for saying, for example, that Israelite children had agency and were active learners is textual, and beyond the chapters of Deuteronomy we do not know the degree to which this may or may not have been true. Our world of understanding is bound and limited, just as the Deuteronomists lived in a given time and place and lacked a crystal-clear picture of what took place many centuries earlier.

- In the inscription process, Israelite children had agency and were active learners, with the power to pose questions as in 6:20.
- The children's questions could critique the system of their own enculturation if there were dissonance, for example, between the legendary realm of Moses and the contemporary context of the child and his parent.
- Although the questioning child in 6:20 makes a cameo appearance, he plays a significant role, like the widow's son in 2 Samuel 4:6, whose one utterance is a proclamation of fulfilment with implications for social justice.
- Reading Deuteronomy 6 through a childist lens makes clear that the enculturation of youth involves a certain reciprocity because the child's forebears as well are led to examine the Deuteronomic tradition more critically.

In terms of the five points, it is intriguing to compare Deuteronomy 6 to certain Christian instructional texts that were developed in the medieval period, the Reformation and the Counter-Reformation. The catechisms, as they were often called, were a pedagogical means of preparing children for fuller incorporation into the community of faith. In the mid-16th century, for example, a catechism was included in the Book of Common Prayer in order to prepare children for confirmation via public examination. Moreover, whereas Deuteronomy 6 is instruction that elaborates the commandments (or Decalogue) given in 5:6–21, catechetical texts typically expounded upon the Ten Commandments, and other topoi as well. Coincidentally, the catechisms often used a question-and-answer format featuring a child interlocutor. In England, the Small Catechism of George Joye (1529) featured 'a dialogue wherein the Child, asked certain questions, answers to the same.'[30] While Joye has a father ask questions of his child, in a subsequent edition the roles are reversed and the child asks the questions while the father replies. The text makes no reference to Deuteronomy 6, but the parallel is striking.

The catechisms of the Roman Catholic Church were no less fond of the question-and-answer format. The 18th-century priest Richard Challoner worked from the Doway Catechism of a century earlier, which contained 109 questions. Challoner's catechism increased the number of questions to 290, although his questions covered traditional catechetical content such as the Creed, the Our Father, the commandments, and the medieval

---

[30] The Joye catechism is described in B.L. Marthaler, *The Catechism Yesterday and Today: The Evolution of a Genre* (Collegeville: Liturgical Press, 1995), 74.

lists of virtues and vices.[31] Challoner proved innovative, however, in appending chapters such as 'The Christian's Rule of Life' and 'The Christian's Daily Exercises.' These original tracts emphasized love of God and love of neighbour, or in other words the Shema of Deuteronomy 6:4–5 as interpreted by Jesus (Matthew 22:39; Mark 12:30–31). Challoner described how Christians should begin the day with morning prayer, make holy their actions throughout the day, and conclude the day with prayer. The rituals loosely recall the mezuzot and tefillin of 6:7b–9. In these and other respects, the catechetical tradition descends from Deuteronomy and other ancient sources, and on that point there is no question.

---

[31] Marthaler, *Catechism Yesterday and Today*, 88.

THE QUESTIONS IN EZRA AND NEHEMIAH

Bob BECKING
Utrecht University

1. Which questions will be dealt with?

This contribution does not deal with the medieval apocryphal text known as the Questions of Ezra. That composition is only known in two slightly different Armenian versions. That text discusses questions about good and evil souls and what will happen to them at the end of time.[1] These questions are more than a little bit removed – as a result of the post-biblical Ezra-tradition – from the questions we find in the biblical Books of Ezra and Nehemiah. Secondly, I will not concentrate on the questions, or problems that these books pose to the modern reader, but on the questions posed within the narratives, with which I mean interrogative clauses. My approach is relatively simple. I just read both books, note questions, and discuss them. I will not enter into a discussion on sources, redactions, and composition, although I am aware of the complex pre-history of the present two books.[2]

2. A warning question by the King of Persia

A first question is encountered in Ezra 4:22. Ezra 4:17–22 contains the text of an Aramaic message written by an anonymous Persian king[3] to two leading officers in Samaria:[4]

> *Be warned of being negligent in acting this out;*
> *why should damage increase to the detriment of the kings?*[5]

---

[1] For a recent edition, see M. Stone, "A new Edition and Translation of the Questions of Ezra," in: Z. Zevit, S. Gitin and M. Sokoloff (Eds.), *Solving Riddles and Untying Knots* (FS J.C. Greenfield; Winona Lake: Eisenbrauns, 1995), 293–316; recent translation in J. Leonhardt-Balzer, *Fragen Esras* (JSHRZ 1,5; Gütersloh: Gütersloher Verlagshaus, 2005); see also L.S. Fried, *Ezra and the Law in History and Tradition* (Columbia: University of South Carolina Press, 2014), 108–109.
[2] See B. Becking, *Ezra – Nehemiah* (HCOT; Leuven: Peeters, 2018); this commentary forms the basis of my reflections in this contribution.
[3] Probably Artaxerxes, see Ezra 4:11.
[4] Rehum the commander, to Shimshai the scribe.
[5] New American Standard Bible.

This message is a reply to a letter sent from Samaria to Artaxerxes. Both should be read against the background of a conflict. The narrative Ezra 3–6 relates the attempt of Judaeans who, after their return from the Babylonian exile, started the rebuilding and reconstruction of the temple in Jerusalem, which lay in ruins. Their endeavours, however, meet opposition from the side of Yahwists in Samaria who had recently built a sanctuary for Yhwh on Mount Gerizim.[6] In the development of the narrative plot these Samarians[7] use the correspondence with the Persian court as a leverage to hamper the rebuilding of the temple in Jerusalem. After minute research in their archives, the Persians arrive at the conclusion that Jerusalem has of old been a rebellious city and that the inhabitants of that city should not be allowed to rebuild their temple. The Persian court urges the Samarian elite to have the work in Jerusalem stopped. Their message ends with a rhetorical question: 'why should damage increase to the detriment of the kings?'.[8]

Whether or not this correspondence is historically trustworthy, the effect of the question is as assumed. It had performative force. The leaders in Samaria take action:

> *Then as soon as the copy of King Artaxerxes' document was read before Rehum and Shimshai the scribe and their colleagues, they went in haste to Jerusalem to the Jews and stopped them by force of arms.* (Ezra 4:23)

Within the narrative plot of Ezra 3–6, the royal question and its Samarian 'answer' – not in words but in writing a letter to the Persian court – has brought the plot to rock-bottom. The aim of the narrative, to have a functioning temple for Yhwh in Jerusalem, now seems unreachable. It is only by prophetic intervention in Ezra 5 that it again comes within arm's reach.

---

[6] See Y. Magen and H. Misgav and L. Tsfania, *Mount Gerizim Excavations: Volume 1 The Aramaic, Hebrew and Samaritan Inscriptions* (Judea and Samaria Publications 2; Jerusalem: Israel Antiquities Authority, 2004); B. Hensel, "On the relationship of Judah and Samaria in post-exilic times: A farewell to the conflict paradigm," *JSOT* 44 (2019): 19–42.

[7] Not yet Samaritans; see G.N. Knoppers, *Jews and Samaritans: The Origins and History of Their Early Relations* (Oxford: Oxford University Press, 2013); B. Hensel, *Juda und Samaria: Zum Verhältnis zweier nachexilischer Jahwismen* (FAT 110; Tübingen: Mohr Siebeck, 2016).

[8] See T. Zewi, "Rhetorical Questions and Negative Clauses in Biblical Hebrew," in: G.R. Kotzé, C.S. Locatell and J.A. Messarra (Eds.), *Ancient Texts and Modern Readers* (SSN 71; Leiden: Brill, 2019), 196–210.

3. An irate inimical question

The next question is found in the section just after the rebuilding of the temple had been resumed after the prophetic intervention in Ezra 5:1–2. Due to the prophecies of Haggai and Zechariah, the people in Jerusalem are seized by the building project. As could be expected, this act met with opposition from Samaria. Almost immediately, Tattenai, the governor of the satrapy 'across the river,' and Shethar-bozenai travelled to Jerusalem accompanied by officials. With a composed voice they put a question to the rebuilders:

> *Who issued you a decree to rebuild this temple and to complete its woodwork?*[9] (Ezra 5:3)

The inspection by Tattenai has, at first sight, no hostile character. He enquires after the authority behind the plans. The idiom שִׂים טְעֵם *to give an order, to command* in the Hebrew Bible always has a human as subject.[10] This demand for human authorization stands, therefore, in contrast to the prophetic motivation just narrated in Ezra 5:1–2. Within the narrative frame of Ezra 3–6, Tattenai's question, however, is not harmless. His composed voice veils powerful antipathy and animosity. His question is functional in the development of the plot. By his indirect denial of the presence of a decree behind the building activities, he aims at receiving the answer 'None!' that could lead to the definitive cessation of the rebuilding.

Due to what the narrator construes as divine caring vigilance it is – ironically – vocalized by Tattenai:

> *But the eye of their God was on the elders of the Judaeans, and they could not have them stop until a report should come to Darius, and then a written reply be returned concerning it.*

Tattenai then sends a report to the Persian court out of anger for not getting a clear answer from the Judaeans. (Ezra 5:5)

---

[9] The architectural term אֻשַּׁרְנָא *woodwork* is derived from the Old Iranian **uščarana, material*. The Aramaic noun – also known from the papyri of Elephantine – refers to materials for construction or repair, mostly made from wood. See C.G. Tuland, "'Uššayyā' and 'Uššarnâ: A Clarification of Terms, Date, and Text," *JNES* 17 (1958): 269-75; H.G.M. Williamson, *Ezra, Nehemiah* (WBC 16; Waco: Word Books, 1985), 70.

[10] See also Ezra 4:21; 5:9, 13; 6:1, 3, 12; Dan 3:10; and in the Elephantine papyri.

4. Report and repetition

In his report to the Persian King Darius (Ezra 5:6–17), Tattenai is presented as the almost ideal civil servant. He does not just make decisions but listens to all parties involved and consents to the appropriate investigation of certain claims by the competent authority. The letter has a clear structure. After the indication that what is coming is a copy (5:6), a discussion of the cause follows: the renewed construction of a temple in Jerusalem and the question of the authority behind it. Next, a relatively detailed description of the response of the elders in Jerusalem is given. This response is largely a reference to historical events and includes a claim that a decree by Cyrus had provided them with the right to rebuild the temple. The letter ends with a clear request to Darius about whether such a decree actually might be found in the archives.

In his report to Darius, Tattenai repeats his question to the leaders of the building project in Jerusalem almost verbatim:

> *Who issued you a decree to rebuild this temple and to complete its woodwork?* (Ezra 5:9)

The author of the narrative Ezra 3–6 included the answer given by the people of Jerusalem to Tattenai's question. It is remarkable that such a question, as found in 5:9, is absent in the previous section of the narrative. In view of the fact that Ezra 3–6 does not give an objective report on the events, but should be construed as an ideological narrative, it is far from certain that Ezra 5 presents the answer as it might have been given in reality. In fact, Ezra 5:11–16 presents the view of a specific group of Yahwists in Jerusalem, namely those who would opt for an exclusive form of Yahwism in which no room was available for dissenters, such as the people in Samaria or the offspring of those who had remained in the land and who had been married to 'strange women.'[11]

The answer supposedly given by the leaders in Jerusalem and assumedly written in a letter to the Persian court contains a condensed history of the period of the Babylonian exile. The wrath of God had caused the end of the cult in the former temple. Nebuchadnezzar had deported the Judaeans to Babylon. Due to the renewed grace of God, a new king – Cyrus of Persia – gave permission to return to Jerusalem and to rebuild the temple. Furthermore, this king returned the precious temple vessels

---

[11] See Becking, *Ezra – Nehemiah*.

which had been removed from Jerusalem by Nebuchadnezzar. In short, it was a decree by Cyrus that made the rebuilding of the temple possible.[12]

This historical summary clearly unveils the point of view of those Judaeans who had returned from exile and who were striving at a pure cult for Yhwh. As a result of the report by Tattenai, a search was made through the archives in Ecbatana, where a document was found that supported the claim of the Judaeans (Ezra 6:1–5). The question by Tattenai had an opposite effect. Instead of being forced to cease the rebuilding, the Judaeans received permission to rebuild (6:6–12), as they indeed do in the narrative (6:13–15).

5. A question for lack of words

The next question in the book of Ezra is found in prayer. Astonished by the news about the mixed-marriages, Ezra prays to Yhwh. This is not the place to enter into a discussion on the character of the marriages to 'strange women' or to linger on the historical situation against which Ezra 7–10 can best be read.[13] The discovery of the undesirable marital relations provokes a crisis within Jerusalem. Ezra uses his position as envoy from the Persian court to mend the crisis. He starts with a penitential prayer to God.[14]

---

[12] On the 'historicity' of the narrative Ezra 3–6, see L.L. Grabbe, "The 'Persian Documents' in the Book of Ezra: Are They Authentic?," in: O. Lipschits and M. Oeming (Eds.), *Judah and the Judaeans in the Persian Period* (Winona Lake: Eisenbrauns, 2006), 531–570.

[13] Elsewhere, I have argued for the view that (a) the marriages that are condemned in Ezra 9–10 were intra-Judaean bonds between people adhering to different forms of Yahwism and (b) that Ezra 7–10 should be construed as a pseudepigraphic pamphlet with which a group of people whose ancestors had been in exile claim their form of Yahwism to be the correct one; see Becking, *Ezra-Nehemiah*.

[14] Several penitential prayers are known from the post-exile period: 2 Chron 33:13; Ezra 9; Neh 1:5–11; 9:6–37; Dan 9:4–19; Bar 1:15–3:8. On this kind of prayer see R.A. Werline, *Penitential Prayer in Second Temple Judaism: The Development of a Religious Institution* (Atlanta: SBL Press, 1998); H.W.M. van Grol, "Exegesis of the Exile – Exegesis of Scripture?," in: J.C. de Moor (Ed.), *Intertextuality in Ugarit and Israel* (OTS 40; Leiden: Brill, 1998), 31–61; R.J. Bautch, *Developments in Genre between post-exilic penitential prayers and the Psalms of communal lament* (AcBib 7; Atlanta: SBL Press, 2003); M.W. Duggan, "Ezra 9:6–15: A Penitential Prayer within Its Literary Setting," in: M.J. Boda and D.K. Falk and R.A. Werline (Eds.), *Seeking the Favor of God: Vol. 1, The Origins of Penitential Prayer in Second Temple Judaism* (EJL 21; Atlanta: SNL Press, 2006), 165–178.

The prayer of Ezra is to be understood as a text directed to Yhwh, but aimed at changing the community in and around Jerusalem.[15] In the text, Ezra repents, while all the while expounding the trespasses of a group within the community – those who married 'strange women' – to the whole of the community, including himself, and places the people's guilt in a historical perspective. He summarizes the history of Israel as a history of continuous human guilt contrasted with God's kindness. In the development of the plot of Ezra 7–10, this prayer sits at a narrative node. Since the textual unit refers back to previous elements (the mentioned crisis) and anticipates forthcoming measures (the dissolution of marriages), the prayer is instrumental in seeking a way out of this crisis. Besides, it is fundamental as the basis of the author's desired community.[16] The prayer has clear performative power: the words of Ezra encourage the community to act.[17] This explains the absence of a request directly addressed to their deity.

After the retrospection, Ezra seeks words to formulate a proper request to God and/or his countrymen:

And now, our God, what can we say after this? (Ezra 9:10a)

This, again, is a rhetorical question that functions as a summons for reflection and behavioural change in the audience of Ezra's prayer: 'What to do?'; 'How to get out of the stalemate?'. The past performance of the people – to which Ezra sees himself as an accomplice – is briefly summarized in the words: 'after all, we have forsaken your commandments' (9:10b).

Despite the rhetorical question and contrary to its contents, Ezra continues his prayer with an anthology of lines from the *tôrah* that summon not to mingle with the original inhabitants of Canaan.[18] This mixed bag of text is followed by a declaration of acceptance. Speaking on behalf of the people – or at least on behalf of the orthodox faction – Ezra accepts

---

[15] See also Werline, *Penitential Prayer*; Van Grol, "Exegesis of the Exile;" R.A. Werline, "Prayer, Politics, and Power in the Hebrew Bible," *Int* 68 (2014): 5–16; R. Heckl, *Neuanfang und Kontinuität in Jerusalem: Studien zu den hermeneutischen Strategien im Esra-Nehemia-Buch* (FAT 104; Tübingen: Mohr Siebeck 2016), 289–301.

[16] See also Van Grol, "Exegesis of the Exile," 33; Duggan, "Ezra 9:6–15," 166–167; Th. Willi, *Esra: Der Lehrer Israels* (Biblische Gestalten 26; Leipzig: Evangelische Verlagsanstalt, 2012), 150–155.

[17] See J.C. Hogewood, "The Speech Act of Confession: Priestly Performative Utterance in Leviticus 16 and Ezra 9–10," in: Boda, Falk and Werline (Eds.), *Seeking the Favor of God*, 69–82.

[18] Ezra 9:11–12; this section contains references and allusions to Lev 18:24–30; Deut 7:1–3; 11:8; 23:6.

the exile as God's punishment for the trespasses of the ancestors. This compliance, however, leads to a follow-up question.

6. Shall we relapse?

In view of the past performance of Israel and Judah, Ezra is not immediately optimistic about their conduct in the near future. He therefore poses a rhetorical question directed to God, but intended for his countrymen:

> *Should we again break your commandments and intermingle with the peoples who commit these abominations? Would you not be angry with us to the point of destruction, until there is no remnant nor any who escape?* (Ezra 9:14)

Ezra clearly aims at a change of the behaviour of the Judaeans involved in the crisis.[19] In the previous verse, he pointed out the mildness of God. In the eyes of the narrator, the Babylonian exile is a fair punishment for the guilt of the people. However, the measure of punishment was milder than the extent of the guilt.[20] The exile turned out not to be the definite end of Israel as a nation. God's care did not drown in the rivers of Babylon. God gave a פְּלֵיטָה *escape, liberation*. This noun is derived from the verb פלט, which almost everywhere in the Hebrew Bible refers to salvation out of difficult situations.[21]

The intended message seems clear. The people in Jerusalem are summoned not to continue trespassing and hence refrain from intermingling with 'strange' elements. The suggestion is that God will prove to be less mild a next time. The appeal turns out to be very effective. Even during the prayer of Ezra, a large crowd gathers around him weeping bitterly.[22] Shechaniah the son of Jehiel, one of the sons of Elam, answers Ezra and comes up with a proposal. A בְּרִית *binding agreement* will be made לֵאלֹהֵינוּ *in front of our God* (10:3).[23]

---

[19] H.W.M. van Grol, " 'Indeed, Servants We Are': Ezra 9, Nehemia 9 and 2 Chronicles 12 Compared," in: B. Becking and M.C.A. Korpel, *The Crisis of Israelite Religion: Transformations of Religious Tradition in Exilic & Post-Exilic Times* (OTS 42; Leiden: Brill, 199), 209–227, here 211–213.

[20] See Bautch, *Developments in Genre*, 77–78.

[21] See, for example, 2 Sam 22:44 = Ps 18:44; Mic 6:14; Ps 22:5, 9; 31:2; 37:40; 71:2; with J. Hausmann, *Israels Rest: Studien zum Selbstverständnis der nachexilischen Gemeinde* (BWANT 124; Stuttgart: Kohlhammer, 1987), 200; P.J. Williams, "The Difference between the Roots mlṭ and plṭ," *ZAW 114* (2002): 438–442.

[22] Ezra 10:1.

[23] And not 'with God,' as is the view in almost all commentaries. In Ezra 10:3 God is made a witness to the human agreement.

The content of this binding agreement is the dismissal of women and children. This sentence is somewhat elliptically formulated and is intended to refer to the dissolution of undesirable bonds, but only after an investigation. This proposal is implemented and the 'mixed marriages' crisis is done with.

7. Questions in Ezra, what about Nehemiah?

The half dozen questions in the book of Ezra play an important role in the development of the two narratives in which they occur. The first set of questions, in a way, guides the process that leads to the completion of the rebuilding of the temple in Jerusalem. The second set of questions is instrumental in solving the 'mixed marriage' crisis. I will now turn to the book of Nehemiah with a question in mind: do the questions in this book play a comparable role? The central plot-line in the book of Nehemiah is, in my view, the removal of the vulnerability of the community in Jerusalem. To that aim, the inhabitants of that city are in need of a reinforced wall and a clear religious identity. Within the book of Nehemiah both are realized due to the deeds and doings of its main character.

8. An empathic king

The first question appears in Nehemiah 2:2 where the Persian king asks Nehemiah:

Why is your face sad though you are not sick?

In the previous parts of the narrative, Nehemiah is introduced as a leading figure in the exilic community in Susan who received a delegation of Judaeans living in Jerusalem. They report to him about the dire situation in the streets of Jerusalem. The wall of the city is broken and the city lies open to all sorts of inimical activity. This report brings Nehemiah into deep distress. His first act is a prayer to God in which he asks for compassion both with himself and for the city of Jerusalem.[24]

After that, the reader is informed that he functions as a cupbearer to the king (Nehemiah 1:11c). At the Persian court, the cupbearer had an

---

[24] Neh 1:5–11; see B. Becking, "The Image of God and the Identity of the Community: Remarks on the Prayers of Nehemiah," in: M. Häusl (Ed.), *Denkt nicht mehr an das Frühere! Begründungsressourcen in Esra/Nehemia und Jes 40–66 im Vergleich* (BBB 184; Göttingen: Vandenhoeck & Ruprecht, 2018), 45–54.

important and trusted function.[25] This officer oversaw all wine-pourers and test-drinkers. The cupbearer himself was responsible for the king's wine, which he drank from a special egg-shaped bowl.[26]

Nehemiah must await a favourable opportunity to approach the king with a request. The event is very precisely dated and localized. The meeting takes place in the first month of the twentieth year of the king and at the table during a banquet. Nehemiah had to act regularly as a royal cupbearer. A cupbearer was not supposed to show his emotions. He has now arrived at the point where he can no longer control his emotions. There is evidence that at the Persian court it was the custom to accept requests from servants on special festive occasions.[27] Nehemiah is in a bad mood; he is רַע, in the sense of *sad, discouraged*.[28]

Artaxerxes notices the mood of his cupbearer and makes three short remarks. Firstly, he enquires into the reason of his sadness. Then he asks a rhetorical question: 'You are not sick?,'[29] and finally he diagnoses Nehemiah to be inflamed by sadness. The royal questions evoke serious fear in Nehemiah.

9. A ruined city evokes a troubled soul

Nevertheless, Nehemiah dares to speak to the Persian monarch. He answers the king in courteous and diplomatic words, while in the meantime showing some courage.[30] His answer gives the king room to act in complete freedom.[31] Court-officials were considered not to be per-

---

[25] See P. Briant, *Histoire de l'Empire Perse: De Cyrus à Alexandre* (Paris: Fayard, 1996), 274–275; L. Llewellyn-Jones, *King and Court in Ancient Persia 559 to 331 bce* (Edinburgh: Edinburgh University Press, 2013), 44–48.137–143; L.L. Grabbe, "The Use and Abuse of Herodotus by Biblical Scholars," in: A. Fitzpatrick-McKinley (Ed.), *Assessing Biblical and Classical Sources for the Reconstruction of Persian Influence, History and Culture* (Classica et Orientalia 10; Wiesbaden: Harrasowitz, 2015), 56–57.

[26] See Xenophon, *Cyropaedia* 1.3.9; 8.4.3.

[27] See Esth 2:18; 5:6; *1 Esdras* 5:6; Herodotus, *Hist.* IX 110; and S. Amigues, "Pour la table du Grand Roi," *Journal des Savants* 1 (2003): 3–59; C. López-Ruiz, "The King and the Cupbearer: Feasting and Power in Eastern Mediterranean Myth," in: J. Blánquez and S. Celestino Pérez (Eds.), *Patrimonio cultural de la vid y el vino* (Madrid: UAM Ediciones, 2013), 133–151.

[28] Gen 40:7; Prov 25:20; Neh 2:1–2; see *DCH* 8 (2011) 507.

[29] The Hebrew could also be rendered with: 'Why are you looking so sad, you don't look sick to me?' This does not affect the narrative strain.

[30] S. Burt, *The Courtier and the Governor: Transformations of Genre in the Nehemiah Memoir* (Journal of Ancient Judaism Supplements 17; Göttingen: Vandenhoeck & Ruprecht, 2014), 127.

[31] Williamson, *Ezra, Nehemiah*, 179.

mitted to speak to the king.³² After the polite standard phrase 'the king lives forever,' Nehemiah confirms the king's observation. He then gives the reason for his sadness. He adopts the words of Chanani from Nehemiah 1:3 in a somewhat changed form and turns it into a rhetorical question:

> *Why should my face not be sad when the city, the place of the tombs of my fathers, lies desolate and its gates have been consumed by fire?* (Nehemiah 2:3)

Remarkably, Nehemiah does not mention the name of the city of Jerusalem.

10. Royal request

Apparently, Nehemiah has hit the right chord. The king immediately takes action by posing a question. He does not make diplomatic detours but comes directly and professionally to the heart of the matter:

> *What would be your request?* (Nehemiah 2:4)

Nehemiah's response to the king's question has a complex communicative structure. He prays to God but speaks to the king. The fact that he prays to the 'God of Heaven' forms a connection with his prayer in Nehemiah 1.³³ The content of the prayer in Nehemiah 2:4 is not given. Perhaps, the words to the Persian king may be seen to be the content of the prayer. This complex communication shows that, for the narrator of Nehemiah too, there was a collaboration between the heavenly and earthly powers. The combination of prayer to God and speaking to the king functions narratively as the beginning of the opening of a door to the solution of the problem sketched.

With courteous politeness, Nehemiah hopes that his proposal might gain royal approval. The content of his request – to go to Judah – repeats the words from verse 3. Again, the name of the city of Jerusalem is not mentioned. The last word of the clause וְאֶבְנֶנָּה *that I will (re)build her* (verse 5) is intriguing. The antecedent of the suffix third person feminine

---

³² See Llewellyn-Jones, *King and Court*, 44–48.
³³ See also M. Häusl, „,Ich betete zum Gott des Himmels" (Neh 2,4): Zur kontextuellen Einbettung der Gebete in Neh 1–13," in: C. Diller, M. Mulzer, K. Ólason and R. Rothenbusch (Eds.), *Studien zu Psalmen und Propheten: Festschrift für Hubert Irsigler* (HBS 64; Freiburg: Herder, 2010), 47–64, here 52–53; D.J. Shepherd and C.J.H. Wright, *Ezra and Nehemiah* (The Two Horizons Old Testament Commentary; Grand Rapids: Eerdmans, 2018), 52–53.

singular is unclear, since there is no feminine noun in the clause. Is Nehemiah referring to the city, the tombs of his ancestors, or the walls? Or does the narrator diplomatically leave that somewhat veiled?

11. A practical question

The king reacts immediately. He, however, shifts from the emotional to the practical. While his spouse[34] is sitting next to him, Artaxerxes directly starts the negotiations:

> *How long will your journey be, and when will you return?* (Nehemiah 2:6)

In a subtle way, the monarch gives his permission. Nehemiah answers politely and gives good reasons as to the duration of his voyage to Jerusalem and the necessary preparations and precautions that will give him a safe journey. As a result, Nehemiah sets off to Judah to inspect and take measures (Nehemiah 2:7–9). Again, a set of questions has helped the plot to unfold.

12. Asking for his true identity

On arrival in Jerusalem, Nehemiah is not warmly welcomed by all his compatriots. There is resistance to his plan especially from the side of Samaria. When three men in power in Samaria hear about the exploits of Nehemiah, they start to mock and despise Nehemiah and his companions.[35] Sanballat the Horonite, Tobiah the Ammonite servant and Geshem the Arab pose a question to Nehemiah:

> *What is this thing you are doing? Are you rebelling against the king?* (Nehemiah 2:19)

The question whether the inhabitants of Jerusalem want to revolt against the Persian king is provocative and ironic at the same time. Indeed, the reader knows what Sanballat, Tobiah and Geshem do not know: Nehemiah will restore the walls with the king's approval. The verb מרד *to revolt, to rebel* is used in the Hebrew Bible to describe all kinds of

---

[34] The word used, שֵׁגָל, is not entirely equivalent to מַלְכָּה *queen*. The Persian kings lived in polygamy. The noun שֵׁגָל is a loanword from Akkadian, *ša ekalli*, literally *her from the palace* and refers to one of the concubines; see A.R. Millard, "ᶠ*ša ekalli – šgl – ᵈsagale*," *UF* 4 (1972): 161–162.

[35] The verb לעג *to mock* indicates a derision of the other, usually by saying preposterous things (see also Job 21:3; Psalm 22:8). The verb בזה *to despise* indicates that the leaders in Samaria looked down on Nehemiah's actions.

rebellion against a higher power, mostly against an earthly king, but also against God (Numbers 14:9, Joshua 22:16, 18, 29; Ezekiel 2:3; Daniel 9:9).

Nehemiah's reply is clear and diplomatic. He refers to his mission by the God of heaven. He seemingly avoids a conversation about the theme of royal approval. His answer is full of confidence and humility. His adversaries do not dare to respond, at least they do not react at this point in the narrative. Nehemiah's answer, however, is not the end of the hostilities between Samaria and Jerusalem.

13. Mocking questions

Nehemiah 3 narrates the conscription of a multitude of volunteers to help Nehemiah in rebuilding the wall of Jerusalem. These activities evoke resistance and incomprehension with Sanballat and his allies. In rage, he poses a set of mocking questions:

> *What are these feeble Judaeans doing?*
> *Will they restore it for themselves?*
> *Will they sacrifice?*
> *Will they finish up in a day?*
> *Will they revive the stones out of the heaps of rubbish,*
> *and burned ones at that?* (Nehemiah 3:34 [ET 4:2])

A few things are remarkable. Firstly, Sanballat calls the Judaeans 'weak'. The word אֲמֵלָל only occurs here in the Hebrew Bible. It is derived from a verb אמל to *be weak* (Ezekiel 16:30). It is unclear whether Sanballat targets physical or emotional weakness. Secondly, the subsequent rhetorical questions question the ability of the Judaeans to restore the walls. The verb form הַיְחַיּוּ *will they revive...?* underscores the view of Sanballat that the destruction of Jerusalem is irreparable.[36] Thirdly, within the narrative context, his questions are part of a kind of power-play. By belittling his Judaean adversaries, he construes himself as in full control and able to stop the rebuilding of the wall.

The Judaeans, clearly the underdogs, act courageously. They pray to God for support and understanding, while continuing the rebuilding. Meanwhile, they take a set of defensive measures to safeguard their work from inimical military threat. The reader, who is urged to sympathize with Nehemiah is hoping for a positive outcome.

---

[36] Williamson, *Ezra, Nehemiah*, 216.

14. Reminding about the rules for redistribution

The book of Nehemiah narrates the construction of a faithful community. To that end, the walls of Jerusalem are rebuilt. The community, however, needs to be rebuilt socially too. Nehemiah 5 informs about measures taken by Nehemiah in times of a drought.[37] The historical connection with the rebuilding is unclear. The conceptual connection, however, is evident. Within the walls there will only be place for loyal and Godfearing Judaeans. As a result of the drought, hunger, poverty, and despair have risen. Some have had to take drastic measures to remain alive: 'We are having to pledge our fields, our vineyards, and our houses in order to get grain during the famine' (5:13). Others have had to borrow money against high interest rates to be able to pay their taxes. On the other hand, a small elite was taking advantage of the situation by buying up acres for low prices and asking too much interest on the loans.

This enrages Nehemiah. He is struck by the lack of solidarity among the people of God and addresses the elite with a reprimanding question:

> *The thing that you are doing is not good. Should you not walk in the fear of our God, to prevent the taunts of the nations, our enemies?* (Nehemiah 5:9)

He does not remain emotional but proposes concrete measures. Contrary to the prevailing ideology, he presents measures that economically reflect a redistribution. The essence of redistribution is that income, prosperity and risks are redistributed, whether successful or 'beneficial,' for example through progressive taxation for the financing of collective goods or services, with most contributing parties not necessarily being those who will profit most. Redistribution is threatened because the relationship between private 'offer' and private 'profit' is not directly visible and therefore evokes much free-riding behaviour (tax evasion, for example). Therefore, redistribution mechanisms are often dependent upon prophetic and ideological safeguards and defences, unless they can, of course, be enforced by (structural) power.[38] What Nehemiah proposes is a redistribution of property that must ensure that the community as a whole can

---

[37] See B. Becking, "Coping with Drought and Famine in some Post Exilic Texts," in: E. Ben Zvi and C. Levin (Eds.), *Thinking of Water in the Early Second Temple Period* (BZAW 461; Berlin: de Gruyter, 2014), 229–255.

[38] On redistribution see H. Uusitalo, "Redistribution and Equality in the Welfare State: An Effort to Interpret the Major Findings of Research on the Redistributive Effects of the Welfare State," *European Sociological Review* 1 (1985): 163–176; G. Tullock, *Economics of Income Redistribution* (Studies in Public Choice 11; Boston: Springer, 1997).

have a future. In addition, Nehemiah reverts to the old idea of the שְׁמִטָּה *remission* (Exodus 23:10–11; Deuteronomy 15).[39] With his proposal, he honours the complaint of the impoverished with the principle of equality in ancient Israel and he safeguards the inner cohesion of the community.

15. A steadfast builder

The leaders in Samaria continue to thwart the rebuilding of the temple. To that aim, they invite Nehemiah for a meeting in Hakkephirim in the plain of Ono (6:2). Nehemiah, however, assuming that they want to harm him, does not leave his post as taskmaster at the rebuilding project. He answers – up to four times – the invitation with a rhetorical question:

> *Why should the work stop while I leave it and come down to you?* (Nehemiah 6:3)

After this fourfold refusal, the clan around Sanballat takes another road by accusing Nehemiah of a rebellion and striving for kingship in Jerusalem. This allegation is then countered by Nehemiah with his declaration that he is certainly not a rebel but obedient to the Persian throne. Then, his opponents try to ambush him in the temple – forbidden ground for a non-priest. Nehemiah reacts with a rhetorical question:

> *Should such a man as I run away?*
> *And what man such as I could go into the temple and live?* (Nehemiah 6:11)

Nehemiah does not answer the question. His reaction is given in the form of a declaration: 'I will not go in!,' implying the answer is 'No!' Despite all temptations, he remains steadfast in his role as rebuilder of the walls of Jerusalem.

16. Tithes for the Levites

The last question in the book of Nehemiah is to be found almost at the end of the text. After the rebuilding of the walls and their festive

---

[39] See, e.g. N.P. Lemche, "The Manumission of Slaves: The Fallow Year, the Sabbatical Year, the Jobel Year," *VT* 26 (1976): 38–59; R. Albertz, *Religionsgeschichte Israels in alttestamentlicher Zeit* (Grundrisse zum Alten Testament 8.1–2; Göttingen: Vandenhoeck & Ruprecht, 1992); E. Otto, *Theologische Ethik des Alten Testaments* (Theologische Wissenschaft 3.2; Stuttgart: Kohlhammer, 1994), 249–256; W. Dietrich, *"Theopolitik": Studien zur Theologie und Ethik des Alten Testaments* (Neukirchen-Vluyn: Neukirchener, 2002), 184–193.

inauguration, Nehemiah took a variety of measures to regulate the coherence of the community. One of them was the collection of tithes for the maintenance of the Levites serving at the temple. During a second mission, Nehemiah finds out that, despite the solemn oaths of the people, much of his measures have not been taken seriously. The Levites did not receive their life-maintenance and had to return to their fields. This results in a bitter question:

Why is the house of God forsaken? (Nehemiah 13:11)

The absence of the Levites caused the interruption of the cult. Nehemiah takes decisive and effective measures. He holds those who had paraded with him in two groups over the walls of Jerusalem at the feast of dedication responsible. He blames them for their lack of supervision resulting in the 'abandonment' of the temple. Nehemiah restores the Levites to their functions even before the payment of tithes is restored. As a result of his actions, all of Judah brings the gifts again. With this *totum pro parte* all those Judeans are meant who are part of the community. As a result, the cult could continue.

17. Conclusion

As in the book of Ezra, interrogative clauses are present at the crossroads of the narratives in Nehemia.[40] Remarkably, most of them are rhetorical questions that do not receive a formal answer, but turn out to be decisive for the development of the plot. The questions in Nehemiah open a window to the future, both at the level of the story and in the history of ancient Israel.

---

[40] An interesting proposal as to the narrative plot of Ezra-Nehemiah has been developed by T.C. Eskenazi, *In an Age of Prose: A Literary Approach to Ezra-Nehemiah* (SBLMS 36; Atlanta: Scholars Press, 1988).

'WHO AM I TO DISOBEY MY LORD?' (JUDITH 12:14)
Asking Questions in the Book of Judith

Barbara SCHMITZ
University of Würzburg

1. Introduction

The book of Judith tells an amazing story about how the 'Assyrian' King Nabouchodonosor wants to conquer the world and wants to be worshipped as the one and only God. This Jewish novel[1] that was originally written in Greek around 100 BCE,[2] explores in a fictional setting how to deal with the claim of the 'Assyrian' King Nabouchodonosor to be worthy of being worshipped as God. He and his general Holofernes – as the story goes – conquer the whole world and destroy the temples and shrines in all the countries they capture. Therefore, the temple in Jerusalem is in great danger. The whole narrative deals with the question: Who is God: Nabouchodonosor or the God of Israel? This question is not posed from the beginning, rather, it is developed in the narrative step by step.

Regarding questions in the Bible, it is interesting to explore how a narrative, the main topic of which is a question itself (Who is God: Nabouchodonosor or the God of Israel?) deals with questions. For the following, I consider questions in a narrowly defined, syntactical way as

---

[1] L.M. Wills, *The Jewish Novel in the Ancient World* (Ithaca: Cornell Univ. Press, 1995), 132–157.
[2] H. Engel, "Der HERR ist ein Gott, der Kriege zerschlägt: Zur Frage der griechischen Originalsprache und der Struktur des Buches Judith," in *Goldene Äpfel in silbernen Schalen*, ed. K.-D. Schunck und M. Augustin (BEATAJ 20; Frankfurt: Lang, 1992), 155–168; J. Joosten, "The Original Language and Historical Milieu of the Book of Judith," in *Meghillot: Studies in the Dead Sea Scrolls V–VI: A Festschrift for Devorah Dimant*, ed. Moshe Bar-Asher and Emanuel Tov (Haifa: University of Haifa / Bialik Press, 2007), 159–176; J. Corley, "Imitation of Septugintal Narrative and Greek Historiography in the Portrait of Holofernes," in *A Pious Seductress: Studies in the Book of Judith*, ed. Géza G. Xeravits (DCLS 14; Berlin: De Gruyter, 2012), 22–54.

those sentences that begin with an interrogative pronoun such as τίς, πόθεν, ποῦ, etc.[3] Considering these sentences as questions, there are altogether sixteen questions in the book of Judith: in Judith 5:3–4 (six times), 6:2 (twice); 8:12, 14; 10:12 (three times), 19 and 12:3, 14. These questions can be divided into different groups. There are questions that are 'real' questions, defined as those questions that seek information and therefore want to have enlightening and helpful answers. Others, however, ask a question but without really expecting an answer. These 'rhetorical' questions only really trigger an answer that is (or seems to be) clear and obvious to the addressees. As the following considerations will show, there are ten 'real' questions (Judith 5:3–4 [six times]; 10:12 [three times] and 12:3), five 'rhetorical' questions (6:2 [twice]; 8:12, 14; 10:19) and one ('rhetorical') question of trickery (see 12:14) in the book of Judith.

Furthermore, the arrangement of the real questions on one hand and the 'rhetorical' or trickery questions on the other is quite interesting. The different types of questions are arranged pairwise, meaning that 'real' questions are followed by 'rhetorical' questions in the same scene (Judith 5:3–4 → 6:2; Judith 10:12 → 10:19; Judith 12:3 → 12:14).

Only the two 'rhetorical' questions in Judith 8:12, 14 are not preceded by a 'real' question.

Therefore, the sixteen questions are split among four scenes and each of them has a different questioner as the following table shows.

Holofernes	5:3–4	→	6:2
Judith			8:12, 14
the Assyrian soldiers	10:12	→	10:19
Judith	12:3	→	12:14

2. Asking Questions: Holofernes (Judith 5:3–4 and Judith 6:2)

The reader encounters the first questions in the narration (Judith 5:3–4) when Holofernes meets with the first resistance. The Israelites had fortified their villages and occupied all the summits of the high mountains (4:5) because they were not willing to submit themselves to the Assyrian King by choice as the other people in the west did (3:7–8). Surprised and angry about this resistance of the Israelites, Holofernes

---

[3] See T. Muraoka, *A Syntax of Septuagint Greek* (Leuven: Peeters, 2016), 91–94.

summoned his council of war (5:2) and asked them a series of six questions:[4]

³ Ἀναγγείλατε δή μοι, υἱοὶ Χανάαν, τίς ὁ λαὸς οὗτος ὁ καθήμενος ἐν τῇ ὀρεινῇ, καὶ τίνες ἃς κατοικοῦσιν πόλεις, καὶ τὸ πλῆθος τῆς δυνάμεως αὐτῶν, καὶ ἐν τίνι τὸ κράτος αὐτῶν καὶ ἡ ἰσχὺς αὐτῶν, καὶ τίς ἀνέστηκεν ἐπ' αὐτῶν βασιλεὺς ἡγούμενος στρατιᾶς αὐτῶν, ⁴ καὶ διὰ τί κατενωτίσαντο τοῦ μὴ ἐλθεῖν εἰς ἀπάντησίν μοι παρὰ πάντας τοὺς κατοικοῦντας ἐν δυσμαῖς.	³ *'Tell me now, Canaanites, who is the people who lives in the highlands? What cities do they inhabit? What is the size of their army and in what does their might and strength lie? Who rules as king over them and leads their army?* ⁴ *Why have they, of all people living in the west, disdained to come and meet me?'*

Hearing Holofernes' voice for the first time, the reader gets to know him as a military leader, as all his questions concern military and political knowledge, which a general must and should have when facing military resistance. His six questions – who ... what ... what ... in what ... who ... why – concern the people, their cities, the army, the power, their leadership, and their reason for resistance. The second question about the cities they live in is, regarding biblical literature, a direct allusion to Numbers 13:19.[5] These questions resemble those of the spies who have a similar task of investigating the military strength of the land of Canaan (Numbers 13:17–21). The closest parallels, however, are the sequences of questions in two works of non-biblical literature: in Aeschylus' *The Persians* (230–245)[6] and in the conversation between Xerxes and the Spartan King Demaratus in Herodotus' *Histories* (7.101–104).[7]

In the book of Judith, the answers to these questions are given by Achior, the leader of Ammon, who gives a long speech. His speech (Judith 5:5, 6–19, 20–21),[8] however, does not pick up on the questions directly. Instead, he responds to only a few of them, at least at first

---

[4] The translation follows D. Levine Gera, *Judith* (Commentaries on Early Jewish Literature; Berlin: De Gruyter, 2014), for the book of Judith, and NETS for other biblical quotations.

[5] It is interesting to note that the Greek of the book of Judith in 5:3 is more idiomatic than in Num 13:19 which is an aspect in favour of an originally Greek-written text, for this see Joosten, "Original Language," 162.

[6] Gera, *Judith*, 196.

[7] B. Schmitz, "Zwischen Achikar und Demaratos: Die Bedeutung Achiors in der Juditerzählung," *BZ* 48 (2004): 19–38.

[8] See B. Schmitz and H. Engel, *Judit* (HThKAT; Freiburg: Herder, 2014), 168–170.

glance. Achior neither explains what cities the people inhabit nor who their king and the general of their army are. On the contrary, he gives a lengthy speech on the history of Israel from the very beginning to the contemporary situation. By recounting the history of Israel with his own very special and perspective-bound narration, he gives an answer to the first, fourth and fifth questions. It is *his* answer who this people is, in what their might and strength lie and who rules as king over them.

In contrast to Holofernes' agent-focused questions about king and military leaders, Achior replies without mentioning a single name: neither Abraham, Isaac, Jacob, Moses, Joshua, David nor any others are recalled. The only agent Achior names is the people as a whole and then God as the one who governs history. For this, Achior interprets the ambiguous fourth question in his own way: whereas Holofernes asked 'in *what* does their might and strength lie' (ἐν τίνι neuter), referring to military strength, Achior interprets the Greek interrogative pronoun as masculine 'in *whom* does their might and strength lie' (ἐν τίνι masculine).[9] By this, Achior presents his own version of the history of Israel, in which strength and power can be traced back to neither weapons and military tactics, nor to kings and powerful leaders. Instead he offers a different concept of political leadership than Nabouchodonosor and Holofernes do. Achior deduces his *theopolitical* principle from his recount of Israel's history (Judith 5:17–18):

[17] καὶ ἕως οὐχ ἥμαρτον ἐνώπιον τοῦ θεοῦ αὐτῶν, ἦν μετ' αὐτῶν τὰ ἀγαθά, ὅτι θεὸς μισῶν ἀδικίαν μετ' αὐτῶν ἐστιν.	[17] *As long as they did not sin before their God, they prospered, because a God who hates wickedness is with them.*
[18] ὅτε δὲ ἀπέστησαν ἀπὸ τῆς ὁδοῦ, ἧς διέθετο αὐτοῖς, ἐξωλεθρεύθησαν ἐν πολλοῖς πολέμοις ἐπὶ πολὺ σφόδρα καὶ ἠχμαλωτεύθησαν εἰς γῆν οὐκ ἰδίαν, καὶ ὁ ναὸς τοῦ θεοῦ αὐτῶν ἐγενήθη εἰς ἔδαφος, καὶ αἱ πόλεις αὐτῶν ἐκρατήθησαν ὑπὸ τῶν ὑπεναντίων.	[18] *But when they rebelled from the path he prescribed for them, often they were utterly destroyed in numerous battles and became captives in a land not theirs. The temple of their God was razed to the ground and their cities were captured by their opponents.*

Surprisingly, Achior, the leader of Ammon, presents Israel's behaviour towards God as the decisive parameter, one that decides the way history goes for Israel. God's criterion, however, is justice: as a God who hates injustice, his people experience good when they don't sin, but whenever they lose their God-focused way, they suffer military conquest, destruction and captivity. Achior, then, applies his conclusion of Isra-

---

[9] Gera, *Judith*, 198.

'WHO AM I TO DISOBEY MY LORD?' (JUDITH 12:14)

el's history to the present situation and to Holofernes' opening questions (Judith 5:20–21):

²⁰ καὶ νῦν, δέσποτα κύριε, εἰ μὲν ἔστιν ἀγνόημα ἐν τῷ λαῷ τούτῳ καὶ ἁμαρτάνουσιν εἰς τὸν θεὸν αὐτῶν καὶ ἐπισκεψόμεθα ὅτι ἔστιν ἐν αὐτοῖς σκάνδαλον τοῦτο, καὶ ἀναβησόμεθα καὶ ἐκπολεμήσομεν αὐτούς ²¹ εἰ δ' οὐκ ἔστιν ἀνομία ἐν τῷ ἔθνει αὐτῶν, παρελθέτω δὴ ὁ κύριός μου, μήποτε ὑπερασπίσῃ ὁ κύριος αὐτῶν καὶ ὁ θεὸς αὐτῶν ὑπὲρ αὐτῶν, καὶ ἐσόμεθα εἰς ὀνειδισμὸν ἐναντίον πάσης τῆς γῆς.	²⁰ *Now, my master and lord, if there is any error in this people and they are sinning against their God, let us find out what their misdeed is and then go up and fight them.* ²¹ *But if there is no lawlessness in their nation, let my lord pass over them, lest their Lord and their God defend them and we shall be out to shame before the entire world.*

Quite unsurprisingly for the reader, this is not the advice that Holofernes has in mind. Therefore, not only do the other members of the council of war protest, saying that the Israelites have neither the power nor the strength for a battle (Judith 5:23: λαὸς ἐν ᾧ οὐκ ἔστιν δύναμις οὐδὲ κράτος εἰς παράταξιν ἰσχυράν), but Holofernes himself also responds to Achior by opening his own reply with another two questions (6:2):

² Καὶ τίς εἶ σύ, Ἀχιὼρ καὶ οἱ μισθωτοὶ τοῦ Ἐφράιμ, ὅτι ἐπροφήτευσας ἐν ἡμῖν καθὼς σήμερον καὶ εἶπας τὸ γένος Ἰσραὴλ μὴ πολεμῆσαι, ὅτι ὁ θεὸς αὐτῶν ὑπερασπιεῖ αὐτῶν; καὶ τίς ὁ θεὸς εἰ μὴ Ναβουχοδονοσόρ;	² *Who are Achior – and the mercenaries of Ephraim – that you have acted the prophet among us today and said that we should not make war upon the people of Israel, because their God will defend them? Who is God, if not Nabouchodonosor?*

It is quite obvious that both questions are rhetorical. The answers to both are clear: Achior is nothing and Nabouchodonosor everything! By contrasting Achior[10] with his master, the Assyrian King, Holofernes shows that he perfectly understands Achior's advice but at the same time strongly rejects it.[11] His rationale is not based upon political or military factors, but upon theological logic. There is just one God and this God is Nabouchodonosor (Judith 6:2). This is the strongest articulation of Nabouchodonosor's being God, presented as an acknowledgement in the speech of Holofernes: he claims Nabouchodonosor not as a god, but Nabouchodonosor to be the one and only God. Thereby, concerning the

---

[10] For the first question cf. Exod 5:2; Jdg 9:28; 1 Sam 25:10; 26:14–15.
[11] Close biblical parallels for the harsh rejection of a wise prophet are the reaction of Balak to Balaam (Num 22–24) and King Ahab to Micaiah (1 Kgs 22).

Babylonian King, the Assyrian general expresses a monotheistic creed, which was never held by an Assyrian or a Babylonian, but developed by Israel during and after its exile in Babylon. Holofernes' wording recalls the six rhetorical questions in Deutero-Isaiah on the incomparability of Yhwh in implicit contrast to other gods, especially Marduk, in Isaiah 40:12–13 (see also the rhetorical questions on the incomparability of God in Job 38:4–7) or in Isaiah 41:26; 44:7 and 48:17 (see Exodus 15:11).[12] In Judith 6:3–4, Holofernes repeats Nabouchodonosor's speech in Judith 2:5–13 in which he explicitly claims himself to be king of the whole world and implicitly to be God,[13] and then taken up explicitly in 3:8. Therefore, Nabouchodonosor's claim to being worthy of being worshipped as God takes up the Hellenistic emperor cult but in a specific Jewish monotheistic interpretation as the one and only God. The exclusivity of the monotheistic concept is the decisive aspect: whereas, in a polytheistic concept in which one god can exist beside another or in competition with each other, there can only be one true God within a monotheistic belief: either the God of Israel or Nabouchodonosor. As king and God, Nabouchodonosor is able to send his might (κράτος) in order to conquer Israel, at least according to Holofernes (Judith 6:2–3). With the word 'might' (κράτος) Holofernes takes up his fourth question: in what does Israel's might and strength lie (5:2)? Thus, Holofernes himself answers his own question in a way that suits him.

3. Asking Questions: Judith (Judith 8:12 and 8:14)

The question of the book – Nabouchodonosor or the God of Israel? – comes to a head in the following chapters: the Assyrian army besieges the fictive, Judean town Bethulia to which Achior was delivered. The consequences are a shortage of water, fainting and revolt against the leaders of Bethulia (Judith 7:19–29). Therefore, the elders of the city negotiate a five-day ultimatum in order to give God time to rescue his people (7:30–32). This is when Judith, as a new character, appears on the scene. She is a beautiful, rich, well-educated and obviously powerful woman who calls in the elders of the city to give them a speech in which she denounces the decision of the town leaders, demonstrating that their position is theologically incorrect.

---

[12] J. Blenkinsopp, *Isaiah 40–55: A New Translation with Introduction and Commentary* (AB 19A; New York: Doubleday, 2000), 191. For rhetorical questions in Deutero-Isaiah see Isa 40:18, 26–27; 41:2, 4, 26; 42:23; 43:9, 13; 45:21; 46:5 etc. Cf. Sir 1:1–3; 18:4–5.

[13] Schmitz and Engel, *Judit*, 109–110.

Judith's two questions open up the long middle part of her tripartite speech (Judith 8:11, 12–23, 24–27), the long middle part being divided into two sections (8:12–16, 17–23).[14]

After having requested their attention and having reopened the topic (Judith 8:11), Judith first deconstructs the position of the elders theologically by questioning their attitude: Who are you (τίνες ἐστὲ ὑμεῖς)?

[12] καὶ νῦν τίνες ἐστὲ ὑμεῖς, οἳ ἐπειράσατε τὸν θεὸν ἐν τῇ ἡμέρᾳ τῇ σήμερον καὶ ἵστασθε ὑπὲρ τοῦ θεοῦ ἐν μέσῳ υἱῶν ἀνθρώπων;	[12] Who are you, now, that you put God to the test today and take the place of God among mortals?

Her opening question is the counterpart to Nabouchodonosor's opening question to Achior 'who are you?' (τίς εἶ σύ, Judith 6:2). Both question the position of a human being versus that of God. Achior, the insightful pagan, however, is right and Nabouchodonosor turns out to be not-God, whereas the Israelite elders are wrong, but their God turns out to be the only and all-powerful God of the whole world (16:13–17).

Judith's question (Judith 8:12) could be considered the abstract of her whole speech. In Judith's point of view, the elders appropriate the position of God and put God to the test by taking an oath between God and themselves, saying that they will surrender the city if God does not help them within the next five days (8:11, cf. 7:30–32). By opening her argumentation with this rhetorical question, the answer of her speech is clear from the beginning: the elders are completely wrong by dispossessing God and empowering themselves through appropriating a God-like position. The reciprocal motif of testing God and being tested by God is one of the central leitmotifs of her speech and it frames the speech as an opening question (8:12) and a conclusion (8:25–27).

With her opening question, Judith alludes to the biblical narratives that tell how human beings question God and thereby test him. The paradigmatic story of testing God is another shortage-of-water story, the story of the water from the rock in the book of Exodus (Exod 17:1–7[LXX]; cf. Ps[LXX] 77:40–41, 56; 94:9).[15] The parallels to this story are close: in both stories, there is an extreme crisis because of the shortage of water, so much so that people are in danger of dying. Therefore, in both stories, the people revolt

---

[14] Schmitz and Engel, *Judit*, 239–230.
[15] See J.W. van Henten and S. Castelli, "Massah and Meribah Re-interpreted: Biblical Accounts, Judith and Josephus," in: *The Early Reception of the Torah*, ed. Kristin De Troyer, Barbara Schmitz, Joshua Alfaro, and Maximilian Häberlein (DCLS 39; Berlin: De Gruyter, 2020), 19–48.

against their leader and in both the situations are described as testing God (πειράζω Exod 17:2, 7^LXX; Judith 8,12). The difference between both stories is that in Exod 17 Moses asks God for help and trusts him, whereas the leaders in the book of Judith decide of their own accord what to do. Due to this parallel, Judith, however, is portrayed as a new Moses who is able to save her people in a desperate situation.

This difference is deepened in Judith 8:13–14 where the fundamental difference between God and human beings is emphasized through asking a second question:

¹³ καὶ νῦν κύριον παντοκράτορα ἐξετάζετε καὶ οὐθὲν ἐπιγνώσεσθε ἕως τοῦ αἰῶνος. ¹⁴ ὅτι βάθος καρδίας ἀνθρώπου οὐχ εὑρήσετε καὶ λόγους τῆς διανοίας αὐτοῦ οὐ διαλήμψεσθε καὶ πῶς τὸν θεόν, ὃς ἐποίησεν πάντα ταῦτα, ἐρευνήσετε καὶ τὸν νοῦν αὐτοῦ ἐπιγνώσεσθε καὶ τὸν λογισμὸν αὐτοῦ κατανοήσετε; μηδαμῶς, ἀδελφοί, μὴ παροργίζετε κύριον τὸν θεὸν ἡμῶν.	¹³ *You are now scrutinizing the Lord Almighty, even though you will never know anything.* ¹⁴ *For you shall not plumb the depths of the human heart nor shall you grasp the thoughts of human minds. How then can you inquire after God who created all these things or know his mind or perceive his reasoning? Do not, brothers, persist in angering the Lord, our God.*

In her *a fortiori* argument, Judith contrasts the omnipotence of the *kyrios pantokrator* with the inability of human beings to understand themselves, let alone understanding anything else. The second question in the speech, therefore, is also a rhetorical one: there is no need for an answer; the warning 'do not / never!' (μηδαμῶς) is enough.

At the end of her speech, Judith comes back to the testing motif, but she offers a new interpretation of the desperate situation in Bethulia. She takes up her opening interpretation – the elders putting God to a test – by turning it upside down: instead of their testing God, God is testing the people of Bethulia (Judith 8:25–26).

²⁵ παρὰ ταῦτα πάντα εὐχαριστήσωμεν κυρίῳ τῷ θεῷ ἡμῶν, ὃς πειράζει ἡμᾶς καθὰ καὶ τοὺς πατέρας ἡμῶν. ²⁶ μνήσθητε ὅσα ἐποίησεν μετὰ Αβρααμ καὶ ὅσα ἐπείρασεν τὸν Ισαακ καὶ ὅσα ἐγένετο τῷ Ιακωβ ἐν Μεσοποταμίᾳ τῆς Συρίας ποιμαίνοντι τὰ πρόβατα Λαβαν τοῦ ἀδελφοῦ τῆς μητρὸς αὐτοῦ.	²⁵ *In the view of all this let us be grateful to the Lord our God, who is testing us, as he did to our fathers.* ²⁶ *Remember all he did with Abraham, and how much he tested Isaac, and all that happened to Jacob in Syrian Mesopotamia when he herded the flocks of Laban, his mother's brother.*

Judith exchanges subject (who tests…?) and object (whom?) and thereby recalls other biblical stories of how God put his people to a test (πειράζω Judith 8:25, 26). She explicitly recalls how God tested Abraham, Isaac, and Jacob (8:25–27), although the biblical literature provides only one story for testing Abraham (Genesis 22:1) and none for Isaac or Jacob. The idea that God tests human beings, however, is well known in the biblical literature (see Exodus 15:25; 16:4; 20:20; Deuteronomy 4:34; 8:2–16; 13:4; Judges 2:22; 3:1–4; 2 Chronicles 32:31; Daniel 12:10).

Judith's argumentation, though, is more than just a reversal. She contextualizes her interpretation – God has put the people to a test – with the insight that God's actual aim of testing is to educate his people (Judith 8:27):

²⁷ ὅτι οὐ καθὼς ἐκείνους ἐπύρωσεν εἰς ἐτασμὸν τῆς καρδίας αὐτῶν, καὶ ἡμᾶς οὐκ ἐξεδίκησεν, ἀλλ᾽ εἰς νουθέτησιν μαστιγοῖ κύριος τοὺς ἐγγίζοντας αὐτῷ.	²⁷ *He has not set us an ordeal by fire as he did with them to test their hearts, nor has he taken revenge upon us, but the Lord chastises those close to him as a warning.*

This explanation of the situation in Judith's speech is in line with the Jewish literature of the Second Temple period in which the idea of testing people is taken up vividly,[16] but Judith's explanation is a reinterpreted way in which God offers the testing as an occasion for learning (see e.g. Wisdom 11:9–10; 12:2; 16:6; Sirach 4:17; see Psalm 25:2[LXX]) for which Abraham is presented as an example (Sirach 44:19–20; see 1 Maccabees 2:52; 4 Maccabees 16:18–20). Judith 8:27 combines the testing of hearts by God and their purification in the fire that is taken up in Wisdom 3:4–6.[17]

4. Asking Questions: the Assyrian Soldiers (Judith 10:12 and 10:19)

After presenting her theological position (Judith 8) in which she announces her intended deed (8:32–34), Judith prepares herself by

---

[16] See Wis 1:2; 2:17, 24; 3:5; 11:9; 12:26; 18:20, 25; 19:5; Sir 2:1; 4:17; 6:7; 13:11; 18:23; 27:5, 7; 37:27; 39:4; 44:20; Tob 12:13ˢ etc.

[17] Wis 3:4–6: ⁴καὶ γὰρ ἐν ὄψει ἀνθρώπων ἐὰν κολασθῶσιν, ἡ ἐλπὶς αὐτῶν ἀθανασίας πλήρης· ⁵καὶ ὀλίγα παιδευθέντες μεγάλα εὐεργετηθήσονται, ὅτι ὁ θεὸς ἐπείρασεν αὐτοὺς καὶ εὗρεν αὐτοὺς ἀξίους ἑαυτοῦ· ⁶ὡς χρυσὸν ἐν χωνευτηρίῳ ἐδοκίμασεν αὐτοὺς καὶ ὡς ὁλοκάρπωμα θυσίας προσεδέξατο αὐτούς. "⁴For even if in the sight of human beings they were punished, their hope is full of immortality, ⁵and having been disciplined a little, they will be greatly benefited, because God tested them and found them worthy of himself; ⁶as gold in the furnace, he tested them, and as a sacrificial whole burnt offering, he accepted them." See H. Engel, *Das Buch der Weisheit* (NSKAT 16; Stuttgart: Katholisches Bibelwerk, 1998), 82–83; L. Mazzinghi, *Weisheit* (IEKAT 21; Stuttgart: Kohlhammer, 2018), 112–114.

praying (chapter 9) and by beautifying herself (10:1–4). Then she leaves Bethulia together with her maid (10:5–10). Going through the valley in the direction of the Assyrian camp, Judith is taken by Assyrian soldiers, who interrogate her (Judith 10:12):

¹² καὶ συνέλαβον αὐτὴν καὶ ἐπηρώτησαν	¹² *They took hold of her and asked,*
Τίνων εἶ	*'To what people do you belong?*
καὶ πόθεν ἔρχῃ	*Where are you coming from*
καὶ ποῦ πορεύῃ;	*and where are you going?'*

The first of the three questions is used in Homer's questioning of a stranger (Il. 21.150; Od. 1.170; 10.325 etc.).[18] The second and third questions reflect Genesis 16:8^LXX, because not only are the questions of the angel of God to Hagar identical, but also the answers of both women are that they are running away (ἀποδιδράσκω).

Judiths replies to these questions by answering them precisely:

¹² καὶ εἶπεν	¹² *she replied,*
Θυγάτηρ εἰμὶ τῶν Ἑβραίων καὶ ἀποδιδράσκω ἀπὸ προσώπου αὐτῶν, ὅτι μέλλουσιν δίδοσθαι ὑμῖν εἰς κατάβρωμα.	*'I am a daughter of the Hebrews and I am fleeing from them, because they are about to become your prey.*
¹³ κἀγὼ ἔρχομαι εἰς τὸ πρόσωπον Ὀλοφέρνου ἀρχιστρατήγου δυνάμεως ὑμῶν τοῦ ἀπαγγεῖλαι ῥήματα ἀληθείας καὶ δείξω πρὸ προσώπου αὐτοῦ ὁδὸν καθ' ἣν πορεύσεται καὶ κυριεύσει πάσης τῆς ὀρεινῆς,	¹³ *I am on my way to the commander of your army, Holofernes, in order to bring him a trustworthy message. I will show him the path he can follow and capture the entire hill country.*
καὶ οὐ διαφωνήσει τῶν ἀνδρῶν αὐτοῦ σὰρξ μία οὐδὲ πνεῦμα ζωῆς.	*Not a single man of his shall perish, not a living soul.'*

As a daughter of the Hebrews (first question), Judith says, she flees them (second question) in order to go to Holofernes (third question). Two aspects in her answer are striking. Firstly, her announcement that Israel will become the Assyrian prey is true regarding the actual situation and fits well with what is expected in Holofernes' war council (see Judith 5:24). Secondly, Judith answers a fourth question that wasn't asked (something like 'what are you going to do?') in revealing her plans to the soldiers.

---

[18] See Gera, *Judith*, 338.

The effect on the soldiers is immediate, although it is not motivated by her particular answers, but instead by the beauty of her appearance (Judith 10:14). It seems to be that the interrogation is part of their professional routine as soldiers, whereas her beauty has caught the soldiers as men. Her beauty, moreover, also saves her from being mistreated or even raped; on the contrary, the soldiers escort the beautiful Judith directly to Holofernes.

At Holofernes' tent, the second question scene takes place (Judith 10:19):

¹⁹ καὶ ἐθαύμαζον ἐπὶ τῷ κάλλει αὐτῆς καὶ ἐθαύμαζον τοὺς υἱοὺς Ἰσραὴλ ἀπ' αὐτῆς, καὶ εἶπεν ἕκαστος πρὸς τὸν πλησίον αὐτοῦ Τίς καταφρονήσει τοῦ λαοῦ τούτου, ὃς ἔχει ἐν ἑαυτῷ γυναῖκας τοιαύτας; ὅτι οὐ καλόν ἐστιν ὑπολείπεσθαι ἐξ αὐτῶν ἄνδρα ἕνα, οἳ ἀφεθέντες δυνήσονται κατασοφίσασθαι πᾶσαν τὴν γῆν.	¹⁹ *They were astounded by her beauty and astounded by the Israelites because of her. They said to one another, 'Who will look down upon this nation, who has women such as these? It is not good if even a single one of their men survives, for if they are left alone they will be able to outwit the entire world.'*

Like the soldiers outside the camp, the soldiers in the camp come together, and, like the first group (cf. Judith 10:14: καὶ ἦν ἐναντίον αὐτῶν θαυμάσιον τῷ κάλλει σφόδρα), they are also astounded by her beauty. Even more, their reaction is reciprocal. They draw conclusions about the Israelites from Judith's beauty and ask one another a (rhetorical) question that they answer immediately: they should not disdain the Israelites who have women such as Judith! Unlike Holofernes' council of war who thought that Israel would easily be conquered (5:23–24; 7:8–16), the soldiers realize the danger. They draw their conclusion through an *a minore ad maius,* or *qol wa-homer*, rationale: if a nation has women such as this, its men will outwit the whole world even more. And, again, the Assyrians are wrong. As the reader knows from reading the book of Judith so far, the men of Israel would not be able to outwit the world: either they act defensively, as the High Priest of Jerusalem did by occupying mountain passes (cf. 4:6–7), or they just sit around waiting for God as the elders of Bethulia (7:30–32) do. 'Outwitting the whole world' – and here the verb κατασοφίζομαι comes into play – refers to the beginning of the Exodus story, because in the LXX the verb is used only three times, once in Exod 1:10^{LXX} and twice in Judith 5:11; 10:19. In Exod 1:10^{LXX} it refers to the Egyptian King who is afraid of the Israelites living in Egypt and is scared that they could outwit the Egyptians. The book of Judith is well aware of this link, as Exod 1 is explicitly alluded to in Judith 5:11 by referring to the story and by using the verb κατασοφίζομαι. Therefore, the repetition of the verb κατασοφίζομαι clearly brings up Exod 1 and thereby parallels the fear of the Assyrian soldiers with the xenophobic attitude of the Egyptian King. The Assyrian soldiers, smart as they are, are however mistaken in thinking of the Israelite men as the dangerous enemies, ignoring that it is precisely Judith who will be the one to outwit the huge and dangerous Assyrian army. As shown in the preceding paragraph (cf. Judith 8:12), Judith is again implicitly portrayed as a new Moses, the one who will save Israel.

5. Asking questions: Holofernes and Judith (Judith 12:3 and 12:14)

Right after the thoughtful question of the Assyrian soldiers, Judith gains Holofernes' attention, again because of her beauty (cf. Judith 10:23) and her speech (11:20–23). During her negotiation concerning the circumstances of her living in the Assyrian camp, Holofernes asks one question (Judith 12:3):

| ³ καὶ εἶπεν πρὸς αὐτὴν Ὀλοφέρνης Ἐὰν δὲ ἐκλίπῃ τὰ ὄντα μετὰ σοῦ, πόθεν ἐξοίσομέν σοι δοῦναι ὅμοια αὐτοῖς; | ³ *And Holofernes asked her, 'If what you have with you runs out, where will we get similar food to give you?'* |

In her answer, Judith points out quite correctly and more precisely than Holofernes can guess that God will have done what he plans by her hand before her food runs out (Judith 12:4).

This question links to the next dining scene, the invitation of Judith by Bagoas to Holofernes' private party given on the fourth day of Judith's stay in camp because Holofernes is afraid that there could be doubts about his virility (Judith 12:10–12).

Bagoas, his servant (Judith 12:11), invites Judith by pointing out that she should drink wine with them for good cheer and to become one of the Assyrian women (12:13). Judith then replies to this straight and quite unambiguous invitation with a question (Judith 12:14):

| ¹⁴ Καὶ τίς εἰμι ἐγὼ ἀντεροῦσα τῷ κυρίῳ μου; ὅτι πᾶν, ὃ ἔσται ἐν τοῖς ὀφθαλμοῖς αὐτοῦ ἀρεστόν, σπεύσασα ποιήσω, καὶ ἔσται τοῦτό μοι ἀγαλλίαμα ἕως ἡμέρας θανάτου μου. | ¹⁴ *'Who am I to disobey my lord? I shall hasten to do everything that is pleasing in his eyes and this will be a source of joy to me until the day I die.'* |

This last question of the book of Judith is not only a rhetorical one, but also a question of trickery, because Judith does not identify whom she has in mind when speaking of 'my lord' (τῷ κυρίῳ μου). In the context of the scene itself, Bagoas has to identify 'my lord' as Holofernes, because Holofernes is also 'his' lord and Judith has already referred to Holofernes as 'lord' (κύριος Judith 11:10, 11, 17). In the book of Judith, the 'lord' (κύριος) is an important leitmotif. Nabouchodonosor is the 'lord'[19], but also the God of Israel is the 'lord.'[20] Achior, Bagoas and his other soldiers call Holofernes their 'lord.'[21] The question of the book – who is God: Nabouchodonosor or the God of Israel? – deals with the biblical double meaning of 'lord' (κύριος) that not only connotes a hierarchical relationship between two human beings, but also is the 'translation' of the Hebrew tetragrammaton Yhwh in the Greek Bible. Therefore, Holofernes is the 'lord' of his soldiers and of Bagoas, just as Nabouchodonosor is the 'lord' of the Assyrian army and of Holofernes, but of course he is not *kyrios* / Lord in the biblical sense of the word. Judith plays on this double meaning: speaking to Holofernes and to Bagoas she speaks ambiguously of *kyrios* so that those who listen to her in the narrative scene and those who read the book can decode it in different ways. For example, Judith promises Holofernes that God will be with Holofernes and that 'my lord will not fail in any of his undertakings' (καὶ οὐκ ἀποπεσεῖται ὁ κύριός μου τῶν ἐπιτηδευμάτων αὐτοῦ 11:6). Holofernes will apply 'my lord' to himself, but readers knowing the language of the Greek Bible could also apply it to the God of Israel. The same is true for Achior in 5:21[22] and Judith in 11:6; 12:4 or 12:14. In 12:14, Judith promises that she will not disobey 'my lord' (τῷ κυρίῳ μου). Again, Bagoas will apply 'my lord' to Holofernes, but readers will apply it to the God of Israel. With this double-bind language, Judith does not lie but uses trickery. In the Assyrian camp, Judith is the powerless, inferior woman who is always in danger of being mistreated or raped. The only power she has are her words.

As Judith 12:14 is furthermore a rhetorical question, this sentence is not only tricky but also deeply ironic. No matter how the question is read (either as Holofernes or the God of Israel), the answer is the same: Bagoas expects her to obey Holofernes; the reader expects her to obey God. In this double sense, Judith, of course, will hasten to do everything

---

[19] κύριος Jdt 2:5, 13, 14, 15; 6:4; 11:4, 22.
[20] κύριος Jdt 4:2, 11, 13, 14, 15; 6:19; 7:19, 28, 29, 30; 8:11, 13, 14, 16, 23, 25, 27, 31, 33, 35; 9:1, 2, 7, 8; 12:8; 13:4, 7, 15, 16, 18; 15:8, 10; 16:5, 12, 13, 16, 17.
[21] κύριος Jdt 5:5, 20, 21; 6:13; 10:15; 12:13; 13:1; 14:13.
[22] In Jdt 5:21 Achior speaks in the same sentence of "my *kyrios*" (ὁ κύριός μου) referring to Holofernes and of "their *kyrios* and their God" (ὁ κύριος αὐτῶν καὶ ὁ θεὸς αὐτῶν) referring to the God of Israel.

that is pleasing in 'his,' that is, either Holofernes' or God's, eyes, as she promises in 12:14.

Her announcement that her deed will be 'a source of joy to me until the day I die' is prophetic, whatever way the double-bind sentence is read.

And, last but not least, this rhetorical, tricky, and ironic question is also a highly intra-textual one, referring to Judith 6:2. Therefore, 12:14 is the counterpart of Holofernes' acknowledgement in 6:2.

6. Conclusion

Reading the book of Judith with respect to the questions that are raised in the narrative, it becomes obvious that the theme of the book of Judith – who is God: Nabouchodonosor or the God of Israel? – is narratively developed by questions. These questions raised through the story draw a line from Judith 5:2, 3–6:2 to 8:12 to 10:12–10:19 to 12:3–12:14.

Holofernes' opening ('real') questions (Judith 5:3–4) trigger Achior's unwanted advice that Holofernes himself rejects with two rhetorical questions (6:2–3) that are the answer – at least in his eyes – of his request. The dynamic of questions and answers in this scene puts the whole theme of the book in a nutshell: Nabouchodonosor or the God of Israel?

In Judith 8, there are no 'real' questions, only rhetorical ones. This does not seem to be chance but, rather, the syntactical expression for the content of Judith's speech: she does not have any 'real' questions, but a powerful and sophisticated position. Her (rhetorical) questions, therefore, do have pedagogical purposes. At first glance, they serve as a rhetorical tool to convince the elders of her position. But the leaders of Bethulia are unable to understand Judith's argumentation. At second glance, however, the rhetorical questions are meant for the reader who is prepared by these questions for Judith's prayer (Judith 9) and her following deed (Judith 10–13). By asking these rhetorical questions, the reader understands that God does not want to test the Bethulians but, rather, wants to motivate them to act on their own as Judith will do.

The sequence of questions by the Assyrian soldiers is opened again by a 'real' question (Judith 10:12) followed by a rhetorical one (10:19). The latter question, 'Who will look down upon this nation, who has women such as these?,' shows that the questioners have the right instinct, although they underestimate the impact of their question. Therefore, they function as true, but unheard, alarms.

The last question in the book of Judith, 'Who am I to disobey my lord?' (Judith 12:14), is the most complex one and summarizes at the same time the topic of the whole book. This was already the case with 6:2, but this time it is more complex as it can be read in different ways: characters within the narrative decode 'lord' as Holofernes, but the readers decode 'lord' as the God of Israel. These different levels of understanding between the characters in the story and the reader are ironic and tricky at the same time.

The question, 'Who is God, if not Nabouchodonosor?' (Judith 6:2), which most explicitly acknowledges Nabouchodonosor as God, draws a line to the last question, 'Who am I to disobey my lord?' (12:14), as an ironic question and a question of trickery that outwits the overwhelming Assyrian power. The reader knows that Judith, of course, will disobey 'her lord' Holofernes! Therefore, the Assyrian soldiers are right in asking the far-reaching question: 'Who will look down upon this nation, who has women such as these?' (10:19).

DO CONTRADICTORY READINGS OF THE QUESTION BY JOB'S WIFE REALLY MATTER?

Sehoon JANG
Kukje Theological University

1. Introduction

The book of Job presents the story of the unparalleled suffering of a non-Israelite from the land of Uz that has been the subject of a great deal of discussion in Joban studies. This God-fearing man is abruptly overwhelmed by a series of tragic calamities; the loss of all his material wealth and the death of all his children, followed by an assault on his own body: terrible sores on his skin. As if to rub salt in the wounds, Job's three friends, whose ostensible purpose of visiting him was to console him, each in turn respond to him with severe criticism, suggesting that Job is being punished for any sins that merit this misery. Such grave misjudgement does nothing but increase his unendurable agony. However, no matter how many ordeals he has undergone, in the end, Job is able to experience God's final vindication and his restoration, while his three interlocutors are condemned for their misapplication of the theory of reward and retribution. Given his unswerving commitment to God, even during his undeserved suffering, it is not too much to say that Job is a paragon of piety in the biblical books.

Though Job is the protagonist throughout the entire book and though his friends play major roles, his wife is marginalized in this book. For instance, she is only identified with the expression, 'his wife' (Job 2:9), without her name. This nameless woman disappears from the scene immediately after speaking only six (Hebrew) words (עֹדְךָ מַחֲזִיק בְּתֻמָּתֶךָ; בָּרֵךְ אֱלֹהִים, וָמֻת) to her husband in the second half of the prologue (Job 2). She is nowhere to be found in the rest of the book of Job other than in Job's references to her twice in the poetic section (Job 19:17; 31:10), and no attention is paid to her even in the epilogue in which the divine restoration of Job is highlighted. Given her disappearance from the text after Job 2, as well as the fact that no information on her identity and her origin is given, it may be fairly asserted that Job's wife is one of the most enigmatic women in the Old Testament. In particular, her seemingly ambiguous speech in Job 2:9 has triggered a variety of interpretations of what she utters in its own context.[1]

It is interesting to observe that the three-word question of the first part of her whole speech in the original Hebrew (עֹדְךָ מַחֲזִיק בְּתֻמָּתֶךָ) is so obscure that one finds it extremely difficult to choose between various possible meanings. Some commentators have considered rendering it as an unfavourable utterance while other exegetes deem it positive or sympathetic.[2] It should be noted that the significance of this equivocal question is surely bound up with what Job's wife intends by the question. Thus, many suggestions have been made to explicate what the genuine intent of her question is, but no agreement has yet been reached. My interest is not to fully engage myself in these countless debates about the meaning of her somewhat ambivalent question. Instead, my chief concern

---

[1] For a negative understanding of Job's wife as a bad or wicked woman, see L. Wilson, *Job* (The Two Horizons Old Testament Commentary; Grand Rapids: Eerdmans, 2015), 38–39. See also D. Penchansky, "Job's Wife: The Satan's Handmaid," in: D. Penchansky and P.L. Redditt (Eds.), *Shall Not the Judge of All the Earth Do What is Right?: Studies on the Nature of God in Tribute to James L. Crenshaw* (Winona Lake: Eisenbrauns, 2000), 223–228; V. Sasson, "The Literary and Theological Function of Job's Wife in the Book of Job," *Bib* 79 (1998): 86–90; J.E. Hartley, *The Book of Job* (NICOT; Grand Rapids: Eerdmans, 1988), 83–84; F.I. Andersen, *Job* (TOTC; Leicester: IVP, 1976), 92–93. For a full-fledged feminist reading of Job's wife, see F. Rachel Magdalene, "Job's Wife as Hero: A Feminist–Forensic Reading of the Book of Job," *BibInt* 14 (2006): 209–258. See also D. Clines, "Why is There a Book of Job, and What Does it Do to You if You Read it?," in: W.A.M. Beuken (Ed.), *The Book of Job* (Leuven: Peeters, 1994), 2–20. For a helpful study of Mrs. Job's contribution to Job's transformation, see P.K.K. Cho, "Job 2 and 42:7–10 as Narrative Bridge and Theological Pivot," *JBL* 136 (2017): 857–877. See also P. Kirkpatrick, "Curse God and Die – Job's Wife and the Struggle for Job's Transformation," in: B. Ego and U. Mittmann (Eds.), *Evil and Death: Conceptions of the Human in Biblical, Early Jewish, and Greco-Roman and Egyptian Literature* (DCLS 18; Berlin: de Gruyter, 2015), 43–55; D. Penchansky, "Job's Wife," 223–228; E. van Wolde, "The Development of Job: Mrs. Job as Catalyst," in: Athalya Brenner (Ed.), *A Feminist Companion to Wisdom Literature* (Sheffield: Sheffield Academic Press, 1995), 201–221. For a treatment of the reception history of Job's wife, see K. Low, *The Bible, Gender, and Reception History: The Case of Job's Wife* (LHBOTS 586; London: T&T Clark, 2013). See also A.W. Stewart, "Job's Wife and Her Interpreters," in: C.A. Newsom, S.H. Ringe and J.E. Lapsley (Eds.), *The Women's Bible Commentary* (London: SPCK, 2014), 216–220; E.O. Gravett, "Biblical Responses: Past and Present Retellings of the Enigmatic Mrs. Job", *BibInt* 20 (2012): 97–125; K.R. Suomala, "The Taming of Job in Judaism, Christianity, and Islam," *Word & World* 31 (2011): 397–408. For a fresh understanding of Job's wife as a female victim of sexual discrimination in a male dominated society, see K.G. Wilcok, "Job, his Daughters and his Wife," *JSOT* 43 (2018): 303–315.

[2] See Stewart, "Job's Wife and Her Interpreters," 97–125.

is to elaborate how her question plays a pivotal role in steering Job onto a new path that he has never attempted to take, no matter what the import of her question is.[3] In this article, I will focus on two current interpretations of the question by Job's wife that appear to be in conflict with each other. I will concentrate on the functional significance of her question since the question has a crucial impact on the swift change in Job's attitude towards God; a change that can be found in the transition between Job 2 and 3. Then I will argue that contradictory readings of her question are unproblematic if they are understood in relation to the functional significance of the question within the text.

2. Reading the Question as an Invective against Impenitence and Hypocrisy

There has been a traditional description of Job's wife as an ally of Satan, who frantically seeks to nullify Job's piety; a negative approach to her that was initiated by the early Church Fathers when they dealt with her as 'an unthinking fool, an irritating nag, a heretic, a tempter, an unwitting tool of the devil, or even a personification of the devil himself.'[4] For instance, Augustine tended to regard her as *adiutrix diaboli* ('devil's assistant') in *Enarratio in Psalmum* 29 II 7, an unfavourable rendering of Job's wife that was maintained by a great number of theologians such as Calvin who identified her with *organum Satani* ('Satan's instrument') and that has remained influential in modern Joban studies.[5] Over the past decades, it has often been taken for granted that the short question of the first part of her speech about Job's integrity ('Do you still persist in your integrity?') immediately accompanied by her desperate advice ('Curse

---

[3] I do not deny that the dramatic grieving of Job's friends, immediately preceding Job's own lament, may have played some role in Job's response. However, there is strong support for an argument that the words of Job's wife are the primary factor. Her words are the very first words from a human being to be heard by Job and to be quoted in the text, but the grieving of the three friends in Job 2 is only described by the narrator. Job's friends raised their voices and wept aloud at the extremity of Job's suffering, but "no one spoke a word to him" (Job 2:13). This is a crucial detail. Of course, spoken (as well as written or transcribed) words are central to the biblical text. Words and their power are a common theme. Whether or not the wordless grief of Job's friends may have an effect, the words of Job's wife – her question and imperative – are critical in evoking both Job's expression of devotion to God and his words of lamentation.

[4] C.L. Seow, "Job's Wife," *Engaging the Bible in a Gendered World*, ed. Linda Day and Carolyn Pressler (Louisville: Westminster John Knox Press, 2006), 141.

[5] See C.L. Seow, *Job 1–21: Interpretation and Commentary* (Grand Rapids: Eerdmans, 2013), 304–305.

God and die') implies that she has now become a spokesperson solely manipulated by Satan. According to this view, the role of the Adversary in the heavenly realm has been replaced by that of Job's wife in the earthly realm.[6] To put it another way, the role of the Adversary in heaven who attempted to wear down Job's piety has been replaced by that of a human being who is now forcefully urging Job to relinquish his integrity. As Paul Cho points out,

> *In short, the words of Job's wife echo both the satan and God and, in this way, replicate the heavenly dialogue on earth. In terms of narrative technique, it is an efficient means of changing the scene and perspective of the drama: the satan and God find their counterpart and are, in a sense, replaced by Job's wife. No longer will the debate concerning human piety and suffering happen in heaven among divine beings from a divine perspective but on earth among human interlocutors from a human perspective.*[7]

In this regard, Job's wife is deemed a merciless shrew who is not so much a comforter as a torturer who speaks with acrimony, with a spiteful tongue that only intensifies the affliction of her husband, who is struggling with the problem of unprovoked suffering. According to this approach to Job's wife, she is nothing more than a means of fulfilling what Satan is eager to anticipate.

It has been argued, furthermore, that Job's wife appears as a precursor of the three foolish advocates of the retribution theology, from the perspective of which they respond to Job with savage and poignant denunciation in the poetic section of the book of Job. Lindsay Wilson argues that the statement made by Job's wife in Job 2:9 is rooted in the traditional principle of retribution, which is subsequently shared by Job's three friends whose erroneous conviction is that Job's suffering undoubtedly results from his hidden sins.[8] He observes:

> *Her reference to his 'integrity' reminds us that God used this same description of Job in 2:3. She appears to believe that Job's suffering will continue until he acknowledges his sin, so that insisting on his*

---

[6] According to Thomas Aquinas, the Satan spares Job's wife in the misfortune that befalls her family so that she could be manipulated to tempt Job. See J. Boss, *Human Consciousness of God in the Book of Job: A Theological and Psychological Commentary* (London: T&T Clark, 2010), 30.

[7] Cho, "Job 2 and 42:7–10 as Narrative Bridge," 871.

[8] Cho also argues that "Job's wife also introduces a theology of defiance that challenges the piety of the Joban tale and anticipates the theological agon of the poetic core." (Cho, "Job 2 and 42:7–10 as Narrative Bridge," 871.)

integrity equals refusing to repent. If so, she is expressing a traditional understanding of the doctrine of retribution.[9]

It is Wilson's contention that the words of Job's wife play a pioneering role in urging Job to reflect on the sins that he has committed. However, it is doubtful whether her words clearly indicate that his suffering is a dire consequence of his sin. More particularly, one calls into question whether her speech indeed ought to be rendered as a forceful call to penitence, since the text itself remains silent as to whether her speech reveals her one-sided retribution theology.[10] It seems to me that Wilson's understanding of Job's wife as expressing retribution theology in the book of Job is highly hypothetical and not supported by textual evidence.[11]

More recently, it has been proposed that the question by Job's wife plays a crucial role in calling Job's attention to what can be viewed as his hypocritical piety. Several interpreters have actively been engaged in discussing another portrayal of Job's wife, namely as the one who is not only disillusioned with, but also willing to divulge Job's hidden hypocrisy which eventually disqualifies him from challenging God's justice. An example of such a commentator is David Penchansky, whose argument about the speech by Job's wife in Job 2:9 should not be overlooked. Having taken a scrupulous look at the two traditional interpretations of Job's wife as 'an evil woman doing the Satan's bidding' and 'some sort of feminist saint,'[12] Penchansky attempts to propose an alternative way of reading her statement that holds these two renderings ('both the Augustinian and the feminist')[13] in tension. To the extent that Job's wife is portrayed as 'the Satan's handmaid,' he tends to accommodate one traditional reading of Job's wife as espoused by the older Christian

---

[9] Wilson, *Job*, 38.
[10] It seems likely that the question by Job's wife does not necessarily suggest a call to repentance, since her subsequent injunction to "curse God and die" can be seen as undercutting the idea of the value of repentance.
[11] It should be noted that in the epilogue the three interlocutors are condemned while the narrator does not give any comments about Job's wife. If the unknown woman who gives birth to ten children in the epilogue is the same person as Job's wife in the prologue, it would be a natural assumption that she is finally vindicated like Job in the last stage of her life. On the other hand, in several ancient traditions, especially the *Testament of Job*, there are two different wives of Job. After his first wife Sitis dies, Job marries Dinah, daughter of the biblical patriarch Jacob, and this couple has another ten children. For a helpful analysis of Job's wives in the *Testament of Job*, see M.C. Legaspi, "Job's Wives in the *Testament of Job*: A Note on the Synthesis of Two Traditions," *JBL* 127 1 (2008): 71–79.
[12] Penchansky, "Job's Wife: The Satan's Handmaid," 223.
[13] Penchansky, "Job's Wife: The Satan's Handmaid," 227.

exegetes such as Augustine.[14] Nonetheless, his particular attention is given to the role of her speech as a call for abandoning Job's hypocrisy. He argues that Job's wife's words, especially her imperative, 'curse God and die' plays an important role in leading Job to face his hypocritical piety. He proceeds to contend that Job's 'notion of integrity is inextricably linked with his pious refusal to curse God under any circumstances.'[15] According to Penchansky, Job wrongly believes that responding to God with a robust complaint is a complete abandonment of integrity. Instead, he asserts that Job's wife sees Job's integrity as being bound up with a tendency to repress his emotions and that she is urging him to lay bare the anger, grief and sadness that he deeply feels during his suffering. Significantly, it is not until after Job's wife poses her stimulating question that Job reconsiders what he has, till then, thought of as integrity. Penchansky observes:

> *One must also note that the wife's comments do effect the birthing of Job's new stance (as evidenced in the poetic center of the book of Job), wherein he rediscovers his integrity through promethean valor. She embodies what Job becomes or what he wishes to become. She is Dame Wisdom, teaching Job a hard lesson, one that he finally seems to learn.*[16]

As the Satan's handmaid, Penchansky remarks, Job's wife 'transforms herself into the crone, the destroyer, the despair who swallows everything up.'[17] In other words, her satanic speech effectively spurs Job to blaspheme God; a blasphemous utterance that could result in the irrevocable punishment of death. Ironically, as Penchansky puts it, 'Job did blaspheme God: but did not die. Finally this is his integrity.'[18] Given the fact that her speech is immediately accompanied by Job's vehement protest against God, the undeniable contribution of Job's wife to her husband's integrity, according to Penchansky, is that she drives Job to go beyond the one barrier to his integrity, namely his hypocritical piety.

Regardless of his thought-provoking approach to Job's wife, I am hesitant to endorse Penchansky's affirmation that Job did blaspheme God by cursing him. I wonder if his conclusion that Job's complaints and challenges to God ought to be understood as blasphemous is in harmony with God's dealing with Job in the divine speeches set forth in Job 38:1–42:7. It needs to be pointed out that these divine speeches make it clear

---

[14] Penchansky, "Job's Wife: The Satan's Handmaid," 224.
[15] Penchansky, "Job's Wife: The Satan's Handmaid," 227.
[16] Penchansky, "Job's Wife: The Satan's Handmaid," 227.
[17] Penchansky, "Job's Wife: The Satan's Handmaid," 227.
[18] Penchansky, "Job's Wife: The Satan's Handmaid," 228.

that God's charge is not that Job complains about his suffering against God, but that his utterances about God's dealing with His universal order of creation are made without knowledge. More specifically, God is not intolerant of Job's lament and intense complaining, but rather of what Job has wrongly judged regarding God's justice, and indeed has done based on his limited wisdom, which is incapable of fully fathoming the depth of God's plan for the universe. In this respect, it seems problematic to embrace Penchansky's contention that Job's complaint to God in the dialogue between Job and his interlocutors is nothing less than blasphemy against God.

However, I am sympathetic with Penchansky's observation that the question by Job's wife about her husband's integrity plays an important role in alerting Job to the fact that he is in urgent need of giving vent to his repressed emotions. Perhaps Job thought it would surely be blasphemous if he were to respond to God with the vigorous complaints from which he is restraining himself. Even if Job longs to pour out his interminable agony, overwhelmed as he is by a series of calamities, he may feel obliged to resist any unrestrained anger towards God with his outcry. Regardless of whether the direct speech by Job's wife, especially her question about integrity, is rendered as an invective against impenitence or hypocrisy, this question serves as a stimulus for motivating Job to unleash his repressed emotions in a blistering outburst.

3. Reading the Question as a Sympathetic Lament

Over the last few decades, there has been a growing interest in the presentation of Job's wife as a victim of Job's torment.[19] Some commentators such as Robert L. Alden have eschewed any tendency to treat Job's wife as Xanthippe.[20] Many biblical interpreters have been actively involved in feminist readings of Job's wife that draw our attention to the image of her as a sacrificing wife, without whose continuous support her disabled husband would not have been able to extend his life. This sympathetic approach to Job's wife appears to stem from the description of her in the Septuagint, which, unlike the Hebrew Bible, has a long addition in

---

[19] See Stewart, "Job's Wife and Her Interpreters," 216–220.
[20] Alden says, "One must remember that though she was not physically afflicted, she also suffered the loss of children and wealth. Now it appears that she would lose her husband. Let us not be too hard on her." See R.L. Alden, *Job* (NAC; Nashville: B&H Publishers, 1993), 66.

Job 2:9. In this regard, the expansion of the statement made by Job's wife in the Greek reading of Job comes to the fore.

> *Then after a long time had passed, his wife said to him, 'How long will you persist and say, 'Look, I will hang on a little longer, while I wait for the hope of my deliverance?' For look, your legacy has vanished from the earth—sons and daughters, my womb's birth pangs and labours, for whom I wearied myself with hardships in vain. And you? You sit in the refuse of worms as you spend the night in the open air. As for me, I am one that wanders about and a hired servant—from place to place and house to house, waiting for when the sun will set, so I can rest from the distresses and griefs that now beset me. Now say some word to the Lord and die!'*[21]

It is undeniable that this expanded version is more sympathetic to Job's wife, who is identified with an Edomite Queen from Arabia (42:17 LXX). The somewhat longer speech attributed to the female sufferer in the Geek rendering invites us to take a considerable look at why she poses a sardonic question and makes a long lament to her husband who remains afflicted. According to the Septuagint, her life seems to have been full of tribulation due to the loss of all the possessions and all her children. Perhaps, in view of her extreme misfortunes, she has in no way been able to avoid social ostracism. Nonetheless, she is sacrificing her entire life for her physically disabled husband since, without her constant support, he would on no account be able to prolong his life. She must not only manage her household but must also hunt for a menial job in order to cope with their pitiful plight. In this sense, there can be little doubt that the addition in the Greek version is designed to portray Job's wife as a victim of Job's torment and as a devoted companion. This is in stark contrast to the aforementioned presentation of her as an evil puppet.

Moving from the Septuagint to the *Testament of Job*, one can see a more important role for Job's wife – here named Sitis. The *Testament of Job* is a Greek text from the first century BCE or CE generally thought to have been authored by an Egyptian Jew who had a good command of Greek. In this Greek text, Job is described as an Egyptian king who not only does good to the poor but also eschews any practice of idol worship. When Job seeks to eradicate an idol in a local shrine, God predicts that Job will be overwhelmed by Satan's devastating attack. When Job undergoes a severe ordeal caused by Satan, Job's wife has to be employed as a maidservant for many years in order to earn bread to feed herself and

---

[21] "IOB", trans. C.E. Cox, *New English Translation of the Septuagint*, eds. A. Pietersma and B.G. Wright (Oxford: Oxford University Press, 2014), 671.

her husband. When she encounters Satan, who has disguised himself as a bread seller, Satan tells her that he will give her three loaves of bread in exchange for her hair. After losing her hair, Job's wife feels humiliated and desperately laments:

> *Observe, this is she who used to have clothing woven from linen with gold:*
> *But now she bears rags and gives her hair in exchange for loaves!*
> *See her who used to own couches of gold and silver: But now she sells her hair for loaves!*
> *'Job, Job! Although many things have been said in general, I speak to you in brief:*
> *In the weakness of my heart, my bones are crushed. Rise, take your loaves, be satisfied.*
> *And then speak some word against the Lord and die. Then I too shall be freed from weariness that issues from the pain of your body* (T. Job 25:7–10).[22]

Here, special attention must be paid to Job's acknowledgment that his wife's reaction was inevitably born of the calamities that have befallen him. Despite Sitis' failure to be aware of the deception of Satan, Job fully sympathizes with her enduring sacrifice on his behalf in the face of financial and personal ruin. Though Job gives short shrift to her speech in the *Testament of Job* 25:10, he on no account downplays the depth of her suffering, but comes to the realization that his wife is also destined to suffer his miserable tragedy. Thus, Job says that 'I do indeed suffer these things, and you suffer them too: the loss both of our children and our goods' (*T. Job* 26:3). In this regard, the characterization of Job's wife as a victim of calamities that befall her husband in the *Testament of Job* makes it evident that she is a loyal caring wife, in spite of her falling for Satan's manipulation. From the perspective of the author of the *Testament of Job,* Job's wife is by no means perfect but is nonetheless a very devoted wife.[23] This sympathetic approach to Job's wife makes it clear

---

[22] The quotation is taken from trans. R.P. Spittler, *The Old Testament Pseudepigrapha*, Vol. 1, ed. J.H. Charlesworth (New Haven: Yale University Press, 1983).

[23] The sympathetic presentation of Job's wife has dramatically been emphasized and even enhanced by her various favourable images in the reception history in forms such as novels and paintings. For instance, the bulk of a series of engraved prints illustrating the Book of Job published in 1826 by William Blake depicts her as a dependable wife who stands by her husband's side. This positive portrayal of Job's wife may also be seen in the painting, the *Jabach Altarpiece* by Albrecht Dürer, in which she is painted as Job's spouse beside him, pouring water over Job's neck, a depiction portraying her as a devoted companion who tends to her suffering husband. See Low, *The Bible, Gender, and Reception History: The Case of Job's Wife*, 135–194; Stewart, "Job's Wife and Her Interpreters," 218–220.

that her question in Job 2:9 does not have to be rendered sarcastically or tauntingly but can be understood to be emotionally motivated by sympathy and compassion rather than by disfavour and odium. Her question is not a malicious utterance intended to undermine Job's integrity but a pathetic lament driven by a loving desire to see the end of his suffering.

The past few decades have witnessed prolific publications with a far more favourable portrayal of Job's wife. Her role has been revisited by modern commentators who are inclined to depict her positively. In particular, the Hebrew word ברך in Job 2:9 has been hotly debated amongst Joban scholars who understand that the meaning of the speech by Job's wife is highly dependent on that particular word.[24] One reason for the difficulty with her statement to Job is that it is reminiscent of both God's assertion in Job 2:3 ('he still persists in his integrity'/וְעֹדֶנּוּ מַחֲזִיק בְּתֻמָּתוֹ) and Satan's prediction in Job 2:5 ('he will curse you to your face'/אִם־לֹא אֶל־פָּנֶיךָ יְבָרֲכֶךָּ), a fact that indicates that there may be two divergent ways of translating this Hebrew word in its own context.

Whereas most English translations tend to treat this word negatively and read 'curse,' some commentators such as Samuel Balentine are willing to read it literally ('bless'), painting Job's wife more sympathetically. Having had a scrupulous look at the Hebrew verb ברך, Balentine resists the traditional interpretation that reads it negatively. He asserts:

> *The prevailing assumption that 'bless' (barak) is a euphemism for 'curse' is, however, open to question. There is no clear evidence that 'bless' is a standard or automatic substitution for 'curse,' either in the language of the ancient Near East or in the Hebrew Bible. Apart from Job, three additional examples of this substitution are sometimes cited (1 Kings 21:10, 13; Psalm 10:3), but serious questions in each text make the translation less than certain.*[25]

Although he acknowledges the ambiguity of the meaning of the Hebrew word ברך in Job 2:9 that flummoxes readers when they have to decide whether to read it as 'curse' or 'bless,' he seeks to adhere to the latter option.[26] If this is the case, the words of Job's wife in Job 2:9 would be

---

[24] For a detailed analysis of the use of this verb, see T. Linafelt, "The Undecidability of ברך in the Prologue to Job and Beyond," *BibInt* 4 (1996): 154–172.

[25] S.E. Balentine, *Job* (Smyth & Helwys Bible commentary; Macon: Smyth & Helwys, 2006), 49.

[26] As observed in the Septuagint and the *Testament of Job*, some scholars, who paint Job's wife positively, prefer the word "curse" since they think that cursing God would result in death that ultimately relieves Job from suffering. In this case, the main point made by them is that Job's wife advises Job out of compassion, even though she uses the word, "curse." See Stewart, "Job's Wife and Her Interpreters," 216–220.

understood in this manner: 'You have indeed maintained your integrity through everything thus far; now continue on, bless God, even though you may die.'[27] Undoubtedly, according to Balentine, these words may not be dealt with as a temptation or a voice from Satan designed to thwart Job's integrity. Rather, her speech could play an important role in affirming Job's integrity in the face of his tragic condition.

However, one calls into question whether Balentine's translation of her speech ('bless God even though you may die') can be maintained since Job's rejection of her words in 2:10[28] indicates that Job views her speech negatively or unfavourably.[29] As Penchansky puts it, 'the text, I contend, will not allow us this sympathetic view. Job's wife tells him to 'curse God,' an activity so dangerous, many biblical texts imply, that immediate death results.' I prefer to render the Hebrew verb ברך negatively ('curse') though the literal interpretation of the verb ('bless') may not be dismissed. Whether the Hebrew word is construed non-literally or literally, more emphasis should be placed upon the fact that it is only after the words of Job's wife – her question, followed by an imperative – that Job commences his outburst of bitter complaints to God. To put it another way, it must be noted that the speech by Job's wife plays a significant role in urging Job to take a radical step that he has never attempted. This understanding of her speech leads us to consider the significance of the role of the question in the first part of the speech about Job's integrity ('Do you still persist in your integrity?'), which has a critical impact on the dramatic change in Job's attitude towards God in the transition between Job 2 and 3.

4. What Happens after the Question?

I now want to turn to recent approaches to Job's wife's statement in Job 2:9, notably advocated by several feminist critics including Patricia G. Kirkpatrick whose current reading of the speech by Job's wife differs from the two above-mentioned interpretations. Kirkpatrick seeks to re-evaluate her speech and presents a somewhat different understanding of

---

[27] Balentine, *Job*, 63.
[28] The Hebrew word (הַנְּבָלוֹת) for "a foolish woman" in 2:10, according to Seow, indicates "a theological-ethical lapse." It refers not to a woman who lacks intellectual sense, but to a woman who "speaks, acts, or is simply outside the acceptable theological, ethical, and social norms, most frequently, someone who flagrantly disregards the community's dictates." (See Seow, *Job 1–21*, 296)
[29] Penchansky "Job's Wife: The Satan's Handmaid," 224. According to Seow, her words are "outrageous." (Seow, *Job 1–12*, 296–297)

the meaning of the Hebrew verb ברך. While she finds the literal interpretation of the verb ('bless') appealing, she is more inclined to accept the observation made by Michael C. Legaspi who seeks to render it as 'bid farewell.'[30] She then goes on to suggest that the speech by Job's wife ought to be read in an alternative way to underscore her 'sincere attempt to have Job bid farewell to his belief in God and accept the inevitable metaphoric death which is practically upon him anyways.'[31] According to Kirkpatrick, what Job's wife urges Job to do is to abandon his prior understanding of God, which Job has desperately clung to. She asserts:

> *Mrs. Job of the prologue did not ask Job to abandon God but rather to abandon his preconceived notions of how God should act. It may in fact mean that Job will have to die a metaphoric death or rather a death to his old religious beliefs. Mrs. Job does not supply him with anything else except to act as a spur to grate against his conscience.*[32]

It is clear that without his wife's advisory speech, Job would not have undergone a transformation of his faith, which ultimately culminates in Job's encounter with God, followed by his confession that 'I had heard of you by the hearing of the ear, but now my eye sees you' (Job 42:5). It is important to note that from the outset of chapter 3, Job immediately begins to express his bitter complaint against God after the interchange between him and his wife at the end of chapter 2. For some critical interpreters who have paid considerable attention to reconstructing a compositional history of the book of Job,[33] it is doubtful whether chapter 2 of the prose prologue and chapter 3 of the poetic core can be read continuously.[34] This is because the radical change in Job's attitude towards God

---

[30] Legaspi argues that "the command to 'bless God,' instead of being a euphemism for cursing God, as most English translations suggest, may amount to a suggestion from Job's wife that Job bid farewell (i.e., 'bless God') and accept his fate ('die')." See Legaspi, "Job's Wives in the *Testament of Job*," 71.

[31] Kirkpatrick, "Curse God and Die," 43.

[32] Kirkpatrick, "Curse God and Die," 53.

[33] Over the past decades, historical-critical approaches have tended to deal with the book of Job as a collection consisting of separate independent components such as the prose frame (chs. 1–2/42:7–17), the poetic dialogue (chs. 3–31), a wisdom poem (ch. 28), the Elihu episode (chs. 32–37) and the divine speeches (38:1–42:6). They have attempted to reconstruct the process by which these various literary components arrived at the present form of the book. In particular, a great deal of proposals have been suggested to explain what parts of the present composition were original or authentic and which were added later. For a concise treatment of these critical issues in Joban studies, see Cho, "Job 2 and 42:7–10 as Narrative Bridge and Theological Pivot," 857–859.

[34] The past few decades have witnessed a dramatic shift away from diachronic to synchronic readings. The focus has moved from reconstructing a compositional history of the book of Job to reading the book as a literary and theological whole. My position is

seemingly alludes to the discontinuity between these two chapters, both of which not only conclude the prose prologue but also open up the poetic discourse. In fact, the exemplary portrait of Job who adheres to integrity even in times of affliction in the prose prologue, is no longer found in the poetic core, from the outset of which Job is depicted as a peevish protestor complaining that God treats him unjustly.[35]

It has been taken into account, nevertheless, that the narrator's comment, 'he does not sin in what he said' (בְּכָל־זֹאת לֹא־חָטָא אִיּוֹב, בִּשְׂפָתָיו) in 2:10 provides a decisive clue to the continuity between chapter 2 and 3.[36] A great deal of emphasis has particularly been placed upon the phrase, 'in what he said' (בִּשְׂפָתָיו) which should be translated more correctly as 'with his lips,' a reference to Job's lips, that clearly distinguishes between 1:22 and 2:10.[37] In fact, the phrase is omitted in the narrator's earlier evaluation of Job in 1:22 (בְּכָל־זֹאת לֹא־חָטָא אִיּוֹב וְלֹא־נָתַן תִּפְלָה לֵאלֹהִים)[38] – it is used only in 2:10 – which may lead us to consider what Job has thought 'in his heart.' This does not necessarily mean, as many scholars, including the medieval Jewish commentator Ibn Ezra, suggest, that the phrase must imply that Job would sin later.[39] Still, the reference to 'with his lips' in 2:10 may play a vital role in anticipating Job's outburst of sorrow and indignation commencing from the outset of chapter 3. Gerald Wilson is correct when he observes:

> *One ought not to make too much of the specificity of the evaluation that Job did not sin in what he said (בִּשְׂפָתָיו 'with his lips'). This does not imply that Job may have sinned in action if not in words. The*

---

that the book of Job needs to be read as a unitary whole no matter what distinctive components are contained in the book of Job, a fact that indicates that the last chapter of the prose epilogue (Job 1–2) cannot be separate from the first chapter of the poetic core (3:1–42:6). Fox is correct when he remarks, "the prologue and the epilogue, whether composed by the main author or borrowed and adapted from a folktale, are integral to the book." See M.V. Fox, "The Meaning of the Book of Job," 9. For a helpful treatment of a synchronic reading of Job, see D. Timmer, "God's Speeches, Job's Responses, and Problem of Coherence in the Book of Job: Sapiential Pedagogy Revisited," *CBQ* 71 (2009): 287–289. For a reading of the book of Job as a canonical final form, see G.H. Wilson, *Job* (NIBC; Peabody: Hendrickson, 2007), 11–16.

[35] Polak also points out that "the attitude of Job seems problematic since the hero of the prose tale accepts his fate (1:21; 2:9–10), while the poetic sections center on Job's emotional expression of his doubts concerning divine justice." (F.H. Polak, "On Prose and Poetry in the Book of Job," *JANESCU* 24 (1996): 61.

[36] Seow, *Job 1–21*, 298; T.E. Fretheim, *God and World in the Old Testament* (Nashville: Abingdon Press, 2005), 225.

[37] See E. van Wolde, *Mr and Mrs Job* (London: SCM, 1997), 25–27; J. Boss, *Human Consciousness of God in the Book of Job*, 31–32; Seow, *Job 1–21*, 297–298.

[38] The text only says, "In all this Job did not sin or charge God with wrongdoing."

[39] Seow, *Job 1–21*, 298.

> *statement does, however, leave an unanswered question regarding Job's thoughts which have yet to be spoken, and in this way the phrase prepares the reader for the outpouring of Job's inner reflection and pain in the dialogue to come.*[40]

Given the fact that Job's response to God abruptly changes from praising to protesting God between chapter 2 and 3, it would be unavoidable to surmise that the words of Job's wife, especially her question that prefaces them, 'Do you still persist in your integrity?' has a critical impact upon the swift change in Job's response to his situation and his dealing with God.[41] In this sense, the functional significance of her question in the transition between the prose prologue and the poetic core is obvious. That is to say, whatever her question intends, it plays a significant role in motivating Job to take a drastic step towards openly expressing what he is feeling in his heart during an unbearable ordeal, a step that finally leads him to the encounter with God that ultimately transforms him.

5. Concluding Remarks: Do Contradictory Readings of the Question Really Matter?

As noted earlier, Job's wife's question could be read either as an invective against impenitence and hypocrisy, or it could be rendered as a sympathetic lament. These two readings of the question appear to be undeniably incongruous. Nonetheless, the incongruity between them is in no way problematic if the functional significance of the question is fully grasped. In addition, the reader is invited to consider the implications of the functional significance of the question by Job's wife for situations in which he or she may be undergoing severe trials. If the reader is wrestling with suffering, he or she may hesitate to express pent up emotions in the midst of hardship. Still, the reader ought to be aware that an outburst of sorrow and complaint is not optional but requisite for coping with suffering. In the end, the reader may be encouraged to respond to God appropriately with lamentable cries in the face of bitter agony, even

---

[40] Wilson, *Job*, 32.
[41] Fretheim draws more attention to the distinction between 1:21 and 2:10 and understands the impact of her question on the sudden change in Job's attitude towards God in this manner: "A careful comparison of 1:21 and 2:10 reveals important differences. Job's second response [2:10] begins to break away from the piety of 1:21 and moves toward the complaints of the dialogue. Job's wife's remarks (2:9) may encourage Job in this important move to lament/complaint, and hence it may be said that her challenge to Job to 'curse God, and die' sets up the rest of the book." (T.E. Fretheim, *God and World in the Old Testament*, 225.)

if a voice is heard from someone like Job's wife, urging him or her to abandon hope and die. This voice could be a deadly temptation from Satan who is hell-bent on frustrating integrity or it could be a sympathetic call for release from suffering. Whether designed to mock or to commiserate does not matter. This is because the recognition of the functional significance of the question by Job's wife leads the reader to fully appreciate the validity of expressing outwardly what is emotionally present in the heart. Interpretive conflicts inevitably occur if the question by Job's wife is construed in various and even contradictory ways due to its uncertainty and ambiguity. However, contradictions would be unproblematic if any rendering of her question is understood in relation to its functional significance within the text. Do contradictory readings of the question really matter? They never matter at all.

IN SEARCH OF GOD
Asking Questions in the Psalms

Harm van Grol
Tilburg University

1. Introduction: Question and Request

The focus of this contribution will be question-word questions in the Psalms, but we would like to stress from the start that this focus is a drastic reduction. Question clauses need interrogatives, but asking questions in Biblical Hebrew does not necessarily involve question clauses. In fact, the majority of questions are not question clauses but imperative clauses, at least in the Psalms. This book abounds with prayers and supplications, pleas and appeals, and their marked form is that of the imperative clause with the jussive clause as an alternative.

One could enter into a boring argument about the difference between a question and a request, but let us look at actual language usage. The Babylonian captors of Psalm 137 *ask* the exiles for words of song, for joyfulness – the poet writes שאלונו – and they use an imperative clause: שירו לנו משיר ציון *Sing for us one of the songs of Zion!* And, this is not even a request, it is a command. Genesis 32:30 has a polite request, using the verb שאל *to ask*, followed by an imperative clause: וישאל יעקב ויאמר הגידה־נא שמך *Jacob asked: Please tell me your name*. The verb שאל *to ask* is used for all types of questions including the imperative request.

The book of Psalms is a discursive text, so that it is lacking in those narrative introductions with the verb שאל, *to ask*. Yet, all the pleas and supplications in the laments and all the hymnic calls to praise are instances of the same act of asking. The Psalms are marked more by these requests than by the question-word questions we will study below, both structurally and thematically.

There are 59 psalms with one or more question-word questions in the book of Psalms. Three parties are involved, God, the psalmist/Israel, and the enemy/enemies/nations. The last two parties ask questions, mostly about God, sometimes about each other. Many questions are of a debunking or deriding nature. The suggestive questions of the enemies/nations about God's active presence are paralleled by the sorrowful questions of the psalmist/Israel regarding the same issue. The poems contain reflective questions about the nature of human kind or the intended behaviour of the righteous of Israel. Expository questions are mostly about the nature and/or behaviour of God. All these questions are part of a debate, so they are partisan and biased and frequently of a rhetorical nature.

We will study three illustrative psalms, Psalm 113, 114, and 115, and we will focus on the poetic, rhetorical and especially communicative functions of the questions asked in these poems.

2. Psalm 113: Comparing God

The rhetorical question *Who is like YHWH our God?!* is found in the middle line of Psalm 113. The psalm has three strophes of each three verse lines, and verse 5 is the second line of the second strophe. We will discuss the precise wording of this question, moreover, its position in the middle of a strophe, and, last, its communicative function.

A Translator's Handbook on the Book of Psalms does not discuss the structure of verses 5–6.[1] It just follows RSV: 'Who is like the LORD our God, / who is seated on high, / who looks far down / upon the heavens and the earth?' and TEV:[2] 'There is no one like the LORD our God. / He lives in the heights above, / but he bends down / to see the heavens and the earth.' In this reading, verse 6 is one clause: *who looks far down upon the heavens and the earth*. This is a fine clause syntactically seen, but it is – the *Handbook* admits – an unusual figure: 'Yahweh is so high above all creation that he must bend down in order to see the heavens and the earth.'

This reading does not reckon with poetry and prosody on the one hand and with stereotyped language on the other. We will start with the latter. Hermann Gunkel's observation is curt but concise: '5b und 6a gehören zusammen, 6b passt gut zu 5a (vgl. Dt 3,24)'.[3] Colon 6b does not belong to the preceding participle clause but is part of the question under discussion: 'Who is like YHWH our God in heaven and on earth?!' Compare Deuteronomy 3:24: מי אל בשמים ובארץ אשר־יעשה כמעשיך וכגבורתך – 'For what god is there *in heaven or on earth* who can do the deeds and mighty

---
[1] R. Bratcher and W. Reyburn, *A Translator's Handbook on the Book of Psalms* (Helps for Translators; New York: United Bible Societies, 1991), 965.
[2] TEV: Today's English Version.
[3] H. Gunkel, *Die Psalmen* (Göttinger Handkommentar zum Alten Testament II/2; Göttingen: Vandenhoeck & Ruprecht, 1926), 492–493.

works you do?'[4] 1 Kings 8:23: יהוה אלהי ישראל אין־כמוך אלהים בשמים
ממעל ועל־הארץ מתחת – 'LORD, the God of Israel, there is no God like
you *in heaven above or on earth below.*' Psalm 73:25: ועמך לא־חפצתי בארץ
\מי־לי בשמים – 'Whom have I *in heaven* but you? / *And earth* has nothing
I desire besides you.' The combination of the formula of divine incomparability with the phrase 'in heaven and on earth' is conventional.[5]

Poetry and prosody may corroborate our reading. Expectation is part of
the reading process. Having read המגביהי לשבת and reading המשפילי the
reader will expect another infinitive, and when the infinitive לראות has
satisfied this expectation, parallelism has come to a closure. A restart is
possible but not probable. Thus, the parallelism of cola 5b and 6a confirms
the association of cola 5a and 6b. The verses have a chiastic structure:[6]

5a	Who is like YHWH our God	A
5b	– he is sitting so high,	B
6a	he is seeing so low –	B
6b	(who) in heaven and on earth?!	A

The chiastic reading of verses 5–6 is bolstered by the chiastic parallelism
of verses 2–3. Again a case of expectation. The first strophe consists of
one linear parallel line and two lines that together constitute a chiastic
parallelism.

1a	*Praise, servants of YHWH,*	//
1b	*praise the name of YHWH!*	
2a	*Let the name of YHWH be blessed*	A
2b	*from now on and to eternity.*	B
3a	*From the rising of the sun to its setting*	B
3b	*(let) the name of YHWH (be) praised.*	A

The second strophe has the same structure. First a linear parallel line and then
two lines that together constitute a chiastic parallelism.

4a	*YHWH is exalted above all nations,*	//
4b	*his glory (is exalted) above the heavens:*	
5a	Who is like YHWH our God	A
5b	– he is sitting so high,	B
6a	he is seeing so low –	B
6b	(who) in heaven and on earth?!	A

---

[4] We will quote the *New International Version* here and elsewhere, but the translation of Psalms 113–115 is our own.
[5] L. Allen, *Psalms 101–150* (WBC 21; Waco: Word Books, 1983), 99.
[6] Our translation avoids the repetition of 'who:' 'who is sitting...' The construction of cola 5b and 6a is discussed in GKC § 114n and note 2: '(...) the principal idea is properly contained in the infinitive, whilst the governing verb strictly speaking contains only a subordinate adverbial statement.'

The precise wording of the question under discussion is hereby established with an appeal to poetry and prosody on the one hand and stereotyped language on the other.[7]

That brings us to our second point: Questions may open a new syntactic unit (paragraph),[8] but our question is found in the middle of a strophe and in fact, it is dependent on verse 4. Clause 5a/6b is a nominal clause like those in verse 4, and the subject matter of these clauses is the same: they are describing or evaluating YHWH. They are even saying the same: YHWH is above all *nations* / there is no one on *earth* like him, and he is above the *heavens* / there is no one in *heaven* like him.

But what would be the point of stating God's incomparability twice? Verse 4 is a general statement and verses 5–6 are elaborating on it. This elaboration is not found in the question itself but in the clauses that are enclosed by it, cola 5b and 6a, and then of course especially in colon 6a and its contrast to colon 5b: 'he is sitting so high, // he is seeing so low.' This thematic structure is confirmed by that of the first strophe. In that strophe, verse 1 contains a general appeal and verses 2–3 are elaborating on it, while the point of this elaboration is found in the middle cola 2b and 3a: 'from now on and to eternity / from the rising of the sun to its setting.'[9]

Our third point will be the function and meaning of the question under discussion. The question is a rhetorical one. It animates the text because it involves the readers. One could say that a rhetorical question does not need an answer. That may be true on the level of meaning but not on that of communication. The answer is given (implicitly), but the readers will give it nonetheless.

The question 'Who is like YHWH our God in heaven and on earth?!' is even more explicit in involving the readers by adding 'our God' to

---

[7] Some commentaries that have chosen the same reading: Allen, *Psalms 101–150*; T. Booij, *Psalmen: Deel IV* (POT; Kampen: Kok, 2009); F.-L. Hossfeld and E. Zenger, *Psalmen 101–150* (HThKAT; Freiburg: Herder, 2008).

[8] Questions may open a syntactic unit, but will be accompanied by a vocative in that case. See H. van Grol, *Een parallel syntagma: Verkenningen in het grensgebied van versbouw en tekstsyntaxis* (Theologische Perspectieven Supplement Series 20; Bergambacht: 2VM, 2017), 107–109, 125–127, 135–136.

[9] Some scholars do not recognize the threefold division of the psalm (verses 1–3, 4–6, 7–9). Their fourfold one (verses 1–2, 3–4, 5–6, 7–9) combines verses 3 and 4, notwithstanding the prosodic and thematic structures described above. They do not recognize the chiastic arrangement of verses 2–3 and the ellipsis in verse 3, taking verse 2 as a wish but verse 3 as a descriptive clause. In their view, the question under discussion opens the second part of the psalm.

'Yhwh.' The incomparability of Yhwh is not a theoretical issue but a personal matter. It is about us against 'the nations' (colon 4a). This rhetorical question will bolster the identity of the readers and their pride in belonging to this God and his people.

The desired praise of Yhwh has a worldwide scope (horizontal – the first strophe), only surpassed by the dimension of Yhwh's power (vertical – the second strophe), but the point of this praise is המשפילי לראות, that he is seeing the poor and the barren, as the third strophe, verses 7–9,[10] elaborates. The rhetorical question is built around this paradoxical image of God, 'sitting so high >< seeing so low'. The text-immanent readers, spoken to as 'servants of Yhwh' (colon 1a) and evoked as 'we' in the rhetorical question (colon 5a), may find this hopeful, because, at the end, they are the poor and the barren.

3. Psalm 114: Asking the Victims

Four parallel questions make up the third strophe of Psalm 114:

5a *What is the matter with you, sea, that you flee,*
5b *Jordan, that you run backwards,*
6a *mountains, that you leap like rams,*
6b *hills, like lambs?*

These questions ask for explanation about the behaviour of the four personified natural beings that are addressed. We may recognize the Sea of Egypt, the River Jordan and, because of the sequence, the mountains and hills of the Promised Land. They show signs of intense fear.

To understand the nature of these questions we like to know the situation in which they are asked. Moreover, we want to know who is asking these questions. And finally, what do the addressees answer?[11]

The situation is given in verses 1–4, but, strangely enough, it is an historical one. The questions suggest an event that happens in the present, but verses 1–4 describe an event in the past. Of course, our surprise should be vice versa: coming from a narrative text about the exodus from

---

[10] For those who are curious about the structure of this strophe: again, it is made up of one line and two lines that belong together, but now in the reversed order and without chiastic parallelism, first the two lines (verses 7–8) and then the other line (verse 9). The deviations mark the third strophe as the last one.

[11] See also: A.L.H.M. van Wieringen, "Two Reading Options in Psalm 114: A Communication-Oriented Analysis," *RB* 122 (2015): 46–58.

Egypt and the entrance into the Land we are plunged into a discursive text about something that happens now.

1a	*When Israel left Egypt,*
1b	*the house of Jacob this babbling people,*
2a	*Judah came to be his sanctuary,*
2b	*Israel his royal domain.*
3a	*The sea – it saw and it fled,*
3b	*the Jordan – it ran backwards,*
4a	*the mountains – they leaped like rams,*
4b	*the hills – like lambs.*

This story, which is a traditional one, is rather unsurprising, but has several lacunae. The first gap is a linguistic one. The possessive adjective 'his' in verse 2 must refer to God – he as king has Israel as his royal domain – but this referent is not mentioned, against the grammatical rules. The second omission is a theological one. The first clause, 'when Israel came out of Egypt,' gives Israel the initiative, whereas the correct presentation should be *when Y<small>HWH</small> brought Israel out of Egypt*. God has a kind of hidden presence in the first strophe.

The second strophe sketches the reaction of nature according to other stories and poems about the described events, but it gives a lot of attention to the four personified natural beings. Do they deserve this attention? Moreover, there is a rather irritating lacuna again. The first clause states that 'the sea saw,' and the next clauses say by way of ellipsis that the other natural beings saw the same, but what did they see? Some translations suggest they 'saw them,' others propose 'it' – whatever that may be – but they miss the point. They should have left it open, knowing that all these lacunae point to this one person who may not yet be mentioned.

The mini story is done with and the third strophe brings us a present time discursive text: 'What is the matter with you, sea, that you flee...?' Many translations refuse to make the transition and go on with past tenses: 'What alarmed you, o sea, that you fled...?'[12] or 'What happened, Sea, to make you run away?'[13] In this reading, the four questions are the opening of a (therapeutic) session to evaluate past behaviour and feelings.

---

[12] *The Book of Psalms: A New Translation according to the Traditional Hebrew Text* (Philadelphia: JPS, 1997).

[13] *Good News Translation* (GNT), formerly known as *Today's English Version* (TEV).

What are the linguistic facts?

verse	A-colon	B-colon
1	a בְּ־ infinitive clause	ellipsis
2	a *qatal* clause	ellipsis
3	a subject-*qatal* clause plus wayyiqtol	a subject-*yiqtol* clause
4	a subject-*qatal* clause	ellipsis
5	מַה־לְּךָ plus a *yiqtol* clause	a *yiqtol* clause
6	a *yiqtol* clause	ellipsis

The mini story uses past tenses except in colon 3b. The deviating *yiqtol* clause may be explained as a poetic variation in the B-colon. The third strophe uses present tenses, without doubt.

The comments and the advice of *A Translator's Handbook on the Book of Psalms* are rather interesting: 'RSV and some others [other translations; HvG] use the present tense (NAB, BJ, NJB, TOB), as though the psalmist were present and seeing the events; this is a superb poetic device, but in translation it may convey the idea that the events are still taking place. So it is better to use the past tense, as TEV and others do.'[14] Bad advice, but great comments!

People would think that the events are still taking place. That could be the purpose of the composition, in a sense. The past of the story changes into a present. The narrator becomes a reporter asking questions. And in the process, the reader becomes a real time witness of the events. He is pulled into a faraway story, so that he himself is standing at the shore of the Sea, going through a dried up River and exploring the Land. This is not only 'a superb poetic device' but, on a communicative level, it is a dramatization of the own history of the reader.

What is the point of the questions asked by our reporter in the field? Is he mocking them for their fear of Y<small>HWH</small>?[15] Improbable, because their fear is substantial. He asks them questions because they have an intimate knowledge of the events. That is the reason he gives them a lot of attention. They are the choicest persons to reveal the essence of the exodus from Egypt and the entrance into the Land, because they are victims and, therefore, have a certain objectivity.

---

[14] Bratcher and Reyburn, *A Translator's Handbook*, 970.
[15] Bratcher and Reyburn, *A Translator's Handbook*, 970.

The answer is given in the last strophe:

7a *From the presence of Adon – tremble, o land! –* 7b   *from the presence of the God of Jacob,*
8a *who turns the rock into a puddle,*
8b *a flinty stone into a fountain.*

Most readers interpret colon 7a as an imperative clause: 'Tremble, O earth, at the presence of the LORD' (JPS), but the Hebrew word order is strange with the imperative at the end, and the prepositional phrase מלפני does not match the verb חול *to tremble*,[16] so that the imperative clause 'tremble, o land!' will be an interjection into an otherwise verbless clause. Thus, the answer to the question 'What is the matter with you, sea, that you flee?' is 'From the presence of Adon, / from the presence of the God of Jacob'. Given the elliptical nature of the psalm these incomplete clauses may be read as elliptical ones with the verb נוס left out:[17] '*I flee* from the presence of Adon, / (*I flee*) from the presence of the God of Jacob.' In fact, the prepositional phrase מלפני does match the verb נוס *to flee*.[18]

The revelation of the sea *cum suis* corresponds to the lacunae of the verses 1, 2, and 3. It is God who is the hidden force behind the exodus of Egypt and the entrance into the Land. The sea and its companions are no push-overs and know what they fear: 'he turns the rock into a puddle, / a flinty stone into a fountain.' Not a fine perspective for the mountains and hills of Israel.

What for the Land is a reason to tremble, is a reason for the text-immanent reader to sing. The hymnic participle clauses in verse 8 make some incidental handling of rocks in the desert into something characteristic of this God. He is the Transformer. He turns rocks into potable water. At this point, the poet is referring us back to the first strophe,[19]

---

[16] The verb חול never has a prepositional phrase. The variant verb חיל may be accompanied by the phrases מפני and מלפני (once). Ps 96:9 // 1 Chr 16:30 looks like Ps 114:7, but 'all the earth' refers to all human beings and not to the earth itself or the land.

[17] Ps 114 is very 'elliptical,' having more clauses with an ellipsis than full clauses. See the overview of the linguistic facts in verses 1–6 above.

[18] The verb נוס is accompanied by the preposition מ/מן, often by the prepositional phrase מפני and once by the phrase מלפני (1 Chr 19:18). One could question the imperative interjection. It may be a corruption of כל־הארץ so that colon 7a originally read: 'From the presence of the master *of the whole earth*,' an epithet known from, inter alia, Josh 3:11, 13 (cf. Allen, *Psalms 101–150*, 103–104).

[19] The poem has four strophes in a chiastic arrangement: A.B//B.A. The A-strophes are connected by the name יעקב and by the dynamic prepositions מ/מן- and -ל.

and we are remembering that other transformation and understanding that this God has turned Judah into his sanctuary, Israel into his royal domain.

The questions of Psalm 114 are used as part of a dramatization of the founding events of Israel. This kind of dramatization is characteristic of Pesach (Exodus 12:24–27; 13; Joshua 4:19–24). The anamnestic ritual has at least three elements. There has to be (1) a question and (2) the answer will draw the participant of the ritual into the past. He is present in the narrated events (3) to witness, he himself, what God did or, even better, does.

Joshua 4:19–24: »On the tenth day of the first month the people went up from the Jordan and camped at Gilgal on the eastern border of Jericho. And Joshua set up at Gilgal the twelve stones they had taken out of the Jordan. He said to the Israelites, 'In the future when your descendants ask their parents, 'What do these stones mean?' tell them, 'Israel crossed the Jordan on dry ground.' For the LORD your God dried up the Jordan *before you until you* had crossed over. The LORD your God did to the Jordan what he had done to the Red Sea when he dried it up *before us until we* had crossed over. He did this so that all the peoples of the earth might know that the hand of the LORD is powerful and so that you might always fear the LORD your God.« (italics: HvG)

The prescribed answer in Joshua 4 is historically nonsense. The fathers never crossed the Sea of Reeds and the children never crossed the Jordan. But they do in this ritual, a ritual which tells them who they are.

4. Psalm 115: Framing the Nations[20]

The first strophe of Psalm 115 contains a double question:

2a *Why should the nations say:*
2b *Where, now, is their god?!*

The subordinate question is a deriding question that ridicules Israel and its God. The main one is argumentative, implying that it is not really necessary that the nations will act in this way.

---

[20] A full analysis of the syntactic and prosodic structures of Ps 115, with the title 'Psalm 115: Syntax and Versification,' is found on my website www.harmvangrol.nl.

The double question is stereotyped. It is also part of the collective lament Psalm 79:

10a *Why should the nations say: Where is their god?!*
10b *Let it be known among the nations before our own eyes:*
10c *the vindication of the spilled blood of your servants.*

And it is the climax of the priestly appeal in Joel 2:17:

17a *Between the portico and the altar,*
17b *let the priests weep,*
17c *the ministers of Y*HWH*, let them say:*
17d *Spare your people, Y*HWH*!*

17e *Do not make your inheritance a derision*
17f *a byword among the nations.*
17g *Why should they say among the nations:*
17h *Where is their god?!*

The double question is an appeal to God, inciting him to act on behalf of his people by suggesting that he himself is the object of scorn among the nations. His own name is at stake. After all, gods are known to be busy elsewhere: 'Perhaps he is deep in thought, or busy, or traveling. Maybe he is sleeping and must be awakened' (1 Kings 18:27). The God of Israel should be present and active, defending his people.

We would like to know how this stereotyped appeal is used in Psalm 115. Who is speaking? What does Israel expect God to do? Is the appeal, being part of the first strophe, of any importance in the other six strophes?

The immediate context of the appeal is the first strophe:

1a *Not to us, Y*HWH*, not to us,*
1b *but to your name bring glory,*
1c *for your* חסד, *for your* אמת.
2a *Why should the nations say:*
2b *Where, now, is their god?!*
3a *Our God is in heaven, isn't he?!*
3b *Whatever he pleases, he makes.*[21]

The first line is already stating the appeal, in more or less plain language: please, bring glory to your name, that is, show your חסד, show your אמת. The double question follows on this appeal and does not add substance but it does add emotion. It should trigger God's ego, his pride.

---

[21] The awkward translation with 'to make' visualizes the connection with the same verbal root in verses 4, 8 and 16.

The appeal does not specify God's glorious behaviour, probably because that is not the point. In fact, the third line (verse 3) drops the appeal and starts a discussion. Line 1 addresses God, line 3 makes God into the topic of debate. Line 2, the double question, belongs to both communicative domains. It is the emotional climax of the appeal (verses 1–2) and it is – at the same time – the starting point of a discussion about God (verses 2–3).

This structure is strange, to say the least. The point of the appeal is to get God working. The suggested question of the nations 'Where, now, is their god?!' is not to be taken seriously, but the writer of this psalm makes an issue out of it. Of course, to get to his real point, but still, discussing God's greatness detracts from the appeal. And so, the strophe comes to its surprising conclusion: This God does not need any incentive to act.

Within three verse lines supplication changed to hymn. 'Our God is in heaven,' that is, he is not hand*made* as the idols of the nations (verses 4–8), and, in fact, he is the creator himself, '*maker* of heaven and earth' (verses 15–16). 'Whatever he pleases, he *makes*,'[22] whereas the idols of the nations are unable to do anything (verses 4–8). The verb 'to make' (√ עשׂה) is avoided in the description of these idols, even negatively, and only used to describe the activity of the idol-*makers* (verses 4, 8), and they will become like their handiwork, dead.

Us against the nations. Notwithstanding the negations, the first colon is very much about participant WE: 'Not to us, YHWH, not to us'. The first stanza opposes participant WE and 'our God' (the first strophe) to the NATIONS and 'their idols' (the second and third strophe, verses 4–6, 7–8). The members of participant WE are invited to assent to the hymn of verse 3. Their counterpart in the community of the NATIONS is 'everyone who trusts in them (cf. the idols)' (colon 8b).

Trust is the theme of the second stanza.

9a   *Israel, trust in YHWH!*
9b   *– he is their help and their shield.*
10a *House of Aaron, trust in YHWH!*
10b *– he is their help and their shield.*
11a *You who fear YHWH, trust in YHWH!*
11b *– he is their help and their shield.*

---

[22] The [qatal]clauses in colon 3b are not retrospective but have the time perspective of the nominal clause 3a and describe expected behaviour. Probably, qatal is chosen to express confidence and certainty. See for this pragmatic use of qatal J. Joosten, *The Verbal System of Biblical Hebrew: A New Synthesis Elaborated on the Basis of Classical Prose* (JBS 10; Jerusalem: Simor, 2012), 206–208.

12a *Y*HWH *has remembered us – he will bless,*
12b *he will bless the house of Israel,*
12c *he will bless the house of Aaron,*
13a *he will bless those who fear Y*HWH,
13b *both the small and the great.*

'Israel,' 'house of Aaron,' and 'You who fear YHWH' are invited to trust in YHWH. Halfway through the stanza, the community as a whole is mentioned in *us* (colon 12a), to be split up again in the remainder of the stanza, which formulates the material object of trust, that is, 'he will bless.' The invitation to trust is based on the conviction that 'YHWH has remembered us.' This central clause confirms that the appeal to God to act on behalf of his people is not a very urgent one – he is already active. His remembrance shows the substantial relevance of his attributes or epithets חסד and אמת (colon 1c).

The psalm is marked by a rapid succession of communicative domains. The second stanza gives the impression of a liturgy, with an antiphony and a litany, but then the supposed antiphony should have read: *he is our help and our shield*. Alternatively, the speaker, member of participant WE, could have continued his address: *Israel, trust in Y*HWH! */ – he is your help and your shield*. Instead of all this, Israel (etc.) is third person in the repeated clauses 'he is *their* help and *their* shield' and 'he will bless *Israel* (etc.),' which is rather strange in combination with clauses that address the same community (cola 9a, 10a, 11a), and with a clause that includes them in a first person *us* (colon 12a). The third person clauses have no addressee. The stanza combines personal communication with objective language.

Why does the poet prefer this detached, observational language? The rationale of his choice lies in the comparison of the God of Israel with the idols of the nations. The God of Israel is described in the same way as the idols of the nations (verses 4–8). Compare the nominal clauses: 'Their idols are silver and gold' over against 'he is their help and their shield,' and the verbal clauses: 'They cannot even groan...' as opposed to 'he will bless (them).' The third person clauses belong to the debate that started in verse 3. The difference between this God and those idols becomes obvious with this objective language. So, the second stanza combines appeal and debate, just like the first one.

The blessings mentioned in verses 12–13 are found in the third stanza.

14a *May Y*HWH *give you increase,*
14b *you and your sons!*
15a *May you be blessed by Y*HWH,

15b *maker of heaven and earth!*
16a *The heavens are heavens of Y*HWH,
16b *but the earth he has given to the sons of man.*

17a *The dead cannot praise Y*AH,
17b *all those who go down into silence,*
18a *but we will bless Y*AH,
18b *from now on to eternity.*

Again, this stanza has a combination of personal communication and descriptive language, of appeal and discussion. The community is addressed in verses 14–15 (*you* plural) and is again mentioned in verse 18 (*we*). The description is in the middle, verses 16–17.

The blessing gives special attention to the future of the community: 'May YHWH give you increase,' which is strengthened by the double address 'you and your sons,' a rephrasing of 'both the small and the great' in colon 13b. The blessing ends with the phrase 'maker of heaven and earth,' an epithet which is stereotypically used in blessings like this and discussions of God's help, but the description of heaven and earth which follows, is a special extension. It looks like an obvious statement, but it leaves us with a question. The word 'sons' is used for the second time in this strophe. What is the point of the inclusive 'sons of man' in a psalm which contrasts Israel and the nations from the start, and in a strophe which is about the future of Israel ('your sons')?

The next verse line about the dead seems to belong to the description of heaven and earth. Verses 16–17 show a threefold sequence of YHWH, the sons of man, and the dead as the inhabitants of respectively heaven, earth, and she'ol, although the last place is only suggested by the phrase 'those who go down.' But again, what is the point of such an obvious description in this psalm?

In fact, the verse line about the dead belongs to the second strophe of the stanza, with verse 18. The verses contrast participant WE with the dead. A strange contrast, because members of participant WE will certainly die, but it is bolstered by the addition 'from now on to eternity.' This absolute association of participant WE with life is prepared for by the special attention to future generations in the first strophe of this stanza.

But, if participant WE is associated with life, who, then, is associated with death? Verse 17 points to verses 4–8. The [YIQTOL-לא]clauses, which observe the inability of the dead to praise YHWH, were previously used to describe the inability of the idols to do anything. The word כל *everyone/all* is used in colon 8b for another human personage: '*all those* who go down into silence' may remind the reader of '*everyone* who trusts in them,' although the syntax differs. The silence of the dead brings back the impotence of the idols: 'They cannot even groan with their throat,' the climax of the description in colon 7b. So, verse 17 points to the idols of the nations and to those who trust in them. Verse 8 has already made clear that the latter will become like the former.

Now we may understand verse 16. The sons of man, who got the earth, consist of the two participants WE and the NATIONS, but in fact, the NATIONS, who trust in idols, will go down into silence, and WE will inhabit the earth and praise YHWH. The others are dead, a rather absurd statement if taken literally, but a strong perspective on the world. This psalm frames the NATIONS as impotent and dead.

Those who trust in YHWH, and thus are blessed by him, will reverse the blessing from now on to eternity, they and their sons. Those who trust in the idols of the nations are dead, because they will be blessed by no one and have no future. Therefore, God has given the earth to all who trust in him, the others will go down.

The psalm started with a deriding statement of the nations: 'Where, now, is their god?!' and continued by debunking their idols, but concludes by framing the nations as being nowhere: 'Where, now, are the nations?!' The question of the nations has been developed to its full potential.

5. Conclusion

We studied three illustrative texts, Psalm 113, 114, and 115, which happen to be adjacent texts, and which belong to the Pesach Hallel. The questions asked in these psalms differ formally. That of Psalm 113 is a rhetorical question, that of 114 an informative one, and that of 115 a deriding one. Their literary functions are similar. That of 113 opens up a description of God, that of 114 discloses God, and that of 115 starts a debate about God. Each of these questions affects the rest of the psalm in an important way. The three psalms are close in discussing YHWH as the God of life, and Israel as its recipient. Maybe the question of Psalm 116 concludes the series: 'How will I return to YHWH / all his generosities to me?!'

ASKING QUESTIONS IN THE BOOK OF BEN SIRA
Their Form and Function

Pancratius C. BEENTJES
Tilburg University

1. Introduction

Investigating particular aspects of the book of Ben Sira – in this case the occurrence and function of questions – immediately poses a methodological problem, since we do not have a complete Hebrew text at our disposal. To date, about three-quarter of the Hebrew text of Ben Sira has been recovered.[1] As a consequence, at least the Greek translation should always be at hand. However, as Benjamin Wright has convincingly argued, this translation can hardly be considered a faithful rendering of the Hebrew original.[2]

Ben Sira was a Jewish sage living in Jerusalem, who between 190–180 BCE published a book of wisdom. For at least three reasons it is a special document. Firstly, it was written in Hebrew, whereas in those days Aramaic was the common language in Judea. Secondly, this document is the first and only biblical book in which the *real* author presents himself: 'Wise instruction and apt proverbs of Simeon, the son of Jeshua, the son of Eleazar, the son of Sira' (Sirach 50:27).[3] And thirdly, this Hebrew writing was translated into Greek by a next of kin, viz. Ben Sira's grandson.

---

[1] See P.C. Beentjes, *The Book of Ben Sira in Hebrew: A Text Edition of all Extant Hebrew Manuscripts & A Synopsis of all Parallel Hebrew Ben Sira Texts* (VTSup 68; Leiden: Brill, 1997), 13–19.

[2] B.G. Wright, *No Small Difference. Sirach's Relationship to its Hebrew Parent Text* (SCS 26; Atlanta: Scholars Press, 1989), 231–250.

[3] Greek: "Instruction in understanding and knowledge I have written in this book, Jesus the son of Sirach, son of Eleazar, of Jerusalem." In other biblical books, such as Psalms, Proverbs, Song of Songs, Qohelet, and Wisdom, anonymous authors present themselves as 'David' or 'Solomon' in order to acquire authority. See D.G. Meade, *Pseudonymity and Canon* (WUNT 39; Tübingen: Mohr Siebeck, 1986), 44–71.

Since we almost know the exact date at which the Hebrew text of Ben Sira was translated into Greek by his grandson, viz. 'in the thirty-eighth year, in the reign of Euergetes the king,'[4] which is either 132 BCE or 117–116 BCE,[5] it is always appropriate to be alert whether and in what way the grandfather's Hebrew text – after a two generations' interval – was rendered in the grandson's Greek text or meanwhile underwent changes to content and meaning as compared to its Hebrew parent text.

Two major aspects must be kept in mind. First, aspects relating to *historical* circumstances. Halfway between 190–180 BCE, on the one hand, and 132–116 BCE, on the other hand, the campaign of Antiochus Epiphanes IV and the religious rejuvenation caused by the Maccabean revolt against the Seleucid Empire (167 BCE) took place. These events might in some way have influenced the grandson's translation. Therefore, the Hebrew book of Ben Sira, dating *before* this period, and its Greek translation, dating *after* these events, in fact represent two different documents. Second, aspects relating to *cultural* circumstances. Ben Sira's document originated in a Jewish context (Juda, Jerusalem; Hebrew), however, the grandson's translation was realized in a Hellenistic society (Egypt, most probably Alexandria; Greek).

Finally, a statement as to methodology is required. As a basic principle, we start from the point of view that the Hebrew text, as well as the Greek and Syriac translation(s), will be treated as they have been handed down. That is to say, any effort to (re)construct a new text by combining these textual witnesses is not allowed, since in that case a text is created that did not exist.

2. Different types of questions

At a rough estimate, a question is posed more than seventy times in the book of Ben Sira. Apart from 'regular questions,' three types of questions are especially worth mentioning: (1) questions introduced by the formula 'Do not say' (e.g. Sirach 5:3–4; 11:23–24; 16:17); (2) questions

---

[4] Prologue, line 27. For a text critical edition of the Greek, see J. Ziegler, *Sapientia Iesu Filii Sirach* (Septuaginta XII/2; Göttingen: Vandenhoeck & Ruprecht, 1965).

[5] R. Smend, *Die Weisheit des Jesus Sirach* (Berlin: Georg Reimer, 1906), 3 favours the year 132 BCE, whereas P.W. Skehan and A.A. Di Lella, *The Wisdom of Ben Sira* (AB 39; New York: Doubleday, 1987), 134–135 favour "the interval between 132–117." J. Marböck, *Jesus Sirach 1–23* (HThKAT; Herder: Freiburg, 2010), 39 on the other hand, favours 116 BCE.

followed by the answer (e.g. 10:19; 39:20–21), and (3) rhetorical questions, a type that is in the majority.

2.1. *Regular questions*

It turns out not to be easy to label a question in the book of Ben Sira as 'regular'. Moreover, there are only a very few of this type to be found. Sirach 13:23 might be an example:

> 'The rich speaks and all are silent,
> his wisdom they extol to the clouds.
> The poor speaks and they say, 'Who is that?'.
> If he stumbles they knock him down'.[6]

Sirach 13:17–23 describes how the rich and the poor are treated quite differently. In these statements, Ben Sira has at least created the impression that he has chosen the poor one's side. Therefore, in 13:24 a statement is added in which the author wants to correct the impression that not all wealth is wrong, nor all poverty good:

> 'Wealth is good if it be without sin,
> and poverty is evil if it come from arrogance' (13:24).[7]

Sirach 14:15 might be another example:

> 'Do you not want to leave your wealth to another
> and your earnings to them that cast lots?'

This verse is part of a section (14:11–19) in which Ben Sira urges his pupil to take advantage of the good things in life and to share one's prosperity with his brothers and friends, before death strikes hard and there will be a row about the inheritance.[8] The main argument: 'For in Sheol, there is no pleasure to seek' (14:16).

---

[6] Skehan and Di Lella, *Wisdom*, 251.
[7] For a detailed analysis of Ben Sira Chapter 13, see P.C. Beentjes, "How can a Jug be Friends with a Kettle?: A Note on the Structure of Ben Sira Chapter 13," *BZ* 36 (1992): 87–93 [= P.C. Beentjes, "Happy the One who Meditates on Wisdom" (Sir. 14,20), in: *Collected Essays on the Book of Ben Sira* (CBET 43; Louvain: Peeters, 2006), 77–85].
[8] Mind the strong resemblance, both in terminology and context, between Sir 14:15 and Ps 49:11. Maybe, the opening הלא is an indication by Ben Sira that he is indeed referring to this specific verse in Psalm 49. See the comment on Sir 46:4 below.

2.2. *'Do not say'* + *question*

2.2.1. Sirach 5:3–4 (Ms A)[9]

5:3 אל תאמר מי יוכל כחו כי ייי מבקש נרדפים
5:4 אל תאמר חטאתי ומה יעשה לי מאומה כי אל ארך אפים הוא
[אל תאמר רחום ייי וכל עונותי ימחה]

First, a translation of the wider context (Sirach 5:1–8) is offered:

5:1   Do not rely on wealth; do not say: 'There is power in my hand'.[10]
5:2   Do not rely on your strength; to walk after the desires of your soul.
5:3   *Do not say: 'Who can endure my strength?'*
      for Yhwh will surely avenge.
5:4   *Do not say: 'I have sinned, yet did anything happen to me?'*
      for Yhwh is slow to anger.
5:5   Regarding forgiveness, do not trust to add sin upon sin;
5:6   and say: 'His mercies are great; he will forgive my many sins'.
      For mercy and anger are with him, and upon the wicked will rest his wrath.
5:7   Do not delay in turning back to him; do not put it off from day to day.
      For suddenly his wrath comes forth, and in the time of vengeance you will be snatched away.
5:8   Do not trust in deceitful riches, for they will not help on the day of wrath.[11]

When Sirach 5:1–8 has been stripped of its commonly accepted doublets (vv. 2a, 2d, 4c–d),[12] there is a passage left over composed of exactly ten *distichoi*.[13] Within this group of prohibitions, the particular formula 'Do not say' strikes the eye.[14] First of all, it is the only formula with אל which, throughout this pericope, is repeated several times (5:1b, 3a, 4a

---

[9] In Ms C., only the first half of Sir 5:4 is found: אל תאמר חטאתי ומה יהוה לו כי ייי אריך אפים הוא.
[10] The "Do not say"–formula in 5:1 is not followed by a question and is, therefore, not included in this paragraph.
[11] Translation by R.A. Argall, *1 Enoch and Sirach: A Comparative Literary and Conceptual Analysis of the Themes of Revelation, Creation and Judgment* (EJL 8; Atlanta: Scholars Press, 1995), 221, with some small alterations of my own (PCB).
[12] See H.P. Rüger, *Text und Textform im hebräischen Sirach: Untersuchungen zur Textgeschichte und Textkritik der hebräischen Sirachfragmente aus der Kairoer Geniza* (BZAW 112; Berlin: De Gruyter, 1970), 13–14, 35–38.
[13] Elsewhere in the book of Ben Sira, this feature of ten *distichoi* appears to be a structural literary principle; see J. Haspecker, *Gottesfurcht bei Ben Sira: Ihre religiöse Struktur und ihre literarische und doktrinäre Bedeutung* (AnBib 30; Rome: Päpstliches Bibelinstitut, 1967), 113–118.181–185; N. Peters, *Das Buch Jesus Sirach oder Ecclesiasticus* (EHAT 25; Münster: Aschendorf, 1913), 332, 341, 363.
[14] For a full analysis of Sir 5:1–8, see: P.C. Beentjes, "Ben Sira 5:1–8. A Rhetorical and Literary Analysis," in: E.G.L. Schrijver et al. (Eds.), *The Literary Analysis of Hebrew Texts* (Publications of the Juda Palache Institute VII; Amsterdam: Univ. of Amsterdam, 1992), 45–59 [= Beentjes, "Happy the One", 49–60].

[4c; cf. 6a]). Secondly, one should attach some importance to the fact that nowhere else in the wider context the formula אל תאמר is again used by the author.[15] In 5:1–8, the opening formulae 'Do not say,' therefore, build a structural element that offers this passage both coherence and unity to a high degree.

What is going on in this passage? As a matter of fact, Ben Sira enters into argument with his contemporary opponents, either real or fictive, about crucial issues relating to God. In his monograph dealing with the problem of theodicy in the book of Ben Sira, Gian Luigi Prato has coined this passage as 'un compendio di teodicea' (*a compendium of theodicy*), since according to his view its structure is characteristic of theodicy (objection – answer – exhortation with motivation).[16]

It can hardly be a coincidence that the expression 'Do not say' is used a number of times besides this instance in the book of Ben Sira, always dealing with the theologically explosive notion of *theodicy* (Sirach 15:11a; 16:17; 34[31]:12c).[17] This would even be more apparent, if we include similar formulae like אין לאמר (39:21) and οὐκ ἔστιν εἰπεῖν (39:17):

- 'No one can say, "What is this?" or "Why is that?" – for everything has been created for its own purpose' (39:21).[18]
- 'No one can say, "What is this?" or "Why is that?" – for at the appointed time all such questions will be answered' (39:17).

The mere fact that Ben Sira quite often uses the particular debate-formula 'Do not say' and 'No one can say' followed by a question is a serious indication that the issue of theodicy was vehemently debated in his days and could also have been a major theological issue for him personally.[19] This might to a high degree be inferred from the observation that, as compared to other biblical wisdom literature, the book of Ben Sira contains a remarkably larger number of passages in which this formula is

---

[15] The first occurrence after 5:1–6 is to be found in 11:23–24.
[16] G.L. Prato, *Il problema della teodicea in Ben Sira: Composizione dei contrari e richiamo alle origini* (AnBib 65; Rome: Biblical Institute Press, 1975), 367–369.
[17] J.L. Crenshaw, "The Problem of Theodicy in Sirach: On Human Bondage," *JBL* 94 (1975): 47–64, also draws attention to "Do not say"–utterances in some Egyptian texts, such as the Instruction of Ani and the Instructions of 'Onchsheshonqy, which also question the problem of theodicy!
[18] Its echo is found in 39:34 – "No one can say, 'This is not as good as that,' for everything proves good in its appointed time."
[19] See P.C. Beentjes, "Theodicy in Wisdom of Ben Sira," in: *Theodicy in the World of the Bible*, ed. A. Laato and J.C. de Moor (Leiden: Brill, 2003), 509–524 [= Beentjes, "Happy the One," 265–279].

used. For in Qohelet and Proverbs the formula 'Do not say' followed by a rhetorical question is to be found only three times in total (Qohelet 7:10; Proverbs 20:22; 24:29).[20]

2.2.2. Sirach 11:20–26

Since the Hebrew text of Sirach 11:18–26 (Ms A.) is incomplete or damaged, the Greek text is to be preferred here.

11:20 Στῆθι ἐν διαθήκῃ σου καὶ ὁμίλει ἐν αὐτῇ καὶ ἐν τῷ ἔργῳ σου παλαιώθητι.
11:21 μὴ θαύμαζε ἐν ἔργοις ἁμαρτωλοῦ, πίστευε δὲ κυρίῳ καὶ ἔμμενε τῷ πόνῳ σου· ὅτι κοῦφον ἐν ὀφθαλμοῖς κυρίου διὰ τάχους ἐξάπινα πλουτίσαι πένητα
11:22 εὐλογία κυρίου ἐν μισθῷ εὐσεβοῦς, καὶ ἐν ὥρᾳ ταχινῇ ἀναθάλλει εὐλογίαν αὐτοῦ.[21]
11:23 μὴ εἴπῃς Τίς ἐστίν μου χρεία, καὶ τίνα ἀπὸ τοῦ νῦν ἔσται μου τὰ ἀγαθά;
11:24 μὴ εἴπῃς Αὐτάρκη μοί ἐστιν, καὶ τί ἀπὸ τοῦ νῦν κακωθήσομαι;
11:25 ἐν ἡμέρᾳ ἀγαθῶν ἀμνησία κακῶν, καὶ ἐν ἡμέρᾳ κακῶν οὐ μνησθήσεται ἀγαθῶν
11:26 ὅτι κοῦφον ἔναντι κυρίου ἐν ἡμέρᾳ τελευτῆς ἀποδοῦναι ἀνθρώπῳ κατὰ τὰς ὁδοὺς αὐτοῦ.

11:20 Stand by your agreement and attend to it, and grow old in your work.
11:21 Do not wonder at the works of a sinner, but trust in the Lord and keep at your job; for it is easy in the sight of the Lord to make the poor rich suddenly, in an instant.
11:22 The blessing of the Lord is in the reward of the pious, and quickly God causes his blessing to flourish.
11:23 *Do not say, 'What do I need, and what further benefit can be mine?'*
11:24 *Do not say, 'I have enough, and what harm can come to me now?'*
11:25 In the day of prosperity, adversity is forgotten, and in the day of adversity, prosperity is not remembered.
11:26 For it is easy for the Lord on the day of death to reward individuals according to their conduct.[22]

The opening Στῆθι ἐν διαθήκῃ σου (11:20), as well as the Latin *Sta in testamento tuo* (11:21 [Vetus Latina]) are difficult to understand, just as the NRSV translation 'Stand by your agreement' is. The Syriac (11:20), however, has *bry qwm 'l 'wrḥk* ('My son, keep to your way [of life]')

---

[20] In Qoh 5:5; Prov 3:28; 20:9; 24:12; 30:9, the formula "Do not say" is not followed by a rhetorical question.
[21] In spite of all Greek manuscripts, Ziegler, *Sapientia*, 177, altered εὐλογίαν (11:22b) into εὐοδία ('prosperity').
[22] Translation from NRSV with Apocrypha, 75. Sir 11:22–26 is missing in the Syriac.

which better suits the context and reflects the meaning of the Hebrew parent text ב[ני] ע[מד] בחוקך (Ms A).[23] Of course, in the book of Ben Sira the Hebrew noun חוק is correctly rendered διαθήκη at least five times (42:2; 44:20; 45:5, 17; 47:11). In 11:20, however, the noun should be rendered 'duty,' specifically referring to the fulfilment of the commandments. And in this vein, the Greek and Latin translations are understandable.

That the opening statement is about obeying God's commandments is, indeed, elaborated in the next verses. One should avoid the works of the sinner, be pious, and trust in the Lord. This latter aspect – trust in the Lord – is explicitly substantiated in the two 'Do not say' sentences (11:23–24).

Sirach 11:20–26 is part of a larger paragraph (11:7–28) that Skehan–Di Lella have characterized as 'Providence and Trust in God,' directly relating, therefore, to the theme of theodicy. An excellent summary of its purport is to be found earlier, viz. in 11:14, 'Good and evil, life and death, poverty and riches – all are from the Lord.' And precisely the two 'Do not say' questions (11:23–24) are an affirmative response to that statement.

2.3. *Question + Answer*

The literary form of question + answer fits very well into the purpose and setting of Ben Sira's book: the education of young pupils, who, therefore, are frequently addressed 'My son'(בני)[24] or 'Child' (τέκνον).[25] The most obvious type consists of a question:

> *'Why is one day more important than another,*
> *when all light of the year is from the sun?'*

which is immediately followed by the answer:

> *'By the wisdom of Yhwh they are separated,*
> *some of them to be special feasts.*
> *Some of them he blessed and sanctified,*
> *and others he appointed as ordinary days'* (Sirach 33:7–9).

In fact, this question and answer are part of a large section (Sirach 32:14–33:18) in which Ben Sira comments upon the behaviour and lifestyle of the pious, i.e. the one who fears the Lord and studies the Torah, as opposed to the conduct of the wicked. In 33:7–15, the author makes

---

[23] In the Syriac, Sir 11:22–26 is missing.
[24] Sir 3:8, 12, 17; 4:1, 20; 10:28; 11:10, 18; 14:11; 37:27; 38:9, 16; 40:28.
[25] Sir 2:1; 3:1, 12, 17; 4:1; 6:18, 23, 32; 10:28; 11:10; 14:11; 16:24; 18:15; 21:1; 37:27; 38:9, 16; 40:28.

a brilliant move, since the opposition between the pious and the wicked is connected with the divine ordering of the cosmos:

> 'Some of them He blessed and exalted,
> and some he sanctified and brought near to himself.
> Others He cursed and laid low,
> and expelled them from their place' (33:12).[26]

2.3.1. Sirach 10:19

Unfortunately, the Hebrew text of Sirach 10:19 is incomplete, both in Ms A and in Ms B.[27] As a consequence, the Greek translation has to be the basis for comment.[28]

10:19a Σπέρμα ἔντιμον ποῖον; σπέρμα ἀνθρώπου.
10:19b σπέρμα ἔντιμον ποῖον; οἱ φοβούμενοι τὸν κύριον.
10:19c σπέρμα ἄτιμον ποῖον; σπέρμα ἀνθρώπου.
10:19d σπέρμα ἄτιμον ποῖον; οἱ παραβαίνοντες ἐντολάς.

10:19a Whose offspring are worthy of honour? Human offspring.
10:19b Whose offspring are worthy of honour? Those who fear the Lord.
10:19c Whose offspring are unworthy of honour? Human offspring.
10:19d Whose offspring are unworthy of honour? Those who break the commandments.[29]

These lines are the opening of a poem about honour and contempt towards human beings (10:19–11:6). The anaphoric lay-out of this opening statement undoubtedly echoes two characteristic notions of the book of Ben Sira.

The first couple of lines (10:19a-b) reaches its climax in 'those who fear the Lord'. Here we come across the most central theological theme of the book of Ben Sira: 'Fear of the Lord.' The most elaborated passage devoted to this notion is found in the opening chapter of the book (1:11–30).[30] Spread over the book of Ben Sira, references to 'fear of the Lord' can be found more than fifty times in total.[31]

---

[26] For a detailed analysis of Sir 33:7–15, see Beentjes, "Theodicy."
[27] See A.A. Di Lella, *The Hebrew Text of Sirach* (Studies in Classical Literature 1; The Hague: Mouton, 1966), 60–63; Rüger, *Text und Textform*, 54–56.
[28] The interrogative form of the sentences has disappeared in the Vetus Latina, and the Syriac, whereas the famous Greek Codex 248 has a completely different text. See J.H.A. Hart, *Ecclesiasticus: The Greek text of Codex 248* (Cambridge: University Press, 1909), 13.
[29] Translation adopted from NRSV with Apocrypha, 1995, 73.
[30] A.A. Di Lella, "Fear of the Lord as Wisdom: Ben Sira 1:1–10," in: P.C. Beentjes (Ed.), *The Book of Ben Sira in Modern Research* (Berlin: De Gruyter, 1997), 113–133.
[31] See Haspecker, *Gottesfurcht*, 48–50.

Whereas the notion 'fear of the Lord' in the book of Ben Sira, as well as in Job and Proverbs, has a strong positive meaning, in our modern perception 'fear' has negative connotations. Sirach 2:15–16, however, with the help of a fruitful *parallelismus membrorum*, offers a clue to transcending this:

> 'Those who fear the Lord do not disobey his words;
> those who love him keep his ways.'
> 'Those who fear the Lord seek to please him,
> those who love him are filled with his law.'[32]

The second couple of lines (10:19c–d) holds the negative counterpart: 'those who break the commandments.' And it goes without saying that 'keeping the commandments' is also a widespread theme in the book of Ben Sira.[33] That 'fear of the Lord' and 'keeping the commandments' are the most important theological couple indeed, is beautifully said in 23:27 – 'and all shall understand that nothing is better than the fear of the Lord, nothing sweeter than keeping the commandments of the Lord.'

2.4. *Rhetorical questions*

In the book of Ben Sira, more than fifty per cent of all questions can be typified as 'rhetorical questions'. A rhetorical question does not expect an answer, since the author (and his readers) very well know(s) the answer. The answer is common knowledge and not open to doubt. The aim of a rhetorical question is to convince the addressee(s) 'by implying that the answer is self-evident or known to everybody and therefore not to be doubted or discussed.'[34] No wonder that rhetorical questions are often used in debate. Moreover, it is very appropriate in a wisdom setting where pupils are being taught.

2.4.1. Sirach 31[34]:28–31

31:28 εἷς οἰκοδομῶν, καὶ εἷς καθαιρῶν· τί ὠφέλησαν πλεῖον ἢ κόπους;
31:29 εἷς εὐχόμενος, καὶ εἷς καταρώμενος· τίνος φωνῆς εἰσακούσεται ὁ δεσπότης;

---

[32] See R. Egger-Wenzel, "'Faith in God' rather than 'Fear of God' in Ben Sira and Job: A Necessary Adjustment in Terminology and Understanding," in: J. Corley and V. Skemp (Eds.), *Intertextual Studies in Ben Sira and Job: Essays in Honor of Alexander A. Di Lella* (CBQMS 38; Washington: Catholic Biblical Association of America, 2005), 211–226.
[33] E.g. Sir 1:26; 6:37; 15:15; 23:27; 32[35]:2, 23.24; 37:12.
[34] S. Bar-Efrat, *Narrative Art in the Bible* (JSOTSub 70; Sheffield: Sheffield Academic Press, 1989), 211.

31:30 βαπτιζόμενος ἀπὸ νεκροῦ καὶ πάλιν ἁπτόμενος αὐτοῦ, τί ὠφέλησεν ἐν τῷ λουτρῷ αὐτοῦ;
31:31 οὕτως ἄνθρωπος νηστεύων ἐπὶ τῶν ἁμαρτιῶν αὐτοῦ καὶ πάλιν πορευόμενος καὶ τὰ αὐτὰ ποιῶν· τῆς προσευχῆς αὐτοῦ τίς εἰσακούσεται; καὶ τί ὠφέλησεν ἐν τῷ ταπεινωθῆναι αὐτόν;

31:28 When one builds and another tears down, what do they gain but hard work?
31:29 When one prays and another curses, to whose voice will the Lord listen?
31:30 If one washes after touching a corpse, and touches it again, what has been gained by washing?
31:31 So if someone fasts for his sins, and goes again and does the same things, who will listen to his prayer? And what has he gained by humbling himself?[35]

These lines are part of a larger section (Sirach 31[34]:21–31) relating to a person's proper conduct of offering sacrifices (vv. 21–27) in a sincere religious way (vv. 28–31).[36] This set of five rhetorical questions reveals a beautiful structure:

28a	εἷς ... καὶ εἷς		
28b		τί ὠφέλησαν	
29a	εἷς ... καὶ εἷς		
29b			εἰσακούσεται
30a			καὶ πάλιν
30b		τί ὠφέλησεν	
31a	οὕτως		
31b			καὶ πάλιν
31c			εἰσακούσεται
31d		καὶ τί ὠφέλησεν	

Whereas vv. 21–27 describe factual unwanted offerings, vv. 28–30 describe the impossibility of true religious behaviour if opposite conditions were valid at the same time. Each of the opposite pairs (28a, 29a, 30a) is concluded with a rhetorical question (28b, 29b, 30b) that reveals the undesirability of such situations. An extensive sentence introduced with οὕτως (31a) and repeating the elements of all three previous rhetorical questions (καὶ πάλιν; εἰσακούσεται; καὶ τί ὠφέλησεν) is undoubtedly to be considered the climax of this passage.

It can hardly be a coincidence that in the subsequent sections of Ben Sira the notions of true worship (35:1–16), God's actions in favour of

---

[35] Translation adopted from NRSV with Apocrypha, 1995, 102.
[36] For Sir 31[34]:21–32[35]:20, see H. Stadelmann, *Ben Sira als Schriftgelehrter. Eine Untersuchung zum Berufsbild des vor-makkabäischen Sōfēr unter Berücksichtigung seines Verhältnisses zu Priester-, Propheten- und Weisheitslehrertum* (WUNT 2. Reihe 6; Tübingen: Mohr Siebeck, 1980), 68–83.

the oppressed (35:17–26), and prayer to God (36:1–17) are an elaboration and comment on the rhetorical questions in 31[34]:28–31.

2.4.2. Sirach 46:3–4

Rhetorical questions are not only found in the wisdom-oriented part of the book of Ben Sira (Sirach 1–43), but they also occur in the so-called *Laus Patrum* (Sirach 44–50), Ben Sira's personal view of Israel's 'heroes'. Three times the author offers a portrayal of a biblical character with the help of a rhetorical question: Joshua (46:3–4), Elijah (48:4); Zerubbabel (49:11) and Jeshua, son of Jozadak (49:12). Let us take Joshua as an example. The rhetorical question relating to Joshua is found in a passage (46:1–8) into which a lot of biblical material has been incorporated.[37]

46:3 מי הוא לפניו יתיצב כי מלחמות ייי נל[חם]
46:4 הלא בידו עמד השמש יום אחד [היה לשנים]

46:3   Who could withstand him, when he fought the battles of Yhwh?
46:4   Was it not by his hand that the sun stopped, that one day became like two?

The way Ben Sira has composed his portrayal of Joshua (Sirach 46:1–8) can be characterized as 'structural use of Scripture'. It is a phenomenon where a passage in a deuterocanonical or non-canonical Jewish writing is largely structured by elements from one or two already existing biblical texts.[38] Joshua 10:11–14 is the Old Testament passage that forms the outline for Ben Sira's description of Joshua. And it is not by chance, therefore, that both passages follow the same sequence of narrative elements. Within Ben Sira's pericope, the solstice as described in Joshua 10:13 receives particular emphasis, since it is introduced in Sirach 46:4 with the help of הלא ('Was it not?').[39]

---

[37] See, e.g., T.R. Elßner, *Josua und seine Kriege in jüdischer und christlicher Rezeptionsgeschichte* (Theologie und Frieden 37; Stuttgart: Kohlhammer, 2008), 24–56; J. Corley, "Canonical Assimilation in Ben Sira's Portrayal of Joshua and Samuel," in: J. Corley and H. van Grol (Eds.), *Rewriting Biblical History: Essays on Chronicles and Ben Sira in Honor of Pancratius Beentjes* (DCLS 7; Berlin: De Gruyter, 2011), 57–77.

[38] See P.C. Beentjes, "Structural Use of Scripture in the Book of Ben Sira," in: J. Corley and G.D. Miller (Eds.), *Intertextual Explorations in Deuterocanonical and Cognate Literature* (DCLS 31; Berlin: De Gruyter, 2019), 57–78.

[39] In the book of Ben Sira, the particle הלא is found seven times (14:15; 31[34]:19; 35[32]:15; 37:2; 38:5; 42:22; 46:4). In 14:15; 35[32]:15; 38:5, and 46:4 it is the introduction to a biblical reference. See P.C. Beentjes, *Jesus Sirach en Tenach* (Nieuwegein: Selbstverlag, 1981), 21–29.

Ben Sira, however, gives his own twist to the solstice of Joshua 10:13. For in the biblical narrative, it is *God* who makes it happen. In the Ben Sira passage, however, the miracle is transferred to *Joshua* ('by his hand'). In order to embed this 'deviant' action, when introducing Joshua, Ben Sira makes him a prophet – 'a minister of Moses in the prophetic office' (46:1b) – so that he is included in the succession of prophets. This fits into the framework of the *Laus Patrum* in which more than once prophets are portrayed as 'heroische Persönlichkeiten, die sich vor allem in staunenswerten Wundertaten manifestierten'.[40] See, e.g., 48:21 where it is not 'the angel of Yhwh' (as in 2 Kings 19:35), but the *prophet Isaiah* who struck the camp of the Assyrians.

3. Conclusion

Within a wisdom setting, the literary form of posing questions is an excellent and workable method for teaching pupils. In the book of Ben Sira a question is posed about seventy times. The majority of these occurrences are phrases shaped as rhetorical questions.

If we try to find a kind of pattern in these rhetorical questions, it comes to light that, without exception, they refer to topics that play a prominent role in the book of Ben Sira: God;[41] Creation and Cosmos;[42] Wisdom;[43] Fool/Wise;[44] Poor/Rich;[45] and Friend/Enemy.[46] It means that Ben Sira is continually emphasizing that both sincere religious behaviour and harmonious human relations are indispensable ingredients for a well-balanced life.

Apart from the large group of rhetorical questions in the book of Ben Sira, three more types are to be distinguished: 'regular questions';

---

[40] M. Hengel, *Judentum und Hellenismus: Studien zu ihrer Begegnung unter besonderer Berücksichtigung Palästinas bis zur Mitte des 2. Jh.s v. Chr.* (WUNT 10; Tübingen: Mohr Siebeck, 1988³), 248. Cf. 'il ne voit dans les prophètes que les faiseurs de miracles'; E. Jacob, "L'histoire d'Israel vue par Ben Sira," in: *Mélanges Bibliques rédigés en l'honneur de André Robert* (Travaux de l'Institut Catholique de Paris; Paris: Bloud & Gay, 1956), 288–294 (quotation 291).

[41] Sir 2:10, 14; 16:20–22, 18:4–8.

[42] Sir 1:2–3; 18:4–8; 42:25; 43:3. The interrelationship between God and Cosmos is amply studied in the recent monograph by A.J. Schmidt, *Wisdom, Cosmos, and the Cultus in the Book of Ben Sira* (DCLS 42; Berlin: De Gruyter, 2019).

[43] Sir 1:6–7; 51:24.

[44] Sir 22:10, 14; 38:25.

[45] Sir 13:2, 17–18, 23; 14:3, 15.

[46] Sir 37:2–3, 8. Friendship is a major topic in the book of Ben Sira. See J. Corley, *Ben Sira's Teaching on Friendship* (Brown Judaic Studies 316; Brown University: Providence, 2002).

questions introduced by the formula 'Do not say,' and questions followed by an answer. Specifically, the 'Do not say'–sentences that are followed by a question catch the eye, since they nearly always refer to the theologically explosive notion of *theodicy*.

QUESTIONS IN ISAIAH'S WOE ORACLES AGAINST THE RULERS OF HIS PEOPLE (ISAIAH 10:1–4) AND THE ASSYRIAN POWER (ISAIAH 10:5–15)[1]

Joachim ECK
Rhenish Friedrich Wilhelm University of Bonn

1. Preliminary Reflection on Questions and Their Role in Isaiah 1–12

For a study interested in types, characteristics and functions of questions in the book of Isaiah, chapter 10 is highly relevant as it contains more questions than any other chapter in Isaiah 1–12. In this first larger section of the book, the role of questions varies significantly from chapter to chapter. No questions, understood as a specific form of speech, occur in Isaiah 4, 9, 11 and 12. Several chapters use one question to mark a specific point, see 2:22b; 3:15aα (if מַלְכֶּם is read as a form of מַה־לָּכֶם); 7:13; 8:19. There are two questions in chapters 5 (v. 4) and 6 (vv. 6 and 11). The opening chapter of the book comprises three questions. One of these (besides Isaiah 1:11aα, 12b) is 1:5a, a rhetorical question linked with a short comment: עַל מֶה תֻכּוּ עוֹד תּוֹסִיפוּ סָרָה *Where else shall you yet be beaten? You will continue to revolt [anyway]!* The prophet here tries to make the Lord's people aware that the many blows which have struck and severely wounded them are a consequence of their stubborn recalcitrance against the Lord.

The example of 1:5a can be useful for defining what precisely is understood by a rhetorical question in this article. As Archibald van Wieringen[2] points out with reference to Manfred Pfister, a question as such implies a discrepancy in information. This means the person asking lacks a piece of information he or she would like to have. The

---

[1] I would like to thank the École bibilique et archéologique française de Jérusalem (EBAF) and the German Academic Exchange Service (DAAD Postdoc Program), which, by their generous support, allowed me to complete this study during a research stay in Jerusalem.

[2] See the contribution of Archibald van Wieringen in this present volume.

person asked may or may not be able and willing to compensate for the discrepancy in information by giving a suitable answer. The particularity of a rhetorical question, however, is that no discrepancy in information occurs in this case. The person asking already knows the answer to the question. Instead, a rhetorical question is a specific way of making a statement. It proposes something to the addressee in the form of a question. In accordance with this observation, Adina Moshavi defines a rhetorical question 'as a question that indirectly expresses an assertion and marks it as obvious; for example, the question "Isn't the sky blue?" expresses something like "As everyone knows, the sky is blue."'[3] Yet, a question which is rhetorical because it obviously does not seek an answer to compensate for a discrepancy in information cannot simply be considered as the same as a straightforward assertion because it maintains an interrogative quality.[4] A statement clad in the form of a rhetorical question always implies an invitation to give an answer because the pragmatic effect of provoking an answer is precisely what makes a question a question – although the content of the answer is already pre-defined due to its rhetorical character. This typical structure of rhetorical questions guides the person being asked towards an answer affirming the position of the person asking. At the same time, the fact that the latter uses the form of a question although the answer is already pre-defined may well trigger genuine questions in many situations. If someone asks 'Isn't the water wet?' it is obvious that the negative answer 'No, it's dry' would make no sense at all. Yet, the implicit statement 'The water is wet' is so self-evident that, depending on the context, it is likely to provoke a questioning response like 'Of course, it is! Why do you ask this?' Thus, the rhetorical question may lead to increased attention and interest as well as a certain insecurity on the part of the person asked, who feels there must be some actual point behind the self-evident assertion and would like to know it.

It is very typical of rhetorical questions that they can intermingle aspects of a question with aspects of an assertion. A full analysis of the

---

[3] A. Moshavi, "Between Dialectic and Rhetoric: Rhetorical Questions Expressing Premises in Biblical Prose Argumentation," *VT* 65 (2015): 136–151, here 137. See also J.K. Kuntz, "The Form, Location, and Function of Rhetorical Questions in Deutero-Isaiah," in: Craig C. Broyles and Craig A. Evans (Eds.), *Writing and Reading the Scroll of Isaiah: Studies of an Interpretive Tradition* (VTSup 70/1; Leiden: Brill, 1997), 121–141, here 121, who states that genuine questions request information whereas rhetorical questions provide it.

[4] See the brief discussion in Kuntz, "Rhetorical Questions," 121–122.

interplay between these aspects is only possible in the specific context in which a rhetorical question occurs. The question in 1:5a עַל מֶה תֻכּוּ עוֹד reveals itself as rhetorical for two reasons.[5] First, the context of the situation described in 1:5–6 shows that the community being addressed has already suffered so many disastrous blows that it resembles a body covered with wounds from the feet to the head (1:6a). Therefore, the question as to where else the addressees can still be beaten implies there is not a spot not yet struck by a blow. They are wounded everywhere. Second, since no one, particularly no one having suffered repeated blows (cf. עוֹד in v. 5a), *wants* to be beaten, the question where they shall yet be beaten anticipates a reaction like '*nowhere* else, please!' or 'no more! stop it, please!'

Connected with this aspect, a true question lies beneath the interrogative statement of 1:5a which could be put as follows: 'Why do you keep behaving in a way that will inevitably provoke more and more blows to be struck against you?' At the same time, even this true question, which resembles a doctor's question to a patient in order to find out what therapy might be adequate for the ailment, also has a rhetorical quality as it implies the exhortation to stop this kind of behaviour immediately. Yet, the context of 1:5aα, especially the preceding section 1:2–4 and the subsequent statement 1:5aβ תּוֹסִיפוּ סָרָה *you will continue to revolt*, causes the addressed Israelites to appear as completely hopeless cases. As a result, the rhetorical quality of the question in 1:5aα is emphasized. Since they will not cease to rebel anyway, the sad truth is that further blows are inevitable although they have suffered more than enough.

While the core message of 1:5a could also be expressed by a straightforward phrase like 'Stop rebelling so that no further blows will hit you!,' the rhetorical question in v. 5aα guides the addressees to reflect on their situation in order to make them realize that their current desperate situation is actually due to their rebellious attitude. Therefore, the most important and genuine question in the background of the rhetorical question is whether the addressees are willing to acknowledge that they are being struck by disasters because of their stubborn opposition to the Lord, and to change their negative behaviour.

---

[5] For a comprehensive exegesis of Isa 1:5a and its context, see J. Eck, *Jesaja 1 – Eine Exegese der Eröffnung des Jesaja-Buches: Die Präsentation Jesajas und JHWHs, Israels und der Tochter Zion* (BZAW 473; Berlin: De Gruyter, 2015), 290–293.302–318.

2. Macrostructure and Context of Isaiah 10:1–15

Before turning to the issue of questions, a discussion of the structure of 10:1–15 will be useful because, as we have seen above in the case of 1:5aα, the context of questions in general and rhetorical questions in particular is of crucial importance. The passage consists of two different texts[6] which both comprise woe oracles. The first one ranges from verse 1 to 4 and condemns influential circles who abuse their power in the legal system of the Kingdom of Judah,[7] increasing their wealth to the detriment of the poor. 10:1–4 is in various ways connected to preceding texts. Beginning with a הוֹי *woe!* addressed to certain leaders of the prophet's people (cf. עֲנִיֵּי עַמִּי *the poor of my people* in v. 2, and יָדוֹ *his hand* in v. 4b referring to Yhwh in third person), it continues the series of woe oracles pronounced in 5:8–10, 11–12, 18–19, 20, 21, 22–23 against the upper class of Judah.[8] At the same time, there is also a connection with the first chapter. The first woe oracle in the book of Isaiah is proclaimed in 1:4a, here not only against certain political stakeholders, but against the sinful people as a whole, and the grievance

---

[6] This is generally acknowledged, see e.g. W.A.M. Beuken, *Jesaja 1–12* (HThKAT; Freiburg: Herder, 2003), 258; P. Höffken, *Das Buch Jesaja: Kapitel 1–39* (NSKAT 18/1; Stuttgart: Katholisches Bibelwerk, 1993), 113–114; P.R. Ackroyd, "Isaiah I–XII: Presentation of a Prophet," in: *Congress Volume: Göttingen 1977: International Organization for the Study of the Old Testament* (VTSup 29; Leiden: Brill, 1978), 16–48, here 44. Yet, M.C.A. Korpel, "Structural Analysis as a Tool for Redaction Criticism: The Example of Isaiah 5 and 10.1–6," *JSOT* 69 (1996) 53–71, proposes to regard 10:5–6 as an integral part of an original composition comprising chapter 5 and 10:1–6 (with redactional expansions only in 5:8–10, 24c–25; 10:4b).

[7] This assignment to Judah is based on the literary setting of Isa 1–12, which due to the explicit references to Judean kings in 1:1; 2:1; 7 is situated in the Judean kingdom of the eighth century. The text-inherent setting is independent of the question when 10:1–4, 5–15 was composed. For a discussion of the different options see H.G.M. Williamson, *Isaiah 6–12: A Critical and Exegetical Commentary on Isaiah 1–27 in Three Volumes* (ICC; London: Bloomsbury T&T Clark, 2018), 468–469. It also remains true if Isa 10:1–3, 4b were an extremely late redactional addition dating from the fourth century, as U. Becker, *Jesaja – von der Botschaft zum Buch* (FRLANT 178; Göttingen: Vandenhoeck, 1997), 155–159, thinks.

[8] E.g. J.D.W. Watts, *Isaiah 1–33* (WBC 24; Nashville: Nelson, 2005), 181. On the proposal that 10:1–4a originally followed immediately after the woe oracles 5:8–24 and was secondarily postponed after 9:20, see recently J.J.M. Roberts, *First Isaiah: A Commentary* (Hermeneia; Minneapolis: Fortress, 2015), 85. J. Blenkinsopp, *Isaiah 1–39: A New Translation with Introduction and Commentary* (AB 19; New York: Doubleday, 2000), 208–212, varies this hypothesis arguing that 10:1–4 originally preceded 5:8, thus opening the series of woe oracles. For discussion of the most important ones of the many proposals on this question, and arguments for an ultimate rejection of the displacement hypothesis, see Williamson, *Isaiah 6–12*, 463–469.

that widows and orphans are deprived of their legal rights (10:2b) is also an issue in 1:17, 23.[9]

The second part of the chapter comprises 10:5–15.[10] From a formal point of view, this section continues 10:1–4 as it is another, albeit unusually long,[11] woe oracle (see v. 5 הוֹי).[12] Yet, contrary to the preceding woe oracles, it is not spoken against Judah or Israel but against Assyria and its great king, who is sent by the Lord to punish Israel (6aα בְּגוֹי חָנֵף אֲשַׁלְּחֶנּוּ). However, the Assyrian denies his dependence on the God of Israel, or, in fact, any other transcendent power, and deems himself invincible due to his own wisdom and strength. His arrogant heart moves him to annihilate other nations and plunder their wealth in order to increase his own political influence. The woe oracle is Yhwh's response to this hubris, announcing doom against the haughty one.

Although the two texts, 10:1–4 on the one hand and 10:5–15 on the other hand, concern different areas of human affairs, namely the interior politics of the small Kingdom of Judah and global foreign politics in a world dominated by the Assyrian superpower, it is no accident that these two texts form a sequence and belong to one and the same chapter. Oppression of weaker neighbours, unjustified appropriation of goods belonging to others, egocentric greed for more power and wealth, and abuse of a mission given by God are important issues in both cases. To learn about the mission that Yhwh had given to the unfaithful rulers of 10:1–4, one has to go back as far as the Vineyard Song in 5:1–7. There, 5:7b says that Yhwh expected his vineyard (alias Israel) to yield justice and righteousness (מִשְׁפָּט and צְדָקָה) but they only brought about oppression. So, the mission of God's people as a whole, and in particular of the responsible leaders, would have been to establish justice and righteousness. Since the society of Judah has fulfilled the very opposite of this mission, the woe oracle against the leaders of Yhwh's people in 10:1–4 resumes and concludes, by its social-critical contents, the series of six woe oracles proclaimed after the Vineyard Song in 5:8–23. The mission of the Assyrian power is clearly stated in the corresponding woe oracle itself in 10:6, where Yhwh says that he sends the Assyrian against his

---

[9] Cf. Beuken, *Jesaja 1–12*, 267–268.
[10] Concerning the delimitation of 10:5–15 as a literary unit, see e.g. E. Haag, "Jesaja, Assur und der Antijahwe: Literar- und traditionsgeschichtliche Beobachtungen zu Jes 10,5–15," *TThZ* 103 (1994) 18–37, here 19–20.
[11] Williamson, *Isaiah 6–12*, 498, with reference to Hans Wildberger.
[12] Based on this observation, Korpel, "Structural Analysis," proposes to regard 10:5–6 as the concluding part of the preceding section.

people, a godless nation (בְּגוֹי חָנֵף אֲשַׁלְּחֶנּוּ) which has incited divine wrath. More specifically, the Assyrian's task is to 'seize plunder, carry off loot, and to trample them like the mud of the street' (note שׁלל and בזז in 10:6 לִשְׁלֹל שָׁלָל וְלָבֹז בַּז וּלְשִׂימוֹ מִרְמָס כְּחֹמֶר חוּצוֹת). This means, he is called by Yhwh to commit against the unfaithful people exactly the same crimes which the tyrannical Judean rulers of 10:1–2 have committed against widows and orphans. The intention of their unjust decrees had been to make 'widows their plunder and orphans their prey' (see שׁלל and בזז in 10:2 לִהְיוֹת אַלְמָנוֹת שְׁלָלָם וְאֶת־יְתוֹמִים יָבֹזּוּ).

The sense of the juxtaposition of the last woe oracle against the Judean upper class and the woe oracle against the Assyrian power can be summed up as follows. God's people had been called to bring forth justice and righteousness but, instead, has caused injustice and oppression. Already in Isaiah 6, Yhwh had called a prophet who was commissioned to harden the heart of the people so that their ways of stubborn iniquity would lead them towards their final punishment, which would take the form of a complete disaster (6:11).[13] The hardening of the people's heart in itself already constituted the interior side of the imminent disaster since the people was thus barred from returning to its divine protector Yhwh. Complementary to this, the Assyrian was called to punish their crimes by the means of military invasion, plundering and destruction. He, however, deemed himself to be more powerful than the God of Israel who had sent him, and abused his mission for the purpose of exploiting the nations and seizing power over the whole world as if he were himself a supreme divinity.

3. The Structure of Isaiah 10:1–4

The section 10:1–4 can be further subdivided into verses 1–2, which constitute the actual woe oracle, a commenting subsection consisting of

---

[13] For a broader discussion of the functions of chapters 5; 6; 7 and 10 in the whole context of 1–12, where the announcement of the revelation of Yhwh's absolute sovereignty on his Day in 2:10–22 is followed by the proclamation of an approaching judgement in chapter 5, and the execution of the judgement is effected by the hardening of the heart of the people in chapter 6, and the sending of the Assyrian as destructive power against Judah/Israel in chapters 7–10, see J. Eck, "Metamorphoses of a Tyrant: Isaiah 14:4b–21 Read in Its Wider Context," in: T. Hibbard and J. Stromberg (Eds.), *The History of Isaiah: The Formation of the Book and its Presentation of the Past* (FAT 150; Tübingen: Mohr Siebeck, 2021), 407–429, here 421–425; J. Eck, "The Song of the Unfruitful Vineyard (Isa 5:1–7): Its Position in the Book of Isaiah and Its Reception in Late Layers of Isaiah and the Twelve," in: R.J. Bautch, J. Eck and B.M. Zapff (Eds.), *Isaiah and the Twelve: Parallels, Similarities and Diffrences* (BZAW 527; Berlin: de Gruyter, 2020), 159–183, here 163–170.

QUESTIONS IN ISAIAH'S WOE ORACLES AGINST THE RULERS   131

verses 3–4a, and a concluding passage in verse 4b.[14] Within the woe oracle of 10:1–2, verse 1 condemns in direct speech those in Judah who are guilty of making unjust legal decrees and decisions. Verse 2 describes what intentions they realize by such unjust means. Their reckless schemes cause the poor and needy to be deprived of their rights and goods so that the responsible rulers can appropriate these as their loot. In verse 3, a series of three questions follows, confronting the persons responsible for enacting unjust statutes and writing oppressive decrees (v. 1) with the expectation of an imminent judgement, a יוֹם פְּקֻדָּה *day of visitation* (v. 3) that will reduce them to utter helplessness. Verse 4a comments on this word by warning that any attempt to avert the severe judgement is useless. This general sense is reasonably clear, although the grammatical construction of the verse presents difficulties.[15] Thus, the use of בִּלְתִּי poses questions in the given context,[16] and the Masoretic punctuation suggests a Qal *perfect* third person masculine *singular* for כרע in 4aα whereas the verb יפלו in 4aβ is a Qal *imperfect* third person masculine *plural*. Taking בִּלְתִּי as a negation equivalent to לֹא, as it also exceptionally appears to be the case in the nominal clause of 1 Samuel 20:26bβ בִּלְתִּי טָהוֹר הוּא *he is not clean*, the Masoretic reading obviously combines a retrospective with a contrasting future perspective. The *perfect* in v. 4aα seems to look into the past so that בִּלְתִּי כָרַע תַּחַת אַסִּיר might be translated as *one has not sunk beneath the captive*, and the continuation in v. 4aβ, which is introduced by a *waw adversativum*, considers the oppressors' fatal end in the future so that וְתַחַת הֲרוּגִים יִפֹּלוּ can be rendered as *but they will fall beneath the slain*. A more consistent and elegant reading with a minimal change of the vowel punctuation was proposed by Hugh Williamson.[17] Taking בִּלְתִּי as a poetic variant of לְבִלְתִּי, he considers כרע in 4a as an *infinitivus constructus* (כְּרֹעַ) and יפלו in v. 4aβ as an asyndetic

---

[14] Cf. Beuken, *Jesaja 1–12*, 267–268.
[15] Cf. Höffken, *Jesaja 1–39*, 114: "angedroht wird wohl der Tod mitten unter Erschlagenen." For a discussion of the textual difficulties of v. 4a, see Beuken, *Jesaja 1–12*, 261, and above all the very thorough work of Williamson, *Isaiah 6–12*, 460–463.
[16] Usually, בִּלְתִּי is either a preposition meaning *except, without* (e.g. Gen 21:26: בִּלְתִּי הַיּוֹם *except today*), or it occurs as the combination לְבִלְתִּי followed by an *infinitvus constructus* and then expresses the negation of the infinitive (e.g. Ex 8:25: לְבִלְתִּי שַׁלַּח אֶת־הָעָם *so as not to send the people away*). But sometimes לְבִלְתִּי is also followed by a finite verb. Thus, note the *imperfect* form in 2 Sam 14:14bγ (לְבִלְתִּי יִדַּח מִמֶּנּוּ נִדָּח) and the *perfect* forms in Jer 23:14aγ (לְבִלְתִּי־שָׁבוּ אִישׁ מֵרָעָתוֹ) and Ezek 13:3bβ (וּלְבִלְתִּי רָאוּ). Also, the combination עַד־בִּלְתִּי *until not* is followed by a finite *perfect* form, see e.g. Num 21:35; Deut 3:3; Josh 8:22. On the problem of בִּלְתִּי in Isa 10:4a, see the discussion by Williamson, *Isaiah 6–12*, 461–462.
[17] Williamson, *Isaiah 6–12*, 460–463.

relative clause equivalent to אֲשֶׁר יִפֹּלוּ, and interprets the entire verse 4a as a continuation of the preceding rhetorical question of 3bβ (וְאָנָה תַעַזְבוּ כְּבוֹדְכֶם), which results in the following translation: [3bβ] *and where will you leave your treasured possessions,* [4a] *so as to avoid crouching among the prisoners and among the slain who have fallen?*[18]

The last subsection is verse 4b. Repeating the refrain of the poem of Yhwh's outstretched hand (see 9:11, 16, 20 as well as already 5:25), it concludes the composition comprising 9:7–20 and 10:1–4 and creates a structure integrating the woe oracle 10:1–4a into this preceding poem.

While 10:1–2 is an outcry against the present arrogance of the addressees, who abuse their authority, the questions following in verse 3, which will be discussed in detail in an extra point below, depict the situation of these rulers at the moment when they will be punished for their crimes. 10:3a וּמַה־תַּעֲשׂוּ לְיוֹם פְּקֻדָּה וּלְשׁוֹאָה מִמֶּרְחָק תָּבוֹא *What will you do when facing the day of visitation, the desolation which comes from afar?* implies that a superior power will come and overwhelm them in order to hold them responsible for their deeds. Then, the unjust rulers, who currently still have the power to impose their unlawful plans upon God's people, will be unable to exert any control over the situation. Next, 10:3bα asks עַל־מִי תָּנוּסוּ לְעֶזְרָה *To whom will you flee for help?* This question indicates that, after the sudden breakdown of the addressed rulers' dominance, there will be no one to grant them asylum or help.[19] The third question concerns the good to which the addressees currently attach a higher estimation than to anything else: their כָּבוֹד *glory,* which in the given context means their influence and wealth gained by illegitimate means.[20] וְאָנָה תַעַזְבוּ כְּבוֹדְכֶם *And where will you leave your glory?* 10:3bβ asks, possibly continuing in verse 4a with a statement indicating a fruitless attempt to avoid a fatal and inevitable judgement. The general statement implicit in this rhetorical question is that the accused ones will have nowhere to store their wealth in order to retrieve it when the storm is over. The day of visitation and disaster mentioned in the first question will force them to definitely abandon their כָּבוֹד *glory.* There will be no safe place to keep it, rather it will be lost once and forever because the judgement will reveal the rotten foundations on which the corrupt leaders' house of glory was built.

---

[18] Williamson, *Isaiah 6–12*, 457.
[19] Cf. Williamson, *Isaiah 6–12*, 476, who underlines there will be no escape for the evildoers.
[20] On this implication of כָּבוֹד in the given context, see Williamson, *Isaiah 6–12*, 478.

The section of 10:1–4 is set off from 10:5–15 by several characteristics. As mentioned, 10:4b takes up the refrain of the prophetic poem of 9:7–20. This refrain marked in 9:11, 16, 20 the conclusion of each of the poem's three stanzas by stating: בְּכָל־זֹאת לֹא־שָׁב אַפּוֹ וְעוֹד יָדוֹ נְטוּיָה *For all this, his wrath is not turned away and his hand is still stretched out!* Although the woe oracle of 10:1–4 is probably not an original and integral part of this prophetic poem because it differs in form and contents while corresponding to the series of woe oracles found in 5:8–23, the fact that the refrain of 9:11, 16, 20 is also repeated in 10:4b indicates a redactional intention to link the conclusion of the woe oracle of 10:1–4 with the preceding poem while setting it off from the subsequent context.[21] But, as already explained above, this redactional intention coincides with other elements in the text which clearly create parallels between the sections 10:1–4 and 10:5–15. Moreover, the fact that the same refrain occurs once more in 5:25b as the final part of 5:24–25, the concluding section of the woe oracles of 5:8–23, shows that it is simultaneously used as a tool for connecting not only 10:1–4 but also the woe oracles of 5:8–23 to the prophetic poem of 9:7–20. As has often been seen, these texts are thus firmly tied to the material found in Isaiah 6; 7; 8; 9:1–6.[22] In sum, the woe oracles of 5:8–23; 10:1–4a and the poem of Yhwh's outstretched hand as found in 5:25b; 9:8–20; 10:4b are a framework around and an indispensable hermeneutic key to the so-called *Jesaja-Denkschrift*, and simultaneously they also correlate the leaders of Judah with the Great King of Assyria, who are both, though in different ways, guilty of insolent arrogance against Yhwh, the divine King of Israel and the universe.[23]

4. The Structure of Isaiah 10:5–15

The single woe spoken against the Assyrian in 10:5 seems quite modest compared to the seven woes spoken against the upper class of Judah.[24]

---

[21] See R.E. Clements, *Isaiah 1–39* (The New Century Bible Commentary; Grand Rapids: Eerdmans, 1980), 62; W.P. Brown, "The So-Called Refrain in Isaiah 5:25–30 and 9:7–10:4," *CBQ* 52 (1990) 432–443, here 439. Yet, Becker, *Jesaja*, 155–159, considers 10:1–3, 4b (to which v. 4a was added secondarily) not as an Isaianic text but as a late redactional text specially created for its present context.

[22] See e.g. C.E. L'Heureux, "The Redactional History of Isaiah 5.1–10.4," in W. Boyd Barrick and John R. Spencer (Eds.), *In the Shelter of Elyon: Essays on Ancient Palestinian Life and Literature in Honour of G.W. Ahlström* (JSOTSub 31; Sheffield: JSOT Press, 1984), 99–119.

[23] Cf. Williamson, *Isaiah 6–12*, 467.

[24] See הוֹי in 5:8, 11, 18, 20, 21, 22; 10:1.

Whereas the people of God is guilty of a countless number of sins, the Assyrian is guilty of a seemingly infinite arrogance (cf. 10:7–11, 13–14). This requires divine sanctions as soon as Assyrian power has fulfilled Yhwh's mission to punish the faithlessness of Israel (10:5–6, 12).[25] Whereas the woe oracle of 10:1–2 against the Judean rulers immediately points out their crime and their evil intentions, the woe oracle against the Assyrian combines the interjection הוֹי *woe!* with a description of the commission to which Yhwh had called him. Thus, verses 5–6 characterize him as the rod of Yhwh's wrath (10:5a הוֹי אַשּׁוּר שֵׁבֶט אַפִּי), into whose hands the divine anger was given as a staff for beating Yhwh's people (v. 5b וּמַטֶּה־הוּא בְיָדָם זַעְמִי). Due to the cruelty of the Assyrian enemy, God's people are exposed to violent deeds which are of the same category as those which they had themselves inflicted upon the poor among them. As they plundered and looted those who lacked the power to defend themselves, they now have to suffer the Assyrian's plundering and looting.[26]

Only the next section 10:7–15 explains his guilt, and it does this in a very elaborate way comprising several subsections. Verse 7 states the general reproach that the Assyrian denies his dependence on Yhwh, who gave him a specific mission, but pursues destruction as a purpose in itself.[27] 10:8–11 proves this reproach by quoting the Assyrian King's own words. This passage contains a series of five questions, which give evidence of his conceit from his own mouth. The questions are rhetorical insofar as they are not motivated by the wish to obtain an instructive answer giving some missing information, but intend to impress the listener. Since the series of questions in 10:8–11 only quotes what the Assyrian had spoken, the speaker of the whole part comprising 10:5–11 is Yhwh.

After the detailed description of the Assyrian's guilt, verse 12a announces in the voice of the prophet that something will happen (וְהָיָה) when Yhwh will have completed the judgement against Jerusalem. In verse 12b, Yhwh's own voice (אֶפְקֹד *I will visit*) continues the announcement and states that he will punish the haughtiness of the King of Assyria. The reasons are again pointed out using a quotation of the delinquent's own words in 10:13–14. Whereas the first quotation of the Assyrian

---

[25] Concerning the thesis that 10:12 is probably a later addition, see Williamson, *Isaiah 6–12*, 495; Brown, "The So-Called Refrain," 441. If he is right to assume that the oracle was originally addressed mainly to Samaria, and verse 12 added later, this redactional supplement would contribute to the intention observed above to describe the sins of God's people as a whole as a form of hubris which is equivalent to that of the Assyrian King.

[26] Cf. Williamson, *Isaiah 6–12*, 476; Brown, "The So-Called Refrain," 440.

[27] See Haag, "Jesaja, Assur und der Antijahwe," 28–29.

King's words in 10:8–11 mainly consisted of rhetorical questions, the second quotation in 10:13–14 is a series of statements confirming and interpreting his arrogant attitude already expressed in the preceding quotation. Taken together, they both give full evidence of his hubris.

In order to reveal the sinful distortedness of the Assyrian King's words and actions, Yhwh concludes the unusually long woe oracle in verse 15[28] with a pair of questions that are again rhetorical as they obviously do not express any discrepancy of information,[29] followed by a pair of comparisons which illustrate the absurdity of the Assyrian King's arrogant self-perception. Whereas the Assyrian intended by his rhetorical questions in 10:8–11 to demonstrate his god-like superiority, Yhwh unmasks this as an entirely unwise and foolish conception. 'Will the axe boast against the one who hews with it?' he asks in 15aα. In 15bβ–γ, he adds in conclusion that it would be equally foolish to think 'a rod (שֵׁבֶט) could sway even the one who lifts it,' or to say 'a staff (מַטֶּה) could lift the one who is not wood:' כְּהָנִיף שֵׁבֶט וְאֶת־מְרִימָיו כְּהָרִים מַטֶּה לֹא־עֵץ. Since the word pair שֵׁבֶט rod and מַטֶּה staff was also used in verse 5, it forms an *inclusio* surrounding the whole composition.[30] This special link between verses 5 and 15 emphasizes the obvious absurdity of the ideas expressed by the Assyrian King. In verse 5, Yhwh had clarified that the latter is nothing else than the rod of his wrath (5a הוֹי אַשּׁוּר שֵׁבֶט אַפִּי), the instrument by which he punishes the sins of his people. This means that also the power of the Assyrian, by which he is able to terrorise the world, is nothing else than a gift of Yhwh, who gave the power of the divine anger into his hand, as verse 5b states: וּמַטֶּה־הוּא בְיָדָם זַעְמִי 'and the staff, the one in their hand, is my anger.'[31]

---

[28] On the question who speaks in 10:15, see the careful analysis of the speech domains in 10:5–15 by A.H.L.M van Wieringen, *The Implied Reader in Isa 6–12* (BibInt 34; Leiden: Brill, 1998), 165–169, who discusses three possible variants and comes to a result in line with our above analysis (pp. 168–169).

[29] H. Wildberger, *Jesaja 1–12* (BKAT 10/1; Neukirchen-Vluyn: Neukirchener, 1972), 400, underlines the subtleness of these questions as they oblige the addressees to give themselves an answer which reveals the foolishness of the Assyrian's arrogance.

[30] Cf. Williamson, *Isaiah 6–12*, 504, who notes that this word pair also occurs in 9:3; 10:24; 14:5; 28:27; 30:31–32. On the role of the word pair שֵׁבֶט/מַטֶּה in intertextual relationships between chapters 1–12 and 13–14, see Eck, "Metamorphoses of a Tyrant," point 4.

[31] This translation seems to me the most probable interpretation of the syntactically difficult text of v. 5b MT, which is the main object of interest in this article. I understand הוּא בְיָדָם as an asyndetic relative clause, see Beuken, *Jesaja 1–12*, 274; Siegfried Mittmann, "Wehe! Assur, Stab meines Zornes" (Jes 10,5–9.13ab–15), in: V. Fritz, Karl-Friedrich Pohlmann and Hans-Christoph Schmitt (Eds.), *Prophet und Prophetenbuch: Festschrift für Otto Kaiser zum 65. Geburtstag* (BZAW 185; Berlin: de Gruyter, 1989), 111–133, here 114–115. Concerning the history of the text, Williamson, *Isaiah 6–12*,

In the context of the Assyrian's fundamental dependence on Yhwh, the two rhetorical questions and comparisons in the final divine speech of verse 15 effectively prove the foolishness of the Assyrian's preceding boisterous speeches. In particular, verse 15 unmasks the preceding praise of his own strength and wisdom in verse 13 as utterly unwise since it is precisely this type of hubris that exposes him to an approaching divine judgement forever extinguishing his power.

The structure of 10:1–15 can be summed up as follows:

Isaiah 10:1–4 Woe oracle against Judean leaders

vv. 1–2 – Proclamation of woe against unjust rulers who deprive the poor of their rights and goods

vv. 3–4a – **Rhetorical questions** and announcement indicating the far-reaching extent of the judgement

v. 4b – Refrain of Yhwh's outstretched hand (cf. 9:7–20) excluding the judgement to end soon

Isaiah 10:5–15 Yhwh's woe oracle against the Assyrian

vv. 5–11 – *Yhwh's first speech against the Assyrian*
vv. 5–6 – Assyria as fallen instrument of judgement in the hand of Yhwh
v. 7 – The Assyrian's plan to dominate the nations by means of destruction
vv. 8–11 – The Assyrian's arrogance expressed in **rhetorical questions**
vv. 12–15 – *Yhwh's second speech against the Assyrian*
v. 12a – Introduction spoken by the prophet: announcement of events after the completion of Yhwh's work against Jerusalem
v. 12b – Beginning of Yhwh's second speech: announcement of doom against the Assyrian King's arrogance
vv. 13–14 – Quotation of the Assyrian King's self-glorification in view of his military success
v. 15 – Yhwh's unmasking of the Assyrian's hubris and foolishness by **rhetorical questions** and *comparisons*

481–482, who offers a detailed discussion of the readings proposed, and Wildberger, *Jesaja 1–12*, 391, will be correct to assume that הוּא בְיָדָם is a late addition in the form of a gloss. This means that, in an earlier stage of text growth, שֵׁבֶט אַפִּי of v. 5a had an exact parallel in v. 5b, which consisted of the construct chain וּמַטֶּה זַעְמִי. The late addition of הוּא בְיָדָם changed the synonymous parallelism into a synthetic one as it supplemented a different but complementary theological aspect. Verse 5a emphasizes the Assyrian as nothing but an instrument of punishment in the hand of the Lord, who controls everything he does. V. 5b underlines that the Assyrian has no power of his own but his only, yet effective, weapon, which was handed over to him when the Lord sent him against his people (v. 6), is the anger of the Lord. This means that the entire Assyrian army and war machine are not an achievement of the Great King, but nothing else than a manifestation of Yhwh's anger given into the Assyrian's hands.

5. Exegesis and Function of the Questions in 10:3

After crying out his woe against the legislators and scribes who deprive the poor and needy of their rights in 10:1–2,[32] the prophet poses them three rhetorical questions in 10:3. The first one, verse 3a, pretends to take interest in the oppressors' plans for the future by asking what they are going to do: וּמַה־תַּעֲשׂוּ. Yet, what follows reveals this to be ironic. With regard to the announced day of visitation and desolation approaching from afar (לְיוֹם פְּקֻדָּה לְשׁוֹאָה מִמֶּרְחָק תָּבוֹא), there is nothing which the guilty oppressors can do. They will have to face the doom[33] that their crimes have conjured up. The question as to what they will do in a situation where nothing can be done expresses a certain mockery.[34] Those who deemed themselves powerful are now exposed to the unalterable consequences of their irresponsible use of authority. The future helplessness of the lawless legislators and scribes is dramatically intensified by the next two rhetorical questions. 10:3bα עַל־מִי תָּנוּסוּ לְעֶזְרָה *To whom will you flee for help?* recalls the fact that, one day not far off, the former oppressors will lose their influence and need to look for protection. Until now, other persons, namely those deprived of their rights, were suffering and hoping for someone to defend them against the addressees' corrupt government. But someone saw their pain – Yhwh, the God of Israel. In his name, the prophet Isaiah announces a יוֹם פְּקֻדָּה *day of visitation* which will bring about a turnaround of the situation.[35]

The question in 10:3bβ וְאָנָה תַּעַזְבוּ כְּבוֹדְכֶם *And where will you leave your wealth?* indicates that in this coming situation, the wealth, or *glory* כָּבוֹד, gathered by the corrupt rulers will be irretrievably lost as they will have no place to keep it. It appears that כָּבוֹד has a double meaning here. As already explained above in the discussion of the structure of 10:1–4, the dominant sense of כָּבוֹד is economic here so that it is usually translated as *wealth* that the rulers gathered by corrupt methods. Therefore, the rhetorical question means that, on the day of judgement, they will lose anything they have, including their land. They will be homeless

---

[32] The terms עמל/און, the described situation of injustice, and relevant contexts are discussed by Beuken, *Jesaja 1–12*, 268–269. The most important point appears to be that educated and influential Israelites/Judeans abused administrative and legal instruments for gaining unlawful profit from fellow citizens who had no means to defend themselves. The story of Naboth's vineyard in 1 Kgs 21 may serve as an illustration of the problem.
[33] On פקדה *visitation* as a prophetic expression for divine judgement over human acts in the course of history, see Beuken, *Jesaja 1–12*, 269.
[34] On further aspects of irony in chapter 10 see Brown, "The So-Called Refrain," 439–440.
[35] Beuken, *Jesaja 1–12*, 269.

refugees or exiles who are unable to possess anything beyond what they can carry on themselves. The alternative translation of כָּבוֹד as *glory* makes sense as well because the announced doom will also destroy the high reputation that they were able to acquire dishonestly in Judean society. 'Where will you leave your glory?' is a question which then also indicates that there will be no social location where they can keep their undeserved glory, which will turn into shame when the society of the Kingdom of Judah breaks up. Since the whole context has an ironic dimension, as was seen above with verse 3a, *glory* can be understood as an ironic reference to the addressees' wealth and influence, which in the end proves to be useless.

In the light of the subsequent verse 4a, which announces to them a fate worse than captivity as they will suffer an unworthy death when they וְתַחַת הֲרוּגִים יִפֹּלוּ *fall under the slain*, the rhetorical question of verse 3bβ assumes an even darker meaning. The corrupt rulers will have no place where they can leave their glory because they will die and be covered by the unclean bodies of the slain. This implies that they will have no proper burial and thus will share the fate of the fallen tyrant of Babylon as described in 14:19–20, who is covered by slain bodies outside his grave (v. 19 וְאַתָּה הָשְׁלַכְתָּ מִקִּבְרְךָ כְּנֵצֶר נִתְעָב נְתֻעָב לְבוּשׁ הֲרֻגִים) while all other 'kings of the nations lie in glory, each in his tomb' according to 14:18 (כָּל־מַלְכֵי גוֹיִם כֻּלָּם שָׁכְבוּ בְכָבוֹד אִישׁ בְּבֵיתוֹ).

In sum, the three rhetorical questions in 10:3 have the primary intention of announcing doom to the corrupt rulers with increasing intensity. First, a day of judgement will come, against which they can do nothing.[36] Second, there will even be no person to help them. Third, they will lose everything, including their – dubious – honour. The rhetorical form of the questions contributes to the alarming character of this message as they confront the addressees with problems they can neither avert nor resolve because their past and irreversible deeds have conjured up the present situation. In reply to the questions, the unjust rulers can only admit that neither their power nor their social relationships nor their possessions will protect them in any way against the coming doom. They either have to realize that all the corrupt endeavours upon which they built their lives has brought them into an absolute impasse, an absolute nowhere, or, in an attempt to ignore all this, they will simply make themselves deaf and blind in accordance with the commission the Lord gave to his prophet Isaiah in 6:9–10.

---

[36] Cf. Beuken, *Jesaja 1–12*, 269.

6. Exegesis and Function of the Questions in 10:8-11, 15

After three rhetorical questions have been posed to Judean rulers in 10:3, the woe oracle against the Assyrian King 10:5–15 contains another seven rhetorical questions. Five of these are spoken by the Assyrian ruler who is quoted by Yhwh in 10:8–11, and the last two questions come from the mouth of Yhwh himself in 10:15, the concluding section of the oracle.

The Assyrian King's five questions are structured in a specific way. הֲלֹא שָׂרַי יַחְדָּו מְלָכִים *Are not my commanders all kings?* asks the first one in verse 8b. The anticipated answer is 'no, not a single commander of yours is of lower rank than a king.' By this indirect method of bragging that his commanders, who are obliged to serve and obey him, are all kings,[37] the Assyrian King portrays himself as King of kings. This role is traditionally reserved to gods in the Ancient Near East. In the context of Isaiah 1–12, Yhwh appears to Isaiah in 6:1–5 as divine king and is praised by the Seraphim in 6:3 as the Holy One, whose glory is the fullness of the earth. This includes that also the kings on earth are called to glorify Yhwh. The Assyrian King, by contrast, sees himself as Lord of earthly kings who serve his glory. He denies Yhwh's kingship over the fullness of the earth. This is also underlined when he boasts to have achieved his military conquests by his own hand (יָדִי in vv. 10, 13, 14) although Yhwh's outstretched hand in 10:4b is the actual reason why the Assyrian is commanded to serve as rod of Yhwh's wrath (10:5a) and sent against Israel (10:6).[38]

The next three questions in verse 9 are linked to each other, with the first question in 9a being supplemented by two similar questions in 9bα and 9bβ: הֲלֹא כְּכַרְכְּמִישׁ כַּלְנוֹ אִם־לֹא כְאַרְפַּד חֲמָת אִם־לֹא כְדַמֶּשֶׂק שֹׁמְרוֹן *Is not Kalno like Carchemish? Or is not Hamath like Arpad? Or is not Samaria like Damascus?* Verse 9a is introduced by the interrogative particle הֲלֹא *is not?*, and verses 9bα and 9bβ are connected to the preceding questions by אִם־לֹא *or not?* Each question is an independent comparative nominal clause juxtaposing two toponyms by means of the preposition כְּ. In terms of content, the three questions list three pairs of place names in geographical order, descending from North to South.[39] While Ernst Haag assumed the toponyms refer to places where different Assyrian kings had

---
[37] Cf. Höffken, *Jesaja 1–39*, 115.
[38] Beuken, *Jesaja 1–12*, 283; cf. Höffken, *Jesaja 1–39*, 115–116.
[39] H. Liss, "Undisclosed Speech: Patterns of Communication in the Book of Isaiah," in: *JHS* 4 (2002) Article 4, DOI: 10.5508/jhs.2002.v4.a4, points 3.1.2–3; Höffken, *Jesaja 1–39*, 115; Williamson, *Isaiah 6–12*, 514.

beaten their opponents at different times,[40] Williamson plausibly details in his recent commentary that, since at least four of the cities mentioned in verse 9 had taken part in the anti-Assyrian alliance fighting against Sargon II in 720 B.C., and Kalno had been annexed by the same Assyrian king only three years later, 'it is highly likely that the verse refers to events that were all related to a single Assyrian king and that took place within a short span of time.'[41] Nonetheless, Haag's conclusion that the Assyrian king who speaks in first person voice in verse 9 is a metahistorical figure[42] seems not entirely out of place because, although the historical events mirrored in verse 9 probably do relate to Sargon II, the style in which the Great King is represented here implies above all a general critique against the Assyrian kingship as an institution.

Again, the three questions in verse 9 are rhetorical,[43] since the quoted speaker, the King of Assyria, does not expect to learn something he does not yet know. Instead, he expects the addressee to agree that Kalno is indeed like Carchemish, Hamath like Arpad, and Samaria like Damascus. An interesting point is that these rhetorical questions require a considerably high level of historical knowledge in order to be fully understood. Someone who does not know that the Assyrian kings won battles against local kings at Carchemish, Kalno, Arpad, Hamath, Damascus and Samaria, would certainly not agree that all these cities enumerated by the Assyrian King were simply one like the other. They are situated in different areas and belong to different peoples, so they are not the same. In fact, they are only comparable under one aspect: they were all places of Assyrian victories. Even during the time of the prophet Isaiah himself, knowledge of these political events could not be anticipated among average people like e.g. illiterate peasants living in the countryside of Judah. Rather, such knowledge required an educated audience informed about the Assyrian politics of expansion. Thus, the quotation of the Assyrian King's speech in 10:8–11 evokes a fictive setting where the Great King

---

[40] Haag, "Jesaja, Assur und der Antijahwe," 32–33. See also Liss, "Undisclosed Speech," point 3.1.2, who details that Carchemish was annexed by Sargon II in 717, Kalno by Tiglath-Pileser III in 739/38, Arpad by Tiglath-Pileser III in 740, Hamath by Sargon II in 720, Damascus by Tiglath-Pileser III in 733/32, and Samaria by Salmanazar V in 722. Yet, the earlier annexation did not prevent at least four of these cities from participating in the above-mentioned anti-Assyrian alliance, see Williamson below.

[41] Williamson, *Isaiah 6–12*, 516, with reference to Otto Procksch.

[42] Haag, "Jesaja, Assur und der Antijahwe," 33: "Daß die Aufzählung vier Städte nennt, die Assur zu verschiedenen Zeiten und durch verschiedene Herrscher bezwungen hat, ist deutlich ein Hinweis auf das übergeschichtliche Ich des hier zu Wort kommenden Sprechers, [...]."

[43] Williamson, *Isaiah 6–12*, 495.

speaks to a high-ranking and educated audience such as an assembly of kings or their ambassadors. This anticipated setting is in line with the contents of the preceding question in 10:8, where the Assyrian presents himself as King of kings. The three rhetorical questions in 10:9, with their enumeration of three pairs of defeated royal cities in the Levante, demonstrate that no kingdom on earth is able to defeat or even defend itself against the power of the army of the god-like Assyrian Great King. In the context of this threatening scenario, the series of toponyms, by describing a military movement from Carchemish in the North to Samaria in the South, implies that the next campaign could at any time advance further to the South and result in an attack against Jerusalem, the next royal city in the neighbourhood of Samaria.[44]

This point, implicit already in 10:9, is explicitly stated in the next question, 10:11: הֲלֹא כַּאֲשֶׁר עָשִׂיתִי לְשֹׁמְרוֹן וְלֶאֱלִילֶיהָ כֵּן אֶעֱשֶׂה לִירוּשָׁלַם וְלַעֲצַבֶּיהָ *As I have done to Samaria and her gods, shall I not do the same to Jerusalem and her idols, too?* Again, this question is rhetorical. Instead of a genuine answer, the Assyrian aims at an affirmation of his position expressed indirectly. Since he has conquered Samaria, he is positive that he is able to defeat Jerusalem whenever he wants. Addressing his audience in the form of a question, he challenges any person present who would dare to speak up against his obvious superiority. The effect of the rhetorical question is increased by the preceding verse 10. In verse 11, the Assyrian King compares Jerusalem only to Samaria and emphasizes that the Judean capital is no greater challenge to him than the one of Northern Israel. Yet, in verse 10 he brags that his hand found לְמַמְלְכֹת הָאֱלִיל וּפְסִילֵיהֶם מִירוּשָׁלַם וּמִשֹּׁמְרוֹן *idolatrous kingdoms and their images, which outnumbered Jerusalem and Samaria.* By invoking the weight of the many Assyrian victories over other kingdoms, including those listed in verse 9, this statement tries to prove that any attempt to give a negative answer to the Great King's question in verse 11, about whether he could not easily defeat Jerusalem like he had Samaria, must appear ridiculous. The Assyrian King's rhetorical strategy, as quoted by Yhwh in 10:8–11, leaves no room for contradiction or even doubt but only permits either confirmation of his superiority, or – and above all – utterly helpless silence. His claim to absolute power is further underlined by the fact that he deems himself to be Lord even over the gods of the kingdoms he defeated when he speaks of מַמְלְכֹת הָאֱלִיל *idolatrous kingdoms* in verse 10; kingdoms that had more cultic images than Jerusalem

---

[44] See already Haag, "Jesaja, Assur und der Antijahwe," 33.

and Samaria. In verse 11, he shows himself convinced his victory over Samaria includes a victory over her gods, and the same would apply to the gods of Jerusalem.

The whole statement in form of a question includes multiple perspectives of meaning. The first one is that a good part of the discourse of the Assyrian King mirrors general beliefs which were common all over the Ancient Near East. Second, some implicit aspects of the statement fiercely criticize the hubris of the Assyrian King. Third, some other aspects contain a critique of religious practices common both in Samaria and Jerusalem. Fourth, one negative aspect which both the Assyrian King and Samaria and Jerusalem have in common is that none of them acknowledges Yhwh as the only divine King of heavens and earth. Therefore, none of them shows any awareness of Yhwh being the divine ruler of history, who grants and limits the power of the Assyrian King in order to realize his own divine plans. These four perspectives of meaning are interwoven and interact with each other. When the Assyrian King states in verse 10 that his hand found kingdoms with more cultic images of gods than Jerusalem and Samaria, and when he mentions a plural of gods venerated in Samaria and Jerusalem in verse 11, then he presents the natural view of the polytheistic type of religions that used to be standard in the Ancient Near East. He takes for granted that there are many gods who can accept ritually dedicated cultic images as real embodiments of their being, and he assumes that a kingdom worshiping a larger number of gods is usually more powerful than one with a smaller number of gods, since the first one is supported by more powerful representatives of the transcendent world than the latter one.[45] Moreover, the Assyrian King is characterized as a foreigner who does not know about the monolatric relationship between Yhwh and Israel, and therefore just relates what he has seen in Samaria, namely a considerable number of idols (verse 11a), and expects the same custom to hold for Jerusalem (verse 11b), without explicitly commenting on or criticizing the religious illegitimacy of such polytheistic practices in Israel.[46] Thus, without being aware of it, the Assyrian King speaks as an objective witness against Samaria and Jerusalem, who are unfaithful to Yhwh.

---

[45] Cf. Haag, "Jesaja, Assur und der Antijahwe," 33.
[46] Haag, "Jesaja, Assur und der Antijahwe," 33, goes so far as to qualify the Assyrian King's statement in vv. 10–11 as blasphemous because he allows himself to judge Yhwh, the God of Israel, using the categories of idols. In my opinion, this goes too far as the Assyrian King cannot be expected to know that the Israelite monolatric religion forbids comparing the God of Israel with other gods.

Although the words of the Assyrian, as they are quoted by Yhwh, do not explicitly state that the polytheistic customs in Samaria and Jerusalem are a wrong against Yhwh, the vocabulary he uses for other gods, i.e. אֱלִיל *idol* (10a), the plural אֱלִילֶיהָ *her idols* (11a) as well as the terms פְּסִילֵיהֶם *their images* (10b) and עֲצַבֶּיהָ *her statues* (11b), has clearly negative undertones.[47] The function of these disrespectful implications is twofold. On the one hand, the Assyrian King reveals himself to be a ruler who does not respect the gods of the nations he defeated and takes an arrogant attitude towards them.[48] From the point of view of traditional polytheistic religions, this is impious and unwise because he will provoke the gods of the defeated nations to seek revenge against him. Therefore, in a general sense, he has no fear of God, which implies that he has no wisdom either. This aspect of meaning in 10:10–11 is a possibility which the text offers to listeners or readers with a polytheistic background. This shows that Isaiah's message may have a specific profile which allows non-Israelite or non-Yahwistic addressees to find meaning in the text on the basis of their own hermeneutical background.[49]

On the other hand, the Assyrian King's arrogant attitude against the gods of the defeated nations specifically includes his despise for Yhwh, the God of Israel. From the point of view of a Yhwh-believer, Isaiah's text offers other and further aspects of meaning. Although Yhwh sent him to punish his chosen people (see v. 5), the Assyrian neither knows nor fears the God of Israel. Instead, he most generally and wrongly speaks of the gods of Samaria and Jerusalem and considers them as utterly inferior in comparison with his own power. Thus, he completely ignores Yhwh although he owes his political and military successes to no one else than him. Nonetheless, the pejorative vocabulary used in the Assyrian King's speech carries a specific meaning which remains hidden to the ignorant Assyrian speaker but directly brings home an important message to Israelite listeners or readers who believe in Yhwh. In fact, they are confronted with a harsh criticism of Israelite polytheistic practices. Although the Assyrian is an example of godless hubris, he is right when he states that idols and their cultic images are void and have no power whatsoever.[50]

---

[47] For פְּסִילֵיהֶם, see e.g. 21:9; 30:22; for אֱלִיל (an exceptional singular) and אֱלִילֶיהָ, see e.g. 2:8, 18, 20; 19:1; 31:7; for עֲצַבֶּיהָ, see e.g. 46:1; cf. 48:5. See also Williamson, *Isaiah 6–12*, 518–520.
[48] Cf. W.A.M. Beuken, *Jesaja 13–27* (HThKAT; Freiburg: Herder, 2007), 283.
[49] Thus, Liss' observation in "Undisclosed Speech," point 3.1.5, that Assyrian ideology was pursuing both internal and external purposes might also be true for 10:5–15.
[50] See already Beuken, *Jesaja 13–27*, 284.

Understood in this context, the quotation of the Assyrian King's speech contains an irony which the quoted speaker unconsciously pits against himself. As he speaks of powerless wooden images that his hand found in idolatrous kingdoms, including Samaria and, as he anticipates, also Jerusalem, it is clear that his victory over such non-existent gods is not a greater achievement than Don Quixote's victory over harmless windmills. This is all the more true as, according to a common view in the Ancient Near Eastern world, any victory or defeat in war is primarily considered as the result of divine action and intervention, whereas human efforts and achievements are mere consequences of these. While the discussed ironic undertones can be perceived in between the lines, the statement expressed by the Assyrian King through his rhetorical question in verses 10–11 clearly characterizes him as a ruler who interprets his numerous military victories as a fruit of his own strength and skills. He does not refer himself to any god who would have bestowed upon him royal prerogatives and commissioned him to act in his name, but he rather emphasizes that his own hand has taken possession of other kingdoms (v. 10 מָצְאָה יָדִי לְמַמְלְכֹת הָאֱלִיל). He alone is the responsible author of what he did (עָשִׂיתִי) to Samaria and her gods, and of what he intends to do (אֶעֱשֶׂה) to Jerusalem and her idols.

This self-perception is confirmed by a second quotation of a speech of the Assyrian King in verses 13–14, which is again introduced by Yhwh as evidence of the Assyrian's hubris (see v. 12). This quotation contains no further rhetorical questions but straightforward statements. Here, he brags that he accomplished all his deeds, i.e. his conquests, his plundering and his measures against the defeated nations (v. 13b), by the power of his own hand and by his own wisdom (v. 13a: בְּכֹחַ יָדִי עָשִׂיתִי וּבְחָכְמָתִי). Comparing himself with a man who plunders a bird's nest (v. 14), he claims that his own hand found (v. 14a: יָדִי ... וַתִּמְצָא) the wealth of the nations with no one even trying to prevent him from doing so (v. 14b). It is noteworthy that the Assyrian's plundering of the wealth of the nations like eggs from an unguarded bird's nest[51] implies the fulfilment of the prophecy of 10:3bβ that the corrupt rulers of Judah will have no place where they can store their wealth when the day of judgement comes upon them. Moreover, the Assyrian takes away from them what they had unlawfully taken as loot from the poor among God's people.

---

[51] Concerning the imagery, in particular the metaphor of plundering a bird's nest, and other characteristics of vv. 13–14, Liss, "Undisclosed Speech," point 3.1.4, assumes that Isaiah adopts the style of Neo-Assyrian Royal Inscriptions. See also the text example in Beuken, *Jesaja 1–12*, 286.

In 10:15, Yhwh comments on the quoted speech of the Assyrian King with two rhetorical questions and two comparisons, which prove the Assyrian's arrogance to be foolish. It is against the most obvious laws of creation to assume that a tool like an axe could itself be the master of a work for which it has been used. The merit of achieving a work with the help of an axe belongs to the master who wields it. The Assyrian is nothing more than a tool like an axe in the hand of Yhwh. Therefore, the deeds he has performed have no merit of their own. He had been raised like a rod by the Lord (v. 15b מְרִימָיו) so all his claims to his own greatness and glory are stolen from the God of Israel, whom he despises and ignores (cf. v. 11b). Another aspect of the images of the axe and saw in verse 15 lies in the fact that these tools are necessary in order to fulfil the prophecy of doom, which the Lord had announced in the Song of the Unfruitful Vineyard in 5:5–6. The Hebrew גַּרְזֶן *axe* is a tool which can be used both for cutting wood like vines (cf. Deuteronomy 20:19), or for hewing stone (cf. 1 Kings 6:7).[52] Both meanings are relevant in the case of the destruction of the Lord's vineyard, which not only has vines but also a wall to be broken down (5:5). Thus, the image of the Assyrian being an axe in Yhwh's hand fits the image of God's people being an unfruitful vineyard that will be destroyed. This is all the more plausible as 10:6 contains another reference to the Vineyard Song, 5:5, where Yhwh states that he is sending the Assyrian against עַם עֶבְרָתִי *the people of [his] wrath* in order to have it trampled down: לְשִׂימוֹ מִרְמָס. The text here not only corresponds to the contents of the prophecy of 5:5, but also uses the same rare noun מִרְמָס *trampling down*.

The specific value of the pair of rhetorical questions in 10:15a-bα (הֲיִתְפָּאֵר הַגַּרְזֶן עַל הַחֹצֵב בּוֹ אִם־יִתְגַּדֵּל הַמַּשּׂוֹר עַל־מְנִיפוֹ), which recalls proverbial literature,[53] comprises several aspects. First, by confronting the addressee with a question about an absolutely simple truth known to everybody, his lack of even the most basic wisdom is revealed. At the same time, he is forced to give himself an answer which unmasks his utter hubris: never ever will an axe or saw wield its master. Third, the proposed absurd image of a man struggling with an axe which causes him to hit things he does not want to hit, and prevents him from hitting things he wants to hit, and determines the moments when all this is to happen, is highly comical. By consequence, the addressee is depicted as a high-ranking fool and rendered an object of mockery.

---

[52] Williamson, *Isaiah 6–12*, 529–530; Beuken, *Jesaja 1–12*, 286–287.
[53] Roberts, *First Isaiah*, 166–167.

7. Conclusion

What conclusions can be drawn from the present study on the role of the rhetorical questions in 10:3; 10:8–11 and 10:15? In 10:3 and 10:15, the questions are spoken by Yhwh and belong to the concluding comments of a woe oracle. Their principal intention is in both cases to demonstrate to the text-internal addressees, which are the Judean leaders abusing the law in 10:3 and the haughty Assyrian King in 10:15, that their relentless egocentrism, their abuse of superior political power, their denials of Yhwh's divine sovereignty, and the resulting forms of hubris will be utterly void when they are confronted with the doom Yhwh has decided against them. This intention is reached by the specific character of the questions, which leaves them no other option than to acknowledge God's absolute sovereignty.

Interestingly, the announced doom will not come simultaneously over both the Judean leaders and the Assyrian King. Rather, the Assyrian remains the instrument of doom striking the Judeans as commanded by God until he has fulfilled his mission, and only then will it be his turn to be punished for his unmeasurable arrogance (see Isaiah 36–37).

Corresponding to this difference, the questions used vary in their specific effect. In 10:3, they illustrate how the dishonest wisdom of the Judean leaders will reach its absolute end when they are called to responsibility in a divine judgement. The questions in 10:15 push the critique against a godless use of wisdom to its extreme when they unveil the utter foolishness of the Assyrian King, who praises his own wisdom (v. 13b), and mockingly expose his infinite lack of understanding. Embedded in between these questions, which prove Yhwh's divine sovereignty, the five rhetorical questions of the King of Assyria in 10:8–11 testify to his hubris. Yet, these are not directly addressed by the speaker to his audience. Instead, Yhwh quotes them as evidence against his opponent before refuting his arrogant position as a whole in 10:15. This art of using questions as a highest form of argumentation is an indirect proclamation of God's infinite wisdom. This divine wisdom is also perceivable in how Yhwh arranges the order of the questions in his speech.

It is noteworthy that in 10:5–15 questions do not provoke answering statements, but statements called into question provoke answers in the form of rhetorical questions. Within 10:5–11, Yhwh describes the Assyrian's mission in the form of a statement in verses 5–6, which is answered by the Assyrian in the form of rhetorical questions. Yet, since this questionable answer in the form of questions is a quotation within

Yhwh's speech, it is at the same time evidence against the Assyrian, who tries to imitate God. In 10:12–15, Yhwh first quotes statements made by the Assyrian in verses 13–14, which he then answers in the form of rhetorical questions. Since these demonstrate the foolishness of the Assyrian's attitude, it also becomes evident that the whole rhetoric strategy applied by the Great King in verses 8–11, where he reacts to the mission imposed upon him by Yhwh with rhetorical questions glorifying himself, is an equally foolish attempt to copy the wisdom of Yhwh by imitating his art of providing answers in the form of questions.

THE QUESTION OF THE WORD OF GOD
The Communicative Function of the Questions in Amos 3:3–8

Archibald L.H.M. van Wieringen
Tilburg University

1. Introduction: towards a definition of 'question'

Questions are a very intriguing issue. What a question is seems like a simple question, but it is not. Most descriptions of what a question is are only taxonomic, i.e. based on undefined semantic categories.[1] In my view, however, questions always have to do with a discrepancy in the information supplied.[2] This is of course obvious, but nevertheless also very complicated.

A discrepancy concerning information offered, gives rise to two topics we have to research:

1. What is this information, which contains a discrepancy, about?
2. For whom does the discrepancy exist?

The standard situation is not difficult. Someone does not know something and therefore makes enquiries about it to someone who has the relevant knowledge. This standard situation occurs many times in daily life, for instance in educational settings. A student does not know the root of the verbal form וַיִּקְטֹל and asks his teacher: 'What is the root of the verbal form וַיִּקְטֹל?' And the teacher will answer: 'The root is קטל.' There is an information discrepancy between the student and teacher regarding the root of the verbal form וַיִּקְטֹל. By asking the question, this information

---

[1] Although from a syntactical perspective the use of interrogatives is important as objective markers of questions, traditional grammars nevertheless deal merely with questions in a semantic way instead, e.g.: *IBHS*, especially 315 [§ 18.1 a].

[2] I derive the idea of 'information discrepancy' from: M. Pfister, *Das Drama* (Uni-Taschenbücher 580; München: Fink, 2001). For a first application of Pfister's theory, see: A.L.H.M. van Wieringen, "Jesaja 40,1–11: eine drama-linguistische Lesung von Jesaja 6 her," *BN* 49 (1989): 82–93.

discrepancy becomes visible. By giving the answer, this information discrepancy is nullified. Both the one who asks the question (in my example the student) and the one who gives the answer (in my example the teacher) play their own role.

2. Rhetorical questions

However, the situation becomes complex if rhetorical questions are involved. The answer to a rhetorical question is already determined: there is no other option than to answer with the expected 'yes' or 'no'. For example, during a guided tour through the old city of Amsterdam, the guide asks: 'Amsterdam is a beautiful city, isn't it?' You are not supposed to react: 'No, it is not.'[3]

If the answer is already determined, what does the discrepancy in information offered then entail? The one who asks the question, already knows that Amsterdam is a beautiful city. If there is a discrepancy of knowledge about the beauty of the city of Amsterdam, this discrepancy is not situated with the one who asks the question, but with the one who has to answer the question.

To mark rhetorical questions Henry Denham, a famous English printer from the 16th century, invented the inverted question mark '⸮'. However, this inverted question mark has never become part of the punctuation of the English language or of any other language.

The reason for this might be that it is far from clear whether a question is a rhetorical question. If you search for an example of a rhetorical question on the Internet, the first example you will find is: 'Is the pope Catholic?'[4] The answer seems to be obvious: 'Yes, he is.' Nevertheless, there are nowadays some cardinals for whom this question is not a rhetorical question at all. Or maybe it is, but in a different way: 'No, he is

---

[3] In fact, this issue is much more complex. Although the answer is determined in the example I give, i.e. determined in a syntactical way (the addressee can ignore this from a communicative, pragmatic point of view), this kind of question is specific for the English language and known as *tag question*. See e.g. S. Nässlin, *The English Tag Question: A Study of Sentences containing Tags of the Type* isn't it?, is it? (Stockholm Studies in English 60; Stockholm: Almqvist & Wiksell, 1984).

[4] See: https://examples.yourdictionary.com/rhetorical-question-examples.html [visited September, 24th, 2019]. This type of question is also known as a *retort question*; see D. Beth Schaffer, "Can Rhetorical Questions Function as Retorts?: Is the Pope Catholic?," *Journal of Pragmatics* 37 (2005): 433–460; C. Clay Doyle, "Archer Taylor Memorial Lecture 2006: Is the Pope Still Catholic?: Historical Observations on Sarcastic Interrogatives," *Western Folklore* 67 (2008): 5–33.

not.' Even the so-called most obvious examples of rhetorical questions may not be rhetorical questions.

In fact, we only have the syntax to help us determine whether a question is a rhetorical question or not. In English we use tags at the end of the line, to make clear what the expected answer should be, but in the communicative situation we can never actually force the desired answer.

In biblical Hebrew, we also have a syntactical element to mark rhetorical questions: the particle הֲלֹא, constructed from the interrogative particle הֲ and the negation לֹא. It always requires an affirmative answer: 'Is it not that…?' – 'Yes, it is….'

3. Amos 3:3–8

I would like to discuss the questions in Amos 3:3–8. The text of Amos 3:3–8, with working translation, is as follows:

3a	הֲיֵלְכוּ שְׁנַיִם יַחְדָּו	Do two go together	3a
3b	בִּלְתִּי אִם־נוֹעָדוּ	without having met?	3b
4a	הֲיִשְׁאַג אַרְיֵה בַּיַּעַר	Does a lion roar in the forest	4a
4b	וְטֶרֶף אֵין לוֹ	but there is no prey to him?	4b
4c	הֲיִתֵּן כְּפִיר קוֹלוֹ מִמְּעֹנָתוֹ	Does a young lion raise his voice from his den	4c
4d	בִּלְתִּי אִם־לָכָד	without having caught?	4d
5a	הֲתִפֹּל צִפּוֹר עַל־פַּח הָאָרֶץ	Does a bird fall into a folding net on the ground,	5a
5b	וּמוֹקֵשׁ אֵין לָהּ	but there is not bait for him?	5b
5c	הֲיַעֲלֶה־פַּח מִן־הָאֲדָמָה	Does a folding net go up from the ground,	5c
5d	וְלָכוֹד לֹא יִלְכּוֹד	but it does absolutely not catch?	5d
6a	אִם־יִתָּקַע שׁוֹפָר בְּעִיר	If a shofar is blown in the city,	6a
6b	וְעָם לֹא יֶחֱרָדוּ	would a people then not tremble?	6b
6c	אִם־תִּהְיֶה רָעָה בְּעִיר	If there is an evil in the city,	6c
6d	וַיהוָה לֹא עָשָׂה	should the Lord then not have made (it)?	6d
7a	כִּי לֹא יַעֲשֶׂה אֲדֹנָי יְהוִה דָּבָר	For should the Lord God not make a word,	7a
7b	כִּי אִם־גָּלָה סוֹדוֹ אֶל־עֲבָדָיו הַנְּבִיאִים	or reveal his confidential talk to his servants the prophets?	7b
8a	אַרְיֵה שָׁאָג	The lion has roared,	8a
8b	מִי לֹא יִירָא	who would not be afraid?	8b
8c	אֲדֹנָי יְהוִה דִּבֶּר	The Lord GOD has spoken,	8c
8d	מִי לֹא יִנָּבֵא	who would not prophesy?	8d

3.1. *The syntax of the questions in Amos 3:3–8*

All commentaries are of the opinion that this text passage is a collection of various rhetorical questions, interrupted by a remark in verse 7.[5] However, these verses are much more complicated than such a description suggests.

In the verses 3–8 the particle הֲלֹא, the syntactical marker of a rhetorical question, is not used. Instead of הֲלֹא, we see different kinds of formulations of the questions.

In the verses 3–5, five questions are formed by using the interrogative particle הֲ. The negation is not present in the particle, but in the second part of the question: בִּלְתִּי *without* is used for the first and third question (verses 3b and 4d),[6] the noun עֵץ *in statu constructo* in the second part of the second and fourth questions (the verses 4b and 5b), and the negation לֹא in the fifth question (verse 5d). The five questions in the verses 3–5, therefore, could be considered to be rhetorical questions, syntactically marked as such in an alternative way.

The two questions in verse 6 do not have an interrogative particle, neither הֲלֹא nor הֲ. They are introduced by עִם, which actually constitutes an 'if..., then...'-construction. The reason these two questions should be interpreted as questions, is the semantic role of the negation לֹא in the 'then...'-part of the two statements. The statement 'if a shofar is blown in a city, then a people will not tremble' does not make sense. Therefore, this statement should be understood as being a question: 'if a shofar is blown in a city, would a people then not tremble?' Due to the parallelism between the verses 6a-b and 6c-d the second statement should be read as a question as well: 'if there is an evil in a city, should the Lord then not have made it?'

---

[5] For example: Y. Gitay, "A Study of Amos's Art of Speech: A Rhetorical Analysis of Amos 3:1–15," *CBQ* 42 (1980): 293–309, here 296, 302; A. Schenker, "Steht der Prophet unter dem Zwang zu weissagen, oder steht Israel vor der Evidenz der Weisung Gottes in der Weissagung des Propheten?: Zur Interpretation von Amos 3,3–8," *BZ* 30 (1986): 250–256, here 253; K. Möller, *A Prophet in Debate: The Rhetoric of Persuasion in the Book of Amos* (JSOTSub 372; Sheffield: Sheffield Academic Press, 2003), 228; cf. P. Bovati and R. Meynet, *Le Livre du Prophète Amos* (Rhétorique Biblique 2; Paris: Cerf, 1994), 106–107. R. Reed Lessing, *Amos* (ConcC; Saint Louis: Concordia Publishing House, 2009), 215 is of the opinion that the rhetorical questions in the verses 3–6 are answered in the verses 7–8. Instead of 'rhetorical questions' A.W. Park, *The Book of Amos as Composed and Read in Antiquity* (StBibLit 37; New York: Peter Lang, 2001), 83 uses the expression 'didactic disputation speech.'

[6] Cf. Gitay, "Amos's Art of Speech," 303.

Verse 8 also contains two questions.[7] In fact, they are recognisable only because of the use of an interrogative in the second element, being twice מִי *who?* (the verse 8b and 8d). Due to the use of the negation לֹא in the second element, following the interrogative מִי, the two questions in verse 8 look like rhetorical questions, although they are not syntactically marked as such.

And what about verse 7? The construction כִּי לֹא ... כִּי אִם is unique in the Hebrew Bible and, as such, does not indicate a question. The *versiones*, too, do not consider verse 7 being a question; they stress the function of the opening word כִּי as an emphatical particle, marking the sentence as a statement. In Biblical Hebrew, nevertheless, questions without any interrogative marker do occur, especially in so-called polar-questions, to which the answer is yes or no. For example: 2 Samuel 18:29 שָׁלוֹם לַנַּעַר לְאַבְשָׁלוֹם *is the young man Absalom all right?*[8] Two additional observations may change the idea that verse 7 cannot be a question. First, verse 7 is part of an enumeration of questions starting in verse 3 and ending in verse 8. Verse 7 not being a question would come as a surprise. Second, the first part contains the negation לֹא that is used in the questions both before and after verse 7. Therefore, I intend to interpret verse 7 as a question as well: *for should the Lord God not make a word, or reveal his confidential talk to his servants the prophets?* At least, in my view, verse 7 is ambiguous.

In conclusion, from a syntactical point of view, it is not fully clear whether the questions in the verses 3–8 are rhetorical questions. They can be read as such, but not necessarily. This implies that the answer to these questions is not as pre-determined as in the case of rhetorical questions.

3.2. The semantics of the questions in Amos 3:3–8

After the above-mentioned syntactical observations, I would like to discuss the semantics of the questions in Amos 3:3–8. At first glance, most of the questions, if not all of them, seem to be simple, almost silly questions and easy to answer: a lion is dangerous – we all know that; you need a trap to catch a bird – we all know that; a shofar is an instrument used to sound the alarm – we all know that. And in the same way, we are all able to know about the Lord God. However, I do not believe that

---

[7] However, van Hoonacker, *Petits Prophètes*, 228 seems to interpret the questions in verse 8 as a form of exclamations in order to make clear the connection to the statements in verse 7.
[8] *IBHS*, 684–685 [§ 40.3].

the semantics of these verses is quite that simple. In my view, the verses 3–8 use semantics that are very confusing.[9]

Wild animals and birds are a *topos* in the Hebrew Bible.[10] Lions and birds, as we can find in our text passage, form a variation on this *topos*. This *topos*, however, is not used in our text passage just to indicate danger.

An *adult lion*, אַרְיֵה, is mentioned in the verses 4a-b. A lion hunts silently, without making any sound, because otherwise the intended prey will flee. After having caught its prey, a lion roars to indicate that it is his prey and no one else's. In fact, a roaring lion as such is no longer quite so dangerous.[11]

The verses 4c-d deal with a *young lion*, כְּפִיר. A lion cub does not make any sound, otherwise it reveals where the den is. Young animals are fragile, and might be prey for other animals, so they keep silent. But if there is food to eat, the cubs make sounds to indicate that they want to eat.

Verse 5 discusses a *trap*, a *folding net*, פַּח, used to catch birds. A trap only moves if there is prey in it, otherwise it does not move. It is precisely because it does not move, that it is dangerous and the prey can end up in it. The traps described in verse 5 are no longer dangerous.

The verses 4–5 refer to the world of shepherds, to the semi-nomadic life. Because of this, I would also interpret verse 3 from the shepherd's life. In a city you can accidentally bump into someone, but not in the pastures. In order to meet someone there, you have to make an appointment.[12]

Whereas the verses 3–5 reflect rural life, verse 6 makes use of urban life. Blowing the shofar is part of the question in the verses 6a-b. Because the words חרד *to tremble* in verse 6b and רָעָה *evil* in verse 6c are used, the blowing of the shofar is not linked to a liturgical festival, but to

---

[9] *Pace*: W. Nowack, *Die kleinen Propheten* (Göttinger Handkommentar zum Alten Testament 3/4; Göttingen: Vandenhoeck & Ruprecht, 1922), 131: "Jener Satz ist nichtssagend, weil selbstverständlich." Cf. in contrast to this statement: Möller, *Prophet in Debate*, 232.

[10] M.L. Barré, "Of Lions and Birds: A Note on Isaiah 31.4–5," in: Ph.R. Davies and D.J.A. Clines (Eds.), *Among the Prophets: Language, Image and Structure in the Prophetic Writings* (JSOTSub 144; Sheffield: Sheffield Academic Press, 1993), 55–59, here 56.

[11] Although this semantical problem has hardly been noticed in the exegesis on Amos the last decades, it was already present among the older exegetical studies, e.g.: A. van Hoonacker, *Les Douze Petits Prophètes* (EBib; Paris: Gabalda, 1908), 225.

[12] N.H. Snaith, *The Book of Amos* (Vol. 1: Introduction; Study Note on Bible Books; London: Epworth Press, 1945), 32.

military circumstances. The shofar is used in two different military settings: attacking or fleeing.[13] Both situations imply that the city is being besieged by a hostile army. If the shofar indicates attacking, the verb חרד in verse 6b indicates *routing* an army; if the shofar indicates fleeing, the verb חרד indicates *fearing* the hostile army. In both cases a dangerous situation is at issue: in a positive way in the case of attacking and in a negative way in the case of fleeing. The first question in verse 6 leaves open which situation is the case.

The second question in verse 6, however, situates the *evil*, רָעָה, בְּעִיר *in the city*, whereas in the case of a siege the hostile army is situated outside the city, surrounding the city. If the enemy is already inside the city, the city is doomed. There is no possibility of escape. There is probably not even time to blow the shofar as a signal to flee. The surprising climax is verse 6d: the Lord appears to be responsible for the fall of the city.[14] Whereas a city's deity is considered to defend the city and to protect it against enemies, the Lord does exactly the opposite. Is this a rhetoric question that people are supposed to affirm almost automatically, as is most often the case for rhetorical questions?

3.3. *Sounds and their interpretation: the discrepancy of information*

The verses 7–8 conclude the enumeration of questions by applying them to the Lord. This conclusion is connected to יהוה *the Lord* in verse 6d, the only time the Lord / God is mentioned in the questions in the verses 3–6. The name יהוה *the Lord* forms an inclusion of the verses 7–8: אֲדֹנָי יהוה is mentioned in the first element of verse 7 as well as in the second question of verse 8.

Besides the name יהוה, only a very few words from the verses 3–6 are repeated in the concluding verses 7–8. The verb עשׂה *to make* in verse 6d is repeated in verse 7a. In this way, at the end of the series of questions, the name יהוה and the verb עשׂה, are immediately re-used in verse 7a. The words אַרְיֵה *lion* and שׁאג *to roar* in verse 8a chiastically refer to verse 4a.

Nevertheless, there are other semantic relations between the verses 3–6 and 7–8. Sounds are expressed by using the words שׁאג *to roar* (the verses 4a, 8a), נתן קוֹל *to raise the voice* (verse 4b), תקע שׁוֹפָר *to blow the shofar* (verse 6a) and דבר *to speak* (verse 8c) and probably also the nouns דָּבָר *word* (verse 7a) and סוֹד *confidential talk* (verse 7b).

---

[13] R. de Vaux, *Les Institutions de l'Ancien Testament* (Vol. 2; Paris: Cerf, 1959), 62–67.
[14] See: Gitay, "Amos's Art of Speech," 304.

The word דָּבָר in combination with the verb עשׂה usually means: to do *something*. Because sounds are at issue and the word סוֹד in verse 7b is parallel to the word דָּבָר in verse 7a, the word דָּבָר seems to mean *word*. In my view, therefore, verse 7 is not only saying that the Lord God does not do anything without informing his prophets, but that what God does, is already communicative as such.

However much sound is at issue here, the sound itself is not easy to interpret. What is the meaning of the sound of the various lions? What is the meaning of the sound of the shofar? Maybe one can easily answer the questions affirmatively, but one cannot easily interpret the meaning of these sounds. If the interpretation of the sound of the lions and shofar is obscure, the interpretation of the sound of the Lord's words is even more obscure. The questions that sound in the text are rather a trap for those who intend to answer them too easily.

The questions clearly show a discrepancy in information between the one who asks them and the ones who have to answer them. There appears to be a sound, having great significance, known to the one who asks the questions, but the revelation of the sound's meaning remains hidden for the ones who are supposed to answer the questions positively. The discrepancy in information is not yet negated in the text.

In fact, the text deepens the discrepancy in information offered. The five questions in the verses 3–5 assume a prior event. This prior event is indicated in the second part of the question, not as a fact, but as a condition. This changes in verse 6. In verse 6a, the second half is not prior to the sound of the shofar, but is the result of it. In verse 6b, the prior event is rendered as a fact. This means that verse 6d, that the Lord is the one who עָשָׂה *made* it, is emphasised. However, the interpretation of the word the Lord עָשָׂה *made*, is still not revealed.

Not only is the expression אֲדֹנָי יהוה *the Lord God* repeated in the verses 7–8, but also the word נָבִיא *prophet*. There is a close relationship between the Lord and the prophet. The words סוֹד *confidential talk* as well as עֶבֶד *servant* in verse 7b, both constructed with a suffix third person singular, indicating the Lord, express this.

This idea of a close relationship in verse 7 refers to the start of the series of questions in verse 3. The two, having met each other, and then going along together, appear to be the Lord and his prophet.[15]

---

[15] See also the interpretative options mentioned by A. Neher, *Amos: Contribution à l'Étude du Prophétisme* (Bibliothèque d'Histoire de la Philosophie; Paris: Vrin, 1981), 15.

The questions in verse 8 do not focus on a prior event, but on the consequences of the sound-event,[16] in the activities of being fearful and of prophesying, expressed by the verbs ירא and נבא. This implies that the interpretation of the sound-event is presupposed. The activity is consequently beyond the interpretation of the sound.

The final question forms the climax: אֲדֹנָי יהוה דִּבֶּר מִי לֹא יִנָּבֵא *the Lord has spoken, who would not prophesy?*[17] The question is formulated in such a way, that the answer can only be: no one. If it is about the Lord, there is only one single possible option of activity based upon the sound, i.e. the word, דָּבָר, of the Lord and its interpretation: to prophesy. This implies that everyone can become a prophet, and can become part of the Lord's close and confidential circle. However, the text also suggests that, although everyone can become a prophet, hardy anyone will.

3.4. *Who is talking to whom in Amos 3:3–8?*

After having examined the discrepancy in information present in the questions in Amos 3:4–8, I would like to discuss the issue regarding between whom in the text this discrepancy of information occurs.

Generally speaking, two different options are advocated in the exegetical literature. Many exegetes believe that these questions are uttered by the character Amos, the prophet-character in the text. A couple of them even considers the text as the Amosian variant of the call-narratives in for example Isaiah and Jeremiah.[18]

Because the character Amos is speaking in the verses 3–8, the addressee is considered to be Judah and/or Israel, the last two nations mentioned in the so-called Oracles Against the Nations. Amos is, more or less, sharing with Judah/Israel his experience of being addressed by the Lord and having no other option than becoming the Lord's prophet.

---

[16] Cf. Schenker, "Amos 3,3–8," 254.
[17] Cf. T.S. Hadjiev, *The Composition and Redaction of the Book of Amos* (BZAW 393; Berlin: De Gruyter, 2009), 141. Cf. the figure of speech 'hermeneia' mentioned by E.W. Bullinger, *Figures of Speech Used in the Bible: Explained and Illustrated* (London: Messrs. Eyre & Spottiswoode, 1898; repr., Grand Rapids: Baker Book House, 2004²⁴ [= 1968¹]), 402.
[18] See: P.R. House, *The Unity of the Twelve* (JSOTSub 97; Sheffield: Almond Press, 1990), 192. Cf. J.A. Motyer, *The Day of the Lion: The Message of Amos* (London: Inter-Varsity Press, 1974), 69 who suggests that Amos addresses himself in Am 3:3–8.

By telling this through the asking of questions, he offers the people of Judah/Israel, God's people, to also participate in the word of the Lord.[19]

Reading from 1:2–3:2, this interpretation is not without validity. Judah and Israel form the climax of the Oracles Against the Nations. In contrast to the foreign nations mentioned in 1:3–2:3, the Lord's accusation is about the decline of the relation his people have with him. It is exactly this relationship that is at issue in the questions Amos asks in 3:3–8.

From this perspective, the image of two partners having met each other and then going along with each other in verse 3 can easily be understood as the Lord and his people.[20] In the end, however, in accordance with the Lord's accusations, it appears not to be the Lord with Judah/Israel, but the Lord with his prophet. The questions, formulated by Amos, intensify the accusation against the Lord's people.

The second option is that Amos, who indeed starts speaking in 1:2a, indicated by the *wayyiqtol*-form וַיֹּאמַר *and then he said*, addresses the text-immanent reader.

Reading from 1:2–3:2, this interpretation is also not without validity. In the Oracles Against the Nations in 1:3–2:9 no one is addressed. The foreign nations are discussed in these oracles. They are present in the text only as a third person plural. Even Judah and Israel are not addressed. They, too, are only present in the text as a third person plural.

In contrast to all these third persons plural, a second person plural is used in 2:10a. By using this second person plural, not Judah and/or Israel are simply addressed, but the text-immanent reader, forming a ninth 'nation' within the so-called Oracles Against the Nations.[21] The Lord, explicitly present in the separate personal pronoun אָנֹכִי *I*, and the text-immanent reader, present in the second person plural אֶתְכֶם *you*, are related to each other in the activity expressed using the verb הלך, the same verb that opens the series of questions in 3:3. From this perspective, the two going along with each other, are the Lord and the text-immanent reader.[22]

---

[19] S.J. Bramer, "Analysis of the Structure of Amos," *BSac* 156 (1999): 160–174, here 163–164, suggests that the nations are addressed.
[20] See e.g.: van Hoonacker, *Petits Prophètes*, 226; M. Holland, *Die Propheten Joel, Amos und Obadja* (Wuppertaler Studienbibel; Wuppertal: Brockhaus, 1991), 124.
[21] A.L.H.M. van Wieringen, "The Prophecies Against the Nations in Amos 1:2–3:15," *EstBib* 71 (2013): 7–19, here 16–17.
[22] Cf. Möller, *Prophet in Debate*, 233 who states that, due to the rhetorical questions, the addressee becomes co-speaker of the addresser's words.

4. Amos 3:3–8 within the book of Amos

In both above-mentioned options regarding who is talking to whom, Amos is present as the one asking the questions. A close look at 3:3–8 makes clear that these verses reflect both the heading in 1:1 and Amos' direct speech in 1:2b–e, and are also a preparation for the questions asked further on in the book of Amos and the narrative about the clash between Amos and Amaziah in 7:10–17.

The heading starts with the word דָּבָר *word*. They are mentioned as the דִּבְרֵי עָמוֹס *words of Amos*, but these words are implicitly related to the Lord in the activity of seeing, expressed by the verb חזה (verse 1c). It is exactly the word of the Lord that is at issue in the questions in 3:3–8, as it is at issue every time the call to listen to the word is present in the text (3:1; 4:1; 5:1; 7:16a).

In the heading, Amos is characterised as one of the shepherds.[23] The rural background is also present in the questions, especially in the first one in verse 3, because two shepherds do not meet each other by chance, but by appointment.

Furthermore, the semantics of trembling, present in the word רַעַשׁ (1:1c) which can refer to an earthquake,[24] is re-used in the verb חרד (3:6b).

The direct speech text passage in 1:2b–e has the image of roaring in common with the questions in 3:3–8.[25] The verbs שׁאג *to roar* and נתן קוֹל *to raise the voice* occur in both 1:2b.c and 3:4a.c. The parallelism between אַרְיֵה *lion* (3:8a) and יהוה *the Lord* (3:8c) gives the Lord the characteristics of a lion. The lion has already raised his voice, the roaring has already taken place, and the character Amos has already answered the raised voice. The correct answers can be seen in what precedes the questions.

The questions in 3:3–8 also form a preparation to the questions further on in the book of Amos. Two sorts of questions can be found. Belonging to the first sort is a question asked by the prophet. In 5:18, the prophetic

---

[23] Ph.J. King, *Amos, Hosea, Micah: An Archaeological Commentary* (Philadelphia: Westminster Press, 1988), 129. Cf. also: R. Hunziker-Rodewald, *Hirt und Herde: Ein Beitrag zum alttestamentlichen Gottesverständnis* (BWANT 155; Stuttgart: Kohl-hammer: 2001), 46-47, 77.
[24] Cf. H. Schmoldt, "רַעַשׁ rāʿaš," *ThWAT* 7 (1993) c. 612–616.
[25] See also: H. Weippert, "Amos: Seine Bilde rund ihr Milieu," in: H. Weippert and K. Seybold and M. Weippert (Eds.), *Beiträge zur Prophetischen Bildsprache in Israel und Assyrien* (OBO 64; Freiburg: Universitätsverlag 1985), 1–29, here 17; Möller, *Prophet in Debate*, 161.

voice asks the question: לָמָּה־זֶּה לָכֶם יוֹם יהוה *what for you will be the day of the Lord?*[26] This question differs in two ways from the questions in 3:3–8. First, an explicit second person plural is present in the question. The question is not an outsider's question. The 'you,' the second person plural, is directly involved. Second, the question is certainly not a rhetoric question, as if the answer is already clear. However, there is no possibility of giving any answer, because the prophetic voice itself answers its own question, although without using a second person: הוּא־חֹשֶׁךְ וְלֹא־אוֹר *it's darkness, no light*. Whereas the addressees are involved in the question, they are absent in the answer. From the perspective of 3:3–8, this suggests that, whereas there was a possibility to give the correct answer to the series of questions about the Lord's word, there is no further possibility to give an answer regarding the day of the Lord.

Belonging to the second sort are questions asked of the prophet, by the Lord. These questions occur in the visions before and after the narrative in 7:10–17. In both the third vision in 7:7–9 and the fourth vision in 8:1–3b, the Lord asks the prophet: מָה־אַתָּה רֹאֶה *what do you see?* (7:8b; 8:2b). By using the prophet's proper name עָמוֹס *Amos* (7:8c; 8:3c) the relationship between the Lord and the prophet is emphasized. This relationship lies beyond the sound that can be heard, and is about dialogue, thus reflecting, from the perspective of the series of questions in 3:3–8, the confidential talk, סוֹד (3:7b), between the Lord and his prophets, even at the moment that the prophet is not able to change the Lord's plans as he was able to do in the first and second vision (7:1–3, 4–6).[27]

In between these two visions, there is the narrative about the clash between Amos and Amaziah (7:10–17). Again, the word and the prophecy are at issue. Amaziah sends a message to the King in which he negatively criticizes all the words of Amos (verse 10e אֶת־כָּל־דְּבָרָיו *all his words*) as if these words could not come from the Lord. In contrast, Amos confronts Amaziah with a word from the Lord: וְעַתָּה שְׁמַע דְּבַר־יהוה *well then, hear the word of the Lord* (verse 16a). Because Amaziah rejects Amos, he wishes to prevent him from prophesying (the verb נבע in verse 13b). But Amos makes clear that he is not a prophet of his own accord, saying לֹא־נָבִיא אָנֹכִי *a prophet I am not* (verse 14c), but that it was

---

[26] Many exegetes do describe the rhetoric effect of 5:18, but without mentioning the fact that a question is used in the text and, moreover, in a very specific way; e.g.: Lessing, *Amos*, 353–357.

[27] See: H. Schüngel-Straumann, *Gottesbild und Kultkritik vorexilischer Propheten* (SBS 60; Stuttgart: Katholisches Bibelwerk, 1972), 72–74; H. Moltz, "A Literary Interpretation of the Book of Amos," *Hor* 25 (1998): 58–71, here 69–70.

the Lord who sent him and commissioned him to prophesy, saying וַיֹּאמֶר אֵלַי יהוה לֵךְ הִנָּבֵא אֶל־עַמִּי יִשְׂרָאֵל *then the Lord said to me: 'Go and prophesy against my people Israel'* (the verses 15b–d).[28] The first task of going is expressed by using the verb הלך, which is also used at the start of the series of questions in 3:3 indicating the Lord and the prophet going along together.

5. Some concluding remarks

Amos 3:3–8 does not contain an explicit second person. The questions are asked using a third person, not a second person. Even in verse 6. The question is not: if a shofar is blown in the city, would you not tremble? It seems that the one asking the question and the one being addressed by the question are outsiders, observing the (hypothetical) situation from a safe distance: would a people not tremble? Nevertheless, a second person, and thus an addressee, is presupposed by formulating questions. After all, a question always assumes an addressee, at least a hypothetical one.

In my view, the text forms a layered communicative pattern, in which the characters Judah/Israel, i.e. the Lord's people, and the text-immanent reader, i.e. also the Lord's people, are both involved. Amos, being a prophet, appears to be the example par excellence for both Judah/Israel and the text-immanent reader as to how to react to the word of the Lord, how to interpret the sound of the Lord's word, how to negate the discrepancy of the information offered and, thus, how to become a prophet of the Lord.[29]

---

[28] Cf. D.A. Garett, *Amos: A Handbook on the Hebrew Text* (Baylor Handbook on the Hebrew Bible; Waco: Baylor University Press, 2008), 224. Cf. also T. Bulkeley, "Amos 7,1–8,3: Cohesion and Generic Dissonance," *ZAW* 121 (2009): 515–529, here 525.

[29] I am greatly indebted to Drs. Maurits J. Sinninghe Damsté (Breña Baja, Santa Cruz de Tenerife, Spain) for his correction of the English of this article.

Q DOCUMENT MEANS 'QUESTION DOCUMENT'

Form and Function of Jesus' Questions in the Sayings Source

Ruben ZIMMERMANN
University of Mainz

1. Introduction

In the most comprehensive study on questions in the New Testament, Douglas Estes states that 15 percent of the NT consists of questions.[1] In the Q document about 40 percent of the *logoi* include questions. If we narrow the inquiry to the individual speech acts of Jesus, then the percentage is even higher.[2] These observations alone may be sufficient to justify the title of this article. But even more important than the quantitative findings is the fact that the questioning technique is obviously one of Jesus' preferred ways of speaking. While scholarship on the historical Jesus often classifies Jesus' speech as proclamation or promise, looking at the oldest layer of the Jesus tradition, one can see that he uses fewer propositions than questions to articulate his message. The Q document provides amazing insight into this phenomenon. It may therefore seem justified, contrary to the usual designation,[3] to speak here of the oldest, postulated source of the Jesus tradition as the 'Question document.'

One may argue that these statistics and considerations fail in light of the ongoing debate on the existence of the Q document[4] and its possible

---

[1] D. Estes, *Questions and Rhetoric in the Greek New Testament: An Essential Reference Resource for Exegesis* (Grand Rapids: Zondervan, 2017), 24.
[2] Here, *logoi* refers to a unit that is defined by a specific content and tradition and is presented with its own section in the Critical Edition of Q: J.M. Robinson, P. Hoffmann and J.S. Kloppenborg, *The Critical Edition of Q: Synopsis Including the Gospels of Matthew and Luke, Mark and Thomas with English, German, and French translations of Q and Thomas* (Hermeneia; Minneapolis: Fortress, 2000). If we count the sentences as individual speech acts, we find that more than 50% of Jesus' Sayings are questions.
[3] Q comes from the German word *Quelle* (source).
[4] See, e.g.: M. Goulder, "Self-Contradiction in the IQP," *JBL* 118 (1999): 506–517; M. Goodacre and N. Perrin (Eds.), *Questioning Q* (London: SPCK 2004); W. Kahl,

reconstruction.[5] This is true to a certain extent. However, even if one may not share in viewing the Q hypothesis as a separate, scriptural source, an intertextual reading of the so-called 'double tradition' (where Matthew and Luke overlap without Mark) also reveals that a strikingly large number of Jesus' Sayings in this layer consists of questions.[6] It does not even require a precise reconstruction of the wording of the Q document to hold to this observation. Even though the wording varies between the Matthean and the Lukan tradition, sentences with interrogative pronouns can be classified as questions. In Q 11:11, for instance, Matthew 7:9 (τίς ἐστιν ἐξ ὑμῶν ἄνθρωπος, ὃν αἰτήσει ὁ υἱὸς αὐτοῦ...) differs from Luke 11:11 (τίνα δὲ ἐξ ὑμῶν τὸν πατέρα αἰτήσει ὁ υἱός...), both texts, however, include the interrogative paricle τίς/τίνα to demonstrate the interrogative character of this utterance. Similarly, even if the particles are as varied as the interrogative pronoun τίς and the interrogative adjective ποῖος,[7] the interrogative character is nevertheless clearly recognizable in both utterances. There are also statements where the interrogative character is more uncertain, but Estes puts these margins at about 3 percent (based on questions in the entire New Testament).[8] Although one can often only decide by the context and meaning of the sentence whether it is a question or not, it may be surprising that the numbers presented in scholarship are relatively similar after all: Reinhard von Bendemann, for instance,

---

"Erhebliche matthäisch-lukanische Übereinstimmungen gegen das Markusevangelium in der Triple-Tradition: Ein Beitrag zur Klärung der synoptischen Abhängigkeitsverhältnisse," *ZNW* 103 (2012): 20–46.

[5] See the overview in: M. Tiwald, *Die Logienquelle: Text, Kontext, Theologie* (Stuttgart: Kohlhammer, 2016), 35–39.

[6] This is also true for the Jesus tradition as derived in the Gospel of Mark, see: R. von Bendemann, "'Was wollt ihr, dass ich euch tue?' (Mk 10,36): Zur Gestalt und Funktion von Fragen im Markusevangelium," in: K. Schiffner, S. Leibold and M. Frettlöh (Eds.), *Fragen wider die Antworten: Festschrift Jürgen Ebach* (Gütersloh: Gütersloher Verlagshaus, 2010), 418–432; J.H. Neyrey, "Questions, Chreiai, and Challenges to Honor: The Interface of Rhetoric and Culture in Mark's Gospel," *CBQ* 60 (1998): 657–681. See the limited number of investigations on questions in the Jesus tradition in C.G. Müller, "Leserorientierte Fragen im Erzählwerk des Lukas," *TGl* 93 (2003): 28–47; L. Wanak, "Jesus' Questions," *Evangelical Review of Theology* 33 (2009): 167–178; M. Leutzsch, "„?"-„?" – Biblische Theologie der Gegenfrage," in: K. Schiffner, S. Leibold and M. Frettlöh (Eds.), *Fragen wider die Antworten: Festschrift Jürgen Ebach* (Gütersloh: Gütersloher Verlagshaus, 2010), 405–417; R. Zimmermann, "Fragen bei Sokrates und Jesus. Wege des Verstehens – Initiale des Weiterfragens," in: H. Lindner and M. Zimmermann (Eds.), *Schülerfragen im (Religions-)Unterricht: Ein notwendiger Bildungsauftrag heute?!* (Neukirchen-Vluyn: Neukirchener Verlag, 2011), 33–59.

[7] Cf., e.g.: Matt 5:46: ἐὰν γὰρ ἀγαπήσητε τοὺς ἀγαπῶντας ὑμᾶς, τίνα μισθὸν ἔχετε; versus Luke 6:32: καὶ εἰ ἀγαπᾶτε τοὺς ἀγαπῶντας ὑμᾶς, ποία ὑμῖν χάρις ἐστίν;

[8] Estes, *Questions and Rhetoric*, 25.

recognizes 167 questions in Matthew and 151 in Luke, while Estes identifies 169 in Matthew and 154 in Luke.[9]

From my point of view, therefore, it is possible to carry out an investigation on the questions of Jesus in the double tradition, despite the uncertainties mentioned. Without being able to go into the reasons in detail at this point, I assume in the following that there was an independent, definable source Q, which is accessible to us through the double tradition in Matthew and Luke.[10] Following the basic decisions of the 'Mainz Approach,'[11] however, I would like to refrain from reconstructing the exact wording of a Q text. Even without reconstructing the exact wording of Q, I contend that it is nevertheless possible to gain textual insights. What has already proven to be a possible approach with regard to metaphors, especially spatial metaphors, characters and parables,[12] can, in my view, also be demonstrated in the speech act of questions. Thus, after a brief orientation on the types of questions that can be found in the Q document, I would like to focus on different groups of questions that play a major role in mapping out the field of questions in the Sayings Source Q, in particular the μήτι οὐχί-questions, the τίς ἐξ ὑμῶν-questions, and questions in parables. In a concluding section of this paper, I will provide a brief interpretation that will elucidate the significance of this question technique for this early layer of the Jesus tradition.

2. Different Types of Questions in the Q document

When asking about the different types of questions in the Q document, one first needs to define the object for which we are searching. Estes, in his study on questions in John, lists no less than eighteen answers from

---

[9] On this, see: Von Bendemann, "Was wollt ihr, dass ich euch tue?," 420–421. The counting differs with Estes, *Questions and Rhetoric*, 26.

[10] See J. Kloppenborg, *Q, the Earliest Gospel: An Introduction to the Original Stories and Sayings of Jesus* (Louisville: WJK, 2008); P. Hoffmann and C. Heil, *Die Spruchquelle Q: Studienausgabe. Griechisch und Deutsch* (Darmstadt: WBG, ⁴2013); more recently: A. Kirk, *Q in Matthew: Ancient Media, Memory, and Early Scribal Transmission of the Jesus Tradition* (LNTS 564; London: T&T Clark, 2016); M. Tiwald, *Die Logienquelle*; also M. Tiwald, *Kommentar zur Logienquelle* (Stuttgart: Kohlhammer, 2019).

[11] See R. Zimmermann, "Metaphorology and Narratology in Q Exegesis: Literary Methodology as an Aid to Understanding the Q Text," in: D.T. Roth, R. Zimmermann, and M. Labahn (Eds.), *Metaphor, Narrative, and Parables in Q* (WUNT 315; Tübingen: Mohr Siebeck, 2014), 3–30; A. Bork, *Die Raumsemantik und Figurensemantik der Logienquelle* (WUNT II/404; Tübingen: Mohr Siebeck, 2015), 22–29; D.T. Roth, *The Parables in Q* (LNTS 582; London: T&T Clark, 2018), 39–55.

[12] See the studies by Bork, *Raumsemantik*; Roth, *Parables*.

literature to the question 'what is a question.'[13] He himself suggests the following working definition: 'A question is any utterance with interrogative force that asks not says, that always applies some rhetorical effect, and that invites a reply of some sort.'[14]

This is a broad definition, which makes it difficult to use it as a precise tool for identifying questions in the text. However, Estes is right when he draws attention to the 'holophrastic' character of the questions, which means 'that they can be asked in abbreviated form with only one word: "Food?"'[15] In other words, not only 'any utterance,' but a single word could be used as a question. In the Q document we find these kinds of questions, for example in Q 7:24–26:

Q 7:24–26 (CEQ)

τί ἐξήλθατε εἰς τὴν ἔρημον θεάσασθα;	What did you go out into the wilderness to look at?
κάλαμον ὑπὸ ἀνέμου σαλευόμενον;	A reed shaken by the wind?
ἀλλὰ τί ἐξήλθατε ἰδεῖν;	What then did you go out to see?
ἄνθρωπον ἐν μαλακοῖς ἠμφιεσμένον;	A man dressed in soft (robes)?
ἀλλὰ τί ἐξήλθατε ἰδεῖν;	What then did you go out to see?
προφήτην;	A prophet?

This carefully composed section consists of six questions in three pairs. The first question with the interrogative pronoun τί is repeated three times with small variations: 'What did you go out (into the desert) to see?' In each of the three intervening questions, possible objects are offered: (a) a reed, (b) a man, (c) a prophet? The first two are further expanded by participles (*shaken by the wind*; *wrapped in soft clothes*), while (c) is just the single word προφήτην; (*a prophet?*). The phrastic form of the second-question parts is here contextually secured. Due to the fact that the first-question part is introduced with the particle τί, the elliptical following section can be easily recognized as a question. Furthermore, this whole saying is nothing other than a series of questions, according to Estes a 'question string.'[16] In view of the strict parallel form, it is all the more striking that the first two short questions expect a negative answer, while the last one suggests a positive one. This change can only be explained by the closer and wider context in which the questions

---

[13] See D. Estes, *The Questions of Jesus in John: Logic, Rhetoric and Persuasive Discourse* (BibInt 115; Leiden: Brill, 2013), 39–42.
[14] Estes, *Questions and Rhetoric*, 20.
[15] Estes, *Questions and Rhetoric*, 22.
[16] Estes, *Questions and Rhetoric*, 316–330.

are integrated. Thus, the first two mentions (reed, man in soft clothes) are allusions to Herod Antipas, who serves here as a contrasting figure.[17] The last option ('prophet'), on the other hand, is confirmed by Jesus' subsequent sentence. Yes, the Baptist is even more than a prophet.

Therefore, we realize that the quest for questions can mostly not be answered on the level of a single word. It leads to the level of phrase, a sentence within context or more precisely, the speech act, which indicates the 'interrogative force' that the utterance 'asks but does not say.' One can further ask, why does a text (or parts of a text) present itself as a question? Are there specific linguistic criteria[18] that signal or at least hint that this utterance should be read as a question and more precisely as a special kind of question? What role does the reader play in the question-answer-game, for questions are always part of an act of communication or speech act ('rhetorical effect;' 'invitation to reply')?

In order to capture the different levels more precisely, Estes has distinguished three categories in which the interrogative character can be recognized: the syntactic, semantic, and pragmatic levels; this differentiated approach, however, has – as Estes notes[19] – heuristic intent, because each of the questions includes syntactic, semantic, and pragmatic aspects to a certain extent. I will follow these categories and explain them with examples from Q.[20]

2.1. *Questions Driven by Syntax*

In New Testament Koinè Greek, as well as in Classical Greek, questions do not have to be marked either by interrogative particles or by a specific word order.[21] Nevertheless, there are signals on the level of *syntax*, which

---

[17] For details, see M. Tiwald, *Kommentar*, 72–73.
[18] As we know, the punctuation as it is given in the critical editions of the Greek text and even more so in the translations, is not found in the oldest manuscripts. The majuscules or minuscules even present the Greek text in many cases continuously, without spacing between the words, see K. Aland und B. Aland, *Der Text des Neuen Testaments: Eine Einführung in die wissenschaftlichen Ausgaben* (Stuttgart: Deutsche Bibelgesellschaft, ²1989), 290–291.
[19] See Estes, *Questions and Rhetoric*, 147.
[20] A content driven grid of categories is presented by Wanak (referring to the Jesus tradition in general). He distinguishes eight types of questions: (1) Questions for Focus and Clarification; (2) Questions from Deep Disappointment; (3) Questions Challenging Tradition and Authority; (4) Questions about his own Nature and Identity; (5) Questions Challenging Values; (6) Questions that are Evasive; (7) Questions to Activate Faith and Commitment; (8) Deeply Penetrating Questions; see Wanak, "Jesus' Questions," 170–177.
[21] Cf. F. Blass, A. Debrunner and F. Rehkopf, *Grammatik des neutestamentlichen Griechisch* (Göttingen: Vandenhoeck & Ruprecht, ¹⁹2020), § 440.

indicate the question:[22] An initial starting point is to orient oneself to the interrogative particles which are quite common in Greek, such as the π-questions like ποῦ (*where*), πόθεν (*whence*), ποῖ (*whither*) πότε (*when*), πῶς (*how*).[23] Similarly, one recognizes questions by the usage of interrogative adjectives like ποῖος (*which*) or πόσος (*how much*). Furthermore, questions introduced with the indefinite pronoun, used as interrogative particles τίς (*who*) and τί (*what*), are equally clear.

Most of the questions in the Q document are easily identified by such signal words. In the sample above (Q 7:24–26) three questions with τί + infinitive can be found. There are also a number of questions introduced by π-words, such as Q 6:42: πῶς δύνασαι λέγειν τῷ ἀδελφῷ σου...; (*How can you say to your brother...?*).

However, in some cases it turns out that though an interrogative particle, such as ὅπου, is used in an indirect question, it does not indicate a question with certainty in the main clause. The sentence Q 17:37 remains ambivalent:

ὅπου ἐὰν ᾖ τὸ πτῶμα ἐκεῖ συναχθήσονται οἱ ἀετοί (Matthew 24:28)
ὅπου τὸ σῶμα, ἐκεῖ καὶ οἱ ἀετοὶ ἐπισυναχθήσονται (Luke 17:37)

It can be taken either as a question[24] (*Where the corpse is, will the vultures gather there?*) or as a statement (*Wherever the corpse is, there the vultures will gather*). The latter dominates in the tradition of interpretation.

2.2. *Questions Driven by Semantics*

With regard to *semantics*, Estes' second category, there can also be signals driven by meaning. In narratives, for instance, one can find explicit introductory verbs (*verba quaerendi*), such as ἐρωτᾶν (*to ask*) and, more often, composites such as ἐπερωτᾶν (*to ask*). Yet, many direct questions are simply introduced by λέγειν (*to say*), which was common in both Classical and Hellenistic Greek.[25] In the reconstructions of the Q document, however, those introductory parts are regularly assumed to be part of the 'redaction' of the Evangelists Matthew and Luke. Therefore, we

---

[22] Estes mentions 12 different aspects in his general chapter on 'Question and Syntax,' and five categories applied to the NT: (A) Polar Questions; (B) Variable Questions; (C) Alternative Questions; (D) Set Questions; (E) Composite Questions; see Estes, *Questions and Rhetoric*, 37–60, 93–145.
[23] See a more comprehensive list by Estes, *Questions and Rhetoric*, 50–51.
[24] See Estes, *Questions and Rhetoric*, 154.
[25] See Estes, *Questions and Rhetoric*, 65 (with examples from Classical and Hellenistic Greek).

cannot identify questions by means of introductory verbs. Following Estes, the main focus of semantics with regard to questions addresses the semantic qualities of the questions. 'Determining the semantic goals of a question cuts to the heart of what the question is trying to ask (about).'[26] Out of the wide range of semantic attitudes in different questions,[27] I will pick two types and demonstrate with samples from Q: first, the so called 'riddle questions,' which use semantics to create ambiguous situations, often by means of word play, poetic language, and simple ideas. They appeal to or even tease the listener (or reader).

Q 6:39:

μήτι δύναται τυφλὸς τυφλὸν ὁδηγεῖν;   *Can the blind lead the blind?*

The proverbial motif of a 'blind guide' is well-known in antiquity.[28] In Jesus' saying this motif is driven to the extreme: not only is the leader blind, the one being led is also blind. According to Estes such a clause hints at a wordplay and makes the audience feel the riddle. 'The question is a riddle-like puzzle from which no good answer can come.'[29]

Second, I want to give an example of the so-called 'Counterfactual Questions.' These questions propose a possibility based on a premise that runs counter to established reality and truth.[30]

Q 14:34

ἐὰν δὲ καὶ τὸ ἅλας μωρανθῇ,   *If salt has lost its taste,*
ἐν τίνι [ἀρτυ]θήσεται;   *(thus,) by means of what will it be made tasty?*

Salt can never become saltless because of its chemical structure. In this respect, the question is based on an assumption that is 'counterfactual.' The function of such a question is to urge the addressees to take reality seriously and to act accordingly. They no longer have the obvious in view and must first be pushed back to it by the question. By identifying themselves with the salt, the question of their own identity is raised. The addressees should also behave according to the unchangeable realities:

---

[26] Estes, *Questions and Rhetoric*, 147.
[27] Estes lists seven categories in his introductory chapter on "Questions and Semantics," and 23 categories applied to the NT, such as (A) Open Questions; (G) Proof Questions; (O) Dilemma Questions; (U) Biased Questions; see Estes, *Questions and Rhetoric*, 61–71, 147–272.
[28] See, for instance, Plato, *Resp.* 8, 554B; Philo, *Virt.* 7; Babrius, *Fab.* 134.
[29] Estes, *Questions and Rhetoric*, 220.
[30] Estes, *Questions and Rhetoric*, 229.

they should be like salt. What this means in a positive sense is not specified in detail. In the Q context, the idea of 'being thrown out' carries with it the idea of judgement.[31] Thus, in this instance a counterfactual question creates avenues for evaluating oneself and for ethics.

2.3. Questions Driven by Pragmatics

Questions can also be driven by *pragmatics*. According to Estes, this third category 'is the most rhetorically powerful of all three but also the hardest to identify within a written text. ... With questions driven by pragmatics, it is tempting for the reader to evaluate the pragmatic qualities of the question by ways of replies.'[32] This includes, however, some kind of interpretative fallacy, since readers do not exactly know what kind of reply is actually being offered. Estes differentiates three main areas of pragmatic questions embedded within a context: turn, position, and repetition.[33] All three evaluate the role of the question within a dialogue or discourse, in particular the potential pragmatic effects. In a 'first-turn question,' for instance, the question is the first utterance of a dialogue sequence. Among this group are 'expository questions,'[34] which introduce a topic or information. According to Estes the expository question must be followed by exposition from the asker (not another speaker). In other words: the asker gives the answer himself. In the Q document we find three prominent questions of this kind. It is significant that the two kingdom of God parables of the Sayings Source are introduced with an expository question:[35]

Q 13:18

| τίνι ὁμοία ἐστὶν ἡ βασιλεία τοῦ θεοῦ (Matt: τῶν οὐρανῶν) καὶ τίνι ὁμοιώσω αὐτήν; | *What is the kingdom of God (in Matthew 'of heavens') like, and with what shall I compare it?* |

---

[31] See Roth, *Parables*, 211–219.
[32] Estes, *Questions and Rhetoric*, 273.
[33] Estes distinguishes in detail the following: (A) First-Turn Questions; (B) Second-Turn Questions; (C) Middle-Position Questions; and (D) Question strings; see Estes, *Questions and Rhetoric*, 273–330.
[34] See Estes, *Questions and Rhetoric*, 282–287.
[35] It is noteworthy that in the Matthean versions the questions are turned into propositions: ὁμοία ἐστιν ἡ βασιλεία τῶν οὐρανῶν ...; see Matt 31:31, 33. This is most likely due to the composition of the parable discourse in Matt 13, where this introductory formula is used 10 times; see R. Zimmermann, "Parables in Matthew: Tradition, Interpretation and Function in the Gospel," in: G. Van Belle and J. Verheyden (Eds.), *An Early Reader of Mark and Q: New and Old on the Composition, Redaction, and Theology of the Gospel of Matthew* (BTS 21; Leuven: Peeters, 2016), 159–185.

Q 13:20
Καὶ πάλιν εἶπεν· τίνι ὁμοιώσω τὴν βασιλείαν τοῦ θεοῦ;   *(And again,) with what shall I compare the kingship of God?*

The introductory question is found here in the parables on the mustard seed (Q 13:18) and leaven (Q 13:20f.). Like a heading, the question gives a metaphorical transfer signal that unmistakably provides the key to understanding right at the beginning of the parable. The following text is not about specific questions of sowing or dough preparation. Rather, the areas mentioned from the everyday life of the addressees are used to formulate statements about the kingdom of God. This kingdom of God is the actual goal; to define it in more detail is the task of the following parable. The message of the kingdom of God is considered central for Jesus' message. It also plays an important role in the Q document.[36]

The fact that Jesus formulates this assignment here as a question is nevertheless striking: The kingdom of God itself is a metaphor to be clarified, it cannot be 'defined' though. Jesus leaves it to the openness of figurative language to evoke ideas in the minds of the listener (and readers of Q) about the realm and rules of God's new world and reality after the overthrow of Satan.[37] The pragmatically effective impulse of the question now consists more closely in the fact that the following parables are by no means simple propositions. The metaphorical language draws the recipient into a process of understanding. One has to go in search of meaning. Exactly this pragmatic is already set on track by the introductory question. The recipients are supposed to start searching for an answer.

A striking example of 'repetitive questions' can be seen in the sample mentioned above (Q 7:24–26) including six questions in close succession. Estes, who calls such a density of multiple questions 'Question strings,' speaks of a 'battery of rhetorical effects on their audience… The overall effect is both dramatic and overwhelming.'[38]

Interestingly there is a side note on the Q tradition in Estes' statement that 'these types of questions are not a natural occurrence in conversations; they are created by speakers purely for rhetorical and persuasive

---

[36] See the occurrences of βασιλεία in Q 4:5; 6:20; 7:28; 10:9; 11:2, 17, 18, 20, 52; 12:31; 13:18, 20, 28; 16:16.

[37] Cf. the excursus 1.1. "Die Königsherrschaft Gottes," in Tiwald, *Kommentar*, 176–184, who closely links this motif to the 'Son of Man'-proclamation and the change of dominion including the overthrow of Satan.

[38] Estes, *Questions and Rhetoric*, 326.

effect.'³⁹ Thus, the Sayings Source Q – at least in the form it is derived – is carefully composed, if not edited as a written document.⁴⁰

3. Exemplary Groups of Questions in Q

It is not possible within the scope of this article to analyse all the questions in Q in more detail. Instead, I would like to focus on three groups of questions that reveal basic functions of the questions in the Sayings Source.

3.1. μήτι and οὐχί-Questions

A strikingly large number of the questions in the Sayings Source are formulated with the negation particles μή(τι) and οὐ(χί). Since μή(τι) normally requires the subjunctive, μή(τι) with indicative can be assumed to be a question.⁴¹ The negation particles have a specifically rhetorical function in questions because they indicate the rhetorical nature of the question. They are so-called 'rhetorical questions' that intend to suggest a particular answer. Basically, the principle is that οὐχί (not...?) expects an affirmative answer (yes!), while μήτι aims at a negation (of course not!).⁴² The following μήτι and οὐχί-questions can be found in the Q document:⁴³

Q 6:32:   οὐχὶ καὶ οἱ τελῶναι τὸ αὐτὸ ποιοῦσιν;
Q 6:34:   οὐχὶ καὶ [οἱ ἐθνικ]οὶ τὸ αὐτὸ ποιοῦσιν;

---

[39] Estes, *Questions and Rhetoric*, 326.
[40] On the issue of orality, secondary orality, and written document, see R. Derrenbacker, "The Medium is the Message: What Q's Content Tells Us about its Medium," in: D.T. Roth, R. Zimmermann and M. Labahn (Eds.), *Metaphor, Narrative, and Parables in Q* (WUNT 315; Tübingen: Mohr Siebeck, 2014), 207–219, here 218 (Derrenbacker himself suggests a Codex/Memory tradition); more recently: Kirk, *Q in Matthew*, 157–183, here 182–183, with his solution of a 'cultural text' alternating the debate by insights from memory theory. See also the summary in Tiwald, *Die Logienquelle*, 30–32. Tiwald, *Die Logienquelle*, 30 also argues for scripturality: 'Der einheitliche theologische und narrative Duktus der Logienquelle (s. u. III 1.) legt solch eine abschließende, formgebende kompositionelle Redaktion nahe.' Furthermore: Kirk, *Q in Matthew*, 157–174.
[41] See: Blass, *Grammatik des neutestamentlichen Griechisch*, §440.
[42] In German, the rhetorical character of μήτι is emphasized by including 'etwa.' For example, 'Kann *etwa* ein Blinder einen Blinden führen?'
[43] With regard to this issue, I will refer to the Critical Edition of Q: Robinson, *The Critical Edition of Q*. We do not find μήτι and οὐχί in both sources of the double tradition in all examples. See, e.g., Luke 6:39 which has μήτι and οὐχί, and Matt 15:14 which does not; Matt 6:25–26 has οὐχί, whereas Luke 12:23–24 does not.

Q 6:39a: μήτι δύναται τυφλὸς τυφλὸν ὁδηγεῖν;
Q 6:39b: οὐχὶ ἀμφότεροι εἰς βόθυνον ἐμπεσοῦνται;
Q 6:44: μήτι συλλέγουσιν ἐξ ἀκανθῶ σῦκα ἢ ἐκ τριβόλων σταφυλ[άς];
Q 10:15: καὶ σύ, Καφαρναούμ, μὴ ἕως οὐρανοῦ ὑψωθήσῃ;
Q 11:11: τίς ἐστιν ἐξ ὑμῶν ἄνθρωπος, ὃν αἰτήσει ὁ υἱὸς αὐτοῦ ἄρτον, μὴ λίθον ἐπιδώσει αὐτῷ;
Q 11:12: ἢ καὶ ἰχθὺν αἰτήσει, μὴ ὄφιν ἐπιδώσει αὐτῷ;
Q 12:6: οὐχὶ [πέντε] στρουθία πωλοῦνται ἀσσαρί[ων δύο];
Q 12:23: οὐχὶ ἡ ψυχὴ πλεῖόν ἐστιν τῆς τροφῆς καὶ τὸ σῶμα τοῦ ἐνδύματος;
Q 12:24: οὐχ ὑμεῖς μᾶλλον διαφέρετε τῶν πετεινῶν;
Q 12:28: οὐ πολλῷ μᾶλλον ὑμᾶς, ὀλιγόπιστοι.
Q 15:4: οὐ[χὶ ἀφή]σει τὰ ἐνενήκοντα ἐννέα [ἐπὶ τὰ ὄρη] καὶ πορευ[θεὶς ζητεῖ] τὸ [ἀπολωλός];

Through this questioning technique, the answer is virtually already put into the mouth of the addressee: Of course, a father will not give his son a stone if he asks for bread (Q 11:11) and a snake if he wants to receive a fish (Q 11:12). The answer to these μή-questions can only be 'No!' In the series of questions Q 12:23–28, the three οὐχί-, οὐχ- and οὐ-questions accordingly expect a positive answer: Life is obviously more valuable than food and people are more important than birds or plants. Within the little parable in Q 6:39, questions are asked using both particles (μήτι and οὐχί):

| μήτι δύναται τυφλὸς τυφλὸν ὁδηγεῖν; | *Can the blind lead the blind?* |
| οὐχὶ ἀμφότεροι εἰς βόθυνον πεσοῦνται; | *Will not both fall into a pit?* |

The first question 'Can the blind lead the blind?' requires a negative answer: 'No, this cannot happen,' or if it does, the result will be a catastrophe. Whereas the second question 'Will not both fall into a pit?' expects a positive answer: 'Yes, this will happen.' The rhetoric function of this double question is a strong confirmation from both perspectives: The listeners or readers are invited to agree with the speaker. The interrogative rhetoric will be even stronger than a propositional utterance. The addressees are not only invited to agree with a statement of the speaker, but to articulate their own responses. Thus, they do not only copy the speaker's opinion, but the speaker makes them feel as if the opinion is their own.

What can be seen with clarity in Q 6:39 is also true for the other μήτι and οὐχί-questions. They appeal to the identity of the addressees to experience them as members of an inner group. The rhetoric of the questions thus serves in a special manner to form the identity of the Q-group.

3.2. τίς ἐξ ὑμῶν-Questions in the Q Document

The distinct phrase τίς ἐξ ὑμῶν is very rare in Greek literature and the LXX.[44] Therefore, it is striking that the phrase occurs three times within the Q document, all of them as questions:[45]

Q 11:11: τίς ἐστιν ἐξ ὑμῶν ἄνθρωπος, ὃν αἰτήσει ὁ υἱὸς αὐτοῦ ἄρτον, μὴ λίθον ἐπιδώσει αὐτῷ;

Q 12:24: τίς δὲ ἐξ ὑμῶν μεριμνῶν δύναται προσθεῖναι ἐπὶ τὴν ἡλικίαν αὐτοῦ πῆχυν...;

Q 15:3:   τίς < > ἄνθρωπος ἐξ ὑμῶν < > ἔχ< > ἑκατὸν πρόβατα καὶ [ἀποστέλας] ἓν ἐξ αὐτῶν, οὐ[χι] ἀφήσ]ει τὰ ἐνενήκοντα ἐννέα [ἐπὶ τὰ ὄρη] καὶ πορευ[θεὶς ζητεῖ] τὸ [ἀπολωλός];

The phrase τίς ἐξ ὑμῶν consists of an indefinite pronoun and prepositional complement with a 2nd person plural personal pronoun. Taken by itself, the phrase could also be translated as 'any of you' or 'a certain one among you.'[46] Within the discourse, however, the interrogative character becomes obvious.

We will attempt to elicit the semantic content of the question. What meaning is being conveyed here? The question *Is there anyone among you?* presupposes two things: on the one hand, a collective audience, which is addressed as a homogeneous group ('you'); on the other hand, a separation of an individual from this group ('who'/'one'), which is additionally emphasized by the actually dispensable preposition ἐκ (*from, of, among*).[47]

---

[44] There are only a few occurrences in Greek literature; see: *Historia Alexandri Magni*, Recensio α I 37:8; 39:9; Recensio β I, 37:29; II 16:8; Recensio γ I 37:37; Soph., *Oed.* 70: ἆρ᾽ ἄν τις αὐτῷ πομπὸς ἐξ ὑμῶν μόλοι; Aristoph., *Daidalos* frg. 1:1 (here τις ὑμῶν); Demosth., *2 Aphob.*, 18:1 (τίς δ᾽ οὐκ ἂν ὑμῶν); Dion. Hal., *De Demosthenis dictione* 43:17 ('Εἰ δέ τις ὑμῶν). The formulation occurs in the Septuagint in 2 Chr 36:23; Ezra 1:3; Isa 42:23; 50:10; Hag 2:3 and translates מִי־בָכֶם (*who/which of you*).

[45] It is also used in parables from Luke's *Sondergut* with corresponding answers: 11:5–8: 'Which of you ...?' (answer positive: he will rise and give to his friend); 14:28–30: 'for which of you ... will not ... reckon?' (answer: everyone will reckon); 14:31–32: 'or which king ... will not take counsel ...?' (answer affirmative: every king will consult); 15:8–10: 'or what woman ...?' (answer positive: she will search until she finds the coin); 17:7–10: 'which of you who has a slave ... will ...?' (Answer: no one). On this issue, see also R. Zimmermann, "Form und Funktion der Frageparabeln des erinnerten Jesus," in: J. Schröter, K. Schwartz, and S. Al-Suadi (Eds.), *Gleichnisse und Parabeln in der frühchristlichen Literatur: Methodische Konzepte, religionshistorische Kontexte, theologische Deutungen* (WUNT; Tübingen: Mohr Siebeck, 2021), 99–117, here 108–112.

[46] See Blass, *Grammatik des neutestamentlichen Griechisch*, § 301, 250f.: 'τις τι as Pronomina Indefinita.' The (missing) accent (for interrogative pronouns with accent: τίς) stated by Blass-Debrunner-Rehkopf as a criterion of distinction is of course meaningless in view of the non-accented majuscule manuscripts.

[47] According to Blass, *Grammatik des neutestamentlichen Griechisch*, § 164 1a (p. 135) it would be sufficient to combine the *Genetivus Partitivus* with τίς without the preposition.

This specific combination of group and individual addressees is a characteristic of the τίς ἐξ ὑμῶν-questions. On the one hand, there is an appeal to everyday knowledge and community ethos; on the other hand, each person is addressed individually, much as if he or she represents the group and is primarily responsible. Estes sees the strongest rhetorical effect of these questions in the personalization that arises from the comparison with the others.[48]

Let us concretize the issue in the light of the example of the plea (Q 11:9–13). The τίς ἐξ ὑμῶν-question appears in the context of a discourse on performing prayers. Jesus wants to credibly assure the answering of prayers and therefore draws on family experience. Even if food were scarce, parents would not deny a starving child a request for food. The rhetorical question is combined with an exaggerated scene: It is not just a matter of denying the child a request, but imagines a father (or mother) offering a lifeless stone or possibly a poisonous snake instead of basic food to the child. The imagination of the scene and the specific question type thus work together to reinforce the rhetorical effect: There is no way any of us would act like this!

Now that a basic emotional stance has been created, the transfer into the realm of the religious can take place all the more effectively: 'If you then, who are evil, know how to give good gifts to your children, how much more will the Father in heaven give good things (Luke 11:13 *the Holy Spirit*) to those who ask him!' (Q 11:13).

Estes, who classifies the τίς ἐξ ὑμῶν-question as a 'set question,' argues: 'These questions – generally speaking – are *set questions* that occur in *middle position* as part of a *question string*. This is the most important feature; the questions serve the rhetorical effect of bringing home the issue in light of a comparison with others for the hearer/reader to make him ready to accept the argument coming in the next utterances. The *inapposite* content, and to a lesser extent, shades of *testing* and occasional *bias*, reinforce this rhetorical effect. It seems to me these questions are designed to personalize the issues so the hearer will 'feel' the point but without making him defensive at the opening of the argument.'[49]

While the syntactic classification lies with the 'set questions,' one recognizes at the same time the direction of the pragmatic goal, which lets

---

[48] According to his email to me on April 16, 2018.
[49] This statement is taken from a personal email dated April 16, 2018. On 'set questions,' see chapter 3.D in Estes, *Questions and Rhetoric*, 115–122.

this question most likely be assigned to the 'biased or leading questions.'[50] 'Biased questions convey an expectation, or bias, on the part of the speaker toward a specific answer to the question.'[51] The answer already lies suggestively in the question itself: 'Who would not act like that?' or in case of negative expectation: 'Who would act like that?' Accordingly, the answers must be, 'Any of us would!' Or, 'None of us would!' This specific kind of question thus urges affirmation and partisanship.

On the level of content, we note that the generally accepted and well-known everyday ethos is used to address theological problems. A child's request for basic provisions, which is answered as a matter of course, is supposed to encourage people to pray (Q 11:9–13). The beauty and unconcern of the lilies and ravens is applied to the (superfluous) concern for people's food and clothing (Q 12:22–31). Seeking a single lost sheep from the flock becomes an image of the divine shepherd going after each and every lost one (Q/Luke 15:5–7). The interpretations mentioned here are of course only one possible variant within polyvalent possibilities of interpretation.[52]

In general, the message of these questions is about an immediate orientation to a single reader/listener, who is invited by the specific form of this question not only to better understand the theological promise against the background of everyday experiences, but also to personally accept it for oneself.

3.3. *Questions in Q-Parables*

As a final group, I would like to discuss questions that can be found clustered in a specific genre. Of the 28 parables in the Q-document,[53] 15

---

[50] Cf. Estes, *Questions and Rhetoric*, 257: 'A biased question is asked to provide a strong rhetorical push at the audience... Biased questions convey an expectation, or bias, on the part of the speaker toward a specific answer to the question.'

[51] Estes, *Questions and Rhetoric*, 257.

[52] On this openness as a constitutive feature of the interpretation of parables, cf. Zimmermann, *Puzzling the Parables: Methods and Interpretation* (Minneapolis: Fortress Press, 2015), 163–174.

[53] The number varies depending on the definition of the parables or even the integration of parables of John the Baptist and the Centurion. See Zimmermann, *Puzzling the Parables*, 214. Roth, *Parables*, 20–21, who excludes in comparison to the *Kompendium der Gleichnisse* Q 10:22 par John 5:19–23, Q 11:34–35, Q 12:54–56, and Q 13:25–27, but includes two parables of John the Baptist (Q 3:9; 3:17) and one of the Centurion (Q 7:8), thus tabulating 27 parables in all. See also the survey of scholarship in P. Foster, "The Q Parables: Their Extent and Function," in: D.T. Roth, R. Zimmermann and M. Labahn (Eds.), *Metaphor, Narrative, and Parables in Q* (WUNT 315; Tübingen:

are connected with questions in different ways: some have the explicit form of a question, others include one or more questions. Some of these texts have already been discussed above, in such a way that the connection between question and parable also has a summarizing character here.

Q 6:39 Parable of the Blind Leading the Blind
μήτι δύναται τυφλὸς τυφλὸν ὁδηγεῖν;
οὐχὶ ἀμφότεροι εἰς βόθυνον ἐμπεσοῦνται;

Q 6:41–42 Parable of the Splinter and the Beam
v. 41: τί δὲ βλέπεις τὸ κάρφος τὸ ἐν τῷ ὀφθαλμῷ τοῦ ἀδελφοῦ σου, τὴν δὲ ἐν τῷ σῷ ὀφθαλμῷ δοκὸν οὐ κατανοεῖς;
v. 42: πῶς ... τῷ ἀδελφῷ σου· ἄφες ἐκβάλω τὸ κάρφος [ἐκ] τ[οῦ] ὀφθαλμ[οῦ] σου, καὶ ἰδοὺ ἡ δοκὸς ἐν τῷ ὀφθαλμῷ σου;

Q 6:43–44 Parable of a Tree Being Known by Its Fruits
v. 44: μήτι συλλέγουσιν ἐξ ἀκανθῶ σῦκα ἢ ἐκ τριβόλων σταφυλ[άς];

Q 7:31–35 Parable of the Children in the Marketplace
v. 31: τίνι ... ὁμοιώσω τὴν γενεὰν ταύτην καὶ τίνι ἐ<στ>ὶν ὁμοί<α>;

Q 11:9–13 Parable of Asking of a Father
v. 11: τίς ἐστιν ἐξ ὑμῶν ἄνθρωπος, ὃν αἰτήσει ὁ υἱὸς αὐτοῦ ἄρτον, μὴ λίθον ἐπιδώσει αὐτῷ;
v. 12: ἢ καὶ ἰχθὺν αἰτήσει, μὴ ὄφιν ἐπιδώσει αὐτῷ;

Q 11:14–20 Parable of a Kingdom Divided against Itself
v. 18: καὶ εἰ ὁ σατανᾶς ἐφ' ἑαυτὸν ἐμερίσθη, πῶς σταθήσεται ἡ βασιλεία αὐτοῦ;
v. 19: καὶ εἰ ἐγὼ ἐν Βεελζεβοὺλ ἐκβάλλω τὰ δαιμόνια, οἱ υἱοὶ ὑμῶν ἐν τίνι ἐκβάλλουσιν;

Q 12:23–28 Parable of The Fowl and the Flowers
v. 23: οὐχὶ ἡ ψυχὴ πλεῖόν ἐστιν τῆς τροφῆς καὶ τὸ σῶμα τοῦ ἐνδύματος;
v. 24: οὐχ ὑμεῖς μᾶλλον διαφέρετε τῶν πετεινῶν;
v. 28: οὐ πολλῷ μᾶλλον ὑμᾶς, ὀλιγόπιστοι.
μὴ [οὖν] μεριμνήσητε λέγοντες· τί φάγωμεν; [ἢ]· τί πίωμεν; [ἢ] τί περιβαλώμεθα;

Q 12:42–46 Parable of the Faithful or Unfaithful Slave
v. 42: τίς ἄρα ἐστὶν ὁ πιστὸς δοῦλος [καὶ] φρόνιμος ὃν κατέστησεν ὁ κύριος ἐπὶ τῆς οἰκετείας αὐτοῦ τοῦ δο[ῦ]ναι [αὐτοῖς] ἐν καιρῷ τὴν τροφήν;

Mohr Siebeck, 2014), 255–285. Foster identifies 17 units that various scholars have classified as Q parables.

[[Q 12:54–56 Parable of Time and Weather
v. 56: τὸ πρόσωπον τοῦ οὐρανοῦ οἴδατε διακρίνειν, τὸν καιρὸν δὲ οὐ δύνασθε;]]

Q 13:18 Parable of the Mustard Seed
v. 18: τίνι ὁμοία ἐστὶν ἡ βασιλεία τοῦ θεοῦ (Matt: τῶν οὐρανῶν) καὶ τίνι ὁμοιώσω αὐτήν;

Q 13:20 Parable of the Leaven
v. 20: Καὶ πάλιν εἶπεν· τίνι ὁμοιώσω τὴν βασιλείαν τοῦ θεοῦ;

Q 14:34 Parable of the Salt
v. 34: ἐὰν δὲ τὸ ἅλας μωρανθῇ, ἐν τίνι [ἀρτυ]θήοεται;

Q 15:4–7: Parable of the Lost Sheep
οὐ[χὶ ἀφή]σει τὰ ἐνενήκοντα ἐννέα [ἐπὶ τὰ ὄρη] καὶ πορευ[θεὶς ζητεῖ] τὸ [ἀπολωλός];

Q 17:37 Parable of the Vultures around a Corpse
v. 37: ὅπου τὸ πτῶμα, ἐκεῖ συναχθήσονται οἱ ἀετοί.

Q 19:12–26 Parable of the Entrusted Money
v. 22: λέγει αὐτῷ· πονηρὲ δοῦλε, ᾔδεις ὅτι θερίζω ὅπου οὐκ ἔσπειρα καὶ συνάγω ὅθεν οὐ διεσκόρπισα;

The list shows that the questions have a very different function and position in the parables. There are 'expository questions:' in addition to those already mentioned above in the parables of the mustard seed (Q 13:18) and leaven (Q 13:20), such a question is found in the parable of the children in the marketplace Q 7:31–35.

Matthew 11:16
  τίνι δὲ   ὁμοιώσω   τὴν γενεὰν ταύτην;
Luke 7:31
  τίνι οὖν ὁμοιώσω τοὺς ἀνθρώπους   τῆς γενεᾶς ταύτης καὶ τίνι εἰσὶν ὅμοιοι;

Though we see a slightly different wording in Matthew and Luke, 'it is clear that the query involves the question of 'to what' this generation is to be compared.'[54] Like a superscription, the question gives a metaphorical transfer signal that unmistakably provides the key to understanding right at the beginning of the parable. However, it is by no means clear with which characters from the parable (or framing verses) 'this generation' is related. Both a one-sided identification with the inviting children and with the uncooperative ones fail for different reasons.[55] Also, the difference in lifestyle between John and Jesus outlined subsequently

---

[54] Roth, *Parables*, 148.
[55] See the arguments in Roth, *Parables*, 151–53.

cannot be retrospectively related to the two groups of children. Thus, the most likely solution remains that the group of children as a whole is the point of comparison. 'This generation' is like the entire group of children who 'sit' in the marketplace and cannot play.[56] Thus, the parable explains the eschatological critique of 'this generation.' In speaking of 'this generation' an Early Jewish apocalyptic pattern (1 Enoch 93; 1QpHab 2:1–10) is taken up, which is expanded in Q by the frequent repetition (Q 11:16, 29–32, 50–51) of one of the load-bearing lines of meaning of the Sayings Source. With Tiwald, however, it is not a specific Jewish group that is criticized here as an opponent. Rather, there is a malevolent generation in the end times (see Q 11:29 γενεὰ πονηρά) that opposes the children of wisdom (Q 11:35).[57] Unlike Q 11:29, the function of the parable is not to announce judgement, but rather to comfort the righteous whose preaching is rejected.[58] The introductory question underscores this pragmatic move. The expository question and the parable work together rhetorically to bring the children of wisdom to a reassessment of their situation with comforting purpose.

In a similar way, parables and questions work hand in hand within the kingdom of God parables. Though being a basic motif within the theological message of Q, it is not clear what the kingdom of God actually is. The readers, however, are pushed by the question to form an idea of some aspects of this unknown reality. The answer, however, given by the parable, remains open and multivalent. What does it mean to compare the kingdom of God with the process of leaven? Is it about the power of the small, is it about the temporal dimension, or even about working in secret? Answers through parables are not definitions, not determinations. They instead leave room for further questions, even provoke them. Therefore, it is not surprising, that questions also play a major role in the corpus of the parables.

---

[56] With Roth, *Parables*, 153: 'The entire group, including those who called out and those who refused, is a 'not playing' group and is thus cast in a negative light.'

[57] See also M. Labahn, *Der Gekommene als Wiederkommender: Die Logienquelle als erzählte Geschichte* (Arbeiten zur Bibel und ihrer Geschichte 32; Leipzig: Ev. Verlagsanstalt, 2010), 424: '(...) diese Generation (ist) die entscheidende Chiffre zur Kennzeichnung der Oppositionsgruppe für Jesus, den Menschensohn, und für seine Anhänger.'

[58] See Tiwald, *Kommentar*, 77–78.108–109, and his Exkursus 4.1.2 on 'Diese Generation' (Tiwald, *Kommentar*, 200–202). See also M. Tiwald, "Die proteptische, konnotative und performative Valeur der Gerichts- und Abgrenzungsmetaphorik in der Logienquelle," in: D.T. Roth, R. Zimmermann and M. Labahn (Eds.), *Metaphor, Narrative, and Parables in Q* (WUNT 315; Tübingen: Mohr Siebeck, 2014), 115–137.

In part, the whole parable consists of nothing but two questions like Q 6:39 (The Blind Leading the Blind, see above). It has been doubted whether these questions can be classified as a 'parable' at all, since no story is told in the strict sense, such that one might miss the criterion of narrativity.[59] At least Luke explicitly recognized this text as a παραβολή in Luke 6:39.[60] In pragmatic terms, the questions in particular stimulate a process of comprehension that reveals a two-stage narrative with multiple characters. The recipient imagines a blind man taking another blind man by the hand and guiding him. However, in trying to visualize this tentative attempt at mutual help by the helpless, one repeatedly comes to the point of inevitable failure. How will the two reach their goal? What if there are obstacles in the way? No matter how one pictures it, the two suggestive questions with μήτι and οὐχί (see above) do not allow any other conclusion, and the addressees give themselves the answers: Yes, certainly this attempt must fail! Applied to religious leaders, one can conclude: One who does not have knowledge himself only leads others into misfortune. Or turned positively: It requires the ability to see and to recognize, in order to be able to lead others, who perhaps do not yet have this recognition.

In addition to such extremely reader-oriented interrogative parables, there are parables that pose questions and answer them themselves, or that make the appeal implicit in the question. This is the case with the proverbial parable of the speck and the beam (Matthew 7:3–4; Luke 6:41–42):

> τί δὲ βλέπεις τὸ κάρφος τὸ ἐν τῷ ὀφθαλμῷ τοῦ ἀδελφοῦ σου,
> τὴν δὲ ἐν τῷ σῷ (Luke 6:41: ἐν τῷ ἰδίῳ) ὀφθαλμῷ δοκὸν οὐ κατανοεῖς;
> πῶς [Matthew: ἐρεῖς; Luke: πῶς δύνασαι λέγειν] τῷ ἀδελφῷ σου
> Matthew: ἄφες ἐκβάλω τὸ κάρφος ἐκ τοῦ ὀφθαλμοῦ σου,
> Luke: ἀδελφέ, ἄφες ἐκβάλω τὸ κάρφος τὸ ἐν τῷ ὀφθαλμῷ σου,
> Matthew: καὶ ἰδοὺ ἡ δοκὸς ἐν τῷ ὀφθαλμῷ σοῦ;
> Luke: αὐτὸς τὴν ἐν τῷ ὀφθαλμῷ σου δοκὸν οὐ βλέπων;

> Why do you see the speck in your brother's eye,
> but do you not see the beam in your own eye?
> How can you say to your brother:
> (Brother), let me pull the speck out of your eye, and behold, the beam is in your eye?

---

[59] According to my definition of a parable, there are six criteria: (1) Narrativity, (2) Fictionality, (3) Relationship to Reality, (4) Metaphoricity, (5) Appeal Dimension, (6) Contextuality; see Zimmermann, *Puzzling the Parables*, 138–150.

[60] See the introduction in Luke 6:39: Εἶπεν δὲ καὶ παραβολὴν αὐτοῖς·... (*He also told them a parable:* ...).

The two questions vary the same message with the same repertoire. The speck in the eye of the brother is put in a contrastive juxtaposition with the beam in one's own eye. To this is added the action opposite to the size of material in the eye. The first question focuses on the sensitivity towards the brother and the blindness towards oneself. The second processes the literal speech to the brother to help him. Thus, now the ethical character of this parable becomes evident. Both questions allow only one possible answer, more precisely one single call to action, which is then explicitly stated:

> Luke 6:42: ὑποκριτά, ἔκβαλε πρῶτον τὴν δοκὸν ἐκ τοῦ ὀφθαλμοῦ σου, καὶ τότε διαβλέψεις τὸ κάρφος τὸ ἐν τῷ ὀφθαλμῷ τοῦ ἀδελφοῦ σου ἐκβαλεῖν.
> Matthew 7:5: ὑποκριτά, ἔκβαλε πρῶτον ἐκ τοῦ ὀφθαλμοῦ σοῦ τὴν δοκόν, καὶ τότε διαβλέψεις ἐκβαλεῖν τὸ κάρφος ἐκ τοῦ ὀφθαλμοῦ τοῦ ἀδελφοῦ σου.
> *You hypocrite! First pull the beam out of your eye, and then you will see clearly enough to pull the speck out of your brother's eye* (Q / Luke 6:42b).

The questions in the parable have a direct ethical function here. They point the recipient to the right action by 'questioning' the presupposed action and thus only open up the possibility for the commanded action. The form of the rhetorical question again corresponds with the imagined content of the parable. There may be experience with splinters in the skin and perhaps rarely also in the eye. A 'beam in the eye,' on the other hand, is a gross exaggeration. Nevertheless, it is a particularly effective image in terms of its emotional impact. Thus, the recipients are urged by rhetorical questions ('How can you…?') and stylistic devices involving exaggeration which lead to ethical insight and a change in attitude: First one must put one's own life and actions in order, then one may give advice and help to others.

The generally accepted and known everyday ethos is in parables first and foremost used to refer to theological messages. In the metaphorical shift, the carelessness of the lilies and ravens is transferred to trust in God, also for daily needs, such as food and the clothing of the people (Q 12:22–31). The use of salt (Q 14:34–35) appeals to the identity of the disciples, or the observation of the weather (Q 12:56) is directed toward an eschatological horizon. A child's request for basic provisions, answered as a matter of course, is meant to encourage the disciple to pray (Q 11:9–13). The search for a single lost sheep from the flock then becomes the image of the divine shepherd who goes after every single lost one (Q 15:5–7). In all cases, everyday knowledge and experiences are so self-evident that one would also agree to the transferred message which refers to theological truths. Through the connection to this realm of experience, the impenetrable speech about the kingdom of God or about God becomes comprehensible.

Rhetorical questions reinforce the 'appeal-character' inherent to parables. Questions have a similar rhetorical effect as the parables themselves. They make the addressees pause by including disturbing elements. They also have an irritating effect, which questions apparent clarity. Thus, questions interwoven in parables are thought experiments and riddles, which are supposed to challenge the audience to a high degree.

4. Conclusion

Questions play an essential role in the Q document. The variation of the questions in form, position in the discourse, and rhetorical function requires that their meaning be determined in each individual case, which has been demonstrated in this article with rudimentary examples. However, the various questions do share some overarching dimensions. Thus, it is significant that only one question is addressed to Jesus from the perspective of John's disciples, 'Are you the one who is to come, or are we to wait for another?' (Q 7:19). Although this question certainly strikes at the Christological heart of the Sayings Source as a whole,[61] the Son of Man issue tends not to be unfolded in questions. Rather, all the remaining questions are Jesus' questions addressed to the people with a specific intent. They demand an answer, they urge the addressees to make a judgement themselves (agreeing or disagreeing), to evaluate their attitude towards Jesus and his message. The questions thus fulfil a missionary cognitive function, which evokes and confirms theological insight and makes faith possible. This faith is not a given, but should be developed and should grow like a mustard seed (Q 17:6; cf. 13:18). With introductory, direct and indirect, open and rhetorical questions, the addressees are urged to give their own answers. Even more, by suggestive questions they are drawn into a new worldview, in which they develop a new group identity. The rhetorical effect (and success) of the Q document is to a certain extent based on this questioning technique, which makes the Sayings Source more akin to a real 'Question document.'

---

[61] See the main thesis in Labahn, *Der Gekommene*, 570–587.

QUESTIONS IN THE GOSPEL OF MARK
Two Examples (1:24; 16:3)

Geert VAN OYEN
UC Louvain

1. Introduction

This article is not the first attempt to focus on questions in Mark, although it is surprising, considering the large number of questions in this Gospel, that there are only a few publications on this intriguing issue.[1] This stands in contrast to the publications on the concept of questions in general and their different functions in rhetoric.[2] No one studying 'questions in the New Testament' today can ignore the monograph *Questions and Rhetoric in the Greek New Testament* by Douglas Estes,[3] but no publication treating the complete range of questions in Mark exists.[4] This contribution will therefore inevitably suffer from the same weakness as the earlier ones: it is a reflection on only a couple of questions in Mark, more

---

[1] Exegesis on questions in Mark is mostly found in the commentaries *in loco*. There are not so many studies on the questions in Mark as a whole. See, e.g. F. Neirynck, *Duality in Mark: Contributions to the Study of the Markan Redaction* (BETL 31; Leuven: University Press, 1988, second edition), 54–63 ('Double Questions and Antithetic Parallelism'), R.M. Fowler, *Let the Reader Understand: Reader-Response Criticism and the Gospel of Mark* (Augsburg: Fortress, 1991), passim [see Index: 'Questions']); J.H. Neyrey, "Questions, *Chreiai*, and Challenges to Honor: The Interface of Rhetoric and Culture in Mark's Gospel," *CBQ* 60 (1998): 657–681; D.M. Rhoads, J. Dewey and D. Michie, *Mark as Story: An Introduction to the Narrative of a Gospel* (Minneapolis: Fortress, third edition, 2012), 55–56; R. von Bendemann, "‚Was wollt ihr, dass ich euch tue?' (Mk 10,36): Zur Gestalt und Funktion von Fragen im Markusevangelium," in: K. Schiffner (Ed.), *Fragen wider die Antworten* (Gütersloh: Gütersloher Verlagshaus, 2010), 418–432; J. Schwiebert, "Jesus's Question to Pilate in Mark 15:2," *JBL* 136 (2017): 937–947.

[2] See the literature mentioned in von Bendemann, "‚Was wollt ihr, dass ich euch tue?'," 418–419, nn. 2–3.

[3] D. Estes, *Questions and Rhetoric in the Greek New Testament* (Grand Rapids: Zondervan, 2017).

[4] See for the Gospel of John, D. Estes, *The Questions of Jesus in John: Logic, Rhetoric and Persuasive Discourse* (BibInt 115; Leiden: Brill, 2013); for 1 Corinthians, see W.H. Wuellner, "Paul as Pastor: The Function of Rhetorical Questions in First Corinthians," in: A. Vanhoye (Ed.), *L'Apôtre Paul: Personnalité, style et conception du ministère* (BETL 73; Leuven: University Press, 1986), 49–77.

precisely on the first one (1:24) and the last one (16:3). I will examine how they function as a means of communication in the story and between the text and the reader.

Paying attention to questions in a first century story like Mark's is not a strange thing to do. Ancient rhetoric contemporary to Mark's Gospel was always interested in questions, as can be illustrated by a famous passage in Quintilian's *Institutio oratoria* (9.2.6–16).[5] As Quintilian already noted, questions can have many functions. Especially rhetorical questions – 'to affirm or deny a point by asking a question that does not invite a response'[6] – are a useful strategy in rhetorical discourses, although it is difficult to give a clear definition of a rhetorical question.[7] Anyway, it may not be surprising to find many questions in New Testament writings (although not all of the twenty-seven books have questions!), since they were written within the context of the rhetoric of the Mediterranean Roman-Hellenistic world.[8] Estes wrote his monograph on questions in the New Testament, because 'thanks to modern linguistics and related disciplines, we have an opportunity to interpret them [i.e. questions] with greater skill and acuity than ever before.'[9] The first part of his book explains the *formation* of the questions on three levels: syntax (with twelve different aspects), semantics (seven aspects), and pragmatics (nine aspects). Then follows a second part on *contents*, in which Estes presents thirty-two categories of questions distributed over the three main forms (five categories of questions driven by syntax, twenty-three by semantics, four by pragmatics), but with the possibility of a question belonging to more than one main genre. The book ends with a summary of the four

---

[5] The passage begins as follows: 'For what is more common than interrogation or questioning? We use the two terms indiscriminately, although the latter is designed to obtain knowledge and the former to prove a point. Whichever name it is given, the process involves a positive multiplicity of Figures (…).' More is quoted in a master thesis: E. van Emde Boas, *Ποῖον τὸν μῦθον ἔειπες; – Rhetorical Questions in Ancient Greek* (Amsterdam [University of Amsterdam], 2005), 14–15 (see https://eprints.illc.uva.nl/179/1/PP-2006-04.text.pdf, accessed January 3, 2021).

[6] See *erōtēma* in M.J. MacDonald, *The Oxford Handbook of Rhetorical Studies* (Oxford: University Press, 2017), 781.

[7] See the criticism by Estes, *Questions and Rhetoric*, 23–24, on rhetorical questions: 'All questions are asked – and this includes questions asked in ancient texts – for someone to give some answer somehow. When dealing with "rhetorical questions," there is a difference between saying "rhetorical questions don't ask an answer" and saying "rhetorical questions don't need an explicit answer".' (23)

[8] See the schedule and the comments on the exact repartition of the questions in the New Testament in Estes, *Questions and Rhetoric*, 25–28. I do not want to say that ancient rhetoric is the only influence on the Gospels or the epistles in the New Testament.

[9] Estes, *Questions and Rhetoric*, 18.

functions of questions in the Greek New Testament: narrative, dramatic, rhetorical and dialectical. In his book, Estes wants to make clear that paying special attention to questions changes the interpretation of the text in many instances. He illustrates his thesis with several examples in which he compares traditional exegesis with a new interpretation taking seriously the questions as questions.

2. Questions in Mark

In his monograph, Estes mentions around sixty questions from Mark, of which some receive a short comment and five are presented in a more or less detailed way as a case study.[10] Before presenting in this article two specific Markan passages, I would like to give some general comments on questions in Mark. Firstly, for several reasons it is difficult to determine the exact number of questions. Questions are not always recognizable by an interrogative pronoun, but sometimes by their tone and word order (for instance 1:27b); and sometimes it is not clear if there is a single or a double question.[11] I have composed a list of 111 questions that could be classified according to different criteria.[12] The list, with some explanation of the data in the columns, is given at the end of this article. Secondly, a quick look at this table reveals some interesting phenomena. Statistically, it is clear that most questions (more than half) are put by Jesus and that the recipients are the disciples (or a group of them) and the opponents (or a group of them). The opponents and the disciples are also the groups that ask the most questions to Jesus. This interaction of people asking questions and responding to questions confirms that the triangle Jesus–disciples–opponents is at the heart of the plot of the Gospel narrative. This is no surprise at all, because these characters are the ones that are present from (almost) the beginning until (almost) the end. Thirdly, when one

---

[10] The questions with a short comment (with reference to the page number between parentheses) are 1:24 (320); 1:27 (195–6); 2:24 (105); 3:33 (215–6); 4:21 (321); 8:23 (238); 8:27, 29 (211, 213); 8:36 (158–9); 9:22–23 (304); 10:17 (279); 12:24 (270); 13:2 (98); 14:60 (258–9); 16:3 (80). The five case studies are 4:40 (187–8); 7:18 (100); 9:19 (102–3, 322–3); 12:37 (222–3); 14:12 (258–9).

[11] For a list of double questions as a characteristic of Markan redactional style, see Neirynck, *Duality in Mark*, category 25. Among the discussable references to double questions are, e.g., 1:27; 3:4; 6:2; 14:60. And, what to do with the series of questions in 8:17–21?

[12] Estes counts 114 questions, but he does not give an overview (*Questions and Rhetoric*, 26). It would be interesting to classify the questions according to his 32 criteria (cf. above), but this would need more time and space.

looks at the patterns of questions-and-answers, sometimes a question is asked to a person or a group of persons, but a third party answers. This is for instance the case in 5:35 where people ask the bystanders: 'Why trouble the teacher any further?' It is Jesus who answers and not the bystanders: 'Do not fear, only believe.' In many other instances, we see that many of the answers (about 15) are again questions. In the terminology of Estes, we could call them 'second turn questions' in reaction to 'first turn questions.'[13] Especially when Jesus replies, he does so by asking a counter question.[14] This is a significant element with regard to the characterization of Jesus.[15] Finally, some real questions (more than 30) do not receive any explicit answer at all.[16]

In light of what Estes has written about the complexity of the functions and forms of questions and because of the large number of questions in Mark, it is difficult to make *general* statements about their narrative and rhetorical functions. Each question is different and needs a specific analysis and evaluation within its context. I will focus on the role of a question in two passages of Mark and, where possible, indicate the impact on the reader.

3. Two Questions in Mark

3.1. *Mark 1:24 (καὶ ἀνέκραξεν) λέγων· τί ἡμῖν καὶ σοί, Ἰησοῦ Ναζαρηνέ; ἦλθες ἀπολέσαι ἡμᾶς;*

The exorcism of a possessed man in the synagogue of Capernaum in 1:23–26 is the first story of a powerful act by Jesus and it is framed by the theme of authority (ἐξουσία) in 1:22 and 1:27. This framework about authority creates a setting of conflict between two opposite views on religion, one represented by Jesus and another one by the authorities. In 1:22 the *narrator* describes the effect on the audience of Jesus' authority compared to the one of the scribes ('not as the scribes'). Later discussions in the Gospel between Jesus and the religious authorities on the sabbath,

---

[13] Estes, *Questions and Rhetoric*, 288–311.
[14] See B.J. Koet's "Counter-questions in the Gospel of Luke: An Assessment" in this volume.
[15] For question as answer, see in the list at the end of this contribution, nos. 6–7, 12, 24, 25, 34, 39, 64, 80–81, 84, 88, 92–93. Sometimes the question is a partial element of the answer.
[16] No answers nos. 1–2, 3, 13, 23, 29, 42–45, 52–53, 55, 56, 57–58, 61, 62, 72, 85–86, 89, 90, 93, 99, 100, 102, 105, 106, 108, 109–110, 111. As we mentioned above, it is not clear if the category of 'rhetorical question' can be applied to (all) these questions.

the purity laws, the temple, and divorce confirm this difference in perspective. In 1:27 the *bystanders* themselves speak about Jesus' authority, but the emphasis is more on the fact that Jesus was able to heal the possessed man than on the comparison of the teaching with the scribes. The difference between the two manifestations of authority is not only a matter of the contents of their teaching. Jesus makes the deepest impression because he is able to act according to his teaching. This is well and succinctly summarized by Eduard Schweizer: 'Sein Wort ist Tat.'[17]

The ABA' structure (authority – exorcism – authority) is a form of indirect communication with the reader and suggests that the opposition is not limited to a conflict between human characters (a possessed man versus Jesus). On the one hand, Satan and his band try to rule the world; on the other, God and his associates attempt to install the Kingdom of God. The link between the two parts A (authority) and B (exorcism) is strengthened by the absence of concrete teaching by Jesus. The exorcism *is* the teaching. The story is a concrete illustration of the almost mythical confrontation between Satan and Jesus in the desert at the end of the prologue of the Gospel (1:12–13).[18] Two diametrically opposite interpretations of existence in this world are at play in Mark's Gospel. This is the real issue of the 'good news' (1:1 and 1:14). And it is a matter of life and death (ἦλθες ἀπολέσαι ἡμᾶς;) as will become clear as the story continues.[19] Jesus' arrival 'signifies the presence of God's powerfully effective reign which leaves no room for opposition to God by Satan and his demons.'[20] There is a fascinating play of power in a complex web going on in this story, with different characters who all have their own explicit or implicit strategy: the possessed man (not actively), the demon, the authorities, Jesus, the people in the synagogue. Jesus' action of liberating a possessed man in the synagogue on a sabbath goes against the

---

[17] E. Schweizer, *Das Evangelium nach Markus* (NTD 1; Göttingen: Vandenhoeck & Ruprecht, 1967), 27.
[18] R.A. Culpepper, *Mark* (SHBC 20; Macon: Smyth & Helwys, 2007), 56: 'Having been tempted by Satan in the wilderness, Jesus is now confronted by an unclean spirit, lending further evidence that Mark characterizes Jesus' ministry as warfare with the power of Evil.'
[19] The verb ἀπόλλυμι is used in the strong sense of 'eliminate' in different contexts in the Gospel: 2:22; 3:6; 4:38; 8:35; 9:22; 11:18; 12:9. The irony in the question is certainly intentional: while the demon knows that Jesus has come to destroy 'them,' the earthly religious leaders who have far less authority than Jesus in the eyes of the people are intending to destroy Jesus.
[20] E.J. Schnabel, *Mark* (TNTC; Downers Grove: IVP Academic, an imprint of InterVarsity Press, 2017), 58.

fossilized application of the legal norms and the attitude of the religious leaders.[21]

In this pericope we find the first question in Mark, which is in fact a double question: τί ἡμῖν καὶ σοί, Ἰησοῦ Ναζαρηνέ; and ἦλθες ἀπολέσαι ἡμᾶς; It is rarely written in commentaries on Mark that the first words spoken in direct discourse by a character other than Jesus after he has started his ministry (1:14–15), are these two questions by an unclean spirit. Estes is right when he says scholars have focused too much on the answers and have forgotten about the importance of questions. In 1:23–26, too, for instance, commentators rapidly switch from the questions of the possessed man to the answer of Jesus, who is then presented as the stronger one, the Holy One of God, who has authority. Immediately, the meaning of the pericope is oriented towards Christological issues. A closer look at the question, however, reveals to the reader the seriousness of what is at stake in that first conflict during a public action, and it has an impact on the interpretation of the rest of the Gospel: 'when one reads a narrative and comes across a question – even if the question is not put to the reader but a character in the story – it elicits a pause and a momentary shift in thinking in the reader.'[22]

The place of these two questions in the beginning of the Gospel, their formulation and the fact that a double question is used, accentuate that the Gospel is about a conflict between two worldviews and that the presence of Jesus is at the heart of the conflict. The tone of the rest of the Gospel is set by this first confrontation: the narrator creates a tension between two forces. Interpreters do not comment very much on the function of the first of the two questions τί ἡμῖν καὶ σοί, Ἰησοῦ Ναζαρηνέ; – an expression that is used elsewhere in the New Testament (Mark 5:7; John 2:4). They refer to parallel expressions in the Hebrew Bible (Judges 11:12; 2 Samuel 16:10; 19:22; 1 Kings 17:18; 2 Kings 3:13), they mention different opinions with regard to the origin (Semitic or Greek?)[23] and the intention of the question (submission or attack?),[24] and they

---

[21] Compare the 'unmasking' of the rigid attitude of the chief of the synagogue in the exegesis of Luke 13:10–17 (also a story of liberation in a synagogue on a sabbath) in A. Wénin, "Le chef de synagogue de Lc 13,14–17: Un exemple biblique de cléricalisme?," *RTL* 51 (2020): 15–34.

[22] Estes, *The Questions of Jesus in John*, 10.

[23] R.H. Gundry, *Mark: A Commentary on His Apology for the Cross* (Grand Rapids: Eerdmans, 1993), 75.

[24] A. Yarbro Collins, *Mark* (Hermeneia; Philadelphia: Fortress, 2007), 169. Very strongly in R. Pesch, *Das Markusevangelium* (HThKNT 2/1; Freiburg: Herder, 1976), 122: 'Abwehrformel.'

make judgements about the relationship between the evil spirit and Jesus (is there any kind of 'positive' relationship or only conflict)?[25] The translations of this first question reflect these debates. They go in different directions and vary between an open question ('What have you to do with us?')[26] and a strong refusal of interference ('Que te mêles-tu de nos affaires?').[27] The meaning of the question clearly depends on its context and 'when addressed to an actual or potential aggressor it has the force of 'Go away and leave me alone.''[28] Some commentators point to the use of the plural form ἡμῖν because from the perspective of the possessed man, 'this particular demon speaks in this initial encounter on behalf of the whole threatened fraternity,'[29] and from the perspective of Jesus, 'Jesus' attack is on the whole community or realm of evil.'[30] The expression has an undeniable link with 5:7 (Τί ἐμοὶ καὶ σοί, Ἰησοῦ υἱὲ τοῦ θεοῦ τοῦ ὑψίστου;) where the singular ἐμοί conceals the multiple identity of the name 'Legion.'

Especially in light of the many questions that will follow in Mark, it is surprising that the rhetorical and narrative function of this first one is overlooked. The question is formally, as well as with regard to the content, extremely important for the rhetoric of the narrative. Estes mentions the first question as an example of 'phatic questions.'[31] Phatic means something like small-talk that is oriented towards not only giving information or towards rhetorical effects, but that functions as an expression of social interaction. In the definition of Estes, 'informational and rhetorical purposes are secondary to the social purposes of the question.' They emphasize 'social interest over grammatical correctness,' are 'ambiguous in content,' and are a kind of 'narrative slang.' In a narrative discourse the rhetorical effect is the emphasis on the relation between the

---

[25] C. Focant, *L'évangile selon Marc* (Commentaire biblique: Nouveau Testament 2; Paris: Cerf, 2004), 88: 'la méfiance et le rejet de toute relation avec Jésus.'

[26] Culpepper, *Mark*, 57; Gundry, *Mark*, 75 (as a possible translation: 'What do we and you have to do with each other?'). The order can also be inverted, cf. G. Guttenberger, *Das Evangelium nach Markus* (ZBK 2; Zürich: Theologischer Verlag, 2017), 50: 'Was haben wir mit dir zu tun?'

[27] Focant, *Marc*, 86.

[28] R.T. France, *The Gospel of Mark* (NIGTC; Grand Rapids: Eerdmans, 2014), 103.

[29] France, *Mark*, 103; Peter Dschulnigg, *Das Markusevangelium* (TKNT 2, Stuttgart: Kohlhammer, 2007), 81: 'damit bringt er wohl zum Ausdruck, dass die ganze Welt der Dämonen gegen Jesus steht und von ihm bedroht ist.'

[30] B. Witherington III, *The Gospel of Mark: A Socio-Rhetorical Commentary* (Grand Rapids: Eerdmans, 2001), 91. Among many others, Schweizer, *Markus*, 28, gives a modern psychological interpretation: 'Persönlichkeitsspaltung.'

[31] Estes, *Questions and Rhetoric*, 203–207 (quotations are from these pages).

asker and the recipient. The language is indeed strange: there is no verb and it almost sounds like a popular greeting as if Jesus and the demon know each other. This is confirmed by the next sentence: the demon seems to know the name of Jesus, and not only his earthly origin, but also his relationship with God. But in reality, the question expresses fear and uncertainty. Jesus enters into the world of the demons – on a sabbath and in a synagogue – and they do not want to be known by him! That is why their recognition of Jesus in what comes after the two questions ('I know who you are: The Holy One of God') is a very confusing 'confession' for the readers.[32] There is a kind of ambiguity in the juxtaposition of the knowledge the demon has about who Jesus is and his desire to keep at a distance. Of course, the naming of the opponent in exorcism stories is a means to try to be his superior. But it is a correct expression of who Jesus is according to the narrator (1:1) or God (1:9; 9:7). The demon wants to say that there is *no* relationship at all, but in putting this question in connection with his use of the title, he already says that Jesus and he have something in common. They both have the same concern: they have a reign to announce or to defend (see 3:22–30 for the reign of Beelzebul). The demon exists because of the existence of Jesus.

If one thinks of this pericope as an oral performance, one would understand even better that the rhetorical strength of the question lies in its communicative value with the audience. Whitney Shiner, who wrote a kind of personal performance critical commentary on Mark, uses the Roman gesture techniques from the handbooks of ancient rhetoric to explain how he would perform Mark. There is a short passage on 1:24 in which he considers the question as an expression of the aggressive attitude on behalf of the demon: 'Belligerence is shown by forming a fist and raising it to the level of the face. The demon probably makes this gesture in 1:24, "What have you to do with us, Jesus of Nazareth?" Stoop down a little bit and shake your fist slightly, and you should feel properly demonic.'[33]

---

[32] See the commentary on Mark 5:7 in the unpublished dissertation by L. Marulli, *Le Gérasénien et le(s) jeune homme(s): Perspectives synchroniques et diachroniques sur le récit de Marc 5,1–20* (Strasbourg, 2020), 103: 'Du point de vue narratif, le lecteur est confronté une fois de plus [in 5,7], à la nature ambiguë de l'interaction entre Jésus et le démoniaque. […] Le lecteur se retrouve ainsi déboussolé: tout d'abord, son point d'encrage empathique narratif, à savoir les disciples, disparaît; ensuite, c'est de la bouche d'un démoniaque que sort la vérité sur l'identité Jésus [*sic*], à laquelle le lecteur est appelé à adhérer. À ce dévoilement correspond, néanmoins, comme en 1,24, la méfiance et l'hostilité du démoniaque qui n'est pas en train de proclamer une profession de foi mais plutôt de déployer une stratégie d'affaiblissement de son adversaire.'

[33] W. Shiner, *Proclaiming the Gospel: First-Century Performance of Mark* (Harrisburg: Trinity Press, 2003), 132.

One of the insights of such a performance critical approach to the pericope is that, when focusing on the demon's question, not only the performer, but also the audience make the demon's question their own. The question thus becomes the articulation of how and what many people – possessed or not – would think about Jesus. It is difficult to find out which emotion is the most dominant one in the words of the demon (fear, submission, enmity, defence, mistrust), but there is no doubt that he fears an intervention from the Holy One of God. He feels threatened because Jesus of Nazareth is considered as one who enters into his realm. If exegesis pauses at the moment of reading or hearing the question, equal attention is paid to the demon's question as to Jesus' answer. If the audience thinks that Jesus' answer also has a meaning for them, then they have to ask the same question as the demon. Through that question every hearer/reader of the Gospel looks into the mirror and asks: 'What is there between you and me after all, Jesus of Nazareth?' It is only in light of this question that the enigmatic and exceptional presence of Jesus can become clear.[34] As the first question of the Gospel, it is a sign for everyone who hears it that s/he has to pass through that door before even thinking of entering the Kingdom of God. The plural ἡμῖν implies that demons can be everywhere: they are those elements in a person that try to prohibit the acceptance of Jesus and his message (see 3:22–30). As a variable question – and not a polar question with only the possibility to answer yes or no – the first part of the double question offers the reader a whole range of answers, as we mentioned already when referring to the variety of possible emotions from the side of the demon.

Instead of jumping directly towards the Christological interpretation of Jesus as an exorcist, listening to the first question in Mark creates the opportunity to hear the voice of those who receive the word. Through its colloquial, popular, direct, and challenging open formulation it creates an openness for all kinds of emotions and attitudes towards Jesus' words and deeds.

If the first part of the double question works as an ambiguous one, but with a clear tendency to be aggressive towards Jesus, the second one is

---

[34] See L. Marulli, *Le Gérasénien et le(s) jeune homme(s): Perspectives synchroniques et diachroniques sur le récit de Marc 5.1-20* (Strasbourg: Université de Strasbourg, 2020), 102 on Mark 5:7: 'Au cœur de cette tension, le lecteur voit jaillir une des nombreuses questions par certains personnages du deuxième évangile et laissées sans réponse explicite: τί ἡμῖν καὶ σοί, Ἰησοῦ …; (v. 7). La stratégie narrative de Marc demande de remplir ce *blanc* pour se positionner personnellement face à l'identité du héros du récit.' This is true as well for the question in 1:24.

a direct accusation. Commentators and translators debate whether it is a question or a statement: 'Have you come...?' or 'You have come...'[35] The form of a question expresses more the fear and the existential uncertainty of the demon. For several reasons the most striking word here that merits attention is ἀπόλλυμι, which occurs ten times in Mark.[36] First of all, there is irony in the use of this word, since the demon is telling the truth. Jesus has come to destroy the evil forces (see 1:12–13). Secondly, ἀπόλλυμι continues this idea of deadly opposition between the two forces. The first encounter in the public arena in Mark announces a battle to the death. The verb will be used again in 3:6 and 11:18 where it is said that the authorities want to destroy Jesus. And they will succeed. So, the irony is double: the demon speaks the truth (Jesus has come to destroy them), but Jesus will be 'destroyed' by his enemies. Thirdly, and this may be surprising, Jesus himself also uses this verb, in the paradoxical saying in 8:35: 'For those who want to save their life, will lose it [ἀπολέσει αὐτήν], and those who lose their life [ὃς δ' ἂν ἀπολέσει] for my sake, and for the sake of the Gospel, will save it.' The plot of the Gospel is based on conflict and the story will end with the death of the hero. But at the centre of the plot, the hero himself interprets in a very personal and unique way the meaning of life and death, including his own life and death. In this paradox (see also 9:35; 10:43–44) we have the same radical opposition between two incompatible ways of life as we have found between the demon and Jesus. The narrator is not very explicit about what it exactly means 'to lose your life.' In verse 36 we learn that everything that is not in accordance with the Gospel and with Jesus is considered 'to gain the world' (8:36) and does not belong to the Kingdom of God announced by Jesus. The meaning of the expression 'to lose one's life' can only be found through a reading of the whole of Mark's story. And in relation to 1:23–26, 'losing one's life' could mean to 'destroy' the evil demons that prohibit hearing the message of Jesus. Those who do not accept or understand this are still setting their minds on 'human things' and not on 'divine things,' as Jesus explained just before to Peter (8:33) when he opposed Jesus' suffering as part of the good news. And, therefore, Jesus called Peter 'Satan,' comparing him to the demons and their opposition to the Gospel.

---

[35] Here are two opinions. Guttenberger translates it as a question, which is the most common interpretation, but 'die Wortstellung schließt einen Aussagesatz nicht aus' (*Markus*, 50). According to Pesch the sentence is a 'Feststellung... (... kaum als Frage aufzufassen)' (*Markusevangelium*, 122).

[36] 1:24; 2:22; 3:6; 4:38; 8:35 (2×); 9:22; 9:41; 11:18; 12:9.

The fact that the first spoken words in direct discourse during Jesus' public ministry are formulated in a double question to start a dialogue with Jesus, makes the story very lively, and from the beginning creates a tension in the plot that will only be resolved at the moment of Jesus' death. These questions, especially the colloquial style of the first one, also stimulate the communication between story and audience, especially when there is oral performance that supports the emotions by tone and gestures. The voice of the demon thus challenges the audience to become aware of their own perspective on Jesus. The question of the demon ('What have you to do with us, Jesus of Nazareth?') may sound very awkward for members in the audience who think about themselves as being very familiar with Jesus. But the question is there and everyone who hears it should try to answer it, no matter whether it is a demon posing it or not.

3.2. *Mark 16:3 καὶ ἔλεγον πρὸς ἑαυτάς· τίς ἀποκυλίσει ἡμῖν τὸν λίθον ἐκ τῆς θύρας τοῦ μνημείου;*

The last question in the Gospel of Mark is a summary of the conversation of the women as they walked to the tomb when the Shabbat was over. At first sight, the question does not seem to be very special and is a little bit awkward (Matthew and Luke will not mention it in their version of the empty tomb story). Firstly, if the women ask the question among themselves, why did they not think of it before and look for someone who could help?[37] It 'adds an almost humorous, homely touch to the scene.'[38] Secondly, the place of 'for it was great' (v. 4b) after the remark that the stone 'had already been rolled back' (v. 4a) is also strange: the delayed explanatory γάρ-clause[39] has to do with their question in v. 3 and is not an explanation of the fact that the stone is rolled away. Therefore, some manuscripts have changed the order of verse 4a and 4b. Scholars try to interpret these two 'problems' in different ways. In order to solve the idea that the women had forgotten such an important issue as the stone in preparing their visit, Joel Marcus thinks that we have here a

---

[37] For Gundry, who interprets the story on a historical level, the women ask the question because it was early in the morning and, 'not yet noticing that the stone has been rolled away,' they could not find anyone near the tomb to help them (*Mark*, 996-997).

[38] France, *Mark*, 678.

[39] See F. Neirynck, "The Apocryphal Gospels and the Gospel of Mark," in: J.-M. Sevrin (Ed.), *The New Testament in Early Christianity* (BETL 86; Leuven: Peeters, 1989), 123–175, here 149–152. Compare other instances: 11:13 (ὁ γὰρ καιρὸς οὐκ ἦν σύκων); 12:12 (ἔγνωσαν γὰρ ὅτι πρὸς αὐτοὺς τὴν παραβολὴν εἶπεν).

rhetorical question that expresses vivid emotion: they are not asking for help, they are lamenting.[40] Adela Yarbro Collins adds the dimension of the communication at discourse level with the audience: 'The evangelist... is less interested in reporting how things would ideally happen than in constructing a dramatic narrative. The question creates dramatic tension and leads the audiences to expect something extraordinary to occur.'[41] The exegesis of 'dramatic tension' and of 'extraordinary' intervention is frequently found in commentaries on Mark.[42] But, here again, the focus of scholars has been on what comes after the question. The question itself has been considered as 'only' setting the stage for the women looking up and seeing that the stone is rolled away;[43] scholars see already in the wording (τίς, 'who') and the placement of the size of the stone a way 'to draw attention to the wonder of God's action,'[44] although Richard France correctly notices that '[w]e are not told how or when the stone had been removed, since the passive ἀποκεκύλισται does not reveal the agency (contrast Matthew 28:2), nor whether it was removed in order for Jesus to come out.'[45] The interpretation of the question is limited to the level of the story (characterization of the women), and when the discourse level of the relation between text and readers is considered it is only because the question prepares for God's saving action. Consequently, although these interpretations are helpful to understand the development of the plot, they do not take the question very seriously as a question. Therefore, as we did with the first question in 1:24, we would like to see what happens to the reader when we take the function of the last question in the whole of the process of communication seriously. Before doing so, we will summarize what Estes has written on the type of question like the one in 16:3.

---

[40] J. Marcus, *Mark 8–16* (AB 27A; New Haven: Yale University Press, 2009), 1079–1080, with reference to BDF §496; cf. Deut 5:29; Ps 55:6 [LXX 54:7]; Jer 9:1.

[41] Collins, *Mark*, 794.

[42] B. Standaert, *Evangile selon Marc: Commentaire* (Pendé: Gabalda, 2010), vol. 3, 1180: 'Marc se révèle ici maître dans l'art de raconter et de dramatiser une scène;' J.R. Donahue and D.J. Harrington, *The Gospel of Mark* (SP 2; Collegeville, 2002), 458: '... to prepare for the surprise they encounter when they finally get to the tomb;' Focant, *Marc*, 595: '... la place, à première vue étonnante, de cette remarque ['car elle était très grande'] ... serait plutôt une façon d'indiquer que l'ouverture du tombeau n'est pas l'œuvre d'une force humaine, mais bien d'une force divine' (with reference to G. Kittel).

[43] Gundry, *Mark*, 990.

[44] Culpepper, *Mark*, 584.

[45] France, *Mark*, 678.

Estes mentions the question in 16:3 on two occasions.[46] According to traditional genre theory, he says, the verse is a part of 'narrated speech within a narrative genre, a generic situation that encourages – but not mandates – the reading of the question to have a stronger informational quality and a weaker rhetorical quality.'[47] Modern rhetorical genre studies are not based on the form of the work but 'on the rhetorical situation in which that work appears. … Rather than asking what form of text the question is embedded in, we ask what way each question is used within the discourse, and to accomplish what purpose. In [Mark 16:3], the question is used by Mark to create reported dialogue between characters in the story. Thus, its purpose is to show interaction and character attitudes on a topic, more than to state anything to the reader of the text. This type of characterization reveals the question to be about openness of dialogue, and therefore it is a classic open-question type.'[48] Estes' analysis of the question offers an explanation why there is little focus on the question itself as a rhetoric element in the whole of the Gospel. The question is formulated as a kind of *dialogue intérieur* between the women and therefore there is no direct communication with the audience.

Further on in his book he explains what 'Open Questions' are and mentions 16:3 as an example.[49] Some elements of the theory on open questions are noteworthy and help to understand the specificity of the women's question. Open questions 'are asked without any push toward or expectation of a possible answer. … [T]hey are so open as to not elicit any definitive replies from the audience. … In order to be an open question, the question under consideration must be asked without any rhetorical pretense on the part of the asker.' As regards the formation of these questions, the most indicated introductory variable words of an open question are *who* or *where* (and not *how* or *why*) without – in theory – any semantic or pragmatic limiters that orientate the answer in a certain direction. As regards the rhetorical effect of open questions on the audience, this is minimal. They 'have almost no persuasive power and are not formed to assert any influence over hearers.' Apart from the fact that they admit ignorance on the part of the asker, open questions have 'the mild

---

[46] Estes, *Questions and Rhetoric*, 81–83 (short commentary) and 154 (only a reference in the context of 'Open Question').
[47] Estes, *Questions and Rhetoric*, 80.
[48] Estes, *Questions and Rhetoric*, 80–81.
[49] Estes, *Questions and Rhetoric*, 149–154 (quotations in this paragraph are from these pages). Open questions are the first case out of twenty-three kinds of 'Questions driven by Semantics.'

rhetorical effect on the hearer ... that it may cause them to raise the same question or at least in their mind suggest possible answers to the question.'

Estes' insights make us better understand that the different interpretations of the commentators on 16:3 are all reader responses to fill in the gap that is created through the open question that *in se* has very little rhetoric impact. Commentators make links between the question and its context, but there is no real orientation in the question that leads the hearer/reader to precise answers.[50] It is, for instance, not at all certain that the word τίς ('who') points to a divine intervention.

What happens if we consider seriously the question by itself within the whole of the pericope and of the Gospel? The question has a function in the story: it creates almost unintentionally the theme of the resurrection by repeating the existence of the stone (see 15:46) and accentuating its heaviness. The stone becomes the symbol of death at the end of the story, and it is with emotions overshowed by death that the women go to the tomb. They are convinced that Jesus is dead and they come to anoint his dead body. The problem of the stone is solved in the story ('it has been rolled away'), but the question itself does not receive an answer. We do not hear 'who' rolled away the stone: 'God? An angel? The resurrected Jesus? Even at the risk of letting his audience think first of graverobbers, Mark does not say (contrast Matthew 28:2).'[51] But this gap in the story, created by the fact that the agent or the reason of the stone being rolled away is not told, creates new questions: where is the body? And how to interpret the emptiness of the tomb? In other words, the question itself is never solved and stands as a question even as we reach the end of the pericope and of the Gospel. The 'simple' explanation of a *passivum*

---

[50] In this regard, one should read the section on the 'Rhetorical-Shift Principle' (Estes, *Questions and Rhetoric*, 87–89) in which Estes explains that informational questions (which we consider the open question in 16:3 to be) can undergo a rhetorical shift when they are integrated in a highly charged rhetorical environment. Two remarks should be made. (1) We are not sure that the context of the question in 16:3 is 'highly rhetorical.' Estes is thinking more about, e.g., the Pauline letters. (2) Estes himself concedes that 'even with the shift, information-leaning questions will still hold onto many of their information-leaning qualities. Persuasion is a force that taints – not transmutes – utterances'.

[51] Gundry, *Mark*, 990. Cf. Donahue and Harrington, *Mark*, 458: 'Was it the "young man" of 16:5, the risen Christ, or God?' Contrast to other scholars like, e.g., Marcus, *Mark*, 1084: 'In the present instance, too, divine power has removed an obstacle that was very large (...);' Dschulnigg, *Markusevangelium*, 412, who speaks of an angel (!) 'der wohl als der ersehnte Helfer zu verstehen ist' (following Rudolf Pesch; cf. Matt 28:2).

divinum is too easy to solve the problem.[52] This aspect of a question that does not receive an explicit answer in the story reinforces the Markan idea of a paradoxical presence of God in the story. On the one hand, there is no story of Mark without God's presence, on the other hand, God does not 'act' in the story.[53]

Looking again at the question in 16:3 as an open question without any clear answer, we can only conclude that it expresses the natural reaction of common people – like the question of the demon who possessed a man in 1:21-28. If we take a pause to hear the women's question (instead of passing immediately to the answer of a 'miraculous' intervention), it becomes the question of any reader or hearer. It becomes our question. Through the question, the narrator offers his audience the most logical down to earth question people can ask. Through the narrative strategy of emotional identification of the audience with the women, the question of the latter becomes the question of the former.[54]

The fact that the issue of the presence of the stone is presented in the form of a question is of great importance. It colours the whole of the pericope and of the Gospel. As Corina Combet-Galland has written comparing the longer ending of Mark (16:9-20) with the shorter one in 16:8: 'The longer ending of Mark, with the Easter appearance stories and the proclamation based upon them in 16:9-20, seems to create a *genealogy of believers* and a story which takes the form of an answer. Does the shorter ending of the empty tomb not tell the story of a *genesis* [of faith] in adopting the form of a question?'[55] In this sense, the narrator does not

---

[52] To mention only one example of such an interpretation, see Gundry, *Mark*, 992: 'This passive meaning, in turn, suggests divine action: God has raised Jesus;' Donahue / Harrington, *Mark*, 458: 'The aorist passive (...) is a theological or divine passive (that is, God raised Jesus from the dead).' For a critical evaluation of the notion *passivum divinum* in general, see P.-B. Smit and T. Renssen, "The *passivum divinum*: The Rise and Future Fall of an Imaginary Linguistic Phenomenon," *Filología Neotestamentaria* 27 (2014): 3-24; with regard to 16:6, see B. Pascut, "The So-Called Passivum Divinum in Mark's Gospel," *NovT* 54 (2012): 313-333, here 322: 'So the passive voice is used because it emphasizes the action whose doer is irrelevant in the present context.'

[53] For a more thoroughgoing analysis of the characterization of God in Mark, see G. Van Oyen, "Dieu, un personnage surprenant," in: A. Wénin and G. Van Oyen (Eds.), *La surprise dans la Bible: Hommage à Camille Focant* (BETL 247; Leuven: Peeters, 2012), 191-208; G. Van Oyen, "Du secret messianique au mystère divin," in: G. Van Oyen (Ed.), *Reading the Gospel of Mark in the Twenty-First Century: Method and Meaning* (BETL 301; Leuven: Peeters, 2019), 1-37.

[54] Michael R. Withenton, "Feeling the Silence: A Moment-by-Moment Account of Emotions at the End of Mark (16:1-8)," *CBQ* 78 (2016): 272-289.

[55] C. Combet-Galland, "L'évangile selon Marc et la pierre qu'il a déjà roulée," in: O. Mainville and D. Marguerat (Eds.), *Résurrection: L'après-mort dans le monde ancien et le Nouveau Testament* (MdB 45; Genève: Labor et Fides, 2001), 93-109, here

'close' the beginning (ἀρχή 1:1).[56] The tension between the stone that is rolled away and the attitude of the women who do not seem to understand the consequences of this should not be polished away in this short ending of Mark. It is not clear whether they think that God has acted in this scene, and their final attitude of flight, silence and fear is at least very ambiguous. The question in 16:3 keeps its 'information-leaning quality' of ... just asking the question and sharing it with the audience.

4. Conclusion

The first and the last question in Mark's Gospel are at first sight very simple questions with a minor function in the rhetorical strategy of the narrator. As examples of a phatic and an open question, commentators have struggled with the meaning and interpretation of these questions in the story but they have neglected to search for the impact of these questions on the response of the audience. We have seen in both cases (1:24 and 16:3) that these questions fit perfectly in the broader narrative concepts of the Markan narrator and that through their open character they invite a wide range of possible thoughts from the audience.

---

100): '(...) les apparitions pascales et la proclamation qu'elles fondent [16:9–20] semblent susciter une *généalogie* de croyants en un récit qui prend la forme d'une réponse. Le récit court [16:1–8] du tombeau vide ne dessine-t-il pas plutôt une *genèse* en adoptant la forme d'une *question*?' (my translation into English).

[56] See this final remark by Combet-Galland, "L'évangile selon Marc," 103: 'L'inachevé, constitutif des commencements, prend ici toute son envergure' (The unachieved, the unfinished, which is a characteristic of all 'beginnings,' takes on its full scope here).

Questions in the Gospel of Mark

Number	Questions in Greek	Double/Triple	Asker	Recipient
1-2	1 καὶ ἀνέκραξεν ²⁴ λέγων· τί ἡμῖν καὶ σοί, Ἰησοῦ Ναζαρηνέ; ἦλθες ἀπολέσαι ἡμᾶς; see 5,7	D	demon	Jesus
3	1 ²⁷ καὶ ἐθαμβήθησαν ἅπαντες ὥστε συζητεῖν πρὸς ἑαυτοὺς λέγοντας· τί ἐστιν τοῦτο; διδαχὴ καινὴ κατ' ἐξουσίαν·[:] see 6,2	[D]	people	(deliberative)
4-5	2 ⁷ τί οὗτος οὕτως λαλεῖ; βλασφημεῖ· τίς δύναται ἀφιέναι ἁμαρτίας εἰ μὴ εἷς ὁ θεός;	D	scribes	(deliberative)
6-7	2 ⁸ καὶ εὐθὺς ἐπιγνοὺς ὁ Ἰησοῦς τῷ πνεύματι αὐτοῦ ὅτι οὕτως διαλογίζονται ἐν ἑαυτοῖς λέγει αὐτοῖς· τί ταῦτα διαλογίζεσθε ἐν ταῖς καρδίαις ὑμῶν; ⁹ τί ἐστιν εὐκοπώτερον, εἰπεῖν τῷ παραλυτικῷ· ἀφίενταί σου αἱ ἁμαρτίαι, ἢ εἰπεῖν· ἔγειρε καὶ ἆρον τὸν κράβαττόν σου καὶ περιπάτει;	D	Jesus Jesus	scribes
8	2 ¹⁶ καὶ οἱ γραμματεῖς τῶν Φαρισαίων ἰδόντες ὅτι ἐσθίει μετὰ τῶν ἁμαρτωλῶν καὶ τελωνῶν ἔλεγον τοῖς μαθηταῖς αὐτοῦ· ὅτι μετὰ τῶν τελωνῶν καὶ ἁμαρτωλῶν ἐσθίει;		scribes	disciples
9	2 ¹⁸ Καὶ ἦσαν οἱ μαθηταὶ Ἰωάννου καὶ οἱ Φαρισαῖοι νηστεύοντες. καὶ ἔρχονται καὶ λέγουσιν αὐτῷ· διὰ τί οἱ μαθηταὶ Ἰωάννου καὶ οἱ μαθηταὶ τῶν Φαρισαίων νηστεύουσιν, οἱ δὲ σοὶ μαθηταὶ οὐ νηστεύουσιν;		«people»	Jesus
10	2 ¹⁹ καὶ εἶπεν αὐτοῖς ὁ Ἰησοῦς· μὴ δύνανται οἱ υἱοὶ τοῦ νυμφῶνος ἐν ᾧ ὁ νυμφίος μετ' αὐτῶν ἐστιν νηστεύειν; ὅσον χρόνον ἔχουσιν τὸν νυμφίον μετ' αὐτῶν οὐ δύνανται νηστεύειν.		Jesus	people

11	2 ²⁴ καὶ οἱ Φαρισαῖοι ἔλεγον αὐτῷ· ἴδε τί ποιοῦσιν τοῖς σάββασιν ὃ οὐκ ἔξεστιν;		Pharisees	Jesus
12	2 ²⁵ οὐδέποτε ἀνέγνωτε τί ἐποίησεν Δαυὶδ ὅτε χρείαν ἔσχεν καὶ ἐπείνασεν αὐτός καὶ οἱ μετ' αὐτοῦ[;] 2 ²⁶ πῶς εἰσῆλθεν εἰς τὸν οἶκον τοῦ θεοῦ ἐπὶ Ἀβιαθὰρ ἀρχιερέως καὶ τοὺς ἄρτους τῆς προθέσεως ἔφαγεν, οὓς οὐκ ἔξεστιν φαγεῖν εἰ μὴ τοὺς ἱερεῖς, καὶ ἔδωκεν καὶ τοῖς σὺν αὐτῷ οὖσιν;	[D]	Jesus	Pharisees
13	3 ⁴ καὶ λέγει αὐτοῖς· ἔξεστιν τοῖς σάββασιν ἀγαθὸν ποιῆσαι ἢ κακοποιῆσαι,[;] ψυχὴν σῶσαι ἢ ἀποκτεῖναι; οἱ δὲ ἐσιώπων.	[D]	Jesus	Pharisees – Herodians
14	3 ²³ Καὶ προσκαλεσάμενος αὐτοὺς ἐν παραβολαῖς ἔλεγεν αὐτοῖς· πῶς δύναται σατανᾶς σατανᾶν ἐκβάλλειν;		Jesus	scribes
15	3 ³³ καὶ ἀποκριθεὶς αὐτοῖς λέγει· τίς ἐστιν ἡ μήτηρ μου καὶ οἱ ἀδελφοί [μου];		Jesus	people
16	4 ¹³ Καὶ λέγει αὐτοῖς· οὐκ οἴδατε τὴν παραβολὴν ταύτην [;], καὶ πῶς πάσας τὰς παραβολὰς γνώσεσθε;	[D]	Jesus	disciples
17–18	4 ²¹ Καὶ ἔλεγεν αὐτοῖς· μήτι ἔρχεται ὁ λύχνος ἵνα ὑπὸ τὸν μόδιον τεθῇ ἢ ὑπὸ τὴν κλίνην; οὐχ ἵνα ἐπὶ τὴν λυχνίαν τεθῇ;	D	Jesus	disciples – people
19	4 ³⁰ Καὶ ἔλεγεν· πῶς ὁμοιώσωμεν τὴν βασιλείαν τοῦ θεοῦ ἢ ἐν τίνι αὐτὴν παραβολῇ θῶμεν;		Jesus	disciples – people
20	4 ³⁸ καὶ ἐγείρουσιν αὐτὸν καὶ λέγουσιν αὐτῷ· διδάσκαλε, οὐ μέλει σοι ὅτι ἀπολλύμεθα;		disciples	Jesus
21–22	4 ⁴⁰ καὶ εἶπεν αὐτοῖς· τί δειλοί ἐστε; οὔπω ἔχετε πίστιν;	D	Jesus	disciples
23	4 ⁴¹ καὶ ἐφοβήθησαν φόβον μέγαν καὶ ἔλεγον πρὸς ἀλλήλους· τίς ἄρα οὗτός ἐστιν ὅτι καὶ ὁ ἄνεμος καὶ ἡ θάλασσα ὑπακούει αὐτῷ;		disciples	(deliberative)

QUESTIONS IN THE GOSPEL OF MARK

24	5 ⁷ καὶ κράξας φωνῇ μεγάλῃ λέγει· τί ἐμοὶ καὶ σοί, Ἰησοῦ υἱὲ τοῦ θεοῦ τοῦ ὑψίστου; ὁρκίζω σε τὸν θεόν, μή με βασανίσῃς. See 1,24			demon	Jesus
25	5 ⁹ καὶ ἐπηρώτα αὐτόν· τί ὄνομά σοι; καὶ λέγει αὐτῷ· λεγιὼν ὄνομά μοι, ὅτι πολλοί ἐσμεν.			Jesus	demon
26	5 ³⁰ καὶ εὐθὺς ὁ Ἰησοῦς ἐπιγνοὺς ἐν ἑαυτῷ τὴν ἐξ αὐτοῦ δύναμιν ἐξελθοῦσαν ἐπιστραφεὶς ἐν τῷ ὄχλῳ ἔλεγεν· τίς μου ἥψατο τῶν ἱματίων;			Jesus	people
27	5 ³¹ καὶ ἔλεγον αὐτῷ οἱ μαθηταὶ αὐτοῦ· βλέπεις τὸν ὄχλον συνθλίβοντά σε καὶ λέγεις· τίς μου ἥψατο;			disciples	Jesus
28	5 ³⁵ Ἔτι αὐτοῦ λαλοῦντος ἔρχονται ἀπὸ τοῦ ἀρχισυναγώγου λέγοντες ὅτι ἡ θυγάτηρ σου ἀπέθανεν· τί ἔτι σκύλλεις τὸν διδάσκαλον;			people	Jairus
29	5 ³⁹ καὶ εἰσελθὼν λέγει αὐτοῖς· τί θορυβεῖσθε καὶ κλαίετε; τὸ παιδίον οὐκ ἀπέθανεν ἀλλὰ καθεύδει.			Jesus	people
30	6 ² καὶ γενομένου σαββάτου ἤρξατο διδάσκειν ἐν τῇ συναγωγῇ, καὶ πολλοὶ ἀκούοντες ἐξεπλήσσοντο λέγοντες· πόθεν τούτῳ ταῦτα, καὶ τίς ἡ σοφία ἡ δοθεῖσα τούτῳ[;] καὶ αἱ δυνάμεις τοιαῦται διὰ τῶν χειρῶν αὐτοῦ γινόμεναι; see 1,27	[D]		people	Jairus
31–32	6 ³ οὐχ οὗτός ἐστιν ὁ τέκτων, ὁ υἱὸς τῆς Μαρίας καὶ ἀδελφὸς Ἰακώβου καὶ Ἰωσῆτος καὶ Ἰούδα καὶ Σίμωνος; καὶ οὐκ εἰσὶν αἱ ἀδελφαὶ αὐτοῦ ὧδε πρὸς ἡμᾶς; καὶ ἐσκανδαλίζοντο ἐν αὐτῷ.	D		people	Jesus? (deliberative)
33	6 ²⁴ καὶ ἐξελθοῦσα εἶπεν τῇ μητρὶ αὐτῆς· τί αἰτήσωμαι; ἡ δὲ εἶπεν· τὴν κεφαλὴν Ἰωάννου τοῦ βαπτίζοντος.			daughter H	mother
34	6 ³⁷ ὁ δὲ ἀποκριθεὶς εἶπεν αὐτοῖς· δότε αὐτοῖς ὑμεῖς φαγεῖν. καὶ λέγουσιν αὐτῷ· ἀπελθόντες ἀγοράσωμεν δηναρίων διακοσίων ἄρτους καὶ δώσομεν αὐτοῖς φαγεῖν;			disciples	Jesus

35	6 ³⁸ ὁ δὲ λέγει αὐτοῖς· πόσους ἄρτους ἔχετε; ὑπάγετε ἴδετε. καὶ γνόντες λέγουσιν· πέντε, καὶ δύο ἰχθύας.		Jesus	disciples
36	7 ⁵ καὶ ἐπερωτῶσιν αὐτὸν οἱ Φαρισαῖοι καὶ οἱ γραμματεῖς· διὰ τί οὐ περιπατοῦσιν οἱ μαθηταί σου κατὰ τὴν παράδοσιν τῶν πρεσβυτέρων, ἀλλὰ κοιναῖς χερσὶν ἐσθίουσιν τὸν ἄρτον;		Pharisees, scribes	Jesus
37–38	7 ¹⁸ καὶ λέγει αὐτοῖς· οὕτως καὶ ὑμεῖς ἀσύνετοί ἐστε; οὐ νοεῖτε ὅτι πᾶν τὸ ἔξωθεν εἰσπορευόμενον εἰς τὸν ἄνθρωπον οὐ δύναται αὐτὸν κοινῶσαι (see 8,17 and 8,21) ¹⁹ ὅτι οὐκ εἰσπορεύεται αὐτοῦ εἰς τὴν καρδίαν ἀλλ' εἰς τὴν κοιλίαν, καὶ εἰς τὸν ἀφεδρῶνα ἐκπορεύεται, καθαρίζων πάντα τὰ βρώματα;	D	Jesus	disciples
39	8 ⁴ καὶ ἀπεκρίθησαν αὐτῷ οἱ μαθηταὶ αὐτοῦ ὅτι πόθεν τούτους δυνήσεταί τις ὧδε χορτάσαι ἄρτων ἐπ' ἐρημίας;		disciples	Jesus
40	8 ⁵ καὶ ἠρώτα αὐτούς· πόσους ἔχετε ἄρτους; οἱ δὲ εἶπαν ἑπτά.		Jesus	Disciples
41	8 ¹² καὶ ἀναστενάξας τῷ πνεύματι αὐτοῦ λέγει· τί ἡ γενεὰ αὕτη ζητεῖ σημεῖον; ἀμὴν λέγω ὑμῖν, εἰ δοθήσεται τῇ γενεᾷ ταύτῃ σημεῖον.		Jesus	Pharisees?
42–44	8 ¹⁷ καὶ γνοὺς λέγει αὐτοῖς· τί διαλογίζεσθε ὅτι ἄρτους οὐκ ἔχετε; οὔπω νοεῖτε οὐδὲ συνίετε; πεπωρωμένην ἔχετε τὴν καρδίαν ὑμῶν; (see 7,18 and 8,21)	T	Jesus	disciples
45	8 ¹⁸ ὀφθαλμοὺς ἔχοντες οὐ βλέπετε[;] καὶ ὦτα ἔχοντε[;] οὐκ ἀκούετε;	[D]	Jesus	disciples
46–47	καὶ οὐ μνημονεύετε, 8 ¹⁹ ὅτε τοὺς πέντε ἄρτους ἔκλασα εἰς τοὺς πεντακισχιλίους, πόσους κοφίνους κλασμάτων πλήρεις ἤρατε; λέγουσιν αὐτῷ· δώδεκα. 8 ²⁰ ὅτε τοὺς ἑπτὰ εἰς τοὺς τετρακισχιλίους, πόσων σπυρίδων πληρώματα κλασμάτων ἤρατε; καὶ λέγουσιν [αὐτῷ]· ἑπτά.	D	Jesus	disciples

48	8 ^{21} καὶ ἔλεγεν αὐτοῖς· οὔπω συνίετε; (see 7,18 and 8,17)	D	Jesus	disciples
49	8 ^{23} καὶ ἐπιλαβόμενος τῆς χειρὸς τοῦ τυφλοῦ ἐξήνεγκεν αὐτὸν ἔξω τῆς κώμης καὶ πτύσας εἰς τὰ ὄμματα αὐτοῦ, ἐπιθεὶς τὰς χεῖρας αὐτῷ ἐπηρώτα αὐτόν· εἴ τι βλέπεις;		Jesus	blind man
50	8 ^{27} Καὶ ἐξῆλθεν ὁ Ἰησοῦς καὶ οἱ μαθηταὶ αὐτοῦ εἰς τὰς κώμας Καισαρείας τῆς Φιλίππου· καὶ ἐν τῇ ὁδῷ ἐπηρώτα τοὺς μαθητὰς αὐτοῦ λέγων αὐτοῖς· τίνα με λέγουσιν οἱ ἄνθρωποι εἶναι;		Jesus	disciples
51	8 ^{29} καὶ αὐτὸς ἐπηρώτα αὐτούς· ὑμεῖς δὲ τίνα με λέγετε εἶναι; ἀποκριθεὶς ὁ Πέτρος λέγει αὐτῷ· σὺ εἶ ὁ χριστός.		Jesus	disciples
52–53	8 ^{36} τί γὰρ ὠφελεῖ ἄνθρωπον κερδῆσαι τὸν κόσμον ὅλον καὶ ζημιωθῆναι τὴν ψυχὴν αὐτοῦ; 8 ^{37} τί γὰρ δοῖ ἄνθρωπος ἀντάλλαγμα τῆς ψυχῆς αὐτοῦ;	D	Jesus	disciples – crowd
54	9 ^{11} Καὶ ἐπηρώτων αὐτὸν λέγοντες· ὅτι λέγουσιν οἱ γραμματεῖς ὅτι Ἠλίαν δεῖ ἐλθεῖν πρῶτον;		disciples	Jesus
55	9 ^{12} ὁ δὲ ἔφη αὐτοῖς· Ἠλίας μὲν ἐλθὼν πρῶτον ἀποκαθιστάνει πάντα· καὶ πῶς γέγραπται ἐπὶ τὸν υἱὸν τοῦ ἀνθρώπου ἵνα πολλὰ πάθῃ καὶ ἐξουδενηθῇ;		Jesus	disciples
56	9 ^{16} καὶ ἐπηρώτησεν αὐτούς· τί συζητεῖτε πρὸς αὐτούς;		Jesus	crowd
57–58	9 ^{19} ὁ δὲ ἀποκριθεὶς αὐτοῖς λέγει· ὦ γενεὰ ἄπιστος, ἕως πότε πρὸς ὑμᾶς ἔσομαι; ἕως πότε ἀνέξομαι ὑμῶν; φέρετε αὐτὸν πρός με.	D	Jesus	disciples – crowd
59	9 ^{21} καὶ ἐπηρώτησεν τὸν πατέρα αὐτοῦ· πόσος χρόνος ἐστὶν ὡς τοῦτο γέγονεν αὐτῷ; ὁ δὲ εἶπεν· ἐκ παιδιόθεν.		Jesus	father of the boy
60	9 ^{28} Καὶ εἰσελθόντος αὐτοῦ εἰς οἶκον οἱ μαθηταὶ αὐτοῦ κατ' ἰδίαν ἐπηρώτων αὐτόν· ὅτι ἡμεῖς οὐκ ἠδυνήθημεν ἐκβαλεῖν αὐτό;		disciples	Jesus

61	9 ³³ Καὶ ἦλθον εἰς Καφαρναούμ. Καὶ ἐν τῇ οἰκίᾳ γενόμενος ἐπηρώτα αὐτούς· τί ἐν τῇ ὁδῷ διελογίζεσθε;	Jesus	disciples
62	9 ⁵⁰ καλὸν τὸ ἅλας· ἐὰν δὲ τὸ ἅλας ἄναλον γένηται, ἐν τίνι αὐτὸ ἀρτύσετε; ἔχετε ἐν ἑαυτοῖς ἅλα καὶ εἰρηνεύετε ἐν ἀλλήλοις.	Jesus	disciples
63	10 ³ ὁ δὲ ἀποκριθεὶς εἶπεν αὐτοῖς· τί ὑμῖν ἐνετείλατο Μωϋσῆς;	Jesus	Pharisees?
64	10 ¹⁷ Καὶ ἐκπορευομένου αὐτοῦ εἰς ὁδὸν προσδραμὼν εἷς καὶ γονυπετήσας αὐτὸν ἐπηρώτα αὐτόν· διδάσκαλε ἀγαθέ, τί ποιήσω ἵνα ζωὴν αἰώνιον κληρονομήσω;	rich man	Jesus
65	10 ¹⁸ ὁ δὲ Ἰησοῦς εἶπεν αὐτῷ· τί με λέγεις ἀγαθόν; οὐδεὶς ἀγαθὸς εἰ μὴ εἷς ὁ θεός.	Jesus	rich man
66	10 ²⁶ οἱ δὲ περισσῶς ἐξεπλήσσοντο λέγοντες πρὸς ἑαυτούς· καὶ τίς δύναται σωθῆναι;	disciples	Jesus
67	10 ³⁶ ὁ δὲ εἶπεν αὐτοῖς· τί θέλετέ [με] ποιήσω ὑμῖν; (see 10,51)	Jesus	James and John
68	10 ³⁸ ὁ δὲ Ἰησοῦς εἶπεν αὐτοῖς· οὐκ οἴδατε τί αἰτεῖσθε. δύνασθε πιεῖν τὸ ποτήριον ὃ ἐγὼ πίνω ἢ τὸ βάπτισμα ὃ ἐγὼ βαπτίζομαι βαπτισθῆναι;	Jesus	James and John
69	10 ⁵¹ καὶ ἀποκριθεὶς αὐτῷ ὁ Ἰησοῦς εἶπεν· τί σοι θέλεις ποιήσω; ὁ δὲ τυφλὸς εἶπεν αὐτῷ· ραββουνί, ἵνα ἀναβλέψω. (see 10,36)	Jesus	blind man
70	11 ³ καὶ ἐάν τις ὑμῖν εἴπῃ· τί ποιεῖτε τοῦτο; εἴπατε· ὁ κύριος αὐτοῦ χρείαν ἔχει, καὶ εὐθὺς αὐτὸν ἀποστέλλει πάλιν ὧδε.	Jesus	(monologue)
71	11 ⁵ καί τινες τῶν ἐκεῖ ἑστηκότων ἔλεγον αὐτοῖς· τί ποιεῖτε λύοντες τὸν πῶλον;	people	disciples
72	11 ¹⁷ καὶ ἐδίδασκεν καὶ ἔλεγεν αὐτοῖς· οὐ γέγραπται ὅτι ὁ οἶκός μου οἶκος προσευχῆς κληθήσεται πᾶσιν τοῖς ἔθνεσιν; ὑμεῖς δὲ πεποιήκατε αὐτὸν σπήλαιον λῃστῶν.	Jesus	(bystanders?)

QUESTIONS IN THE GOSPEL OF MARK

73–74	11 ²⁸ καὶ ἔλεγον αὐτῷ· ἐν ποίᾳ ἐξουσίᾳ ταῦτα ποιεῖς; ἢ τίς σοι ἔδωκεν τὴν ἐξουσίαν ταύτην ἵνα ταῦτα ποιῇς;		authorities	Jesus
75	11 ³⁰ τὸ βάπτισμα τὸ Ἰωάννου ἐξ οὐρανοῦ ἦν ἢ ἐξ ἀνθρώπων; ἀποκρίθητέ μοι.		Jesus	authorities
76	11 ³¹ καὶ διελογίζοντο πρὸς ἑαυτοὺς λέγοντες· ἐὰν εἴπωμεν· ἐξ οὐρανοῦ, ἐρεῖ· διὰ τί [οὖν] οὐκ ἐπιστεύσατε αὐτῷ;		authorities	(deliberative)
77	11 ³² ἀλλὰ εἴπωμεν· ἐξ ἀνθρώπων; - ἐφοβοῦντο τὸν ὄχλον· ἅπαντες γὰρ εἶχον τὸν Ἰωάννην ὄντως ὅτι προφήτης ἦν.		authorities	(deliberative)
78	12 ⁹ τί [οὖν] ποιήσει ὁ κύριος τοῦ ἀμπελῶνος; ἐλεύσεται καὶ ἀπολέσει τοὺς γεωργούς καὶ δώσει τὸν ἀμπελῶνα ἄλλοις.		Jesus	(deliberative)
79	12 ¹¹ παρὰ κυρίου ἐγένετο αὕτη καὶ ἔστιν θαυμαστὴ ἐν ὀφθαλμοῖς ἡμῶν;		Jesus	authorities
80–81	12 ¹⁴ καὶ ἐλθόντες λέγουσιν αὐτῷ· διδάσκαλε, οἴδαμεν ὅτι ἀληθὴς εἶ καὶ οὐ μέλει σοι περὶ οὐδενός· οὐ γὰρ βλέπεις εἰς πρόσωπον ἀνθρώπων, ἀλλ' ἐπ' ἀληθείας τὴν ὁδὸν τοῦ θεοῦ διδάσκεις· ἔξεστιν δοῦναι κῆνσον Καίσαρι ἢ οὔ; δῶμεν ἢ μὴ δῶμεν;	D	Pharisees – Herodians	Jesus
82	12 ¹⁵ ὁ δὲ εἰδὼς αὐτῶν τὴν ὑπόκρισιν εἶπεν αὐτοῖς· τί με πειράζετε; φέρετέ μοι δηνάριον ἵνα ἴδω.		Jesus	Pharisees – Herodians
83	12 ¹⁶ οἱ δὲ ἤνεγκαν. καὶ λέγει αὐτοῖς· τίνος ἡ εἰκὼν αὕτη καὶ ἡ ἐπιγραφή; οἱ δὲ εἶπαν αὐτῷ· Καίσαρος.		Jesus	Pharisees – Herodians
84	12 ²³ ἐν τῇ ἀναστάσει [ὅταν ἀναστῶσιν] τίνος αὐτῶν ἔσται γυνή; οἱ γὰρ ἑπτὰ ἔσχον αὐτὴν γυναῖκα.		Sadducees	Jesus
85–86	12 ²⁴ ἔφη αὐτοῖς ὁ Ἰησοῦς· οὐ διὰ τοῦτο πλανᾶσθε μὴ εἰδότες τὰς γραφάς μηδὲ τὴν δύναμιν τοῦ θεοῦ; 12 ²⁶ περὶ δὲ τῶν νεκρῶν ὅτι ἐγείρονται οὐκ ἀνέγνωτε ἐν τῇ βίβλῳ Μωϋσέως ἐπὶ τοῦ βάτου πῶς εἶπεν αὐτῷ ὁ θεὸς λέγων· ἐγὼ ὁ θεὸς Ἀβραὰμ καὶ [ὁ] θεὸς Ἰσαὰκ καὶ [ὁ] θεὸς Ἰακώβ;	D	Jesus	Sadducees

87	12 ²⁸ Καὶ προσελθὼν εἷς τῶν γραμματέων ἀκούσας αὐτῶν συζητούντων, ἰδὼν ὅτι καλῶς ἀπεκρίθη αὐτοῖς ἐπηρώτησεν αὐτόν· ποία ἐστὶν ἐντολὴ πρώτη πάντων;		one of the scribes	Jesus
88	12 ³⁵ Καὶ ἀποκριθεὶς ὁ Ἰησοῦς ἔλεγεν διδάσκων ἐν τῷ ἱερῷ· πῶς λέγουσιν οἱ γραμματεῖς ὅτι ὁ χριστός ἐστιν υἱὸς Δαυίδ ἐστιν;		Jesus	crowd in temple
89	12 ³⁷ αὐτὸς Δαυὶδ λέγει αὐτὸν κύριον, καὶ πόθεν αὐτοῦ ἐστιν υἱός; Καὶ [ὁ] πολὺς ὄχλος ἤκουεν αὐτοῦ ἡδέως.		Jesus	crowd in temple
90	13 ² καὶ ὁ Ἰησοῦς εἶπεν αὐτῷ· βλέπεις ταύτας τὰς μεγάλας οἰκοδομάς; οὐ μὴ ἀφεθῇ ὧδε λίθος ἐπὶ λίθον ὃς οὐ μὴ καταλυθῇ.		Jesus	one of the disciples
91	13 ⁴ εἰπὸν ἡμῖν, πότε ταῦτα ἔσται καὶ τί τὸ σημεῖον ὅταν μέλλῃ ταῦτα συντελεῖσθαι πάντα;	D	4 disciples	Jesus
92	14 ⁴ ἦσαν δέ τινες ἀγανακτοῦντες πρὸς ἑαυτούς· εἰς τί ἡ ἀπώλεια αὕτη τοῦ μύρου γέγονεν;		«people»	(deliberative)
93	14 ⁶ ὁ δὲ Ἰησοῦς εἶπεν· ἄφετε αὐτήν· τί αὐτῇ κόπους παρέχετε; καλὸν ἔργον ἠργάσατο ἐν ἐμοί.		Jesus	«people»
94	14 ¹² Καὶ τῇ πρώτῃ ἡμέρᾳ τῶν ἀζύμων, ὅτε τὸ πάσχα ἔθυον, λέγουσιν αὐτῷ οἱ μαθηταὶ αὐτοῦ· ποῦ θέλεις ἀπελθόντες ἑτοιμάσωμεν ἵνα φάγῃς τὸ πάσχα;		disciples	Jesus
95	14 ¹⁴ καὶ ὅπου ἐὰν εἰσέλθῃ εἴπατε τῷ οἰκοδεσπότῃ ὅτι ὁ διδάσκαλος λέγει· ποῦ ἐστιν τὸ κατάλυμά μου ὅπου τὸ πάσχα μετὰ τῶν μαθητῶν μου φάγω;		disciples (Jesus in story)	(monologue)
96	14 ¹⁹ ἤρξαντο λυπεῖσθαι καὶ λέγειν αὐτῷ εἷς κατὰ εἷς· μήτι ἐγώ;		disciples one by one	Jesus
97–98	14 ³⁷ καὶ ἔρχεται καὶ εὑρίσκει αὐτοὺς καθεύδοντας, καὶ λέγει τῷ Πέτρῳ· Σίμων, καθεύδεις; οὐκ ἴσχυσας μίαν ὥραν γρηγορῆσαι;	D	Jesus	Simon (disciple)

99	14 ⁴⁸ Καὶ ἀποκριθεὶς ὁ Ἰησοῦς εἶπεν αὐτοῖς· ὡς ἐπὶ λῃστὴν ἐξήλθατε μετὰ μαχαιρῶν καὶ ξύλων συλλαβεῖν με;		Jesus	authorities – Judas
100	14 ⁶⁰ καὶ ἀναστὰς ὁ ἀρχιερεὺς εἰς μέσον ἐπηρώτησεν τὸν Ἰησοῦν λέγων· οὐκ ἀποκρίνῃ οὐδὲν[·] τί οὗτοί σου καταμαρτυροῦσιν;	[D]	highpriest	Jesus
101	14 ⁶¹ ὁ δὲ ἐσιώπα καὶ οὐκ ἀπεκρίνατο οὐδέν. πάλιν ὁ ἀρχιερεὺς ἐπηρώτα αὐτὸν καὶ λέγει αὐτῷ· σὺ εἶ ὁ χριστὸς ὁ υἱὸς τοῦ εὐλογητοῦ;		highpriest	Jesus
102	14 ⁶³ ὁ δὲ ἀρχιερεὺς διαρρήξας τοὺς χιτῶνας αὐτοῦ λέγει· τί ἔτι χρείαν ἔχομεν μαρτύρων;	D with v. 64	highpriest	authorities
103	14 ⁶⁴ ἠκούσατε τῆς βλασφημίας· τί ὑμῖν φαίνεται; οἱ δὲ πάντες κατέκριναν αὐτὸν ἔνοχον εἶναι θανάτου.		highpriest	authorities
104	15 ² Καὶ ἐπηρώτησεν αὐτὸν ὁ Πιλᾶτος· σὺ εἶ ὁ βασιλεὺς τῶν Ἰουδαίων; ὁ δὲ ἀποκριθεὶς αὐτῷ λέγει· σὺ λέγεις.		Pilate	Jesus
105	15 ⁴ ὁ δὲ Πιλᾶτος πάλιν ἐπηρώτα αὐτὸν λέγων· οὐκ ἀποκρίνῃ οὐδέν; ἴδε πόσα σου κατηγοροῦσιν.		Pilate	Jesus
106	15 ⁹ ὁ δὲ Πιλᾶτος ἀπεκρίθη αὐτοῖς λέγων· θέλετε ἀπολύσω ὑμῖν τὸν βασιλέα τῶν Ἰουδαίων;		Pilate	crowd
107	15 ¹² ὁ δὲ Πιλᾶτος πάλιν ἀποκριθεὶς ἔλεγεν αὐτοῖς· τί οὖν [θέλετε] ποιήσω [ὃν λέγετε] τὸν βασιλέα τῶν Ἰουδαίων;		Pilate	crowd
108	15 ¹⁴ ὁ δὲ Πιλᾶτος ἔλεγεν αὐτοῖς· τί γὰρ ἐποίησεν κακόν; οἱ δὲ περισσῶς ἔκραξαν· σταύρωσον αὐτόν.		Pilate	crowd
109–110	15 ³⁴ καὶ τῇ ἐνάτῃ ὥρᾳ ἐβόησεν ὁ Ἰησοῦς φωνῇ μεγάλῃ· ελωι ελωι λεμα σαβαχθανι; ὅ ἐστιν μεθερμηνευόμενον· ὁ θεός μου ὁ θεός μου, εἰς τί ἐγκατέλιπές με;	D	Jesus / narator	God
111	16 ³ καὶ ἔλεγον πρὸς ἑαυτάς· τίς ἀποκυλίσει ἡμῖν τὸν λίθον ἐκ τῆς θύρας τοῦ μνημείου;		women	(deliberative)

COUNTER-QUESTIONS IN THE GOSPEL OF LUKE

An Assessment[1]

Bart J. KOET
Tilburg University

1. Introduction

Socrates and Jesus are often compared.[2] Most of the time this comparison deals with the similarities between their (sham) trial, their violent death and the accusation that their teachings were against the religious practices of their society. However, less attention has been paid to their similar teaching styles. It is common knowledge that Socrates teaches by asking questions. However, less attention is given to the fact that according to all the Gospels, Jesus, like Socrates, also frequently uses questioning as a strategy for learning and teaching.[3] In other words, although Jesus is primarily a teacher, through his questions, he is, in a certain sense, also a learner, as rabbis are in the later Rabbinic literature.[4] How essential questions are for both Socrates and Jesus is manifested by the fact that

---

[1] Paper presented at a symposium on "Questions in Religious Authoritative Texts," on the occasion of the Tenth Anniversary of the RSCS Research Institute, Louvain-la-Neuve, 11 September 2019 and at the Luke-Acts Society (the Netherlands/Belgium). Thanks are due to the participants of both colloquia for their constructive comments. I also thank my students Rieks Hekman and Joachim Oude Vrielink for their comments. Finally, I have also greatly benefited from the comments of Dr. Douglas Estes. Greek references are taken from NA[28].

[2] See for example the classic study by I.F. Stone, *The Trial of Socrates* (New York: Anchor Books Double Day, 1988), 3.

[3] R. Zimmermann, "Fragen bei Sokrates und Jesus: Wege des Verstehens – Initiale des Weiterfragens," in: Heike Lindner (Ed.), *Schülerfragen im (Religions-)Unterricht: Ein notwendiger Bildungsauftrag heute* (Neukirchen-Vluyn: Neukirchener Theologie, 2011), 33–59.

[4] D. Estes, *Questions and Rhetoric in the Greek New Testament: An Essential Reference Resource for Exegesis* (Grand Rapids: Zondervan, 2017), 20 argues that it is hard to answer the question what a question is. He gives as working definition: 'A question is any utterance with interrogative force that asks not says, that always applies some rhetorical effect, and that invites a reply of some sort'.

they both continue to ask questions during their trial.[5] Even in that situation they remain faithful to their method of stimulating other people to think by their questions. The fact that Jesus so often asks questions in the Gospels has up until now been too often overlooked.[6] In this article I will start to examine the way Jesus asks questions in more detail in only one Gospel, that of Luke, but because of the limitations of this article I will concentrate on only one specific category of questions, counter-questions: those questions one asks in response to the questions one is asked.

2. Questions in the New Testament? Previous research

Jesus' questioning mode of teaching in all the Gospels has rarely been discussed and has rarely been subjected to a systematic examination.[7] In one of these rare examples, a layman booklet by Martin Copenhaver, the writer claims that Jesus is not the answer, but the question.[8] Copenhaver says that Jesus asks 307 questions in the New Testament and gives only eight answers.[9] Douglas Estes, in his seminal scholarly study of the phenomenon of questions in the NT, argues that 15 percent of the NT consists of questions.[10] His basic assumption is that scholars have overlooked the importance of questions in their study of the New Testament. Questions are too often treated as assumptions, or even as statements and propositions. Overlooking the dynamics of questions frequently comes at

---

[5] For only one example in Socrates' trial, see *Apol.* 12. For Jesus' trial, see only John 17:21, 23, 34.

[6] Estes, *Questions and Rhetoric*, 15.

[7] For example, R. Riesner, *Jesus als Lehrer: Eine Untersuchung zum Ursprung der Evangelien-Überlieferung* (WUNT 7; Tübingen: Mohr, 1981 [²1984, erweitert: ³1988]) here and there points out the importance of asking questions in Jesus' role as a teacher in the context of Jewish teaching traditions. He (167) refers to Ben Sira who uses questions in his didactics. Riesner (395–396) also refers to the fact that there are prophetic parallels to emphatic questions like τίς ἐξ ὑμῶν (Matt 7:9).

[8] M.B. Copenhaver, *Jesus Is the Question: The 307 Questions Jesus Asked and the 3 He Answered* (Nashville: Abingdon Press, 2014), XVIII, even argues that Jesus seems to prefer to ask questions rather than to provide direct answers.

[9] Copenhaver, *Jesus Is the Question,* XVIII. Copenhaver refers to J. Dear, *The Questions of Jesus: Challenging Ourselves to Discover Life's Great Answers* (New York: Doubleday, 2004), xxii, who argues that in the four Gospels Jesus asks 307 different questions, while he is only asked 183 questions. Dear even suggests that Jesus answers only 3 of these questions. Dear's book is a meritorious and original meditation book. Although Copenhaver uses the number three in the title of his booklet, according to his count, Jesus directly answers eight of the questions he is asked (see XVIII of the introduction of his book).

[10] Estes, *Questions and Rhetoric*, 24. By the way, the Koran seems to be even more composed of questions, around 20 percent.

the expense of understanding the dynamics of those texts in the NT in which questions play a (major) role. Estes categorizes different features of question-asking, and he distinguishes four formations of questions driven by syntax.[11] In addition to these categorizations he also gives a list of questions driven by semantics.[12] An important category which Estes also describes are the questions driven by pragmatics.[13]

Estes earlier wrote a book about questions in the Gospel of John and this is one of the few studies that try to systematically tackle the phenomenon of asking questions in one, specific New Testament book.[14] A thorough study of the questions in the other Gospels still seems to be lacking, although there are some articles that deal with questions in a particular passage.[15] An example of this is an article by Deborah Thompson Prince about rhetorical questions in Luke 24.[16] There are at least two articles that have given a first impetus to an assessment of Luke's use of questions throughout the entire Gospel. The first one is that of Paul Elbert, who focuses on – what he describes as – two-clauses questions: 'that is, they have a dual focus determined either by two verbal expressions or two distinct concepts.'[17] He states that there are 152 questions in the third Gospel, of which he typifies sixty-five as two-clauses questions.[18] His main thesis is that 'Luke fully realized that appropriately composed narrative-rhetorical questions can have a direct bearing on the comprehension of future words that are to be recorded after them.'[19] Elbert's article is more focused on the place of questions in Luke-Acts than on the rhetorical function of questions in that corpus.

---

[11] Variable questions, polar questions, alternative questions and set questions: see Estes, *Questions and Rhetoric*, 93–146
[12] Estes, *Questions and Rhetoric*, 147–272.
[13] Estes, *Questions and Rhetoric*, 273–330.
[14] D. Estes, *The Questions of Jesus in John: Logic, Rhetoric and Persuasive Discourse* (BibInt 115; Leiden: Brill, 2012).
[15] P. Elbert, "An Observation on Luke's Composition and Narrative Style of Questions," *CBQ* 66 (2004): 98–109, here 99 notices that at the time of the writing of his article he does not know of any literature that explicitly deals with Luke's use of questions!
[16] D. Thompson Prince, ""Why Do You Seek the Living among the Dead?" Rhetorical Questions in the Lukan Resurrection Narrative," *JBL* 135 (2016): 123–139.
[17] Elbert, "An Observation on Luke's Composition," 100.
[18] Elbert, "An Observation on Luke's Composition," 100 gives as example Luke 8:25b: 'Who then is this man, that he commands even the winds and the water and they obey him.' Elbert argues that the primary concern of the question is to get an answer about Jesus' identity. The second part of the question makes a topical connection with 8:24 where it is told that Jesus rebukes the wind and the water and that they cease.
[19] Elbert, "An Observation on Luke's Composition," 104.

In his article, Christoph Müller distinguishes three kinds of questions in the Gospel of Luke.[20] The first species is the 'decision question' (*Entscheidungsfrage*). As examples Müller mentions Luke 14:3; 20:22; 22:49.[21] A second kind of question is according to Müller the 'supplementary question' (*Ergänzungsfrage*). However, he does not give any examples of this. The third type of question is the rhetorical question. He mentions as examples: 6:39; 7:24, 25; 11:11, 12; 13:2, 4; 14:5, 28, 31; 17:9; 18:7; 22:27; 23:39. Müller argues that questions are a means of communication and that they are often the beginning of a conversation.[22] He notes that the biographical nature of a Gospel has as a consequence, that there are quite a few apophtegms and *chreias*. In such a *chreia* one can often find questions and these questions are the triggers for the subsequent biographical episode. Müller claims that Luke has further elaborated on the motif of questions and answers.[23] He observes that in Luke-Acts Jesus often answers a question with a counter-question. He gives a number of examples in a footnote, but does not elaborate on them.

This review of the limited literature on questions in the New Testament and especially on those in the Gospel of Luke shows that the task to make a thorough inventory and evaluation of all the questions in that Gospel still lies open.[24] Considering the amount of questions involved, for a first assessment it is a good idea to limit ourselves. To mark out a responsible limitation, we will first discuss a special form of questioning: the counter-question.

3. Question and counter-question

Martin Leutzsch points out in a short, but important article that one way of asking questions has been even less studied than other ways of asking questions: counter-questions ('Gegenfrage').[25] In this pattern, the one who

---

[20] C.G. Müller, "Leserorientierte Fragen im Erzählwerk des Lukas," *TGl* 93 (2003): 28–47.
[21] See for this classification, Müller, "Leserorientierte Fragen," 30.
[22] Müller, "Leserorientierte Fragen," 30.
[23] Müller, "Leserorientierte Fragen," 31.
[24] We saw above that Elbert, "An Observation on Luke's Composition," 100, counts 152 questions in Luke's Gospel! Estes, *Questions and Rhetoric*, 26, counts 154 in the Nestle Aland[28]. The difference in number is related to the fact that some statements in the Gospel can be interpreted as statements and/or as questions. For a list of possible questions in the English translation of Luke, see Dear, *The Questions of Jesus*, 298–302.
[25] Cf. M. Leutzsch, "»?« – »?« Biblische Theologie der Gegenfrage," in: K. Schiffner (Ed.), *Fragen wider die Antworten: Festschrift Jürgen Ebach* (Gütersloh: Gütersloher Verlagshaus, 2010), 405–417.

has received a question and who is expected to give an answer, reacts to the question by posing a question. Leutzsch points out that precisely these kinds of questions in biblical texts are important and that they are even central to biblical theology! The bulk of his article is a commentary on Mark 10:17–19. He sketches how a man walks towards Jesus, runs towards him and falls to his knees and asks a question: 'Good Master, what shall I do that I may inherit eternal life?' (King James Version). Leutzsch argues that this description typifies the man as someone who is a rather dependent person and who puts his fate into the hands of Jesus. He seems to be asking for healing rather than for a wise lesson. With Jesus' counter-question that only deals with the way he is addressed by the man (the meaning of 'good') and that therefore does not give an answer to the man's question, Jesus stimulates the man to think. Leutzsch concludes that the counter-question in Mark 10:18 is a professional expression of a teacher in a learning situation. As a didactic tool, the counter-question wants to problematize the problem initiated by the question.[26]

Leutzsch's remarks are in line with those of Estes, but where Leutzsch seems to assume that it is clear what a 'Gegenfrage' is, Estes categorizes the phenomenon of a question as an answer to an earlier question (a 'counter-question'), in the context of what he calls Second-Turn Questions. In his section on these questions he describes such a question as 'any question asked by the second speaker within the second utterance of a dialogue sequence.'[27] He argues that speakers can use Second-Turn Questions as a reaction to any type of First-Turn Utterance, but that they are more dramatic used after First-Turn Questions.[28] Estes makes some clear distinctions in these Second-Turn Questions, which we cannot discuss in detail here.[29] However, we have to mention that the different types also have different relationships with the First-Turn Question and that their rhetorical effects are also diverse. I will give just two examples of Second-Turn Questions here: the Opposing-Turn Question and the Echo Question. Estes describes Opposing-Turn Questions as those 'asked in response to a question asked in the preceding dialogue turn.'[30] He mentions that these questions

---

[26] Leutzsch, "»?« – »?«," 412.
[27] Estes, *Questions and Rhetoric*, 288–311, here 288.
[28] Estes, *Questions and Rhetoric*, 288.
[29] For a chart of the six types of Second-Turn Questions, see Estes, *Questions and Rhetoric*, 289–290.
[30] Estes, *Questions and Rhetoric*, 289; Estes sketches the formation and the rhetorical effects of Opposing-Turn Questions in *Questions and Rhetoric*, 289–293.

have to be loosely related to the question it is opposing and that they tend to be short and blunt.[31] He argues that the rhetorical effect can be quite forceful and even suggests that the person who uses an Opposing-Turn Question violates the rules of a dialogue.[32] A quite specific form of an Opposing-Turn Question is an Echo Question. Such a question has a matching relation with the First-Turn Question, and an Echo Question is somehow an imitation or an echo of the first question.[33] The most obvious rhetorical effect of an Echo Question is that it raises questions about the original question.[34]

Leutzsch claims that it is especially in the Gospel of Mark that Jesus is characterized as someone who asks counter-questions.[35] When he briefly discusses the other Gospels, however, he cites a few examples, which indicate that Luke demonstrates in his own material, and in his own way, that counter-questions are an important part of Jesus' learning strategies.[36] Because counter-questions are a special form of asking questions and because

---

[31] Estes, *Questions and Rhetoric*, 290.

[32] Estes, *Questions and Rhetoric*, 289.

[33] For a description of Echo Questions, *Questions and Rhetoric*, 301–304.

[34] The distinction between the different types of questions is not watertight. In his discussion of Matt 15:2-3 Estes shows that the boundaries between the Opposing-Turn Question and the Echo Question are fluid: Estes, *Questions and Rhetoric*, 293. The boundaries are fluid, because they are rhetorical creatures!

[35] Leutzsch, "»?« – »?«," 413–414: There are six passages where Mark has a counter-question and the parallel passage in Luke has one too: besides his prime example 1) 10:17–19 (parallel to Luke 18:18–19), Leutzsch mentions 2) the healing of the paralytic (Mark 2:1–12; where Jesus asks two questions in 2:8–9 in response to 2:7; see the parallel to Luke 5:17–26); 3) the question about fasting (Mark 2:18–21, with a question of Jesus in 2:19 as response to 2:18; parallel to Luke 5:33–39); 4) Jesus' disciples plucking grain on the Sabbath (Mark 2:23–28 with Jesus' long question in 2:25 as response to 2:24; parallel to Luke 6:1–5); 5) the questions about Jesus' authority (Mark 11:27–33 with the question in 11:29 in response to 11:28; parallel to Luke 20:1–8; here we see that Jesus is presented as somebody who reflects about his own way of dealing with questions; he explicitly declares that he will ask them a question (11:29); in Luke 20:3 Luke explicitly introduces Jesus' counter-question as a response to the question of 20:2); and 6) the question about paying tribute to Caesar (Mark 12:13–17 with Jesus' question in 12:15 as a response to 12:14; parallel to Luke 20:20–26 where 20:24 is a response to 20:22).

Note: In some Lukan parallels to passages where one can find counter-questions in Mark, the pattern question-counter-question disappears. While in Mark 2:18 Jesus is questioned about his attitude towards fasting, the Pharisees and their *grammatikoi* (see Luke 5:30; basic level teachers) in Luke 5:33 do not ask a question but postulate that Jesus' disciples do not fast. Jesus responds to this statement with a question, but that is no longer a counter-question. In the discussion about divorce in Mark 10:2–12, Jesus' counter-question in 10:12b is a response to the question in 10:1a; but there is no parallel in Luke. Compare also Mark 12:24 with Luke 20:34. Mark 8:10–11 is a possible case of a counter-question, but here there is also no parallel in Luke.

[36] Leutzsch, "»?« – »?«," 415–416.

there are fewer of them, an inquiry into only those kinds of questions is a responsible limitation for an inquiry into the questions in that Gospel.

However, if we are looking for the way in which counter-questions are asked in Luke's Gospel, it is a good idea to also take into account a different classification: in addition to a division into possible types of questions in the Gospel, another division is also relevant. After all, questions in the Gospel of Luke can also be divided into at least three categories: questions that we also find in the material that Luke has in common with Mark and Matthew, questions that can also be found in Q, the material that Matthew and Luke have in common in general, and finally questions in Luke's *Sondergut*. However, also this classification is not entirely satisfactory because there are also questions that can be found in the Q material in the Gospel of Luke and not in the Gospel of Matthew.[37] When researching the proper role of questions in the work of Luke, keeping this differentiation in view can be of aid in clarifying this proper role and thus we will assess the counter-questions in Luke using different categories, starting with those counter-questions that Luke has in common with the other synoptics.

4. Counter-questions in Luke with parallels in Mark

Looking at the pericopes that Luke shares with Mark, we can see that in most passages of Mark where there is a question followed up by a counter-question, we can also find the same in the parallel in Luke's Gospel.[38] In the following we will assess these passages.

Leutzsch discusses Mark 10:17–22 most extensively. Just as in this passage (see also the parallel in Matthew 19:16–22), in Luke 18:18–23 Jesus answers a question with a counter-question, but this counter-question will be the steppingstone for Jesus' answer to the question:

> *Question: 18:18 And a certain superior asked him, saying: Good Master, what shall I do to inherit eternal life?*
> *Counter-question: 18:19 And Jesus said to him: Why do you call me good? None is good, save one, that is, God.*[39]

---

[37] M. Goulder, *Luke: A New Paradigm* (Vol. 1, JSNTSup 20; Sheffield: JSOT Press, 1989), 86–128 describes the Lukan style. He notes (90) three cases where in Luke there is a question where in the parallel with Matthew there is none: Luke 12:41; 13:23 and 17:20. The last reference is not so convincing, while there is nearly no parallel in Matthew. However, also in Luke 3:10–14 we can find several questions, where the parallel material in Mark and/or Matthew has no questions. If we compare the performance of John the Baptist in the three synoptics, Luke is the only one to have the crowd ask John questions.
[38] For the parallels, see footnote 35 above.
[39] For this passage in Mark, see Leutzsch, "»?« – »?«," 406–411.

Whereas in Mark, according to Leutzsch, the man is a supplicant who, while he makes a *proskunesis* for Jesus, almost begging for some kind of healing instead of advice to live well, in the Gospel of Luke it is a man from the elite (τις ἄρχων) who, like in Mark, addresses Jesus as a good teacher and asks quite/nearly objectively what he must do to inherit eternal life (18:18). Jesus' counter-question is his reaction to the use of the word 'good' in the man's way of addressing him.[40] The counter-question is not the end of Jesus' reaction (18:19a), because he is going to refute this form of address (18:19b). Only God is good! In the next verses Jesus answers the man's question by referring to the commandments. When the man says he has kept the commandments since his youth (18:21), Jesus says he must sell all his possessions and give them to the poor (18:22). The man then becomes sad, both in Mark 10:22 and in Luke 18:23.

The personal relationship that seems to arise in the passage of Mark (the man addresses Jesus again as 'master' [διδάσκαλε 10:20] and it is said of Jesus that he looks at the man and loves him [Ο δὲ Ἰησοῦς ἐμβλέψας αὐτῷ ἠγάπησεν αὐτὸν 10:21]) clearly plays a less important role in Luke's work. There is another important difference between the Markan version and that of Luke. Because in Luke 18:23 it is not explicitly said that the man, contrary to Mark 10:22, leaves the place where Jesus is, he, possibly being a rich person, becomes one of the people who will be addressed in the following verses. Jesus responds to the sadness of the man (18:24; cf. Mark 10:22, where the man is also depicted as sad and only then is it disclosed that the man has many possessions) by speaking about the difficulty for the rich in entering the Kingdom (18:24–27). The counter-question (18:19) in this passage is more a kind of objection (to the way the man addressed Jesus) than a real question that stimulates the other to reflect.[41]

There are three other passages in which we can find the pattern question – counter-question in Mark as well as in Luke.

Luke 6:1–5 (parallels: Mark 2:23–28 and Matthew 12:1–8) is an example of a counter-question as the first step of an answer to questioners. When one Sabbath Jesus was going through the grainfields, his disciples began to pick some heads of grain, rub them in their hands and eat the kernels. Some of the Pharisees ask them, why they are doing something that would be against the Law: 'Why are you doing what is

---

[40] Cf. Estes, *Questions and Rhetoric*, 279, who describes the counter-question in Mark 10:18 as a rebuttal.

[41] Jesus' question is probably an expository question, see Estes, *Questions and Rhetoric*, 280. The question introduces the topic and then Jesus can explain his idea about God.

unlawful on the Sabbath?' It is the teacher and not the disciples, who reacts. His reaction is in Luke 6:3 and is described as an answer (ἀποκριθεὶς πρὸς αὐτοὺς εἶπεν; Mark 2:25 does not describe Jesus' reaction as an answer), but it is in fact a quite long question: 'Have you not (or not even) read what David did when he and his companions were hungry?' After this, Jesus describes, as an element of that question, what David did and this becomes the basis of his argument that 'The Son of Man is Lord of the Sabbath.'[42] Fitzmyer argues that the Lukan version is more ironical than the Markan one. Of course, this is related to the determination of what kind of question this question is. The question is clearly a polar question ('answer is yes or no') but is it also a rhetorical question? It can also be a confirmation question: of course they did! Probably different interpretations are possible. No matter how one regards the exact function of this question, one thing is clear. The counter-question is an introduction to a story taken from a biblical tradition, which is a shared source, and which can be seen as an authority both by the questioners and by Jesus. Using a counter-question in combination with a reference to the written example of David, Jesus takes the lead in the conversation and puts the questioners to work. Luke 20:1–8 (see Mark 11:17–33 and Matthew 21:23–27) is an example of a passage where, like in Mark, the counter-question is the only reaction to an earlier question:

> [2] *'Tell us by what authority you are doing these things,'* they said. *'Who gave you this authority?'* [3] *Answering, he said* (ἀποκριθεὶς εἶπεν), *'I will also ask you a word. Tell me:* [4] *John's baptism, was it from heaven, or of human origin?'*

Jewish leaders put two questions to Jesus about his authority and he answers them with a counter-question. In this passage the counter-question is not related to any explanation, but is only a question about two alternatives, and thus the original questioners have to start thinking for themselves. After the questioners have discussed matters among themselves, they say to Jesus that they do not know. The passage is here, as

---

[42] This passage is one of the examples from the New Testament where Jesus asks a question and then combines it with narrative elements: in this passage it is a reference to a passage from the Old Testament about what King David did (1 Sam 21:1–6); elsewhere Jesus tells a parable. For a first attempt at an assessment of the relationship between question and parable, see Bart J. Koet, "An Uncomfortable Story from the New Testament: About Making Friends with the Mammon (Luke 16:1–13)," in Myriam G.P. Klinker-De Klerck, Arco den Heijer, and Jermo van Nes (Eds.), *Troubling Texts in the New Testament: Essays in Honour of Rob van Houwelingen* (CBET 113; Leuven: Peeters, 2022), 55-64.

well as in Mark, an example of how a person who asks a counter-question can take the initiative. In this case, Jesus' question (which, as we indicated in the quotation above, is characterized in 20:3 as an answer; see Matthew 21:24) forces the questioners to consider possible answers not only to the dilemma which Jesus sketches by his question, but also to their own question. In Luke 20:5–6 // Mark 11:31–33 we can hear these considerations and reflections. Interesting about their deliberations is that they realize that if they answer that John the Baptist got his authority from heaven (thus, from God), Jesus will ask a next question: Why did you not believe (trust) him?' (Luke 20:5).

After their final answer that they do not know (which is in a certain sense not an answer, but only a response or reply), Jesus says to them that he will also not tell them by what authority he does what he does (20:8).[43]

Here the counter-question plays an important role in the interaction. The effect of the counter-question is that the first question does not have to be answered, thus defusing the negative intention, because the questioners are embarrassed by Jesus' move.[44]

The passage about paying tribute to Caesar (20:20–26) is another example of a counter-question being the only reaction to an earlier question. The people who ask the question (20:21) were sent by teachers and other high religious leaders, so that Jesus could be caught (20:19–21). After requesting a denarius, Jesus asks in Luke 20:24 whose image and epigraph/inscription it has.[45] The questioners answer the question by saying that Caesar is depicted on it. Jesus then answers that they must give the emperor 'that' of the emperor and that which belongs to God, to God. What happens in all these three passages is that Jesus takes the initiative from the spying questioners by asking for a denarius and by the accompanying counter-question. Interestingly, in his version, Luke makes the amazement about Jesus that Mark depicts,

---

[43] Their non-answer is in indirect speech. It is not so easy to differentiate between response, reply and answer. Here I cannot go into defining these terms, but here I consider an answer as giving the information, which is asked for in a question. Thus, I can typify here their final words as a *response* and not an *answer*. Perhaps it is written in Luke indirectly because it is merely a response?

[44] Note that after this dialogue Jesus tells the parable of the tenants of a vineyard. At the end he asks the people about their interpretation of the stone which the builders rejected but which has become the cornerstone (see Ps 118:22; Luke 20:17). Luke 20:1–19 is framed by the references to the high priests and their companions (20:1, 19) as a unity.

[45] In the parallel texts in Mark 12:13–17 and Matt 22:15–22 Jesus reacts to the question about paying taxes to Caesar with two counter-questions ("What are you testing me?"; see Mark 12:15 // Matt 22:18) and the question about the image on the denarius (12:16; cf. tribute money in Matt 22:19).

in a way even more specific.[46] He mentions that the listeners are so surprised (θαυμάσαντες; 20:26) about Jesus' answer that they remain (or even become) silent.[47]

The fact that Jesus responds with a counter-question not only to explicit questions, but also to implicit ones, can be found in another example where the text of Luke has a parallel in Mark (5:17–26 // Mark 2:1–12). In Luke 5:21–22 such an interaction is described:

> [21] *And the scribes and the Pharisees began to question, saying, 'Who is this who speaks blasphemies?* (question 1) [22] *Who can forgive sins but God alone?'* (question 2) *When Jesus perceived their thoughts, he answered them,* (again: ἀποκριθεὶς εἶπεν) [23] *'Why do you question in your hearts?* (counter-question 1) *Which is easier, to say, 'Your sins are forgiven you,' or to say, 'Rise and walk'?'* (counter-question 2)

When Jesus recognizes the considerations in their thoughts, he starts to give an answer to their implicit ideas (at least that is how it is in Luke's case), but that answer consists, in the first instance, of two questions. First, he asks a more or less open question about what they are thinking in their hearts. Next, he gives a question that places those who question his attitude or, worse still, criticize him, in a dilemma. They will have to choose between two positions, both of which are not entirely obvious. When looking at how this text can be seen from the perspective of semantics this seems to fit Estes' description of a dilemma question.[48] However, from the perspective of pragmatics, Jesus' questions are clearly Opposing-Turn Questions.

The several types of counter-questions we have discussed here function in slightly different ways. In his article, Leutzsch describes the way Jesus responds to the question of the person asking what he has to do to inherit eternal life as a strategy to irritate his questioners. He claims that in order to change the expectation horizon of those seeking instruction, a teacher must irritate.[49] Later in his article he describes the

---

[46] Often people think that they were amazed at his answer because of the content of the answer, but the content still must be conveyed linguistically, and so the amazement may also have to do with *how* he answered the question and not just the *what* that was in his answer.

[47] In some manuscripts 5:33 is parallel to Mark 2:18 (a question). Then Luke 5:34 could be another example of a counter-question. After answering his audience with a question and then explaining his answer, he also tells a parable (5:36–39).

[48] Estes, *Questions and Rhetoric*, 223.

[49] Leutzsch, "»?« – »?«," 407: 'Um dem Erwartungshorizont der um Belehrung Nachsuchenden zu verändern, muss eine Lehrperson irritieren.' It must be said that in German the verb *irritieren* is slightly less negative than in Dutch or English. It can also mean something like 'to create disorientation'.

counter-question as part of Markan Jesus' didactic strategy of bluffing, a strategy that should eventually lead to a broader horizon for the questioners.[50] Rather than applying the characterization of irritation or bluff strategy, I prefer to characterize counter-questioning as a kind of deregulation strategy, which should open up the questioner to start thinking himself or herself and probably even open the questioner up to a different way of thinking.

Estes describes quite aptly what happens when a counter-question really functions only as a question.[51] Counter-questions do not meet the expectations of a question that has just been asked. After all, there is no answer. By answering the question with a question, the ball is returned to the first questioner, but in such a way that he or she is no longer the most decisive person in the dialogue. Instead of getting an answer, the questioner should start thinking for himself or herself. Of course, it depends on the nature of the first question to what extent the counter-question does provide an answer. This is the case when the counter-question – like what is usually called a rhetorical question – suggests an answer to the first questioner.

However, also when a speaker starts an argument with a counter-question, like Jesus does in Luke 6:3, it appeals to the original questioner(s) to return to their/his/her own question, in order to critically reflect on this question. At the same time, they are offered another perspective and taken in the direction of what is being told. A question like 'Haven't you read?' involves the questioners in the answer and appeals to what they may already know, while Jesus can assume that they know the story about David. Jesus' question stimulates them to actively think along with the person asking the counter-question, which is the beginning of a further explanation.[52]

Leutzsch does not mention Mark 3:1–6 as an example of a counter-question, but that passage also more or less contains the pattern of a question followed by a counter-question. Mark 3:1–6 sketches the deliberations of the people in the synagogue and these deliberations concern the question whether Jesus will heal on the Sabbath (3:2). Jesus 'reads' this question, lets the man with a withered hand rise and then asks a

---

[50] Leutzsch, "»?« – »?«," 414–415.
[51] Estes, *Questions and Rhetoric*, 291–293.
[52] Again, using the threefold idea of a response, a reply, and an answer; a counter-question technically cannot provide an answer in the truest sense, but it is certainly a response, and it can be a reply, in that it suggests certain directions or expectations for the conversation.

question which is more or less a counter-question to the implicit question of his audience. When his audience does not answer, Jesus heals the man. Also, in Luke 6:8 it seems that Jesus responds to the deliberations of the 'Grammaticians' and the Pharisees by first letting the man rise and then letting him stand in the middle. Jesus asks a question in 6:9 and heals the man (// Mark 3:4).[53]

5. Counter-questions, only in Luke

It is remarkable that one Q pericope that Luke has in common with Matthew contains a counter-question in Luke, which is a 'normal' question in the Matthean parallel. After Jesus in 12:36–40 (// Matthew 24:42–44) has told a parable about a gentleman coming home from a wedding, we hear in Luke 12:41 how Peter asks whether Jesus has told the parable only to his disciples, or to all? Because Jesus then asks a question (τίς ἄρα ἐστὶν ὁ πιστὸς οἰκονόμος ὁ φρόνιμος, ὃν καταστήσει ὁ κύριος ἐπὶ τῆς θεραπείας αὐτοῦ τοῦ διδόναι ἐν καιρῷ [τὸ] σιτομέτριον; 12:42), it becomes in the Lukan text a counter-question while in the text of Matthew this question is just a part of Jesus' argument.[54]

In his own material Luke presents Jesus again and again as someone who uses questions as part of his teaching strategy. For example, in 12:13–21 (*Sondergut*) Jesus answers a request concerning whether he wants to be judge over a brother (12:13) with a question (12:14) and with a parable (12:16–21).[55]

---

[53] That it is a question gets extra emphasis in Luke because the question word Ἐπερωτῶ is used! Also, elsewhere in Luke, Jesus asks questions of his audience, when they are observing him. For Jesus' use of questions and parables as pedagogic tools in Luke 14, see my "Who Do you Have to Invite to the Table? A Dropsy Certainly; About Luke 14,1–24 as a Literary Unit" (forthcoming).

[54] We can find a question in the Q material in Luke 13:22–30. The question in 13:23 cannot be found in the parallels of the Q material in the Gospel of Matthew. However, there are also quite a few questions in the Q material of Matthew where Luke has no questions, see for example Matt 6:25, 26, 31 // Luke 12:23, 24, 29. Compare also Matt 12:22–30, esp. 12:23 (with the question whether Jesus is the son of David) with Luke 11:14–23 (where there is no question in 11:14).

[55] The combination of question and parable can also be found in Luke 13:18–19, with synoptic parallels. The combination of a question and a parable we also find in the *Sondergut* of Luke for example in Luke 7:36–50 in verses 41–42. Jesus tells his host a parable about two debtors and asks him which of the debtors will most love the man they owe money to. The combination is not surprising because both the parable and a question try to make listeners active. In Luke 4:22 the audience asks whether Jesus is not the son of Joseph. Jesus answers with a parable. It would be worthwhile

One of the most explicit examples of the Lukan Jesus using counter-questions, can be found in Luke 10:25–38, a *Sondergut* passage, often titled the Good Samaritan. In response to a question from a lawyer (νομικός) about what he has to do to receive eternal life, Jesus answers with two questions:

> ²⁵ *And behold, a lawyer* (νομικός) *stood up to put him to the test, saying, 'Teacher, what shall I do to inherit eternal life?'* (First-Turn Question) ²⁶ *He said to him, 'What is written in the Law? How do you read it?'* (Second-Turn Questions).

After the νομικός has answered by connecting two passages from the Scriptures (10:27), he gets a compliment and some advice from Jesus (10:28). This is not the end of the dialogue, for the νομικός asks a new question: 'And who is my neighbour?' We could typify this question as a Third-Turn Question, and it is then the second counter-question. After Jesus recounts the parable of the Good Samaritan (10:30–36), he adds to this story a question, which can be seen as the fourth counter-question in this dialogue. This question is directly related to the lawyer's second question, because after telling the story Jesus repeats in his question the word 'neighbour': 'Which of these three, do you think, proved to be a neighbour to the man who fell among the robbers?' (10:36). When the lawyer has given an answer to Jesus' last question, it turns out that Jesus has reframed the question from 'Who is my neighbour?' to a question of how to become a neighbour to people in need and distress. By answering Jesus' second counter-question at the end, the questioner has given an answer to his own question and now he knows how he can become a neighbour and fulfil the Law and thus inherit internal life. This passage shows how apt the Lukan Jesus is in his asking of counter-questions in combination with telling stories like parables. We also have to note that in this passage Luke presents a more complex pattern of questions than we can find in Mark.

This is also the case in the following example. In the last part of his Gospel, Luke describes a meeting between the risen Jesus and two disciples, using a complex pattern of questions. In the well-known Emmaus story, there are two counter-questions. The encounter between Jesus and the two disciples can be seen as a special form of a learning-process. The problems of the disciples are, as I have tried elsewhere to demonstrate, related to their failure to understand what happened to Jesus in relation

---

to further explore the pedagogical similarities between the use of asking questions (and especially counter-questions) and telling parables, for a first assessment, see Koet, "An Uncomfortable Story."

to their interpretation of the Scriptures.⁵⁶ This is clear because, among other things, their interaction is characterized by Luke with συζητεῖν and ὁμιλεῖν (24:14–15).⁵⁷ Jesus starts the conversation with a question: *What are these words that you in turn throw to one another, while you were walking?*⁵⁸ Cleopas, the only one of the two who gets a name, answers the question with a counter-question (= Second-Turn Question): *Are you alone as a stranger in Jerusalem, not knowing that what happened in her* (= Jerusalem) *in these days?* Jesus answers this counter-question with a very short counter-question (which is a Third-Turn Question): *Which?* The disciples then tell a lot about Jesus the Nazarene (24:19–24). After a short description of the disciples, Jesus asks another question: *Was it not necessary that the Christ should suffer these things and enter into his glory?* (24:26). Then he starts with an explanation of the relation between what happened to him and what is said in the Scriptures (which the readers do not hear, by the way!). In Luke 24 the risen Jesus is still a teacher and in Luke 24:13–35 he enables, by his asking questions and his explanation, the two disciples to understand the Scriptures.

We have shown in the above that Luke presents a Jesus who makes his audience think using counter-questions. This is in line with what he does in the Gospel of Mark. However, it seems that Luke uses more complex patterns of questioning than Mark does.⁵⁹

That Jesus is someone who is good at asking questions is no surprise to the reader/hearer of Luke's Gospel, because this is already announced in the beginning of the Gospel in Luke 2:40–52.

---

[56] See my "Some Traces of a Semantic Field of Interpretation in Luke 24,13–35," *Bijdr* 46 (1985) 59–73; reprinted in: *Five Studies on the Interpretation of Scripture in Luke-Acts* (SNTA 14; Leuven: Peeters, 1989), 56–72.

[57] This verb συζητεῖν is used ten times in the New Testament and almost all times in the context of Jesus' contacts with people in which explanations of the Scriptures play a role: for example about learning in the synagogue (Mark 1:27; see 1:21); see my "Markus 12,28–34: Übereinstimmung über das Wichtigste," in: C.M. Tuckett (Ed.), *The Scriptures in the Gospels* (BETL 131; Leuven: Peeters, 1997), 513–523; see also the article mentioned in footnote 56 above.

[58] In classical Greek περιπατέω became particularly associated with 'walking and talking' or 'walking and teaching.' This happened to such an extent that Peripatetics were recognized as a unique philosophical group. Specifically, the Peripatetics were associated with Aristotle, who delivered his lectures 'walking'.

[59] A first assessment of Matthew shows that Luke also uses more complex patterns than that evangelist. Such an initial assessment of Matthew's material also suggests that Jesus makes less use of counter-questions in those passages. Perhaps the two questions in the special passage about the Temple tax (and the coin in the fish's mouth) come closest to that pattern.

6. Luke 2:40-52: foreshadowing Jesus as somebody who is capable of asking questions

Elsewhere I have written several times how Luke 1–2 discloses what Jesus and his teachings will signify for Israel and the other peoples. Luke 2:29–32 is a disclosure of Jesus' mission as seen by Luke.[60] However, the passage about Jesus staying behind as a child in the Temple of Jerusalem can also be seen as a preview of what Jesus will do in the remainder of the Gospel. This passage is seen, for example by Tannehill, as a demonstration of Jesus' wisdom and of the special favour of God which rests upon him. However, it is also a narrative introduction to *what kind of teacher Jesus will be*.[61] There are two elements in this pericope that announce the fact that asking questions is an important part of Jesus' pedagogical stance in the Gospel of Luke. First of all, Jesus is presented as a disciple who asks questions. He is a παῖς (2:43), sitting in the midst of the teachers (2:46), listening to the teachers and asking them questions (καὶ ἐπερωτῶντα αὐτούς). Asking questions is part of being a disciple and the fact that in this passage Jesus is a disciple is also suggested because it is said that the listeners are amazed by his answers. Asking the right questions and giving answers that lead to amazement or even bewilderment makes a person a special learner. However, asking the right questions is also a characterization of a good teacher. And as we have seen above, that is exactly one of the characteristics of Jesus as a teacher.

We have seen that both in the synoptic tradition and in Luke's own material Jesus quite often poses counter-questions. It is therefore significant that Jesus' first words in the Gospel of Luke are counter-questions. His mother asks him: *Child, what did you do thus unto us?* Jesus answers: with two counter-questions. The first is: *What is it that you sought me?*[62] The second is: *Did you not know that I had to be among those (=teachers) of my father*.[63] These questions prepare the reader for the fact that Jesus will quite often ask counter-questions in the Gospel.

---

[60] See for example my "Simeons Worte (Lk 2:29–32, 34c–35) und Israels Geschick," in: F. Van Segbroeck (Ed.), *The Four Gospels 1992: Festschrift Frans Neirynck* (BETL 100; Peeters, Leuven, 1992) 1549–1569; reprinted in B.J. Koet, *Dreams and Scripture in Luke-Acts. Collected Essays* (CBET 43: Leuven: Peeters, 2006), 99–122.

[61] Cf. J.J. Kilgallen, "Luke 2:41–50: Foreshadowing of Jesus, Teacher," *Bib* 66 (1985): 553–559, here 553: 'One can expect to see played out in the central part of the Gospel the theme ideas of the Finding in the Temple.'

[62] Jesus' reply begins with the same word as Mary's question: τί.

[63] An interesting interpretation of ἐν τοῖς τοῦ πατρός μου can be found in N. Riemersma, *Het Lucasevangelie onder de loep: Opbouw, stijl en theologie* (Middelburg: Skandalon, 2018), 50–59. Riemersma argues that ἐν τοῖς does not refer to things, but to persons,

7. A case of avoiding counter-questions in Luke's passion narrative

During the interrogation at Jesus' trial, it is only in Luke that Jesus says something which in a very special way shows that sometimes it is better to refrain from asking questions. In Mark we can find the trial in 14:53–65: Jesus is led away to the High Priest and to the chief priests, the elders and the scribes. When no witnesses can be found to testify against Jesus, he is accused with the help of false witnesses (14:57–59). This makes the trial a violation of the Jewish Law, which says that one may not give false testimony. The accusation of these witnesses is that they heard him say that he would destroy the Temple and would then build another one within three days (14:58), but because their testimony does not agree, it is not valid (14:59). It is the High Priest who then starts asking Jesus about himself (14:60). Jesus remains silent after the first question, but when the High Priest asks him whether he is the Christ, the Son of the Blessed, Jesus answers (14:62). For the High Priest his answer is the reason that he rips his clothes and asks the audience two questions. In the version of Mark, the High Priest therefore asks four questions: two to Jesus and two to those present.[64]

In the Lukan version of the passion narrative the interaction between Jesus and his opponents is different. In Luke, the High Priest 'disappears' into a larger collective, the presbyterium (τὸ πρεσβυτέριον; 3 × New Testament; here in 22:66, in Acts 22:5 and 1 Timothy 4:14).[65] There are also fewer questions and the question in Mark 14:62 takes the form of a request in Luke: If you are the Christ, tell us (Luke 22:66).[66] Jesus' answer in Luke's version is longer and consists of two parts. First, he says: *If I*

---

and translates: *Wist u niet dat ik onder die van mijn vader moet zijn?* (= Didn't you know that I have to be among those of my father?). I can imagine that with the persons indicated by ἐν τοῖς πατρός μου is also, perhaps or even especially, meant the Jewish teachers, in whose midst Jesus is in Jerusalem's Temple.

[64] Questions addressed to Jesus: 'Do You make no answer? What is it that these men are testifying against You? ... Are You the Christ, the Son of the Blessed *One*?' (Mark 14:60–61 NAS); questions to those present: 'What further need do we have of witnesses? You have heard the blasphemy; how does it seem to you?' (Mark 14:63–64 NAS). The version of Matthew follows more the version of Mark.

[65] Although most of the modern translations follow the Vulgate and translate τὸ πρεσβυτέριον with a plural (*seniores;* 'the elders' [KJV]) we have to note that this is collective and that we can translate it probably better with a singular: the council of *presbuteroi* or like in some German translations: *Ältestenrat*. Luke explains later that they are the ἀρχιερεῖς (which is a cultic term and not, like the Greek word οἱ πρεσβύτεροι, an indication of the leadership functions of elderly people).

[66] The lapse of time in Luke is different from Mark's version. In Luke's version, the question comes the next day.

said so to you, you wouldn't believe me. But then there is, in the version of Luke, a special addition: *If I also ask* you, *ye will not answer me...*[67]

Jesus is presented by Luke here as someone who, even in the context of his trial, could take the initiative by asking questions. In ancient Athenian trials, the accused was the one who was allowed to ask questions of his accusers.[68] Jesus, as accused, does not ask questions, but announces that he will not remain an accused person, but will become a judge (22:69; there is a parallel in the synoptics). However, Luke depicts Jesus as someone who, at a low point in his life, alludes to what Luke said he was doing both at the beginning of his Gospel (Luke 2:46; see also below) and at the end of his life (Luke 24:13–35): he was a striking questioner. Jesus asks questions over and over again and these questions are usually part of his way of being a teacher. However, if he were to answer the council with a question, Jesus knows that he will not get an answer.

We have seen above that counter-questions are about getting the questioners to participate in a thought process. Because it is clear that here in the trial against Jesus there are false witnesses involved and that therefore probably no openness to a joint thought process is to be expected, Jesus states very explicitly that he sees no salvation in asking questions. For a real conversation a certain honesty is a prerequisite. If Jesus were to have asked questions, then the questions coming from the council would have been counter-questions. Precisely because Luke explicitly says that Jesus will not ask any questions, Luke plays with a pattern of questions and counter-questions in a subtle way and, with that, this dialogue is characterized as the more or less explicit absence of a question and counter-question pattern.

8. Conclusions

We have seen how in Luke 10:25–37 a combination of a complex pattern of questions and telling a parable eventually helps the questioner both to get an answer to his question and to deepen his question. In the literature on parables it has often been pointed out that parables invite the hearers/readers to think for themselves and that different interpretations of parables are therefore possible. In the New Testament parables are part of the

---

[67] There are interesting text variations, such as the addition that he will not only not get an answer, but that he will not be released either. In this context, I cannot comment on these variants.

[68] In ancient Athens there was no lawyer in court, but the accused had to ask questions to his accusers.

pedagogical teaching strategy of Jesus; they make his listeners think.[69] They appear to have this in common with the counter-questions Jesus poses in the Gospel.

Estes has shown how many strategies can be used when someone asks a question. Also, when asking counter-questions, different strategies play a role. Even though there are different forms of asking counter-questions (for example, a counter-question as an introduction to a narrative element and a counter-question that has no accompanying text), all counter-questions have in common that they more or less get the listeners thinking.

To answer a question with a counter-question is to make the first questioner think about his own question. In this way, questions become a bridge to the world of the recipients (first in the text and then with the readers).[70] In Luke 10:25–37 it is ultimately the questioner who gives the answer to his own question. This could indicate one of the primary aims of a counter-question. It encourages questioners to think for themselves as much as possible, sometimes even to the extent that they will give the answer themselves, like in Luke 10:25–37.

It seems that in the Gospel of Luke there is more emphasis on the fact that counter-questioning is part of Jesus' teaching strategy than in the other two synoptics. One argument for this is that the first words of Jesus in Luke are two counter-questions (2:40–52). In a way, one of Jesus' last performances, the meeting on the way to Emmaus, is also a very clear example of his posing of counter-questions as part of his pedagogical strategy. These passages also provide another argument for the thesis that Luke puts more emphasis on counter-questions; both in Luke 24:13–35 and in Luke 10:25–37, Luke presents a more complex pattern of question and counter-question asking than one can find in the other synoptics.

In a sense, it seems that counter-questions and the telling of parables or other narrative elements in the communication of the teacher Jesus with very different groups all have a similar purpose: to stimulate his audience to think for themselves first and perhaps then to act.[71]

---

[69] See R. Zimmermann, *Puzzling the Parables of Jesus: Methods and Interpretation* (Minneapolis: Fortress Press, 2015), 152–179.

[70] In this article I cannot elaborate on how important these counter-questions are for the text-immanent reader/listener. A PhD-student of the Tilburg School of Catholic Theology, Maurits Sinninghe Damsté, will give attention in his dissertation to the connection between questions in Luke 1–2 and the text immanent reader/listener.

[71] For the relationship between learning and doing in different pericopes of Luke-Acts, see my "Luke 10,38–42 and Acts 6,1–7: A Lukan Diptych on Diakonia," in: J. Corley and V.T.M. Skemp (Eds.), *Studies on the Greek Bible: Essays in Honor of Francis T. Gignac, S.J.* (CBQMS 44, Washington: Catholic Biblical Association of America 2008), 163–185.

UNASKED QUESTIONS IN THE GOSPEL OF JOHN
Narrative, Rhetoric, and Hypothetical Discourse

Douglas ESTES
Tabor College

1. Introduction

Like many narratives, the Gospel of John uses questions to tell its story. The most evident use of questions in the Gospel comes when one character asks another character a direct question. For example, Jesus, the protagonist of John's Gospel, utters his first words as a question in which he asks the two disciples who start to follow him, 'What are you seeking?' (1:38a). If we start with just the question itself, the question's syntax shows it to be a *variable question* (as it prompts the hearer to solve the variable *x*, which in this case is 'what'). Building up from the syntax, the question is semantically a type of *speculative question* (as it pushes reflection in the hearer), although it also acts to some degree as both a *test question* and a *loaded question* (as its intent is both hidden and suggestive).[1] Pragmatically, the question serves as a *governing question* (as it 'governs' the subsequent dialogue). These syntactic, semantic, and pragmatic descriptors explain the purpose of the question building

---

[1] In my first book on interrogatives, *The Questions of Jesus in John*, I held John 1:38a to be primarily a *sequence question* based on its semantics. In writing my second book on interrogatives, *Questions and Rhetoric in the Greek New Testament*, I expanded my field of study significantly which allowed me to sharpen my descriptive categories. As a result, I have come to limit sequence questions to those questions that more narrowly ask "how" (πῶς), although my overall discussion of the reflective purpose of John 1:38a in *The Questions of Jesus in John* remains unchanged. I mention this to underscore an important point about questions: while we may use semantic and pragmatic categorization to describe how questions work, questions are not statements – their rhetorical qualities make them far more malleable and thus resistant to categorization. Thus, any one question may exhibit multiple semantic and pragmatic qualities in various degrees. For further discussion on John 1:38a, see D. Estes, *The Questions of Jesus in John: Logic, Rhetoric and Persuasive Discourse* (BibInt 115; Leiden: Brill, 2013), 104–107; D. Estes, *Questions and Rhetoric in the Greek New Testament: An Essential Reference Resource for Exegesis* (Grand Rapids: Zondervan, 2017), 17, 210, 267, 282.

up from syntax and moving to its function in discourse. They are useful for qualifying how a speaker *might* use the question in context, or *does* use the question in context, but they cannot always predict how a speaker *will* use the question in context.

In contrast, it is also possible to evaluate questions in narrative use by starting at the discourse level and working down to syntax. While the bottom-up approach (as exampled above with 1:38a) is worthwhile for most questions found in most narratives, there are a few unusual scenarios where a top-down approach may provide a better understanding. For example, a top-down approach is more advantageous when the usage of the question appears to be at odds with its linguistic structure.[2] One type of question that occurs in complex narratives for which the top-down approach will work is the *unasked question*. The Gospel of John contains a number of unasked questions, and these unusual questions reveal much about both the unasked questions themselves as well as the some of the overall narrative and rhetorical goals for questions in the Gospel.

2. Questions in Narratives

Narratives tell stories. In fact, 'narrative,' 'tell,' and 'story,' are all concepts related to the same idea – what we refer to in English as 'storytelling.' Yet there are more ways to tell a story than to tell a story. And, there are things that stories do more than simply tell. Sometimes, stories show. Sometimes, stories ask. Sometimes stories seem to ask, but never do.

The simplest narratives narrate events in a temporal sequence.[3] These basic narratives only tell; there are no questions explicitly involved.

(a) Bridget went to her room, closed the door, and started reading her book.

Since questions (interrogatives) tend to perform two major operations in discourse – request information and encourage a different perspective – there is no real need for questions in a simple narrative that merely tells.[4] This is especially the case once we consider the nature of narration and

---

[2] Two examples include the *phatic question* and the *retort question*; see Estes, *Questions and Rhetoric*, 203–207, 288.

[3] E.M. Forster, *Aspects of the Novel* (San Diego: Harvest, 1927), 27; and for a list of the many theorists who make similar arguments, see D. Estes, *The Temporal Mechanics of the Fourth Gospel: A Theory of Relativity in the Gospel of John* (BibInt 92; Leiden: Brill, 2008), 9.

[4] Estes, *Questions and Rhetoric*, 23–24, 65–69.

characterization; in the above simple narrative, there are only two existents: Bridget (a character) and the narrator. Bridget performs the action while the narrator tells the action.[5] Since there is only one character, there is no dialogue, and only the potential for monologue.[6] Likewise, because the narrator is a hidden narrator, there is no dialogue with the audience,[7] only monologue (narration). Statements can exist in purely monological environments, but questions cannot.[8] Questions require dialogue.[9] To be convincing, narrative dialogue expects questions.

Once a narrative becomes complex enough to have direct dialogue, one character speaking to another character, or the narrator speaking to the narratee, then questions become more common. Characters may at first speak to each other in statements, but as narrative complexity grows, the more likely that the audience will encounter other types of utterances beyond statements. The same is true in the case of the narrator; the narrator may at first speak to the narratee (and be heard by the audience) only in statements, but as narrative complexity grows, the more likely that the audience will encounter other types of utterances beyond statements. Thus, characters may pose questions to other characters, and the narrator may pose questions to the audience.[10] Although Aristotle (384–322 BC) demoted the value of utterances that were not assertive,

---

[5] Equally well-established is that every narrative has a narrator; see for example, W.C. Booth, *The Rhetoric of Fiction*, 2nd ed. (Chicago: University of Chicago Press, 1983), 152; I.J.F. de Jong, "Narratological Theory on Narrators, Narratees, and Narrative," in: I. de Jong, R. Nünlist and A. Bowie (Eds.), *Narrators, Narratees, and Narratives in Ancient Greek Literature: Studies in Ancient Greek Narrative, Volume One* (Mnemosyne Bibliotheca Classica Batava Supplementum 257; Leiden: Brill, 2004), 1.

[6] Narratology has well established that narrators are themselves often characters in narrative, either explicitly or implicitly. However, even when the narrator is also openly a character (a *homodiegetic narrator*), the narrator acts as a special type of character. For simplicity's sake, I draw a clear but artificial line between the narrator and the character. For more discussion of the narrator as character, see G. Prince, *A Dictionary of Narratology*, rev. ed. (Lincoln: University of Nebraska, 2003), 40–41.

[7] I use the term *audience* to denote any possible group of hearers or readers of a text, without distinction. Thus, audience can include the narratee, the implied reader, real readers, historical readers, or any other user of the text.

[8] If a character in a story speaks to themselves, and in doing so asks a question of themselves (a *deliberative question*), then that is not a monologue in the purest sense since the person has (artificially) created a dialogue with themselves. Likewise, if a character adds a so-called 'rhetorical question' to a monologue, the asking implies an audience, and therefore this also is not a monologue in the purest sense.

[9] D. Estes, "Questioning Why God Questions," *Christianity Today*, August 18, 2017.

[10] In less common situations, the narrator may pose questions to characters, and characters may be made to pose questions to the audience.

non-assertive utterances such as questions tend to make a narrative much more interesting – yet no less truthful.[11]

As narrative complexity grows, so too does the way characters and narrators speak – the reader encounters various kinds of discourse such as indirect discourse. In contrast to questions in direct discourse (b), indirect discourse occurs when the narrator speaks for the character, summarizing the words of the character (c):

(b) Violet went to her teacher and asked, 'Where can I find the book?'
(c) Violet went to her teacher and asked where she can find the book.

Both of these situations are common in narrative. Less common is *free indirect discourse*, a situation where the narrator assumes the speaking role to represent a character's speaking (d).[12]

(d) Violet looked at her teacher. Would she know where the book was?

Though its origins are subject to much debate, free indirect discourse does seem to occur in ancient and medieval narratives.[13] Another uncommon speech representation is *free direct discourse* (e),[14] which functions in a way that is similar to *interior monologue*.[15]

(e) Violet went to her teacher. Where is my book? She stood and waited.

From a narrative perspective, (e) raises a hard question: How does the narrator know what Violet was thinking? These entanglements increase the complexity of the narrative.

---

[11] Aristotle did this as a consequence of how he believed speakers convey truth – statements can convey truth but questions and other forms of utterances cannot; see Aristotle, *Int.* 17a1–8.

[12] We may also think of these categories as direct speech, indirect speech, free direct speech, and free indirect speech.

[13] M. Fludernik, *The Fiction of Language and the Languages of Fiction: The Linguistic Representation of Speech and Consciousness* (London: Routledge, 1993), 79–100; D. Beck, "The Presentation of Song in Homer's Odyssey," in: E. Minchin (Ed.), *Orality, Literacy and Performance in the Ancient World* (OLAW 9; Leiden: Brill, 2012), 29. For counter argument, especially relating to classical Greek, see C. Bary and E. Maier, "Unembedded Indirect Discourse," *Proceedings of Sinn und Bedeutung* 18 (2014): 77–94.

[14] For an extended definition and discussion of free direct discourse, see Prince, *Dictionary of Narratology*, 34; A. Palmer, *Fictional Minds* (Lincoln: University of Nebraska Press, 2004), 54–55; and D. Cohn, *Transparent Minds: Narrative Modes for Presenting Consciousness in Fiction* (Princeton: Princeton University Press, 1978), 63.

[15] S. Marnette, *Speech and Thought Presentation in French: Concepts and Strategies* (Pragmatics & Beyond NS 133; Amsterdam: John Benjamins, 2005), 244–245; and R. Scholes, J. Phelan and R. Kellogg, *The Nature of Narrative*, 40th anniv. ed. (Oxford: Oxford University Press, 2006), 177–186.

These types of complex situations are found on the discourse level and flavour the narrative to make it more engaging for the hearer or reader. But they also shape how the narrator will and must construct the narrative on levels below the discourse level. When it comes to questions, simple narratives may be able to get by with merely *open questions* and *decision questions* (two uncomplicated types of questions), but more complex narratives will require questions that are also more complex in their syntax (form), semantics (meaning), and pragmatics (use).[16] Thus, discourse drives pragmatics, semantics, and syntax, just as the integration of syntax, semantics, and pragmatics culminates in discourse. These complex questions will then intersect with complex discourse. Understanding a decision question in direct discourse is one thing; deciphering a *counterfactual question* in an interior monologue is something else altogether.

As with so many questions in the Greek New Testament, it is all too quick and easy for a modern reader to read past questions with limited concern for their role and purpose in the narrative. Although the Gospel of John is an ancient Greek text that is both short in length and simple in register, it displays a level of narrative complexity that open questions and decision questions alone will not satisfy. Evaluating the questions in John based on their syntax, semantic, and pragmatic features reveals that there are a variety of types of questions. Beyond open questions (e.g. 18:29) and decision questions (e.g. 21:15), the Johannine narrator and characters also use many other types of questions such as *focus-shifting questions* (e.g. 2:18), *echo questions* (e.g. 7:20), and *negative polar questions* (e.g. 3:10), each instance of which contributes to the creation of the overall story and influence of the Gospel. One thing that unites the latter three types of questions, though, is that they bring complexity to the discourse in their syntactic, semantic, and/or pragmatic features. This means that we see their complexity from the bottom-up.

Occasionally, however, readers will encounter questions where the most notable effect of the question is pragmatic, or even more unusually, where the purpose of the question derives as much or more from its function in discourse than it does from its syntactic and semantic qualities. In these situations, it is often questions with simple syntactic or semantic qualities that are put to complex uses. For example, if a postmodern

---

[16] The types of questions discussed in this essay originate from my work, *Questions and Rhetoric in the Greek New Testament*, wherein I analyse the nearly one thousand questions in the Greek New Testament along syntactic, semantic, and pragmatic lines. This builds on my preliminary work on Hellenistic Greek interrogatives in *The Questions of Jesus in John*.

narrative with an unreliable narrator asks a question of a personal nature – formed as an open question – directly to the narratee, or even, to the readers themselves, the most notable feature of the question is likely not found either in its syntax or semantics, nor even in its pragmatics, but primarily in its discourse use:

> (f) I watched as Ken got up and moved toward the door. Jason was still nowhere to be seen. Ken peeked outside, hesitantly. 'Where are you?' Ken seemed to ask, imploring a response. There was only silence. It was a question that needed asking: 'Where are you?' Still no response came.

Both questions in (f) are simple in their syntactic and semantic qualities, and the first one is also unremarkable in its pragmatic qualities. But the second question here is most notable for its role on the discourse level. In (f2), the narrator jumps from one *diegesis* to another – from the Ken-Jason narrative frame to the narrator-narratee narrative frame – which disrupts the flow of the story for the audience. This creates *metalepsis*, or the crossing or blurring of two or more narrative diegeses.[17] What is more, the narrator uses the second question as an intentional echo of the original question. Since we locate the purpose of the question on the pragmatic and discourse levels, evaluating this question from the top-down will prove effective. It also reveals that the narrator is not merely narrating but also actively pushing the reader.

This is not to say that this diminishes the other linguistic qualities of the question – the syntax, semantics, and pragmatics still very much contribute to what the question asks. Furthermore, the informational and rhetorical qualities of this type of question is every bit as relevant. However, when a question such as (f2) makes an impact on the discourse level, it is more 'heard' by the audience than other questions, in part because it creates surprise and in part because it speaks more directly to the audience.[18] The reader takes note of question (f2) far more than (f1). As a rule of thumb, the more macroscopic the interrogative logic affects (syntax → semantics → pragmatics → discourse), the more 'higher pitched' (disruptive) the question becomes. This is one reason some questions in texts stand out more than others, an example of which we consider below.

---

[17] M. Fludernik, "The Diachronization of Narratology," *Narrative* 11 (2003): 331–348, here 339.

[18] Questions not only induce surprise, they also are often the response to surprise; see A. Celle, A. Jugnet, L. Lansari, and T. Peterson, "Interrogatives in Surprise Contexts in English," in: N. Depraz and A. Celle (Eds.), *Surprise at the Intersection of Phenomenology and Linguistics* (C&E 11; Amsterdam: John Benjamins, 2019), 117–137.

3. Unasked Questions in John

Within the narrative of the Fourth Gospel there are approximately one hundred seventy-two direct questions.[19] Among these, there are a few that are unique in the way they affect the discourse. For example, the Gospel of John makes use of a *retort question* (11:9), a kind of utterance with a rather singular focus that is exceedingly rare in the ancient world.[20] This question is notable primarily for its pragmatic features as a type of second-turn question.[21] It also says something about the protagonist that effects a reading of the greater story. Since ancient hearers and readers would have recognized it as a kind of aphorism that is in some ways unrelated to the narrative dialogue, the retort question stands out from the rest of the dialogue. This occurs, generally speaking, whenever a narrative tries to make an external reference that shifts the audience's focus from the narration itself.

Another unusual phenomenon in the Gospel of John is the *unasked question* – a question that is thought by a character or narrator but never actually asked with voice. At first glance, an unasked question sounds like an oxymoron, akin to a 'devout atheist,' 'paid volunteer,' or perhaps 'eternal life.' Yet it is another type of complex question that a narrator may select to convey their story. Within any narrative, there are always numerous gaps in the story – events that occurred (either in the story world or real world) but did not make the final cut for the story. We know they exist in theory because of how narratives are made, but also practically because some narratives make either direct or oblique references to events that are not narrated, words that are never spoken, and characters that fail to appear. Sometimes this is an error in narration (often the discussion of modern film criticism, where the editing process was flawed), but sometimes it is by design. Within these missing events there occurs a phenomenon called *disnarration*, a term coined by literary theorist Gerald Prince to describe 'all the events that *do not* happen but, nonetheless, are referred to (in a negative or hypothetical mode) by the

---

[19] Figuring the number of questions in ancient Greek texts is always an approximation for several reasons, including the general lack of punctuation in most ancient texts and the tension between information structure and usage of interrogative pronouns/adverbs (π-words); see Estes, *Questions and Rhetoric*, 25–30.

[20] Estes, *Questions of Jesus in John*, 140–144; C. Clay Doyle, "Is the Pope Still Catholic? Historical Observations on Sarcastic Interrogatives," *Western Folklore* 67 (2008): 5–33.

[21] Estes, *Questions of Jesus in John*, 288–289.

narrative text.'[22] In less common situations, a narrative may narrate disnarration; for example:

(g) Wyatt never thought he would say, 'I want more homework,' but today, here he is, looking for more homework.

Here the character never actually says, 'I want more homework,' nor does he think it, but the narrator still feels it important to tell the narratee about this unrealized thought (an utterance that did not happen). When 'future, possible, imaginary, or counterfactual' utterances are made within narrative, the narrative shows an instance of *hypothetical discourse*.[23] Within hypothetical discourse, there occurs what Meir Sternberg calls *negated quotations* as the example in (g).[24] Negated quotations, within hypothetical discourse, disnarrated in stories, have largely been overlooked in the study of narrative and language. Even more overlooked, though, are negated interrogatives disnarrated in hypothetical discourse – or more simply, unasked questions.

In John, there are eight unasked direct questions embedded in the dialogue between characters (1:19; 4:27a, 27b; 12:27; 21:12, 17, 20, 23).[25] We can describe these eight down by their general use: one is a disnarrated future utterance (1:19),[26] four are thought-not-asked (4:27a, 27b; 12:27; 21:12), and the final three are thought-not-asked reiterations of previously narrated questions (21:17, 20, 23, notably all three in John's epilogue).[27] If we consider these eight against the one hundred seventy-two in the Gospel, it suggests that approximately 4.6% of the questions in John's Gospel are unasked. Comparatively, a large-scale study of modern British narratives found that 4% of direct and indirect speech falls

---

[22] G. Prince, "The Disnarrated," *Style* 22 (1988): 1–8, here 2; and see also, M. Lambrou, *Disnarration and the Unmentioned in Fact and Fiction* (London: Palgrave Macmillan, 2019), 20.

[23] E. Semino, M. Short and M. Wynne, "Hypothetical Words and Thoughts in Contemporary British Narratives," *Narrative* 7 (1999): 307–334, here 308.

[24] M. Sternberg, "Proteus in Quotation-Land: Mimesis and the Forms of Reported Discourse," *Poetics Today* 3 (1982): 107–156, here 143.

[25] For the sake of this essay, I limit my study to explicit examples of disnarrated questions. This excludes direct questions that imply disnarration – such as questions asked to and from the same group (for example, 7:35; 11:56), multiple iterations of questions summarized as one (for example, 8:25; 11:47), or paraphrased questions (for example, 8:33).

[26] A minority of critical editions view 1:19 as an indirect question; this debate, however, does not impact my principal argument and is beyond the scope of this essay.

[27] Of these eight, I consider two to be special cases: the question as narrative projection in 1:19 and the hypothetical deliberative in 12:27.

with the category of hypothetical discourse.[28] Though this data is a bit apples to oranges, I surmise that the percentage of unasked questions in John is slightly higher than expected, but within an acceptable range for a narrative written in an Indo-European language.[29] Why would a narrative such as John employ a question that is never actually asked? Why would the narrator believe it important to include it?

4. Unasked Questions: Formation and Effects

An unasked question is any question that a narrative represents as being asked but is not actually asked. The representation of asking can occur in both free direct discourse, example (e), and free indirect discourse, example (d).[30] What makes an unasked question unusual is that it is an utterance which could be more economically made through normal indirect discourse. For example:

(h) Everett sat by the fire and wondered who would bring him the marshmallows. He watched, waited, but said nothing.
(i) Everett sat by the fire and wondered, 'Who would bring the marshmallows?' He watched, waited, but said nothing.
(j) Everett sat by the fire and wondered. Who would bring him the marshmallows? He watched, waited, but said nothing.

Here example (h) is a relatively common way for a narrator to express the inner question and concerns of a character. We consider narration of this type to be indirect discourse, and the question within it we label an *indirect question*. Therefore, the indirect question (h) is *not* an unasked question. However, in (i), instead of the narrator describing the character's thoughts, which could be possible from a reliable narrator, the narrator instead expresses the character's thoughts explicitly and literally, which is not probable unless the narrator is omniscient (or perhaps, very, very reliable). The same situation occurs in (j), except that the narrator's mode of representation is different (free indirect discourse versus interior monologue). At first glance (h), (i), and (j), may seem identical in meaning, but the erotetic logic and narrative function of the (i) and (j) thoughts are distinct from the (h) thought, much the same way that a summary of

---

[28] Semino, Short and Wynne, "Hypothetical Words and Thoughts," 313.
[29] The strongest evidence for this is that disnarration is not disruptive in the Gospel. A full-scale study of disnarration, hypothetical discourse, and unasked questions in Hellenistic literature may be in order.
[30] E. Maier, "Quotation and Unquotation in Free Indirect Discourse," *Mind and Language* 30 (2015): 345–373, here 347.

a speech is different from the wording of a speech. Thus, (d), (e), (i), and (j) are all examples of unasked questions.

4.1. Formation

Because unasked questions are defined by their role in narrative context, they cannot be identified via syntax or semantics. Unasked questions are formed from the narrative situations that allow their asking to occur. They must be placed as a type of direct speech in either free direct or free indirect discourse, and then 'negated' by the narrator. This negation creates a situation wherein the reader must understand that this is not represented speech, as with normal narrative interaction, but hypothetical represented speech.[31] Unasked questions have no syntactic requirements; thus, an asker can form an unasked question using any of the four primary formations, and with either positive or negative polarity.[32]

There is also little limit on the type of semantic qualities that an unasked question can convey, although some question types as defined by their semantics (for example, *leading questions* and *dilemma questions*) would be unlikely to be found in interior monologue.

Instead, we can only identify unasked questions by their pragmatics (the way a writer uses them) and discourse function (the way a writer relates them to the whole text). Readers may expect unasked questions to be brief, and while this is most commonly the case, it is not mandated. Too many, however, will tax the reader.[33] It is also possible for unasked questions to carry other pragmatic qualities, such as in the case of a double question placed by the narrator as an unasked question.

4.2. Rhetorical Effects

As a type of hypothetical discourse, unasked questions have weak informational qualities and strong rhetorical qualities.[34] However, the rhetorical effects of unasked questions are different than most questions because they exist only within hypothetical discourse. Instead of affecting the diegesis of

---

[31] G. Myers, "Unspoken Speech: Hypothetical Reported Discourse and the Rhetoric of Everyday Talk," *Text* 19 (1999): 571–590, here 574.

[32] For the four primary formations of questions based on syntax, see Estes, *Questions and Rhetoric*, 93–94.

[33] Cf. M.W.G. Stibbe, "Protagonist," in: D. Estes and R. Sheridan (Eds.), *How John Works: Storytelling in the Fourth Gospel* (RBS 86; Atlanta: SBL Press, 2016), 133–150, here 149.

[34] Myers, "Unspoken Speech," 587–588.

the level that the question exists on, unasked questions seem to move their impact 'upward' into the next diegesis level (see the more literal occurrence of this in (f) above). Restated more plainly, a typical question asked by Character A in a typical story interacts informationally and rhetorically with other characters in the same story; but an unasked question asked by Character A in a typical story interacts informationally and rhetorically with a character at the next level of the story (which, in most cases, is the narratee, as heard by the audience). So, for example, a narrator has Character A ask a decision question in direct discourse to influence Character B; but later the same narrator has Character A ask an unasked question in hypothetical discourse to influence the audience, not any character in the story itself. Of course, these types of influences are complex, and often uneven, but there are two rhetorical effects that unasked questions create.

First, unasked questions colour characters and scenes. While it is true that any utterance made by a character helps to shape the audience's perspective on that character, unasked questions shape this perspective in a different way by allowing the audience to peer into the mind and thoughts of a character. This is akin to the way that an internal description of characters – the narrator sharing with the reader how the character feels or what they believe – tends to shape characters in a stronger way than direct discourse utterances.[35] Even more so, hypothetical discourse, because it is a form of direct speech, represents one of the more direct lines of sight from character to audience that can exist in narrative. This line also becomes more clear if it moves from unasked questions in free indirect speech to unasked questions in direct speech; free direct speech unasked questions such as (i) colour the character more than free indirect speech unasked questions such as (j).[36] Thus, unasked questions are one narrative discourse feature that rounds a character.[37] As with other questions that are noted for their pragmatic qualities, unasked questions can heighten the drama of the scene.[38]

---

[35] A style of characterization that is uncommon in John's Gospel; see M.W.G. Stibbe, *John's Gospel* (New Testament Readings; London: Routledge, 1994), 9; J.L. Resseguie, "Point of View," in: D. Estes and R. Sheridan (Eds.), *How John Works: Storytelling in the Fourth Gospel* (RBS 86; Atlanta: SBL Press, 2016), 79–96, here 89.

[36] Semino, Short and Wynne, "Hypothetical Words and Thoughts," 307–308.

[37] P. Sellew, "Interior Monologue as a Narrative Device in the Parables of Luke," *JBL* 111 (1992): 239–253, here 239; and cf. C. Bennema, "A Comprehensive Approach to Understanding Character in the Gospel of John," in: C.W. Skinner (Ed.), *Characters and Characterization in the Gospel of John* (LNTS 461; London: Bloomsbury, 2013), 48.

[38] J. Sams, "Quoting the Unspoken: An Analysis of Quotations in Spoken Discourse," *Journal of Pragmatics* 42 (2010): 3147–3160, here 3157; and cf. Myers, "Unspoken Speech," 573.

Second, unasked questions project their influence from the diegesis of their occurrence to the next higher diegesis. Put more simply, within the circumstance of most narratives, when a character asks an unasked question, the rhetorical effects of the question does not impact another character as much as it impacts the narratee (and transfers to the audience). Even though the narrator selects all utterances (even in historical narratives), unasked questions are specifically selected because their occurrence is essentially unnecessary to accomplish the narrative's goals. Unasked questions are useful for the narrator to engage the audience directly without alerting the audience to this engagement.[39] When a character asks an unasked question, the question projects itself and is internalized by the audience.[40] Using the previous example (i), when Everett wonders who will bring the marshmallows, and the narrator gives this unasked question an uttered form, the verbalizing of this encourages the audience to ask the same question: 'Who *will* bring the marshmallows?' This particular rhetorical effect is stronger for unasked questions than most other questions – especially questions best described by their syntactic and semantic qualities – because the hypothetical nature of the discourse prevents interference between the character asking and the character being asked to respond. In short, since an unasked question does not appear to be 'aimed' at any other character, it is more likely to be picked up by the audience.

5. Case Study: John 21:12

> λέγει αὐτοῖς ὁ Ἰησοῦς, Δεῦτε ἀριστήσατε.
> οὐδεὶς δὲ ἐτόλμα τῶν μαθητῶν ἐξετάσαι αὐτόν, Σὺ τίς εἶ; εἰδότες ὅτι ὁ κύριός ἐστιν.
>
> *Jesus says to them, 'Come eat breakfast.'*
> *But none of the disciples dared to question him, 'Who are you?' – having known it was the Lord.*

After these things (μετὰ ταῦτα), or an indeterminate time later, Jesus again appears to some of the disciples (21:1).[41] These seven disciples go out to fish, and by the morning, have caught nothing. Jesus stands on the shore, calling out to the disciples; 'however the disciples didn't know it was

---

[39] Cf. Myers, "Unspoken Speech," 576.
[40] Cf. Semino, Short and Wynne, "Hypothetical Words and Thoughts," 316.
[41] For discussion of the arrangement of the scenes of the Gospel of John, see D. Estes, "Time," in: D. Estes and R. Sheridan (Eds.), *How John Works: Storytelling in the Fourth Gospel* (RBS 86; Atlanta: SBL Press, 2016), 41–58.

Jesus' (21:4). Jesus points the disciples where to fish and a miraculous catch is made. This leads the Beloved Disciple to claim, 'It is the Lord' (21:7). With Peter swimming, and the others coming by boat, the disciples come to shore to find Jesus by a charcoal fire with fish and bread. Peter brings the remaining fish, one hundred fifty-three in total. Now Jesus tells them, 'Come eat breakfast.' But none of the disciples dared to question him – 'Who are you?' – knowing it was the Lord (21:12).

The first, and most important, issue of interpretation is to determine if the question in 21:12 is direct speech or indirect speech. If direct speech, then the question functions as (b) and (i) or (d) and (j), above. If indirect speech, then the question functions as (c) and (h), above – and is not an unasked question, nor hypothetical discourse, but merely an indirect question. Although the translators and editors of almost all modern translations and Greek critical editions have rendered the utterance σὺ τίς εἶ as a direct question,[42] the concern is serious enough that it warrants further investigation. After all, narrative-complex elements such as unasked questions, hypothetical discourse, and free (in)direct speech are harder to identify in ancient texts – if and when they occur. Though the narrative placement suggests direct speech, the question itself is found as an adjunct clause following the infinitive of a communication verb (ἐξετάζω); in the Greek New Testament, it is very common for an indirect question to be introduced by this type of infinitive (for example, Matthew 16:1).[43]

Often there is no easy way to determine whether an utterance in the Greek New Testament is direct or indirect. This includes both statements and questions. When it comes to questions, variable questions are usually easier to determine than polar questions. Although the question in John 21:12 uses the expected interrogative variable word τίς, the writers of the New Testament created their texts within an uncomfortable age – a time when indirect π-words (ὅστις, ὅπου, ὁπότε, ὁποῖος, ὅπως, ὅθεν, ὁπόσος, ὁποδαπός, ὁποσάκις) were falling into less consistent use and punctuation had not yet been invented (or certainly, implemented).[44] To

---

[42] Every major modern translation in English, German, and French renders this question as a direct question. Further, major critical editions such as the UBS[5] and the NA[28] do so as well. Finally, historically significant translations such as the Vulgate, Lutherbibel, Tyndale, Wycliffe, and the Geneva Bible are also all united in translating this as a direct question. The only evidence I can find where the editor or translator rendered this question indirectly is in the Patriarchal Greek New Testament (PATr).

[43] D.B. Wallace, *Greek Grammar Beyond the Basics: An Exegetical Syntax of the New Testament* (Grand Rapids: Zondervan, 1996), 603–605.

[44] J. Hope Moulton, *A Grammar of New Testament Greek*, with W.F. Howard and N. Turner, Volume 3 (London: T&T Clark, 1963), 48; Estes, *Questions and Rhetoric*, 57.

wit, when an indirect π-word occurs in the Greek New Testament, it occurs in an indirect question; but when a direct π-word occurs, it is almost as likely to be used in an indirect question as a direct question.[45] As a result, New Testament writers did use direct π-words to introduce indirect questions. Therefore, the clause σὺ τίς εἶ could be direct speech because it contains a direct interrogative variable word, but that is not a given.

Unusually, this clause does not front its interrogative variable word (it is π-*in-situ*). Since Greek has a regular word order with variable questions – with 95% occurrence of fronted interrogative variable words in direct questions – this raises the question of the formation of this question. However, of the 5% of questions that do not conform to expectations, most are in Luke-Acts and John, and many are variations of this same question (for example, John 1:19; 8:25, Romans 14:4).[46] In particular, the question 'Who are you?' is notably π-*in-situ* in a few situations not only in the Greek New Testament but also in the Septuagint (for example, Job 35:2; Jeremiah 4:30) and beyond.[47] Because indirect questions also front their indirect interrogative variable word in almost all situations, the primary conclusion that we can draw is that the utterance σὺ τίς εἶ is something of a colloquial expression whose information structure is set up either due to cultural expectation (for example in English, 'It's when?' instead of 'When is it?') or for emphasis (for example in English, 'You're who!?' instead of 'Who are you?').[48]

---

[45] Based on previous research into the use of ποῦ / ὅπου and πόθεν / ὅθεν in the Greek New Testament. I have not calculated the percentages for all π-word pairs. For further discussion, see Estes, *Questions and Rhetoric*, 54–61.

[46] D. Estes, "The Exceptions to the Rule: What Non-π-fronted Questions Reveal about Information Structure in Biblical Greek" (paper presented at the Annual Meeting of the Society of Biblical Literature, Boston, 18 November 2017). Further, see the extensive use in *T. Sol.* 7.3, 12.2, 14.2, 17.2, 18.2, 18.4, 22.19, 25.1.

[47] For example, Epictetus, *Diatr.* 3.1.22; cf. E.A. Abbott, *Johannine Grammar* (London: Adam and Charles Black, 1906), 597. But the question is not always π-*in-situ*; for example, the LXX of Gen 27:18; 27:32, and Ruth 3:9 front the π-word as expected (plus see the following footnote).

[48] An example of this seems to occur in Aristophanes' *The Birds*, where Peisthetaerus asks τίς δ' εἶ σύ; (which correctly fronts the π-word), but then receiving an inappropriate response (an *opposing-turn question*), asks ἀλλὰ σὺ τίς εἶ; (which is π-*in-situ*) presumably for emphasis or emotional effect (exasperation or frustration); see Aristophanes, *Av.* 1497–99; as well as the emphatic translation in Aristophanes, *The Birds*, trans. B. Bickley Rogers (LCL; London: William Heineman, 1927), 268. A similar phenomenon where the formation of this question switches from π-fronted to π-*in-situ* is also found in *T. Sol.* 2.1, 3.6, 5.1–2, though contrast with 10.2, 13.2–3, where it is not always clear where the variation is emphatic, or possibly, for literary ornament (esp. 13.2–3).

There is also the placement of the clause in the text. The shift in case from the third person to the second person in the indexical σύ suggests that the question is meant to be heard as a direct question. If so, this partially resolves the potential anacoluthon in the εἰδότες clause; the direct question is interior monologue, which renders the placement: 'But none of the disciples dared to question him [since they] knew it was the Lord.' In this case, the unasked question functions almost like a Johannine aside – an intentionally inserted metaleptic feature of the text.

Turning to ancient evidences, an examination of many of the earliest Greek codices, such as Codex Vaticanus (ca. early 4th century), Codex Washingtonianus (ca. 4th or 5th century), and Codex Bezae (ca. 5th century), does not reveal notable evidence for either reading. In Codex Cyprius (ca. 9th century), the use of punctuation in the manuscript could suggest the thought-utterance is an indirect question, but the overall evidence is mixed.[49] In contrast, punctuation in the Codex Sangallensis (ca. 9th century) and Lectionary 1533 (ca. 9th century) suggest the utterance is a direct question.

Therefore, the conclusion is that the question in John 21:12 is a form of direct speech. For the sake of the argument here, it is not necessary to determine with precision whether the question is direct speech or free indirect speech; either way, the question is an unasked question that interrupts the flow of the narrative for reasons that are essential to the overall narrative of the Gospel of John.

From the standpoint of syntax, the typical way for the writer of the Gospel to narrate this event would be to use an indirect question: 'But none of the disciples dared to question who he was, knowing it was the Lord.' But the narrator of the Fourth Gospel is no typical, detached narrator; instead, the Gospel's narrator intrudes on the narrative every so often to push the audience in a preferred direction. In this scenario, the narrator intrudes on the scene to insert an unasked question into the thoughts of characters, privileging the audience to hear these character's thoughts. This utterance helps set up the aside in 21:12b.[50] The narrator forms the question

---

[49] The manuscript places a high stop (στιγμὴ τελεία) after εἶ for the π-question in 21:12, but in contrast, it places a question mark (;) after ἔχετε for the polar question in 21:5. That could lead one to conclude that the utterance is indirect. However, a survey of scribal marks at the end of John suggests that other direct π-questions, such as the two questions in 20:15, also terminate with a high stop; whereas other polar questions, such as those in 21:15 and 21:17, bear what could be described as a modified question mark (mid stop comma). One possible, and tentative, conclusion is that Codex Cyprius recognizes the difference between the syntax of polar and π-questions in its irregular punctuation.

[50] J.J. O'Rourke, "Asides in the Gospel of John," *NovT* 21 (1979): 210–219.

as a *variable question*, and its semantics are what would be expected of a *speculative question*. Yet, the question is unasked; its narrative function largely supersedes other semantic and pragmatic factors.

Though the narrator need not use an unasked question to tell the interior monologue of the disciples, the narrator does so as a rhetorical act to speak to the audience. First, the unasked question colours the character of the disciples, bringing their thoughts and feelings to the surface. The unasked question creates a palpable sense of expectation, transmitting the emotional see-saw that the disciples felt in both their excitement and their fear. It is a kind of 'disputing with their hearts' that prompted interior monologue in Homer and the classical Greek tradition.[51] The audience can 'hear' the question even though it is never asked.

Second, the question causes the audience to connect with similar echoes earlier in the Gospel. 'Who are you?' is 'the question that characterizes the dialogues of the Gospel.'[52] This is the same question as the very first question of the Gospel – the priests and Levites openly (but hypothetically) ask John the Baptist, 'Who are you?' (1:19). And it is the same question that some of the Judeans ask Jesus during his public ministry, 'Who are you?' (8:25). And a moment before, the Beloved Disciple answered the question, saying 'It is the Lord' (21:7). Building on these echoes, here the narrator takes it a step further; instead of character-to-character interaction, the unasked question creates a scenario wherein the audience is more plainly confronted with this question, 'Who are you?' Because unasked questions trigger metalepsis, and skip from one narrative discourse level to the next, the question seems as much intended for the audience as it does for the characters within the narrative. The rhetorical function of the unasked question is to add colour to the characters while at the same time push the audience to ask the critical question, 'Who are you?' – which the aside answers, about the disciples, maybe the reader, 'they knew it was the Lord.'

6. Conclusion

With almost two hundred asides,[53] the Gospel of John conditions its audience to expect explicit communication from the narrator. Thus, it comes as little surprise that the Gospel would engage in other implicit strategies

---

[51] Sellew, "Interior Monologue," 240.
[52] J.-A.A. Brant, *John* (Paideia; Grand Rapids: Baker Academic, 2011), 283.
[53] T. Thatcher, "A New Look at Asides in the Fourth Gospel," *BSac* 151 (1994): 428–439.

for the narrator to communicate directly with the audience. One of those implicit strategies is the use of unasked questions. Although statements and questions may occur in hypothetical discourse, the rhetorical quality of questions lends them to not only colour the character asking the unasked question but also plant the question suggestively in the mind of the audience. Unasked questions perform a similar metaleptic movement as do asides, yet the effect is implicit, not explicit.

While small in quantity, the use of unasked questions in the Gospel point to a number of larger factors that shape the Johannine narrative. The Gospel's rhetorical scheme is complex, using antithesis, paradox,[54] questions, riddles, *peristaseis*,[55] syllogistic logic, and much more throughout the text. The Gospel's narrative scheme is also complex, using metalepsis, epic language, asides, scene-setting, unasked questions, and much more throughout the text. The conclusion drawn from this is that the Gospel of John is audience-focused. The questions asked in John are often repetitive, asking the same questions in slightly different variations, over and over again.[56] Though they may come from the mouth of characters, the questions in the Gospel of John are asked with a view of their impact on the audience. Sometimes when we read stories, we feel as though the story is speaking to us. This is even true where the story is asking questions; at times, we may feel it is even questioning (ἐξετάζω) us. This is less true in simple narratives, such as the fiction underlying modern films, where the primary goal is often to tell a story for the sake of the story. It is more true in complex narratives, such as the Fourth Gospel, where the primary goal is to persuade the audience of the truth of the story (20:31).

Unasked questions are a first step in decoding why questions can be so powerful *for the reader* even when the text is not 'speaking' to them. They reflect as much as what the narrator wants to ask the audience as much as it does the characters themselves. Rather than merely telling a story about the life of Jesus, the narrative and rhetorical features in John work together to push the audience in the direction that the narrator wants the audience to go – or more specifically, to believe.

---

[54] D. Estes, "Dualism or Paradox? A New 'Light' on the Gospel of John," *JTS* 71 (2020): 90–118.

[55] D. Estes, "Rhetorical *Peristaseis* (Circumstances) in the Prologue of John," in: K. Bro Larsen (Ed.), *The Gospel of John as Genre Mosaic* (Studia Aarhusiana Neotestamentica 3; Göttingen: Vandenhoeck & Ruprecht, 2015), 191–207.

[56] See especially the discussion of the cumulative effect of question asking in John in Estes, *Questions of Jesus in John*, 163–172.

A QUESTION OF MISUNDERSTANDING OR A MISUNDERSTOOD QUESTION?

Exegetical Comments on Acts 1:6

Arie W. ZWIEP
Free University Amsterdam

1. Introduction

The book of Acts opens with a question that has hopelessly divided interpreters over the centuries.[1] Responding to Jesus' command not to leave Jerusalem but to wait for the promise of the Father, that is, the outpouring of the Spirit 'not many days from now' (οὐ μετὰ πολλὰς ταύτας ἡμέρας, Acts 1:4–5), the assembled disciples[2] ask: 'Lord, is this the time when you will restore the kingdom to Israel?' (κύριε, εἰ ἐν τῷ χρόνῳ τούτῳ ἀποκαθιστάνεις τὴν βασιλείαν τῷ Ἰσραήλ; v. 6), a question that seems to make good sense after the forty days during which the risen Jesus had instructed the apostles 'concerning the things of the kingdom of God' (τὰ περὶ τῆς βασιλείας τοῦ θεοῦ, v. 3) and had announced the coming of the eschatological Spirit (v. 4; cf. Luke 24:49).[3] Jesus, however, responds more or less indirectly to

---

[1] Paper presented at a symposium on "Questions in Religious Authoritative Texts," on the occasion of the Tenth Anniversary of the RSCS Research Institute, Louvain-la-Neuve, 11 September 2019, and at the *Amsterdam New Testament Colloquium* (Nieuwtestamentisch Werkgezelschap), 13 September 2019. Thanks are due to the participants of both colloquia for their constructive comments. Greek references are taken from NA[28]; unless otherwise indicated, English translations are from NRSV.

[2] With C. Kingsley Barrett, *A Critical and Exegetical Commentary on the Acts of the Apostles* (Vol. 1; ICC; Edinburgh: T&T Clark, 1994), 75, I take οἱ μὲν οὖν συνελθόντες (v. 6) as a continuation of the previous verses, that is, with no change of subject implied: *"They, then, when they had assembled"* (italics original). Says Barrett: 'Thus it is the apostles who raise the question of this verse, as they were those addressed in v. 5.' Also S.G. Wilson, *The Gentiles and the Gentile Mission in Luke-Acts* (SNTSMS 23; Cambridge: Cambridge University Press, 1973), 88–89.

[3] I take the imperfect ἠρώτων as an iterative ('they were repeatedly asking,' or 'they were continuously asking'), thereby stressing the urgency of the disciples' question. But cf. Barrett, *Acts*, 75: '[A]s in classical usage, the imperfect is used for a question

the disciples' question by saying: 'It is not for you to know the times or periods that the Father has set by his own authority' (οὐχ ὑμῶν ἐστιν γνῶναι χρόνους ἢ καιροὺς οὓς ὁ πατὴρ ἔθετο ἐν τῇ ἰδίᾳ ἐξουσίᾳ). In other words, it is not their business. He then sketches an alternative scenario for days to come: 'But you will receive power when the Holy Spirit has come upon you; and you will be my witnesses in Jerusalem, in all Judea and Samaria, and to the ends of the earth' (ἀλλὰ λήμψεσθε δύναμιν ἐπελθόντος τοῦ ἁγίου πνεύματος ἐφ' ὑμᾶς καὶ ἔσεσθέ μου μάρτυρες ἔν τε Ἰερουσαλὴμ καὶ [ἐν] πάσῃ τῇ Ἰουδαίᾳ καὶ Σαμαρείᾳ καὶ ἕως ἐσχάτου τῆς γῆς, vv. 7–8).

Question and answer have been strategically placed at the beginning of Luke's second volume and are, as many exegetes have correctly observed, programmatic.[4] Apparently, the book of Acts is about the Spirit-empowered mission of the apostles as witnesses of/to Jesus from Jerusalem to the ends of the earth. Many interpreters have taken verses 7 and 8 as some sort of table of content of the Acts: the first five chapters describe the apostolic witness in Jerusalem, chapters 6–12 are about the witness in Judea and Samaria, and chapters 13–28 about the witness from Antioch 'to the ends of the earth' (NRSV, ἕως ἐσχάτου τῆς γῆς, which does not mean 'to the end of the world,' as Richard Pervo aptly remarks).[5] Such a table of content was not unusual in Graeco-Roman and Jewish-Hellenistic historiography of the time.[6]

---

because the action of questioning is incomplete until an answer is given.' This is questioned by M.C. Parsons, M.M. Culy and J.J. Stigall, *Luke: A Handbook on the Greek Text* (Baylor Handbook on the Greek New Testament; Waco: Baylor University Press, 2010), 7: '[t]he fact that this verb is used in the aorist tense in analogous passages ... make such a claim questionable.'

[4] J.A. Fitzmyer, *The Acts of the Apostles: A New Translation with Introduction and Commentary* (AB 31; New York: Doubleday, 1998), 200; R.I. Pervo, *Acts: A Commentary* (Hermeneia; Minneapolis: Fortress, 2009), 43; D.W. Pao, "Jesus's Ascension and the Lukan Account of the Restoration of Israel," in: D.K. Bryan and D.W. Pao (Eds.), *Ascent into Heaven in Luke-Acts: New Explorations of Luke's Narrative Hinge* (Minneapolis: Fortress, 2016), 114–115; A.W. Pitts, *History, Biography, and the Genre of Luke-Acts: An Exploration of Literary Divergence in Greek Narrative Discourse* (BibInt 177; Leiden: Brill, 2019), 81.

[5] Pervo, *Acts*, 41. Cf. on the expression ἕως ἐσχάτου τῆς γῆς also Barrett, *Acts*, 1:80; Pao, "Jesus's Ascension," 144–145.

[6] See, e.g., Philo, *Prob.* 1.1–2 (445); LCL 363:10–11 (Colson): Ὁ μὲν πρότερος λόγος ἦν ἡμῖν, ὦ Θεόδοτε, περὶ τοῦ δοῦλον εἶναι πάντα φαῦλον, ὡς καὶ διὰ πολλῶν καὶ εἰκότων καὶ ἀληθῶν ἐπιστωσάμεθα· οὑτοσὶ δ' ἐκείνου συγγενής, ὁμοπάτριος καὶ ὁμομήτριος ἀδελφὸς καὶ τρόπον τινὰ δίδυμος, καθ' ὃν ἐπιδείξομεν, ὅτι πᾶς ὁ ἀστεῖος ἐλεύθερος, 'Our former treatise, Theodotus, had for its theme 'every bad man is a slave' and established it by many reasonable and indisputable arguments. The present treatise is closely akin to that, its full brother, indeed, we may say its twin,

In practice, the average reader and/or exegete will normally pay more attention to the answer than to the question. Once the question has been answered and has performed its rhetorical task (that is, creating an opportunity for the answer), the question is usually left for what it is, as if it were a station passed. But that does not seem to be a wise strategy if the *connection* (or *correlation*) between question and answer is not well understood, and the answer leaves much to be desired. And this is precisely the case here. How the answer exactly relates to the question has given rise to widely varied interpretations *of the question*, with significant implications for understanding Luke's answer and for understanding the nature of his project as a whole. Unfortunately, in his ground-breaking work on *Questions and Rhetoric in the Greek New Testament*, Douglas Estes does not discuss this particular question.[7] In what follows I will

---

and in it we shall show that every man of worth is free.' Josephus, *C. Ap.* 2.1; LCL 186:292–293 (Thackeray): Διὰ μὲν οὖν τοῦ προτέρου βιβλίου, τιμιώτατέ μοι Ἐπαφρόδιτε, περί τε τῆς ἀρχαιότητος ἡμῶν ἐπέδειξα, τοῖς Φοινίκων καὶ Χαλδαίων καὶ Αἰγυπτίων γράμμασι πιστωσάμενος τὴν ἀλήθειαν καὶ πολλοὺς τῶν Ἑλλήνων συγγραφεῖς παρασχόμενος μάρτυρας, τήν τε ἀντίρρησιν ἐποιησάμην πρὸς Μανεθῶνα καὶ Χαιρήμονα καί τινας ἑτέρους. ἄρξομαι δὲ νῦν τοὺς ὑπολειπομένους τῶν γεγραφότων τι καθ' ἡμῶν ἐλέγχειν, 'In the first volume of this work, my most esteemed Epaphroditus, I demonstrated the antiquity of our race, corroborating my statements by the writings of Phoenicians, Chaldaeans, and Egyptians, besides citing as witnesses numerous Greek historians; I also challenged the statements of Manetho, Chaeremon, and some others. I shall now proceed to refute the rest of the authors who have attacked us.' For more examples and discussion, see V. Larrañaga, *L'Ascension de Notre-Seigneur dans le Nouveau Testament*, trans. from Spanish by G. Cazaux (Scripta Pontificii Instituti Biblici 50, Rome: Pontifical Biblical Institute, 1938), 294–333; L. Alexander, *The Preface to Luke's Gospel: Literary Convention and Social Context in Luke 1.1–4 and Acts 1.1* (SNTSMS 78; Cambridge: Cambridge University Press, 1993), 142–146; Eadem, "The Preface to Acts and the Historians" (1999), repr. in *Acts in Its Ancient Literary Context: A Classicist Looks at the Acts of the Apostles* (LNTS 298; London: T&T Clark, 2006), 21–42; D.W. Palmer, "Acts and the Historical Monograph," in: B.W. Winter and A.D. Clarke (Eds.), *The Book of Acts in Its Ancient Literary Setting* (BAFCS 1; Grand Rapids: Eerdmans; Carlisle: Paternoster, 1993), 1–29, esp. 21–26; Barrett, *Acts*, 1:67; Craig S. Keener, *Acts: An Exegetical Commentary*, vol. 1: *Introduction and 1:1–2:47* (Grand Rapids: Baker Academic, 2012), 708–710 ("An Outline for Acts?"); Pitts, *History, Biography, and the Genre of Acts*, 112–119.

[7] Douglas Estes, *Questions and Rhetoric in the Greek New Testament: An Essential Reference Resource for Exegesis* (Grand Rapids: Zondervan, 2017). A reference to the question of Acts 1:6 is also absent from D.B. Wallace, *Greek Grammar beyond the Basics: An Exegetical Syntax of the New Testament* (Grand Rapids: Zondervan, 1996), 789 (*s.v.* questions), 811 (Scripture index). Nor is R. Dean Anderson's otherwise very helpful *Glossary of Greek Rhetorical Terms Connected to Methods of Argumentation, Figures and Tropes from Anaximenes to Quintilian* (CBET 24; Leuven: Peeters, 2000), of much help.

therefore review a few older and more recent interpretations of the question and then offer my own.[8]

2. Classical interpretations

According to many scholars (perhaps a majority), the question arises from *ignorance* or *misunderstanding* on the part of the disciples. They ask a foolish question and Jesus answers (corrects) them by exposing their foolishness and lack of understanding. John Chrysostom (c. 349–407 CE), for instance, suggested in his commentary on Acts that the disciples 'had not any clear notion of the nature of the kingdom (τίς ποτε ἦν ἡ βασιλεία); for the Spirit had not yet instructed them ... they were still affected towards sensible objects (τὰ αἰσθητά), seeing they were not yet become better than those who were before them.'[9]

In a similar vein, Martin Luther, in a sermon from 1531, declared that the disciples were weak (*schwach*) and carnal (*carnales*) and that they

---

[8] Disregarding minor textual variations in the Greek manuscript tradition of Acts 1:6 [for which see R.J. Swanson (Ed.), *The Acts of the Apostles*, New Testament Greek Manuscripts: Variant Readings arranged in Horizontal Lines against Codex Vaticanus (Sheffield: Sheffield Academic Press, 1998), 3], M.-É. Boismard and A. Lamouille have, based on D, Augustine, and a Coptic version, reconstructed the Western text as follows: Οἱ μὲν οὖν συνελθόντες ἐπηρώτων αὐτὸν λέγοντες· κύριε, εἰ ἐν τῷ χρόνῳ τούτῳ ἀποκατασταθήσῃ καὶ πότε ἡ βασιλεία τοῦ Ἰσραήλ; In other words, the question is twofold: 'Is this the time that you will reinstate?' and 'When (comes) the kingdom of Israel?' Marie-Émile Boismard, *Le texte occidental des Actes des Apôtres: Édition nouvelle entièrement refondue* (EBib NS 40; Paris: Gabalda, 2000), 52–53: 'Eux donc, étant rassemblés, l'interrogeaient en disant: "Seigneur, est-ce en ce temps-ci que tu seras rétabli, et à quand le royaume d'Israel?"' [also M.-É. Boismard and A. Lamouille, *Les Actes des deux Apôtres*, vol. 1: *Introduction – textes* (EBib NS 12; Paris: Librairie Lecoffre, Gabalda, 1990), 64, and P. Faure, *Les Actes des Apôtres: Texte occidental reconstitué* (EBib NS 79; Leuven: Peeters, 2019), 6–7.] This reading is found in Augustine, *Fund.* 9 (LLT): 'interrogabant eum dicentes: domine, si hoc in tempore repraesentaberis, et quando regnum israhel' (trans. NPNF[1] 4:133: 'When they had come, they asked him, saying, Lord, wilt Thou at this time manifest Thyself? And when will be the kingdom of Israel?') and in G[67]. Different: Augustine, *Fel.* 1.4 (LLT): 'illi ergo conuenientes interrogabant eum dicentes: domine, si in hoc tempore praesentabis regnum israhel?' Possibly, the reading arose under the influence of Luke 17:20 (πότε ἔρχεται ἡ βασιλεία τοῦ θεοῦ). The *Amsterdam Database of New Testament Conjectural Emendation* does not instance any conjecture on Acts 1:6–8. See J. Krans, B.J. Lietaert Peerbolte et al. (Eds.), *The Amsterdam Database of New Testament Conjectural Emendation* (http://ntvmr.uni-muenster.de/nt-conjectures, accessed 16 July 2019).

[9] John Chrysostom, *Hom. Act.* 2: Ἐμοὶ δὲ δοκεῖ οὐδὲ τετρανῶσθαί πως αὐτοῖς, τίς ποτε ἦν ἡ βασιλεία· οὔπω γὰρ ἦν τὸ Πνεῦμα διδάξαν αὐτούς (...) Ταῦτα οὕτω πυνθάνονται, ὅτι περὶ τὰ αἰσθητὰ ἔτι διέκειντο, εἰ καὶ μὴ ὁμοίως ὡς πρότερον (LLT); trans. *NPNF[1]* 11:11.

could not understand (*begreiffen*) that Jesus was speaking about spiritual things: 'Ideo non *kundens versthen* quam de corporali regno, et tamen praedicavit, postea cum spiritus sanctus venit, bene intellexerunt.'[10] It was only after Pentecost that they arrived at a correct understanding.

Likewise, John Calvin, to mention one more telling and quite influential example, did not have a good word for the disciples' behaviour. He took their question as the ultimate proof of their inadequacy and incapability: '[T]hey declared thereby how bad scholars they were under so good a Master' (*ostendunt, quam male profecerint sub optimo magistro*).[11] The question, so he argued, arose not from the stupidity of an individual, a loner, but from 'the common consent of them all' (*non unius aut alterius stultitia esse motam, sed simul omnium*), as if they spoke from one mouth.[12] '[M]arvellous is their rudeness, that when they had been diligently instructed by the space of three whole years, they betray no less ignorance than if they had heard never a word. There are as many errors in this question as words' (*Mira vero illorum fuit ruditas, quod tam absolute tantaque cura per triennium edocti non minorem inscitiam produnt, quam si nullum unquam verbum audissent. Totidem in hac interrogatione sunt errores quot verba*).[13]

In the seventeenth century, the Anglican scholar John Lightfoot (1602–1675), one of the first scholars to relate knowledge of the rabbinic tradition systematically to the New Testament,[14] argued – albeit less vigorously than Calvin – that the disciples' question arose from ignorance on their part. In his (posthumously published fourth volume of) *Horae*

---

[10] Martin Luther, *In Vigilia Ascensionis Domini, Act. 1*, WA 34/1 (Predigten 1531), 404–405: '*Da wird widder maniche hubsche predigt gefallen sein*, quae etiam non scriptae, quanquam *hin und widder* in Euangelio, quod ipsi *sind* [Apg. 1,6] *schwach* et interrogant: *Num in tempore?* Ipse loquitur de regno dei, sed non intelligunt, quia Regnum dei *heist*, ut ipse dicit, quod Iohannes [Luk. 24,47] baptizat. Et in Luca: Ite et praedicate in toto mundo 'poenitentiam et remissionem pecca torum,' *das sind ander wort* quam dicere, quomodo *krieg, harnisch sol fueren, heuser bauen*. Sed de regno dei, ut homines *mogen leben und selig* et liberati a morte, peccatis, de quo *wird er manig schone predigt gethan,* sed erant carnales, non poterant *begreiffen*. Ideo non *kundens versthen* quam de corporali regno, et tamen praedicavit, postea cum spiritus sanctus venit, bene intellexerunt' (bold font replaced by italics; references added by the editors of WA).

[11] John Calvin, *Commentariorum in Acta Apostolorum liber primus*, ed. Helmut Feld (Ioannis Calvini Opera omnia Series II Opera Exegetica Veteris et Novi Testamenti 12/1; Geneva: Droz, 2001), 25; trans. John Calvin, *Commentary upon the Acts of the Apostles*, vol. 1, trans. Henry Beveridge (Edinburgh: Calvin Translation Society, 1894), 43.

[12] Calvin, *Acta Apostolorum*, 1:24; trans. Beveridge, *Acts*, 43.

[13] Calvin, *Acta Apostolorum*, 1:24; trans. Beveridge, *Acts*, 43.

[14] A.W. Zwiep, *Tussen tekst en lezer: een historische inleiding in de bijbelse hermeneutiek, deel 1: De vroege kerk – Schleiermacher* (Amsterdam: VU University Press, 2009, 2021[5]), 326–330.

Hebraicae et Talmudicae, he wrote: 'It is very apparent, that the apostles had the same fanciful conceptions about the earthly reign of Christ with the rest of that nation: but yet they seem here a little to doubt and hesitate, either as to the thing itself, or at least as to the time.'[15] And when it comes to Jesus' answer to the question, Lightfoot observed that the answer 'does not in the least hint any such kingdom ever to be; but he [the Saviour] openly rebukes their curiosity in inquiring into the times, and in some measure the opinion itself...'[16]

In modern scholarship suchlike explanations have been defended by such diverse scholars as F.F. Bruce and Hans Conzelmann, among others.[17] More recently, Richard Pervo claimed that 'the question is excruciatingly inept.'[18] He then proceeded: 'Literary tradition permitted pupils to ask dull or inappropriate questions so that teachers could promulgate the correct view.' This may well be the case (although Pervo fails to substantiate this claim), but the question is whether it is indeed such 'an excruciatingly inept question' in the first place.[19] This is often posited

---

[15] J. Lightfoot, *Acts–1 Corinthians*, vol. 4 of *A Commentary on the New Testament from the Talmud and Hebraica*, repr. from *Horae Hebraicae et Talmudicae*, ed. R. Laird Harris (Peabody: Hendrickson, [1979] 2003), 10.

[16] Lightfoot, *Commentary*, 4:10. Cf. also H. Robinson, *Acta Apostolorum variorum notis tum dictionem tum materiam illustrantibus suas adjecit* (Cambridge: Deighton, 1824), 3 n. 6: 'Respicitur forsan ad Mic. iv.8. ubi *regnum prius* ad filiam Zionis *rediturum esse* praedicitur. Apostoli igitur, praejudicatis opinionibus involuti, avidè expectabant, Christum *terrestre regnum* esse instauraturum' (italics original).

[17] Cf. F. Fyvie Bruce, *The Book of the Acts: Revised Edition* (NICNT; Grand Rapids: Eerdmans, [1954] 1988), 36: 'Their present question appears to have been the last flicker of their former burning expectation of an imminent theocracy with themselves as its chief executives;' H. Conzelmann, *Die Apostelgeschichte* (HNT 7; Tübingen: Mohr Siebeck, 1963, 1972²), 26: 'Lk läßt die Jünger ihre Frage aus den jüdischen Voraussetzungen formulieren, *um sie zu korrigieren* und eine Auskunft über den Termin der Parusie *grundsätzlich zu verweigern*' (my emphasis). Cf. J. Zmijewski, *Die Apostelgeschichte*, (RNT; Regensburg: Pustet, 1994), 56: 'Lukas [läßt] Jesu Jünger hier bewußt eine "unverständige" Frage stellen.'

[18] Pervo, *Acts*, 41. A brief and somewhat apologetic survey of various negative interpretations of the question can be found in A. Buzzard, "Acts 1:6 and the Eclipse of the Biblical Kingdom," *EvQ* 66 (1994): 197–215. Buzzard himself opts for a positive interpretation.

[19] In the history of interpretation, the episode of the election of Matthias as a successor to Judas Iscariot (Acts 1:15–26) has sometimes been explained in similar terms, viz. as an inappropriate and premature action taken by the eleven apostles on their own initiative. Rather than casting lots, so the argument runs, they should have waited for the guidance of the Spirit. Paul, not Matthias, should have been the God-ordained successor to complete the circle of the Twelve. Bruce, *Book of Acts*, 47–48, refers to this question only to dismiss it: 'It has sometimes been suggested that the apostles were wrong in co-opting Matthias to complete their number, that they should have waited until, in God's good time, Paul was ready to fill the vacancy.' He refers to R. Stier and

rather than proven. It only carries conviction if there is (con)textual evidence that this is the best way to explain the data.

According to another classical interpretation the question did not arise from ignorance or misunderstanding but from *impatience* on the part of the disciples. The question is a legitimate one, or at least a reasonable one, but it is premature. J.B. Lightfoot (1828–1889), the famous bishop of Durham, not to be confused with the earlier mentioned John Lightfoot, comments in his recently discovered and published commentary on Acts: 'It is not the expectations of the disciples but their impatience to which the answer is directed.'[20] The question then relates first and foremost to the *timing* of the expected 'restoration of the kingdom to Israel,' not to the expectation as such.[21]

3. Methodological Issues

In the narrative world of Acts the disciples are the questioners and Jesus the one who gives a response.[22] However, both question and answer have

G. Campbell Morgan. In Bruce's *The Acts of the Apostles: Greek Text with Introduction and Commentary* (Grand Rapids: Eerdmans; Leicester: Apollos, [1951] 1990³), this question is not addressed nor is reference made to these authors. See also A.W. Zwiep, "Putting Paul in Place with a Trojan Horse: Luke's Rhetorical Strategy in the Acts of the Apostles in Defence of the Pauline Gospel," in: A.W. Zwiep, *Christ, the Spirit and the Community of God: Essays on the Acts of the Apostles* (WUNT 2/293; Tübingen: Mohr Siebeck, 2010), 167–168, and on the passage in general, A.W. Zwiep, *Judas and the Choice of Matthias: A Study on Context and Concern of Acts 1:15–26*, (WUNT 2/187; Tübingen: Mohr Siebeck, 2004).

[20] J.B. Lightfoot, *The Acts of the Apostles: A Newly Discovered Commentary*, vol. 1 of *The Lightfoot Legacy*, ed. B. Witherington III and T.D. Still (Downers Grove: IVP Academic, 2014), 78.

[21] Cf. J.A. McLean, "Did Jesus Correct the Disciples' View of the Kingdom?," *BSac* 151 (1994): 215–227; D.L. Bock, *Acts* (BECNT; Grand Rapids: Baker Academic, 2007), 61: 'Many Jewish texts, as well as OT hope in general, expected that in the end Israel would be restored to a place of great blessing (…) The question is a natural one for Jews who have embraced the messianic hope.' J.D.G. Dunn, *The Acts of the Apostles* (Epworth Commentaries; Peterborough: Epworth, 1996), 10: 'It is important to note that the hope of the kingdom in these terms is corrected or qualified by Jesus, but not denied or rejected.' Barrett, *Acts*, 1:77, points to the absence of 'of God' (not denying that this is implied in the expression) and suggests: 'In this verse the word βασιλεία stands by itself and probably means simple *sovereignty*; the apostles inquire whether Israel is once more to enjoy the wide dominion that it enjoyed in the time of David.' See further also J. Maston, "How Wrong Were the Disciples about the Kingdom? Thoughts on Acts 1:6," *ExpTim* 126 (2015): 169–178; Pao, "Jesus's Ascension," 143–145.

[22] Cf. C.R. Holladay, *Acts: A Commentary* (NTL; Louisville: Westminster John Knox, 2016), 74: 'Although [*sic!*] the apostles' question in verse 6 is set within the early part of the first century, given earlier Jewish history, it has an authentic ring. Having conquered death, can the risen Lord now establish a new era of Jewish rule comparable to

been 'framed' by the implied author ('Luke') with a view to his implied readers. In the classical treatments of the issue this has often been ignored or negated. When Luke put the question in the mouth of the disciples at this precise point of the narrative, he did so with a view to his implied audience, knowing well (or at least making the reasonable guess) that the question of the disciples was *their* question, and that the answer was pertinent to *them*. So the question to be answered is how the question of the disciples (and the answer provided by Jesus) functions on the level of Luke, and how it relates to his larger narrative concern c.q. his and his readers' theological convictions.[23] So what can be said about the question of the disciples from the perspective just sketched? Let me try to define the nature of the question in a few steps.

3.1. *The question is a* layered *question, not a* composite *question*

Gerhard Lohfink, to whom I shall turn below, has argued quite circumstantially that the response of the Lukan Jesus implies that the question consisted in fact of three questions, one about timing, one about the role of Jesus and one about the future of Israel.[24] Others have argued that the question of the disciples consisted of at least two questions.[25] If so, either

---

the Hasmonean dynasty or the earlier Davidic-Solomonic dynasty? Instead of feeding these political hopes, however, the risen Lord redirects the apostles' attention toward an alternative vision of the future, in which the Holy Spirit is the defining presence.'

[23] Methodologically, I find Collingwood's model of a 'logic of question and answer,' and his preference for 'questions that arise' [R.G. Collingwood, *The Idea of History: Revised Edition with Lectures 1926–1928*, with an Introduction by J. van der Dussen (Oxford: Oxford University Press, 1946, 1993/1994²); R.G. Collingwood, *An Autobiography and Other Writings, with Essays on Collingwood's Life and Work*, ed. D. Boucher and T. Smith (Oxford: Oxford University Press, 2013)], and U. Eco's model of textual interpretation, including the notion of *isotopy* as a means to disclose textual meaning [U. Eco, *Lector in fabula: La cooperazione interpretativa nei testi narrativi* (TBomp 27; Milano: Bompiani, 1979, 2010¹¹); Dutch trans. *Lector in fabula: De rol van de lezer in narratieve teksten*, Y. Boeke and P. Krone (Amsterdam: Bert Bakker, 1989)] helpful tools to tackle the questions of this article. The work of Estes, *Questions and Rhetoric*, helps to make abstract philosophical and semiotic questions relevant for practical exegetical purposes.

[24] G. Lohfink, *Die Himmelfahrt Jesu: Untersuchungen zu den Himmelfahrts- und Erhöhungstexten bei Lukas* (SANT 26; München: Kösel, 1971), 153–158.

[25] So G. Schneider, *Die Apostelgeschichte*, vol. 1: *Einleitung, Kommentar zu Kap. 1,1–8,40* (HThKNT 5; Freiburg: Herder, 1980), 201: 'Die Frage enthält die beiden Aspekte, die in der Antwort begegnen (VV 7f.). Es geht um den Zeitaspekt ('in dieser Zeit') und um die Erstreckung des Reiches ('für Israel').' So already H.H. Wendt, *Die Apostelgeschichte* (KEK III; Göttingen: Vandenhoeck und Ruprecht, 1880, 1899⁸), 66: 'Bemerkenswert ist, dass sich die Frage sowohl auf die *Zeit* der Reichserrichtung, als auch auf

way, technically speaking, the question would be a *composite* question.[26] However, from a syntactical perspective, it is obvious that Luke has formulated the question as a *single* question: 'Is this the time (ἐν τῷ χρόνῳ τούτῳ, fronted for emphasis) that you will restore the kingdom to Israel?' As such it is a straightforward question about the timing of what is to come.[27] But straightforward does not mean simple. The question of the disciples is a classic example of what the speech-act theorist H. Paul Grice has called 'conversational implicature,' conclusions which come with an utterance although these are not explicitly stated: the question presupposes or implies a number of facts as being true or given.[28] It may not be a composite question but at least it is a *layered* question. What that means for the interpretation of the question, I will explain in what follows.

3.2. *The question has been formulated from the answer, not vice versa*

This observation is not a novel one. Rudolf Pesch in his commentary on Acts observes in passing that 'die Frage ... schon mit Rücksicht auf die Antwort formuliert [ist].'[29] Gerhard Lohfink in particular has argued that, despite its brevity, the question is very complex (*sehr vielschichtig*) in that it seeks, as I just mentioned, to address three issues at one stroke: it has a temporal, a spatial and a Christological dimension.[30] Each of these aspects or motifs, so the arguments runs, has its counterpart in the answer: 'Die Jüngerfrage liefert das Stichwort, auf das hin die Aussagen

---

  die Bestimmung des Reichs *für Israel* richtet. Auf beide Punkte bezieht sich nachher die Antwort Jesu' (wide spacing replaced by italics).
[26] On composite questions, see Estes, *Questions and Rhetoric*, 122–146.
[27] So already J.A. Bengel, *Gnomon Novi Testamenti in quo ex nativa verborum vi simplicitas, profunditas, concinnitas, salubritas sensuum coelestium indicatur*, ed. E. Bengel (Tübingen: Schramm, 1742, 1773³), ed. P. Steudel (Stuttgart: Steinkopf, 1891⁸), 435: 'Apostoli, re praesupposita, quaerebant de tempore' (spaced setting replaced by italics).
[28] On conversational implicature, see H.P. Grice, "Logic and Conversation" (1975), repr. in: H.P. Grice, *Studies in the Way of Words* (Cambridge: Harvard University Press, 1989), 22–40. See also S.C. Levinson, *Pragmatics* (Cambridge Textbooks in Linguistics; Cambridge: Cambridge University Press, 1983, 1985²), 97–166, and Zwiep, *Tussen tekst en lezer*, 2:276–278.
[29] R. Pesch, *Die Apostelgeschichte (Apg 1–12)* (EKKNT 5; Solothurn: Benziger; Neukirchen-Vluyn: Neukirchener, 1986, 1995²), 68. Also D. Marguerat, *Les Actes des Apôtres (1–12)* (CNT 5a; Geneva: Labor et Fides, 2007), 40.
[30] Lohfink, *Himmelfahrt Jesu*, 153–158. Followed by Zmijewski, *Apostelgeschichte*, 56–57. Zmijewski reads the second question as: 'Wird das Reich (*nur*) *'für Israel'* wiederhergestellt? Anders gefragt: Bleibt das eschatologische Heil auf die Juden beschränkt' (57) (first italics added, second original).

der Verse 7–8 erfolgen können.'[31] First, according to Lohfink, the question is about timing: 'is it *in this time* (now) that you will restore the kingdom to Israel?' Second, the question is about spatiality: 'that you will restore the kingdom *to Israel*.' Third, the question is about Christology: 'is it *you* who will restore the kingdom to Israel?'[32] Now Lohfink is certainly correct in pointing out the congruence between question and answer – Luke has carefully construed them, one in view of the other. However, this must not be taken in the sense that the disciples are actually asking three questions, three different questions in one. It is rather *one* question, as I just suggested – the question about *timing*, as is clear from the fronting of the time marker ἐν τῷ χρόνῳ τούτῳ – which implicates the spatial and Christological aspects *as already given*. That the kingdom will be restored *to Israel* and that *Jesus* will assume an active role in its restoration, is taken for granted (and can be reasonably inferred by Luke's audience from the Gospel, e.g., from the Birth Narratives). The spatial and Christological aspects implied in the question are not problematized, at any rate, nor are they significantly or substantially corrected in the answer.[33]

3.3. *The question responds to an issue in the time of Luke and his readers*

The problem of imminent expectation (*'Naherwartung'*) is not a specifically early-Christian concern.[34] *In nuce* it is already found in the Hebrew Bible, e.g. in Habakkuk 2:2–3 ('If [the end] seems to tarry, wait for it; it will surely come, it will not delay'), and in the ministry of John the Baptist (Matthew 3:10 // Luke 3:9 (Q): 'Even now the axe is lying at the root of the trees'). However, the fall of Jerusalem and the destruction of the temple must have ignited an apocalyptic fever among Jews and Christians alike.

---

[31] Lohfink, *Himmelfahrt Jesu*, 154.
[32] This is the weakest point of Lohfink's argument. The Greek has ἀποκαθιστάνεις, with no emphatic σύ.
[33] So also J. Jervell, *Die Apostelgeschichte* (KEK III; Göttingen: Vandenhoeck & Ruprecht, 1998), 114: 'Es wird nicht danach gefragt, *ob* das Reich für Israel wiederhergestellt werden soll, denn das ist selbstverständlich. Dies wird ja auch in der Antwort Jesu nicht korrigiert (...). Die Frage ist nicht, *ob* das Reich für Israel kommen wird, sondern ausschliesslich: *Wann* kommt das Reich ...?' (italics original).
[34] See A. Strobel, *Untersuchungen zum eschatologischen Verzögerungsproblem auf Grund der spätjüdisch-urchristlichen Geschichte von Habakuk 2,2ff.* (NovTSup 2; Leiden: Brill, 1961). A different assessment is given by K.R. Jones, *Jewish Reactions to the Destruction of the Temple in 70 A.D.: Apocalypses and Related Pseudepigrapha* (Supplements to the Journal for the Study of Judaism 151; Leiden: Brill, 2011).

Contemporary Jewish apocalypses such as *4 Ezra* and *2 Baruch*, and texts from the Dead Sea scrolls were written in the conviction that the End was near, or at least from the conviction that the non-arrival of the Day of Judgement was problematic and demanded an explanation.[35]

3.4. *Question and answer reflect a typical Lukan theological (eschatological) concern*

As I have argued elsewhere, there is a firm element of imminent expectation in Luke's Gospel.[36] Without any apparent sign of embarrassment, Luke passes on some of the harshest *Naherwartungslogia* preserved in the Jesus tradition (Luke 9:27 // Mark 9:1 ['Some of those standing here will not taste death until they see that the kingdom of God has come with power']; Luke 21:32 // Mark 13:30 ['This generation will not pass away until all these things have taken place']; Luke 22:18 // Mark 14:25 ['I will never drink the fruit of the vine until that day when I drink it new in the kingdom of God'; cf. John 6:53]). Although Luke mitigates the stress on judgement in Q considerably, the apocalyptic-eschatological preaching of John the Baptist is still characterized by the expectation of an impending eschatological wrath (Luke 3:7, 9, 17). The Seventy(-two) disciples are to announce the imminent coming of the eschatological kingdom of God (Luke 10:9, 11; cf. 21:31). And in the Parable of the Unjust Judge (Luke 18:1–8), which comes immediately after a set of eschatological instructions (Luke 17:20–37), God is promised to act 'quickly, speedily' (ἐν τάχει, 18:8) on behalf of his elect, that is, at the parousia of the Son of Man. Texts that are usually put forth in support of a 'delay' theory (e.g. Luke 12:38, 45; 13:6–9; 19:11, 12; 20:9; 21:8)

---

[35] W. Harnisch, *Verhängnis und Verheißung der Geschichte: Untersuchungen zum Zeit- und Geschichtsverständnis im 4. Buch Esra und in der syr. Baruchapokalypse* (FRLANT 97; Göttingen: Vandenhoeck & Ruprecht, 1969); Jones, *Jewish Reactions*. E.g. 4 Ezra 4:26: 'the age is hastening swiftly to its end' [trans. B.M. Metzger, in *The Old Testament Pseudepigrapha*, ed. J.H. Charlesworth (New York: Doubleday, 1985), 2:530]; 4 Ezra 4:33–50 (*OTP* 2:531); 8:61 (*OTP* 2:544): 'Therefore my judgment is now drawing near;' 11:44 (*OTP* 2:549): 'And the Most High has looked upon his times, and behold, they are ended, and his ages are completed!;' 2 Bar. 85:10 (trans. A.F.J. Klijn, *OTP* 2:651): 'For the youth of this world has passed away, and the power of creation is already exhausted, and the coming of the times is very near and has passed by. And the pitcher is near the well, and the ship to the harbour, and the journey to the city, and life to its end.'

[36] For what follows see A.W. Zwiep, *The Ascension of the Messiah in Lukan Christology* (NovTSup 87; Leiden: Brill, 1997), 175–181; A.W. Zwiep, "*Assumptus est in caelum*: Rapture and Heavenly Exaltation in Early Judaism and Luke-Acts" (2001), in: *Christ, the Spirit and the Community of God*, 38–67.

may well account for the 'delay' that had *already* occurred at the time of Luke – if Luke wrote in the 80s or 90s of the first century CE the duration of the interval had already been extended to over half a century! – and needed not necessarily be extended very much beyond his own time.[37] Even though Luke's primary interest is in the present, not the future (one is reminded here of his special use of σήμερον 'today'),[38] he cannot be denied a concern with an imminent eschatological expectation. For the implied reader of Luke's Gospel the question of the disciples therefore cannot come as a surprise!

3.5. *Question and answer are a-synchronic*

At first sight, the question of the disciples is a *closed-ended* question, or, in the terminology of Estes, a 'polar question.'[39] Is this the time? can be answered with a simple *yes* or *no* (or *no, not yet*). But the answer does not zoom in on the *timing* itself – the question about timing is blocked. Rather the questioners' right to pose the question (or, as Bengel says, the right to know the answer)[40] is put on the table and problematized: 'It is not for you to know,' or less diplomatic, 'it's none of your business.' The issue is lifted to a meta-level, away from the timing aspect and redirecting the attention to the disciples' responsibility *in the present*. This, incidentally, is also the case with the second question in the book of Acts, in v. 11, which strengthens the impression that this is a particular *Lukan* concern. The angelic question to the witnesses of the ascension, 'Men of Galilee, why do you stand looking up toward heaven?' (ἄνδρες Γαλιλαῖοι, τί ἑστήκατε [ἐμ]βλέποντες εἰς τὸν οὐρανόν;), suggests that it is *not now* appropriate to stand there and look up toward heaven; rather they should now go into the world and proclaim the gospel to all nations.

---

[37] See also A.J. Mattill, *Luke and the Last Things: A Perspective for the Understanding of Lukan Thought* (Dillsboro, NC: Western North Carolina Press, 1979), *passim*; Eric Franklin, *Christ the Lord: A Study in the Purpose and Theology of Luke-Acts* (London: SPCK, 1975), 14–15, 19–20, 26.

[38] Luke 2:11; 3:22; 4:21; 5:26; 12:28; 13:32, 33; 19:5, 9; 22:34, 61; 23:43; Acts 4:9; 13:33; 19:40; 20:26; 22:3; 24:21; 26:2, 29; 27:33. See A. Denaux and R. Corstjens, in collaboration with H. Mardaga, *The Vocabulary of Luke: An Alphabetical Presentation and a Survey of Characteristic and Noteworthy Words and Word Groups in Luke's Gospel* (BTS 10; Leuven: Peeters, 2009), 558.

[39] Estes, *Questions and Rhetoric*, 94–100. Polar questions 'ask for a positive or negative answer (…) the set of answers for polar questions is extremely limited (…) and the question is highly directed by the asker' (94, 95).

[40] Cf. Bengel, *Gnomon*, 435: 'Non dicit non est juris et officii vestri quaerere: sed ait Non vestrum est nosse.'

Of course, the perplexed disciples can hardly be blamed for looking into the sky when they had just seen Jesus disappearing in a cloud and, with the command of Luke 21:28 in mind ('Now when these things begin to take place, stand up and raise your heads, because your redemption is drawing near'), it is the most natural thing to do. But again, there is a temporal issue: it is *not now* appropriate – but it will be in the future.

3.6. *The question fits Luke's (positive) portrayal of the apostolic circle*

Different from Mark's more ambivalent description of the Twelve, Luke demonstrates a more positive attitude toward the apostolic band.[41] They time and again display misunderstanding but in the end *they* are the examples to be followed; *they* are, after all, the leaders to whom the risen Lord entrusted his post-resurrection teaching about the kingdom (1:3). Luke certainly does not paint them in such dark colours as Calvin did. Jesus' response to the disciples' question does *not* entail a stern rebuke, as in Peter's earlier reaction to Jesus's prediction of his imminent death and resurrection reported in Mark 8:33 // Matthew 16:23 ('Get behind me, Satan!'), a text dropped by Luke in the parallel passage.[42] Nor does he blame the disciples for their lack of faith, as in Luke 9:41 ('You faithless and perverse generation, how much longer must I be with you and bear with you?'), nor does he utter a complaint about their slowness of heart as in the case of the disciples from Emmaus (24:25: 'Oh, how foolish you are, and how slow of heart to believe all that the prophets had declared!'). Even in Luke 19:11, where it is said that the disciples 'supposed (implied is: wrongly) that the kingdom of God was to appear immediately,' Jesus does *not* criticize the expectation of the coming of the kingdom as such, but (as here) redirects the disciples' attention to what is to be done in the meantime.[43] Given these precedents, it is telling

---

[41] Zwiep, "Putting Paul in Place," 157–175, esp. 161–162.

[42] H. Schürmann, *Das Lukasevangelium 1,1–9,50* (HThKNT 3; Freiburg: Herder, 1969, 1984²), 536: 'Luk läßt Mk 8, 32f fort, weil er – hier wie sonst häufig – die Jünger schonen will;' J.A. Fitzmyer, *The Gospel according to Luke I–IX: A New Translation with Introduction and Commentary* (AB 28A; Garden City: Doubleday, 1981), 777: Luke 'undoubtedly considered the rebuke unflattering to Peter;' F. Bovon, *L'Évangile selon saint Luc 1–9* (CNT 3a; Genève: Labor et Fides, 1991), 467: 'Luc omet enfin le court sommaire puis l'entretien véhément entre Pierre et Jésus de Mc 8, 32–33, parce qu'il ne voit pas le sens qu'aurait une prédication à ce moment-là et qu'il ne supporte pas la dureté du mystérieux dialogue.'

[43] So, *inter alios*, also D.L. Tiede, "The Exaltation of Jesus and the Restoration of Israel in Acts 1," *HTR* 79 (1986): 278–286 ('Jesus' final words respond positively to the question of restoration,' 278); Buzzard, "Acts 1:6."

that in Acts 1:7 the Lukan Jesus does not accuse the disciples of misunderstanding, faithlessness or slowness of heart, although Luke had a stock repertoire at hand to make such an accusation. In Luke's view, then, the disciples' question does not arise from a structural misunderstanding – the hope of an imminent arrival of the kingdom τῷ Ἰσραήλ[44] still stands; it is the time-table that he finds problematic.[45]

4. Conclusion

That, according to Luke, the disciples' question does not arise from ignorance or stupidity, does not mean that question and answer are perfectly balanced. On the contrary, there still is a fair degree of a-synchronism. However, as both structuralists and poststructuralists argue, meaning

---

[44] I take τῷ Ἰσραήλ as a dative of advantage (*commodi*) [cf. F. Blass and A. Debrunner, *Grammatik des neutestamentlichen Griechisch*, ed. F. Rehkopf (Göttingen: Vandenhoeck & Ruprecht, 2001[18]), § 188.1; D.B. Wallace, *Greek Grammar beyond the Basics: An Exegetical Syntax of the New Testament* (Grand Rapids: Zondervan, 1996), 142–144], *pace* Joachim Eck (Eichstätt-Ingolstadt), who suggested that based on LXX usage it might perhaps be taken as an instrumental dative, indicating the restoration of the kingdom *through* Israel (oral communication d.d. 11 September 2019). However, Luke would almost certainly have used a construction with ἐν or διά. For Luke, Jesus rather than Israel is instrumental in the restoration of the kingdom, Israel is its recipient (cf. Acts 3:26 ὑμῖν πρῶτον ἀναστήσας ὁ θεὸς τὸν παῖδα αὐτοῦ ἀπέστειλεν αὐτὸν εὐλογοῦντα ὑμᾶς, my italics). Codex Bezae reads τοῦ Ἰσραήλ (d: istrahel). On Luke's perspective on Israel and its future, see further M. Neubrand, *Israel, die Völker und die Kirche: Eine exegetische Studie zu Apg. 15* (SBB; Stuttgart: Katholisches Bibelwerk, 2006); M.F. Fuller, *The Restoration of Israel: Israel's Re-gathering and the Fate of the Nations in Early Jewish Literature and Luke-Acts* (BZNW 138; Berlin: de Gruyter, 2006); M.A. Salmeier, *Restoring the Kingdom: The Role of God as the "Ordainer of Times and Seasons" in the Acts of the Apostles* (PTMS 165; Eugene: Pickwick, 2011); C. Schaefer, *Die Zukunft Israels bei Lukas: Biblisch-frühjüdische Zukunftsvorstellungen im lukanischen Doppelwerk im Vergleich zu Röm 9–11* (BZNW 190; Berlin: de Gruyter, 2012); K. Crabbe, *Luke/Acts and the End of History* (BZNW 238; Berlin: de Gruyter, 2019).

[45] Contra E. Haenchen, *Die Apostelgeschichte*, (KEK III; Göttingen: Vandenhoeck & Ruprecht, 1956, 1977[7]), 150: Luke 'hat entschlossen auf die Naherwartung des Endes verzichtet;' E. Grässer, *Das Problem der Parusieverzögerung in den synoptischen Evangelien und in der Apostelgeschichte* (BZNW 22; Berlin: de Gruyter, 1957, 1977[3]), 204–209; E. Grässer, "Die Parusieerwartung in der Apostelgeschichte," in: J. Kremer (Ed.), *Les Actes des Apôtres: Traditions, rédaction, théologie* (BETL 48; Gembloux: Duculot; Leuven, University Press, 1979), 99–127: 'Die fixierte Naherwartung ist nicht nur *geschichtlich überholt. Sie ist Irrlehre* (s. Lk 21,8 im Vergleich mit Mk 13,6) (…) Da Lukas die Durchlässigkeit dieser Konzeption für eine Individualeschatologie mehrmals deutlich markiert hat, ist es *völlig gleichgültig, wie lange die Parusie verzieht. Hypothetisch läßt sie sich sogar für immer streichen*, ohne daß die Heilsökonomie Gottes fundamentalen Schaden nähme' (124–125, my emphasis).

arises through difference (or *différance*).[46] In the answer given in the verses 7–8, the Lukan Jesus redirects the disciples' attention away from the future to the present and their present duty to proclaim the Gospel.[47] How exactly the Father will realize the expected 'restoration of the kingdom to Israel' will be part and parcel of Luke's subsequent narrative. This narrative will show how the 'Biblical' notion of Israel is redefined to include the Jesus story and the Gentile mission.[48] The disciples' question,

---

[46] Cf. Zwiep, *Tussen tekst en lezer*, 2:225, 381–385.

[47] P.W. van der Horst, "Hellenistic Parallels to the Acts of the Apostles (1,1–26)," *ZNW* 74 (1983): 20, instances the following Hellenistic parallels to Acts 1:7: Sophocles, *Fragments*, fragm. 590; LCL 483:296–297 (Lloyd-Jones): (chorus) θνητὴν δὲ φύσιν χρὴ θνητὰ φρονεῖν, τοῦτο κατειδότας, ὡς οὐκ ἔστινπλὴν Διὸς οὐδεὶς τῶν μελλόντωνταμίας ὅ τι χρὴ τετελέσθαι. 'Human nature must think human thoughts, knowing that there is no master of the future, of what is destined to be accomplished, except Zeus.' Plutarch, *Mor. Sera* 4.549–550F, LCL 405:190–191 (De Lacy, Einarson): πλέον γάρ ἐστι τοῦ περὶ μουσικῶν ἀμούσους καὶ πολεμικῶν ἀστρατεύτους διαλέγεσθαι τὸ τὰ θεῖα καὶ τὰ δαιμόνια πράγματα διασκοπεῖν ἀνθρώπους ὄντας, οἷον ἀτέχνους τεχνιτῶν διάνοιαν ἀπὸ δόξης καὶ ὑπονοίας κατὰ τὸ εἰκὸς μετιόντας. οὐ γὰρ ἰατροῦ μὲν ἰδιώτην ὄντα συμβαλεῖν λογισμόν, ὡς πρότερον οὐκ ἔτεμεν, ἀλλ' ὕστερον, οὐδ' ἐχθὲς ἔκαυσεν, ἀλλὰ σήμερον, ἔργον ἐστί, περὶ θεῶν δὲ θνητὸν ῥᾴδιον ἢ βέβαιον εἰπεῖν ἄλλο πλὴν ὅτι τὸν καιρὸν εἰδὼς ἄριστα τῆς περὶ τὴν κακίαν ἰατρείας ὡς φάρμακον ἑκάστῳ προσφέρει τὴν κόλασιν, οὔτε μεγέθους μέτρον κοινὸν οὔτε χρόνον ἕνα καὶ τὸν αὐτὸν ἐπὶ πάντων ἔχουσαν, 'For it is presumptuous enough for those untrained in music to speak about things musical, and for those of no military experience about war; but it is more presumptuous for mere human beings like ourselves to inquire into the concerns of gods and daemons, where we are like laymen seeking to follow the thought of experts by the guesswork of opinion and imputation. It cannot be that while it is hard for a layman to conjecture the reasoning of a doctor – why he used the knife later and not before, and cauterized not yesterday but to-day – it should be easy or safe for a mortal to say anything else about God than this: that he knows full well the right moment for healing vice, and administers punishment to each patient as a medicine, a punishment neither given in the same amount in every case nor after the same interval for all.' And for a parallel to χρόνους ἢ καιρούς: Demosthenes, *Orations* III, *3 Olynth.* 16; LCL 238:50–51 (Vince): τίνα γὰρ χρόνον ἢ τίνα καιρόν, ὦ ἄνδρες Ἀθηναῖοι, τοῦ παρόντος βελτίω ζητεῖτε; 'Why, what better time or occasion could you find than the present, men of Athens?'

[48] Redefined, not replaced or rejected, with Barrett, *Acts*, 1:77–78; cf. with somewhat different emphases R.L. Brawley, *Luke-Acts and the Jews: Conflict, Apology, and Concilliation* (SBLMS 33; Atlanta: Scholars, 1987); J. Jervell, *Luke and the People of God: A New Look at Luke-Acts* (Minneapolis: Augsburg, 1972); J. Jervell, *Apostelgeschichte*; K. Haacker, *Die Apostelgeschichte* (TKNT 5; Stuttgart: Kohlhammer, 2019), 28–32 ("Gottes Königherrschaft ... 'zionistisch zentriert'," 28). Contra H. Conzelmann, *Die Mitte der Zeit: Studien zur Theologie des Lukas* (Beiträge zur historischen Theologie 17; Tübingen: Mohr Siebeck, 1954, 1977⁶), 152: 'Act 1,6 redet vom Reich für Israel. Nicht die Hoffnung darauf wird zurückgewiesen, sondern nur die Berechnung des Zeitpunktes.' But then Conzelmann continues: 'Woran aber Lucas denkt, zeigt V. 8.... An diesen beiden Stellen [= Acts 28:28 and 13:17ff.] wird der Gedanken des Lukas von der *planmäßigen Ablösung der Juden durch die Christen* im Zusammenhang eines Periodenschemas besonders klar' (emphasis mine). Cf. T. Jantsch, *Jesus, der Retter: Die*

then, launches Luke's narrative in a very appropriate way. In a way, the whole book of Acts is Luke's personal attempt to provide an answer to the very question. And, perhaps even more to the point, if I am correct in reading a fair degree of imminent expectation into Luke's work, at the end of Acts (28:28, 31)[49] the disciples' question is still as appropriate and even all the more urgent as it was at the beginning of Acts.[50]

Soteriologie des lukanischen Doppelwerks (WUNT 381; Tübingen: Mohr Siebeck, 2017), 292–294: '[d]iese Erwartung [der Wiedererrichtung des Königtums in Israel] wird grundsätzlich desavouiert' (293).

[49] V. 29 (Καὶ ταῦτα εἰπόντος αὐτοῦ ἀπῆλθον οἱ Ἰουδαῖοι πολλὴν ἔχοντες ἐν ἑαυτοῖς συζήτησιν, see Swanson, *Acts*, 493; Boismard, *Texte occidentale*, 429) is a Western addition (adopted by the Majority text). See on this variant E.J. Epp, *The Theological Tendency of Codex Bezae Cantabrigiensis in Acts* (SNTSMS 3; Cambridge: Cambridge University Press, 1966), 114–115; B.M. Metzger, *A Textual Commentary on the Greek New Testament* (Stuttgart: Deutsche Bibelgesellschaft, United Bible Societies, 1971, 1994²), 444.

[50] Cf. also J.T. Carroll, *Response to the End of History: Eschatology and Situation in Luke-Acts* (SBLDS 92; Atlanta: Scholars, 1988), 127–128: "Luke and his community live ... on the far side of a series of events which have fulfilled scripture (and the promise of the risen Lord as well) and brought the eschaton itself closer to realization. In such a situation, persevering hope in Jesus' return – not in the distant future but at an imminent, while unspecified point in time – becomes especially important. Luke's narration of Jesus' final episode with his followers and his ascension into heaven serves to undergird just such eschatological faith." Contra N.T. Wright's metaphorical interpretation in *The New Testament and the People of God*, vol. 1 of *Christian Origins and the Question of God* (London: SPCK, 1992); *Jesus and the Victory of God*, vol. 2 of *Christian Origins and the Question of God* (London: SPCK, 1996), and *Surprised by Hope* (London: SPCK, 2007). With E. Adams, *The Stars Will Fall from Heaven: "Cosmic Catastrophy" in the New Testament and Its World* (LNTS 347; London: T&T Clark, 2007).

AN ERŌTĒSIS IN ROMANS 8:31–39
On the Importance of Questions and Question Marks

Bert Jan LIETAERT PEERBOLTE
Free University Amsterdam

1. Introduction

In this volume on questions in biblical texts a contribution on Paul is definitely necessary. The Pauline epistles, both the undisputed ones and the disputed letters, clearly show traces of ancient rhetorical conventions and are therefore important for the subject under discussion here. Since a general contribution on Pauline questions would be far too broad in scope, this essay approaches the topic from another angle. Instead of focusing on the general use of questions, it looks at one text in particular, in which Paul applies questions as a rhetorical device: Romans 8:33-34. As will become clear below, the ambiguity of this particular text poses a problem for modern editors of the Greek New Testament, and the current contribution argues that the interpunction in the Modern Critical Text (MCT) should be revised. The verses mentioned appear to contain two questions that are overlooked by the conventional interpunction in modern editions. Before we turn to the text under discussion, however, it is good to begin with some general observations (§ 2). After that, we will turn to the position of Romans 8:31–39 within the whole of the letter to the Romans (§ 3), to then look into the history of printing conventions in editions since Erasmus as well as the manuscript evidence (§ 4). Finally, Augustine of Hippo's analysis of the passage under discussion here will prove to contain a sharp analysis of what is at stake (§ 5). The conclusion will be, as said, that the interpunction of the verses under discussion is in need of revision, and that Paul's use of questions was an even stronger rhetorical instrument than is currently suggested by the MCT.

2. Questions in Paul

2.1. *Paul's letters and the spoken word*

Paul's letters are generally regarded as written versions of spoken communication, and the rules of ancient rhetoric are broadly applied by Pauline scholars in their attempts to understand his oftentimes dense way of arguing.[1] The Epistle to the Romans is perhaps the most polished and the most extensive piece of Pauline rhetoric.[2] The letter is, as is well known, an exception to the rule that Paul wrote his letters to congregations he had founded himself. In Romans, Paul introduces himself and his Gospel to the followers of Jesus Christ in Rome. In a way, Paul has to formulate his own credentials in this letter, which he plans to send to Rome in order to pave the way for him to visit this group or these groups of Christ followers.[3] Obviously, it is unknown how the Gospel took hold in Rome, and who was or were responsible for its arrival in the capital.

The rhetoric of Romans is clearly more polished than, for instance, Paul's first letter to the Corinthians. The letter's opening is longer than usual, and in 1:1–7 Paul introduces the Gospel as rooted in the prophecies of old and for that reason not at all new.[4] Jesus Christ, the Son of God, a descendent of David, rose from the dead, and his fate and ministry thus have meaning for all humankind. In 1:16–17 Paul gives a summary of the Gospel, which he expands in an argument that addresses 'the Jew' and 'the Greek' directly, in the second person singular. Both have shown their inability to reach out to God directly, and thus, Paul argues, God has sent his Son. Romans 3:21–31 presents the Gospel as a universal proclamation of freedom and acquittal. Then, in the long passage of 4:1–8:39, Paul deals with a number of fundamental questions regarding

---

[1] This essay is dedicated to the memory of Robert Jewett (1933–2020). I had the pleasure of sharing an office with him during my 2016 stay in Heidelberg as fellow of the *Forschungszentrum für internationale und interdisziplinäre Theologie* (FIIT), and cherish the memories of the rich encounters with him and the conversations we had on Paul's argumentative techniques.

[2] See e.g. the discussion by B. Witherington III, with D. Hyatt, *Paul's Letter to the Romans: A Socio-Rhetorical Commentary* (Grand Rapids: Eerdmans, 2004), especially 16–25. On the roots of Paul's rhetorical skills, see R.F. Hock, "Paul and Greco-Roman Education," in: J.P. Sampley (Ed.), *Paul in the Greco-Roman World: A Handbook*, Vol. 1 (London.: Bloomsbury T&T Clark, 2016), 230–253.

[3] A.J.M. Wedderburn, *The Reasons for Romans* (Edinburgh: T&T Clark, 1988), 75–87; B.J. Lietaert Peerbolte, *Paul the Missionary* (CBET 34; Leuven: Peeters, 2003), 244–254.

[4] The opening verses of Romans can even be seen as a summary of the Gospel, as is done by G. Agamben, *The Time that Remains: A Commentary on the Letter to the Romans* (Meridian; Stanford: Stanford University Press, 2005).

the Gospel. In 8:31–39 Paul wraps up his argument, and in a lyrical passage he concludes that both Jew and Greek, if they are called by God, cannot be separated from the love of Christ. It is this passage that requires our attention in the current contribution.

2.2. *How to recognize a question?*

Before we tune in to the section under scrutiny in this contribution, it is important to first study the elementary question of how to recognize a question. In any modern edition of the Greek text a question is made recognizable by means of a semicolon (;) that functions as a question mark in Greek, but this is a modern convention that can be seen to reflect the interpretative tradition. Douglas Estes estimates the number of direct questions in the GNT at approximately 980 and counts 87 direct questions in Romans.[5]

In antiquity, Greek was largely written without interpunction, and this remained the common practice until the 9th century, when minuscules came to replace uncial manuscripts. The ancient grammarian Dionysius Thrax mentions three types of *stigme*: 'the final point, the middle point, and the 'under' point (*hypostigme*).'[6] Dionysius explains the function of the *stigme* as follows:

> *The final point is the sign of a completed thought, the middle point is used for the sake of breathing, and the under point is an indicator of sense which is not yet complete. In what respect does the point differ from the under point? In time: the interval is substantial with the point, with the under point it is much less.*[7]

Thus, in order to recognize a question in an uncial manuscript we will have to look at the syntax of a clause as well as the context. If a clause contains an interrogative pronoun, it is likely to be a question, be it direct

---

[5] Only 1 Corinthians exceeds this number: in Estes' count it contains 106 direct questions. For the statistics, see D. Estes, *Questions and Rhetoric in the Greek New Testament: An Essential Reference Resource for Exegesis* (Grand Rapids: Zondervan Academic, 2017). https://search-ebscohost-com.vu-nl.idm.oclc.org/login.aspx?direct=true&db=nlebk&AN=1780524&site=ehost-live. Accessed March 9, 2021.

[6] This quote and the translation of Dionysius Thrax in S. Colvin, *A Brief History of Ancient Greek* (Chichester: Wiley, 2014), 54–55.

[7] A.T. Robertson, *A Grammar of the Greek New Testament in the Light of Historical Research* (London: Hodder & Stoughton, ³1914 [¹1859]), 242, gives a similar description: 'The point at the top of the line (·) (στιγμὴ τελεία, 'high point') was a full stop; that on the line (.) (ὑποστιγμή) was equal to our semicolon, while a middle point (στιγμὴ μέση) was equivalent to our comma.' The footnote Robertson adds, however, indicates that these interpretations were subject to discussion also in the 19th century.

or indirect. This does not mean, however, that a clause without an interrogative pronoun cannot be a question. Here, the context of the clause is decisive, and it will become clear below that this criterion sometimes leads to ambiguity in both the manuscript tradition and in modern editions.

2.3. *Questions in Romans*

It is evident that Paul frequently uses questions in Romans in order to take the readers/hearers by the hand and usher them into his line of thinking. If we focus on Paul's usage of questions in Romans, it is noteworthy that in 3:27 he introduces the figure of an *erōtēsis*, a series of questions, beginning with Ποῦ οὖν ἡ καύχησις; ἐξεκλείσθη.[8] Paul's rhetoric continues with διὰ ποίου νόμου; τῶν ἔργων; οὐχί, ἀλλὰ διὰ νόμου πίστεως. From here until the end of chapter 8 Paul builds a complex argument in which he discusses the meaning of the Gospel, and positions it in the history of humanity, and to be more precise: Israel. Especially the relationship between the Gospel and the Law of Moses is important here, and Paul's move in chapter 5 is to juxtapose Christ not with Abraham or with Moses, but with Adam. Just as all human beings die through the sin of Adam, Paul argues, all human beings in Christ will share in his resurrection.

The rhetorical importance of 8:31–39 is evident if one takes into account that it forms the closing statement of the first main part of the letter and thus also the transition to the discussion of the status of Israel over against Christ in chapters 9–11. In that section, Paul moves away from the themes discussed in the previous part of the letter, but clearly builds his argument on the basis of the idea of God's consistency and God's faithfulness which he praises in 8:31–39. So, on the basis of the rhetorical structure of Romans these verses form a closing statement, but at the same time they introduce the theme of the next part, viz. the faithfulness of God over against Israel.

The rhetorical character of Romans is especially visible in the number of questions Paul uses throughout the letter. The interrogative reference τί οὖν, for instance, occurs eleven times in Romans (3:1, 9; 4:1; 6:1, 15; 7:7; 8:31; 9:14, 19, 30; 11:7) and Paul uses τί without οὖν to introduce a question the same number of times (3:3, 5, 7; 4:3; 9:19, 32; 10:8; 11:2, 4; 14:10 [twice]). This means that the use of questions is

---
[8] For an exact description of an *erōtēsis*, cf. the discussion of Aristotle below.

well attested in Romans, and forms an important element in Paul's rhetoric of this letter, and, as will be argued below, the emphatic use of questions in 8:31–39 is not by accident.

3. Romans 8:31–39 within the whole of the letter

One of the main questions surrounding Romans 9–11 is the question: how do the 'remnant' of Israel, with which Paul opens his argument, and the 'whole of Israel,' that is so crucial to his point in the final verses of chapter 11 relate to each other? Put differently: how does 9:6b (οὐ γὰρ πάντες οἱ ἐξ Ἰσραὴλ οὗτοι Ἰσραήλ) relate to 11:26 (καὶ οὕτως πᾶς Ἰσραὴλ σωθήσεται)? In the opening lines of these three chapters, Paul explains how there are two forms of Israel: on the one hand, there are the followers of Jesus the Messiah, and on the other hand, there are those Israelites who reject him as such. The underlying theme that is foundational for the argument of chapters 9–11 is the point that is introduced in the passage under discussion here, viz. the love of God through Christ for human beings, whether they are Jew or Greek.

There is much to be said in favour of a comparison between 1 Corinthians 8–12 and the argument Paul makes in Romans 9–11. In 1 Corinthians 8 Paul's premise is that everyone is allowed to eat meat sacrificed to idols, and the conclusion of his argument is the opposite: if the result of my eating meat sacrificed to idols is the fall of my brother or sister, I shall never eat that meat again in my life.[9] This rhetorical strategy is copied in Romans 9–11: the premise is that only the remnant of Israel is loyal, but the conclusion is that *all* of Israel will be saved. This is not the place to deal with the question whether that salvation for all of Israel will be the result of the rest of Israel accepting Jesus as the Messiah or not. Paul's position is not very clear in Romans 11: it may be that he expects the whole of Israel to ultimately accept Jesus as the Messiah, it may be that he expects that part of Israel that does not do so to be accepted by God after all. Yet the exact expectation of Paul concerning the redemption of Israel is not the point of this essay. What is important here is that Paul uses a clear rhetorical strategy in Romans 9–11 in which his point of departure is the observation that only a small remnant of Israel accepts Jesus as the Messiah, but that ultimately the whole of Israel will be saved, while God is and will remain faithful to his people. In this view, Romans

---

[9] See also J. Smit, *About the Idol Offerings, Rhetoric, Social Context and Theology of Paul's Discourse in First Corinthians 8:1–11:1* (CBET 27; Louvain: Peeters, 2000).

9–11 reflects deliberate composition on the part of Paul, and this deliberate composition may reflect Paul's *pathos*, but that does not mean that these chapters were written in an emotional state and that Paul may not have realized exactly what he was saying. Hence, the part following on the section under discussion here should be seen as the result of deliberate composition as well, which also goes for 8:31–39, the section that forms the bridge to chapters 9–11.

3.1. Questions in Romans as rhetorical indicators

After the extended opening formula of 1:1–7, Paul continues with the thanksgiving section (1:8–15) to then state the *status causae* of the letter in 1:16–17.[10] Paul clearly summarizes his Gospel by means of his quotation of Habakkuk 2:4, in which he cleverly leaves out the personal pronoun μου from the Septuagint, and thus slightly alters the meaning of the words quoted: 'the righteous will live through faith' (ὁ δὲ δίκαιος ἐκ πίστεως ζήσεται).[11] The next section contains a description of how both Jew and Greek have nothing to boast about over against God, for Jews have the Law, but do not keep it, and Greeks could have come to know God but failed to do so (1:18–3:20). Then, in 3:21–26, Paul gives a second summary of his Gospel, to discuss the effect of this Gospel on Abrahamic ancestry in 3:27–4:25. In this passage he tacitly introduces the topics to which he will return in chapters 9–11. The section 5:1–8:39 subsequently describes the implications of the advent of the Gospel for the followers of Christ.

As argued above, throughout the letter to the Romans Paul makes use of rhetorical devices, and one such device, no doubt taken from the popular style figure of the *diatribe,* is the use of questions. Let us focus on two examples. The first was already mentioned above: in 3:27 Paul starts a description of the consequences of the advent of the Gospel. Having argued that Jew nor Greek has anything to boast about and having subsequently described the Gospel, he continues with a question: 'Then what becomes of boasting?' (ποῦ οὖν ἡ καύχησις;). He answers his own

---

[10] These verses were already identified as such by Philipp Melanchthon; cf. S.J. Chester, *Reading Paul with the Reformers: Reconciling Old and New Perspectives* (Grand Rapids: Eerdmans, 2017), especially 219–224.

[11] The LXX reads ὁ δὲ δίκαιος ἐκ πίστεως μου ζήσεται and since Yhwh is speaking, this should be translated as 'the righteous person will live because of my faithfulness.' Or, as the translation of Pietersma and Wright reads: 'But the just shall live by my faith'; cf. A. Pietersma and B.G. Wright (Eds.), *A New English Translation of the Septuagint and the Other Greek Translations Traditionally Included under that Title* (New York, Oxford, etc: Oxford University Press, 2007).

question ('It is excluded'), and then immediately continues with the next two questions: 'By what law? By that of works?' (διὰ ποίου νόμου; τῶν ἔργων;). Here, Paul makes use of the figure of an *erōtēsis*, a series of questions intended to underline the point he intends to convey to his audience. The verses 3:27–31 contain a series of twelve clauses, half of which are put in the form of questions.

The second example of the importance of questions for understanding Paul's rhetoric in Romans is his use of the repeated question τί οὖν ἐροῦμεν (NRSV 'What then are we to say?'). Paul uses this particular question six times in Romans, each time introducing a new part of his argument. In 4:1 he turns to the Abrahamic descent of the Jews, and then argues how Abraham is in fact the founding father of an inclusive version of Israel, centred around the faith in Christ, since Abraham himself was counted as righteous because of his faith (see especially 4:16–25). After relating this theme to the typology of Adam and Christ in chapter 5, Paul repeats the question τί οὖν ἐροῦμεν in 6:1. Here, it forms the bridge to his description of baptism and the expected sharing of the resurrection for those who have, through this rite, become unified with the death of Christ. In chapter 7, Paul uses the same question to draw the audience's attention to the point that he is making (7:7). He does the same thing in 8:31; 9:14, 30.

Interestingly enough, the structure of Paul's use of τί οὖν ἐροῦμεν is the same in all six cases. On average, this question introduces a state of affairs that Paul subsequently denies. This is fully in line with the description of an *erōtēsis* by Aristotle – in his *Rhetoric* he discusses this particular style and indicates its function: 'As for interrogation (*erōtēsis*), it is most opportune to use it when an opponent has said one thing and, if the right question is asked, an absurdity results.'[12] Aristotle continues by describing the second function of an *erōtēsis*: 'A second situation is when something is self-evident and it is clear to the questioner that the opponent will grant another point.'[13] Either way, the series of questions moves toward a point that should be seen as the concluding statement of the argument in which an *erōtēsis* is used.[14]

---

[12] Rhetoric 1419a; translation: Aristotle, *On Rhetoric: A Theory of Civic Discourse*, Translated with Introduction, Notes, and Appendices by G.A. Kennedy (Oxford: Oxford University Press, ²2007 [¹1991]), 247.

[13] Rhetoric 1419a.

[14] Aristotle's conclusion: 'Thus, one should not ask any further question after drawing a conclusion nor couch the conclusion as a question unless the balance of truth is in one's favor' (Rhetoric 1419a).

Indeed, the six times Paul uses the clause τί οὖν ἐροῦμεν mostly introduce a point that is subsequently rejected, which is in accord with what Aristotle describes as the first function of an *erōtēsis*. In 4:1 it refers to the idea that Abrahamic descent would be reason for the Jew to boast, and this idea is subsequently rejected. In 6:1 the option is introduced and rejected that followers of Christ should 'continue in sin.' In similar guise 7:7 raises the thought 'that the law is sin,' which is immediately rejected. And in 9:14 the state of affairs that is raised and rejected is the thought that there is 'injustice on God's part'. The last time that Paul uses this introductory question, however, does not refer to an observation that is rejected, but to a conclusion that is emphasized by this particular introduction: the fact that Gentiles who did not strive for righteousness did find it through faith whereas Israel failed to obtain it through the Law (9:30–31). This is in line with the second function described by Aristotle. In line with these observations, it makes sense to look at 8:31–39 as containing a full blown *erōtēsis* that underlines the argument which Paul has described in the main part of his letter (5:1–8:39). The passage under scrutiny here is thereby evidently intended as a rhetorical closing statement of that main part of the letter.

3.2. *Romans 8:31–39 as* peroratio *and* inclusio

Though 8:31–39 has been treated as a hymn in the past or as a doxology, Michael Wolter rightly comments that the correct way to understand it is to see it as an 'argumentative text, that applies rhetorical instruments that are mostly used in the Hellenistic *diatribe*.'[15]

In his Hermeneia commentary, Robert Jewett correctly argues that this section contains an *erōtēsis*, a series of questions that intends to evoke the attention of the audience in order to wrap up the argument made in the section 5:1–8:39 in line with the description by Aristotle referred to above. Let us take a closer look at the passage.

Jewett first of all indicates here that these verses echo motifs of the opening lines of the main part of the letter (5:1–11) and thus form the

---

[15] M. Wolter, *Der Brief an die Römer; Teilband 1: Röm 1–8* (EKKNT 6/1; Neukirchen-Vluyn: Neukirchener Verlag; Patmos: Ostfildern, 2014), 539 (translation LP). K. Haacker, *Der Brief des Paulus an die Römer* (THKNT 6; Leipzig: Evangelische Verlagsanstalt, 1999), 173, mentions the same possibility but does not exclude a hymnic character. Cf. also E. Lohse, *Der Brief an die Römer* (KEK 4; Götttingen: Vandenhoeck & Ruprecht, 2003), 255; U. Wilckens, *Der Brief an die Römer*, Vol. 2 (EKKNT 6/2; Zürich et al.: Benziger; Neukirchen-Vluyn: Neukirchener Verlag, 1978), 172.

peroratio of that entire section.[16] The repetition of motifs from 5:1–11 thus creates a rhetorical *inclusio*:

set right	5:1, 9	8:33
suffering	5:3	8:35–37
God's love	5:5, 8	8:35, 39
Christ's death	5:6, 10	8:34
saved from wrath	5:9	8:31–34
Christ's resurrection	5:10	8:34
rejoicing in God	5:11	8:31–39

The questions with which Paul starts the *erōtēsis* lead the hearer to implied negative answers. After the repeated opening question τί οὖν ἐροῦμεν Paul uses the question particle τίς four times to introduce further questions: τίς καθ' ἡμῶν (v. 31), τίς ἐγκαλέσει (v. 33), τίς ὁ κατακρινῶν (v. 34), and τίς ἡμᾶς χωρίσει (v. 35). In Jewett's words:

> An *erōtēsis* containing ten rhetorical questions is arranged in three sections (8:31–32, 33–34, 34–37), of which the last contains seven forms of suffering in a rhetorically effective series linked with 'or' (v. 35). This reflects a Hebraic numerical preference for seven as the number that connotes completeness.[17]

Jewett's full analysis needs not be quoted here, but his conclusion with regard to this passage as a whole should:

> *It is a wonderful, exultant example of Pauline inspiration, driving artistic prose as far as possible in the direction of poetry and providing the 'emotional appeal to the audience' required in a proper peroration.*[18]

The emphasis in this *peroratio* lies on the nearness and reliability of God as shown in Christ. God's nearness is indicated by the fact that he did not spare his own son, but gave him up 'for all of us' (v. 32). This brings Paul to emphasize that no one will be able to condemn the followers of Christ (vv. 33–34), since nothing will ever separate them from the love of Christ (v. 35). In order to substantiate this last point, Paul mentions a catalogue of hardships in which he lists 'seven forms of adversity.'[19] Jewett here mentions examples of similar lists of hardships from both the pagan world and from Jewish authors, indicating that here, too, Paul deploys a well-known stylistic feature.

---

[16] Jewett, *ad loc.*
[17] Jewett, *ad loc.*
[18] Jewett, *ad loc.*
[19] Jewett, *ad loc.*

After a quotation from Psalm 44:22 Paul continues his argument in an elevated tone mentioning ten possible threats that could hypothetically distance the believers from the love of God in Christ to indicate that this is fully impossible. Thus, Romans 5:1–8:39 reaches its rhetorical climax and Paul enables himself to focus on the next point in his letter from 9:1 on.

One often overlooked, but important point in the text of 8:31–39 is the problem posed by 8:33–34. The MCT prints these two verses as two questions each of which is followed by an answer given by Paul himself:

> τίς ἐγκαλέσει κατὰ ἐκλεκτῶν θεοῦ; θεὸς ὁ δικαιῶν· τίς ὁ κατακρινῶν; Χριστὸς [Ἰησοῦς] ὁ ἀποθανών, μᾶλλον δὲ ἐγερθείς, ὃς καί ἐστιν ἐν δεξιᾷ τοῦ θεοῦ, ὃς καὶ ἐντυγχάνει ὑπὲρ ἡμῶν (NA[28]/ UBS[5]/Tyndale/SBLGNT).

Jewett, however, follows Charles Barrett's analysis here and opts for understanding this as a series of four questions:[20]

> τίς ἐγκαλέσει κατὰ ἐκλεκτῶν θεοῦ; θεὸς ὁ δικαιῶν; τίς ὁ κατακρινῶν; Χριστὸς [Ἰησοῦς] ὁ ἀποθανών, μᾶλλον δὲ ἐγερθείς, ὃς καί ἐστιν ἐν δεξιᾷ τοῦ θεοῦ, ὃς καὶ ἐντυγχάνει ὑπὲρ ἡμῶν;

If the argument proposed by Barrett and Jewett is correct, this would require a change in typography in the next edition of the MCT, and it would even further strengthen the case for the use of questions by Paul as a highly effective rhetorical instrument. In order to substantiate the argument, we will have to take a look at modern editions in order to look into the established conventions, and subsequently check those against the available manuscript evidence.

4. Romans 8:33–34 in editions and manuscripts

It is clear that typographic decisions in any modern edition of an ancient text always reflect editorial choices that are based on both existing conventions, and the manuscript evidence. It is, for that reason, worth the effort to look into both the printing conventions of Romans 8:33–34 and the available manuscript readings.

---

[20] Jewett, *ad loc*. Cf. C.K. Barrett, *A Commentary on the Epistle to the Romans* (Black's New Testament Commentaries; London: Black, 1957), 172–173.

4.1. Romans 8:33 in printed editions of the New Testament

In the quest for the history of the interpunction of 8:33–34 it makes sense to start with the first critical edition of the New Testament, Erasmus' *Novum Instrumentum Omne* of 1516. Erasmus prints these two verses as four clauses consisting of three questions, the first of which is followed by an answer. In modern typography, his text reads as follows:

> τίς ἐγκαλέσει κατὰ ἐκλεκτῶν θεοῦ; θεὸς ὁ δικαιῶν. τίς ὁ κατακρινῶν; Χριστὸς Ἰησοῦς ὁ ἀποθανών, μᾶλλον δὲ ἐγερθείς, ὃς καί ἐστιν ἐν δεξιᾷ τοῦ θεοῦ, ὃς καὶ ἐντυγχάνει ὑπὲρ ἡμῶν;

The Latin translation of the text confirms this typography, so it is clearly not by accident that Erasmus chose this option. Already in his second edition of 1519, however, he corrected this by changing the last question mark into a full stop, thereby introducing the typography that is current in the MCT until today. This decision would be continued in his 3rd, 4th, and 5th editions as well.

It is remarkable to see that Robertus Stephanus' 1546 edition chooses differently. Stephanus decides to put a comma after θεὸς ὁ δικαιῶν, thus combining this clause with the next and adds a question mark after it. The fourth clause ends with a full stop:

> τίς ἐγκαλέσει κατὰ ἐκλεκτῶν θεοῦ; θεὸς ὁ δικαιῶν, τίς ὁ κατακρινῶν; Χριστὸς ὁ ἀποθανών, μᾶλλον δὲ ἐγερθείς, ὃς καί ἐστιν ἐν δεξιᾷ τοῦ θεοῦ, ὃς καὶ ἐντυγχάνει ὑπὲρ ἡμῶν.[21]

This particular typography is retained in the subsequent editions of 1549 and 1550, but in 1551 Stephanus changed it and introduced the reading that would become the standard for the *textus receptus*:[22]

> τίς ἐγκαλέσει κατὰ ἐκλεκτῶν θεοῦ; θεὸς ὁ δικαιῶν. τίς ὁ κατακρινῶν; Χριστὸς ὁ ἀποθανών, μᾶλλον δὲ ἐγερθείς, ὃς καί ἐστιν ἐν δεξιᾷ τοῦ θεοῦ, ὃς καὶ ἐντυγχάνει ὑπὲρ ἡμῶν.

Johann Jakob Wettstein prints this reading of the text in his 1751–1752 edition but adds a remark in the critical apparatus stating that already Augustine had proposed to read these clauses as questions, a suggestion

---

[21] Online: http://data.onb.ac.at/rep/10270936, accessed March 3, 2021.
[22] Stephanus' editions can be checked online. Second edition (1549): http://data.onb.ac.at/rep/10270983; third (1550): http://data.onb.ac.at/rep/102800FD; and fourth (1551): https://doi.org/10.3931/e-rara-6036, all sites accessed March 3, 2021. All five major editions of Beza retain Stephanus' interpunction here, though with high points replacing the commas from the third edition onward (1556/57, only in Latin; 1565; 1582; 1588; 1598). The famous Elzevir edition of 1633 retains Stephanus' interpunction.

which we will have to look into at a later point in this essay.[23] As usual in Wettstein's edition, the apparatus reveals his preference, but he prints the traditional text of the *textus receptus*.[24]

In later editions, the typography of the TR is abandoned, and other options are printed. In 1796, Johann Jakob Griesbach turns these two verses into a sequence of seven questions:

> τίς ἐγκαλέσει κατὰ ἐκλεκτῶν θεοῦ; θεὸς ὁ δικαιῶν; τίς ὁ κατακρινῶν; Χριστὸς ὁ ἀποθανών; μᾶλλον δὲ ἐγερθείς; ὃς καί ἐστιν ἐν δεξιᾷ τοῦ θεοῦ; ὃς καὶ ἐντυγχάνει ὑπὲρ ἡμῶν;

He continues along this line in verse 35:

> τίς ἡμᾶς χωρίσει ἀπὸ τῆς ἀγάπης τοῦ Χριστοῦ; θλῖψις; ἢ στενοχωρία; ἢ διωγμὸς; ἢ λιμὸς; ἢ γυμνότης; ἢ κίνδυνος; ἢ μάχαιρα;

Karl Lachmann prints four questions in 1831:

> τίς ἐγκαλέσει κατὰ ἐκλεκτῶν θεοῦ; θεὸς ὁ δικαιῶν; τίς ὁ κατακρινῶν; Χριστὸς [Ἰησοῦς] ὁ ἀποθανών, μᾶλλον δὲ ἐγερθείς, ὃς [καὶ] ἐστιν ἐν δεξιᾷ τοῦ θεοῦ, ὃς καὶ ἐντυγχάνει ὑπὲρ ἡμῶν;

Subsequently, however, the editions of Westcott & Hort, Tischendorf (*octava maior*), Baljon, and Scrivener all print this passage with the typography that is now current in the MCT. In his edition of 1857 Samuel Prideaux Tregelles decided to combine the two clauses θεὸς ὁ δικαιῶν and τίς ὁ κατακρινῶν, and prints a comma between them instead of the colon used in the other editions mentioned.[25]

---

[23] Wettstein, at loc.: '*Augustinus* D.C. III.3.3 (& ex eo *Sedulius* in l.). Illud, quod sequitur, sono interrogantis enuncietur: Deus, qui justificat? Ut tacite respondeatur: non. – rursusque interrogemus; Christus, qi mortuus est? &c.'

[24] On Wettstein's choice to print the received text in his edition and comment on it in his apparatus, see the 2019 Amsterdam dissertation by S. Castelli, *Johann Jakob Wettstein's Principles for New Testament Textual Criticism: A Fight for Scholarly Freedom* (NTTS 62; Leiden: Brill, forthcoming in 2020), 79–83. Especially 83: '... the task of Wettstein's learned reader would not end with the text and the suggested readings at the foot of the text. The editorial choices printed at the bottom of the text would be explained by the first, text-critical apparatus, and read together with a massive number of alternative manuscript readings, references to Fathers and versions, and conjectures.' Based on this verdict, Wettstein's edition can be used as a 3-D hologram of the text of the New Testament.

[25] Most translations render these verses as two rhetorical questions each of which is directly followed by an answer. This is the case in the King James Version, the German Luther bible, the Dutch *Statenvertaling*, but also in the NRSV and the NIV. This choice was already made by Luther in his September Testament of 1522, repeated in the full translation of the Bible in German of 1534: 'Wer wil die auserweleten Gottes beschuldigen? Gott ist hie, der da Gerecht machet. Wer wil verdammen? Christus ist hie, der gestorben ist, ia viel mehr, der auch aufferwecket ist, welcher ist zur rechten Gottes, und vertrit uns.'

All in all, what we can establish here, is that the interpunction of NA[28], UBS[5], Tyndale GNT, and SBLGNT is based on a scholarly convention that arose in the 19th century. Since the mere repetition of an assertion or convention does not equal its truth, it might be good to delve a bit deeper and look if the manuscript evidence gives us any indication whether this convention is correct or not.

4.2. Manuscript evidence

In search of manuscript evidence for the interpunction of this particular passage it makes sense to look at the so-called 'consistently cited witnesses' in NA[28] as far as they are available through the New Testament Virtual Manuscript Room.[26] Papyri 10, 26, 31, 40, 61, 94, 99, 113 and 118 are all listed as such for Romans, but none of these manuscripts contains 8:33–34. The two verses are present in P46, but in fragmentary shape and without any kind of interpunction. This means that P46 is inconclusive with regard to the question to be answered here.

The next group of manuscripts to check are the uncials listed under the consistently cited witnesses of NA[28]. Here, too, the evidence is inconclusive. The verses 8:33–34 are missing from manuscripts 048, 0172, 0209, 0219, 0221, 0278, 0285, and 0289. Unfortunately, the NTVMR does not enable users to check the text of A02, F010, K018, L020, P025, and Ψ044. The uncials that are available are A01, B03, C04, D06, and G012.

A01 has this passage with a form of interpunction. Transcribed, this is the reading of Sinaiticus:

> τίς ἐγκαλέσει κατὰ ἐκλεκτῶν θ,υ θς ὁ δικαιῶν · τίς ὁ κατακρινῶν · χς ις ὁ ἀποθανών · μᾶλλον δὲ ἐγερθείς · ἐκ νεκρῶν · ὅς ἐστιν ἐν δεξιᾷ τοῦ θυ · ὃς καὶ ἐντυγχάνει ὑπὲρ ἡμῶν ·

The *stigme* in these lines has clearly been inserted by a later scribe, who also made a mistake by adding a comma between the letters ΘΥ (ἐκλεκτῶν θεοῦ) instead of after them. Since the function of this middle point is to mark a breathing space, it is unclear whether the clauses that are thus separated should be seen as questions, but the possibility is certainly there.

---

[26] URL: http://ntvmr.uni-muenster.de; accessed daily.

In the re-inked text of B03 the medieval scribe who is responsible for the accents and interpunction uses two different kinds of *stigme* here. He uses both the high point and the middle point, and we can generally assume that the high points here indicate questions, with the clauses closing with a middle point seen as the answers:

> τίς ἐγκαλέσει κατὰ ἐκλεκτῶν θυ· θς ὁ δικαιῶν. τίς ὁ κατακρινῶν· χς ὁ ἀποθανών · μᾶλλον δὲ ἐγερθείς, ὃς καί ἐστιν ἐν δεξιᾷ τοῦ θεοῦ · ὃς καὶ ἐντυγχάνει ὑπὲρ ἡμῶν·

In the interpretation of the medieval scribe whose work we see in the interpunction of B03, the first four clauses should be seen as consisting of two questions and two answers, the latter of which is considerably longer than the former.

Unfortunately, the other uncials are inconclusive: C04 does not contain any interpunction and neither do D06 and G012. In both uncials that do have a form of interpunction here, A01 and B03, the interpunction dates to a much later moment in time than the production of the original manuscripts, is ambiguous and hence also inconclusive.

Since this contribution was written during the social restrictions of the Covid-19 pandemic, the only possible checking of the manuscripts was through the NTVMR in Münster. Unfortunately, it does not contain any publicly accessible images of the minuscules 33, 81, 104, 630, 1175, 1241, 1505, 1739, 1881, and 2464, and neither are lectionaria 249 and 846 available. The one minuscule that can be checked online is the 12th century manuscript 365, and here the interpunction is as follows:

> τίς ἐγκαλέσει κατὰ ἐκλεκτῶν θεοῦ · θεὸς ὁ δικαιῶν τίς ὁ κατακρινῶν · Χριστὸς Ἰησοῦς ὁ ἀποθανών, μᾶλλον δὲ ἐγερθείς, ὃς καί ἐστιν ἐν δεξιᾷ τοῦ θεοῦ · ὃς καὶ ἐντυγχάνει ὑπὲρ ἡμῶν ·

The middle *stigme* can be read as both a full stop or as a question mark, so once again the evidence is inconclusive. What is remarkable, though, is that this interpunction apparently takes θεὸς ὁ δικαιῶν τίς ὁ κατακρινῶν as a unity instead of seeing the first three words as an independent clause.

All in all, the manuscript evidence does not give us the clarity sought after with regard to the status of Romans 8:33–34: is this a sequence of questions only or should we read two clauses as answers to the questions Paul asks? For this reason, it may be good to turn to an ancient authority, who – as we saw above – was referred to and quoted by Wettstein and Tischendorf: Augustine of Hippo.

5. Augustine on Romans 8:33–34

In the second part of his *editio octava critica maior* (1872) Constantin von Tischendorf adds a long Latin footnote to Romans 8:33. He indicates that Griesbach (1796) prints these clauses as questions, refers back to Wettstein (1752), and to the *Quaestiones in Novum Testamentum* by Eucherius of Lyons (ed. 1677), and quotes the source of the suspicion that these clauses should be read as questions: Augustine, *De doctrina christiana* 3,3. It is worth quoting this passage at length here:

> *The points that I have just made about problems of punctuation also apply to the problems of reading aloud. These too, unless they are simply mistakes due to a reader's gross carelessness, are resolved by considering either the rules of faith or the surrounding context. If neither of these methods is used to resolve them they will none the less remain in dispute, but in such a way that the reader will not be wrong however the passages are articulated. If our faith did not prevent it – for we believe that God will not make accusations against his elect and that Christ will not condemn the elect – the following passage might be read in such a way that the question, 'Who will make an accusation against God's elect?' is followed by a sort of answer in the words 'God who justifies them,' and then, similarly, by the question, 'Who is it that condemns them?,' and the answer, 'Christ Jesus who died'. But since it would be crazy to believe this, it will be articulated as a* percontatio *followed by an* interrogatio. *(The difference between these, according to ancient authorities, is that many answers may be given to the former, but only 'yes' and 'no' to the latter.) So it will be articulated in such a way that what follows the* percontatio *('Who will make an accusation against God's elect?') is intoned interrogatively ('God who justifies them?'), expecting the tacit answer 'no'.*[27]

Augustine, who was well trained in ancient rhetoric, is clearly convinced that the passage under discussion here should be seen as an *interrogatio*, in Greek: an *erōtēsis*.

Unfortunately, the lockdown due to the Covid-19 crisis under which this article was written prevented the author from checking the work of Eucherius, and for the sake of completeness, this should still be done. Nevertheless, Augustine's analysis of this passage delivers us the clearest indication that Jewett's reading of the passage under discussion is indeed correct, and the clauses in Romans 8:33–34 should be read and printed as an interrogation.

---

[27] Augustine, *De Doctrina Christiana*, edited and translated by R.P.H. Green (Oxford: Clarendon Press, 1995), 137 (3,3,10–12).

6. Conclusion

In the section of his New Testament grammar on interpunction, Archibald Robertson indicates that adding punctuation is the task of the editors of the New Testament, but this punctuation should be regarded with some freedom by those who use their edition: 'the editor's punctuation may be a hindrance to the student instead of a help. It is the privilege of each N.T. student to make his [or her; LP] own punctuation.'[28]

This student of the New Testament would like to suggest changing the punctuation of Romans 8:33–34 in the MCT by taking into account that these verses contain an *erōtēsis*. The result of this questioning is, according to the instructions given for the use of this style-figure by Aristotle and the interpretation of this particular passage by Augustine, that Paul here rhetorically emphasizes the fact that nobody is able to press any charges against the followers of Christ. In Greek, the likeliest interpunction of these verses would seem to be the following:

> τίς ἐγκαλέσει κατὰ ἐκλεκτῶν θεοῦ; θεὸς ὁ δικαιῶν; τίς ὁ κατακρινῶν; Χριστὸς Ἰησοῦς ὁ ἀποθανών, μᾶλλον δὲ ἐγερθείς, ὃς καί ἐστιν ἐν δεξιᾷ τοῦ θεοῦ, ὃς καὶ ἐντυγχάνει ὑπὲρ ἡμῶν;

In translation, this could be rendered as follows:

> *Who will bring any charge against God's elect? God, who justifies?!?*
> *Who is to condemn? Christ Jesus, who died, yes, who was raised, who*
> *is at the right hand of God, who indeed intercedes for us?!?*[29]

The answer that is implied by these questions is obviously negative: 'no, certainly not!' Read in this way, Paul is pressing the point here that God and Christ would have been the only ones in the position to press any kind of charges, but instead they are doing quite the reverse. The effect of this staggering climax of 5:1–8:39 is the introduction of the quotation from LXX Psalm 43:23.

As is implied by καθώς, Paul inserts the quote from LXX Psalm 43 as an illustration of the hardships mentioned in v. 35. The quoted Psalm speaks about the relationship of Israel with Yhwh, and the second part of the psalm, the part that ends with the verse quoted by Paul, describes how Yhwh has abandoned Israel. This can hardly be the point that Paul has in mind in quoting the words from v. 23, for the whole argument he is making in this passage hinges on the idea that nothing and nobody is able

---

[28] Robertson, *Grammar*, 245.
[29] Based on the NRSV. Cf. the Dutch *Willibrordvertaling* 1978.

to cause distance between the believers and God (and Christ). So, the reason for quoting this particular verse at this particular point in Paul's rhetoric is that he uses it in order to illustrate the hardships he has just mentioned. These hardships cannot take away the effect of the love mentioned in v. 37 (ἀγαπήσαντος) and v. 39 (ἀπὸ τῆς ἀγάπης τοῦ θεοῦ). All in all, the *erōtēsis*, the two hardship catalogues, and the scriptural quotation form the climax of Paul's argument thus far in the letter, and can be summarized by saying that Paul is convinced that nothing will separate the believers from Christ, and that through Christ they are united with God. The aorist tense of ἀγαπήσαντος indicates that Paul had a single moment of love in mind, and this can hardly be anything else that the death and resurrection of Christ. Paul thus arrives at the end of his argument. The juxtaposition of Christ and Adam in chapter 5, the description of the newness of life that comes about by sharing in the death of Christ, by baptism, described in chapter 6, the problematizing of life under the Law by the *prosopopoeia* in chapter 7, and the following description of life in the Spirit in chapter 8, all bring Paul to the passage under discussion here: even the hardships Paul mentions are no refutation of the believers' unity with Christ, but rather form proof of it.

The study of the final lines of Romans 8 clearly indicates that this text is a conscious composition, in which Paul applies a variety of rhetorical devices, among them the repeated figure of the rhetorical question. This has an important consequence. If the passage up to 8:39 should be read as a conscious composition, in which Paul applies a variety of rhetorical techniques, so should the chapters 9–11. This means that the point mentioned above, viz. that Paul had the end of Romans 11 in mind when he began dictating Romans 9, should be credited. The importance of this is, that it leads us to a new reading of these three fundamental chapters. The 'remnant of Israel,' with which Paul starts, is there to lead to 'the whole of Israel' with which Paul finishes his argument. The question of how 'the whole of Israel' will be saved, however, exceeds the scope of this limited contribution and will have to wait for another occasion.

QUESTIONS AS RHETORICAL TOOLS IN 1 CORINTHIANS 11:22

Ignas W. TILMA
Tilburg University

1. Introduction

Questions play an important role in the first letter to the Corinthians. Paul uses about one hundred questions in this letter. Most of them are generally qualified as rhetorical questions. They are characteristic of Paul's rhetorical style in 1 Corinthians.[1] Several passages contain a series of questions, for example 1:20 and 9:1. As will be shown below, this combination of multiple questions could be seen as a typical use of questions in the letter.

Questions can be used as rhetorical tools in many ways to enrich the meaning and dynamics of a text. With regard to Paul's use of questions in 1 Corinthians, many different aspects are mentioned by commentators. These include remarks about the formulation of questions,[2] their overtone[3] and their function within Paul's argumentation.[4] Although these observations offer important insights into the passage at hand, a systematic approach to the questions in the letter seems to be lacking.

It seems that the study of questions in Paul's letters is an area that could be further explored. Two examples of valuable contributions are the articles

---

[1] Cf. J.A. Fitzmyer, *First Corinthians: A New Translation with Introduction and Commentary* (AB 32; New Haven: Yale University Press, 2008), 66. See also Witherington's remark while commenting on 1 Cor 1:13: 'Paul loved to use rhetorical questions;' B. Witherington, *Conflict and Community in Corinth: A Socio-Rhetorical Commentary on 1 and 2 Corinthians* (Grand Rapids: Eerdmans, 1995), 168 (e-pub version). A special formula, used by Paul to introduce important rhetorical questions, is 'Do you not realize that'; cf. Fitzmyer, *First Corinthians*, 202.

[2] E.g. H. Conzelmann, *1 Corinthians: A Commentary on the First Epistle to the Corinthians* (Hermeneia – a critical and historical commentary on the Bible; Philadelphia: Fortress Press, 2008), 152, on 1 Cor 9:1: 'The form of the questions anticipates the answer.'

[3] E.g. Conzelmann, *1 Corinthians*, 195, on 1 Cor 11:22b: 'a reproachful question.'

[4] E.g. Witherington, *Conflict and Community*, 302–303 (on 1 Cor 9:1: 'Rhetorical questions could be used in different ways' and the following) and 409 (on 1 Cor 14:36: 'It was a common rhetorical technique to end a discussion with rhetorical questions').

written by Wilhelm Wuellner[5] and Duane Watson.[6] Both focus on the phenomenon of the rhetorical question. Watson describes the function of the questions in 1 Corinthians 10:23–11:1 using the Graeco-Roman rhetorical handbooks. Wuellner has a broader approach, using categories from classical handbooks as well as more recent approaches to rhetorical criticism to describe Paul's use of questions in 1 Corinthians.

The stimulus for this article was given by the reading of the work of Douglas Estes, *Questions and Rhetoric in the Greek New Testament*.[7] Estes dismisses the term 'rhetorical question' as useful: 'The category of *rhetorical question* is so broad as to be practically meaningless when it comes to understanding the purpose of a question.'[8] Although the term is so common that scholars often do not feel the need to give a description or definition,[9] in the classical period such an overarching category is not mentioned in the rhetorical handbooks.[10] Estes analyses questions using a linguistic approach.

This article focusses on the group of questions in 1 Corinthians 11:22. Commentators describe these questions as rhetorical questions,[11] but little is said about their function as question. Following Estes in his conviction that more can be said about rhetorical questions, this article provides a linguistic and rhetorical analysis of the questions, using the categories provided in Estes' book. The purpose of this analysis is to describe their function within the passage of 1 Corinthians 11:17–34 more precisely. In doing so, this article aims to contribute to the field of rhetorical studies concerning Paul's letters and to call attention to Paul's use of questions as a rhetorical tool.

---

[5] W.H. Wuellner, "Paul as Pastor: The Function of Rhetorical Questions in First Corinthians," in: A. Vanhoye (Ed.), *L'Apôtre Paul: Personnalité, Style et Conception Du Ministère* (BETL 73: Leuven: Peeters, 1986), 49–77.

[6] D.F. Watson, "1 Corinthians 10:23–11:1 in the Light of Greco-Roman Rhetoric: The Role of Rhetorical Questions," *JBL* 108 (1989): 301–318.

[7] D. Estes, *Questions and Rhetoric in the Greek New Testament: An Essential Reference Resource for Exegesis* (Grand Rapids: Zondervan Academic, 2017).

[8] Estes, *Questions and Rhetoric*, 69.

[9] Bullinger offers a clear description of what is generally meant by the term 'rhetorical question'. He does not use the term, but calls it 'erotesis' or 'interrogating.' See E.W. Bullinger, *Figures of Speech Used in the Bible: Explained and Illustrated* (London: Eyre & Spottiswoode, 1898), 943.

[10] Watson offers an overview of different functions questions could have, as reported in classical handbooks. Watson, "1 Corinthians 10," 310–318. This overview confirms Estes' observation that the different functions of questions in classical handbooks do not fit into one overarching category of 'rhetorical questions.'

[11] G.D. Fee, *The First Epistle to the Corinthians* (NICNT; Grand Rapids: Eerdmans, 1987), 591, 601; W. Schrage, *Der erste Brief an die Korinther* (EKKNT 7/3; Zürich: Benziger; Neukirchen-Vluyn: Neukirchener, 1999), 27; Fitzmyer, *First Corinthians*, 435.

The outline of this article is as follows: the first paragraph will offer a brief presentation of Estes' method. In the second paragraph I will describe the immediate context of 1 Corinthians 11:22. The third paragraph provides an analysis of the questions in the verse. In the fourth and final paragraph I will draw some conclusions.

2. Douglas Estes' *Questions and Rhetoric* and rhetorical questions

In his *Questions and Rhetoric* Douglas Estes states his dislike for a 'modern' attitude to biblical texts, in which the focus is on what information the text offers, paying less attention to the rhetorical dynamics of the text.[12] The qualification of a question as a rhetorical question, in Estes' opinion, often facilitates treating those questions as if they were assertions, thereby losing their value and logic as a question. Reading questions as questions, with their own logic and rhetorical force, helps us to understand and determine more fully the meaning of a text.

Although Estes dismisses the term 'rhetorical question,' it is my impression that the term and its definition are, although imprecise, not entirely useless. My reason is practical. Clearly, when the term 'rhetorical question' discards the interrogative force of a question completely, Estes is right in his aversion. Nevertheless, I can imagine that many publications want to avoid technical language or a profound description of the function of a question. With the logic of questions in mind, the term 'rhetorical question' can be used without harm to express some general aspects of these questions, like persuasion and assertion. This article will show that a rhetorical analysis of Paul's letters has to take into account more systematically the different aspects of questions.

3. Structure and translation

3.1. *Delimitation and structure of 1 Corinthians 11:17–34*

In chapters 7–14 of 1 Corinthians, Paul addresses several questions and problems brought to his attention in a letter or reported by messengers

---

[12] Cf. Estes, *Questions and Rhetoric*, 22; with regard to the letters of Paul, Wuellner, "Paul as Pastor," 49, makes a similar remark: 'It is this effect factor which makes us appreciate Paul as pastor in distinction from our long-standing preoccupation with Paul as theologian.' P. Perkins, *First Corinthians* (Paideia commentaries on the New Testament; Grand Rapids: Baker Academic, 2012), 26, is positive about recent development in this area: 'Emphasis on the dynamics of communication is transforming study of the NT letters.'

from the Corinthian community.[13] It is not clear how Paul got his information about the two issues he addresses in chapter 11. The two topics are both related to 'traditions' (cf. verses 2 and 23) and, like chapters 12–14, discuss the proper conduct at gatherings of the community in Corinth.[14]

In the first part of chapter 11, Paul discusses the matter of praying with the head unveiled. Verse 16 creates a closure to this passage.[15] The clause τοῦτο δὲ παραγγέλλων *now in giving this instruction* in verse 17 indicates the transition to a new passage.[16] The passage it introduces, also concerns the gathering of the community, but a new problem is formulated. What should be the 'Supper of the Lord,' does not deserve that name, because 'one is hungry, another is drunk' (verse 21).

The passage could be divided into four sections. In verses 17–22 Paul introduces the problem and expresses his indignation. Then, in verses 23–26, he cites tradition material about the Last Supper and applies it to the Corinthian situation. In verses 27–30, Paul elaborates the subject and brings it to a conclusion in verses 31–34.

The end of the passage is clearly marked by 34d: τὰ δὲ λοιπὰ ὡς ἂν ἔλθω διατάξομαι *the other things I will set in order when I come*. One could argue that 34c already concludes the passage. This would leave 34d as a somewhat solitary remark. The next verse (12:1) begins with περὶ δέ, introducing the next subject of the letter.

The structure of the passage could be rendered schematically as follows:

First section: verses 17–22
17	Introduction of the problem: coming together for the worse
18–19	Specification of the problem: divisions / factions
20–21	Restating the problem: it is no Supper of the Lord
22	Questions to the readers:
	a-c second person plural: questions about the content
	d-f first person singular: relational questions (and one answer)

---

[13] Cf. Fitzmyer, *First Corinthians*, 56. It can be argued that chapter 15 and the first part of chapter 16 also belong to this unit of the letter. See for example C.H. Talbert, *Reading Corinthians: A Literary and Theological Commentary* (Macon: Smyth & Helwys, 2002), 25. For an overview of different hypotheses questioning the integrity of the letter, see Talbert, *Reading Corinthians*, 6–7.
[14] Cf. Talbert, *Reading Corinthians*, 85.
[15] See for example Fitzmyer, *First Corinthians*, 407: 'he invokes church discipline to end the discussion.'
[16] In this article I leave the question open whether the demonstrative τοῦτο *this* in 17a points forward or backwards. Cf. Schrage, *Der erste Brief an die Korinther*, 18.

Second section: verses 23–26
23–25   Tradition material:
             23a-b   introduction
             23c–24   action and words on the bread
             25   action and words on the cup
26   Application of the tradition material

Third section: verses 27–30
27–30   Elaboration of the subject: how to participate in the Supper of the Lord?

Fourth section: verses 31–34
31–32   Exhortation to prevent condemnation
33–34   Conclusion of the passage

Within the passage of 1 Corinthians 11:17–34, only verse 22 contains questions. The next paragraph will provide an analysis of the questions in this verse, but first I will offer the Greek text and my translation.[17]

3.2. *Translation of 1 Corinthians 11:22*

22a	μὴ γὰρ οἰκίας οὐκ ἔχετε εἰς τὸ ἐσθίειν καὶ πίνειν;	*Do you not have houses for eating and drinking?*
22b	ἢ τῆς ἐκκλησίας τοῦ θεοῦ καταφρονεῖτε,	*Or do you despise the church of God*
22c	καὶ καταισχύνετε τοὺς μὴ ἔχοντας;	*and shame those who have not?*
22d	τί εἴπω ὑμῖν;	*What shall I say to you?*
22e	ἐπαινέσω ὑμᾶς;	*Shall I praise you?*
22f	ἐν τούτῳ οὐκ ἐπαινῶ.	*In this I do not praise you.*

With regard to the function of questions, one choice in this translation should be explained. It is difficult to translate the combination of μὴ and οὐκ in 22a.[18] My attempt to reproduce the extra emphasis of the combination (by replacing 'Don't you have' with 'Do you not have') is too weak. Some translations add an interjection (e.g. NRSV: 'What! Do you not have…?') Unfortunately, these translations colour the question as an utterance of surprise or indignation, which is not necessarily the main or

---

[17] The Greek text is from NA[28].
[18] Paul uses the same combination in questions in 1 Cor 9:4–5. Cf. A.T. Robertson, *A Grammar of the Greek New Testament in the Light of Historical Research* (London: Hodder & Stoughton, ³1919), 1173.

only purpose of the question. As this purpose is the subject of this paper, I have decided not to add such an interjection.

4. The questions in 1 Corinthians 11:22

Verse 22 is the concluding verse of the first section of the passage. As explained above, Paul introduces a new problem in verse 17. After a brief digression about the divisions that it causes, he returns to the problem and describes it in more detail in verses 20 and 21. When the Corinthian church gathers for the Supper of the Lord, inequality arises. Some have enough, while others have to do without or with only little food.

It is at this point, that Paul turns to the use of questions. Verse 22 contains four questions (counting 22b and 22c as one), followed by a proposition (22f). In this paragraph I will analyse each question separately, using the syntactical and semantic material from the book of Estes. At the end of the paragraph, I will discuss the pragmatics of these questions.

22a: 'Do you not have houses for eating and drinking?'

The first question μὴ γὰρ οἰκίας οὐκ ἔχετε εἰς τὸ ἐσθίειν καὶ πίνειν; in verse 22 desires affirmation or negation. Although many responses are possible, the question itself desires 'yes' or 'no' as an answer. This is the characteristic of a polar question, often called a yes/no-question.[19] Polar questions are very common. In Koine Greek polar questions are constructed the same way as propositions. They have some syntactical constraints, but don't require specific syntactical elements.[20]

The question in 22a contains a negation, giving it a negative polarity. This is important, because it modifies the effect of the question. Used in questions, negative polarity often brings in a strong rhetorical force.[21] The combination of μή + οὐκ does not create a positive polarity (through double negation), but strengthens the negative polarity and adds bias to the question.[22] The construction expects an affirmative answer.[23]

---

[19] Estes, *Questions and Rhetoric*, 94–100.
[20] Cf. Estes, *Questions and Rhetoric*, 94–98; F. Blass, A. Debrunner and F. Rehkopf, *Grammatik des neutestamentlichen Griechisch* (Göttingen: Vandenhoeck & Ruprecht, 1979), 365 [§ 440].
[21] Cf. Estes, *Questions and Rhetoric*, 47.
[22] Cf. Estes, *Questions and Rhetoric*, 63: 'all NPIs (Negative Polarity Items, IWT) create bias in questions as a result of their oppositional polarity.' Cf. also Fitzmyer, *First Corinthians*, 435: 'With emphasis Paul asks his first rhetorical question.'
[23] Cf. F. Blass, A. Debrunner and F. Rehkopf, *Grammatik des neutestamentlichen Griechisch* (Göttingen: Vandenhoeck & Ruprecht, 1979), 355 [§ 427,2b].

The syntactical construction of the question (a polar question with negative polarity) is the purest form of one of Estes' twenty-three semantic categories: the negative polar question. Negative polar questions come close to assertions through their strong rhetorical quality (the degree of persuasion) and weak informational quality (what the question asks). For this reason verse 22a would be normally labelled as a rhetorical question and be treated more or less as an assertion.[24]

This assertive aspect of verse 22a adds an important element to Paul's argument. The theme of eating and drinking, introduced in the verses 20–21, now gets linked to the function of houses. The question assumes that the reader agrees with this connection. Therefore, another semantic category could be applied here, the endoxical question. This term is derived from the Greek ἔνδοξον, which means 'a generally accepted opinion.' Endoxical questions refer to such an accepted opinion and in doing so create a common ground for writer and reader.[25] The question in 22a therefore functions as a good starting point in Paul's argumentative strategy. In fact, with verse 22a Paul starts to discuss the problem and already points forwards to his conclusion in verse 34.[26]

Nonetheless, verse 22a is formulated as a question, with its own logic and force. By formulating verse 22a as a question, Paul also compels his readers to agree. The combination μὴ + οὐκ is heavily coercive. His readers are forced to consider the purpose of their houses, although this reflection is strongly steered in one direction. The question also has a reproaching overtone.

22b-c: 'Or do you despise the church of God and shame those who have not?'

As I will discuss below in the paragraph about pragmatics, questions can be combined into question strings. On the syntactical level, however, multiple questions can also be combined to form one composite question. In that case, multiple questions are asked at the same time, using a conjunctive or a disjunctive particle. In some cases it is difficult to determine

---

[24] For example Schrage, *Der erste Brief an die Korinther*, 27.
[25] Cf. Estes, *Questions and Rhetoric*, 198–201; cf. 'codes and shared values' in Wuellner, "Paul as Pastor," 63–65; on page 64–65 Wuellner applies this to verse 22a.
[26] Cf. Conzelmann, *1 Corinthians*, 195; Schrage, *Der erste Brief an die Korinther*, 27. Against the generally accepted interpretation, I keep the possibility open that Paul refers here and in verse 34 to the houses in which the community gathers. Cf. Godfrey C. Nicholson, "Houses for hospitality: 1 Cor 11:17–34," *Colloquium* 19 (1986): 1–6. See the discussion in Schrage, *Der erste Brief an die Korinther*, 27, note 444.

which of these two categories applies. This is also true for the three questions in verses 22a-c.

The question in verse 22b begins with the disjunctive particle ἤ.[27] The disjunctive function of this particle is clear: either houses are used by the Corinthians for eating or drinking (verse 22a) or they choose to despise the church of God (verse 22b).

However, verse 22b and verse 22c are also connected, in this case by the conjunction καί. The conjunction is strengthened by a chiastic parallelism, which is most overt in the formation and position of the verbs. Furthermore, the two questions share the same thought. Therefore, the internal coherence of verses 22b-c is stronger than the disjunction between verse 22a and verse 22b. This leads me to describe verses 22b-c as a conjunctive question.[28] The combination of verse 22a and verses 22b-c will be described below as a question string in the next paragraph.

Both questions in verses 22b-c are polar questions with a positive polarity. Although syntactically the questions are neutral, semantically much bias is added. The verbs express attitudes (καταφρονέω *to despise* and καταισχύνω *to shame*) which can only be evaluated negatively. This bias is highlighted by the contrasting positive phrase τῆς ἐκκλησίας τοῦ θεοῦ *the church of God*. Through the chiastic structure this also lends positive value to τοὺς μὴ ἔχοντας *those who have not*. This is one of the rhetorical effects of a conjunctive question: to connect two closely related concerns.[29] By combining two questions this way, Paul urges his readers to consider 'those who have not' as part of the church of God.

On the semantic level Estes distinguishes the category of biased questions. These are questions in which a strong bias comes to the front. The questions in verses 22b-c seem to fit into this category. Biased questions frequently convey opinions and expectations of the asker. They often, to some extent, attack the reader.[30] This is what Paul does in verses 22b-c and therefore the rhetorical nature of verses 22b-c is stronger than it is informational. The questions, however, remain questions. They ask the readers about their attitude towards being the church of God and towards those who have not. The decision, yes or no, is left to the readers.[31]

---

[27] Cf. Robertson, *Grammar of the Greek New Testament*, 1177; Blass, Debrunner and Rehkopf, *Grammatik*, 365 [§ 440,1]; E. van Emde Boas, A. Rijksbaron, L. Huitink and M. de Bakker, *Cambridge Grammar of Classical Greek* (Cambridge: Cambridge University Press, 2017), 673.
[28] Estes, *Questions and Rhetoric*, 124–129.
[29] Cf. Estes, *Questions and Rhetoric*, 127.
[30] Cf. Estes, *Questions and Rhetoric*, 259.
[31] Cf. Estes, *Questions and Rhetoric*, 100.

22d: 'What shall I say to you?'

After asking polar questions in verses 22a-c, Paul now uses a variable question: τί εἴπω ὑμῖν; The easiest way to describe this syntactical type of question is that they start with an interrogative variable word (a *π-word* or, in English, *wh-word*: who / what / where etc.). The logic of variable questions is that they seek to solve this variable word. 'Who' desires a person as an answer, 'Where' desires a location as an answer, etc.[32] The question in verse 22d. starting with 'What,' desires Paul's verbal reaction to the situation in Corinth as an answer.

Paul here employs a first person singular aorist active subjunctive, making verse 22d a deliberative question.[33] Deliberative questions merge writer and reader, because the question is directed to the writer himself and reveals his internal struggle.[34] In this way the question in verse 22d adds drama to the passage. The readers get involved in Paul's deliberation, which creates tension and suspense. This is the rhetorical quality of the question. At the same time, the question asks for information. The question is syntactically an open question. Therefore, the readers are activated in considering all the different reactions Paul could have regarding their gatherings.

22e: 'Shall I praise you?'

In verse 22e Paul returns to the use of a polar question. The question ἐπαινέσω ὑμᾶς; has a positive polarity. It asks for a confirmation or denial from the readers: is the situation praiseworthy? As in verse 22d, the subjunctive mood and the first person singular constitute a deliberative question. This second deliberative question extends and increases the drama of the first. The question in verse 22e creates a dramatic peak. Interestingly the verb ἐπαινέω *to praise* has a positive bias. However, as I will explain below, the pragmatics overtakes the force of the question and in doing so increases the drama.

5. Pragmatics of the questions in 1 Corinthians 11:22

Questions are often coloured by the context in which they are used. The passage under scrutiny here is part of persuasive discourse (1 Cor), so rhetorical force could be expected. The questions are in a middle position

---

[32] Cf. Estes, *Questions and Rhetoric*, 101.
[33] Cf. Robertson, *Grammar of the Greek New Testament*, 934; Van Emde Boas, Rijksbaron, Huitink and De Bakker, *Cambridge Grammar*, 440 and 479.
[34] Cf. Estes, *Questions and Rhetoric*, 166–169; see also 44.

within the passage. Estes explains that negative polar questions tend to be 'much more rhetorically disruptive' than other question types in such a middle position.[35] Through their closed nature (yes or no), the readers are forced to pause and decide. This is why verse 22 functions so well as the transition from the introduction of the problem to Paul's argumentation.[36]

An important aspect of the pragmatics of questions is how questions are combined into a question string.[37] The use of question strings could be seen as a characteristic of Paul's style in 1 Corinthians.[38] Although commentators often point at this phenomenon, only occasionally the coherence and functioning of a question string is discussed. Yet, this would contribute to the understanding of Paul's use of questions. For example, the first three questions in 1:20 are clearly connected by the repetition of ποῦ *where?* (anaphora), with a climax in the third, longer question.[39] Another example is the question string in 4:7, with, according to Hans Conzelmann, a 'chainlike intertwining of the catchwords.'[40] Most commentators do reflect on the question strings in chapter 9 of the letter. The use of questions in this chapter cannot be ignored, because no other chapter in the New Testament has more questions than Paul uses here.[41] Pheme Perkins, for example, describes how the four questions in 9:1 begin similarly with *not* and how each of the questions is a specification of the previous.[42] She also points at the coherence of the three questions in 9:7, in which Paul uses 'commonplace examples.'[43]

The coherence of the questions in 11:22 is less obvious, but not less important to describe. In his handbook Estes differentiates between double questions and multiple questions. At first sight verse 22 seems to fit the latter. In my opinion, however, it is better to consider them as two double questions (22a-c and 22d-e). Both pairs address their own issue.

---

[35] Estes, *Questions and Rhetoric*, 314.
[36] The *inclusio* with verse 17 supports the caesura created by the questions. Cf. Talbert, *Reading Corinthians*, 93. Fitzmyer, *First Corinthians*, 435, also notes the connection with verse 2.
[37] Cf. Estes, *Questions and Rhetoric*, 316–330.
[38] Cf. Conzelmann, *1 Corinthians*, 5. Perkins, *Frist Corinthians*, 26, mentions question strings as part of the diatribe and the *propōsopoeia*.
[39] Cf. Conzelmann, *1 Corinthians*, 43.
[40] Conzelmann, *1 Corinthians*, 86. Cf. Fitzmyer, *First Corinthians*, 217.
[41] Cf. Bullinger, *Figures of Speech*.
[42] Cf. Perkins, *First Corinthians*, 118.
[43] Cf. Perkins, *First Corinthians*, 119.

The questions in verses 22a-c work together to apply strong pressure towards the readers to influence their opinion about the issue at hand.[44] The reference to common knowledge in verse 22a, combined with the negatively biased verbs καταφρονέω *to despise* and καταισχύνω *to shame* in verses 22b-c, give the readers the impression that their situation is fundamentally wrong. They do not get time to answer the questions properly. Following Estes and his boxing terms, Paul almost knocks out his readers before discussing the problem.[45]

The combination of verses 22d-e works differently. The question in verse 22d opens up to all the possible ways Paul could react. The following question in verse 22e limits the possibilities with its focus on praise. Should Paul approve or disapprove of the Corinthians? Here the pragmatics overtakes the force of the question. Because verse 17 has already stated that Paul did not praise the Corinthians, and because of the negative bias in verses 22a-c, the expected answer can only be 'no.' Readers know this is the case. Therefore, putting it as a question increases the tension and drama, before definitively declaring: ἐν τούτῳ οὐκ ἐπαινῶ *in this I do not praise you* (verse 22f).

One additional remark could be made. The questions in verses 22d-e contain the implicit assumption that Paul is qualified to give his opinion about the situation in Corinth. This assumption, however, is implicit in the whole of the letter as well as in the immediate context (cf. verse 17). It does not affect the questions in a strong way. If this would be the case, the questions would qualify as loaded questions, one of Estes' semantic categories.[46] On the pragmatic level, however, Paul's authority is made explicit in verse 23, which can be understood as the answer to the question in verse 22d.

6. Conclusions

This article started with the premise that under the label 'rhetorical question' much more could be discovered. After analysing the syntax, semantics and pragmatics of the questions in 1 Corinthians 11:22, it is indeed possible to describe the function of the questions in the verse more precisely.

---

[44] Cf. Estes, *Questions and Rhetoric*, 321. A possible reading of 'those who have not' complements this clause with the object 'houses' from 22a: 'those who have no house.' In this reading the two questions are even more connected; cf. Fitzmyer, *First Corinthians*, 435.
[45] For the boxing analogy, see Estes, *Questions and Rhetoric*, 319. Perkins, *First Corinthians*, 107, uses a different, military analogy in her discussion of 1 Cor 9: 'composed as a barrage of nineteen rhetorical questions.'
[46] Estes, *Questions and Rhetoric*, 262–268.

The questions in verse 22 form the end of the first section of the passage. Paul has stated the problem in verses 17–21. The questions pause the flow of the argument, involve the readers and, with their compelling nature, point forward to the conclusions in verse 34. This rhetorical effect is caused by Paul's use of questions. They introduce a different dynamic with the reader than mere assertions would.

The readers of the letters are activated by the questions in verses 22a-c. The informational aspect of the questions forces them to decide what their position is in the matter at hand. What is their opinion about the situation during the meals in the community? Where do they stand? The rhetorical aspect compels them to agree with Paul. Paul creates a common ground (*endoxa*) to build his argument. The negative bias and the reproaching overtone of the questions work together to change the readers' attitude and behaviour.

The questions in verses 22d-e involve the readers even more. Using two short questions, Paul places them in his own shoes (informational aspect). However, the rhetorical aspect is leading here. Besides causing tension and suspense, the questions also implicitly convey Paul's authority to intervene in the Corinthian situation.

To reach his goal Paul uses a combination of questions. As I mentioned in the introduction, he applies this technique in other passages as well. Further research could reveal if these combinations follow a similar pattern and serve a similar purpose. The study in this article shows that, in addition to other approaches to questions in the letters of Paul, a rhetorical analysis of his letters cannot do without a systematic analysis of its questions.

ASKING QUESTIONS IN THE REVELATION OF JOHN

Hanna ROOSE
Ruhr University Bochum

1. Introduction

The book of Revelation raises many questions. At least to modern readers, the impression is not so much that the book of Revelation reveals what was once concealed, but rather that it conceals its 'message' in enigmatic visions and auditions. Therefore, the expression 'the book with the seven seals' has become a metaphor for any text that is incomprehensible and leaves the reader with a large number of questions. In the book of Revelation itself, however, not many questions are asked – and all of these questions are answered. The NRSV renders no more than eight (explicit) questions in the whole book, and this concurs with the punctuation offered by the Greek text NA 28th Edition. In order of appearance, the eight questions and their answers are the following:

- In the vision of the divine throne room, the mighty angel asks: 'Who is worthy to open the scroll and break its seals?' (5:2). At first, this question seems to go unanswered, but then we read about the saints singing: 'You are worthy...' (5:9) and the seer hears many voices from 'angels,' 'living creatures' and 'the elders' naming this 'you' in their praise: 'Worthy is the Lamb that was slaughtered...' (5:12).
- When the Lamb opens the fifth seal, John sees the souls of those who have been slaughtered for the word of God. They ask the Lamb: 'How long will it be before you judge and avenge our blood on the inhabitants of the earth?' (6:10) They are told to 'rest a little longer,' until the number will be complete 'both of their fellow-servants and of their brothers and sisters' who will soon be killed (6:11).
- When the Lamb opens the sixth seal, people hide in caves from the one seated on the throne and the Lamb. They call: 'For the great day of their wrath has come, and who is able to stand?' (6:17) In their view, of course, no one is able to stand. However, the reader will soon learn that 144.000 will indeed be spared (7:1–8).

- In another vision in which 'a great multitude,' robed in white, appears before the throne and worships God, John is addressed by an elder who asks him: 'Who are these, robed in white, and where have they come from?' (7:13) John does not answer but hands the question back to the elder who then gives the answer: 'These are they who have come out of the great ordeal; they have washed their robes and made them white in the blood of the Lamb' (7:15).
- When the beast rises out of the sea, the whole earth is amazed. All follow and honour the beast, asking: 'Who is like the beast, and who can fight against it?' (13:4) The praise implies that in fact no one is like the beast, no one can fight against it. However, the reader knows that 'the whole earth' is mistaken: the Son of Man can and will fight the beast and capture it (19:20).
- Those who have conquered the beast sing a song of praise and ask: 'Lord, who will not fear and glorify your name?' (15:4) The implicit answer is, of course, 'nobody,' in other words: everybody will and must praise the Lord. The explicit answer follows in the same verse: 'All nations will come and worship before you.'
- In 17:7, an angel asks John: 'Why are you so amazed?' He then goes on and explains what John has just seen: the judgement of the great whore.
- Confronted with the fall of Babylon (i.e. Rome), 'all shipmasters and seafarers, sailors and all whose trade is on the sea' lament: 'What city was like the great city?' (18:18) In their view, the answer is 'none,' but the reader will soon be allowed a glimpse of the New Jerusalem in all its splendour (21:1–22:5).[1]

This short survey of the questions asked – and answered – in the book of Revelation may, at first glance, discourage any further investigation into this topic. What can we learn about the last book of the Bible by concentrating (only) on the questions? To my knowledge, there has been no scholarly contribution focusing on this aspect in Revelation so far. There might be sound reasons for this reticence. And yet I think that a closer look at the different functions of the questions in Revelation yield valuable insights into some structural and pragmatic as well as theological aspects of this biblical writing.

---

[1] T. Nicklas, "Neue Forschungen zur Johannesapokalypse," *Zeitschrift für Neues Testament* 42 (2018): 5–22, here 19.

2. The apocalyptic drama is set in motion (5:2)

The first question in Revelation marks a strategic point in the narration. In 4:1 John is invited to come up to heaven and see what must happen in the eschatological future. The scene that he then describes is – at first – rather static: thrones, a rainbow, elders sitting on thrones. God's appearance is likened to precious (solid) stones and even the sea is not moving, but is like a 'sea of glass, like crystal' (4:6). The living creatures sing continuously and praise God as the one 'who was, and is, and is to come' (4:8). The whole setting is one of sublime calm. However, ὁ ἐρχόμενος *he who is to come* (1:4) points towards the eschatological future and in 4:9–11 the verbs are in the future rather than in the present tense.[2] Thus, the scene is set into motion and opens the reader's perspective towards what is going to happen. This setting into motion, however, does not run smoothly. It is here that the first question in Revelation is placed. Seals need to be broken for the apocalyptic events to take place. A mighty angel asks who is worthy to do this (5:2) – and the first answer is: 'no one in heaven or on earth or under the earth' (5:3). The seer begins to weep bitterly, he is not (any longer) a detached onlooker, but (gets) directly involved. The narrative drama seems to stall, it seems to have come to an end before it has really begun. In this situation of crisis, one of the elders answers the question that the mighty angel in 5:2 had asked. In doing so, he does not address the angel, however. Rather, he turns to the seer and offers him consolation by pointing to the one (and only!) who is capable to open the seals.

It is interesting to look at how the reader gets involved in this scene. The seer speaks in the first person. With the seer, the reader enters the heavens. He can see through the seer's eyes. When the I-figure gets emotionally involved, the reader gets involved, too. But how, exactly, does he or she get involved? The I-figure in the text gets stuck and does not know how the drama can go on. Does this apply to the reader as well? If we assume that the first readers or listeners were Jesus-followers, we can assume that they could guess: Jesus Christ will, somehow or other, enter the stage. So, at this point, the reader dissociates from the seer because he knows: The drama will go on. But how? And how will this further development fit in with the first reader's present situation? So, the reader's involvement is not quite the same as the seer's involvement.

---

[2] U.B. Müller, *Die Offenbarung des Johannes* (Ökumenischer Taschenbuchkommentar zum Neuen Testament 19; Gütersloh: Gütersloher, 1995²), 141–142.

The reader's involvement is ambivalent. On the one hand, he or she watches the seer being involved and can offer him consolation, just like the mighty angel. On the other hand, he or she is well aware that not all is well in the present, so the question as to the eschatological status of the present remains, at this point, unanswered.

Consequently, this is not fantastic literature with a playful note to it.[3] This is not a fictitious apocalyptic drama for us to enjoy by watching from a safe distance. Everything is at stake, here. The ultimate question that is addressed in 5:2 – and in the following visions – is one that concerns all of us, readers of the text of Revelation, directly: who has power over the destiny of the earth? 'Das mythische Szenario im Himmel verbindet sich mit den geschichtlichen Ereignissen auf der Erde.'[4] In the end, the New Jerusalem itself will come down out of heaven from God (21:10).

In consequence, the first question that is asked in Revelation does not only raise the dramatic tension, it also bridges the distance between heaven and earth, between heavenly beings and mankind: what is going to happen is of imminent importance to all men.[5] This is highlighted by further questions that express (misguided) lament in the face of apocalyptic happenings.

3. Questions as (misguided) lamentations (6:10, 17; 18:18)

Three questions represent a form of a lamentation. These lamentations come from opposing sides: in 6:10, the martyrs ask 'how long' it is going to be until the Lord will judge the earth. In 6:17 this day of judgement has come and 'the kings of the earth, the magnates and the generals' now lament their fate. Similarly, in 18:18 those 'whose trade is on the sea' lament the destruction of Babylon, 'the great city.' This destruction will be contrasted by the coming down of the 'holy city' Jerusalem in

---

[3] M. Frenschkowski, "Applaus im Himmel? Gedanken zum Gott der Apokalypse zwischen Phantastik und Politik," *Zeitschrift für Neues Testament 42* (2018): 109–124, here 123. Differently, A. Stefan, "The Book of Re(ve)lation: How to Read Intertextually," in: J. Verheyden, T. Nicklas and A. Merkt (Eds.), *Ancient Christian Interpretations of "Violent Texts" in the Apocalypse* (NTOA 92; Göttingen: Vandenhoeck & Ruprecht, 2011), 287–303.

[4] Frenschkowski, "Applaus im Himmel?," 122.

[5] H. Konrad, "Jesus Christus – der Erste und der Letzte: Zur Christologie der Johannesapokalypse," in: J. Frey, J.A. Kehlhoffer and F. Tóth (Eds.), *Die Johannesapokalypse* (WUNT 287; Tübingen: Mohr Siebeck, 2012), 435–472; Frenschkowski, "Applaus im Himmel?," 122.

21:2. At its arrival, God will wipe every tear from his people's eyes (21:3). Thus, the three questions are part of a chiastic pattern: in the present, the martyrs lament and long for the day of judgement (6:10) and, once this day has come, the kings of the earth will lament (6:17). In the eschatological future, the seafarers will lament the destruction of the 'great city' (18:18), but God will console his people and live with them in the holy city (21:3).

3.1. *Lamentation by the martyrs (6:10) – Revelation between freedom and predestination*

When the Lamb opens the fifth seal, John sees the souls of those who have been slaughtered for the word of God. They ask the Lamb: 'How long will it be before you judge and avenge our blood on the inhabitants of the earth?' (6:10) They are told to 'rest a little longer,' until the number will be complete 'both of their fellow-servants and of their brothers and sisters' who will soon be killed (6:11). 6:11 narrates an act that is about to happen in the future and that can be considered as an answer to the question asked in 6:10. However, at this point the answer remains rather unspecific. The martyrs are offered consolation by the fact that the remaining time will be short.

On a narrative level, the whole book can be regarded as the more specific answer.[6] Part of this answer has already been provided: the Lamb who, like the martyrs, was slaughtered,[7] is worthy to unroll the apocalyptic drama – God is already in charge (5:2, 9).[8] The following chapters will describe what is going to happen in the near future (cf. 1:19 ἃ μέλλει γενέσθαι μετὰ ταῦτα) in detail. Those who do not fear God will be destroyed, the faithful will be resurrected and the New Jerusalem will come down out of heaven from God (22:1) to the earth. The end of the book of Revelation can be regarded as Jesus' final consoling answer to the question the martyrs ask in 6:10: 'Yes, I am coming soon,' followed by the faithful's call: 'Amen, come, Lord Jesus!' (22:20).

---

[6] Nicklas, "Neue Forschungen zur Johannesapokalypse," 20.
[7] H. Roose, *Das Zeugnis Jesu: Seine Bedeutung für die Christologie, Eschatologie und Prophetie in der Offenbarung des Johannes* (Texte und Arbeiten zum neutestamentlichen Zeitalter 32; Tübingen: Francke, 2000), 67–71.
[8] Cf. M.R. Hoffmann, *The Destroyer and the Lamb: The Relationship between Angelomorphic and Lamb Christology in the Book of Revelation* (WUNT 203; Tübingen: Mohr Siebeck, 2005).

At first glance, the accusing question of the martyrs may be aimed at personal revenge. However, it must be borne in mind that this complaint is based on the awareness that the eschaton has not yet been realized. With the words 'how long' the question takes up an essential stylistic element of Old Testament lament psalms (cf. e.g. Psalm 13:2–3; 73:10; 78:5). An exact correspondence can be found in 4 Ezra 4:35–36, where the souls of the righteous lament in their chambers: 'How long shall we stay here? When will the fruit finally appear on the threshing floor of our reward?' So, the problem that Revelation 6:10 deals with is not that of personal revenge. There is much more at stake, namely the fundamental problem that justice is not realized within the world.[9]

God seems to have withdrawn from the world. At the same time, the martyrs have not given up hope of his intervention. They still trust God to defeat the opposing forces. In the face of God man appears ambivalent: on the one hand he can decide how he wants to position himself before God. The martyrs have chosen God and have been killed because of their confession. They are like the tip of an iceberg, the extreme points of Christian existence in the hostile world (12:17)[10]; hostile because man can also decide against God and even kill people who confess God. In this respect man is free. He is judged according to his works (20:12). On the other hand he is predestined in his destiny – depending on whether he is listed in the book of life from the beginning or not (13:5). Revelation thus creates an image of man between freedom and determinism.[11] This tension also permeates the (misguided) laments of the kings of the earth (6:17) and the sailors (18:18). They are guilty of having made the wrong choice – and they are doomed and have been doomed from the very beginning. In the eschatological future, they will therefore lament their fate.

3.2. *Lamentation by the 'kings of the earth' (6:17): the guilt of mankind*

The opening of the sixth seal causes a cosmic upheaval: the sun turns black, the moon becomes like blood (6:12; cf. Amos 8:9; Isaiah 13:10; Joel 3:4) and the stars fall from the sky (Revelation 6:13). The sky itself

---

[9] Cf. K. Wengst, *„Wie lange noch?": Schreien nach Recht und Gerechtigkeit – eine Deutung der Apokalypse des Johannes* (Stuttgart: Kohlhammer, 2010).

[10] Roose, *Das Zeugnis Jesu*, 52.

[11] T. Nicklas, "Freiheit oder Prädestination? Gedanken zum Menschenbild der Johannesapokalypse," in: A.Y. Collins (Ed.), *New Perspectives on the Book of Revelation* (BETL 291; Leuven: Peeters, 2017), 105–129, here 129.

vanishes, allowing God's throne to come into view. Mountains and islands are moved by an earthquake (cf. Mark 13:8). Nothing stays the way it was (6:14). According to Jewish-apocalyptic tradition (As. Mos. 10:4f.; 4 Ezra 6:14ff.; Sib. Or. 3:80–91, 369–697; cf. Mark 13:24ff.), these events mark the coming of the day of wrath (Revelation 6:17). Whereas in 6:11 the martyrs lamented their fate, we now see the 'kings of the earth and the magnates and the generals and the rich and the powerful and everyone, slave and free' (6:15) hiding (cf. Isaiah 2:10; 19:21) and we hear them lamenting their fate, begging the mountains and the rocks to fall upon them so that they cannot be seen from above.

The enumeration of those who are affected by the anger of the Lamb includes ever larger groups and ends in a general 'everyone' (6:15). All mankind is guilty and doomed – and well aware of it. That is the only reason mankind is afraid of the day of judgement and tries to hide from God and the Lamb. In their view, the question 'Who is able to stand?' is a purely rhetorical one: no one is able to stand, all humanity is guilty.[12] However, the readers of Revelation know better: the martyrs and those who trust in the Lamb *can* stand, they will not be destroyed but will be spared from the eschatological woes (7:1–8).

The glimpse at the day of wrath is proleptic: in the following chapters, Revelation goes back twice and unfolds the eschatological drama in the visions of the seven trumpets and the seven bowls. Each of them ends in a vision of the day of wrath (11:15ff.; 16:17ff.). After the pouring out of the seventh bowl, one of the seven angels addresses John and shows him the judgement of the great whore (17:1ff.), and it is in this context that we encounter the 'shipmasters and seafarers, sailors and all whose trade is on the sea' (18:17) who lament the destruction of Babylon, the great city, by asking: 'What city was like the great city?' (18:18).

3.3. *Lamentation by the seafarers (18:18)*

Again, the question asked in 18:18 is a rhetorical one. Again, the reader knows that the answer implied by those who ask ('no city was like the great city') is wrong: Jerusalem, the 'holy city' (21:2), will surpass Babylon infinitely. Unlike the 'kings of the earth and the magnates and the generals and the rich and the powerful and everyone, slave and free' (6:15), the seafarers are presented as distant spectators. They stand 'far

---

[12] W. Klaiber, *Die Offenbarung des Johannes* (Die Botschaft des Neuen Testaments; Neukirchen-Vluyn: Neukirchener, 2019), 130.

off' (18:17). And yet, what they see regards them directly. They look on, unable to prevent the destruction of Babylon. This destruction of the great city annihilates their business. It shows that what was important to them – trade and riches – is taken from them in an instant. In a way, the riches are transferred to Jerusalem, the holy city that presents itself surrounded by 'a radiance like a very rare jewel, like jasper, clear as crystal' (21:11). Revelation does not criticize wealth as such. It is concerned with the question where wealth should be seen, who should be rich and who should be made poor.

3.4. *Questions as (misguided) lamentations: the reader knows the answer*

We have seen that three questions in Revelation function as lamentations. In all three instances, the reader knows (at least part of) the answer to those questions. However, he or she knows the answer in two different ways:

In 6:11, the martyrs' question 'how long' is an open question that stresses the urgency of God's taking action. The reader knows part of the answer to this question from what has already been narrated in the text. He has just been informed that God has indeed already taken action. The eschatological drama has begun, it is already well under way. However, the complete answer to the martyrs' question has not been provided yet. It will be given to the reader as the apocalyptic drama unfolds and the drama unfolds in the light of the 'Maranatha' in 22:20. However, in 6:10–11, the question 'how long' is not answered directly and thus, for the time being, remains open to the martyrs and to the reader.

In 6:17 and 18:18, the questions are rhetorical ones. They imply certain answers. In both cases, the reader knows that the answers implied by those who ask are wrong. Thus, the questions do not only function as forms of lamentation. They privilege the (historical) reader who knows more than the misguided figures in the text.

On a deeper level, the questions stress how deeply misguided mankind is. Those who belong to the Lamb have to be protected against a world that gets its priorities totally wrong.

4. Questions as (misguided) praise (13:4; 15:4)

In two instances, questions express misguided praise. In 13:3–4, we read that 'the whole earth' worships the beast asking 'Who is like the beast and who can fight against it?' The beast represents the power of the Roman Empire. The τίς ὅμοιος ... τίς δύναται in 13:4 recalls the τίς ἄξιος from

5:2. In 5:3, the angel's question was – at first – answered in the negative: 'no one in heaven or on earth or under the earth' (5:3). Likewise, the answer implied by 'the whole earth' in 13:4 is also in the negative: the (power of) the beast is beyond compare – an aspect that is usually attributed to God.[13] In Exodus 15:11, Moses and the Israelites praise God by asking: 'Who is like you, O Lord, among the gods? Who is like you, majestic in holiness, awesome in splendour, doing wonders?' Just as in Exodus 15:11 the Israelites imply that no one is like the Lord, in Revelation 13:4 the inhabitants of the earth do not expect anyone to be able to resist or fight the beast. However, because of 5:9–10, the reader knows this to be wrong. The beast's era of power is strictly limited to 42 months (13:5). In the end, it will be fought and defeated by God's power (19:20) – a power that does not only compare to the beast's power but that clearly surpasses it. Thus, the text of Revelation creates a parody in which it presents the followers of the beast as followers of the Anti-Christ. The beast representing the Roman Empire is allowed to utter blasphemies against God and to make war on the saints (13:6–7). So superior is God's power that he can allow the beast to act out its wishes for a limited stretch of time. Despite apparent successes of anti-godly powers, God is always in charge.

In many ways, 15:4 can be seen as the counterpart to 13:4. Whereas in 13:4, 'the whole earth' praises the beast, in 15:4 'those who had been victorious against the beast' praise the Lord God by singing: 'Who shall not fear you, Lord and do homage to your name?' Whereas in 13:4, the scene is situated on earth, the vision in 15:4 is located in heaven (15:1). The 'sea of glass' (15:2) recalls the heavenly setting as it is found in chapter 4. However, unlike in 4:6, in 15:2 the 'sea of glass' is 'shot through with fire.' The image refers to lightning and, on a metaphorical level, it refers to the Day of wrath that is near.[14] The characterization of the song as 'the song of Moses, the servant of God, and the song of the Lamb' (15:3) is somewhat enigmatic. It likens the exodus, led by Moses, to the salvation brought about by the Lamb. In both cases, God's power is at work. Just as Moses and the Israelites followed God and praised him for his deeds in Exodus 15, in Revelation 15 those who were victorious against the beast followed the Lamb and praise him for his deeds.

The song in its poetic form recalls Old Testament hymns. They often feature rhetorical questions. Revelation 15:4 goes back to Jeremiah 10:6–7: 'There is none like you, O Lord, you are great, and your name

---

[13] Müller, *Die Offenbarung des Johannes*, 251.
[14] Müller, *Die Offenbarung des Johannes*, 275.

is great in might. Who would not fear you, O King of the nations? For that is your due; among all the wise ones of the nations and in all their kingdoms there is no one like you.' In Revelation 15:4, the hymn falls into three parts: In the first part, the Lord God is described as the 'Almighty' who is 'just and true' and 'king of the nations' (15:3). The last part of the hymn names the consequences of God's greatness: 'All nations will come and worship before you.' (15:4) The rhetorical question is located between those parts. Through its rhetorical force, it highlights the inevitability of what is to come: since everybody will fear God and glorify his name, the nations will have to recognize God's judgments (see above). Again, as in 7:1–8, the heavenly scene is proleptic: it envisages events that are bound to come.

5. Questions as attention-seekers (7:13; 17:7)

Visions are rather typical of apocalyptic literature. Quite often, the visionaries do not understand what they see. Therefore, in Old Testament apocalyptic literature, the seer may ask a heavenly being to explain the meaning of their visions. For example, Zechariah sees a rider on a red horse and behind it more horses (Zechariah 1:8). He asks the Lord: 'What are these, my Lord?' (1:9) The Interpreting Angel provides an explanation (1:10). In these cases, the questions are asked by the visionary and they are 'real' questions: the questioner wants to get an answer from someone who knows. He needs to ask a heavenly being – for example an angel – to explain the visionary images.

However, in Revelation, we do not come across any questions that John addresses to heavenly beings in order to have his visions explained. Most visions lack (detailed) interpretations altogether. In two instances, we do find more detailed interpretations of visions (7:13–15b; 17:7–18). In both cases these interpretations are triggered by a question (7:13; 17:7). But neither of these questions is asked by the seer John. He is the addressee, although he does not know the answer. Thus, the questions are no longer 'genuine' questions. They do not aim at getting information from someone who knows. So, what is their rhetorical function?

5.1. *A didactic question (7:13)*

In 7:13 one of the elders addresses the seer John with the following question: 'Who are these, robed in white, and where have they come from?' The question is embedded in the interpretation (7:13–15) of the preceding vision (7:10–12). It refers to the 'great multitude that no one could count' in 7:9. The seer returns the question: 'My lord, you are the one that knows.' (7:14). The scene is reminiscent of Ezekiel 37:3–4 where we have a similar effect. The Lord asks Ezekiel: 'Mortal, can these bones live?' (37:3). And Ezekiel answers: 'O Lord God, you know.' (37:3)

Thus, the ordinary structure of question and answer is turned upside down: Whereas usually the one who does not know asks the one who knows, here the one who knows, asks the one who does not know. Therefore, it is clear that in Revelation 7:13 – as in Ezekiel 37:3–4 – it is not a question of information with which someone wants to find out something.[15] The function of the question is rather a didactic one. It involves the seer in the event and at the same time makes it clear to him that he needs (and will get) explanations in order to understand what he sees. He will not be left in the dark. The didactic question aims at raising the seer's and the reader's attention.

On a narrative level, the seer's ignorance is astonishing. For in 6:10–11 he saw and heard the martyrs who were given white robes. So at least he could venture an educated guess. But apparently, he does not make the connection and proclaims that he does not know. This provides the opportunity for the elder to give out more information. In fact, those who are wearing white clothes are not only the martyrs that we heard about in 6:11 but all those 'who have come out of the great ordeal' (7:14). If we interpret 'the great ordeal' with reference to Daniel 12:1, we can assume that in Revelation 7:14 the elder refers not only to the martyrs but to all those who belong to the Lamb.

To the historical – and modern – reader, this answer hardly comes as a surprise. So, the question works differently for the seer and for the readers. As far as the seer is concerned, it focusses his attention and provides him with extra information. As far as the readers are concerned, who already know the answer, the question triggers heavenly confirmation of what they already knew.

5.2. A rhetorical question (17:7)

As in 7:13, 17:7 marks the transition from the vision to its interpretation. 17:6 ends with the remark that the seer 'was greatly amazed.' Again, the seer gets emotionally involved. Whereas in 5:4 he was distressed because no one was found to open the seals, in 17:6 he is amazed by the drunken

---

[15] H. Lichtenberger, *Die Apokalypse* (TKNT 23; Stuttgart: Kohlhammer, 2014), 150.

woman he sees.[16] His reaction is noticed by the angel who is with him, and it is not one of fear. He seems to feel safe with the angel – and he knows that a 'great multitude that no one can count' (17:9) will be saved. The angel asks: 'Why are you so amazed? I will tell you the mystery of the woman, and of the beast with seven seals and ten horns that carries her.' (17:7) In this case, the question is a rhetorical one. It implies that there is no need to be amazed by the drunken woman. Amazement is here a symptom of ignorance. It motivates the angel to explain to the seer John – and to the reader – what the vision is about.

6. Conclusion

In the Revelation of John, not many questions are asked. The questions that we do find serve different ends and they are asked by different groups of people. Heavenly beings ask who can set the eschatological drama into motion (5:2) and they address the seer with a didactical (7:13) and a rhetorical question (17:7). All these questions demonstrate that the seer is involved in the apocalyptic drama he is witnessing. Indirectly, this involvement is aimed at the reader or listener: what (s)he is reading or hearing regards his or her eschatological fate. Some questions are asked by those who are misguided and who will see destruction (6:17; 13:4; 18:18). Their questions serve as lamentations over their future fate (6:17; 18:18) or as praise given to the present power of the Roman Empire (13:4). Interestingly, the followers of the Lamb ask questions to the same end, however, the eschatological signs are reversed: They lament their present fate (6:10) and they praise the Lord God because of their future victory over the beast (15:4).

The only person not to ask any questions is the seer. This is all the more striking as Old Testament visionaries are known to ask heavenly beings about the meaning of their visions. John does not do this. He does not need to do so. God reveals everything that he – and the reader – needs to know.

---

[16] Cf. H. Roose, "The Fall of the "Great Harlot" and the Fate of the Aging Prostitute," in: A. Weissenrieder, F. Wendt and P. von Gemünden (Eds.), *Picturing the New Testament* (WUNT 193; Tübingen: Mohr Siebeck, 2005), 228–252, here 228–252.

ASKING QUESTIONS IN QUMRAN LITERATURE

Albert L.A. HOGETERP

University of the Free State Bloemfontein

1. Introduction

The Dead Sea Scrolls from the caves of Khirbet Qumran comprise a richly varied corpus with various categories and genres of texts, including biblical manuscripts, parabiblical and non-biblical texts, and many genres, such as rule texts, sapiential texts, poetic and liturgical texts, apocalyptic and eschatological texts.[1] While the biblical Qumran scrolls may occasionally comprise some interesting examples of variant readings concerning biblical questions,[2] the focus of this essay is on the parabiblical and non-biblical Qumran texts. The latter groups of texts are most distinctive regarding the development of biblical positions in late Second Temple Judaism from the viewpoint of Qumran literature.[3]

---

[1] For literary categorizations of Qumran texts, see D. Dimant, "The Qumran Manuscripts: Contents and Significance," in D. Dimant and L.H. Schiffman (Eds.), *Time to Prepare the Way in the Wilderness* (STDJ 16; Leiden: Brill, 1995), 23–58; D. Dimant, "The Qumran Manuscripts: Contents and Significance," in D. Dimant, *History, Ideology and Bible Interpretation in the Dead Sea Scrolls. Collected Studies* (FAT 90; Tübingen: Mohr Siebeck, 2014), 27–56.

[2] Variant readings may concern (a) *additional questions* as plus materials, e.g. Deuteronomic material, Deut 1:9–18 after Exod 18:24 in 4QpaleoExod^m XIX 7–17, question in line 10, and material comparable to Deut 2:2–6; 3:24–28 after Num 20:13 in 4QNum^b XI, frgs. 13 i–14 ll. 25–30; (b) *substantiation of a biblical question*, regarding 2 Sam 11:3, with the further qualification of Uriah the Hittite as 'the armour-[b]earer of Joab' as represented in 4QSam^a frgs. 90–91. 4 parallel to Josephus, not in MT; (c) *different wordings of questions*, as. In 1QIsa^a XIII 4 // LXX ≠ MT Isa 14:32; 1QIsa^a XXX 17–18 ≠ MT, LXX Isa 37:13; 1QIsa^a XXXIII 13–14 ≠ MT Isa 40:13–14; 1QIsa^a XXXIII 17–18 ≠ MT Isa 40:18; 1QIsa^a XLVIII 1–2 ≠ MT Isa 58:7; (d) *framing as a question what is a jussive in the MT*, in 4QPs^a 19 ii 32 as compared with MT Ps 69:14. For a comprehensive survey of variant readings in the biblical Qumran scrolls in English translation, cf. M. Abegg, P. Flint, and E. Ulrich, *The Dead Sea Scrolls Bible: The Oldest Known Bible Translated for the First Time into English* (San Francisco: Harper, 1999); in Hebrew, see E. Ulrich, *The Biblical Qumran Scrolls: Transcriptions and Textual Variants* (VTSup 134; Leiden: Brill, 2010).

[3] Texts and translations of Quran literature are from F. García Martínez and E.J.C. Tigchelaar, *The Dead Sea Scrolls Study Edition. 1. (1Q1–4Q273). 2 (4Q274–11Q31)* (Leiden: Brill, 2000), unless otherwise mentioned.

No systematic survey of questions appears possible for non-biblical Qumran literature, since, contrary to the biblical corpus, most of these texts have only been preserved fragmentarily.[4] Since, to my knowledge, the subject of asking questions in Qumran literature has not yet been intensively studied,[5] this article will aim to provide a tentative survey of important samples of asking questions in various genres of texts which are represented in Qumran literature. It will aim to highlight how questions function in diverse literary contexts, what they intend to communicate, and which communication process is involved within each text. As such, Qumran literature provides unique evidence of Hebrew and Aramaic texts around the turn of the common era for researching this topic.

Much previous work has been done on asking questions in biblical Hebrew.[6] Adina Moshavi recently surveyed various types of content questions in classical biblical Hebrew prose (Genesis-2 Kings): information-seeking questions, rhetorical questions, pre-directive questions, directive-seeking questions, and commitment-seeking questions. She noted the relatively high frequency of 301 rhetorical questions out of a total of 479 content questions in this biblical corpus.[7] Analogous to the prominence of rhetorical questions in biblical tradition, is the large number of rhetorical questions found in Qumran literature. These rhetorical questions occur across various genres.[8] Yet rhetorical questions, which

---

[4] Among the Dead Sea discoveries, only the early finds from Qumran cave 1 of the great Isaiah Scroll (1QIsa^a), 1QIsa^b, the Hymn Scroll (1QH^a, 1QH^b), the War Scroll (1QM), the Rule scroll (1QS, 1QSa, 1QSb), Pesher Habakkuk (1QpHab), the Genesis Apocryphon (1QapGen ar), as well as the Temple Scroll from Qumran cave 11 (11QT^a) comprise extensively intact texts. Qumran cave 4 yielded a great many texts, but these are usually fragmentarily preserved.

[5] The linguistic and rhetorical subject of asking questions is not an explicit theme in any of the international conference proceedings on the Hebrew of the Dead Sea Scrolls and related literature so far published at Leiden, Brill, edited by T. Muraoka and J. Elwolde, STDJ 26 (1997), 33 (1999), 36 (2000); by J. Joosten and J.-S. Rey, STDJ 73 (2007); by S. Fassberg, M. Bar-Asher and R. Clements, STDJ 108 (2013); and by E.J.C. Tigchelaar and P. Van Hecke, STDJ 114 (2015).

[6] See e.g. K.M. Craig, *Asking for Rhetoric: The Hebrew Bible's Protean Interrogative* (BibInt 73; Leiden: Brill Academic, 2005); A. Moshavi, "The Communicative Functions of Content ('Wh') Questions in Classical Biblical Hebrew Prose," *JNSL* 39 (2013) 69–87; A. Moshavi, "Interrogative Clause, Biblical Hebrew," in: G. Khan (Ed.), *Encyclopedia of Hebrew Language and Linguistics* (Leiden: Brill, 2013), 306–316.

[7] Moshavi, "Communicative Functions of Content Questions," 69–87.

[8] Because of their cross-sectional occurrence, rhetorical questions will receive separate consideration by the end of this article. This article does not consider questions in Qumran exegetical literature (e.g. the Pesharim; 4Q174, 4Q177 (4QMidrEschat^{a-b})), which are part of quoted portions of biblical text. Only questions which are posed separately from biblical texts may illuminate further developments of biblical positions.

have been intensively studied regarding biblical Hebrew,[9] constitute a subject in their own right. Their alleged interrogative or rather assertive function may reportedly vary in each discourse context, where these rhetorical questions occur.[10]

This paper will first survey select Qumran texts as representative of various genres, in order to illustrate a broader spectrum of types of questions which may be asked, literary contexts in which these questions appear, and communicative settings regarding speaker(s) and addressee(s), ranging from characters in narrative texts to text-immanent readers in various genres of texts. The texts from which samples will be discussed concern the following categories and genres: parabiblical literature (*Pseudo-Ezekiel*),[11] sapiential literature (*1–4QMysteries*), and apocalyptic literature (4Q521). These texts have been selected because they are unique to the Qumran corpus[12] and they comprise extended sections in which asking (a) question(s) plays a prominent role. We will then highlight the cross-sectional occurrence of rhetorical questions in various genres of Qumran literature, including their attestation in the longer-known sectarian Qumran texts, before turning to an evaluation and conclusions.

[9] Cf. e.g. L.J. de Regt, "Discourse Implications of Rhetorical Questions in Job, Deuteronomy and the Minor Prophets," in: L.J. de Regt *et al.* (Eds.), *Literary Structure and Rhetorical Strategies in the Hebrew Bible* (Assen: Van Gorcum, 1996), 51–78; A. Moshavi, "Two Types of Argumentation Involving Rhetorical Questions in Biblical Hebrew Dialogue," *Bib* 90 (2009): 32–46 with further bibliography on rhetorical questions (RQs) in various genres, such as poetry, prose, wisdom literature; A. Moshavi, "Can a Positive Rhetorical Question have a Positive Answer in the Bible?," *JSS* 46 (2011): 253–273; A. Moshavi, "Between Dialectic and Rhetoric: Rhetorical Questions Expressing Premises in Biblical Prose Argumentation," *VT* 65 (2015): 136–151; T. Zewi, "Rhetorical Questions and Negative Clauses in Biblical Hebrew," in T. Zewi, *Ancient Texts and Modern Readers* (SSN 71; Leiden: Brill 2019), 196–210.

[10] See A. Moshavi, "Rhetorical Question or Assertion? The Pragmatics of הֲלֹא in Biblical Hebrew," *JANESCU* 32 (2011): 91–105.

[11] Parabiblical Qumran literature comprises a broad set of texts with questions. *Pseudo-Ezekiel* has been selected as an elaborate and prominent example. Yet other examples could be drawn from *4QFour Kingdoms*[a-c] *ar*, in which questions are asked of 'trees,' which symbolically stand for kingdoms (4Q552 1 ii 4, 8, 11 // 4Q553 6 ii 4, 5–6); from the *Visions of Amram* (4Q544 frg. 1 10–14 // 4Q543 6 1–6) regarding questions addressing otherworldly beings (Melchizedek en Melchiresha) who quarrel over the question which of them the protagonist chooses to be ruled by; or from the *Genesis Apocryphon* (1QapGen ar 2.16–17, 20.26 (/ Gen 12:18), 22.32).

[12] Qumran literature also comprises fragments of apocryphal and pseudepigraphical texts, such as Tobit and 1 Enoch, which have been preserved more extensively outside Qumran. These texts also comprise questions, as part of human conversation (Tob 6:7, 4QTob[b] ar 4 i 12; Tob 6:16, 4QTob[a] ar 14 i 8–9 // 4QTob[b] ar 4 ii 12–13; Tob 7:3–5, 4QTob[a] ar 14 ii 8–10 // 4QTob[b] ar 4 iii 5–7) and as part of exchanges between Enoch and an *angelus interpres* (1 Enoch 22:6, 4QEn[e] ar 2 ii 6–7; 1 Enoch 23:3, 4QEn[d] ar 1 i 5; 1 Enoch 27:1, 4QEn[d] ar 1 ii 9).

2. Asking Questions in Parabiblical Literature: Questions Addressing God in *Pseudo-Ezekiel*

Pseudo-Ezekiel is a parabiblical Qumran text in Hebrew, dated around the mid-second century BCE,[13] which is known for its dialogue between Ezekiel as the first-person singular protagonist and God,[14] including questions and answers. One extensively preserved fragment, 4Q385 (4QpsEzek[a]), fragment 2, lines 1–10 // 4Q386 (4QpsEzek[b]), fragment 1, column 1, lines 1–10, which is partly modelled on the vision of the valley of dry bones in Ezekiel 37:1–14, is particularly worth noting regarding the dialectic between questions and answers. This fragment is cited in translation below.[15]

> 1 [for I am the Lord] who redeems my people, giving unto them the covenant. *Vacat*
> 2 [And I said: 'O Lord!] I have seen many (men) from Israel who have loved your Name and have walked 3 in the ways of [your heart.
> Q   And th]ese things when will they come to be and how will they be recompensed for their piety?'
> A   And the Lord said 4 to me: 'I will make (it) manifest[ ] to the children of Israel and they shall know that I am the Lord'. *Vacat*
> 5 [And He said:] 'Son of man, prophesy over the bones and speak and let them be j[oi]ned bone to its bone and joint 6 [to its joint'. And it wa]s so. And He said a second time: 'Prophesy and let arteries come upon them and let skin cover them 7 [from above'. And it was so.] And He said: 'Prophesy once again over the four winds of heaven and let them blow breath 8 [into the slain'. And it was so,] and a large crowd of people came [to li]fe and blessed the Lord Sebaoth wh[o 9 had given them life. *vacat*]
> Q   [and] I said: 'O Lord! when shall these things come to be?'
> A   And the Lord said to m[e: 'Until   ] 10 [after da]ys a tree shall bend and shall stand erect[   ]

This fragment has been characterized by the editor as a pseudepigraphic interpretation of the biblical vision of the valley of dry bones which

---

[13] Editio princeps by D. Dimant, *Qumran Cave 4. XXI: Parabiblical Texts, Part 4: Pseudo-Prophetic Texts* (DJD 30; Oxford: Clarendon Press, 2001), 16, who argues for this date of composition by situating 4Q386 (4QpsEzek[b]) 1 ii against the historical circumstances under the reign of Antiochus IV Epiphanes (175–164 BCE). *Pseudo-Ezekiel* was known already to Qumran scholarship by the time of the preliminary publication of J. Strugnell and D. Dimant, "4QSecond Ezekiel," *RevQ* 13 (1988): 45–58.

[14] Cf. 4Q385 (4QpsEzek[a]) 4 4, ויאמר יהוה אלי לא אש[י]ב פניך יחזקאל, "And the Lord said to *me*: 'I will not re[fu]se you, O *Ezekiel*!'". Text and translation from Dimant, *DJD 30*, 37–38. Cursives are mine.

[15] Text and translation from Dimant, *DJD 30*, 24. Text division and margin indications of question (Q) and answer (A) are mine.

presents 'the future reward for the righteous in the form of resurrection.'[16] Yet the form of interpretation, framed in terms of questions and answers, is also most distinctive in *Pseudo-Ezekiel* as compared with the biblical text. That is, the structure of this fragment is determined by the form of dialogue which interchanges between words of the Lord (4Q385 2 1); a twofold question of Ezekiel addressing the Lord, preceded by an introductory statement (4Q385 2 2–3); the Lord's answer (4Q385 2 3–9) culminating in a prophetic vision of (slain) people coming back to life through divine agency (4Q385 2 8–9); a question of Ezekiel addressing the Lord (4Q385 2 9); and the Lord's (fragmentarily preserved) answer (4Q385 2 9–10).

Before Ezekiel asks any question, our fragment appears to start *in medias res* with the statement of the Lord that he redeems his people in his covenant relationship with them (4Q385 2 1). When we single out the questions of Ezekiel in this fragment, they are threefold:

[וא]לה מתי יהיו, '[And th]ese things when will they come to be?' (4Q385 2 3)

והיככה ישתלמו חסדם, 'and how will they be recompensed for their piety?' (4Q385 2 3)

מתי יהיו אלה, 'when shall these things come to be?' (4Q385 2 9)

It should be noted that the third question (4Q385 2 9) appears to repeat the first question (4Q385 2 3), thus stressing a recurrent concern with time ('when,' מתי) and timeframes for the fulfilment of the Lord's prophecies on the part of the protagonist. The first question, '[And th]ese things when will they come to be?,' implies that the preceding statement of the Lord about redemption for his people is perceived not (only) as a general principle, but as a specific divine intervention in human history.

For Ezekiel the direction of the prophecy is determined by his question about recompense for the piety of many from Israel 'who have loved your Name and have walked in the ways of [your heart]' (4Q385 2 2–3). The answer of the Lord consists of an initial assurance that he will make his theodicy manifest (אראה) to the children of Israel (4Q385 2 3–4), followed by a tripartite prophecy over the bones, the arteries and skin, and the four winds of heaven for breath (4Q385 2 5–6, 6–7, 7–9), perhaps thereby physiologically highlighting distinct parts of human physical existence.[17]

---

[16] Dimant, *DJD 30*, 9; cf. pp. 32–37 on 4Q385 frg. 2 as evidence for the belief in resurrection, also in comparison with biblical texts and other early Jewish literature.

[17] Cf. Dimant, *DJD 30*, 33, who contrasts a three-stage process in this fragment of *Pseudo-Ezekiel* to a two-stage process in the biblical text. Ezek 37:7–8, 9–10 comprises two

The third question (4Q385 2 9) repeats the unceasing concern of Ezekiel with time: 'when shall these things come to be?' Ezekiel thereby asks when the prophecy about a large crowd of people coming back to life will be fulfilled. The prophet thereby further enquires about the time of this recompense for the many in Israel who have been loyal to the Lord (4Q385 2 2–3). Not enough text has been preserved of fragment 2 of 4Q385 to ascertain what the answer is to this third question of Ezekiel.

The composition of *Pseudo-Ezekiel* as a whole provides evidence for a further progression of thought in dialogue. That is, 4Q386 (4QpsEzek[b]), of which fragment 1 column 1 runs parallel to fragment 2 of 4Q385, comprises a second column with further dialogue between God and Ezekiel. 4Q386 1 ii 2–3 adds a fourth question after the Lord has instructed Ezekiel to behold the land of Israel (1 ii 1–2): 'And I said, "I have seen, Lord, and behold it lies waste, and when will you gather them together?".'[18] This fourth question, 'and when will you gather them together?,' ומתי תקבצם (4Q386 1 ii 3), further concerns a projected future return from exile and restoration of Israel. This aspect of the prophetic vision could also echo the interpretive section of Ezekiel 37:11–14, which reflects on the land of Israel and God's return of his people to it.[19] The second column of 4Q386 fragment 1 comprises an extensive answer of God to Ezekiel's fourth question with various indications of an envisioned time of tribulation, including schemes of oppression (4Q386 1 ii 3–4) and divine intervention against wickedness leaving neither survivor nor produce (4Q386 1 ii 4–5), as a setting for the return of a remnant (4Q386 1 ii 6). Yet the sequence in 4Q386 1 ii 7–10 appears ambiguous as to who is concerned by the divine wrath 'from the four corners of the heaven[s]' (ll. 8–9).[20] In any case, God's answer to the prophetic pre-occupation with time (ומתי) makes clear that the fulfilment of the prophetic vision is characterized as a time of tribulation and divine intervention.

Regarding the composition as a whole, divine intervention concerns breath from the four winds of heaven to bring a large crowd of people to

---

instructions for prophecy, one regarding the bones, sinews, flesh and skin (Ezek 37:7–8) and the other regarding the four winds for breath (Ezek 37:9–10).

[18] Translation from Dimant, *DJD 30*, 63.
[19] Cf. Dimant, *DJD 30*, 63 who identifies the use of the verb קבץ as "the standard expression for the ingathering of the exiles, especially in contexts of prophetic forecasts of the future," also with reference to Ezek 37:21.
[20] Dimant, *DJD 30*, 66 on syntactical ambiguity regarding עליהם, theoretically applicable to the "Israelites in Egypt or elsewhere," which would "continue the subject from lines 6–8," or to "the nations – Egypt and Babylon," which would "constitute an abrupt change of subject."

life (4Q385 2 7–9 // 4Q386 1 i 8–10), while the four corners of the heavens are involved in divine wrath (4Q386 1 ii 8–9). Perhaps these are dual aspects of the prophetic vision of divine agency in *Pseudo-Ezekiel*, restoration of a risen crowd of people and resuscitation of divine wrath regarding wickedness and deluded ideas of peace, quiet and continuity with the days of old (4Q386 1 ii 7–8).

Returning to the questions in these fragments of *Pseudo-Ezekiel*, it is time to take stock of this parabiblical composition's distinctiveness vis-à-vis the biblical text of Ezekiel. A significant difference of fragment 2 of *4QPseudo-Ezekiel*[a] with its biblical model consists in the fact that Ezekiel does not pose any questions in Ezekiel 37:1–14, but only follows prophetic instructions from the Lord. In fact, it is God who asks the prophet a question in Ezekiel 37:3: 'And he said to me, Son of man, can these bones live? And I answered, "O Lord God, thou knowest"' (RSV). In the biblical text on the vision of the valley of the dry bones, it does not occur to Ezekiel to ask God any questions. Only God's question opens up prophetic imagination of the previously unimaginable.

The four questions of Ezekiel in the fragments of *Pseudo-Ezekiel* (4Q385 2; 4Q386 1 i–ii) as discussed above include three 'when' (מתי) questions regarding the fulfilment of prophecy. In fact, another fragment, 4Q385 3, may provide a further clue regarding the pre-occupation with time. Here Ezekiel does not ask a question but petitions God: 'Instead of my grief make my soul rejoice and let the days hasten quickly that it be said by men: "Indeed the days are hastening on so that he children of Israel may inherit"' (4Q385 3 1–3).[21] God's answer is affirmative, shortening the days and the years (4Q385 3 4–5). Ezekiel's personal involvement regarding grief and joy is pronounced as compared with biblical formulations.[22]

In sum, Ezekiel's questions about time in *Pseudo-Ezekiel* appear to progress toward a petition to hasten time regarding God's fulfilment of prophecy, so that the children of Israel are restored to their land and may inherit. The personal involvement of Ezekiel in asking questions and petitioning God to change his grief into joy foregrounds the idea that Israel's restoration, framed in terms of resurrection, is presented not as a

---

[21] Translation from Dimant, *DJD 30*, 38. On דין, translated as "grief," cf. M. Jastrow, *A Dictionary of the Targumim, the Talmud Babli and Yerushalmi, and the Midrashic Literature* (New York: The Judaica Press, 1996), 284, 286.
[22] Dimant, *DJD 30*, 38 refers to Ezek 21:11–12 and 24:15–18 for a background to Ezekiel's sorrow, but in these passages it is not Ezekiel who formulates his state of mind or mood, but it is the Lord who gives instructions to Ezekiel as son of man regarding his plight.

unidirectional revelation from God to Ezekiel, but as a vision which unfolds in dialogue between God and his prophet.

3. Asking Questions in Sapiential Texts: Questions for Addressees as Initiates to the Mystery of Existence in *1–4QMysteries*

1–4QMysteries is a fragmentarily preserved composition attested in 1Q27 (1QMyst) and in 4Q299–300 (4QMyst[a-b]), and perhaps tentatively in 4Q301 (4QMyst[c]?), which has been categorized among sapiential literature by its editors and in recent discussion.[23] *1–4QMysteries* has been dated to the last two centuries before the turn of the common era and it comprises a series of rhetorical questions which are 'understood in continuity with the wisdom tradition.'[24]

It is to these rhetorical questions that our survey now turns. These rhetorical questions are most elaborately preserved in 1QMyst 1 i 8–12. These questions have their setting in a preceding context of a digression on the mystery of existence surrounding the vision of ultimate justice and the definite disappearance of darkness and evil (1QMyst 1 i 3–7). The relevant section, 1QMyst 1 i 8–12, which contains an interchange between rhetorical question (RQ) and answer (A), rhetorical questions (RQ) and rhetorical counter-questions (RcQ) indicating contrasting realities, is cited in translation below.[25]

        8 This word will undoubtedly happen, the prediction is truthful. And by this he will show you that it is irrevocable:
RQ[1]   Do not (הלוא) all 9 nations loathe sin?
A   And yet, it is about by the hands of all of them.
RQ[2]   Does not (הלוא) praise of truth come from the mouth of all nations?
RcQ[1]   10 And yet, is there perhaps (היש) one lip or one tongue which persists with it?

---

[23] Editio princeps of 1QMyst by J.T. Milik, *Qumran Cave 1* (DJD 1; Oxford: Clarendon Press, 1955), 102–107, pls. XXI–XXII, and of 4QMyst[a-b] by L.H. Schiffman, *Qumran Cave 4. XV Sapiential Texts, Part 1* (DJD 20; Oxford: Clarendon Press, 1997), 33–112, pls. III–VIII. 4Q301 (4QMyst[c]?) has tentatively been related to *1–4QMysteries*, but it is unclear which parallels in content corroborate the literary relation of 4Q301 to 1QMyst and 4QMyst[a-b]. More recently M. Goff, *Discerning Wisdom: The Sapiential Literature of the Dead Sea Scrolls* (VTSup 116; Leiden: Brill, 2007), 69–103 categorized the Book of Mysteries as 'eschatological wisdom.'

[24] Goff, *Discerning Wisdom*, 96–97 and 99–101, allows for a range of 2nd–1st centuries BCE to date the composition of the Book of Mysteries.

[25] Text and translation from García Martínez and Tigchelaar, *Study Edition. 1*, 68–69. 4Q299 (4QMyst[a]) 1 1–4 runs largely parallel to 1QMyst 1 i 8–12, except for the fact that it lacks RQ[4] and RcQ[2] in the structure noted above.

RQ³   What (מי) people would wish to be oppressed by another more powerful than itself?
RQ⁴   Who (מי) 11 would wish to be sinfully looted of its wealth?
RcQ² And yet, which (מי) is the people not to oppress its neighbour?
RcQ³ Where (איפה) is the people which has not 12 looted [another] of its wea[lth?]

The rhetorical questions introduced by הלוא (RQ¹⁻²) consistently have a positive implied answer, while the rhetorical questions introduced by מי (RQ³⁻⁴) have a negative implied answer. Consistently contrasting realities to the rhetorical questions are asserted in the respective answer (A), and in the rhetorical counter-questions (RcQ¹⁻³) which have negative implied answers. As for RQ²-RcQ¹, biblical tradition also comprises evidence for pairs of rhetorical questions with successive positive and negative implied answers. Moshavi has noted Job 11:2 as an example.[26] As for all four rhetorical questions (RQ¹⁻⁴), we should keep in mind Moshavi's observation of a wide-spread 'justificational use' of rhetorical questions in biblical Hebrew, serving to establish 'common ground between speaker and addressee ("Clearly we both agree on the obvious fact that...").'[27]

What then is the common ground which this fragment of *1–4QMysteries* searches to establish through the succession of rhetorical questions and counter-questions? As the preceding section, 1QMyst 1 i 1–7, has envisioned the disappearance of sin and evil in favour of worldwide justice and knowledge in the end, the section with rhetorical questions, 1QMyst 1 i 8–12, focuses on the persistent reality of evil. That is, these lines provide reflections on the problem of evil in a development of thought through successive rhetorical questions concerning the following issues: the ubiquity of sin (RQ¹-A), the abandonment of (the praise of) truth (RQ²-RcQ¹), oppression among neighbouring peoples (RQ³-RcQ²), and the ongoing looting of wealth among peoples (RQ⁴-RcQ³). All these issues are persistent realities, in spite of the idea that no nation would in principle wish those things to occur to their imagined worlds and to themselves.[28] If this is the common ground for speaker and addressees, the idea presents itself that, from the perspective of *1–4QMysteries*, there is no escape from confronting evil for which an

---

[26] Moshavi, "The Pragmatics of הֲלֹא in Biblical Hebrew," 94.
[27] Moshavi, "The Pragmatics of הֲלֹא in Biblical Hebrew," 101.
[28] The issues, sin, abandonment of (the praise of) truth, oppression, looting of wealth, partly overlap with evildoing noted in 4Q390 2 i 8–9 (domineering for wealth, oppression of one's neighbour) and with matters to abstain from by the sectarian movement in CD-A 6.15–16 (wicked wealth, looting).

eschatological resolution in favour of worldwide justice and knowledge, though shrouded in mysteries of sin and of existence (1QMyst 1 i 2-3), is irrevocable (1QMyst 1 i 8).

4. Asking Questions in Apocalyptic Literature: A Question for Addressees as 'All Those Who Hope in Their Heart' in *4Q521*

4Q521 came to be known in the early 1990s as an apocalyptic text, of which one composite fragment, 2 ii+4, mentions expectations of resurrection (2 ii+4 12) and, perhaps more debatably, a messianic figure ('his anointed one,' 2 ii+4 1).[29] The composition was dated to the second half of the second century BCE by its editor.[30] It is beyond the scope of this discussion to consider its part in the early Jewish tradition history of eschatological, apocalyptic, and messianic ideas[31] or its intertextuality (e.g. Psalm 146:7-8; 1 Samuel 2:6; Isaiah 61:1) in comparison with a Gospel passage (Luke 7:18-23 // Matthew 11:2-4).[32] Our discussion here turns to the issue of asking a question and its implications. There is one prominent question in line 4. The relevant fragment is cited in translation below.[33]

    1 [for the heav]ens and the earth will listen to his anointed one,
    2 [and all th]at is in them will not turn away from the precepts of the holy ones.
    3 Strengthen yourselves, you who are seeking the Lord, in his service! *Blank*
Q   4 Will you not (הלוא) in this encounter the Lord, all those who hope in their heart?
A   5 For the Lord will consider the pious, and call the righteous by name,
    6 and his spirit will hover upon the poor, and he will renew the faithful with strength.
    7 For he will honour the pious upon the throne of an eternal kingdom.

---

[29] É. Puech, "Une apocalypse messianique (4Q521)," *RevQ* 15 (1992): 475–522. Editio princeps by É. Puech, *Qumrân grotte 4. XVIII: Textes hébreux (4Q521–4Q528, 4Q576–4Q579)* (DJD 25; Oxford: Clarendon Press, 1998), 1–38, here 35, noted that 4Q521 speaks "un langage mi-prophétique et mi-apocalyptique". On 'his anointed one,' 4Q521 2 ii+4 1 as a prophetic figure, e.g. M. Becker, "4Q521 und die Gesalbten," *RevQ* 18 (1997): 73–96.

[30] Puech, *DJD 25*, 37.

[31] A.L.A. Hogeterp, *Expectations of the End: A Comparative Traditio-Historical Study of Eschatological, Apocalyptic and Messianic Ideas in the Dead Sea Scrolls and the New Testament* (STDJ 83; Leiden: Brill, 2009), 277–281, 299, 301, 303, 307, 375, 433–434, 446–448, 459, 461–462, 464–466, 470.

[32] Cf. e.g. F. Neirynck, "Q 6,20b–21; 7,22 and Isaiah 61," in: C.M. Tuckett (Ed.), *The Scriptures in the Gospels* (BETL 131; Leuven: Peeters, 1997), 27–64.

[33] Text and translation after García Martínez and Tigchelaar, *Study Edition.* 2, 1044–1045, added by English renderings in cursive of additional readings and reconstructions of Hebrew text by Puech, *DJD 25*, 10.

8 freeing prisoners, giving sight to the blind, straightening out the twis[ted.]
9 And for[e]ver shall I cling [to those who h]ope, and in mercy *he will*[ ]
10 and the fru[it of] *a good [dee]d for humankind will* not be delayed.
11 And the Lord will perform marvellous acts such as have not existed, just as he sa[id,]
12 [for] he will heal the badly wounded and will make the dead live, he will proclaim good news to the poor
13 and *he will make the [poo]r who[le]*, lead *those who are uprooted* and enrich the hungry.
14 *And those who have under[standing* (?)] ο and all *of them like the ho[ly ones?*]
15 *And I will*[

The question in line 4, הלוא בזאת תמצאו את אדני כל המיחלים בלבם, 'Will you not in this encounter the Lord, all those who hope in their heart?,' begins with a negative introduction (הלוא) with a positive implied answer. Yet differently from rhetorical questions, as in *1–4QMysteries*, this question is not a simple yes-no rhetorical question, but it sets the stage for an elaborate exposition which fills in the ways in which the addressees may encounter the Lord.

In order to determine the setting of the question and its answer, it is important to highlight the structure of this passage. Lines 1–2 comprise parallel elements (heaven and earth // all that is in them; will listen to // will not turn away from; representatives of divine agency: his anointed one // the precepts of the holy ones). Lines 3–4 also comprise a parallel feature: seeking the Lord // encounter the Lord. While line 3 stipulates an admonitory directive to strengthen oneself in the search of the Lord, the question in line 4 provides the answer to this seeking in encounters of the Lord for those who hope in their heart. Since בזאת, 'in this' or literally 'in these things' may, strictly speaking, refer to either preceding things or following things, or to both,[34] the referentiality or directionality of the question is at issue here.

If lines 3–4 are taken together as a form of admonition, it should be noted that the subsequent lines reiterate elements, such as strength, בכחו (l. 6), and hope, [במ]יחלים (l. 9), which also occur in lines 3–4 (התאמצו, המיחלים). If בזאת is understood as a plural ('in these things'), subsequent lines may provide elaboration. Lines 5–8 comprise two motivational clauses starting with כי (ll. 5, 7), introducing indications of the Lord's active pres-

---

[34] KBL, 250–251 s.v. זֶה, rubrics 5 and 6. Cf. Puech, *DJD 25*, 12–13 mentions various possible referents for בזאת, such as 'in his service' (l. 3) or 'the precepts of the holy ones' (l. 2), but deems the subsequent expression of hope in terms of messianic and eschatological expectation the more probable referent.

ence. Line 9 even starts with a first-person singular statement of the Lord's union with those who hope, assuring them of the immediate value of the fruit of good deeds (line 10). Line 11 makes a new statement about the Lord's marvellous acts, followed by one further motivational כי-clause (l. 12) which enumerates such acts (ll. 12–13). Lines 14–15 have been preserved very fragmentarily, although the reconstructed reference to 'holy ones,' קד[ושים], in line 14 may reiterate line 2. The intermediate section, lines 3–13, could be understood as an admonition of those who hope in their heart (ll. 3–4). The question about encounters of the Lord in line 4 then leads to an unfolding perspective on the Lord's active presence through two motivational כי-clauses (ll. 5–6, 7–8), a first-person singular statement of the Lord's compassion with the faithful (ll. 9–10), and an *a fortiori* statement about the Lord's marvellous acts 'such as have not existed,' נכבות שלוא היו (l. 11), followed by another motivational כי-clause (ll. 12–13).

In sum, the question asked in line 4 about encounters with the Lord for those who hope in their heart is predetermined by obedience to the Lord's anointed one (l. 1) and to the precepts of the holy ones (l. 2) and by being in the Lord's service (l. 3). Yet the perspective of hope unfolds in the subsequent lines 5–13 regarding the various indications of the Lord's active presence among the righteous and pious, the poor, those on the margins of society, and even extending to acts 'such as have not existed' (ll. 11–13).

5. Asking Rhetorical Questions in Qumran Literature

Non-biblical Qumran literature comprises many rhetorical questions across various genres. Rhetorical questions may be introduced by negative adverbs implying a positive answer or positive adverbs implying a negative answer:

> with an expected positive answer, introduced by הלוא (1QMyst 1 i 9; 4Q185 1–3 iii 11; 4Q302 2 ii 6; 4Q418 55 7–8, 69 ii 3–4, 12, and 14; 4Q423 2 1; 4Q521 2 ii 4) or by ואין (CD-A 9.5)

> or a negative answer, introduced by היש (1QMyst 1 i 10; 4Q381 76–77 9) or by ה (4Q418 55 11; 69 ii 13; 4Q511 30 4) or by אם (4Q511 18 ii 5; 30 4)

Some rhetorical questions may be framed as counter-questions, as we already saw in *1–4QMysteries*. A further example may be discerned in 4Q418 (*4QInstruction*[d]) 69 ii 10–14, which first addresses a group with a question introduced by the words 'how can you say,' איכה תאמרו (10–11),³⁵ and then proceeds to pose rhetorical questions (12–14). Occasionally a rhetorical question serves the admonitory purpose of reminding readers of a scriptural prooftext ('Is it not written that,' CD-A 9.5, followed by a citation of Nahum 1:2). It is beyond the scope of this article to discuss each rhetorical question individually. Yet the following semantic categories of rhetorical questions may be discerned in non-biblical Qumran literature.

'what' – 1QapGen ar 20.26 (/Genesis 12:18); 22.32; 1QS 5.17; 11.20, 11.21; 11.22 (twice); 1QH^a 5.19–20; 5.20; 7.2; 7.24; 9.23; 11.24 (twice); 12.29 (twice); 15.32 // 1QH^b 1 i 6–7; 1QH^a 18.3; 18.5–6 (twice); 18.7; 18.12; 19.3–4; 20.27; 20.31; 20.32; 20.32–33; 20.33–34; 23 bottom 7; 26 bottom 10 // 4QH^a 7 iii 16; 4Q299 (4QMyst^a) 3 ii 7; 4Q381 31 6; 4Q400 2 7; 4Q417 1 i 10 // 4Q416 2 i 5; 4Q418 69 ii 4–5 and 5; 11Q5 24 (Psalm 155) 15

'who' – 1QS 11.20; 1QM 10.8–9, 10.9–11, 13.13–14; 1QH^a 3 bottom 5; 11.24; 15.28 // 1QH^b 1 i 2; 1QH^a 18.10–11; 19.24; 21 top 11; 22 bottom 10; 4Q185 1–2 i 8; 4Q212 (4QEn^g ar) 5.14–16; 5.18–19; 5.20–21; 4Q381 15 6–7 (Psalm 89:7); 31 5; 76–77 10 מי בכם, 'who among you';³⁶ 4Q393 3 5; 4Q401 16 4; 4Q411 1 ii 7; 4Q417 1 i 16; 4Q491c 1 8; 1 9; 1 10 (3 times); 4Q511 2 ii 6; 30 4–5; 11Q5 22 9 and 9–10

'which' – 'which (...) is like (...),' כ (...) מיא, 1QM 13.14; 'which man at all who,' מנו הוא כול אנוש די, 4Q212 (4QEn^g ar) 5.17–18 and 5.22

'how' – 1QH^a 7.17; 7.24; 9.25–26 (3 times); 18.6–7 (twice); 18.7; 20.27–28 (twice); 20.33; 20.34; 20.34–35; 20.35; 21 top 4–5; 21 bottom 6; 21 bottom 12; 4QMyst^a 3 ii 2 and 3; 8 5; 4Q400 2 6 (twice); 4Q417 1 i 16; 4Q418 69 ii 5; 4Q511 30 6

'where' – 1QMyst 1 i 11; 4Q393 3 5

'why' – 4Q185 1–2 ii 2–3; 4Q417 1 i 23 // 4Q418 7 6

'when' – 'until when,' עד [מתי], 4Q380 1 ii 5–6

The 'who' questions often concern rhetorical questions which assert some aspect of God's omnipotence, for instance as creator (1QH^a 3 bottom 5), as incomparable to any heavenly being (4Q381 15.6–7 [Psalm 89:7]), as the sole cause of truth and righteousness (1QH^a 15.28),

---

³⁵ Cf. the epistolary formulation πῶς λέγουσιν ἐν ὑμῖν τινες in 1 Cor 15:12.
³⁶ Cf. τίς ἐξ ὑμῶν in Luke's Greek (Luke 11:5, 11; 12:25; 14:5, 28; 15:4; 17:7. Cf. 4Q301 2 4.

as the one to whom judgement belongs (1QH^a 22 bottom 10; 4Q417 1 i 16), as all-powerful and glorious (1QS 11.20; 1QH^a 18.10–11), as being wrathful (4Q185 1–2 i 7–8), and as unsearchable or inscrutable in his command, words or thoughts (4QEn^g ar 5.14–16). In the *War Scroll*, the rhetorical 'who (is like)' question about God's omnipotence stands in a remarkable parallel position to a subsequent rhetorical 'who (is like)' question about Israel as God's nation (1QM 10.8–9 and 10.9–11).

The rhetorical 'what' questions recurrently concern human transience and insignificance as compared with the divine realm of marvellous works and eternity (e.g. 1QS 11.20–22; 1QH^a 5.19–20; 4Q381 31 6; 4Q400 2 7; 11Q5 24 15).

As compared with the Hebrew Bible, Qumran literature attests a similar relatively high frequency of rhetorical 'what' and 'who' questions. Yet differently from biblical Hebrew, the preserved Qumran evidence does not attest a high frequency of rhetorical 'why' questions.[37]

6. Evaluation and Conclusions

6.1. *Questions in Parabiblical and Non-Biblical Qumran Texts*

Looking back on our survey, it stands to reason that questions that are part of dialogues or conversations occur as a rule in narrative texts. These usually are parabiblical texts (*Pseudo-Ezekiel*, *Visions of Amram*, *4QFour Kingdoms^{a-c} ar*, *Genesis Apocryphon*) or longer-known pseudepigraphic and apocryphal texts which have been fragmentarily preserved in Qumran (1 Enoch; Tobit). *Pseudo-Ezekiel* is a prominent example which illustrates how the asking of questions by a biblical character in dialogue with God shapes the prophetic vision of resurrection and restoration as a matter of progressive revelation concerned with the time of its fulfilment.

In sapiential literature, the asking of rhetorical questions paired with rhetorical counter-questions may structure the development of thought to let readers reflect on a problem. In *1–4QMysteries*, this is the problem of evil and its eschatological resolution.

In apocalyptic literature, a question may be used to admonish addressees to take a certain stand in a text's perspective on steadfastness in

---

[37] Moshavi, "Communicative Functions of Content Questions," 82 table 3 surveys the following numbers for 479 content questions in Gen – 2 Kgs: 147 'what' (31%), 3 'which' (1%), 89 'who' (19%), 48 'where' (10%), 8 'when' (2%), 34 'how' (7%), 3 'how many' (1%), and 147 'why' (31%); she further notes that "most 'why' questions in Biblical Hebrew are rhetorical (133 out of 147, or 91%)."

relation to divine precepts. In 4Q521 this steadfastness concerns hope regarding divine providence and social justice.

The questions asked in sectarian Qumran texts are predominantly, but not exclusively, rhetorical questions. The Temple Scroll comprises some examples of different questions. Sometimes a deliberative, information-seeking question, 'and if you say {to} in your heart «How shall we know the word which YHWH has not spoken?»' (11QT[a] 61.2–3)[38] also occurs, relating to the issue of discerning true from false witness to the word of the Lord. In another case, a pre-directive question is asked of people in the context of preparation for battle (11QT[a] 61.12–62.5): '«Who is a coward and feeble of heart? He should go and return to his house, lest he weaken the heart of his brother like his own heart»' (11QT[a] 62.3–4).[39]

A different case presents itself in the context of an incantation in 11Q11 5.6, where the posing of a question of identification, 'who are you,' is immediately followed by assertion, analogous to a rhetorical question. Yet the function of the question is different: it serves an apotropaic function to ward off an otherwise indeterminate demonic threat by labelling it.

6.2. A Meta-Question: Attitudes to Asking Questions in Qumran Literature

Beyond the matter of asking specific questions, we are left with a meta-question regarding the socio-cultural context of attitudes to asking questions in Qumran literature. We finally turn to this issue with some observations by way of conclusion to this article.

In the hierarchical context of the sectarian Scrolls movement, there were restrictions to uttering speech, including the matter of asking questions, in communal sessions, as illustrated by the *Community Rule*:

> 'And in the session of the Many no-one should utter anything without the consent of the Many, save the Inspector of the Many. And anyone who has something to say to the Many but is not in the position of one who is asking questions (במעמד האיש השואל) to the Community council, that man should stand up and say: «I have something to say to the Many». If they tell him to, he should speak' (1QS 6.11–13).[40]

---

[38] Translation from García Martínez and Tigchelaar, *Study Edition. 2*, 1283.
[39] Translation from García Martínez and Tigchelaar, *Study Edition. 2*, 1285.
[40] Translation from García Martínez and Tigchelaar, *Study Edition. 1*, 85.

Reversely, the strict admission procedures for volunteers into the community involved prolonged *inquiry* about one's insight and one's deeds (ידורשהו, 1QS 6.14), *questioning* about one's affairs (ונשאלו, 1QS 6.15–16), *inquiry* about one's spirit and one's deeds (ידרושהו, 1QS 6.17), and *questioning* about one's affairs, one's insight and one's deeds according to the law (ישאלו, 1QS 6.18).[41]

More broadly speaking, the asking of questions would also be presupposed by the directive of investigating things. Thus, the activity of asking informed questions is implied in labels such as 'searchers of the roots of knowledge' (4Q301 1 2; 2 1) and 'pursuers of knowledge' (4QMyst[a] 8 7; 4Q424 3 2). It further surfaces in an injunction such as 'consider the mystery of existence and grasp the birth-times of salvation' (4Q416 2 i 5–6 // 4Q417 1 i 10–11).[42] The asking of questions is also of primordial importance in the following call for prudence in a sapiential text: 'And a man who judges before investigating (בטרם ידרוש) and who believes before [examining], does not perform his work in a balanced manner' (4Q424 3 1).[43] A final example is the following encouragement to search: [בק]שו ואז תמצא[או], '[se]ek and then you shall fin[d]' (4Q418 107 1).[44]

---

[41] Cf. 1QS 7.21 on prolonged *questioning*, ישאלו and ישאל, of those who have been excluded for two years, in the case of renegades who return to the community (1QS 7.18–20).

[42] Translation from García Martínez and Tigchelaar, *Study Edition*. 2, 849, 855.

[43] Translation from García Martínez and Tigchelaar, *Study Edition*. 2, 891.

[44] Text and translation from García Martínez and Tigchelaar, *Study Edition*. 2, 874–875. This is perhaps not unlike "ask, and it will be given to you; *seek, and you will find*" in Luke 11:9 // Matt 7:7 (RSV). For comparison, see A. Denaux and A. Hogeterp, "*Parallelismus Membrorum* in Luke's Greek: Revisiting a Synoptic Perspective," in: I.M. Gallarte and J. Peláez (Eds.), *In Mari Vita Tua. Philological Studies in Honour of Antonio Piñero* (EFilNeot 11; Córdoba: Almendro, 2016), 317–339, here 331–332.

SOME OBSERVATIONS ON THE IMPORTANCE OF QUESTIONS IN RABBINIC TRADITION AND HALAKHAH

Leon MOCK

Tilburg University

1. Introduction

In the Bible and Rabbinic tradition, we find a twofold view on the Torah. On one hand the Torah is somehow pre-existent in the divine realm as is described in Proverbs 8:22 and 8:30. This Torah is the perfect and precious Tree of Life, pleasant, peaceful and a source of happiness (Proverbs 3:15–18). In Proverbs this is said about Wisdom – but the Rabbis understand the Torah as being the ultimate wisdom and the tool by which God created heaven and earth. It is this Torah, also as God's Law, that is life and the good, and the just (Deuteronomy 4:6; 12:28). On the other hand, the Torah is a law for man on earth[1] in a concrete physical world, as the Deuteronomist poetically explores in Deuteronomy 30:11–14. And not only is the Torah given to the human creature on earth, it also takes into account its imperfections by proposing atonement for sins and procedures for making up for mistakes of different kinds – from monetary issues to accidental manslaughter.

It is especially in this mundane realm of human life, experience and understanding that questions may arise due to uncertainty and a lack of knowledge about the applications of the Torah as law, as is recognized for example in Deuteronomy 17:8. The solution given by the Deuteronomist is to go to the sacred place of God's choice and to posit the question to the priests and judges – people who are inspired by his spirit (judges)[2] and who serve God in his place of worship (priests). Whenever a question arises, man should consult the religious authorities of his days, the priest or the judge, and question them about the matter. They will clarify all questions and provide certainty about all matters, as they are

---

[1] See also Prov 8:31.
[2] See the biblical Book of Judges and also Rabbinic exegesis that explain the word אֱלֹהִים as sometimes referring to 'judges,' Gen. Rab. 26:5 commenting on Gen 6:2.

seated in the place of God's choice (17:8, 10). That is the reason why one ought not to deviate from 'the word' (הדבר *the judgment, statement, verdict*) which they pronounce, 'nor to the right, nor to the left' (17:11). Disobedience will be punished by death (17:12). Although questions arise from a lack of knowledge and uncertainty concerning the right practice or law, this is not considered as being a flaw or major problem. The religious authority, being an inspired body of people residing in a sacred place, is able to solve all problems.

2. Questions and Rabbinical Courts

In the Rabbinic conception of Torah as a dual Torah, it is especially the Oral Torah that is connected with the human, mundane realm, with Halakhah being concerned, for an important part, with daily, human life in all its facets. The Oral Law includes a moral-ethical aspect (Aggadah), a rational-logical one (Talmud) and a practical one (Halakhah).[3] It is especially in this last field, which occupies itself with physical quantitative parameters like measures of time, place, and material, but also with intentions of the human mind ('what is the purpose / goal / intention of a certain action'), that we can expect that questions could arise and be asked – partly also because of the multiple possible and conflicting interpretations.[4] And questions should, if possible, be answered and not left unanswered. Rabbinic traditions use Deuteronomy 17:8–13 for describing a somewhat idealistic system of Halakhic authority, with the Great

---

[3] See also S. Safrai, "Oral Tora," in: S. Safrai and P.J. Tomson (Eds.), *The Literature of the Sages; First Part: Oral Tora, Halakha, Mishnah, Tosefta, Talmud, External Tractates* (Assen: Van Gorcum, 1987), 35–120, here 36–37.

[4] See bEruvin 13b (all the quotes from the Babylonian Talmud in the article are taken from the translation of the Soncino edition): 'in the generation of R. Meir there was none equal to him; then why was not the halakhah fixed in agreement with his views? Because his colleagues could not fathom the depths of his mind, for he would declare the ritually unclean to be clean and supply plausible proof, and the ritually clean to be unclean and also supply plausible proof ... R. Abbahu stated in the name of R. Johanan: R. Meir had a disciple of the name of Symmachus who, for every rule concerning ritual uncleanness, supplied forty-eight reasons in support of its uncleanness, and for every rule concerning ritual cleanness, forty-eight reasons in support of its cleanness.' In the manuscript version of this text from the Talmud in the Vatican, Bibliotheca Apostolica, Ebr 127, the end of the text reads differently: 'R. Meir had a disciple of the name of Symmachus who, for every rule concerning ritual uncleanness, supplied forty-eight reasons in support of its cleanness, and for every rule concerning ritual cleanness, forty-eight [reasons in support of its] uncleanness.' See also the *Midrash Yalkut Shimoni* on Tehillim §658 where it states that on every item of law (דבר) that God told Moses he showed him 49 reasons for purity and 49 reasons for impurity.

Sanhedrin in the 'Hall of Hewn Stones' in the Temple at the top and the local courts around the country at the bottom. When questions or disputes arise, one should consult the court, which will give an answer or give a verdict. Whenever a question is not able to be answered by a lower court, the higher court of the three sitting on the Temple Mount should be consulted. If matters are still not clarified, the second High Court can be addressed, till finally – if necessary – the Court of the Hewn Stones is to be consulted, which will give its final ruling, binding everyone.[5]

The Halakhic Midrash Sifre on Deuteronomy 17:8 presents different fields that may pose a context for questions / disputes in daily life – from laws on impurity and purity that are connected to 'blood' (menstruation, childbirth), monetary issues, cases in which flogging is at issue, or the death penalty, to matters of sanctified Temple property (through vows) and agricultural laws (*pe'a* and the like).[6] In fact the jurisdiction and authority granted to the historic institute of the Sanhedrin was expanded to the Rabbinical Court of Yavne and any later Rabbinical Court and, from then on, included all matters of Oral Law, custom and instituted restrictions (*takanot, gezerot*).[7]

---

[5] Mishnah Sanhedrin 11:2 quoted in bSanhedrin 86b: 'Three courts of Law were there, one situated at the entrance to the Temple Mount, another at the door of the [Temple] Court, and the third in the Hall of Hewn Stones. They [first] went to the Beth Din which is at the entrance to the Temple Mount, and He [the rebellious elder] stated, thus have I expounded and thus have my colleagues expounded; thus have I taught, and thus have my Colleagues taught. If [this first Beth Din] had heard [a ruling on the Matter], they state it. If not, they go to the [second Beth Din] which is at the entrance of the Temple Court, and he declares, thus have I expounded and thus have my colleagues expounded; thus have I taught and thus have my colleagues taught. If [this second Beth Din] had heard [a ruling on the matter]. They state it; if not, they all proceed to the Great Beth Din of the Hall of Hewn Stones whence instruction issued to all Israel, for it is written, "[which they] of that place which the Lord shall choose [shall shew thee]." '

[6] Sifre § 152 on Deut 17:8.

[7] Maimonides (12th century), basing himself on other Rabbinic traditions, describes it in his Codex *Mishneh Torah* as follows: 'The Supreme Sanhedrin in Jerusalem are the essence of the Oral Torah. They are the pillars of instruction from whom statutes [chok] and judgment [mishpat] issue forth for the entire Jewish people. Concerning them, the Torah promises Deuteronomy 17:11: "You shall do according to the laws which they shall instruct you ..." (...) Whoever believes in Moses and in his Torah is obligated to make all of his religious acts dependent on this court and to rely on them. Any person who does not carry out their directives transgresses a negative commandment, as Ibid. continues: "Do not deviate from any of the statements they relate to you neither right or left",' Maimonides, *Laws of the Rebellious Ones* 1:1–2. The authority of the judges and priests of the Bible has been replaced by Maimonides (and the Rabbis) by the Supreme Court, the Sanhedrin. Its status is now not only *ad hoc* – to posit an answer whenever questions and doubts arise – but it is now the regular religious authority, which takes into account the enforcement and making of laws and the issuing of decrees and edicts safeguarding the Torah – apparently all necessary stipulations: '(...) We are obligated to heed their words whether they:

In numerous parts of the Babylonian Talmud, questions play an important role in the discourse – in fact questions form the main core of many Talmudic texts, although, as will be shown, it is important in Rabbinic Judaism to give an answer to (most) questions. In this vision questions and debates are an integral, important part of the Halakhic process. Halakhah is made up of questions that are answered and sometimes decided upon, and even unanswered or undecided questions have a high theological status as Torah – even if not directly practiced.[8]

3. Rabbi Yohanan and Resh Lakish

A famous Talmudic story in Baba Metsia 84a shows the important role of questions and discussion in the process of learning. It is the story of the tragic friendship between two people, a scholar and a former robber. The scholar Rabbi Yohanan convinces the robber Resh Lakish to change his lifestyle and become a Torah-scholar. As a reward he receives Rabbi Yohanan's sister in wedlock. She happens to be a beautiful woman. Rabbi Yohanan and Resh Lakish become dear friends and study-partners for years. In the beginning Rabbi Yohanan is the teacher, but in time the knowledge of Resh Lakish increases so quickly and is so profound that they become colleagues and partners-in-study (*chevruta*). One day, a heated debate on a question, concerning (again) the ritual status of certain kinds of weapons, explodes and takes a personal turn. Rabbi Yohanan reminds Resh Lakish of his past as a robber, during which he used weapons. Hence, he should be more of an expert in this matter than Rabbi Yohanan! Resh Lakish in turn answers something that deeply hurts the feelings of Rabbi Yohanan: what was the point then of making this big change in lifestyle and hence what use was Rabbi Yohanan to him? As a result of the argument Resh Lakish falls ill and dies, while Rabbi Yohanan is plunged into deep grief. He no longer has a partner to study with, like he had before the argument with Resh Lakish, which caused his death. The Rabbis arrange a new partner-in-learning for him in the

---

a) learned them from a heard tradition, i.e., the Oral Torah, b) derived them on the basis of their own knowledge through one of the attributes of Biblical exegesis and it appeared to them that this is the correct interpretation of the matter, c) instituted the matter as a safeguard for the Torah, as was necessary at a specific time. These are the decrees, edicts, and customs instituted by the Sages.' Translation of E. Touger, *Mishneh Torah* (New York: Moznaim Publishing, 1989), Internet version: https://www.chabad.org/library/article_cdo/aid/682956/jewish/Mishneh-Torah.htm.

[8] See C.N. Saiman, *Halakhah: The Rabbinic Idea of Law* (Princeton: Princeton University Press, 2018), 29–43.

person of Rabbi Eleazar ben Pedath, who has a sharp mind. But Rabbi Yohanan is not satisfied with his new partner.

> So, he went and sat before him; and on every dictum uttered by R. Yohanan he observed: 'There is a Baraitha which supports you.' 'Are you as the son of Lakisha?' He complained: 'When I stated a law, the son of Lakisha used to raise twenty-four objections, to which I gave twenty-four answers, which consequently led to a fuller comprehension of the law; whilst you say, "A Baraitha has been taught which supports you:" do I not know myself that my dicta are right?' Thus he went on rending his garments and weeping, 'Where are you, O son of Lakisha, where are you, O son of Lakisha;' and he cried thus until his mind was turned. Thereupon the Rabbis prayed for him, and he died.[9]

The message of this story is that questions play an important role in the learning process, and that even the expert needs a (expert) partner-in-learning. In the dynamic process of initial questioning, answering and then questioning the answers, and so on and on, man's mind is sharpened and his insight deepened – although this 'sharpening' also has a negative potential, as the story about Rabbi Yohanan and Resh Lakish illustrates. On the verse in Proverbs 27:17 'Iron sharpeneth iron; so, a man sharpeneth the countenance of his friend' (KJV), the Talmud comments:

> This is to teach you that just as in the case of one [iron] iron sharpeneth the other so also do two scholars sharpen each other's mind by halachah. Rabbah b. Hanah said: Why are the words of the Torah likened to fire, as it is said (Jer. 23:29), Is not my word like as fire? saith the Lord? This is to teach you that just as fire does not ignite of itself so too the words of the Torah do not endure with him who studies alone. This is in agreement with what R. Jose b. Hanina said: What is the meaning of the verse (Jer. 50:36) A sword is upon the lonely, and they shall become fools? This means, destruction comes upon such scholars who confine themselves to private study...[10]

It is this perspective on questions that is adopted by most parts of the Babylonian Talmud, where questions are the substantial part of every topic that is dealt with. Asking questions for the sake of asking, even if an answer is not present or is never going to be given, is still valuable. Questions and the debates they initiate are a very important part of Talmudic texts, with interrogative words and phrases that express questions, like: 'since when' or 'from when' (מאימתי), 'how' (כיצד), 'when (in which case) are these words said' (במה דברים אמורים), '(does) this

[9] bBaba Metzia 84a.
[10] bTa'anith 7a.

teach(es) that' (זאת אומרת), 'it was asked' (בעא), 'the problem was posed to them' (איבעיא להו), 'a refutation was given' (תיובתא).[11]

4. The Heavenly Academy and Rabbah bar Nachmani

Another Talmudic story in Baba Metsia 86a is even more bold. It portrays a Heavenly Academy that is a mirror of the Rabbinical Academy on earth. In this Heavenly Academy things proceed (almost) like on earth. So, in this Heavenly Academy a debate arises concerning a remote question in the Laws of *Tzara'at* (usually translated as *leprosy*), based on a reading of Leviticus 13:1–3, which deals with signs of purity that become visible on the body of the afflicted.

> Now, they were disputing in the Heavenly Academy thus: If the bright spot preceded the white hair, he is unclean; if the reverse, he is clean. If [the order is] in doubt – the Holy One, blessed be He, ruled, He is clean; whilst the entire Heavenly Academy maintained, He is unclean.[12]

The question is undecided in Heaven, since God and the other members of the Academy are embroiled in a disagreement on this question, which has to be decided upon. So, who is going to give the final answer to the question? According to this story, matters are decided by man – in this case by Rabbah bar Nachmani who is an expert in the Laws of Leprosy. Rabbah bar Nachmani is summoned by the Angel of Death to come to the Heavenly Academy.

> A messenger was sent for him, but the Angel of Death could not approach him, because he did not interrupt his studies [even for a moment]. In the meantime, a wind blew and caused a rustling in the bushes, when he imagined it to be a troop of soldiers. 'Let me die,' he exclaimed, 'rather than be delivered into the hands of the State. As he was dying, he exclaimed, 'Clean, clean!' when a Heavenly Voice cried out, 'Happy art thou, O Rabbah b. Nahmani, whose body is pure and whose soul had departed in purity!'[13]

We may draw a couple of conclusions from this – quite fabulous – story:

- Questions exist even in Heaven and a certain, objective Truth may be non-existent.
- Man has the power to decide questions, not God or (his) absolute Truth. Man's perspective is the leading theme in raising questions and answering them.

---

[11] For other dialectical terms see S. Safrai, "Oral Tora," 95–97.
[12] bBaba Metzia 86a.
[13] bBaba Metzia 86a.

- There are procedures to decide a question. In this story it is the opinion of an expert, who is consulted to decide matters.

5. Rabbi Eliezer and Rabbi Joshua

A further empowerment of man to answer questions in matters of Torah and Halakhah is found in another famous story in the Bava Metzia 59b, dealing with an argument concerning a certain type of oven, called 'The oven of Akhnai,' and whether it is ritually clean or impure. In this argument between Rabbi Eliezer and Rabbi Joshua, the former even produces miracles as proof that he is right.

The story receives another dimension when a heavenly voice declares that Rabbi Eliezer is in fact right! The other scholars though, decide not to heed the heavenly voice, seeing the Torah after the Revelation is a product of man and is decided upon according to man's capacities and faculties: miracles and voices from Heaven are to be ignored. The question of the status of the oven is to be decided upon according to the majority principle – a conclusion to which even God agrees, even if it contradicts the absolute Truth in Heaven. Truth in Heaven is set in opposition to human truth as reached by the majority view (and not the experts' opinion, as in the story of Rabbah bar Nachmani). The conclusion of the story is that questions and debates play an important part in the initial phase of the Halakhic process, but that afterwards consensus should be obtained and persistent deviancy punished – in the story Rabbi Eliezer is punished with excommunication.[14]

6. Maimonides

Furthermore, questions about the Law and debates are not seen by Maimonides as something positive *per se* – in this he is again relying on other Rabbinic traditions, medieval and older. In fact, the Divine Torah

---

[14] On this story of the oven of Akhnai see for example: H.L.M. Ottenheijm, "De 'Oven van Aknai' (b.Bava Metsia 59b) herlezen: Voetnoten bij een Talmudisch verhaal," in: A. Merz and B. Becking (Eds.), *Verhaal als Identiteits-Code: Opstellen aangeboden aan Gert Van Oyen bij zijn afscheid van de Universiteit Utrecht* (Utrechtse Theologische Reeks 60; Utrecht: Universiteit Utrecht, 2008), 242–254; V. Noam, "Traces of Sectarian Halakha in the Rabbinic World," in: S. Fraade, A. Shemesh and R.A. Clements (Eds.), *Rabbinic Perspectives: Rabbinic Literature and the Dead Sea Scrolls: Proceedings of the Eighth International Symposium of the Orion Center for the Study of the Dead Sea Scrolls and Associated Literature, 7–9 January, 2003* (STDJ 62; Leiden, Brill 2006), 67–85.

as received by Moses is univocal and not subject to debate and hence questions are for the expert:

> There can never be any difference of opinion with regard to matters received [through the Oral] tradition. Whenever there arises a difference of opinion with regard to a matter that proves that it was not received in the tradition from Moses our teacher.[15]

Questions about the Law exist because of a lack of knowledge or differing opinions, and law enforcement and the creation of new laws are now regulated by the Supreme Court. Maimonides, nevertheless, still has an optimistic view on the functioning of this Supreme Sanhedrin, residing in the Hall of the Hewn Stones, which manages to unite the law through knowledge or consensus[16] and which is used as a model for later periods. The real crisis was created when the Temple was destroyed and the Sanhedrin abolished. The factor unifying the law and its regulations was then destroyed. The result was a multitude of opinions and debates, and hence unresolved questions, which are a sign of exile.[17]

In fact, Maimonides' reserved attitude towards questions and debate, quoted above, is taken from his *Laws on the Rebellious Ones*, with the 'Rebellious Elder' (זקן ממרא) as the Rabbinic prototype of a scholar who questions the prevailing knowledge and the tradition–paradigm, and who posits different solutions and traditions to problematic situations and questions as discussed in the Talmud tractate Sanhedrin. This phenomenon is considered a threat to (Rabbinic) authority – with in mind, perhaps, Second Temple sectarians – as it may lead to different practices. Rabbinic Judaism, as a tradition which emphasises the study of texts, is

---

[15] Maimonides, *Laws of the Rebellious Ones*, 1:3. Translation of E. Touger, see n. 7.
[16] Maimonides, *Laws of the Rebellious Ones*, 1:4: 'When the Supreme Sanhedrin was in session, there was never any prolonged differences of opinion among the Jewish people. Instead, if a doubt arose ... over any law, he would inquire of the court in his city. If not, the questioner and that court – or its agents – ascend to Jerusalem and ask the court which holds sessions on the Temple Mount. If they know, they will reply to him, if they do not know, everyone comes to the court ... at the entrance to the Temple Courtyard. If they know, they will reply to him, if they do not know, everyone comes to the Chamber of Hewn Stone, ... and presents the question ... they relate the decision immediately.' If, however, the decision was unclear to the Supreme Sanhedrin, they would discuss the matter until a uniform decision was reached, or a vote was taken and the majority decided.
[17] Maimonides, *Laws of the Rebellious Ones*, 1:4 (at the end): 'After the Supreme Sanhedrin was nullified, differences of opinion multiplied among the Jewish people. One would rule an article is impure and support his ruling with a rationale and another would rule that it is pure and support his ruling with a rationale. This one would rule an article is forbidden and this would rule that it is permitted.'

here captured between acknowledging the contribution of questions and debate to the process of learning and the possible threat to unity, consensus and authority posed by these same questions and discussions.

7. Answering Questions

However, not only is the raising of questions important – answering them is no less important, as has already been shown. A real scholar and Sage is expected to not only be able to answer the questions of the common man, but also those of his learned colleagues and experts. The Talmud discusses which qualities a 'student of the Sages' תלמיד חכם and a Sage (חכם) should possess – the discussion takes place in the context of conditions of betrothal. The man assures the bride that he is a student or Sage himself and hence has to meet certain criteria:

> *[If someone marries a woman] 'On condition that I am a disciple [תלמיד חכם],' we do not say, such as Simeon b. 'Azzai and Simeon b. Zoma, but one who when asked a single question on his studies in any place can answer it, even in the Tractate Kallah.*[18] *'On condition that I am a Sage (חכם),' we do not say, like the Sages of Jabneh or like R. Akiba and his companions, but one who can be asked a matter of wisdom in any place and he can answer it.*[19]

A scholar has to have the patience to answer the questions of the layman as is exemplified in a famous story on Hillel. Two people placed a bet on whether they were able to anger Hillel with silly questions, and so one of them disturbed the famous scholar on Friday afternoon, when Hillel was preparing himself for the Sabbath and was washing his hair:

> *He went, passed by the door of his house, and called out, 'Is Hillel here, is Hillel here?' Thereupon he robed and went out to him, saying, 'My son, what do you require?' 'I have a question to ask,' said he. 'Ask, my son,' he prompted. Thereupon he asked: 'Why are the heads of the Babylonians round? 'My son, you have asked a great question,' replied he: 'because they have no skilful midwives.' He departed, tarried a while, returned, and called out, 'Is Hillel here; is Hillel here?' He robed and went out to him, saying, 'My son, what do you require?' 'I have a question to ask,' said he. 'Ask, my son,' he prompted. Thereupon he asked: 'Why are the eyes of the Palmyreans bleared?' 'My son, you have asked a great question, replied he: 'because they live in sandy places.' He departed, tarried a while, returned, and called out, 'Is Hillel here; is Hillel here?' He robed and went out to him, saying, 'My son,*

---

[18] A minor tractate and therefore not studied much.
[19] bKiddushin 49b.

what do you require?' 'I have a question to ask,' said he. 'Ask, my son,' he prompted. He asked, 'Why are the feet of the Africans [negroes] wide?' 'My son, you have asked a great question,' said he; 'because they live in watery marshes.' 'I have many questions to ask,' said he, 'but fear that you may become angry.' Thereupon he robed, sat before him and said, 'Ask all the questions you have to ask...'[20]

The plot of the bet is then revealed and the explicit message of the story is that patience and not losing one's temper are the right character traits for especially a scholar, but for the layman too. Besides that, the implicit message is that even questions that are not strictly related to religious issues should receive a genuine answer by the scholar, even if these are 'silly' questions of the multitude.

8. Characteristics of Asking and Answering Questions

In this story about Hillel no boundaries are set for questions. It shows the importance of asking questions and the expectation of a scholar and Sage to answer them using his best capacities. In the context of two people learning together – as in the story on Rabbi Yohanan and Resh Lakish – the dynamics of asking and answering is almost unlimited. In the context of a scholar teaching several students or a class, or a Sage or head of an Academy who has to answer a large audience, things are, however, different. We find in Rabbinic literature that procedures emerge that are meant to regulate the asking of questions and their answering. In the Talmud we already find that a student should ask his master questions on the subject that is studied by his teacher. Asking 'off-topic' questions leads to the embarrassment of the master-teacher who will not be able to answer such questions correctly.

> *Said R. Hiyya to Rab: Son of illustrious ancestors! Have I not told you that when Rabbi is engaged on one Tractate you must not question him about another, lest he be not conversant with it. For if Rabbi were not a great man, you would have put him to shame, for he might have answered you incorrectly.*[21]

To this the Tosefta adds that one should not ask a Sage a question when he has just come into the Beth Midrash – one should wait till 'his mind is set'.[22] The Tosefta adds other regulations concerning the asking of questions, but these were originally related to the Rabbinical Court and

---

[20] bShabbat 31a.
[21] bShabbat 3b.
[22] Tosefta Sanhedrin 7:10.

its procedures.[23] These regulations are even codified in the medieval codices of Maimonides – the *Mishneh Torah*[24] – and the *Shulchan Aruch* (R. Josef Karo, 16th c.). Maimonides adds that asking questions is also an important tool for teaching and should be used by a rabbi-teacher. He should try to test their sharpness of mind with questions that may confuse them or to use questions to see whether they remember what he has taught them. For this the rabbi-teacher may also use off-topic questions.[25]

In Karo's Laws on The Study of Torah § 246:14 we read there based on the Tosefta:

> *When two came to ask [a question]. If one asks on a current [relevant] topic and the other on a non-current topic, we relate [first] to the one [that asked] on the current topic. [If one asks] on a practical [applicable] topic and the other on a non-practical [theoretic] topic, we relate [first] to the one [that asked] on the practical topic. [If one asks] on a Halakhic topic and the other on an Aggadic topic, we relate [first] to the one [that asked] on the Halakhic topic. If one asks] on an exegetic [Midrash] topic and the other on an Aggadic topic, we relate [first] to the one [that asked] on the exegetic topic...*[26]

In another paragraph[27] Karo's Codex states that the status of the questioner should also be taken into account when two people come together to ask their questions. In this case Karo's Codex prefers to deal first with the one that has a higher status as expressed by his level of knowledge (and not his inherited social status alone). So Karo's Codex prefers to first answer the question of the Sage and after that the illiterate may ask his question, while in other cases the responder may decide himself whom to answer first. While these regulations seem to be directed to the Sage or Rabbi who answers the questions, it prompts and directs the questioner towards practical, relevant and on-topic questions in certain settings, while the more theoretical and off-topic questions should be kept for different, small scale and more intimate settings.

9. Responsa Literature

In fact, a whole genre of Rabbinic literature consists of questions posed to an expert Rabbi and his answer to the questioner. This genre is called

---
[23] Tosefta Sanhedrin 7:6–7.
[24] *Laws on The Learning of Torah*, 4:6–8.
[25] *Laws on The Learning of Torah*, 4:6, based on bMegillah 6b and bHullin 43b.
[26] The translation is my own.
[27] *Laws on The Study of Torah*, § 246:15.

responsa literature (in Hebrew שאלות ותשובות -שו"ת, 'Questions and Answers') and can already be found in the Talmud, in the form of questions from students and colleague-rabbis to great scholars and Rabbis. If a real personal encounter was not possible, the question was sent to the scholar in writing or sometimes orally, through a messenger. This fostered the contacts in Talmudic times between Israel and Babylon and to a lesser degree with other Diaspora congregations.

Responsa literature as a clearly distinct genre arose in the early Middle Ages – initially in Babylon – but afterwards it emerged in North-Africa, Spain, France, Germany, Central- and Eastern Europe, and in other important Jewish Diaspora communities. It became the prominent medium for Rabbinic communication of authority in a Jewish world that had become increasingly fragmented through physical and cultural-religious distances. As a genre it has continued its important role into the modern era and reponsa are written on a daily base. In the technological and digital era, responsa are given by telephone, via the Internet and even by SMS.

In its basic form, a responsum intends to bridge the gulf between theory and the practice of the Jewish Law in 'real life.' It deals with how the theoretical framework should be applied to a specific case, often a new situation, to which the existing principles cannot *a priori* be easily applied. The problem is presented to an expert scholar to make a ruling in this specific case. His ruling in a particular case may subsequently be regarded as jurisprudence for similar problems in the future.[28]

10. Concluding Remarks

This article illustrates the importance of questions in Rabbinic traditions. Questions are an outcome of the process of the implementation of general principles of law to the physical, human world and are part of the dialectical Rabbinic tradition of studying and clarifying the law. Asking questions of each other sharpens the mind and clarifies the dimensions of the Torah and its laws. Answering questions is important too – since persistent debate, discussion and doubts may undermine authority and consensus. Rabbinic tradition had at least two mechanism in dealing with this problem: deciding by majority or accepting the view of an expert as

---

[28] L. Mock, *The concept of 'Ruakh Ra'ah' in post-1945 Rabbinic responsa literature: a case study of the relation between knowledge of the physical world and traditional knowledge* (Tilburg: 2015), 2–7 [Dutch]. The publication of the English version is in process. For examples of response texts, see A.Y. Finkel, *The Responsa Anthology* (Northvale: Jason Aronson, 1990).

binding. It was expected of a scholar and Rabbi that he be able to address and answer the questions of his colleagues, students and the layman. However, procedures emerged that were to regulate the way questions were to be posed to a scholar in a communal, non-private setting. The genre of the responsa literature shows the ongoing importance given to questions and their answers by the Rabbis, right into the modern era: as a way of clarifying the law in new situations and times and as a means of establishing authority.

DISTURBING QUESTIONS
Observations on the Rhetoric of Two Rabbinic Parables[1]

Eric OTTENHEIJM
University of Utrecht

1. Introduction

One of the distinguishing features of Rabbinic Judaism is the prominence it attributes to questions.[2] It is no coincidence that the Mishna, and by extension the Talmud, starts with a question: 'from when does one say the *Shema* in the evening?' (m. *Berakhot* 1:1), and that the night of Passover traditionally opens with the 'Four Sons,' questioning the difference with other nights.

There are two ways of understanding the phenomenon of questions in a philosophical sense. The first is that they may be explained as signalling rational forces engendering a continuous quest for meaning. The second approach validates questions as reinforcing the rhetorical stance of the text as such. In the first approach, questions organically facilitate the adaptation of rituals and laws in changing social and political circumstances. Questions as such are considered as part of a Rabbinic culture of study, debate, and dialogue, the literary dynamics making up the fabric of Talmudic texts and underlying the rise of the Rabbinic elite after the fall of the Temple in Jerusalem.[3] The second approach will be dealt with extensively in this article.

Moreover, questions correlate with a polyphony of voices and dialogue. Indeed, as an answer to its very first question, the Mishna comes

---

[1] This paper is part of an ongoing research project 'Parables and the Partings of the Ways' (funded NWO 2014–2020), based at Utrecht University, Tilburg School of Catholic Theology (Tilburg University) and the Protestant Theological University in Amsterdam/Groningen.
[2] See also the essay by Leon Mock in this volume.
[3] D. Kraemer, *Reading the Rabbis: The Talmud as Literature* (New York: Oxford University Press, 1996) provides an excellent example of this human-centric and rationalist view.

up with a number of halakhic options, several referring to the Temple service, but the issue remains undecided.[4] It is this image of Judaism as a religion accommodating to changing cultural and political regimes, as well as to diasporic conditions, that has dominated scholarly research and public perception. Judaism, in this perspective, becomes a foil for other religions seeking a new 'social contract' with modernity: emphasising the critical stance of the individual, acclaiming questions as engendering learning and reflection and opposing a Christian dogmatism, reflective of a Greek emphasis on truth.[5]

2. Dialectic Monologue instead of Rhetorical Dialogue?

In recent years, this view of Judaism as a religion of plurality and debate has received critical scrutiny and is now yielding a more restrained assessment of the text as being dominated by the monologous voice of the Rabbinic editor. First, any alleged systemic opposition between Jewish and Greek culture should engage with the deep impact of Greek (and Roman) thinking and practice on early Hellenistic and Rabbinic Judaism. This impact has already been assessed in Rabbinic textual discourse by previous generations. Saul Lieberman and David Daube noted similarities between Greek rhetorical terms (both in narratives and in legal debates) and Talmudic discourse. Legal concepts such as intention or legal fictions became standard procedure in halakha.[6]

---

[4] The Babylonian Talmud offers elaborate discussions on the inconsistencies and contradictions within the Mishnah as well as between the Mishna and *baraitot* partly represented in the Tosephta.
[5] This typology, popular in Jewish and Christian theological perceptions of the mid and last part of the 20th Century ce, located an organic and versatile mode of the Jewish tradition as opposed to the universalizing Greek thinking with its emphasis on detached concepts and universalistic outlooks. Christianity, in this view, due to processes of Hellenization, became separated from its Jewish 'roots' and in turn developed into a Romanized state religion, anchored in this Greek predilection for dogma. On this typology as a result of a mutual 'gaze,' S. Heschel, "Jews and Christianity," *Cambridge History of Judaism* 8 (2017): 1063–1092, here 1072.
[6] There is ample literature on this: S. Lieberman, *Greek in Jewish Palestine* (New York: Jewish Theological Seminary, 1942); D. Brodsky, "From Disagreement to Talmudic Discourse: Progymnasmata and the Evolution of a Rabbinic Genre," in: R. Nikolsky and T. Ilan (Eds.), *Rabbinic Traditions between Palestine and Babylonia* (Ancient Judaism and Early Christianity 89; Leiden: Brill, 2014), 173–231. For the role of 'legal fiction' (a legal concept developed in Roman law and applied in Rabbinic halakha as well) and modes of intention in early Jewish legal debates, E. Ottenheijm, *Disputen omwille van de Hemel: Rol en betekenis van intentie in de controverses over sjabbat en reinheid tussen de Huizen van Sjammai en Hillel* (Amstelveen: Amphora, 2004).

Talmudic narrative, like Greek sources, deploy the *chreia*, the combination of a saying and a whimsy story typical for a Sage.[7] Richard Hidary argues for seeing some of the highly theoretical, even absurd legal cases brought forward in the Babylonian Talmud halakha as editorial tools meant to sharpen the mind: their form and function resemble Stoic philosophy with its paradoxical and surreal cases.[8]

It might also be more than merely a matter of parallels or even of influence of form. What could be at stake is the nature of the texts as we read them. Daniel Boyarin, in a highly provocative book, calls attention to the parallels between anecdotal absurdities woven into the serious philosophical discussions of Plato, and the witty 'seriocomic' stories about Rabbis, appearing amidst halakhic or theological debates, and portraying philosophers or Rabbis as human beings responding in embodied, foolish ways to events.[9] These sometimes burlesque stories are to be considered a part of the textual rhetoric, rhetorically bridging the dialectical nature of a revealed (or discovered) truth with the aesthetical expectations of the general public. The editorial rhetoric is not only used to convey an absolute philosophical and theological truth as contained in the revealed Torah, but to do so in the form as taught by the Talmudic Rabbis, thus also inculcating their authority. Boyarin's book sheds serious doubts on our way of engaging the Talmudic texts as dialogical discourse and, by implication, about questions being intended to open up difference and plurality. Reading the Talmud with one eye on Plato, Boyarin builds a case to demonstrate the highly dialectical ways in which Rabbinic storytelling is subsumed under the Mosaic aegis of a revealed truth, encapsulated in the Rabbinic concept of the double Torah, but articulated in the anonymous voice of the text's editor, the *stamma*. Dissent and dialogue, as well as absurd 'low' stories, are mere pretexts and vehicles for discovering this truth, and the *sugya* or Talmudic discussion is less open-ended, but inculcates a specific theology or halakhic point of view.

This is not a dialogical discourse in the real sense of the word, even if contradictory voices may creep into the text and upset the argument.[10]

---

[7] H. Fischel, *Rabbinic Literature and Greco-Roman Philosophy: A Study of Epicurea and Rhetorica in Early Midrashic Writings* (StPB 21; Leiden: Brill, 1973).
[8] R. Hidary, *Rabbis and Classical Rhetoric: Sophistic Education and Oratory in the Talmud and Midrash* (Cambridge: Cambridge University Press, 2018).
[9] D. Boyarin, *Socrates and the Fat Rabbis* (Chicago: University of Chicago Press, 2009).
[10] Boyarin, *Socrates*, 200–201 locates these contradictory, 'creeping' voices as part of the Talmud's authorial voice. In framing dialogue and dialogical, he draws heavily from the work of the Russian literary critic Mikhail Bakhtin.

What was perceived, in reading a Rabbinic dispute, as a dialogical exchange of questions and opinions, exuding individuality and the particularity of diverging world views, now serves as a rhetorical form of the text directed at making the (standard) ideology acceptable, and the dialogue is a bridge inculcating expected patterns of behaviour as well as theological thought.

In short: Rabbinic Judaism is less a plural, open-minded system of discussion and dialogue, and more a variant of any other Late Antique religion, or to put it pointedly: a distinct Jewish form of Platonic, Stoic philosophy. It likewise portrays its heroes as comical figures, but this is a rhetorical tool serving the quest for serious truth.[11]

3. Questions as Dialogical Rhetoric

If I read Boyarin correctly, he (rhetorically?) voices doubts regarding his readings being sufficiently consistent. Moreover, his readings are limited to the Babylonian Talmud. The remainder of this paper seeks to assess how parables may be located in this assessment of Palestinian Rabbinic, haggadic discourse. The choice is deliberate: in my reading, parables are not illustrations of what would otherwise be known anyhow, neither should they be considered only as exegetical tools. As I would like to argue here, (some) parables have the ability to carry questions into the discourse that allow for the possibility of doubt, critique or alternative possibilities. As such they are carriers of questions not explicitly addressed by the Rabbinic discourse, and represent voices destabilizing dominant Rabbinic rhetoric. Parables (some, not all) carry non-dialectical elements into dialectic discourse, and destabilize its core ideology. Such parables are initiated by moments of contestation, even to the brink of questioning issues of Rabbinic authority itself. If this is correct, questions triggering parables insert moments of unresolved doubt or social anxiety into the discourse. Even if this view does not negate Boyarin's assessment of the Rabbinic text, the questions addressed by parables shed new light on their dialogical potential.

In order to make my case, we will discuss one example of Eikha Rabba and a section including a parable from Avot deRabbi Nathan. One involves a Midrashic context, the other involves the combination of a

[11] Boyarin, *Socrates*, 29: 'What characterizes, grosso modo and inter alia, this particular cultural form is its vaunted reliance on rational inquiry as the way to truth. Consequently, the dialogization of such a culture will come rather precisely from a form antithetical to the presentation of its heroes as fully rational beings.'

Rabbinic 'biographical' story with a parable. As we will show, both are expressive of questioning a received interpretation as inaccurate or problematic in light of lived, daily life and experience. It is here that the question 'creeps' into the Talmudic system of establishing authority and revealed truth, questioning it not from above but, so to say, from below. First, however, we will shortly introduce the Rabbinic parable, or *mashal*, as such.

4. On Parables: 'To what does the matter resemble?'

Rabbinic literature is replete with parables, short, fictive stories or similes addressing a specific problem by means of comparison. Mostly, these problems arise from an exegetical question or issue. Some parables convey non-textualized, legal or moral concepts. The standardized opening of all of these parables is the formula 'they told a parable. To what can the matter be compared?' which in itself already sounds like a rhetorical question introducing a specific and expected form, the *mashal*. The opening sentence has become so formulaic, that abbreviations, or mere shortcut formulae, such as 'to' also came into use.

These phenomena suggest a highly standardized technique of parable storytelling, meeting the expectancies of the public or readers as to what is to come when a parable is told. Scholars have discussed the exegetical functions and embedding of the parable in Rabbinic midrash, and crucial is the appearance of the application, or *nimshal*, usually introducing a Scriptural verse.[12]

The intertextuality of these parables is apparent, and their exegetical qualities seem to buttress the general Midrashic discourse they appear in. The *nimshal* not only completes but also informs the *mashal*, and both elements now become a combined narrative. However, this is not mere repetitive biblicism: due to this rhetorical unity, the reading of the biblical text becomes informed by the *mashal* as much as the *mashal* itself is triggered by the *nimshal*. The fact that both the biblical text, adduced in the *nimshal*, and the *mashal* itself are not marked by redundancy of information, but merely by insufficiency – in the forms of gaps and blanks

---

[12] D. Stern, *Parables in Midrash: Narrative and Exegesis in Rabbinic Literature* (Cambridge: Harvard University Press, 1991), 13. The term *nimshal* does not appear before the Middle Ages, but Y. Fraenkel, *Darke ha-aggadah vehamidrash*, 2 vols. (Givataim: Yad La-Talmud Jerusalem, 1991), 323, note 5 aptly notices that the term may be derived from the variant introduction למה נמשלה, *to what can it be compared?*.

– offers rhetorical space for doubts and questions to occupy their place in Rabbinic discourse.[13]

This narrative strategy is highly significant for the teacher or preacher: in this way, the parable invites the reader to question and to fill in the narrative and creates rhetorical space for the listener to enter its narrated world with his or her own experiences and perspectives. Thus, the parable, *mashal* and *nimshal*, becomes a medium, a rhetorical narrative, one that resembles biblical narrative, but bridges biblical revelation with the location of the hearer or reader and the views of the Rabbinic preacher. Indeed, exegesis is part of a complex communicative function of the parable, of which the bearing of the ideology or worldview of the *darshan*, the synagogue preacher, or the teacher in the Beith HaMidrash is also a part: it is this fusion of textual interpretation, as guided or informed by Rabbinic ideology, with the audience's perceptions and experiences that enables the parable to convey its message.[14]

This implies that by merely introducing the question 'to what may it be compared?' the midrash or narrative breaks up its discourse to allow other notions to enter. David Stern, in his reading of parables in the Rabbinic midrash on Lamentations, indeed notices how non-exegetical notions and sensitivities creep into the discourse by means of the parable. Lamentations addresses the loss of Jerusalem and the demise of the Temple, but parables discuss the present day, diasporic situations of the Jewish people.

We will present one, tantalizing, example of this hybridity of exegesis and ideology, which echoes tensions of the social and religious realm: the parable of the reading woman. By locating the parable in the texture of Rabbinic midrash, Stern makes clear that to understand the parable one has to read and understand Rabbinic midrash, but also vice versa: parables not only illustrate what already was known through exegetical operations, they insert emotions, ideas, resistance, or perceptions of reality that are not necessarily provided by the biblical text itself into the midrash. This leads him to offer a balanced definition: 'the Rabbinic *mashal* can be defined as a parabolic narrative that claims to be exegesis and

---

[13] Stern, *Parables in Midrash*, 15.74, 78. A blank is a disparity between *mashal* and *nimshal*: Stern, *Parables in Midrash*, 77. Sometimes gaps or even blanks are trivial from a narratological point of view, and need no elaboration. Compare his discussion of two parables of Yohanan ben Zakkai approaching his death (Semahot deRabbi Hiya 4:1), Stern, *Parables in Midrash*, 207–209. External cultural data creep into the discourse with the character of the Hegemon, which imbues the *midrash* with a Roman political context.

[14] Stern, *Parables in Midrash*, 51.

serves the purpose of ideology.'[15] It is in this dimension of the ad hoc situation that life vibrates within the text.

4.1. *'The Woman reading her* Ketubah': *A Parable on Abandonment*

An example containing perhaps the most gripping hybridity of exegesis and ideology, bearing on the dialectic relation between *mashal* and *nimshal*, and echoing tensions of the social and religious realm, is Stern's discussion of the parable of the reading woman:[16]

> R. Abba bar Kahana said: It is like a King who married a woman and wrote her a large marriage-settlement (כתובה). He wrote her: So many bridal chambers I am building for you; so much jewelry I make for you; so much gold and silver I give you. Then he left her for many years and journeyed through the provinces. Her neighbours used to taunt her and say to her: Hasn't your husband abandoned you? Go! Marry another man. She would weep and sigh, and afterward she would enter her bridal chamber and read her marriage settlement and sigh (with relief). Many years and days later the king returned. He said to her: I am amazed that you have waited for me all these years! She replied: My master, O King! If not for the large wedding-settlement that you wrote me, my neighbors long ago would have led me astray. Likewise: the nations of the world taunt Israel and say to them: Your God does not want you. He has left you. He has removed his presence from you. Come with us, and we will appoint you to be generals, governors, and officers. And the people of Israel enter their synagogues, and houses of study, and there they read in the Torah: 'I will look with favor upon you and make you fertile ... I will establish My abode in your midst, and I will not spurn you.' (Leviticus 26:9.11). And they console themselves. In the future when the redemption comes, the Holy One blessed be He will say to Israel: My children, I am amazed at how you have waited for Me all these years! And they will say to Him: Master of the Universe! Were it not for the Torah You gave us, in which we read when we enter our synagogues and houses of study 'I will look with favor upon you and I will not spurn you,' the nations of the world long ago would have led us away from you. That is what is written: 'Were not your teaching my delight, I would have perished in my affliction (Psalm 119:92). Therefore it says: 'This (זאת) I call to my mind: therefore I have hope' (Lamentations 3:21) (...)
> (Eikha Rabba 3:21, ed. Margulioth 2:635–655)[17]

---

[15] Stern, *Parables in Midrash*, 68.
[16] Stern, *Parables in Midrash*, 57–62. Cf. D. Stern, *Midrash and Theory: Ancient Jewish Exegesis and Contemporary Literary Studies* (Rethinking Theory; Evanston: Northwestern University Press, 1996), 39–54.
[17] We follow the translation as offered in Stern, *Parables in Midrash*, 57–58.

The *mashal* tells about a wife who is left without any reason by her husband and who, in his absence, finds consolation in reading the *ketubah*, the nuptial agreements, where all the bounties promised her are listed. In genre-critical terms, this parable shares an aspect of what some scholars, notably David Flusser, have emphasized as not fitting a proper parable: the identity of religious language in the parable's story and the application, here represented in the *ketubah* as establishing a 'covenant' between man and wife with its promises, and the Torah. Yet, it is not a *ma'aseh*, a case story, neither is it an example story.

A woman featuring in parables is rare, and a woman, metaphorically representing Israel, reading the Torah even less so. It may here be related to the female widow character in Lamentations as informing the parable, but in the Rabbinic system a woman reading Torah is highly irregular, and the metaphorical application should rather be seen in vulnerability due to the absence of the spouse. Indeed, as Stern notices, perhaps the most historical feature of the parable is offered by the neighbour's reaction: whereas the woman sticks to the promises of the text, which represents the Torah, they see a desolate and abandoned wife, which they interpret as divine abandonment.[18]

Stern points to the second Century CE Roman jurist Ulpian, who defended the notion of *maritalis affectio*, the intention to be in a married state, as forming the legal basis for marriage. The neighbours' interpretation of the king's absence, however, also hovers as a possibility above the tale, since it expresses perceptions and emotions that are tangible and understandable within the community as well. And even when the main rhetoric of the parable, as becomes clear in the *nimshal*, is praise and consolation – God will redeem His people in the near future, *lemachar* – the parable evokes more questions than it can most possibly address: why did the king leave his wife deserted, how did the wife feel when being asked by her neighbours, what did she feel and imagine while reading, and under what circumstances and when will the king come back?[19]

The implied interpreter (a figure loosely modelled after the implied reader) is the consort, whose character and person offer the possibility of full identification, especially in her act of reading, an 'interpretive event' for the reader.[20] This feature of parables, offering characters or events, with a figure of 'flesh and blood,' is rhetorically more effective in

---

[18] Stern, *Parables in Midrash*, 46.
[19] Stern, *Parables in Midrash*, 50: lit. 'tomorrow,' the Sephardic version adds כשיבא, *as soon as he will come*.
[20] Stern, *Parables in Midrash*, 52, 53.

creating an interpretative bridge between the canonical text and the reader than intertextual exegesis. However, willingly or unwillingly, in and through the imagery and the narrative deployed, the *mashal* also engenders superfluous meaning, since the *mashal* is in need of commentary and elucidation. This, by necessity, makes such a parable poly-interpretable.

In its narrative gaps, not commenting on motifs of the protagonist or the antagonist, or in creating unexplained time-leaps in the narrative, the parable even shares a literary quality with biblical literature itself, which, in the words of Auerbach, also shows lack of literary explication, and where merely nothing is foregrounded, although against a background 'fraught with meaning.'[21] These 'gaps,' unexplained features and omissions in the narrative, leave enough space for the reader's imagination and offer modes of identification, locate the parable close to biblical narrative and invite the reader to insert private perceptions and emotions into the narrative. It is here that the parable mediates, and its manner of interpreting is a presence 'in between,' bridging the biblical text and the reader.[22]

Applying the approach developed by Ronit Nikolsky, the parable thus channels emotions such as despair, frustration and even anger, and 'translates' these into a desired outcome, namely the Rabbis' own perception as founded in fealty and loyalty to Torah. Neither these emotions nor their direction are clearly present in the biblical text, which laments the fate of Israel after the destruction of the Temple, but they nonetheless arrive with the act of reading the text and do so by means of the parable.[23] This shows in the *nimshal*, especially in the demonstrative pronoun זאת *this* from Lamentations 3:21, 'I remember this.' Stern notices how in Lamentations the verse represents a break in the biblical lament of the man who is haunted, and who now finds comfort in remembering 'this'. The Midrashic technique is conventional: זאת recurs in Deuteronomy 4:44, hinting at the Torah, which for the midrashist provides a direction

---

[21] Stern, *Parables in Midrash*, 51, the actual quote is 'fraught with background,' see E. Auerbach, E.W. Said and W.R Trask, *Mimesis: The Representation of Reality in Western Literature – New and Expanded Edition* (Princeton: Princeton University Press, 2013), 12. This enforces our point in reading parables as pseudo-realistic, yet in a literary sense realistic, intrusion into the text.

[22] Stern, *Parables in Midrash*, 53.

[23] This function of parables, applying cognitive theory, is argued for in R. Nikolsky, "Are Parables an Interpretation?," in: M.M. Piotrkowski and T. Ilan (Eds.), *Sources and Interpretation in Ancient Judaism* (Ancient Judaism and Early Christianity 104; Leiden: Brill, 2018), 289–315.

for reading Lamentations in this sense as well.[24] However, the midrash does not feature the parable in order to merely illustrate this exegesis of a deictic form as hinting at the Torah. This could have been said without further ado. The parable, however, adds emotion, and the possibility of identification by inserting the character of the reading woman, with her despair, and the king, with his inexplicable behaviour. The tenacity of the spouse, sticking to the intimacy of reading her nuptial contract, evokes admiration and raises the natural question of how to justify her socially vulnerable state. In trying to fill gaps in the biblical narrative, the parable narrative reveals much about the situation of the reader.[25]

The unanswerable question as to why the woman was left behind hovers above the midrash as well as above the biblical text. It is this basic question that any faithful reader or hearer will have to confront.

4.2. *'The Man and the Mountain'*: *A Parable on Scriptural Exegesis*

Following these readings, we will now address a parable questioning Rabbinic hermeneutics. This parable needs an introduction and illumination of its textual context. The parable is part of a commentary on a saying of a Second Temple era Sage, Yose ben Yoezer, as recorded in the Mishnaic collection of Wisdom sayings, tractate Avot:[26]

> Yose ben Yoezer said: Let your house be a gathering place for the sages, and cover yourselves with the dust of their feet, and drink in their water thirstily.[27]

---

[24] The verse is quoted in some parallels, see Stern, *Parables in Midrash*, 59–60.
[25] One dimension could be added: since medieval times, the demonstrative pronoun זאת has accompanied a liturgical gesture of all individuals pointing to the Torah Scroll in synagogue liturgy, invoking the verse from Deuteronomy 4:44 present in some manuscripts of the midrash, and it may even be the case that the text hints at this gesture as well: in that case the parable addresses the participants in the synagogue, and identifies them as the reading woman. The parable here becomes a 'textual gesture.' If this is a plausible reading, as we think it is, the *Sitz im Leben* of the parable, the synagogue, strengthens its dramatic impact on the gathered community.
[26] Avot is usually translated as '(Sayings of the) fathers,' but the meaning of 'Principles' might be more appropriate: S. Safrai (Ed.), *The Literature of the Sages First Part: Oral Torah, Halakha, Mishna, Tosefta, Talmud, External Tractates* (CRINT 2/3; Assen: van Gorcum, 1987), 263–264.
[27] Avot deRabbi Nathan a 6; b, 12 [edition H.-J. Becker, *Avot de-Rabbi Natan: Synoptische Edition beider Versionen = Āvôt dĕ-Rabbî Nātān* (TSAJ 116; Tübingen: Mohr Siebeck, 2006), 79–81, 339–340]. We follow the a-version, as this represents the 'canonical' text in the printed editions of the Talmud. Translations follow the *Sefariah* edition (https://www.sefaria.org/Avot_D'Rabbi_Natan?lang=bi) and are slightly adapted where deemed necessary.

Mishna Avot is commented on in Avot deRabbi Nathan, an Amoraic tractate containing biographical narratives, Midrashic expositions as well as sayings, and is handed down in two versions. As a non-canonical tractate, it has become part of the Babylonian Talmud, and version a is printed in the authoritative 19th Century CE Vilna edition. The saying of Yose ben Yoezer adduced an elaborate comment, consisting of three stages. The first is primarily of a practical nature, introduced by a regular introductory term in the Mishnah or the Tosephta ('how so?'), usually signalling a halakhic detailing of a principle, here urging to provide physical space for the community of learners:

> *How so? This teaches us that a person's house should always be open to the sages, and to their students, and their students' students, so that a person should be able to say to his friend: I will save a place for you there!*

In a second move, the commentary focusses on establishing a hierarchical and highly emotion-invested relation towards the Sage:

> *Another explanation: How should your house be a gathering place for the sages? When a student of the sages enters and says: Teach me! – if you have something to teach, teach it, but if not, let him go on his way. He should not sit before you on a bed, or a chair, or a bench. He should sit before you only on the ground. And anything that comes out of your mouth, he should accept with reverence, fear, quaking, and trembling.'*

The awe mentioned in it clearly evokes a repetition of the Sinai experience, now with the Sage in the role of Moses himself, who was the sole person who 'accepted Torah from Sinai' (Avot 1:1) before he handed it down to his disciple Joshua. The experience of the Sinai revelation, as witnessing the revelation of truth, has to be emulated while being seated, literally, at the feet of the Sage. Learning is a spiritual re-enactment of this national, biblical core-experience, and thus learning affiliates the individual with this corporate emotion as well as with social covenantal belonging.[28] There is not much room here for questions, doubts or personal feelings: the emotional regime instilled in this text is one of awe for tradition and a sense of being overwhelmed by the absolute values carried in it.[29] Studying here means listening, interiorizing and repeating

---

[28] Emotions are individual, but also collectively shared, and are culturally inculcated forms of perception. As such they are relevant in social formation: O. Riis and L. Woodhead, *A Sociology of Religious Emotion* (Oxford: Oxford Scholarship, 2010), 47.

[29] This interpretation is repeated, now commenting on the advent of a visiting scholar as well: *'Cover yourself with the dust of their feet'. How so? When a Torah scholar enters*

the handed down 'Torah of Sinai.' This mode of studying also protects against loss of memory, corruption of tradition and deviation. According to the praise of Rabban Yohanan ben Zakkai for his pupil R. Eliezer ('he is like a plastered pit that does not lose a drop,' M. *Avot* 2:8), this model may be labelled the Eliezer model. Indeed, this section closes off with this Sage, and then shifts to Akiva:

> *Another explanation: Cover yourself with the dust of their feet: This refers to Rabbi Eliezer. And drink with thirst their words: this is Rabbi Akiva.*

4.2.1. The Akiva model: exploring hidden meaning

Now, the text comes to discuss the model of learning connected to Rabbi Akiva, the towering figure of Rabbinic Judaism in its formative era, during the early and mid-second Century CE. His influence on the structure and contents of the Mishna is huge, and his pupils (R. Meir, R. Yehuda, R. Shimon, and R. Yosi in particular) are credited with providing the bulk of Mishnaic rules and traditions. R. Akiva is, however, also famous for his hermeneutics, which provide meticulous techniques for reading texts in a non-literal manner, as well as for his personal fate as a martyr during the Bar Kokhba Revolt. Both forms of agency are discussed in the sources as a model for religious practice.[30] Stories as presented here likewise do not aim at biography, but show how tradition typifies a Sage as embodying values representative and relevant for the cultural world of the Rabbis and their audience.[31]

As Azzan Yadin shows, Talmudic tradition features two portrayals of R. Akiva's exegetical work: one, most prominent in earlier sources, shows him as inventively bridging the concepts and laws of the Oral tradition with the biblical text; the second image, conveyed especially by

---

the city, do not say: I don't need him. Instead, go to him. And do not sit next to him on a bed, or on a chair, or on a bench. Rather, sit before him on the ground, and accept upon yourself every word that comes from his mouth with fear and reverence, trembling and sweating, just as our forefathers accepted what they heard at Mount Sinai with fear and reverence, trembling and sweating.

[30] E. Ottenheijm, "Martyrdom as a Contested Practice in Rabbinic Judaism," *NedTT* 69 (2015): 102–118.

[31] E.g. A. Goshen-Gottstein, *The Sinner and the Amnesiac: The Rabbinic Invention of Elisha ben Abuya and R. Eleazar ben Arakh* (Contraversion; Stanford: Stanford University Press, 2000); J.L. Rubenstein, *Talmudic stories: Narrative Art, Composition, and Culture* (Baltimore: Johns Hopkins University Press, 1999); J.L. Rubenstein, *The Culture of the Babylonian Talmud* (Baltimore: Johns Hopkins University Press, 2005).

Talmudic texts, shows him as an ingenuous exegete able to distil meaning even from the crowns and the little diacritic signs of the Hebrew text.[32] It is this second, Talmudic type that we encounter in a narrative about the beginnings of his career:[33]

> What were the origins of Rabbi Akiva? They say that he was forty years old and had still not learned anything. Once, he was standing at the mouth of a cistern and he said: Who hollowed out (חקק) this stone? They said to him: It is from the water, which constantly [falls] on it, day after day. And they said: Akiva, have you not read, 'Water erodes (שחקו)[34] stones' (Job 14:19)? Rabbi Akiva immediately applied this, all the more so, to himself. He said: If something soft can crush something hard, then all the more so, the words of Torah, which are like iron, will engrave (שיחקקו) my heart, which is but flesh and blood.

Rabbi Akiva is portrayed as a simple man, the prototypical *am ha'aretz*, during his first forty years.[35] Only after encountering a natural phenomenon, does he start to fathom the truth of the Torah text.

Crucial are, of course, the questions raised here. It all starts with the experience of a stone cap, covering the pit of a cistern, and hollowed out by the drops of water. The story is associated with the motif of drinking Torah thirstily, and it loosely refers to the narratological function of wells in the Genesis story (see further), but the narrative focusses less on drinking and more on the power of water. The reader of this text already may have associated water with Torah, a recurring metaphor.[36] As such, the question is highly rhetorical, as the outcome focusses on the truth of the revealed text, represented here in the verse from Job.

Being confronted with the fact that this power of nature correlates with the words of the Torah, a verse from Job, Rabbi Akiva applies this logic to his own person: if such is the power of nature, all the more so will Torah change his heart. This ironical and unexplained move of the

---

[32] A. Yadin, *Scripture and Tradition: Rabbi Akiva and the Triumph of Midrash* (Divinations: Rereading Late Ancient Religion; Philadelphia: University of Pennsylvania Press, 2014). The second type is represented by the most famous story on Moses attending the Academy of R. Akiva (b. Menahot 29b).
[33] Unless noted otherwise, we follow the edition princeps, edition Becker 78–81.
[34] The text plays with the relatedness in terms of meaning of the verbs חקק and שחק, as *hollowing out, carving,* or *writing with a stylus.*
[35] The frame of 3 × 40 years follows a biblical pattern (Moses), but the sources differ: see the extensive discussion of the traditions in A. Yadin, "Rabbi Akiva's Youth," *JQR* 100 (2010) 573–597.
[36] See e.g. Mekilta deRabbi Ishmael, *Bahodesh* 5.

plot reiterates a topos told about the non-learned disciple of Hillel who wanted to become a High Priest, but after having read Leviticus learned to apply a biblical logic to himself.[37] The use of the *kal wahomer*, reasoning from light to weighty, is not without a deep sense of irony as it is one of the basic hermeneutical rules applied by the Rabbis themselves, and the motif exudes the rhetoric that the Rabbis deploy common human sense.[38] The story may very well have had a humoristic ring. Indeed, the narrative aggrandizes this non-serious tone of the story by introducing Akiva as being seated next to his son, ushering in his becoming one of the *literati*:

> *He immediately went to start studying Torah. He went with his son and they sat down by the elementary teacher. He said to one: Rabbi, teach me Torah! He then took hold of one end of the tablet, and his son took hold of the other end. The teacher wrote down aleph and bet for him, and he learned them; aleph to tav, and he learned them; the book of Leviticus, and he learned it. And he went on studying until he learned the whole Torah. Scripture and Targum, midrash and halakhot. Then he went and sat before Rabbi Eliezer and Rabbi Joshua. My masters, he said, reveal the reason (תאם) of a mishnah to me. When they told him one law from the Torah,[39] he went off and sat down to work it out for himself. This aleph, what was it written for? That bet, what was it written for? Why was this thing said? He came back, and asked them, and clarified the matter for them (העמידן בדברים).*[40]

The story of the elementary-school teacher reflects an institutionalized study system of the late Amoraic period.[41] The remainder represents a 'mosaic of elements drawn from other sources,' or told in earlier stories in Avot deRabbi Natan, and provides a stylized model rather than history.[42] It takes up a topos present in the story of Hillel and the illiterate

---

[37] Avot deRabbi Natan a 15, edition S. Schechter, *Aboth de Rabbi Nathan* (Hildesheim: Olms, 1979 60–62; b 29, edition Schechter, *Aboth de Rabbi Nathan*, 60–62; b. Shabbat 30b–31a.

[38] The principle probably originated parallel to or under the influence of Hellenistic rhetoric: D. Daube, "Rabbinic methods of interpretation and Hellenistic rhetoric," *HUCA* 22 (1949) 239–264; more cautious: G. Stemberger, *Einleitung in Talmud und Midrash*, 9. Auflage (München: Beck, 2011), 29.

[39] The versions offer 'when they told him a halakha,' but Geniza fragment T-S NS 313–1 probably offers the correct reading: Yadin, *Scripture and Tradition*, 117.

[40] Sefariah offers: 'and silenced them.' We follow Yadin, *Scripture and Tradition*, 117.

[41] Yadin, "Rabbi Akiva's Youth," 580.

[42] A historical discussion of some of its motifs (teacher, poverty) is provided in Yadin, "Rabbi Akiva's Youth," 581, 582. These motifs may be Babylonian elements: M. Kister, *Studies in Avot de-Rabbi Natan: Text, Redaction and Interpretation* (Jerusalem: Hebrew University Press, 1998), 206–212. We are not seeking 'historical

man, who had to trust his teacher that this actually was an *aleph* and that a *bet* here. R. Akiva questions the position of the *aleph* and the *bet* to symbolize an approach driven by holy curiosity and an urge to delve into the hidden sources of the text: why is this *aleph* written here, why this *bet* written there?[43] Unlike the person in the story of Hillel, he is not restrained in his attempts to uncover the text, nor forced to accept the authority of his teachers. Or rather, he is not the person to be restrained: Rabbi Akiva is, what one could say, 'a pain in the ass' for his teachers. There is something daring in his behaviour, and being seated next to his son makes his appearance somewhat grotesque. On the one hand, Akiva's repeated turn to the written text links this story with the rhetoric of study as continuity and repetition, the dominant ideology of this text.[44] It adds, however, a new and dramatic tone to it, in the form of the repeated questioning as to why the text states what it states, and why here. This includes his teachers, who are relegated to the function of offering Scriptural argumentation, to which Akiva in turn dedicates his genius. He transforms from being a pupil to teaching his masters. As Yadin argues, seeking for the 'reason' (תאם) of the oral laws of his teachers can refer either to logical reasons or to Scriptural proof, and it is this twofold dynamics that governs the way Akiva confronts Scripture ('why is this *aleph* written here,' etc.).[45] It is this philosophical mode of study, questioning order and substance and seeking foundational meaning, that emerges as a new meaning of the saying of Yose ben Yoezer: it is radically different to the awe instilled by sitting before a teacher and listening to his words.

4.2.2. The 'Parable of the Stonecutter'

It is at this stage of the text that Akiva's method, bypassing tradition in favour of a renewed reading of the sacred text, is commented upon in a

---

kernels,' but, following Yadin, *Scripture and Tradition*, the Rabbinic typology of Akiva in this text.
[43] Avot deRabbi Natan a 15, edition Schechter, *Aboth de Rabbi Nathan*, 60–62; b 29, edition Schechter, *Aboth de Rabbi Nathan*, 60–62; b. Shabbat 30b–31a.
[44] A.J. Saldarini, *Scholastic Rabbinism: A Literary Study of the Fathers According to Rabbi Nathan* (BJS 14; Chico: Scholars Press, 1982) argues the closeness of this discourse to Graeco-Roman philosophical schools.
[45] Yadin, *Scripture and Tradition*, 117: 'The entire trajectory of the story makes it clear that literacy, not the receipt of traditions, is the key to Rabbi Akiva's genius.'

parable by a later generation.[46] The parable voices disturbing notions on this way of dealing with Revelation:

> Rabbi Shimon ben Elazar[47] said: I will give you a parable. To what can the matter be compared? To a stonecutter who was hacking away at the mountains. One time he took his pickaxe in his hand, and went and sat on top of the mountain,[48] and began to chip small stones away from it. And people came by and asked him: What are you doing?[49] He said to them: I am going to uproot the mountain and throw it into the Jordan! They said to him: You cannot uproot the entire mountain (את כל ההר)![50] But he kept hacking away, until he came to a big boulder. So he wedged himself underneath it, pried it loose, and threw it into the Jordan. And he said to it:[51] Your place is not here, but there!

The parable tells a fascinating but somewhat absurd story of a stonecutter 'uprooting' a mountain. The metaphorical identification of teachers as mountains may be found behind this parable, which would relate to R. Joshua and R. Eliezer as the teachers of Akiva, but the mountain here more probably evokes Sinai and the written Torah.[52] The motif of the Jordan River may be explained from Job 28:11, a Wisdom verse which will appear in the *nimshal*.[53] We saw, however, how the reference to Sinai was already deployed in the explanation of the saying as amounting

---

[46] Shimon ben Eleazar was a contemporary of R. Yehuda haNasi, beginning of the third Century ce; W. Bacher, *Die Agada der Tannaiten*, Band 2: Die Agada der Tannaiten. Bd 2 Von Akiba's Tod bis zum Abschluß der Mischna (Berlin: de Gruyter, 1966), 422–436. Remarkably, Yadin, *Scripture and Tradition*, 114 ff. does not include the parable in his translation or discussion.
[47] In version b, the parable is attributed to Shimon ben Manasia, a second Century ce teacher. Compare Bacher, *Agada der Tannaiten*, 435.
[48] MS New York 10484 and T-S NS 313.1 as well as version b read 'next to (בסד) the mountain.'
[49] T-S NS 313.1: 'what is this?;' version b: 'what are you doing here?'.
[50] This remark is missing in T-S NS 313.1. Version b: 'they said to him: can you succeed? He said: yes!'.
[51] In version b Rabbi Akiva directs these words to the Jordan, followed by a Scriptural quote (*shene'amar*): 'Man sets his hand against the flinty rock. And overturns mountains by the roots' (Job 28:9, JPS).
[52] The Houses of Hillel and Shammai, represented by R. Joshua and R. Eliezer, are depicted as 'mountains' in t. Jevamot 1:10 [edition S. Lieberman, *Talmud Yerushalmi* (Jerusalem: Kedem, 1971), 3]; p. Jevamot 1:6 (3b). The mountain as metonym for Torah is articulated in Tannaitic midrash (e.g. Mekhilta deRabbi Ishmael, Bahodesh 4) and in M. Avot 1:1: 'Moses received Torah from Sinai.'
[53] The parable may have derived its prime motifs (carving, rock, streams, mountain) indeed from Job 28:9–11, the impression of which receives some support from the quote from Job 28:9 in b and 28:11 in a. The motif of the Jordan remains unexplained. It may allude to the blocking of the river and the twelve stones (!) in Joshua 3:15; 4:20. Is Akiva's hermeneutic, so the parable, indicative of a renewed covenantal relation?

to an emotional regime of submissiveness, fear and trembling. Akiva, delving for big rocks to uproot this mountain, has a comical ring, borders on the absurd and maybe even alludes to myth.[54] This is strengthened by the reactions from 'some people,' actually voicing and channelling the hearer's perception as well: who would be able to replace a mountain? Yet this surreal image provides a powerful and emotion-invested picture for a different type of learning: one seeking reasons and principles, and laying these bare for others as well.

In contrast to the starting point of the story, water hollowing out rock, it is now R. Akiva who is using a pickaxe, working slowly but consistently like water, to delve for secrets. In a way, he enacts the principle and the power of Torah he has learned by mere watching. One wonders what the implications are for the Torah itself: like the mountain, it will never again regain its former shape. Crucial is the focalization in the text: 'Your place is not here, but there!' evoking a topical rearrangement of the divine law according to human (rational?) principles.[55]

Moreover, the motif of throwing the stones into the Jordan River may also be read as retroactively invoking the motif of water hollowing out the stone: the river will do its polishing work. There is admiration but also a disturbing atmosphere in these images, especially compared to the Eliezer model, because the dynamics imply queries ('why is this *aleph* written here?'/hacking), destruction and replacement ('this is your place').

A sense of admiration is expressed in the *nimshal*, or application, which is not a biblical verse, but a biographical notion accompanied by a biblical verse:

> This is what Rabbi Akiva did to Rabbi Eliezer and Rabbi Tarfon.[56] Rabbi Tarfon[57] said to him: Akiva, it is about you that the verse says (Job 28:11), 'He stops up the streams so that hidden things may be brought to light.' For Rabbi Akiva has brought to light things which are kept hidden from human beings.

Rabbi Tarfon (or his teacher Eliezer, according to version b) indeed expresses that Akiva was not only dealing with his teacher's words, but

---

[54] There is a slight reminder here of Hercules redirecting the rivers to cleanse the stables of King Augeas.
[55] Only MS New York Rab. 25 offers a confused reading and puts these words in the mouths of the bypassing people, probably due to *homoioteleuton*.
[56] This sentence is missing in version b.
[57] Version b: R. Eliezer.

with Revelation itself. Applying a verse from Job qualifies his actions as emulating man seeking wisdom by turning things upside down.

4.2.3. Questioning the Akiva model

It all started out with questions related to the power of water to hollow out stone, only to be followed by text-related questions on Revelation itself. The laudatory nature of this section notwithstanding, there is social anxiety as well. First, R. Akiva takes away any excuse for a poor person not to learn Torah: there simply is no excuse. Second, it may not be accidental that the text now introduces a second character, the wife of R. Akiva, who parades with garments showing her newly acquired social status. Akiva is critically questioned on this by his disciples.[58] Akiva, however, remains steadfast in his approval of her behaviour: unlike his disciples, it is she who had to endure the troubles of his former poverty. Now, also she is granted the honour of enjoying the material rewards of his Torah-study. This depiction of Rachel follows a romantic love story, with the couple having to wait several years before tasting the material fruits of their marriage, and is loosely based on Jacob and Rachel (Genesis 30) who likewise had to wait several years before she bore children. Nonetheless, the picture of Rachel showing off publicly is not without problems, for ostensive behaviour might not befit an austere Torah-study regime following the model of Eliezer. The love story is, however, crucial for the theological rhetoric of Torah-study in this model: it is no coincidence that R. Akiva is not the teacher of fear and trembling, but the hero of love for God and love for the neighbour.[59]

The discourse changes drastically in its comment on Yose ben Yoezer's saying. Neither Akiva, nor Rachel is seated in dust and in fear and trembling, but a romantic form of companionship reigns instead. The parable marks a point of transition in the text, in comparing an explorative way of study to the fate of Torah itself, and pairs a disconcerting sense with appraisal: Torah-study has become a way of loving God rather than fearing him, but by definition human agency and change is brought

---

[58] *He merited to have his wife Rachel. He was forty years old when he went to study Torah, and after thirteen years, he was teaching Torah to the masses. It was said that he did not leave the world until he had tables full of silver and gold, and he could go up to his bed on golden ladders. His wife would go out in a fancy gown and with golden jewelry with an engraving of Jerusalem on it. His students said: Rabbi, you are embarrassing us with what you have done for her. He said to them: She suffered greatly with me for the sake of Torah.* (Avot deRabbi Nathan a 6)

[59] Bereshit Rabba 24:7; p. Nedarim 30b.

into the system. In providing a questioning person who develops into a teacher unravelling the principles of love, the text subtly curbs the saying of Yose ben Yoezer and the ensuing commentary as well. The parable on the mountain addresses both this fundamental shift with Akiva, as well as the potentially disturbing consequences, social as well as hermeneutical, for a study based on awe and continuity, lauded so emphatically at the start of the discourse.[60]

5. Conclusions

Boyarin may have touched a sensitive nerve: the Rabbis, like other religious elites in Late Antiquity, had a keen interest in propagating a 'serious' ideology and practice that buttressed their authority, centred around their ways of dialectically unravelling Torah. In a certain sense, this is a closed discursive system, and Boyarin's observations limit the alleged dialogical character of Rabbinic discourse. This is the case at least in the Babylonian Talmud, with its articulated theology and developed authority subsuming other modes of study or practice outside Rabbinic realms.[61] Questions serve rhetorical aims, feigning different possibilities of thought or action, but actually introducing a reaffirming entrance of the revealed Torah as embodied by the Rabbinic Sages. Moreover, we should not conflate questions with dialogue.

However, in deploying parables, even with their highly stylized, intertextually fabricated images, perceptions of reality creep into the text that, at times, destabilize this theological rhetoric. They bring unsaid and unarticulated emotions and sensitivities into the textual web. The woman reading her *ketubah* in the absence of her husband raises an age-old anxiety: why did her husband (God) leave her (Israel) in the first place? While this anxiety can at first be seen as recapturing the mood of Lamentations, and, within the midrash, reaffirms a programme of Torah-study and Torah-practice, the question hovers in the air and is not answered.

This question is nonetheless a threat to the system of Torah, as it questions its theodicy. R. Akiva's handling of the Torah amounts to processes that resemble destruction and reconstruction of divine wisdom itself, resulting in a highly human-made fabric of the divine Law. Instead of

---

[60] Yadin, "Rabbi Akiva's Youth," 597: '(…) his ignorance and his poverty early on in his life mark him as a new kind of interpreter: a master of midrash who does not – could not – emerge from the (priestly, *auth.*) elite circles.'
[61] Cf. also Yadin, "Rabbi Akiva's Youth," 595.

sitting in the dust and absorbing tradition, the Torah teacher queries and uproots its foundations, and this amounts to an opposite interpretation of the saying of Jose ben Yoezer.

It is in such moments of instability, produced by the parable and its application, that the questions addressed in the midrashic discourse become tangible. These moments provide us with a glimpse as to why the parable was placed here in the first place. The parable marks the transfer of an emotional regime propelling a Torah-study of fear and awe towards one of love and intellectual curiosity, but also infuses a deep sense of disturbance about this shift. In this light, even the highly conventional 'to what may it be compared?' may, sometimes, be more than a mere literary device: it is a warning sign, signalling incoming traffic from the outer textual or the counter-textual entering the textual discourse. By means of parables, questions aroused by socially lingering doubts and concerns found their place in a monologue-shaped text. In the end, these disturbing questions remained unanswered.

EDUCATIONAL PERSPECTIVES ON QUESTIONS IN BIBLICAL TEXTS

Hanna ROOSE

Ruhr University Bochum

1. Questions in an educational perspective

For a long time, biblical scholars have overlooked the importance of questions in biblical texts. However, in educational contexts, questions have always been considered essential. I will restrict myself to three milestones.

a) Socrates is famous for his way of teaching by asking his interlocutor questions. His maieutic technique 'gives birth' to knowledge that was hidden:

> *The basic principle of Socratic teaching is that the teacher does not simply say what he wants to convey, but that he withholds his knowledge and, by asking questions that are not questions for himself, leads the one being taught to his or her own insights.*[1]

This technique has been adopted by the so-called 'questioning-developing class discussion' ('fragend-entwickelndes Unterrichtsgespräch') which is still widely spread in classrooms today, although it has come under attack for various reasons. It is regarded by many as 'an uneconomic and dishonest pattern of action that disguises the relations of power in the classroom.'[2] It is uneconomic in that it hopes to get from the pupil what could be said more quickly by the teacher; it is dishonest in that the teacher pretends not to know what he or she does know;[3] it disguises the relations of power in the classroom in that it gives the impression of entering into a face-to-face dialogue between pupil and

---

[1] K. Spinner, "Sokratisches Lehren und die Dialektik der Aufklärung. Zur Kritik des fragend-entwickelnden Unterrichtsgesprächs," *Diskussion Deutsch: Zeitschrift für Deutschlehrer aller Schulformen in Ausbildung und Praxis* 23 (1992): 309–321, here 316.

[2] H. Meyer, *UnterrichtsMethoden II: Praxisband* (Weinheim: Beltz, 1989), 287.

[3] In other words, using Archibald van Wieringen's view on questions: be aware of the discrepancy in information (see pages 149-150 of this volume).

teacher without really breaking down the pedagogical asymmetry – it is still the teacher who knows better and who evaluates the answers.

b) Catechisms use questions for purposes of memorizing and interpreting biblical tradition, but also for examining candidates regarding the Christian Creed. However, if we look at Martin Luther's 'Small Catechism' ('Kleiner Katechismus'), it is noteworthy that the question-answer-structure does not quite match typical exam questions. Let us briefly look at the first item.

> *I am the Lord your God. You shall have no other gods besides me. What is this? We are to fear, love and trust God above all things.*

The wording 'what is this?' aims at a better understanding of biblical texts.[4] A question like that could be asked in Religious Education classes (or, for that matter, regarding other subjects) with reference to any given text. However, the 'we' in the answer stands out. It does not say: 'Men are to fear' or 'Jews are to fear' or 'Christians are to fear.' Instead, the speaker locates him- or herself within a community: 'we are to fear.' This implies that further questions derived from this answer will be asked from 'within,' asked by someone as a member of this community, based on what has been passed on. The question then is: does the Catechism leave space for critique, for contradiction? Is it used as a means of merely passing on, of examining younger generations, or as a starting point for open, controversial discussions?

c) Twenty years ago, pedagogy of religion started to plead for a change of perspective:[5] teaching Religious Education, so it was said, should no longer be based on didactical questions asked by the teacher who knows the answer. Instead, it should be based on 'real' questions asked by the pupils, 'big' questions that do not have any given answers but give rise to open discussions,[6] questions as: Where do I come from? How can the universe be infinite? What happens after death? Why do people fight against each other? What is time? What does it look like in heaven?[7] It

---

[4] Cf. also pages 46–47 of this volume.
[5] Cf. A. Wright, "The Integrity of Students' Theological Discourse: Critical Realism and the Variation Theory of Learning," in: G. Yde Iversen, G. Mitchell and G. Pollard (Eds.), *Hovering over the Face of the Deep: Philosophy, Theology and Children* (Münster: Waxmann, 2009), 163–176.
[6] Cf. G. Büttner and L.C. Seelbach, *Kinder und die großen Antworten. Generationsübergreifende Impulse für Schule und Gemeinde* (Stuttgart: Calwer, 2019); H. Kuindersma (Ed.), *Powerful Learning Environments and Theologizing and Philosophizing with Children* (Beiträge zur Kinder- und Jugendtheologie 2; Kassel: University Press, 2013).
[7] Cf. R. Oberthür, *Kinder und die großen Fragen: Ein Praxisbuch für den Religionsunterricht* (München: Kösel, 1995), 14–16.

is this change of perspective that makes – as we will see below – Deuteronomy 6:20–25 so attractive to educational contexts because, for once, it is the child who asks.

This brief sketch of questions in educational contexts can make us more sensitive when we turn to look at questions in biblical texts. Educational questions concerning the Bible and questions in the Bible are both embedded in power structures. They can reinforce an imbalance in power, or they can minimize it.

Educational questions concerning the Bible and questions in biblical texts are both embedded in the process of passing on knowledge. They can consolidate this knowledge or criticize it.

Educational questions concerning the Bible and questions in biblical texts are also both embedded in relations of belonging. They allocate specific social (in the widest sense) positions to the person who asks and to the person who might answer.

Looking back on the contributions in this volume from an educational perspective, several aspects stand out. For reasons of space, I will concentrate on only three aspects that have caught my attention.

2. Between generations

Richard Bautch focusses on Deuteronomy 6:20–25 and reflects on the difference between 'now' and 'then,' between this generation and future generations, between child and adult.

In 6:20–25, the child's question about God's decrees, statutes, and ordinances, gives rise to a 'teaching moment'.[8]

This 'teaching moment' is embedded both in a generation gap and in a gap between 'heritage' and 'contemporary Israel'.

> *In Deuteronomy 6, both the incised child and the questioner represent Israelite society's youngest generation who are learning key elements of their ethnic and cultural heritage. Moreover, they are active learners who apply the lessons of history to their own day and critique contemporary Israel when it is warranted.*[9]

The 'teaching moment' as it is described here, follows the lines of so-called 'evolutionary didactics.'[10] Evolutionary didactics reflect on the

---
[8] See pages 38–44 of this volume.
[9] See page 39 of this volume. Cf. also pages 166–167 of this volume.
[10] A. Scheunpflug, *Evolutionäre Didaktik: Unterricht aus system- und evolutionstheoretischer Perspektive* (Studien zur Schulpädagogik und Didaktik 18; Weinheim: Beltz, 2001).

possibilities and obstacles of transferring ethnic and cultural heritage from one generation to the next. According to evolutionary didactics, this transfer can never be complete. Younger generations partly refuse to simply carry on with what they are being handed down. Youngsters at some point defy their parents. It is this shift in what different generations adhere to that allows for traditions to be modified and contested. Bautch stresses this aspect with regard to Deuteronomy 6:20–25. Children and youngsters locate themselves 'liminally' between two generations. They 'are active learners who apply the lessons of history to their own day and critique contemporary Israel when it is warranted.' Since the times of Deuteronomy, many more generations have passed on the 'lessons of history.' The generation gap has widened. Religious Education has to deal with this gap. In order to do so, it must listen to the questions that learners ask when reading the Bible.

These questions can be asked either from 'within' a Jewish or Christian community or from 'without.' The child in Deuteronomy 6:20–25 'is marked by his belief and his commitment. The child is not outside the community or its faith...'[11] Sometimes, questions from 'within' can afford to be more critical than questions from 'without.' Many of today's school-children are located 'liminally somewhere along the edges of' – in their case – (Jewish or) Christian communities. Quite often, they do not ask questions from 'within' when it comes to the Bible. Many of them are barely influenced by or even acquainted with Jewish or Christian beliefs and they are rarely expected by their families to hand these traditions on. Their encounter with biblical texts is more like that of a tourist exploring new places. The acute need to make this place worthwhile visiting, 'to shore up the credibility of the religious system, especially among youth'[12] has increased. As 'tourists,' children and youngsters are inscribed with their own cultures and experiences. The question as to whether the child 'might ... have something to say' about biblical tradition thus becomes less predictable and proves a challenge to contemporary religious education.

3. Between involvement and reflection

Different types of questions have different rhetorical effects. Two contributions in this volume focus on two types of questions that have opposite

---

[11] See page 38 of this volume.
[12] See pages 38–39, 117–118 of this volume.

aims: Whereas 'unasked questions' in the Gospel of John implicitly involve the reader *in* the narrative, 'counter-questions' in the Gospel of Luke wish to make the reader think *about* the narrative. From an educational perspective, the tension between involvement in biblical texts and reflection on biblical texts is essential. Let us first review the exegetical evidence according to Estes and Koet before considering educational issues.

In his reading of the Gospel of John, Douglas Estes focusses on 'unasked questions.' Thereby, he highlights the reader's involvement in biblical texts.

> *Unasked questions are useful for the narrator to engage the audience directly without alerting the audience to this engagement. When a character asks an unasked question, the question projects itself and is internalized by the audience.*[13]

The involvement is implicit, and it is all the more powerful because the reader is hardly aware of it:

> *Unasked questions perform a similar metaleptic movement as do asides, yet the effect is implicit, not explicit.*[14]

The reader is drawn into the narrative, the story speaks to him/her. At the end, the Gospel of John states clearly where this narrative strategy is aimed: 'the primary goal is to persuade the audience of the truth of the story' (John 20:31). The audience is to be moved, changed, challenged:

> *Rather than merely telling a story about the life of Jesus, the narrative and rhetorical features in John work together to push the audience in the direction that the narrator wants the audience to go – or more specifically, to believe.*[15]

Bart Koet focusses on a different type of question: he looks into 'counter questions' in the Gospel of Luke. 'Counter-questions' are 'those questions one asks in response to the questions one is asked.'[16] These questions do not aim at implicit involvement, but at reflection on the part of the reader. 'all counter-questions have in common that they more or less get the listeners thinking.'[17] 'Counter-questions' reflect on the question that has been asked. Thereby, they encourage 'questioners to think for

---

[13] See page 240 of this volume.
[14] See page 245 of this volume. Cf. also pages 26, 31–32 of this volume.
[15] See page 245 of this volume. See also A.L.H.M. van Wieringen, "Psalm 65 as Non-Appropriation Theology," *Biblica* 95 (2014) 179–197.
[16] See page 210 of this volume.
[17] See page 227 of this volume.

themselves as much as possible, sometimes even to the extent that they will give the answer themselves, like in Luke 10:25-37.'[18]

Koet compares the rhetorical function of 'counter-questions' to the rhetorical function of Jesus' parables:

> *In the literature on parables it has often been pointed out that parables invite the hearers/readers to think for themselves and that different interpretations of parables are therefore possible. In the New Testament parables are part of the pedagogical teaching strategy of Jesus; they make his listeners think. They appear to have this in common with the counter-questions Jesus poses in the Gospel.*[19]

'Counter-questions' and parables are viewed as maieutic techniques to make the reader (or interlocutor) aware of what s/he already knows without yet knowing that s/he knows. In this respect, Jesus' way of teaching can be compared to that of Socrates.

What are we to make of these distinct narrative strategies from the perspective of practical theology? Do we, as ministers or teachers, want to involve the reader *in* the biblical narrative, or do we wish to make the reader think *about* the narrative? The two strategies imply different positions that the reader is meant to take: either *in* the text or *outside* the text; either the reader is a *participant* or he/she is an *observer*.

The question is rather tricky. For in a way, education – and, for that matter, homiletics – aim at both. Sermons are meant to 'teach' (*docere*) *and* to 'move' (*movere*).[20] Listeners should learn and be moved – but: they should not be manipulated (!). They should get involved *and* 'think for themselves.' However, we can hardly do both at the same time. So where should we start? How can we get from one position to the other? In other words: How do these two aims interrelate?

In homiletics, this question is (controversially) discussed: rhetoric can encourage listeners to 'think for themselves,'[21] but it can also be used to manipulate the audience – which would be a problematic way of 'involve-

---

[18] See page 227 of this volume.
[19] See page 226 of this volume. Cf. also pages 170–172 of this volume. For the relation between parables and questions in the Gospel of Luke, see B.J. Koet, "An Uncomfortable Story from the New Testament: About Making Friends with the Mammon (Luke 16:1–13)," in: M. Klinker-De Klerck et al. (Eds.), Troubling Texts in the New Testament (CBET 113; Leuven: Peeters, 2022), 45–64.
[20] I. Karle, *Praktische Theologie* (Lehrwerk Evangelische Theologie 7; Leipzig: Leipziger Verlagsanstalt, 2020), 169.
[21] R. Conrad, *Weil wir etwas wollen! Plädoyer für eine Predigt mit Absicht und Inhalt* (Evangelisch-Katholische Studien zu Gottesdienst und Predigt 2; Neukirchen-Vluyn: Neukirchener Theologie, 2014), 17–41.

ment.' Therefore, some practical theologians prefer the aesthetic paradigm, which views the biblical text – and the sermon – as an open piece of art where the listener decides for him- or herself *how* to get involved.[22]

In religious education, some approaches in biblical didactics aim at drawing the child *into* the biblical text. They are asked to identify with certain biblical characters, to mourn with the Psalmist, to feel with those that ask Jesus for help.[23] This kind of involvement is meant to *prevent* them from asking 'unproductive' questions like: 'did this miracle really happen?' In comparison to this rather common didactic method of involvement via identification, we can spell out the quality of involvement via 'unasked questions' in more detail. Their way of involvement is subtler than asking children to identify with a certain character in the narrative because the 'metaleptic move' creates a (liminal) space between the child and the narrative. It locates the child on the edge of the narrative rather than within it.

Other approaches in biblical didactics aim at encouraging children and youngsters to 'think for themselves' *about* biblical narratives. They stress the distance between their world and the world of the biblical text.[24] According to these approaches, children and youngsters need help in order to learn from biblical texts. Someone has to bridge the gap between the Bible and our world of today. However, this help should be a form of empowerment. The aim is not cultivation, it is not about forming the student from the 'outside,' but 'subjectivation' in the sense of 'the process where, as educators, we encourage students to take up their own subject-ness, that is, to become subjects of their own life, rather than objects of what other people or forces may want them to be.'[25] The question would then be: How do 'counter-questions' make biblical texts more suitable for the purpose of 'subjectification'? And an answer could be: by pointing at a reflexive meta-level where biblical questions are questioned – as much as our own questions about the Bible and ourselves are.

---

[22] M. Nicol and A. Deeg, *Im Wechselschritt zur Kanzel: Praxisbuch dramaturgische Homiletik* (Göttingen: Vandenhoeck & Ruprecht, ²2013).

[23] I. Baldermann, *Einführung in die biblische Didaktik* (Die Theologie; Darmstadt: Wissenschaftliche Buchgesellschaft, ⁴2011), 15–23.

[24] S. Alkier and B. Dressler, "Wundergeschichten als fremde Welten lesen lernen: Didaktische Überlegungen zu Mk 4,35–41," in: B. Dressler and M. Meyer-Blanck (Eds.), *Religion zeigen: Religionspädagogik und Semiotik* (Grundlegungen 4; Münster: Lit, 1998), 163–187.

[25] G. Biesta, "Education, Education, Education: Reflections on a missing dimension," in: G. Biesta and P. Hamman (Eds.), *Religion and Education: The Forgotten Dimensions of Religious Education?* (Leiden: Brill, 2021), 8–19, here 8.

4. Unwanted questions

For obvious reasons, this volume highlights the importance of questions. However, in educational contexts, questions are not always welcome and not all kinds of questions are welcome at all times. I have already mentioned a question that is thought to be 'unproductive' with regard to miracle stories. Leon Mock points out that whereas questions are highly valued in Rabbinic Tradition, there are restrictions as to what kind of questions may be asked at what point of time:

> We find in Rabbinic literature that procedures emerge that are meant to regulate the asking of questions and their answering. In the Talmud we already find that a student should ask his master questions on the subject that is studied by his teacher. Asking 'off-topic' questions leads to the embarrassment of the master-teacher who will not be able to answer such questions correctly.[26]

In a classroom, asking 'off-topic' questions might not only embarrass the teacher, but it might also lead to chaos. Religious Education then runs the risk of being labelled a subject where anybody can say (ask) anything. In order to prevent this from happening, the teacher must guide discussions and pupils must learn to distinguish between 'on-topic' and 'off-topic' contributions. The consequences of this insight are extensive: from an educational perspective, they challenge a one-sided understanding of education as 'subjectification.' In contrast to Alexander von Humboldt who views 'education' very much in the sense of 'subjectification,'[27] Georg Hegel stresses that education aims at a process that he calls 'Sich Allgemein Machen.' Pupils need to learn to become members of society. They need to learn (from) what former generations have achieved. Hegel vividly rejects the concept of 'thinking for oneself' and instead stresses the need of cultivation:

> This inheritance ready at hand must be earned by the individual, i.e., learned. The teacher possesses this treasure; he pre-thinks it. The pupils re-think it.[28]

---

[26] See page 330 of this volume.
[27] Cf. A. Dörpinghaus, A. Poenitsch and L. Wigger, *Einführung in die Theorie der Bildung* (Grundwissen Erziehungswissenschaft; Darmstadt: Wissenschaftliche Buchgesellschaft, ⁴2012), 67–80.
[28] G. Hegel, *Encyclopaedia of the Philosophical Sciences Part One*, § 23 https://hegel.net/en/pdf/Hegel-Enc-1.pdf [accessed 14.04.2021]; cf. Dörpinghaus, Poenitsch and Wigger, *Theorie der Bildung*, 83–87.

5. Concluding remarks

Let us turn back to the child in Deuteronomy 6:20–25. The child asks a pertinent question and it is part of the community: it asks from 'within.' In this respect, the biblical scene can be regarded as an example of learning to be part of the community. At the same time, the child positions itself liminally, at the edge of the community. The question does not simply require a pre-thought answer. Rather, it bears a critical note. In this respect, the scene can be regarded as an example of 'subjectification.'

In a modern educational perspective (at least in mine), asking questions in and about the Bible is all about striking an adequate balance between 'subjectification' *and* 'cultivation.'

INDEX OF REFERENCES

BIBLE

Genesis

6–9	24	15:17–18a	10
6:2	321	15:17–21	10
11:27–25:18	7–20	15:18b–21	11
12:1	17	16	11–12, 19
12:1—3	8–9	16:7	11
12:1–22:19	20	16:8	11, 18, 74
12:2	7–8	16:9	11
12:6–8	8	16:9–12	11
12:7	7–9	16:10	11, 19
12:8	307	16:11	18
12:10-19	8	16:11–12	11
12:11–20	8	16:13	11–12, 18, 20
12:12–16	8	16:14	12
12:18	28	16:15	18
12:18–19	8	15:15–16	12
12:19	317	17:1–22	12–14
13	8–9	17:15–16	12
13:9	8	17:16	13
13:10–12	9	17:18	13,. 18
13:14–15	9	17:18–22	13
13:16	10	17:19	13, 16
13:17–18	10	17:19–21	19
13.18	10	17:20	18
14:18–23	9	17:22	16
15:1	9	17:23	18
15	9–11	17:23–27	13
15:2–3	9–10	18:1–15	12–14, 16
15:4	10	18:9	13
15:4–5	9	18:10	13–14, 16
15:5	10	18:11–12	17
15:6	9	18:12	13–14
15:7	9–10	18:12–15	13, 16
15:8	10	18:13	13–14
15:9	9	18:13-14	17
15:9–11	10	18:13–15	18
15:9–16	9	18:14	14, 16–17, 19, 21
15:13	10	18:15	14
15:13–16	10	18:16–33	14–16
15:15	10	18:16	14
		18:16–23	15
		18:17	15
		18:17–19	15

INDEX OF REFERENCES

18:18	19	32:5	28
18:33	14–15	32:20	97
18:19b	5	40:7	57
18:20	15	44:4	28
18:21	15		
18:25	16	*Exodus*	
18:28	16	1:10	74
19–20	16	3:6–7	12
19:2	28	3:11	17
19:19	28	4:10	28
20:18	16	5:2	69
21:1	16	5:12	28
21:1–2	16	5:22–26	28
21:1–7	14, 16–17, 20	8:25	131
21:3	16	12:24–27	105
21:4	16	12:38	26
21:6	16	15	301
21:6–7	16	15:11	70, 301
21:7	17, 21	15:22	29
21:8–21	18–20	15:25	73
21:10	19	16	27
21:11–13	18	16:4	73
21:13	18	17:1–7	29, 71
21:15–20	18	17:2	72
21:17	18–19	17:3	26
21:18	19	18:24	305
21:19	18–19	19:3	26
21:26	131	20:20	73
22:1	73	23:10–11	62
22:1–19	18–20	34:5	26
22:2	19		
22:3–9	19	*Leviticus*	
22:7	21	13:1–3	326
22:8	19	13:56	12
22:14	12, 19–21	14:36	12
22:15–18	20	18:24–30	54
22:16	20	25:35–38	43
22:17	19		
22:17–18	18	*Numbers*	
22:18	19–20	11:1–3	24, 26
22:19	20	11	23–34
24:7	19	11:4	26–27, 29–30
25:5–9	18	11:4–6	27
25:19–35:19	7, 19	11:4–15	24
26:3	19	11:4–25	23
27:18	242	11:5	26, 27
27:32	242	11:7–9	27
27:45	28	11:11-12	28, 33

11:11–13	27–29	6:4	38
11:12	28	6:4–5	47
11:13	28–29, 33	6:4–6	37
11:14–15	25, 33	6:4–9	35
11:16	23	6:7	35–36, 44
11:16–17	24–25, 29, 31–33	6:7b–9	38, 47
11:18–20	29, 33	6:10–19	38
11:18–24a	24	6:17	38
11:20	29	6:20	35, 38–42, 44–46
11:21–22	30, 33	6:20–25	35–36, 39, 43, 357–
11:21–23	25		358, 363
11:22–23	29–31	6:21	40, 43
11:23	30	6:21–25	38, 40
11:24a	25	6:24	43
11:24b–30	23–24, 31–32	7:1–3	54
11:29	31	8:2–16	73
11:31	24	8:3	27
11:31–34	30	8:16	27
11:31–35	24–25	11:8	54
11:35	25	12:28	321
13:17–21	67	13:4	73
13:18	67	15	62
13:19	67	15:15	40
14:9	60	16:21	40
14:33	26	17:8	321–323
14:41	28	17:8–13	322
20:13	305	17:10	322
21:35	131	17:11	322–323
22–24	69	17:12	322
32:1	26	20:19	145
		23:6	54
Deuteronomy		24:18	40
1:9–18	305	30:11–14	321
2:2–6	305		
3:3	131		
3:24	98	*Joshua*	
3:24–28	305	3:11	104
4:6	321	3:13	104
4:34	73	3:15	350
4:44–49	39	4:19–24	105
4:45	39	4:20	350
5:6	40	8:22	131
5:6–21	46	10:11–14	121
5:15	40	10:13	121–122
5:29	194	11:12	188
6:1	38	22:16	60
6:1–3	37	22:18	60
6	35–47	22:29	60

Judges

2:22	73
3:1–4	73
9:28	69

Ruth

3:9	242
4:16	28

1 Samuel

2:16	314
20:26b	131
18:10	31
21:1–6	217
25:10	69
26:14–15	69

2 Samuel

4:4	28
4:6	46
11:3	305
14:14b	131
16:10	188
18:29	153
19:22	188
22:44	55

1 Kings

8:23	99
17:18	188
18:27	106
18:29	31
21:10	90
21:13	90
22	69

2 Kings

3:13	188
4:1–7	42–43
4:6	42
10:1	28
10:5	28
10:22	17
19:35	122

1 Chronicles

16:30	104
19:18	104

2 Chronicles

32:31	73
33:13	53
36:23	174

Ezra

1:3	174
3–6	50–52
4:11	49
4:17–22	49
4:21	51
4:22	49
4:23	50
5:1–2	51
5	50, 52
5:3	51
5:5	51
5:6	52
5:6–17	42
5:9	51–52
5:11–16	52
5:13	51
6:1	51
6:1–5	53
6:3	51
6:6–12	53
6:12	51
6:13–15	53
7–10	53–54
9	53
9–10	53
9:10a	54
9:10b	54
9:11–12	54
9:14	55
10:3	55

Nehemiah

1:3	58
1:5–11	53, 56
1:11c	56
2:1–2	57
2:2	56
2:3	58
2:4	58
2:6	59
2:7–9	59
2:19	59

INDEX OF REFERENCES 369

3:34	60	13:2–3	298
5:9	61	18:44	55
5:13	61	22:5	55
6:2	62	22:8	59
6:11	62	22:9	55
9:6–37	53	26:2	73
9:15	27	31:2	55
9:20	27	37:40	55
13:11	63	44:22	272
		44:23	278
Esther		44:35	278
2:7	28	49:11	113
2:18	57	55:6	194
5:6	57	69:14	305
		71:2	55
Job		73:10	298
1–2	92–93	73:25	99
1:21	94	78:5	298
1:22	93	78:17–30	24
2	81, 83, 91–93	78:23–25	27
2:3	84, 90	78:27	24
2:5	90	78:40–41	71
2:9	81, 84–85, 88, 90, 94	78:56	71
2:10	91, 93–94	79:10	106
2:13	83	89:7	317
3	91–93	95:9	71
3–31	92	96:9	104
3:1–42:6	93	105:40	27
8:2	17	106:2	17
11:2	313	106:14–15	24
19:17	81–82	113:1a	101
21:3	59	113:1–3	100
28	92	113	98–101
28:9	350	113:2–3	99–100
28:9–11	350	113:3–4	100
28:11	350	113:4	100–101
31:10	81	113:5	98, 101
32–37	92	113:5–6	98–100
33:3	17	113:6	98
35:2	242	113:7–9	100–101
38:1–42:7	86, 92	114:1	104
38:4–7	70	114:1–4	101–102
42:5	92	114:1–6	103–104
42:7–17	92	114	98, 101–105
42:17	88	114:2	102, 104
		114:3	104
Psalms		114:3b	103
10:3	90	114:5–6	101

114:7a	104	25:20	57		
114:7	104	27:17	325		
114:7-8	104	30:9	116		
114:7-9	101				
114:9	101	*Qohelet*			
115:1-2	107	5:5	116		
115:1-3	106	7:10	116		
115	98, 105–110				
115:1c	108	*Isaiah*			
115:2	105	1:1	128		
115:2-3	107	1–12	125–127, 130, 135, 139		
115:3	107–108				
115:4	106–107	1:2–4	127		
115:4-6	107	1:4a	128		
115:4-8	107–109	1:5a	125, 127		
115:7-8	107	1:5-6	127		
115:7b	110	1:6a	127		
115:8	106–107, 110	1:11	125		
115:9a	108	1:12	125		
115:9-13	107–108	1:17	129		
115:10a	108	1:23	129		
115:11a	108	2:1	128		
115:12a	108	2:8	143		
115:12-13	108	2:10	299		
115:15-15	109	2:10-22	130		
115:14-18	108–109	2:18	143		
115:15-16	107	2:20	143		
115:16	106, 110	2:22b	125		
115:16-17	109	3:15	122		
115:17	109–110	4	125		
115:18	109	5:1-7	129		
116	110	5	128, 130		
118:22	218	5:4	125		
119:2	39	5:5	145		
119:22	39	5:5-6	145		
137	97	5:8	128, 133		
146:7-8	314	5:8-10	128		
		5:8-24	128–129, 133		
Proverbs		5:11	133		
3:15-18	321	5:11-12	128		
3:28	116	5:18	133		
8:22	321	5:18-19	128		
8:30	321	5:20	128, 133		
8:31	321	5:21	128, 133		
20:9	116	5:22	133		
20:22	116	5:22-23	128		
24:12	116	5:24-25	133		
24:29	116	5:24c-25	128		

INDEX OF REFERENCES

5:25	132	10:8–11	134–136, 139–147
5:25b	133	10:8b	139
6:1–5	139	10:9	139–141
6	130, 133	10:10a	143
6:3	139	10:10	139, 141, 144
6:6	125	10:10–11	142–144
6:9–10	138	10:10b	143
6:11	125, 130	10:11a	143
7	128, 130, 133	10:11	141–142
7–10	130	10:11b	143, 145
7:13	125	10:12a	134, 136
7:13–14	134	10:12	134, 144
8	133	10:12–15	136, 147
8:19	125	10:12b	134, 136
9:1–6	133	10:13	136, 139, 144, 146
9	125	10:13–14	135–136, 144, 147
9:3	135	10:14	139, 144
9:7–20	132–133	10:15a	135
9:11	132–133	10:15	135–136, 139–146
9:16	132–133	10:15b	135, 145
9:20	128, 132–133	10:24	135
10:1	131, 133	11	125
10:1–2	130–132, 136–137	12	125
10:1–4	128–134, 136–137	13–14	135
10:1–6	128	13:10	298
10:1–15	128–130, 136	14:5	135
10	125, 130	14:18	138
10:2b	129	14:32	305
10:2	128, 130–131	19:1	143
10:3a	132	19:21	299
10:3	131–132, 137–139, 146	21:9	143
		23:8	17
10:3–4a	131, 136	28:27	135
10:3b	132, 137	30:22	143
10:4a	131–132	30:31–32	135
10:4b	128, 131–133, 136	31:7	143
10:5	129, 133–134, 139, 143	36–37	146
		37:13	305
10:5–6	128–129, 134, 136	40:12	17
10:5–11	134, 136	40:12–13	70
10:5–15	4, 128–129, 133–136, 139, 143, 146	40:13–14	305
		40:18	70, 305
10:5b	134–135	40:26	17
10:6a	129	40:26–27	70
10:6	130, 145	41:2	17, 70
10:7	136	41:4	17, 70
10:7–11	134	41:26	17, 70
10:7–15	134	42:23	70, 174

372 INDEX OF REFERENCES

43:9	70	1:2a	158
43:13	70	1:2–3:2	158
44:7	70	1:2b	159
45:21	70	1:2b–e	159
46:1	143	1:2c	159
46:5	70	1:3–2:3	158
48:5	143	1:3–2:9	158
48:17	70	2:10a	158
49:23	28	3:1	159
50:10	174	3:3	153, 156, 158–159, 161
58:7	305		
61:1	314	3:3–5	152, 154, 156
		3:3–6	155
Jeremiah		3:3–8	149–161
4:30	242	3:3b	152
10:6–7	301	3:4a	155, 159
23:14a	131	3:4a–b	154
29:26	31	3:4–5	154
		3:4–8	157
Ezekiel		3:4b	152, 155
2:3	60	3:4c	159
13:3b	131	3:4c–d	154
16:30	60	3:4d	152
21:11–12	311	3:5	154
24:15–18	311	3:5b	152
37:1–14	308, 311	3:5d	152
37:3	303, 311	3:6a	155–1556
37:3–4	303	3:6a–b	152, 154
37:4	303	3:6	152, 154–156, 161
37:7–8	309–310	3:6b	154, 156, 159
37:9–10	309–310	3:6c	154
37:11–14	310	3:6c–d	152
37:21	310	3:6d	155–156
		3:7a	155–156
Daniel		3:7	152–153, 155–156
3:10	51	3:7–8	155–156
9:4–19	53	3:7b	155–156, 160
9:9	60	3:8a	155, 159
12:1	303	3:8	153, 155, 157
12:10	73	3:8b	153
		3:8c	155, 159
Joel		3:8d	153
2:17	106	4:1	159
3:4	298	5:1	159
		5:18	159–160
Amos		7:1–3	160
1:1	159	7:7–9	160
1:1c	159	7:8b	160

7:8c	160	4:13	77
7:10–17	159–160	4:14	77
7:10e	160	4:15	77
7:13b	160	5:2	67, 70, 78
7:14c	160	5:3–4	66–67
7:15b–d	161	5:3–6:2	78
7:16a	159–160	5:5	67, 77
8:1–3b	160	5:6–19	67
8:3c	160	5:11	75–76
8:9	298	5:17–18	68
		5:20	77
Micah		5:20–21	69
6:14	55	5:21	77
		5:23	69
		5:23–24	75
Nahum		5:24	74
1:2	317	6:2	66, 69, 71, 78–79
		6:2–3	70
Habakkuk		6:3–4	70
2:2–3	256	6:4	77
2:4	268	6:13	77
		6:13–17	71
Haggai		6:19	77
2:3	174	6:20–21	67
		7:8–16	75
Zechariah		7:19	77
1:8	302	7:19–20	70
1:9	302	7:28	77
1:10	302	7:29	77
		7:30	77
Tobit		7:30–32	70–71, 74
6:7	307	8	73
6:16	307	8:11	71, 77
7:3-5	307	8:12	66, 70–72, 76, 78
12:13	73	8:12–16	71
		8:12–23	71
Judith		8:13	77
2:5	77	8:13–14	72
2:5–13	70	8:14	66, 70, 77
2:13	77	8:15–27	71
2:14	77	8:16	77
2:15	77	8:17–23	71
3:7–8	66	8:23	77
3:8	70	8:24–27	71
4:2	77	8:25	73, 77
4:5	66	8:25–26	72
4:6–7	75	8:25–27	73
4:11	77	8:26	73

8:27	73, 77	*Wisdom*	
8:31	77	1:2	73
8:32–34	73	2:17	73
8:33	77	2:24	73
8:35	77	3:4–6	73
9:1	77	3:5	73
9	74, 78	11:9	73
9:2	77	11:9–10	73
9:7	77	12:2	73
9:8	77	12:26	72
10:1–4	74	16:6	73
10–13	78	18:20	73
10:5–10	74	18:25	73
10:12	66, 73–74, 78	19:5	73
10:12–13	74		
10:12–19	78	*Ben Sira*	
10:14	75	1–43	121
10:15	77	1:2–3	122
10:19	66, 73, 75, 78–79	1:6–7	122
11:4	77	1:11–30	118
11:6	77	1:13	70
11:10	77	1:26	119
11:11	77	2:1	73
11:17	77	2:10	122
11:20–23	76	2:14	122
11:22	77	2:15–16	119
12:3	66, 76	3:8	117
12:3–14	78	3:12	117
12:4	76–77	3:17	117
12:8	77	4:1	117
12:10–12	76	4:17	73
12:11	76	4:20	117
12:13	76–77	5:1	114
12:14	66, 76–79	5:1–6	115
13:1	77	5:1–8	114–115
13:4	77	5:1b	114
13:7	77	5:3a	114
13:15	77	5:3–4	112, 114–116
13:16	77	5:4a	114
13:18	77	5:4c	115
14:13	77	5:4	114
15:8	77	5:6a	115
15:10	77	6:7	73
16:5	77	6:37	119
16:12	77	10:19a–b	118
16:13	77	10:19	113, 118–119
16:16	77	10:19–11:6	118
16:17	77	10:19c–d	119

10:28	117	33:12	118
11:7–28	117	34:12c	115
11:10	117	35:1–16	120
11:14	117	35:3	17
11:18	117	35:15	121
11:18–26	116	35:17–26	121
11:20	116–117	36:1–17	121
11:20–26	116–117	37:2	121
11:21	116	37:2–3	122
11:22–26	116–117	37:7–15	118
11:23–24	112, 115, 117	37:8	122
13:2	122	37:12	119
13:11	73	37:27	73, 117
13:17–18	122	38:5	121
13:17–23	113	38:9	117
13:23	113, 122	38:16	117
13:24	113	38:25	122
14:3	122	39:4	73
14:11	117	39:17	115
14:11–19	113	39:21	115
14:15	113, 121–122	39:34	115
14:16	113	40:28	117
15:11a	115	42:2	117
15:15	119	42:22	121
16:17	112, 115	42:25	122
16:20–22	122	43:3	122
16:24	117	44–50	121
18:4–5	70	44:19–20	73
18:4–8	122	44:20	73, 117
18:15	117	45:5	117
18:23	73	45:17	117
21:1	117	46:1–8	121
22:10	122	46:1b	122
22:14	122	46:3–4	121
23:27	119	46:4	113, 121
27:5	73	47:11	117
27:7	73	48:4	121
31:19	121	48:21	122
31:21–27	120	49:11	121
31:21–31	120	49:12	121
31:21–32:20	120	50:27	111
31:28–31	119–121	51:24	122
32:2	119		
32:14–33:18	117	*Baruch*	
32:23	119	1:15–3:8	53
32:24	119		
33:7–9	117	*1 Esdras*	
33:7–15	117	5:6	57

INDEX OF REFERENCES

1 Maccabees
2:52   73

4 Maccabees
16:18–20   73

Matthew
3:10   256
5:46   164
6:25   221
6:25–26   172
6:26   221
6:31   221
7:3–4   180
7:5   181
7:9   164
11:2–4   314
11:16   178
12:1–8   216
12:22–30   221
12:23   221
15:14   172
16:1   241
16:23   259
19:16–22   215
21:23–27   217
21:24   218
22:15–22   218
22:18   218
22:19   218
22:39   47
24:28   168
24:42–44   221
28:2   194, 196

Mark
1:1   187, 190, 198–199
1:9   190
1:12–13   187, 192
1:14   187
1:14–15   188
1:21   223
1:21–28   197
1:22   186, 192
1:23–26   186, 188, 192
1:24   184–194, 198
1:27   185–187, 199, 223
1:27b   185

2:1–12   214, 219
2:7   199, 214
2:8–9   186, 199, 214
2:16   199
2:18   199, 214, 219
2:18–21   214
2:19   199, 214
2:22   187
2:23–28   214, 216
2:24   185, 200, 214
2:25   214, 217
2:25–26   186, 200
3:1–6   220
3:2   220
3:4   185–186, 200, 221
3:6   187, 192
3:22–30   190–191
3:23   200
3:33   185, 200
4:13   200
4:21   185, 200
4:30   200
4:38   187, 192, 200
4:40   185, 200
4:41   186, 200
5:7   186, 188–191, 201
5:9   186, 201
5:30   201
5:31   201
5:35   186, 201
5:39   186, 201
6:2   185, 201
6:3   201
6:24   201
6:37   186, 201
6:38   202
7:5   202
7:18   185
7:18–19   202
8:4   186, 202
8:5   202
8:10–11   214
8:12   202
8:17   186, 202
8:17–21   185
8:18   186, 202
8:19-20   202
8:21   203

8:23	203	12:12	193
8:27	185, 203	12:13–17	214, 218
8:29	185, 203	12:14	186, 205, 214
8:33	192, 259	12:15	205, 214, 218
8:35	192	12:16	205, 218
8:36	185, 192	12:23	186, 205
8:36–37	186, 203	12:24	185–186, 205, 214
9:1	257	12:26	186, 205
9:7	190	12:28	206
9:11	203	12:30–31	47
9:12	186, 203	12:35	186, 206
9:16	186, 203	12:37	185–186, 206
9:21	203	13:2	185–186, 206
9:19	186, 185	13:4	206
9:22	187, 192	13:8	299
9:22–23	185	13:24ff	299
9:28	203	13:30	257
9:33	186, 204	14:4	186, 206
9:35	192	14:6	186, 206
9:41	192	14:12	185, 206
9:50	186, 204	14:14	206
10:1a	214	14:19	206
10:2–12	214	14:25	257
10:3	204	14:37	206
10:12b	214	14:48	186, 207
10:17	185–186, 204	14:60	185, 207
10:17–19	213–214	14:60–61	225
10:17–22	215	14:61	207
10:18	204, 213	14:62	225
10:20	216	14:63	186, 207
10:21	216	14:63–64	225
10:22	216	14:64	207
10:26	204	15:2	207
10:43–44	192	15:4	186, 207
11:3	204	15:9	186, 207
11:5	204	15:12	207
11:13	193	15:14	186, 207
11:17	204	15:34	186, 207
11:17–33	217	15:46	196
11:18	187, 192	16:3	184–186, 193–198, 207
11:27–33	214		
11:28	205, 214	16:4a	193
11:29	214	16:4b	193
11:30	205	16:6	197
11:31	205	16:9–20	197
11:32	205		
12:9	187, 192, 205	*Luke*	
12:11	205	1–2	224

2:11	258	11:11	164, 212, 317
2:29–32	224	11:12	212
2:40–52	223–224, 227	11:13	175
2:43	224	11:14	221
2:46	224, 226	11:14–23	221
3:6	256	11:29	214
3:7	257	12:13	221
3:9	257	12:13–21	221
3:10–14	215	12:14	221
3:17	257	12:16–21	221
3:22	258	12:23	221
4:21	258	12:23–24	172
4:22	221	12:24	221
5:17–26	214, 219	12:25	317
5:21–22	219	12:28	258
5:26	258	12:29	221
5:33	214, 219	12:36–40	221
5:33–39	214	12:38	257
5:34	219	12:41	215, 221
5:36–39	219	12:42	221
6:1–5	214, 216	12:45	257
6:3	217, 220	13:2	212
6:8	221	13:4	212
6:9	221	13:6–9	257
6:32	164	13:18–19	221
6:39	172, 180, 212	13:22–30	221
6:41	180	13:23	215, 221
6:41–42	180	13:32	258
6:42	181	13:33	258
7:18–23	314	14	221
7:24	212	14:3	212
7:25	212	14:5	212, 317
7:31	178	14:28	212, 317
7:36–50	221	14:28–30	174
7:41–42	221	14:31	212
8:24	211	14:31–32	174
8:25b	211	14:53–65	225
9:27	257	14:57–59	225
9:41	259	14:48	225
10:9	257	14:49	225
10:11	257	14:60	225
10:25–38	222, 226–227, 360	14:62	225
10:27	222	15:4	317
10:28	222	15:5–7	176
10:30–36	222	15:8–10	174
10:36	222	17:7	317
11:5	317	17:7–10	174
11:5–8	174	17:9	212

17:20	215	24:13–35	223, 226
17:20–37	257	24:14–15	223
17:37	168	24:19–24	223
18:1–8	257	24:25	259
18:7	212	24:26	223
18:8	257	24:49	247
18:18	215–216		
18:18–19	214	*John*	
18:18–23	215	1:19	236, 242, 244
18:19	215–216	1:38a	229–130
18:21	216	2:4	188
18:22	216	2:18	233
18:23	216	3:10	233
18:24	216	4:27a	236
18:24–27	216	4:27b	236
18:19	216	5:19–23	176
19:5	258	6:53	257
19:9	258	7:20	233
19:11	257, 259	7:35	236
19:12	257	8:25	236, 242, 244
20:1	219	8:33	236
20:1–8	214, 217	11:9	235
20:1–19	218	11:47	236
20:2	214	11:56	236
20:3	214, 218	12:27	236
20:5–6	218	17:21	210
20:9	257	17:23	210
20:17	218	17:34	210
20:19	218	20:15	243
20:19–21	218	20:31	245, 359
20:20–26	214	21:1	240
20:21	218	21:4	241
20:22	212, 214	21:5	243
20:24	214	21:7	241, 244
20:26	219	21:12	236, 240–244
21:8	257	21:12b	243
21:28	259	21:15	233, 243
21:31	257	21:17	236, 243
21:32	257	21:20	236
22:18	257	21:23	236
22:27	212		
22:34	258	*Acts*	
22:49	212	1:3	247, 259
22:61	258	1:4	247
22:66	225–226	1:4–5	247
23:39	212	1:7	260–261
23:43	258	1:7–8	248, 256, 261
24	211	1:11	258

1:15–26	252	7	269, 279
3:26	260	7:7	266, 269–270
4:9	258	8	266, 279
6–12	248	8:31	266, 269
13–28	248	8:31–34	271
13:33	258	8:31–39	6, 265–268, 270–272
19:40	258	8:32	271
20:26	258	8:33	271, 273–275, 277
22:3	258	8:33–34	263, 272–278
22:5	225	8:34	271
24:21	258	8:34–37	271
26:2	258	8:35	271, 274
26:29	258	8:35–37	271
27:33	258	8:37	279
28:28	262	8:39	271, 279
28:29	262	9:1	272
28:31	262	9	279
		9–11	266–268, 279
Romans		9:6b	267
1:1–7	264, 268	9:14	266, 269–270
1:8–15	268	9:19	266
1:16–17	264, 268	9:30	266, 269
1:18–3:20	268	9:30–31	270
3:1	266	9:32	266
3:3	266	10:8	266
3:5	266	11	267
3:7	266	11:2	266
3:9	266	11:4	266
3:21-26	268	11:7	266
3:21–31	264	11:26	267
3:27	266, 268	14:4	242
3:27–4:25	268	14:10	266
4:1	266, 270		
4:1–8:39	264	*1 Corinthians*	
4:3	266	1:20	281, 290
4:16–25	269	4:7	290
5:1	271	8	267
5:1–11	270–271	8–12	267
5	266, 269	9:1	281, 290
5:1–8:39	268, 270, 272, 278	9:4–5	285
5:3	271	9:7	290
5:5	271	10:23–11:1	282
5:8	271	11	284
5:9	271	11:2	284
5:10	271	11:16	284
5:11	271	11:17	284, 286, 291
6:1	266, 269–270	11:17–21	292
6	279	11:17–22	284
6:15	266	11:17–34	282–285

11:18–19	284	6:10	293, 296–298, 304
11:20	286	6:10–11	300
11:20–21	284, 287	6:11	293, 297, 300
11:21	284, 286	6:12	298
11:22a	285–288, 291	6:13	298
11:22a–c	284, 288, 290–292	6:14	299
11:22	282–292	6:15	299
11:22b	285–286, 288	6:17	293, 296–300, 304
11:22b–c	287–288, 291	7:1–8	293, 299, 302
11:22c	285–286, 288	7:9	303
11:22d	285, 289, 291	7:10–12	303
11:22d–e	290–292	7:13	294, 302–304
11:22d–f	284	7:13–15b	302
11:22e	285, 289	7:14	303
11:22f	285–286	7:15	294
11:23a–b	285	11:15ff	299
11:23	284, 291	12:17	298
11:23–26	284–285	13:3–4	300
11:23c–24	285	13:4	294, 300–302, 304
11:25	285	13:5	298, 301
11:26	285	13:6–7	301
11:27–30	284–285	15:1	301
11:31–32	285	15	301
11:31–34	284–285	15:2	301
11:33–34	285	15:3	301–302
11:34	287, 292	15:4	294, 300–302, 304
11:34d	284	16:17ff	299
12:1	284	17:7	294, 302–304
12–14	284	17:7–18	302
14:36	281	17:9	304
15:12	317	18:17	299–300
		18:18	294, 296–297, 299–300, 304
1 Timothy			
4:14	225	19:20	294, 301
		20:12	298
Revelation		21:1–22:5	294
1:4	295	21:2	297, 299
1:19	297	21:3	297
4:1	295	21:10	296
4:6	295, 301	21:11	300
4:8	295	22:1	297
4:9–11	295	22:20	297, 300
5:2	293, 295–297, 301, 304		
5:3	295, 301	Q DOCUMENT	
5:4	303		
5:9	293, 297	3:9	176
5:9–10	301	3:17	176
5:12	293	4:4	171

6:20	171	15:3	174
6:32	172	15:4	173
6:34	172	15:4–7	178, 182
6:39	169, 173, 177, 180	16:16	171
6:41–42	177	16:29–32	179
6:42	168	17:6	182
6:43–44	177	17:31–35	178
6:44	173	17:37	168, 178
7:8	176	19:12–26	178
7:19	182		
7:24–26	166, 168, 171		
7:28	171	**DEAD SEA SCROLLS**	
7:31–35	177		
10:9	171	*1QapGen ar*	
10:15	173	2.16–17	307
10:22	176	20.26	307, 317
11:2	171	22.32	307, 317
11:9–13	175–177, 181		
11:11	164, 171, 173–174	*1QH^a*	
11:12	171, 173	3 bottom 5	317
11:13	175	5.19–20	317–318
11:14–20	177	5.20	317
11:16	179	7.2	317
11:17	171	7:17	317
11:18	171	7.24	317
11:20	171	9.23	317
11:29	179	9.25–26	317
11:29–32	179	11.24	317
11:34–35	176	12.29	317
11:35	179	15.28	317
11:50–51	179	15.32	317
11:52	171	18.3	317
12:6	173	18.5–6	317
12:22–31	176, 181	18.6–7	317
12:23	173	18.7	317
12:23–28	173, 177	18.10–11	317–318
12:24	173–174	18.12	317
12:28	173	19.3–4	317
12:31	171	19.24	317
12:42–46	177	20.27	317
12:54–56	176, 178	20.27–28	317
12:56	181	20.31	317
13:18	170–171, 178, 182	20.32	317
13:20	171, 178	20.32–33	317
13:25–27	176	20.33	317
13:28	171	20.33–34	317
14:34	169, 178	20.34	317
14:34–35	181	20.34–35	317

INDEX OF REFERENCES

20.35	317		11.20	317–318
21 top 4–5	317		11.20–22	318
21 top 11	317		11.21	317
21 bottom 6	317		11.22	317
21 bottom 12	317			
22 bottom 10	317–318		*4QEn^d ar*	
23 bottom 7	317		1 1.5	307
26 bottom 10	317		1 2.9	307

1QH^b *4QEn^e ar*
1 1.2   317   2 2.6–7   307
1 1.6–7   317
   4QEn^g ar
1QIsa^a   5.14–16   318
13:4   305
30:17–18   305   *4QH^a*
33:13–14   305   7 iii 16   317
33:17–18   305
40:1–2   305   *4QMyst^a*
         3 2.2   317
1QM   3 2.3   317
10.8–9   317–318   8 5   317
10.9–11   317–318   8 7   320
13.13–14   317
13.14   317   *4QNum^b*
         9   305
1QMyst
1 1.1–7   313   *4QpaleoExod^m*
1 1.2–3   314   29:7–17   305
1 1.3–7   312
1 1.8   314   *4QPs^a*
1 1.8 12   312–313   19 2.32   305
1 1.9   316
1 1.10   316   *4QSam^a*
1 1.11   317   90–91   305

1QpHab   *4QTob^b ar*
2:1–10   179   4 1.12   307
         4 2.12–13   307
1QS   4 3.5–7   307
5.17   317   14 1.8–9   307
6.11–13   319   14 2.8–10   307
6.14   320
6.15–16   320   *4Q185*
6.17   320   1–2 1.7–8   318
6.18   320   1–2 1.8   317
7.18–20   320   1–2 2.2–3   317
7.21   320   1–3 11.1   316

4Q212

5.14–16	317
5.17–18	317
5.18–19	317
5.20–21	317
5.22	317

4Q299

3 2.7	317

4Q301

1 2	320
2 1	320
2 4	317

4Q302

2 2.6	316

4Q380

1 2.5–6	317

4Q381

15 6–7	317
31 4	317
31 6	317–318
76–77 9	316
76–77 10	317

4Q385

2	311
2 1	309
2 1–10	308
2 2–3	309–310
2 2–9	310
2 3	309
2 3–4	309
2 3–9	309
2 5–6	309
2 6–7	309
2 7–9	309, 311
2 8–9	309
2 9	309
2 9–10	309
3.1-3	311
3	311
3 4–5	311
4 4	308

4Q386

1 1.1	310
1 1.1–2	311
1 1.1–10	308
1 1.8–10	311
1 2.1–2	310
1 2.2–3	310
1 2.3	310
1 2.3–4	310
1 2.4–5	310
1 2.6	310
1 2.7–8	311
1 2.7–10	310

4Q393

3 5	317

4Q400

2 6	317
2 7	317–318

4Q401

16 4	317

4Q411

1 2.7	317

4Q416

2 1.5	317
2 1.5–6	320

4Q417

1 1.10	317
1 1.10–11	320
1 1.16	317
1 1.23	317

4Q418

7 6	317
55 7–8	318
55 11	316
69 2.3–4	316
69 2.4–5	317
69 2.5	317
69 2.10–14	316–317
69 2.12	316
69 2.13	316

INDEX OF REFERENCES

69 2.14	316	22:9–10	317
107 1	320	24 15	317–318
4Q423		*11Q11*	
2 1	316	5.6	319
4Q424		*CD-A*	
3 1	320	6.15–16	313
3 2	320	9.5	316–317
4Q491c			
1 8	317	OLD TESTAMENT APOCRYPHA	
1 9	317		
1 10	317	*Assumption of Moses*	
		10:4–5	299
4Q511			
2 2.6	317	*2 Baruch*	
18 2.5	316	85:10	257
30 4	316		
30 4–5	317	*1 Enoch*	
30 6	317	22:6	307
		23:3	307
4Q521		27:1	307
1-15	314–316	93	179
2 2.4	316		
		4 Ezra	
4Q543		4:33–50	257
6.1-6	307	4:35–36	298
		6:144ff	299
4Q544		8:61	257
1.10–14	307	11:44	257
4Q552		*Sibylline Oracles*	
1 2.4	307	3:80–91	299
1 2.8	307	3:369–397	299
1 2.11	307		
		Testament of Job	
4Q553		25:7–10	89
6 2.4	307		
6 2.5–6	307	*Testament of Solomon*	
		2.1	242
11QT^a		3.6	242
61.2–3	319	5.1–2	242
61.12–62.5	319	7.3	242
		10.2	242
11Q5		12.2	242
22 9	317	13.2–3	242

INDEX OF REFERENCES

14.2	242
17.2	242
18.2	242
18.4	242
22.19	242
25.1	242

PHILO AND JOSEPHUS

Philo
De virtutibus 7   169
Quod omnis probus liber
  sit 1.1–2   248

Josephus
Contra Apio-
  nem 2.1   249

RABBINIC LITERATURE

Mishnah
Avot 1:1	350
Avot 2:8	346
Berakhot 1:1	335
Sanhedrin 11:2	323

Tosephta
Jevanot 1:6	350
Sanhedrin 7:6–7	331
Sanhedrin 7:10	330

Talmud Bavli
bBaba Metzia 59b	327
bBaba Metzia 84a	325
bBaba Metzia 86a	326
bEruvin 13b	322
bHullin 43b	331
bKiddushin 49b	329
bMenahot 29b	347
bMegillah 6b	331
bSanhedrin 86b	323
bShabbat 3b	330
bShabbat 30b–31a	349
bShabbat 31a	330
bTa'anith 7a	325

Avot de-Rabbi Natan A
6	344, 352
15	348–349

Avot de-Rabbi Natan B
12	344
29	348–349

Bereshit Rabbah
24:7	352
26:5	321

Eikha Rabbah
3:21	341

Mikilta de Rabbi Ishmael
Bahodesh 4	350
Bahodesh 5	347

Sifre Devarim
152	323

Pesiqta Rabbati
Jevanot	350
Nedarim 30b	352

Semahot de Rabbi Hiya
4:1	340

ANCIENT WORLD

Aeschylus
Persians 230-245   67

Aristophanes
Aves 1497–1499   261

Aristotle
De interpretation
17a1–8	232
Rhetorica 1419a	269

Babrius
Fabulae 134   169

Demosthenes
2 In Aphobum 18.1   174

INDEX OF REFERENCES

3 Olynthiaca 16   261
Orationes III   261

Dionysius of Halicarnassus
De Demosthenis
dictione 43.17   174

Epictetus
Diatribai 3.1.22   242

Herodotus
Histories 7.101-14   67
Histories 9.110   57

Historiae Alexandri Magni
I 37.8   174
I 37.29   174
I 37.37   174
I 39.9   174
II 16.8   174

Homer
Ilias 21.150   74
Odyssea 1.170   74
Odyssea 10.325   74

Plato
Respublica 8, 554B   169

Plutarch
Moralia Sera 4.549–550F   261

Quintilian
Institutio oratoria 9.2.6–16   184

Sophocles
Fragments 590   261
Oedipus Rex 70   174

Xenophon
Cyropaedia 1.3.9   57
Cyropaedia 8.4.3   57

AUGUSTINE

Confessiones
XI 14,17   2

Contra Epistolam Manichaei quam vocant Fundamenti liber unus
9   250

Contra Felicem Manichaeum libri duo
1.4   250

De Doctrina Christiana
III 3,3   274
III 3,10-12   277

Enarrationes in Psalmos
XXIX 2,7   83

INDEX OF MODERN AUTHORS

Abbott, E.A. 242
Abegg, M. 305
Ackroyd, P.R. 128
Adams, E. 262
Agamben, G. 264
Aland, B. 167
Aland, K. 167
Albertz, R. 62
Alden, R.L. 87
Alexander, L. 249
Alfaro, J. 71
Alkier, S. 361
Allen, L. 99–100, 104
Al-Suadi S. 174
Amigues, S. 57
Andersen, F.I. 82
Anderson, R.D. 249
Argall, R.A. 114
Armstrong, K. 40
Arnold, B.T. 2
Ashley, T.R. 25, 27
Auerbach, E. 343
Augustin, M. 65

Bacher, W. 350
Baden, J.S. 24
Bakker, M. de 3-4, 288–289
Baldermann, I. 361
Balentine, S.E. 90–91
Bar-Asher, M. 65, 306
Bar-Efrat, S. 119
Barré, M.L. 154
Barrett, C.K. 247–249, 253, 261, 272
Barrick, W.B. 133
Barton, J. 27
Bary, C. 232
Bautch, R.J. 53, 55, 130, 357–358
Beck, D. 232
Becker, H.-J. 344, 347
Becker, M. 314
Becker, U. 128, 133
Becking, B. 40, 49, 52, 55–56, 61, 327

Beentjes, P.C. 111, 113–115, 118, 121
Ben Zvi, E. 61
Bendemann, R. von 164–165, 183
Bengel, E. 258
Bengel, J.A. 255
Bennema, C. 239
Beth Schaffer, D. 150
Betsworth, S. 44
Beuken, W.A.M. 82, 128–129, 131, 135, 137–139, 143–145
Bickley Rogers, B. 242
Biesta, G. 361
Blánquez, J. 57
Blenkinsopp, J. 70, 128
Block, D.I. 37
Blum, E. 24
Bock, D.L. 253
Boda, M.J. 53–54
Boeke, Y. 254
Boismard, M.-É. 250, 262
Booij, T. 100
Booth, W.C. 231
Bork, A. 165
Boss, J. 84, 93
Boucher, D. 254
Bovati, P. 152
Bovon, F. 259
Bowie, A. 231
Boyarin, D. 337–338
Bramer, S.J. 158
Brant, J.-A.A. 244
Bratcher, R. 98, 103
Brawley, R.L. 261
Brenner, A. 82
Briant, P. 57
Briggs, M.R. 45
Brodsky, D. 336
Brown, W.P. 133–134, 137
Broyles, C.C. 126
Bruce, F.F. 252
Bryan, D.K. 248
Buber, M. 15

Bühlmann, W. 10
Bulkeley, T. 161
Bullinger, E.W. 10, 157, 282, 290
Burt, S. 57
Büttner, G. 356
Buzzard, A. 252, 259

Calvin, John 251
Carpenter, J.E. 23
Carroll, J.T. 262
Castelli, S. 71, 274
Celle, A. 234
Charlesworth, J.H. 89
Chester, S.J. 268
Cho, P.K.K. 82, 84, 92
Choi, J.H. 2
Clarke, A.D. 249
Clements, R.E. 133, 306, 327
Clines, D.J.A. 82, 154
Coats, G. 30
Cohn, D. 232
Collingwood, R.G. 254
Collins, A.Y. 188, 298
Colvin, S. 265
Combet-Galland, C. 197–198
Conrad, R. 360
Conzelmann, H. 252, 261, 281, 287, 290
Copenhaver, M.B. 210
Corley, J. 65, 119, 121–122, 227
Corstjens, R. 258
Cox, C.E. 88
Crabbe, K. 260
Craig, K.M. 3, 306
Crenshaw, J.L. 115
Culpepper, R.A. 187, 189, 194
Culy, M.M. 248

Daube, D. 348
Davidson, A.B. 26
Davies, Ph.R. 154
Day, L. 83
De Troyer, K. 71
Dear, J. 210, 212
Deeg, A. 361
Denaux, A. 320, 258
Depraz, N. 234
Derrenbacker, R. 172
Dewey, J. 183

Di Lella, A.A. 112–113, 118
Dietrich, W. 62
Diller, C. 58
Dimant, D. 305, 308–311
Donahue, J.R. 194, 196–197
Dörpinghaus, A. 362
Doyle, C.C. 150, 235
Dressler, B. 361
Dschulnigg, P. 189, 196
Duggan, M.W. 53–54
Dunn, J.D.G. 253
Dussen, J. van der 254

Eck, J. 127, 130, 135, 260
Eco, U. 254
Egger-Wenzel, R. 119
Ego, B. 82
Elbert, P. 210, 212
Elßner, T.R. 121
Elwolde, J. 306
Emde Boas, E. van 3–4, 184, 288–289
Engel, H. 65, 67, 70–71, 73
Epp, E.J. 262
Eskenazi, T.C. 63
Estes, D. 3, 163–172, 175–176, 183–186, 188–189, 195–196, 209–214, 216, 219–220, 229–231, 233, 235, 238–240, 242, 245, 249, 255, 258, 265, 282–283, 286–291, 359
Evans, C.A. 126

Falk, D.K. 53–54
Farber, Z.I. 38
Fassberg, S. 306
Faure, P. 250
Fee, G.D. 282
Feld, H. 251
Finkel, A.Y. 332
Fischel, H. 337
Fitzmyer, J.A. 248, 259, 281–282, 284, 286, 290–291
Fitzpatrick-McKinley, A. 57
Flint, P. 305
Fludernik, M. 232, 234
Focant, C. 189
Fokkelman, J.P. 13
Forster, E.M. 176, 230
Fowler, R.M. 183

INDEX OF MODERN AUTHORS

Fox, M.V.   93
Fraade, S.   327
Fraenkel, Y.   339
France, R.T   189, 193–194, 197
Franklin, E.   258
Frenschkowski, M.   296
Fretheim, T.E.   27, 93–94
Frettlöh, M.   164
Frey, J.   296
Fried, L.S.   49
Fritz, V.   135
Fuller, M.F.   260

Gallarte, I.M.   320
García Martínez, F.   305, 312, 314, 319–320
Garett, D.A.   161
Garroway, K.H.   36, 38, 44
Gemünden, P. von   304
Gera, D.L.   67–68, 74
Gitay, Y.   152, 155
Gitin, S.   49
Goff, M.   312
Goodacre, M.   163
Goshen-Gottstein, A.   346
Goulder, M.   163, 215
Grabbe, L.L.   53, 57
Grässer, E.   260
Gravett, E.O.   82
Gray, G.B.   24, 27, 32
Green, R.P.H.   277
Grice, H.P.   255
Grol, H.W.M. van   53–55, 100, 105, 121
Gundry, R.H.   188–189, 193–194, 196
Gunkel, H.   98
Guttenberger, G.   189, 192

Haacker, K.   270
Haag, E.   129, 134, 140–142
Häberlein, M.   71
Hadjiev, T.S.   157
Haenchen, E.   260
Hamman, P.   361
Harford-Battersby, G.   23
Harnisch, W.   257
Harrington, D.J.   194, 196–197
Harris, R.L.   252
Hart, J.H.A.   118

Hartley, J.E.   82
Haspecker, J.   114, 118
Häusl, M.   56, 58
Hausmann, J.   55
Heckl, R.   54
Hegel, G.   362
Heijer, A. den   217
Heil, C.   165
Held, M.   28
Hengel, M.   122
Hensel, B.   50
Hens-Piazza, G.   35, 41–43
Henten, J.W. van   71
Heschel, S.   336
Hibbard, T.   130
Hidary, R.   337
Hock, R.F.   264
Höffken, P.   128, 131, 139
Hoffmann, M.R.   297
Hoffmann, P.   163, 165
Hogeterp, A.L.A.   314, 320
Hogewood, J.C.   54
Holladay, C.R.   253
Holland, M.   158
Holzinger, H.   24
Hoonacker, A. van   153–154, 158
Horn, C.B.   44
Horst, P.W. van der   261
Hossfeld, F.-L.   100
House, P.R.   157
Howard, W.F.   241
Huitink, L.   3–4, 288–289
Hunziker-Rodewald, R.   159
Hyatt, D.   264

Ilan, T.   336, 343
Iversen, G.Y.   356

Jacob, B.   11–13, 15, 17
Jacob, E.   122
Janowski, B.   13
Jantsch, T.   261
Janzen, J.G.   18
Jastrow, M.   311
Jervell, J.   256, 261
Jewett, R.   264, 271–272
Jones, K.R.   256–257
Jong, I.J.F. de   231

INDEX OF MODERN AUTHORS

Joosten, J. 65, 107, 306
Jugnet, A. 234

Kahl, W. 163
Karle, I. 360
Keener, C.S. 249
Kehlhoffer, J.A. 296
Kellogg, R. 232
Khan, G. 306
Kilgallen, J.J. 224
King, Ph.J. 159
Kirk, A. 165, 172
Kirkpatrick, P. 82, 92
Kister, M. 348
Klaiber, W. 299
Klijn, A.F.J. 257
Klinker-De Klerk, M.G.P. 217, 360
Kloppenborg, J.S. 163, 165
Knoppers, G.N. 50
Koet, B.J. 1, 6, 36, 186, 217, 222–224, 227, 359–360
Konrad, H. 296
Korpel, M.C.A. 55, 128–129
Kotzé, G.R. 50
Kraemer, D. 335
Krans, J. 250
Kratz, R.G. 39
Kremer, J. 260
Krone, P. 254
Kuenen, A. 24
Kuindersma, H. 356
Kuntz, J.K. 126
Kunz-Lübcke, A. 38

L'Heureux, C.E. 133
Laato, A. 115
Labahn, M. 165, 172, 176, 179, 182
Lambrou, M. 236
Lamouille, A. 250
Lansari, L. 234
Lapsley, J.E. 82
Larrañaga, V. 249
Larsen, K.B. 245
Lefevre, H. 11
Legaspi, M.C. 85, 92
Leibold, S. 164
Lemche, N.P. 62
Leonhardt-Balzer, J. 49

Lessing, R.R. 152, 160
Leutzsch, M. 164, 212–215, 219–220
Levin, C. 61
Levine, B. 25–26, 29
Levinson, S.C. 255
Lichtenberger, H. 303
Lieberman, S. 336, 350
Lietaert Peerbolte, B.J. 250, 264
Lightfoot, J.B. 252–253
Linafelt, T. 90
Lindner, H. 164, 209
Lipschits, O. 53
Liss, H. 139, 140, 143–144
Llewellyn-Jones, L. 57–58
Locatell, C.S. 50
Lohfink, G. 254–256
Lohse, E. 270
López-Ruiz, C. 57
Low, K. 82, 89
Lundbom, J.R. 37
Luther, Martin 251
Lux, R. 38

MacDonald, M.J. 184
Magdalene, F.R. 82
Magen, Y. 50
Maier, E. 232, 237
Maimonides 323, 327–329, 331
Mainville, O. 197
Marböck, J. 112
Marcus, J. 194, 196
Mardaga, H. 258
Marguerat, D. 197, 255
Marnette, S. 232
Martens, J.W. 44
Marthaler, B.L. 46–47
Marulli, L. 190–191
Maston, J. 253
Mattill, A.J. 258
Mazzinghi, L. 73
McLean, J.A. 253
Meade, D.G. 111
Melanchthon, Philipp 268
Merkt, A. 296
Merz, A. 327
Messarra, J.A. 50
Metzger, B.M. 257, 262
Meyer, H. 355

Meyer-Blanck, M.   361
Meynet, R.   152
Michie, D.   183
Milgrom, J.   26, 32
Milik, J.T.   312
Millard, R.A.   59
Miller, G.D.   121
Minchin, E.   232
Misgav, H.   50
Mitchell, G.   356
Mittmann, S.   135
Mittmann, U.   82
Mock, L.   332, 335, 362
Möller, K.   152, 154, 158–159
Moltz, H.   160
Moor, J.C. de   53, 115
Morgan, G.C.   253
Moshavi, A.   126, 306–307, 313, 318
Motyer, J.A.   157
Moulton, J.H.   241
Muddiman, J.   27
Müller, C.G.   164, 212
Müller, U.B.   295, 301
Mulzer, M.   58
Muraoka, T.   66, 306
Myers, G.   238–240

Nässlin, S.   150
Neher, A.   156
Neirynck, F.   183, 185, 183, 314
Nes, J. van   217
Neubrand, M.   260
Newsom, C.A.   82
Neyrey, J.H.   164, 183
Nicholson, G.C.   287
Nicholson-Smith, D.   11
Nicklas, T.   294, 296–298
Nicol, M.   361
Nikolsky, R.   336, 343
Noam, V.   327
Noble, J.T.   18
Nowack, W.   154
Nünlist, R.   231

O'Floinn, G.   1
O'Rourke, J.J.   243
Oberthür, R.   356
Oeming, M.   53

Ólason, K.   58
Olson, D.T.   27
Ottenheijm, H.L.M.   327, 336, 346
Otto, E.   62

Palmer, A.   249
Palmer, D.W.   232
Pao, D.W.   248, 253
Pardee, D.   28
Park, A.W.   152
Parker, J.F.   44
Parsons, M.C.   248
Pascut, B.   197
Peláez, J.   320
Penchansky, D.   82, 85–86, 89, 91
Pérez, S.C,   57
Perkins, P.   283, 290–291
Perrin, N.   163
Person Jr., R.F.   39
Pervo, R.I.   248, 252
Pesch, R.   188, 255
Peters, N.   114
Peterson, T.   234
Pfister, M.   125, 149
Phelan, J.   232
Pietersma, A.   88, 268
Piotrkowski. M.M.   343
Pitts, A.W.   248–249
Poenitsch, A.   362
Pohlmann, K.-F.   135
Polak, F.H.   93
Pollard, G.   356
Prato, G.L.   115
Pressler, C.   83
Prince, G.   231–232, 236
Procksch, O.   140
Puech, É.   314–315

Rad, G. von   39
Redditt, P.L.   89
Regt, L.J. de   307
Renssen, T.   197
Resseguie, J.L.   239
Rey, J.-S.   306
Reyburn, W.   98, 103
Rhoads, D.M.   183
Riemersma, N.   224
Riesner, R.   210

INDEX OF MODERN AUTHORS

Riis, O. 345
Rijksbaron, A. 3–4, 288–289
Ringe, S.H. 82
Roberts, J.J.M. 128, 145
Robertson, A.T. 265, 278, 285, 288–289
Robinson, H. 252
Robinson, J.M. 163, 172
Roose, H. 297–298, 304
Rosenzweig, F. 15
Roth, D.T. 165, 170, 172, 176, 178–179
Rothenbusch, R. 58
Rubenstein, J.L. 346
Rüger, H.P. 114
Runge, S.E. 3

Safrai, S. 322, 326, 344
Said, E.W. 343
Saiman, C.N. 324
Saldarini, A.J. 349
Salmeier, M.A. 260
Sampley, J.P. 264
Sams, J. 239
Sasson, V. 82
Schaefer, C. 260
Schechter, S. 348–349
Schenker, A. 152, 157
Scherer, K. 10
Scheunpflug, A. 357
Schiffman, L.H. 305, 312
Schiffner, K. 164, 183, 212
Schmid, K. 39
Schmidt, A.J. 122
Schmitt, H.-Ch. 135
Schmitz, B. 67, 70–71
Schmoldt, H. 159
Schnabel, E.J. 187
Schneider, G. 254
Scholes, R. 232
Schrage, W. 282, 284, 287
Schrijver, E.G.L. 114
Schröter, J. 174
Schultz, R.L. 37
Schunck, K.-D. 65
Schüngel-Straumann, H. 160
Schürmann, H. 259
Schwartz, K. 174
Schweizer, E. 187, 189
Schwiebert, J. 183

Seelbach, L.C. 356
Sellew, P. 239, 244
Semino, E. 236–237, 239–240
Seow, C.L. 83, 91, 93
Sevrin, J.-M. 193
Seybold, K. 159
Shemesh, A. 327
Shepherd, D.J. 58
Sheridan, R. 238–240
Shiner, W. 190
Short, M. 236–237, 239–240
Skehan, P.W. 112–113
Skemp, V.T.M. 119, 227
Skinner, C.W. 239
Smend, R. 112
Smit, J. 267
Smit, P.-B. 197
Smith, T. 254
Snaith, N.H. 154
Sokoloff, M. 49
Sommer, B.D. 24, 30, 33
Spencer, J.R. 133
Sperling, S.D. 28
Spinner, K. 355
Stadelmann, H. 120
Standaert, B. 194
Stefan, A. 296
Stemberger, G. 348
Stephanus, Robertus 273
Stern, D. 339–344
Sternberg, M. 236
Steudel, P. 255
Stewart, A.W. 82, 87, 89–90
Stibbe, M.W.G. 238–239
Stier, R. 252
Stigall, J.J 248
Still, T.D. 253
Stone, I.F. 209
Stone, M. 49
Strawn, B.A. 37, 40
Strobel, A. 256
Stromberg, J. 130
Strugnell, J. 308
Suomala, K.R. 82
Swanson, R.J. 250, 262

Talbert, C.H. 284, 290
Taschner, J. 7

INDEX OF MODERN AUTHORS

Thatcher, T. 244
Thomas Aquinas 84
Thompson Prince, D. 211
Tiede, D.L. 259
Tigay, J.H. 37
Tigchelaar, E.J.C. 305–306, 312, 314, 319–320
Timmer, D. 93
Tiwald, M. 164–165, 167, 171–172, 179
Tomson, P.J. 322
Tóth, F. 296
Touger, E. 324
Tov, E. 65
Trask, W.R. 343
Tsfania, L. 50
Tuckett, C.M. 223, 314
Tuland, C.G. 51
Tullock, G. 61
Turner, N. 241

Ulrich, E. 305
Uusitalo, H. 61

Van Belle, G. 170
Van Hecke, P. 306
Van Oyen, G. 197
Van Segbroeck, F. 224
Vanhoye, A. 183, 282
Vaux, R. de 155
Verheyden, J. 170, 296

Wallace, D.B. 241, 249, 260
Wanak, L. 164
Watson, D.F. 282
Watts, J.D.W. 128
Wedderburn, A.J.M. 264
Weippert, H. 159
Weippert, M. 159
Weissenrieder, A. 304
Wendt, F. 304
Wendt, H.H. 254
Wengst, K. 298
Wénin, A. 8–9, 12–14, 188, 197
Werline, R.A. 53–54
Westermann, C. 17
Wettstein, J.J. 273–274

Wieringen, A.L.H.M. van 1, 6, 15, 36, 42, 101, 125, 135, 149, 158, 355, 359
Wigger, L. 362
Wilckens, U. 270
Wilcok, K.G. 82
Wildberger, H. 129, 135–136
Willi, Th. 54
Williams, P.J. 55
Williamson, H.G.M. 51, 57, 60, 128–129, 131–135, 139–140, 143, 145
Wills, L.M. 65
Wilson, G.H. 93
Wilson, L. 82, 85, 93–94
Wilson, S.G. 247
Winter, B.W. 249
Withenton, M.R. 197
Witherington III, B. 189, 253, 264, 281
Wolde, E. van 82, 93
Wolter, M. 270
Woodhead, L. 345
Wordsworth, W. 44
Woude, A. van der 42
Wright, A. 356
Wright, B.G. 88, 111, 268
Wright, C.J.H. 58
Wright, J.L. 38
Wright, N.T. 262
Wuellner, W.H. 183, 282–283
Wynne, M. 236–237, 239–240

Xeravits, G.G. 65

Yadin, A. 347–350, 353

Zapff, B.M. 130
Zenger, E. 100
Zevit, Z. 49
Zewi, T. 50, 307
Ziegler, J. 112, 116
Zimmermann, M. 164
Zimmermann, R. 164–165, 170, 172, 174, 176, 179–180, 209, 227
Zlotowitz, M. 14, 17
Zmijewski, J. 252, 255
Zwiep, A.W. 251, 253, 255, 257, 259, 261